German Civil Justice

German Civil Justice

Peter L. Murray
Robert Braucher Visiting Professor
of Law from Practice,
Harvard Law School

Rolf Stürner
Professor *Ordinarius* of Law,
University of Freiburg
Judge of the State Court of Appeals

Carolina Academic Press
Durham, North Carolina

ISBN 1-59460-003-1

LCCN 2003116285

Carolina Academic Press
700 Kent Street
Durham, NC 27701
Telephone (919) 489-7486
Fax (919) 493-5668
www.cap-press.com

Printed in the United States of America

CONTENTS

Foreword

Arthur T. von Mehren

As our world becomes increasingly complex and interconnected, comparative study of law and legal systems is rendered ever more difficult. When I began to study law comparatively more than half a century ago, most legal orders could be seen as shaped by two major legal cultures, the common-law and the civil-law systems, respectively. By now, as the third millennium begins, the tasks faced by comparative study of law have greatly increased in number and complexity. Since "each system functions as a whole[, i]ts general tendencies depend on the interaction in concrete situations...", accordingly "all... [relevant] historical, institutional and social" circumstances must be considered before "comparative generalizations [can safely] be offered".[1]

In the 1950s Benjamin Kaplan, Rudolf Schaefer and I undertook to consider the elements of civil procedure in the Federal Republic of Germany in a study which was ultimately published as "Phases of German Civil Procedure", 71 Harv. L. Rev. 1193 and 1443 (1957, 1958). We described the system of German civil procedure in its own setting but did "not undertake extended comparison with the markedly different American practice...". Nor did we "inquire how far German procedure may be regarded as typical of modern procedural methods in other countries on the continent of Europe".[2] In effect, our effort was to trace the course of procedure in civil cases passing through the regular German courts of first and later instance.

"[C]oncerned with sketching the structure of modern German civil process,... [we] paid scant attention to the historical evolution of procedural norms and practices". Nor did we make broad assessments of "German success or failure in achieving ultimate aims professed by all modern systems:

1. Von Mehren, "The Judicial Process: A Comparative Analysis", 5 Am. J. Comp. L. 197, at 198 (1956).
2. 71 Harv. L. Rev. at 1193.

thoroughness of consideration of the facts and the law, resoluteness, speed, economy and impartiality in the handling of cases".[3]

We sought answers to some of the "classical antinomical questions" raised by German scholarship: *e.g.*, to what extent are case materials to be presented by the parties, to what extent must or may they be searched out by judicial initiative? To what degree do the parties determine the pace of their lawsuit, to what degree does the court control it?

The comparative study of law can be undertaken with various objectives in mind. Students may, for example, seek detailed information on certain areas of foreign substantive and procedural law. Again, their interests can be primarily jurisprudential or historical. Or they may be seeking a better understanding of the institutions and processes of growth of their own legal system. These objectives do not exclude each other – though, of course, differences in emphasis will flow from the student's primary concern. A mastery in fair detail of some part of the law of the legal system under investigation is, in all events, essential before more jurisprudential or historical work can be fruitful. Conversely, a knowledge of the detailed rules of a particular area of substantive or procedural law is of little practical value unless informed by insight into the processes of growth and development of the system under consideration and by an understanding of the habits of thought current in that system.

German Civil Justice presents a synthesis and evaluation of the entire German system that we did not undertake in "Phases of German Civil Procedure". Professors Murray and Stürner study the German system as a whole and at many levels. The work includes an explanation of German civil procedure law ranging from a discussion of the oft-cited principles underlying the doctrine to a detailed description of the processing of law suits in their various instances from the initiation of suit through revision appeal. The authors analyze in some detail those structural elements and role divisions in the processing of German civil litigation, which our earlier study recognized but did not grapple with. The work addresses other features of German civil justice not seriously touched on in "Phases of German Civil Procedure" such as the education and training of German judges and the structure and regulation of the German bar. This work should provide students and practitioners with a comprehensive understanding of the German civil justice system. It also gives comparative law scholars entree to the necessary material to support and enable meaningful comparative work involving German civil procedure law and institutions of civil justice.

3. 71 Harv. L. Rev. at 1470.

Professors Murray and Stürner bring to this formidable task both the scholar's and the practitioner's perspective and experience. *German Civil Justice* is a major addition to comparative-law scholarship in Civil Procedure, one of the most challenging comparative law fields, in which the observer finds it both more necessary and more difficult to combine an understanding of practice and theory than is normally the case.

Finally it should be noted that *German Civil Justice* incorporates description and discussion of the many reforms to the German Civil Procedure Code and practice that have taken place since our work was published in 1958. Some of these reforms have directly affected features of German civil justice that we found worthy of comment. An example is the "Stuttgart" reforms of the late 1970's, which have tended to concentrate German proceedings for oral argument and taking of evidence in a single main hearing. These newer developments, even up to the very recent changes effective January 1, 2002, have all been included in the Murray-Stürner text.

German Civil Justice is an outstanding contribution to comparative scholarship in an especially difficult field of law.

Arthur T. von Mehren

Preface

1. Why This Book Was Written

This book was written to provide jurists in the English-speaking world with a comprehensive description and analysis of the German system of civil justice as seen and interpreted by observers from both German civil law and American common law backgrounds.

Modern Germany has evolved a highly sophisticated and relatively successful system of civil procedure law, constitutional doctrine and institutions of justice for civil litigants in German courts. It is a good example of an efficient and respected system by which the rule of law can be maintained in the everyday world of civil litigation.

Moreover, the modern German system (together with its Austrian counterpart) has had greater influence on civil justice systems worldwide than any other procedural system of the civil law world. In Europe, the civil justice systems of Switzerland, Greece, Turkey, The Czech Republic, Slovakia, Hungary, Poland, and Croatia have been strongly influenced by German and Austrian civil procedural law. In Asia, Japan, South Korea and to a somewhat lesser extent China derive their civil justice systems more or less directly from the German-Austrian model. German procedural law has played significant, although lesser roles, in the development of civil justice systems in the Skandinavian and Baltic countries. Any student interested in the development of institutions of civil justice in general would do well to become familiar with the German system as a prototype of modern continental-European civil justice on which many other systems are founded in whole or in part.

The German civil justice system has been documented, described and critiqued in a voluminous literature of treatises, commentaries, texts and articles which have appeared over the last century. However almost all of the currently extant literature is written and published in German, and hence not accessible to persons not familiar with that language.

Over the last decades English has become an international language for legal discourse among legal professionals from cultures in which English is not the primary national language. By writing this work in English the authors hope to provide a first-hand description and analysis of German civil justice to jurists from common law, civil law and hybrid legal traditions who otherwise would have limited access to relevant explanatory and analytical literature.

One could ask the question, "Why not merely translate some of the excellent treatises on German civil justice which have been written by German legal scholars in German?" While such translations are of great value, the work as translated continues to reflect the cultural and legal perspective of its original author. By writing this work in English the authors hope to lend a more international common-law perspective from which to describe and analyze the German law and institutions of civil justice in a way that will make them more understandable to lawyers, judges and law students from other legal traditions.

The primary purpose of this book is to depict and analyze the German civil justice system, not to compare it in any detail to another specific legal system or tradition. On the other hand, the authors hope and expect that the material in this work will provide bases for readers' comparative analyses of elements of German civil justice with functionally corresponding features of other civil law or common law systems. For these reasons the authors have generally refrained from conscious comparisons in the body of the text. At the end of the work the authors venture some of their own comparative observations on certain salient features of German and Anglo-American civil justice.

As a Member State of the European Union, Germany and its civil justice system have been significantly impacted by the development of a growing body of European law. The significant features of this developing law are included in this description, especially as they relate to international civil procedure.

It is the authors' hope that this work will help foster the inclusion of German legal institutions in the everyday global discussion and comparative analysis of civil justice and its evolution. In that vein the authors would be grateful for the reactions and comments of readers and users of this book to the end that it might achieve greater usefulness over time.

2. Intended Readership

This book is intended to be read by English-speaking judges, lawyers, law academics and law students from all modern legal cultures who seek a basic knowledge of the German system of civil justice. The text is accompanied by sufficient references to source materials to enable interested readers to make more detailed inquiry into areas of specific interest. It can be read as a descriptive, analytical and comparative account or can be used as an entry-level basic reference work in the law office or academic library. German lawyers and law academics may find this text useful in explaining German civil procedure and civil justice institutions to foreign students, colleagues, and clients.

The first chapter, which provides an introductory overview of the German civil justice system, is intended to be suitable for use as a comparative perspective in law school and university courses on domestic civil procedure. Permission is hereby given for non-commercial reproduction of Chapter 1 for use in academic programs at the university or law school level, provided that appropriate attribution accompanies such use.

3. Scope and Coverage

German civil justice is a major topic about which many volumes have been written and about which many more will be written. An explanatory work of this kind must make compromises in both scope of coverage and detail of analysis in the interest of compact presentation.

The authors' aim has been to provide a reasonable description of the key elements of German civil justice with enough detail so that the reader can gain an understanding of the degree of legal sophistication and nicety with which the system operates. The work addresses both the written civil procedure law and the various institutions such as the bench and bar, which put that law into practice.

Both of the authors have practice backgrounds in civil justice to complement their academic perspectives. Visiting Professor Murray actively practiced as an American civil and criminal litigator for over 25 years before entering full-time academics. Professor Stürner served as judge on the German state courts early in his career and continues to serve as part-time judge of the State Appeals Court of Karlsruhe. Professor Murray has gained familiarity with the German civil justice system through academic research, discussions with colleagues, judges and practitioners, and actual observation of and participation in German civil proceedings during visits to Germany over several years for research and teaching as a Fulbright Visiting Professor at the University of Freiburg. Professor Stürner has come to know the Anglo-American systems of civil justice not only through academic study and dialogue, but also through observation and discussion with English and American judges and practitioners as well as through his work as UNIDROIT Reporter of the ALI/UNIDROIT Transnational Principles of Civil Procedure and as Visiting

Professor at Harvard Law School. We are both interested in how things are actually done as well as how they are supposed to take place as a matter of theory. The work includes occasional mention of practical realities when required in order to give a fair description of how the system actually works.

From time to time we have attempted to sketch images of how actual legal proceedings take place. We have included some details of procedure such as the statutory time periods for various legal acts to provide a sense of the "texture" of the system. Such details help portray, for example, the extent to which German civil justice system goes to preserve the right of a fair hearing at all stages of civil proceedings. The aim is to give the reader a sense of the "feel" of German civil justice as well as its legal and institutional features.

We have included a few words of history (Chapter 2) to give some idea of the cultural context from which the modern German civil justice system has developed. Other key elements of the work include a description of the structure and features of the German judicial system (Chapter 3), material on the composition and role of the German bar (Chapter 4), brief analysis of subject matter jurisdiction and venue of the German courts (Chapter 5), and a discussion of certain fundamental principles of German civil justice (Chapter 6). The core of the work is the description and analysis of German civil proceedings starting with the preliminary stages of a law suit (Chapter 7), going on to plenary proceedings and proof (Chapter 8), to judgments and other case dispositions (Chapter 9) and ultimately to appeals (Chapter 10). We also cover certain important special procedures (Chapter 11) and address German civil justice in international matters (Chapter 12) We close the work with a brief evaluation of certain key features of German civil justice in comparison with the Anglo-American civil justice systems (Chapter 13).

We have not been able to cover every conceivable feature of German civil justice in the broad sense. Certain features have been omitted. For instance, we have not given any coverage to practice and procedure in the specialized Labor, Administrative, Social Welfare or Tax Courts, even though collectively these jurisdictions encompass important components of what is considered as civil justice by Anglo-American lawyers. We have omitted covering these specialized jurisdictions because we believe that a more detailed depiction of the operations of the "ordinary courts" will give a better sense of the process of German civil justice than using the space to give briefer descriptions of the activities of the courts of specialized jurisdiction.

Our coverage of other important areas is limited. For instance, this text includes only brief treatment of execution of judgments and the law of bankruptcy although both are major areas of civil procedure law in Germany. In recent years the Federal Constitutional Court has tended to exercise a large influence on civil justice and procedure in Germany. However space has permitted us only a rather brief description of this activity. The same is true of the growing role of the European Court of Justice of the European Union and the European Court of Human Rights, about which there is already some English language literature extant. We are all too conscious of the effects of limited time and space on the completeness of any description and analysis as ambitious as that attempted by this work.

4. Terminology

Although this book is intended to be understandable to readers from every legal culture, it is expected that many of the readers will have some pre-existing familiarity with the Anglo-American civil justice system. Many of the features of the German civil justice system are best understood by Anglo-American lawyers in terms of the legal language and concepts with which they are already familiar, at least to the extent that such language and concepts can be fairly used to describe the German system. At the same time we have tried to avoid arcane language and terms associated only with a particular legal system or tradition.

Some German terms or concepts do not easily translate into Anglo-American legal cognates. In such cases the authors have attempted to explain the German terms and concepts as best we can. Key terms appear parenthetically in German. We have also included the original German language of material quoted in translation so that readers with knowledge of German can have the original terminology available.

The names of the various German courts are translated variously in the currently available English-language sources. Some authors retain the German designations and do not attempt to translate them. We have chosen "neutral" designations designed to describe the actual legal roles of the respective courts without attempting to match them with corresponding courts in any particular Anglo-American jurisdiction. Thus we refer to the lowest level of ordinary court, the German *Amtsgericht*, as the "local court". The German *Landgericht* appears here as "state district court," the *Oberlandesgericht* is the "state appeals court," and the *Bundesgerichtshof* is the Federal Supreme Court. Our aim is to stick with English terminology that accurately describes the functions of the courts referred to, albeit at the expense of elegance of language.

5. Sources, Citations and Bibliography

English-language reference material on post-World War II German civil justice is relatively scanty. The most authoritative systematic analysis that has appeared to date is Kaplan, von Mehren and Schaefer, "Phases of German Civil Procedure," 71 *Harvard Law Review* 1193, 1443 (1958). The insights embodied in this standard work are still of value, although intervening legislative reform and developments at the EU level have rendered some of the specifics out of date.

Professor John Langbein's "The German Advantage in Civil Procedure," 52 *University of Chicago Law Review* 823 (1985) and its progeny of critical and supporting commentary have played an important role in awakening the interest of the American procedural law community to comparative procedural law in general and German civil procedure in specific. These publications do not, however, purport to give comprehensive descriptions or analyses of the German civil justice system.

There are also a few short descriptions of German civil procedure such as Koch, *Civil Procedure in Germany* (Kluwer 1998), as well as a number of English-language articles or chapters in comparative law journals, legal encyclopedias, or books covering German law in general. While these offer interesting glimpses at German civil justice, they do not cover the subject in depth or detail. Several of these articles and other sources are listed in the Brief Bibliography accompanying this text.

The information set forth in this work is based on the original German-language statutory text, commentaries on that text by German legal scholars, and some of the leading German treatises. Rosenberg, Schwab, Gottwald *Zivilprozessrecht* (15th Ed. 1993) is frequently cited in the edition available at the time this book was written. It is thus of somewhat limited usefulness because of its date. Lüke, *Zivilprozessrecht* (7th Ed. 1999) is an easily readable shorter text which is current except for the most recent 2001 reforms. Jauernig, *Zivilprozessrecht* (27th Ed. 2002) includes coverage of the most recent reforms. Geimer, *Internationales Zivilprozessrecht* (4th Ed. 2000) and Schack, *Internationales Verfahrensrecht* (3rd Ed. 2002) provide up to date coverage of international civil procedure. Thomas, Putzo, *Kommentar zur ZPO* (2002), Zoeller, *Kommentar zur ZPO* (2002), and Musielak, *Kommentar* zur ZPO (2002) are the most frequently cited commentaries. The work includes citations to a number of judicial decisions, articles and other sources, chiefly in the German language.

We have adopted a style of citation based largely on the American model. Statutes and other sources in the German legal literature have been abbreviated in accord with German practice. A few frequently cited texts are also abbreviated. However each citation is intended to enable the reader to locate the material referred to. Appended to the Preface is a Table of Abbreviations to assist with abbreviations in references to statutes and other similar material.

6. Acknowledgements

The authors wish to acknowledge with thanks the helpful cooperation of several colleagues, academic assistants, judges, lawyers and others who have contributed to the writing of this work and its preparation for publication.

Professor Murray expresses deep appreciation to colleagues Arthur von Mehren and Detlev Vagts of the Harvard Law School faculty for their encouragement, advice and support of his interest in comparative law. Professor Stürner is grateful to Professor Geoffrey Hazard, University of Pennsylvania Law School, and Professor Neil Andrews, Cambridge University for their encouragement of his undertaking to coauthor an English-language book about German civil justice.

The authors thank Vice President Heribert Veit, Freiburg Amtsgericht, President Klaus Kunath, Ellwangen Landgericht, colleagues of the Freiburg panel of the Karlsruhe Oberlandesgericht, and Vice-President Professor Dr. Horst Hagen of the Bundesgerichtshof for generously providing access to court proceedings and taking time to discuss civil justice issues with the authors. Dr. Wolfgang Schmid and the partners and associates of Bappert, Witz, Selbherr in Freiburg are thanked for arranging several visits to court proceedings. Dr. Robert Schumacher, Prof. Dr. Alexander Bruns, and Axel Dittmann, former academic assistants in the Institut für Zivilprozessrecht, Department 1 at the University of Freiburg helped coordinate Professor Murray's court visits and other work in Freiburg in the early stages of this project.

During the time this work has been "in process" a number of persons have made helpful contributions to portions of the text and notes. At Harvard Law School Moritz Baelz, Anna Cross, Claus Binder, Holger Schelling and Barbara Niederkofler performed helpful research and developed footnotes. In Germany Michael Breyer assisted with late revisions to Chapters 12 and 13 as well as final manuscript review. Nils Meppen prepared the Table of Abbreviations. Christian Nick and Florian Rink researched additional citations for footnotes. Lena Wallenhorst, Nils Meppen, Sven Mossler, Brit Neuburger and Friederike Bauer helped with checking citations and reconciling footnotes. Assistance in proofreading was provided by the foregoing as well as by Christoph Kern, Dr. Marius Kohler, Malte von Bargen, Benjamin Glunz and

Daniel Adloff. The authors thank Victoria Marini for typing a large portion of the manuscript.

The authors acknowledge with gratitude the financial support of the Harvard Law School, European Legal Studies Fund, and the German Academic Exchange Service -Alexander von Humboldt Foundation Transcoop Program, which have jointly funded outlays for travel and research assistance in the course of this project. Without this support it is unlikely that this project could have been completed.

Finally, the authors wish to thank our respective spouses, Deborah Murray and Ursula Stürner, for their continued support, encouragement and understanding of our enterprise and the necessary travel and focus of our energies which it required. This book is dedicated to them, and to our families.

Cambridge, Massachusetts, USA and
Freiburg im Breisgau, Germany
September 2003

Table of Abbreviations

ABA	American Bar Association
AcP	*Archiv für die civilistische Praxis*
AD	*Anno Domini*
ADR	Alternative Dispute Resolution
AfP	*Zeitschrift für Medien- und Kommunikationsrecht* (until 2001: *Archiv für Presserecht)*
AktG	*Aktiengesetz* of September 6, 1965 (BGBl. I, p.1089)
Ala. L. Rev.	Alabama Law Review
ALI	American Law Institute
Am. J. Comp. L.	American Journal of Comparative Law
Am. U. L. Rev	American University Law Review
AMG	*Gesetz über den Verkehr mit Arzneimitteln (Arzneimittelgesetz)* of August 24, 1976 (BGBl. I, pp. 2445, 2448)
AnfG	*Gesetz über die Anfechtung von Rechtshandlungen eines Schuldners außerhalb des Insolvenzverfahrens* of October 5, 1994 (BGBl. I, p. 2911) (*Anfechtungsgesetz)*
AnwBl	*Anwaltsblatt*
AnwZ	*Anwaltszeitung*
ArbGG	*Arbeitsgerichtsgesetz* in the version promulgated on July 2, 1979 (BGBl. I, pp. 853, 1036)
AusfG	*Ausführungsgesetz zum Haager Übereinkommen über die Zustellung gerichtlicher und außergerichtlicher Schriftstücke im Ausland in Zivil- und Handelssachen* of December 12, 1977
AVAG	*Gesetz zur Ausführung zwischenstaatlicher Verträge und zur Durchführung von Verordnungen der Europäischen Gemeinschaft auf dem Gebiet der Anerkennung und Vollstreckung in Zivil- und Handelssachen* of February 19, 2001

B. C. L. Rev.	Boston College Law Review
BauGB	*Baugesetzbuch* of June 23, 1960 (BGBl. I, p. 341) in the version promulgated on August 27, 1997 (BGBl. I, p. 2141)
BB	*Betriebs-Berater*
BBesG	*Bundesbesoldungsgesetz* of May 23, 1975 (BGBl. I, p. 1173) in the version promulgated on August 6, 2002 (BGBl. I, p. 3020)
BBG	*Bundesbeamtengesetz* of July 14, 1953 (BGBl. I, p. 551) in the version promulgated on March 31, 1999 (BGBl. I, p. 675)
BegrRegE	*Begründung des Regierungsentwurfs eines Gesetzes zur Reform des Zivilprozesses*
BER	Brussels Regulation on Cooperation between the Courts of the Member States in the Taking of Evidence in Civil or Commercial Matters, European Union Regulation No. 1206/2001, OJ L 174, 28/05/2001, p.1
BGB	*Bürgerliches Gesetzbuch* of August 18, 1896 in the version promulgated on January 2, 2002 (BGBl. I, p. 42)
BGBl.	*Bundesgesetzblatt*
BGH	*Bundesgerichtshof*
BGHSt	*Entscheidungen des Bundesgerichtshofs in Strafsachen*
BGHZ	*Entscheidungen des Bundesgerichtshofs in Zivilsachen*
BGHZ (GS)	*Entscheidungen des Großen Senats des Bundesgerichtshofs in Zivilsachen*
BinnSchiffG	*Binnenschiffahrtsgesetz* of June 15, 1895 in the version promulgated on June 15, 1898
BMinG	*Gesetz über die Rechtsverhältnisse der Mitglieder der Bundesregierung* of June 17, 1953 (BGBl. I, p. 407) in the version promulgated on July 27, 1971 (BGBl. I, p. 1166)
BNatSchG	*Bundesnaturschutzgesetz* of March 25, 2002 (BGBl. I, p. 1193)
BORA	*Berufsordnung für Rechtsanwälte* of August 1, 1959 (BGBl I, p. 565), as amended
BRAGO	*Bundesgebührenordnung für Rechtsanwälte* of July 26, 1957 (BGBl I, pp. 861, 907), as amended
BRAK-Mitt.	*Mitteilungen der Bundesrechtsanwaltskammer*

BRAO	*Bundesrechtsanwaltsordnung*
BRD	*Bundesrepublik Deutschland*
BRJE	European Union Regulation No. 44/2001 of December 22, 2000 on Jurisdiction and Recognition and Enforcement of Decisions in Civil and Commercial Matters, OJ L 012, 16/12/2001, p. 1
Brussels Evidence Regulation	*see* BER
Brussels Regulation	*see* BRJE
BT-Drs.	*Drucksachen des Deutschen Bundestags*
BT-Drucksachen	*see* BT-Drs.
BVerfGE	*Entscheidungen des Bundesverfassungsgerichts*
BVerfGG	*Gesetz über das Bundesverfassungsgericht* of March 12, 1951 (BGBl. I, p. 243) in the version promulgated on August 11, 1993 (BGBl. I, p. 1473)
Cal. Rev.	California Law Review
C.J.Q.	Civil Justice Quarterly
Cath. U. L. Rev.	Catholic University Law Review
CDS	Criminal Defense Service
cf.	compare
Ch.	Chapter
CISG	United Nations Convention on Contracts for the International Sale of Goods
CLS	Community Legal Service
CMR	Convention on Contracts for the International Carriage of Goods by Road
col	column
COM	Working Documents of the European Commission
Comparative L. Rev.	Comparative Law Review
DB	*Der Betrieb*
DDR	*Deutsche Demokratische Republik*
Denv. U. L. Rev.	Denver University Law Review
DePaul L. Rev.	DePaul Law Review
DM	*Deutsche Mark*
DÖV	*Die Öffentlichen Verwaltung*
DRiG	*Deutsches Richtergesetz* of September 6, 1961 (BGBl. I, p. 1665) in the version promulgated on April 19, 1972 (BGBl. I, p. 713)
DRiZ	*Deutsche Richterzeitung*

EC	European Community
ECHR	European Court of Human Rights
ECJ	European Court of Justice
ECR	Report of Cases before the Court of Justice of the European Communities
ed.	edition *or* editor
EFTA	European Free Trade Association
e.g.	for example
EGGVG	*Einführungsgesetz zum Gerichtsverfassungsgesetz* of January 27, 1877 as amended
EGMR	*Europäischer Gerichtshof für Menschenrechte, see* ECHR
EGZPO	*Einführungsgesetz zur Zivilprozessordnung* of January 30, 1877 as amended
EHRR	European Human Rights Reports
Einl	*Einleitung*
et al.	and other
EU	*Europäische Union* / European Union
EuBVO	*EG-Verordnung Nr. 1206/2001 über die Zusammenarbeit der Gerichte auf dem Gebiet der Beweisaufnahme in Zivil- und Handelssachen* / Council Regulation (EC) No 1206/2001 of 28 May 2001 on cooperation between the courts of the Member States in the taking of evidence in civil or commercial matters, OJ L 174, 27/6/2001
EuGH	*Europäischer Gerichtshof, see* ECJ
EuGRZ	*Europäische Grundrechtszeitschrift*
EuGVÜ	*Brüsseler EWG-Übereinkommen über die gerichtliche Zuständigkeit in Zivil- und Handelssachen* of September 27, 1968
Eur. Ct. HR Rep.	European Court of Human Rights Reports
Euratom	European Atomic Energy Community / *Europäische Atomgemeinschaft*
EU Service Regulation	European Union Regulation of May 29, 2000 on the Service in the Member States of Judicial and Extra-Judicial Documents in Civil or Commercial Matters, European Union Regulation No. 1348/2000 OJ L 160, 29/06/2000, p. 37
F. Supp.	Federal Supplement

F.R.Civ. P.	Federal Rules of Civil Procedure
FamRÄndG	*Gesetz zur Vereinheitlichung und Änderung familienrechtlicher Vorschriften - Familienrechtsänderungsgesetz* of August 11, 1961 (BGBl. I, p. 1221)
FamRZ	*Zeitschrift für das gesamte Familienrecht – Ehe und Familie im privaten und öffentlichen Recht*
ff.	and following
FGG	*Gesetz über die Angelegenheiten der freiwilligen Gerichtsbarkeit* of May 17, 1898 as amended
FGO	*Finanzgerichtsordnung* of October 6, 1965 (BGBl I, p.1477) in the version promulgated on March 3, 2001 (BGBl. I, pp. 442, 2262)
Fla. Cir. Ct.	Florida Circuit Court
Fordham Int'l L. J.	Fordham International Law Journal
F. R. Ev.	Federal Rules of Evidence
GBO	*Grundbuchordnung* of March 24, 1897 in the version promulgated on May 26, 1994 (BGBl. I, p. 1114)
Geo. J. Legal Ethics	Georgetown Journal of Legal Ethics
GG	*Grundgesetz* of May 23, 1949 (BGBl. I, p.1) as amended
GKG	*Gerichtskostengesetz* of June 18, 1878 in the version promulgated on December 15, 1975
GRUR	*Zeitschrift der Deutschen Vereinigung für gewerblichen Rechtsschutz und Urheberrecht GRUR*
GRURInt	*GRUR International - Gewerblicher Rechtsschutz und Urheberrecht, Internationaler Teil, Zeitschrift der Deutschen Vereinigung für gewerblichen Rechtsschutz und Urheberrecht*
GVG	*Gerichtsverfassungsgesetz* of January 27, 1877 in the version promulgated on May 9, 1975 (BGBl. I, p. 1077)
GVGA	*Geschäftsanweisung für Gerichtsvollzieher*
GVO	*Gerichtsvollzieherordnung*
GWB	*Gesetz gegen Wettbewerbsbeschränkungen* in the version promulgated on August 26, 1998, BGBl. I, 2546.
Hague Service Convention	Hague Convention on Service Abroad of Judicial and Extra-Judicial Documents of November 15, 1965
Harv. L. Rev.	Harvard Law Review

Harv. Int'l L.J.	Harvard International Law Journal
Hastings L.J.	Hastings Law Journal
HGB	*Handelsgesetzbuch* of May 10, 1897 as amended
HMSO	Her Majesty's Stationery Office
ICC	International Chamber of Commerce
InsO	*Insolvenzordnung* of October 5, 1994 (BGBl. I, p. 2866)
Int'l J. Legal Prof.	International Journal of the Legal Profession
IPRax	*Praxis des internationalen Privat- und Verfahrensrechts*
JA	*Juristische Ausbildung*
JuS	*Juristische Schulung*
JZ	*Juristenzeitung*
LAB	Legal Aid Board
LG	*Landgericht*
LSC	Legal Services Commission
Mass. Law Quarterly	Massachusetts Law Quarterly
M. R. Civ. P.	Maine Rules of Civil Procedure
Md. L. Rev.	Maryland Law Review
MDR	*Monatsschrift für Deutsches Recht*
Me. L. Rev.	Maine Law Review
Mealey's Int'l Arb. Q. L. Rev.	Mealey's International Arbitration Quarterly Law Review
Mich. L. Rev.	Michigan Law Review
Minn. L. Rev.	Minnesota Law Review
mn.	margin
MRSA	Maine Revised Statutes Annotated
NJW	*Neue Juristische Wochenschrift*
NJW-RR	*NJW Rechtsprechungs-Report Zivilrecht*
Nw. U. L. Rev.	Northwestern University Law Review
NYU Journal of International Law and Politics	New York University Journal of International Law and Politics
OJ	Official Journal of the European Communities / Union
OLG	*Oberlandesgericht*
OLGZ	*Rechtsprechung der Oberlandesgerichte in Zivilsachen, Amtliche Entscheidungssammlung*
PatAnwO	*Patentanwaltsordnung* of September 7, 1966 (BGBl I, p. 557) as amended

PatG	*Patentgesetz* of May 5, 1936 in the version promulgated on December 16, 1980, as amended
p.	page
pp.	pages
Prac. L. Inst.	Practising Law Institute
Prac. L. Inst. / Lit.	Practising Law Institute - Litigation and Administrative Practice Course Handbook Series - Litigation
Rabels Zeitschrift	*Zeitschrift für ausländisches und internationales Privatrecht*
RGZ	*Entscheidungen des Reichsgerichts in Zivilsachen*
RIW	*Recht der Internationalen Wirtschaft*
Rpfleger	*Der Rechtspfleger*
RPflG	*Rechtspflegergesetz*
Rutgers L. Rev.	Rutgers Law Review
S. Ct.	Supreme Court Reporter
SchiedsVfG	*Schiedsverfahren- Neuregelungsgesetz*
Service Regulation	*see* EU Service Regulation
SGG	*Sozialgerichtsgesetz* of September 3, 1953 (BGBl. I, pp. 1953, 1239) in the version promulgated on September 23, 1975 (BGBl. I, p. 2535), as amended
SMU L. Rev.	Southern Methodist University Law Review
StGB	*Strafgesetzbuch* of May 15, 1871 in the version promulgated on November 13, 1998 (BGBl. I, p. 3322)
Tulane J. Int'l and Comp. Law	Tulane Journal of International and Comparative Law
U. C. Davis L. Rev.	University of California, Davis Law Review
U. Chi. L. Rev.	University of Chicago Law Review
U. Chi. Legal F.	University of Chicago Legal Forum
U. Chicago L. Rev.	*see* U. Chi. L. Rev.
U. Pitt. L. Rev.	University of Pittsburgh Law Review
U.C.L.A.	University of California, Los Angeles
U.S.C	United States Code
U.S.C.A.	United States Code Annotated
UHG	*Umwelthaftungs-Gesetz* of December 10, 1990 (BGBl. I, p. 2634)
UKlaG	*Unterlassungsklagengesetz* of November 26, 2001 in the version promulgated on August 27, 2002 (BGBl. I, p. 3422)

UNCITRAL	United Nations Commission on International Trade Law
Unidroit	International Institute for the Unification of Private Law
Uniform L. Rev.	Uniform Law Review
UPA L.Rev.	University of Pennsylvania Law Review
U.S.	United States Reports
UWG	*Gesetz gegen den unlauteren Wettbewerb* of June 7, 1909, as amended
Vand. L. Rev.	Vanderbilt Law Review
VersR	*Versicherungsrecht, Juristische Rundschau für die Individualversicherung*
VerwArch	*Verwaltungsarchiv*
Vol.	Volume
VwGO	*Verwaltungsgerichtsordnung* of January 1, 1960 (BGBl. I, p. 17) in the version promulgated on March 19, 1991 (BGBl. I, p. 686) as amended
Wash. & Lee L. Rev.	Washington and Lee Law Review
Wis. L. Rev.	Wisconsin Law Review
WM	*Wertpapiermitteilungen*
Wm. & Mary Bill Rts. J.	William and Mary Bill of Rights Journal
Wm. & Mary L. Rev.	William and Mary Law Review
WRP	*Wettbewerb in Recht und Praxis*
ZaöRV	*Zeitschrift für ausländisches öffentliches Recht und Völkerrecht*
ZIP	*Zeitschrift für Wirtschaftsrecht*
ZPO	*Zivilprozessordnung* of January 30, 1877 in the version promulgated on September 12, 1950 (BGBl. I, p. 533), as amended
ZPO-RG	*Gesetz zur Reform des Zivilprozesses* of July 21, 2001 (BGBl. I, p.1887)
ZRHO	*Rechtshilfsordnung für Zivilsachen* of October 19, 1956 in the version promulgated on February 26, 1976
ZRP	*Zeitschrift für Rechtspolitik*
ZSEG	*Gesetz über die Entschädigung von Zeugen und Sachverständigen* of July 26, 1957 (BGBl. I, p. 902) in the version promulgated on October 1, 1969 (BGBl. I, p. 1756) as amended

ZustDG	*Gesetz zur Durchführung gemeinschaftsrechtlicher Vorschriften über die Zustellung gerichtlicher und außergerichtlicher Schriftstücke in Zivil- oder Handelssachen in den Mitgliedsstaaten (EG-Zustellungsdurchführungsgesetz)* of July 9, 2001 (BGBl. I, p.1536)
ZustRG	*Gesetz zur Reform des Verfahrens bei Zustellungen im gerichtlichen Verfahren (Zustellungsreformgesetz)* of June 25, 2001 (BGBl. I, p. 1206)
ZVG	*Gesetz über die Zwangsversteigerung und Zwangsverwaltung* of March 24, 1897 in the version promulgated on May 20, 1898, as amended
ZvglRwiss	*Zeitschrift für vergleichende Rechtswissenschaft*
ZZP	*Zeitschrift für Zivilprozeß*
ZZPInt	*Zeitschrift für Zivilprozeß International - Jahrbuch des Internationalen Zivilprozessrechts*

German Civil Justice

CHAPTER 1

Overview of German Civil Justice

Within the Civil Law world, the modern German civil justice system stands out for its pervasive integration in German culture and economic life, its overall size and complexity, its operational efficiency, the high quality of its judicial and legal establishment, and the volume of academic and other literature describing and analyzing its purpose and operations. These attributes make it an ideal subject for study by jurists from all legal backgrounds. The following brief overview is designed to give a brief glimpse of some of the workings of this system and to serve as an introduction to the remainder of this work.[1]

A. Purpose and Constitutional Role of Civil Justice in Modern Germany

The institutions of civil justice play a pervasive role in the modern German political economy. As a "State embodying the rule of law" (*Rechtsstaat*), Germany is committed to the principle that relationships among its citizens and between its citizens and their government are to be governed by a system of public and private law, fairly applied and evenly enforced.

---

1. This initial chapter is designed so that it can also be read separately from the rest of this work as an introduction to the German civil justice system and thereby provide comparative perspective in a course or program with some other primary focus. For this reason the text is somewhat generalized and most footnotes have been omitted. Complete references can be found in subsequent chapters dealing in greater detail with various aspects of the German civil justice system.

Permission is hereby granted for the non-commercial reproduction of Chapter 1 (with correct citation and attribution) for distribution to and use by law students and in similar programs.

1. The Purpose of Civil Justice

Germany's commitment to the principles of governance by law, not men, is demonstrated by the large size and high quality of its legal establishment. In no other country in the world other than perhaps the United States, does the Law, with its various accoutrements of legislature, administration, judiciary, and bar occupy a more prominent place and exercise a greater role.

Within this overall framework, the role of civil justice is important and substantial. Germans are conscious of their rights, whether vis à vis their government, or vis à vis each other. They are ready to resort to litigation to enforce their rights. As will be seen below, the German civil justice system is well adapted to serving them in this respect.

Although like any civil justice system, German civil justice has multiple purposes and functions, its primary purpose and function are seen as the determination and enforcement of private legal rights and obligations. A related purpose is the resolution of private disputes according to the norms of law. To be sure, the determination and enforcement of private rights leads to the ongoing development and improvement of the law itself. However the prevailing view is that improvement of the law is more a by-product than the driving purpose of civil justice.

Although the promotion of the collective public interest is seen as one civil justice goal, which finds expression in statutory "interest group claims" (*Verbandsklage*) in consumer and environmental matters, for example, the limited role such claims currently play bespeaks this function's relatively low priority.

In German civil litigation the discovery and ascertainment of factual truth are seen as important only in the context of determination and enforcement of the rights of the immediate parties. Civil justice has no particular business investigating or publicizing private or public wrongs.

By the same token, the private rights focus of German civil justice is inconsistent with any function of punishment of wrongdoers. As a matter of principle there is no provision for punitive damages in German civil litigation. Awards of damages are limited to redress of private interests injured, and are not generally expected to serve roles of public deterrence or punishment.

2. The State's Constitutional Responsibility for Civil Justice

The provision of civil justice of high quality both systemically and in specific cases is an important responsibility of the German state. The right of the individual citizen against the state for the protection of the law (*Rechtsschutz*) includes the right of access to competent courts for prompt vindication of private rights and responsibilities according to a clear and understandable legal order. This "claim to justice" (*Justizanspruch*) is fundamental to the citizen-state relationship. The citizen's claim to justice has been recognized at least since the 19th Century in German legal doctrine and literature. Although the degree to which it was realized in practice varied, sometimes to extremes, up to the middle of the 20th Century, for the last 50 years it has been firmly embedded in both theory and practice in German legal and political culture.

The citizen's claim to justice finds reflection in several provisions of the modern German Constitution. For instance, Article 97 of the Constitution guarantees the independence of all German judges. Article 101 gives every citizen a right to a "lawful judge" (*gesetzlicher Richter*), whose jurisdiction, powers and case assignments are prescribed by law of general applicability. The "right to be heard" (*rechtliches Gehör*), encompassing several aspects of procedural fairness, is guaranteed by Article 103.

More general provisions of the Constitution have been applied to vouchsafe and reinforce the German citizen's right to justice. For instance, the basic guarantee that "All persons are equal before the law" (*Alle Menschen sind vor dem Gesetz gleich*) set forth in Article 3 of the Constitution has been interpreted to require that parties have equal chances (*Waffengleichheit*) in civil proceedings, including access to legal aid where necessary. Even the basic principle that litigation is under the control of the parties (*Dispositionsmaxime*) finds support in Article 2 of the Constitution, which guarantees citizens the maximum scope of personal freedom consistent with an ordered society.

The Federal Constitutional Court has been vigilant in applying constitutional norms to civil litigation. Its case law, frequently the result of constitutional appeals by individual litigants, has interpreted the general clauses of the Constitution to require a "fair proceeding" in both criminal and civil litigation. Many other constitutional provisions have been interpreted to apply to civil proceedings. In a few extreme cases the Federal Constitutional Court has even set aside manifestly wrong decisions of civil courts as denials of a party's right to a competent and independent judge.

B. The German Civil Justice Establishment

Germany dispenses civil justice through a substantial establishment of courts backed up by a state and federal ministries of justice and a well educated and organized bar. Germans are somewhat litigious and readily resort to their lawyers and courts in order to seek vindication of their rights and interests. Generally the system is able to meet the needs of citizens for determination of their civil disputes in a prompt and efficient manner.

1. The Courts

The heart of the German system of civil justice is composed of the five systems of state and federal courts which hear and decide civil and administrative cases. In each system the courts of first instance and the lower tiers of appellate courts are maintained by the respective German states (*Länder*). The five Supreme Courts as well as the Federal Constitutional Court are organs of the German federal judicial branch.

Four of the five court systems are specialized systems for defined kinds of cases. The system of state Labor Courts (*Arbeitsgerichte*) and the Federal Supreme Labor Court have jurisdiction over cases involving collective bargaining and all aspects of the employment relationship. The various state Administrative Courts (*Verwaltungsgerichte*) and the Federal Supreme Administrative Court hear and decide all matters involving the correctness of administrative decisions and administrative action including non-monetary claims against the state for wrongful administrative action. The state Tax Courts (*Finanzgerichte*) and the Federal Supreme Tax Court exercise jurisdiction over all issues and disputes relating to state and federal taxation. Social welfare and insurance claims are heard by the state Social Welfare Courts (*Sozialgerichte*) with appeals to the Federal Supreme Social Welfare Court.

The fifth and largest system of state and federal courts is the so-called "ordinary" (*ordentliche*) court system, which has jurisdiction over all civil and criminal matters not confided to the jurisdiction of one of the specialized systems. This system exists in three tiers within each German state with final review appeal to the Federal Supreme Court in Karlsruhe.

The numerous local courts (*Amtsgerichte*) in each state form the base of the justice pyramid. These courts exercise jurisdiction over money claims of less than 5000 Euro and an exclusive jurisdiction in family law cases and in residential landlord-tenant matters. The local courts also exercise non-contentious functions such as maintenance of real estate and business registries, probate of decedents estates, garnishment, execution sales and appellate review of executions of judgments of all courts. The local courts sit as single professional judges. Parties may appear in these courts *pro se* and do so in about one-third of the cases heard.

The first-instance courts of general jurisdiction for most civil matters are the state district courts (*Landgerichte*). They hear all cases not specially confided to the local courts' jurisdiction. They also exercise a second-instance appellate jurisdiction over non-family cases originally brought in the local courts.

While the state district courts have traditionally sat as three-judge panels, as a result of recent reforms a large proportion of first instance proceedings and some appeals now take place before single judges. Representation by counsel is required in all district court civil proceedings.

Each German state has at least one state appeals court which hears second instance appeals (*Berufungen*) from decisions of the state district courts and of the local courts in family law matters. These courts generally sit in three judge panels and parties must be represented by counsel.

Second instance appellate decisions of the state appeals courts (and the state district courts on local court appeals) are subject to discretionary review appeal (*Revision*) to the Federal Supreme Court on issues of law or procedure only. Although this court sits in several senates, the number of cases appealed greatly exceeds the capacity of the court to entertain them. Currently review appeals to the Federal Supreme Court require permission of the court whose decision is being appealed or of a panel of the Federal Supreme Court based on the difficulty and general significance of the issue being appealed.

Court fees for civil cases at all levels of the system are prescribed by a detailed federal statute based on the amount in controversy and the stage to which the matter progresses. Depending on the amount in controversy court costs can be substantial. As is the case with attorneys fees, the losing party is required to pay all court costs regardless of which party originally incurred them.

2. The Judges

Germany boasts a numerous, well educated and highly professional state and federal judiciary. All courts are staffed by trained, full time, professional judges. In fact Germany has more professional judges per capita than any other state of today's world.

Judicial service is a highly respected form of public service in Germany. Judges are adequately but by no means excessively compensated. Judicial independence, guaranteed by the Federal Constitution, is maintained by laws and traditions insulating judges from political, economic and other extraneous pressures or influences.

Every person who seeks to become a judge must have a full university education in law of at least seven semesters duration, usually lasting somewhat longer. The university education culminates in a statewide "first state examination" (*erstes Staatsexamen*) given semi-annually in each German state and designed to assess basic knowledge of the law and its theoretical application to hypothetical cases. The next stage is a two-year period of practical training (*Referendariat*) consisting of successive internships in state and federal courts, private law offices, state's attorneys' offices, federal or state administrative agencies and an elective internship in some other foreign or domestic organ of public or private law or the legal profession. This period of practical training is followed by a second state examination which focuses more on practical legal applications. The overall educational program is built around the ideal of developing the "complete jurist" (*Volljurist*) who can thereafter fill any of the various justice roles of judge, public attorney, private attorney or even legal academic.

Judges generally commence judicial service immediately following completion of their practical training and second state examination. Judges of the various state courts are typically appointed by the ministries of justice in the various states upon recommendation of or subject to confirmation by selection committees involving elements of the state parliaments or judiciary. The selection process for new judges is generally competitive resulting in candidates of higher than average academic attainment. Probationary judges are typically assigned to collegial first instance courts where they can learn by observation of their more senior colleagues. Judicial appointees are also usually expected to serve for one or two years as a state's attorney early in their careers. After three years of satisfactory service judges obtain a kind of judicial tenure and are subject to removal or demotion only upon demonstrated serious misconduct confirmed by court decision.

Promotion to higher judicial positions within the state systems and to the benches of most of the Federal courts is based on seniority and demonstrated meritorious service. State court judges are generally selected for promotion by mechanisms combining elements of the state legislative, executive and judicial branches. Most federal judges are elected by a special committee composed of members of the Federal Parliament and state ministers with advice of the appropriate Federal Ministry. There is a special parliamentary selection process for judges of the Federal Constitutional Court. Although political considerations play a role in appointment to the federal courts, they are not as important within the state systems. Judges are not permitted to hold any other office or render legal services for private parties.[2]

There are no juries within the German civil justice system. Some tribunals of the administrative courts, the social welfare courts and the labor courts have lay members who sit on panels with professional judges. Each state district court system includes commercial panels (*Handelskammer*) which hear business and commercial matters. These commercial panels include honorary lay

2. Exceptions are that German law professors may serve as part time judges, usually on state appeals courts, and that judges may serve as neutral arbitrators in private arbitrations with the permission of their state ministries of justice.

judges (*ehrenamtliche Richter*) who bring specialized business and commercial expertise to the deliberations of these courts.

German courts are staffed with a number of other justice functionaries including magistrates (*Rechtspfleger*) who handle subsidiary matters and less contentious jurisdiction, court clerks (*Urkundsbeamter*) who manage court filings and records, and court executors (*Gerichtsvollzieher*) who attend to civil executions. In general court facilities are modern, adequately outfitted with information technology, and accessible to the litigants and public. Most plenary court hearings are open to the public. Litigation files and case records (*Akte*) are subject to inspection and copying by the court, the parties and their lawyers and by other persons (such as academics) who can demonstrate a legitimate special interest in seeing them.

Although not strictly part of the civil justice system, the German Federal Constitutional Court (*Bundesverfassungsgericht*) plays a sometimes important role in German civil justice. When the constitutionality of a German statute becomes a decisive issue in civil litigation other German courts are as a matter of principle required to refer the constitutional issue to the Federal Constitutional Court for its ruling. The Constitutional Court also exercises a kind of appellate jurisdiction over the decisions of other German courts on constitutional issues. This jurisdiction may be invoked by individual civil litigants via constitutional appeal (*Verfassungsbeschwerde*).

In recent years the growing integration of the European Union has resulted in an increased role of the European Court of Justice in the civil justice systems of the Member States. Decisive questions of European law which arise in cases before the highest courts of the EU member states must be referred for decision by the European Court of Justice. Occasionally a civil matter in Germany may involve human rights in a way that the jurisdiction of the European Court on Human Rights in Strasbourg might be invoked to, in effect, review the result reached in Germany.

3. The Lawyers

Lawyers play important roles in all aspects of civil justice in Germany. They advise their clients as to likely merits of their legal claims and defenses. They formulate claims and defenses and organize and designate evidence in pleadings and oral presentations to the court. They argue issues of law and fact at all stages of the proceedings, orally and in writing. They are the partisan strategists, tacticians, and foot-soldiers of litigation. Although German civil justice is sometimes described as "judge-led", in reality German lawyers are largely responsible for the quality and energy of German litigation in court.

German lawyers are educated in the same manner as German judges according to the model of the complete jurist. This high standard of education results in a high level of quality in German legal discourse. A lawyer can be admitted to the bar of a German court following successful completion of the second state examination. Once admitted to the bar of any German state court, a lawyer may appear before any German state first-instance or appellate tribunal. Recent legislation implementing European Union directives has expanded the ability of lawyers from other EU nations to practice in German state courts. The German Federal Supreme Court is the only German court that now has an exclusive bar, which consists of a relative handful of distinguished appellate specialists who confine their practices to matters before that court.

German lawyers practice as solo practitioners and in large and small firms in every city and locality in Germany. Local bar associations in all state appeals court districts have roles in lawyer regulation and discipline as well as continuing legal education and law reform. There are also voluntary bar associations which promote the interests of lawyers in general as well as the interests of specialized segments of the bar.

German lawyers handling litigated matters are entitled to compensation from their clients in accord with a statutory schedule of fees based on the amount in controversy and the stage to which the litigation has progressed. Cases involving larger amounts in controversy bear larger statutory fees. The official table of fees is not based on any kind of hourly rate and does not directly reflect the time expended by the lawyer in handling any particular aspect of the case. Contingency and pure conditional fees are also not permitted.

Although lawyers are free to contract with their clients for compensation in excess of the statutory schedule, in practice this seldom occurs in litigated matters. One reason is that in most cases the loser is required to reimburse the winner of litigation for court costs and attorneys fees as computed according to the official schedule. The principle of "loser pays" is so well ingrained in the German legal culture that few clients are willing to incur fees greater than would be reimbursed if they won their suits. One result of this compensation arrangement is that cases with moderate amounts in controversy may not generate fees sufficient to support a great deal of lawyer activity and may be handled somewhat perfunctorily. Potential liability for or ability to recover court costs and attorneys fees is a significant consideration in litigation strategy and case handling.

Germany has made a significant commitment to effectuate all its citizens' claims to justice by providing civil legal aid (*Prozesskostenhilfe*) at all levels of its court systems. Indigent litigants can apply to the courts for legal aid in order to file or defend civil litigation. If the court finds financial need according to a statutory formula and is of the view that the applicant's position in the litigation is not frivolous, legal aid is granted and the state pays the court costs and attorneys fees of the litigant's counsel, albeit at a slightly reduced rate. Legal aid does not, however, cover reimbursement of the costs of a prevailing opposing party.

In recent years the amount expended in Germany for legal aid in proportion to its population has been second only to the corresponding amount expended in Great Britain and well in excess of the per capita expenditure in the United States. Many Germans are able to minimize their exposures to court costs and attorneys fees by purchasing legal cost insurance to defray these expenditures regardless of who wins. The German system of statutory lump sum fees based on amount in controversy appears to make it possible for insurers to gauge their risks and offer coverage at reasonable rates.

C. Overview of Civil Proceedings

The central figure in German civil procedure is the judge. This is not because German civil procedure is in any way "inquisitorial". A basic principle of German civil procedure law is party control of litigation (*Dispositionsmaxime*). However, under German law the judge bears the responsibility of properly deciding the issues of fact or law presented by the claims asserted and facts alleged by the parties and of guiding the course of proceedings taken to resolve them. German civil procedure is designed to facilitate the performance of this judicial task.

This having been said, German civil litigation is fundamentally adversarial and party driven. It is the parties and their counsel who define the scope of litigation by the claims of the pleadings and by their designation of the expected sources of evidence to sustain or refute those claims. These claims and designated factual material define the scope of action for the court. While the parties may and do argue the applicability of specific provisions and doctrines of law to the claims and facts pled, they are not required to do so. German civil procedure operates under the principle that the judge is presumed to know the law and can decide the claims asserted by applying the correct legal rule to the facts alleged and proof proffered by the parties.

German civil procedure is regulated by the Civil Procedure Code, a federal statute. Courts do not have the authority to adopt general procedural rules.

Most civil cases can be said to consist of two phases, the pleading and preparatory phase and the plenary and evidentiary phase. In recent years there has been a tendency to try to reduce the number of hearings and concentrate plenary and evidentiary proceedings into a single main hearing.

1. The Pleading and Preparatory Phase of a Civil Case

In most cases a civil proceeding is commenced by filing a written complaint (*Klage*) with the first-instance court having subject matter jurisdiction and venue over the claims to be presented. The complaint must set forth with specificity the plaintiff's claims for relief as well as the facts and anticipated sources of evidence on which the plaintiff bases those claims. Frequently the complaint will attach relevant documents, photographs and other portable evidence in support of facts alleged.

The judge to which the case is assigned conducts a preliminary review of the complaint promptly after filing in order to check on legal prerequisites to suit (*Prozessvoraussetzungen*) such as proper jurisdiction, venue, capacity to sue and be sued, and the like. If one of these is plainly lacking, the complaint may be returned to the plaintiff with a suggestion that the defect be corrected.[3] Otherwise, the complaint is sent for service on the defendant. German law permits service by several methods calculated to give the person sued actual and timely notice of the suit so as to enable him to defend it. Fictitious service is not favored because of the risk of offending the constitutional right to be heard.

As part of the initial review of the complaint, the judge usually tentatively decides whether the case will be prepared for disposition by a discussion at a preliminary hearing (*früher erster Termin*) or by filing and exchange of written pleadings and briefs (*schriftliches Vorverfahren*). Although formerly a preliminary hearing was the norm, currently many rather routine cases are ordered prepared by written submissions. In the state district court the initial review also includes a determination of whether the case will be assigned to a single judge for further proceedings and disposition or whether it is the kind of case that must be heard by a three-judge panel.

If the case is to be prepared in writing, the defendant is required to file a notice of intent to defend within a specified time of service of the complaint and accompanying papers on him and an answer (*Klageerwiderung*) to the complaint within a further time interval. The answer must assert a right to dismissal of the complaint and may also assert set-offs and counterclaims. As is the case with the complaint, the answer is supposed to set forth the relevant facts with specificity and may incorporate or attach cited evidence. Either be-

---

3. Such a suggestion would fall within the duty of the court to provide the parties and their counsel with "hints and feedback" (*Hinweise*) to facilitate the presentation of the issues and prevent unfair surprise or other injustice.

fore or after reviewing the answer the court can require the parties to file additional written pleadings or briefs which address and clarify designated issues of fact, law, asserted claims or evidence.

If the case is to be prepared by a preliminary hearing, the court sets a time for the hearing. The court may also require the defendant to file an answer within a further specified interval. The parties and their counsel are summoned to the hearing, which often takes place in the assigned judge's chambers. At the hearing the judge discusses the issues raised by the complaint (and answer if it has already been filed) with the parties and their counsel.

The court can also require that the parties or even third parties produce documentary evidence or allow inspection of things at any stage of the written or oral preparatory proceeding.[4] The aim is to streamline the case and narrow the issues of fact and law so that the case can be disposed of at a single plenary hearing. In some cases the facts or law are such that the case can be disposed of at the preliminary hearing.

If the defendant fails to file a statement of intent to defend or if either party fails to attend a scheduled hearing, a default judgment may be entered dismissing claims raised by the defaulting party or granting relief requested by the opponent without further *ex parte* proceeding. Default judgments in Germany may usually be set aside by the simple filing of an "objection" (*Einspruch*) requesting that the default judgment be lifted so as to permit a defense on the merits. If the default judgment is set aside, the case proceeds as if the default had never been entered, except that the defaulting party must pay the costs occasioned by the default. On the other hand, a second default judgment after one has already been set aside is usually final. If a party fails to file an answer or other requested pleading, or fails to provide clarification of its position when requested by the court, that party may be precluded from later asserting any claims or defenses that could have been disclosed in such pleading or clarification.

German judges have long been under a statutory obligation to facilitate and promote settlement. This duty has recently been reinforced by a requirement that in virtually all civil cases a settlement conference with parties and lawyers must take place before the commencement of plenary proceedings. The German judge's familiarity with the parties' respective contentions and factual and legal proffers enables her to take a relatively creative role in settlement discussions. It is quite common for a judge to propose a particular settlement based on her then view of the case. If a settlement is documented with the court, it has the same effect as a judgment with respect to the availability of

4. The enlarged authority of the court to order production of documents and inspections by third parties is the result of very recent reforms in German civil procedure.

execution. In most cases the settlement agreement provides for the allocation of court costs and attorneys fees among the parties. Otherwise court costs and attorneys fees in settled cases are "suspended" (*aufgehoben*), which means that each party bears its own attorneys fees and court costs are split equally.

2. Plenary Proceedings and Reception of Evidence

German civil proceedings are in a sense continuous in that there are no precisely defined boundaries between preliminary, evidentiary and plenary proceedings. Discussion of the parties' respective claims and the facts and law relating to those claims takes place at all stages of the case. Facts and evidence, whether asserted in and attached to pleadings or independently received, may come in at almost any time, provided that parties are expected to assert facts and designate evidence in good faith and in a manner so as not to delay the proceedings. The court can decline to consider late proffers of proof resulting from negligence or bad faith. Cases can be disposed of at any stage of the litigation.

On the other hand, the trend in recent years has been to concentrate the plenary argument and the evidentiary parts of the proceedings, if possible, to a single main hearing (*Konzentrationsmaxime*). This assumes that there has been sufficient clarification and narrowing of the issues in the preparatory stage so that the remaining issues can be dealt with in a single court session.

Ordinarily both parties and their counsel will attend the plenary hearing. The judge starts out by orally outlining the status of the proceeding and the issues to be addressed. She then addresses the parties, who are asked to state their positions and views on the issues. This direct interaction of judge and parties at this and other stages of the litigation guarantees the parties their right literally "to be heard" by the judge who will decide their case.

If there are material facts remaining in dispute at the plenary stage, the court will likely hear the evidence which the parties have designated with respect to any factual issues. Within the scope of the factual assertions by the parties the court has the power to order production of relevant documents and tangible things on its own motion. However when it comes to live testimony the court is restricted to witnesses named by at least one of the parties. The court can also examine the parties themselves at the request of the opposing parties or on the court's own motion. If it is inconvenient to hear the proof at the plenary hearing, a separate hearing for the reception of evidence (*Beweisaufnahme*) can be scheduled for this purpose.

There are no rules restricting the admission of particular kinds of evidence, which is generally subject to "free evaluation" (*freie Beweiswürdigung*) by the court. The court may receive relevant evidence in the form of inspection of persons, places and things, witness testimony, documentary evidence, expert testimony and the statements or examination of parties. The court may give this evidence such weight as good sense and experience would suggest is appropriate. Certain witnesses and kinds of information are protected from compelled testimony by statutory privileges.

Initial examination of witnesses is by the judge, or the presiding judge in a three-judge court. Witnesses are first asked to make their contributions in their own words. Follow-up questions focus on particular facts and issues. Strongly suggestive questioning like Anglo-American cross examination is hardly ever used. Nor do lawyers intensively prepare third-party witnesses before they appear in court lest the court draw a negative inference about the credibility of the witness's testimony from the fact of such preparation. Parties are not considered witnesses. The results of a formal "party examination" (*Parteivernehmung*) by the court is considered as proof only if other more neutral proof is unavailable or insufficient.

After the judge's initial questioning the parties' lawyers (and sometimes the parties) can ask their own questions to address facts or areas omitted or left unclear by the witness's initial statement or the judge's questioning. The substance of the witness's testimony is summarized by the court in minutes of the hearing (*Protokoll*) which become a part of the case record (*Akte*). Lawyers and parties may suggest revisions or additions to the version dictated by the judge.

If there is a dispute of fact outside the everyday experience of the participants in the litigation the issue will generally be referred to a court-appointed expert witness (*Sachverständige*). The order of referral will request the expert's opinion based on facts disclosed or to be ascertained by the expert. In most cases the expert will file a written report of his investigation (*Gutachten*) which will be reviewed by the parties and by the court. If there is any issue about the expert's conclusion, the expert is subject to oral examination at an evidentiary hearing. Parties may also call expert witnesses of their own. Such experts may cause the court to doubt a contrary opinion of the court-appointed expert, which usually leads to the appointment of another court-appointed expert rather than a reliance on the party expert's findings. The costs of court-appointed experts are treated like other litigation costs and are ultimately borne by the losing party.

The plenary proceeding is also the occasion for oral argument by the parties and their lawyers on the factual and legal issues raised by the case. The court is not supposed to surprise the parties by an unexpected judgment. It is thus common for the court to indicate to the parties its tentative judgment on the issues of the case so that they can attempt to disabuse the court of any misapprehensions of fact or law or correct mis-impressions from the evidence. The court's duty to give hints and feedback requires it to allow the parties to comment on the inferences that the court should draw from any evidence received.

Once all issues of fact and law necessary to reach a decision have been addressed in plenary proceedings, the matter is ripe for decision. Some cases are decided shortly after the conclusion of the plenary hearing. Collegial courts reach their decisions by majority vote after deliberations in chambers. All judges are required to sign the majority decision. In the ordinary civil courts there are no published dissents.

The oral tradition of German civil justice survives in the form of oral rendition of most judgments usually at a special hearing called thereafter for that purpose. The written judgment, including an opinion justifying the decision (*Begründung*) is filed at the time of or shortly after the oral rendition. German judgment creditors have a variety of execution remedies with which to enforce their judgments.

3. Appeals

German civil justice has traditionally been known for the number and intricacy of its appellate remedies. Recently there has been some attempt to simplify and reduce the number of second instance and review appeals.

Virtually all litigants have a right to one second instance appeal (*Berufung*) from a judgment of a first instance court. In a sense, a second instance appeal is considered as a continuation of the first instance proceeding rather than as a totally separate review proceeding. The record of proceedings, which is forwarded from the first instance court, is cumulative rather than discrete. The second instance court may permit the assertion of new facts not asserted below. It has the right to rehear evidence submitted below and can receive evidence that was not proffered at all during the first instance proceeding. Recent reforms have restricted second instance offers of additional facts and evidence if the failure to offer them at the first instance was the result of intentional act or neglect of the moving party. The second instance court is free to disregard the fact findings of the first instance court and reach its own view of the facts as well as its own conclusions of law.

While such a broad scope of second instance appeal may seem unnecessarily redundant, the availability of the remedy permits German courts to reach first instance decisions rapidly and economically. In most cases the litigants will be satisfied with the first instance results. Those litigants for whom the first instance decision is not palatable will have the right to a more thoroughgoing examination at the second instance. Overall such a system may provide greater justice at lower cost than one which provides in every case a more thorough fact examination in the first instance and little or no review of facts on appeal.

A second instance appeal is initiated by filing a notice of appeal with the court to which the appeal is taken. The case record is then forwarded to the appellate court and the case proceeds there in a manner very similar to a first-instance proceeding. The difference is that the second instance court will already have the evidence and record of testimony of the first instance proceeding on which it can rely if it chooses to do so. However if a party can convince the court that justice requires a rehearing of a witness or consideration of additional evidence not considered below, the appellate court is entitled to do so.

Certain interlocutory orders and final decisions other than judgments are subject to miscellaneous appeal (*Beschwerde*). In most cases new facts may be adduced and old facts may be revisited as is the case with the second instance appeal.

Appellate remedies beyond the second instance appeal are limited to review appeals (*Revision* and *Rechtsbeschwerde*) to the Federal Supreme Court. Review appeals may raise only issues of law or of correct procedure. Most facts are taken as established by the findings of the second instance appellate court. If the second instance court agrees to permit a review appeal, or if the Federal Supreme Court decides itself to accept the appeal, the record of the case is forwarded from the second instance court. Preparation for oral plenary proceedings in the Federal Supreme Court is generally by filing and exchange of written briefs arguing the points of law or procedure raised. A preliminary hearing is scheduled only in a rare case. Oral argument before a five judge panel from a senate of the Federal Supreme Court by the specialist attorneys partakes of the flavor of academic discussion as the points are analyzed in dignified exchanges between court and counsel.

Judgments and court orders issued by a court of last instance (frequently a Federal Supreme Court) which are alleged to violate the provisions of the Federal Constitution may be subject to constitutional appeal (*Verfassungsbeschwerde*) to the Federal Constitutional Court. Such appeals are subject to an acceptance proceeding which can result in a summary grant or denial by a three-judge panel of the court. The relatively few appeals which are accepted for plenary disposition are argued to one of the two senates of the Constitutional Court, which may vacate or amend the judgment entered below to the extent required by the Federal Constitution.

German courts may refer decisive issues of European law to the European Court of Justice. Parties who allege violations of the European Convention on Human Rights may also apply to the European Court on Human Rights in

Strasbourg for a declaratory judgment, which may initiate the alteration of a judgment of a national court or even an award of damages.

4. Special Proceedings

The German civil justice system provides a number of specialized procedures designed to address different kinds of problems and cases. For instance, the statutory warning procedure (*Mahnprozess*) can be used to get prompt enforcement of claims for the payment of money which are not likely to be in dispute. Using preprinted forms creditors can cause their debtors to be served with warning notices (*Mahnbescheide*) and notices of impending execution (*Vollstreckungsbescheide*) that will ultimately support executions if timely objections are not filed by the debtors. If a debtor contests the claim asserted in such a warning or execution notice the dispute is processed like any civil law suit.

There is a similar simplified procedure for claims based solely on documentary evidence, especially checks (*Urkundenprozess, Scheckprozess*). This permits rapid and economical processing and determination of such cases without oral evidentiary proceedings, while preserving the right to all forms of proof if other forms of evidence become relevant.

In family cases the local courts sometimes relax the principle of party control of litigation (*Dispositionsmaxime*) in favor of seeking results that are best for all impacted persons, including children. Other civil matters within the noncontentious jurisdiction (*freiwillige Gerichtsbarkeit*) of the local courts are often handled under specialized simplified procedures and are frequently decided, at least initially, by magistrates.

Although procedure in the four specialized court systems in general follows that prescribed by the Civil Procedure Code for the ordinary courts, there are many variations designed to adapt procedures to the particular needs of the specialized jurisdiction. For instance, most actions in the labor courts commence with strictly compulsory conciliation sessions (*Güteverhandlung*) conducted by the presiding judges assigned to the cases. These sessions dispose of a high percentage of cases which would otherwise fill the dockets of the labor courts. Many administrative court cases must be preceded by administrative appeals within the agencies whose decisions are being attacked. There is a corresponding provision for cases in the social welfare courts.

Germany has recently reformed its laws governing arbitration generally in accord with the UNCITRAL Model Law on Arbitration. Arbitration of most civil matters, domestic and international, can freely proceed in accord with the requirements of these laws and the resulting award will be enforceable in Germany.

D. Current Performance of German Civil Justice

German civil justice appears to be working well at fulfilling its assigned role of vindicating private legal rights and applying the norms of law to resolve civil disputes. Some have even suggested that it is working too well, namely that its relatively low cost and high efficiency are actually fostering litigation and causing citizens to resort too readily to the courts. It is also debated whether the currently popular legal costs insurance may be contributing to an increase in litigation.

One of the many strengths of the German civil justice system is its relative promptness. For instance, in 1996 some 48% of the 1,737,202 cases filed in local courts were disposed of within 3 months of filing and the average duration of local court cases, from filing to settlement or decision was 4.6 months. In the same year German state district courts disposed of 414, 579 cases, 38.9% within 3 months of filing, 26.5% within 6 months of filing, 21.7% within 12 months of filing and 9.6% within 24 months of filing, for an average pendency of 6.5 months. Appeals to the state appeals courts in 1996 averaged 5.3 months in duration.[5] These statistics have continued to obtain since then.

It also appears that the German system offers parties access to justice at relatively modest cost. The division of labor between judge and lawyers and the effect of the statutory fee schedule and fee shifting regime combine to moderate the parties' overall costs to conduct litigation in German courts. For example, a simple personal injury case resulting in a first-instance judgment of a German state district court awarding 50,000 Euro to the successful plaintiff would generate statutory attorneys fees of some 3,138 Euro for representation of each party, or a total for both parties of about 13% of the amount in controversy. By way of comparison, in most American jurisdictions contingent compensation of the plaintiff's counsel alone would be at least a third of the amount recovered. Hourly billings of defense counsel could easily reach a similar amount, making a total cost for services of counsel of about two thirds of the amount recovered. The German cost advantage in counsel fees appears to be offset only to a slight degree by higher court costs payable under the German system.[6]

---

5. See Gottwald, "Civil Justice Reform: Access, Cost, and Expedition. The German Perspective", in: Zuckerman (ed.), *Civil Justice in Crisis* (Oxford 1999) 207, 211–213.

6. For an effort to make a comparison of relative costs and efforts expended in German and American civil litigation by analysis of simulated case presentations see Murray, "A Comparative Law Experiment," 8 *Indiana International and Comparative Law Review* 231 (1998).

The apparent efficiency and economy of German civil justice may be a result of a system that assigns the various functions involved in the presentation and disposition of a civil law suit to the participants most able to perform those functions in an efficient and economical manner. For instance, the principle of party control of litigation (*Dispositionsmaxime*) assigns the parties, who know more about their own interests than anyone else, the responsibility for defining the scope of the litigation by formulating their claims for relief, and gives them the power to commence and stop litigation more or less at will. On the other hand, once the litigation is commenced, the court, which must decide the case, is given considerable authority to focus the participants' attention and energy on the key issues and to shape the proceeding to a prompt and efficient disposition.

The parties, who are most familiar with the real-life circumstances of their dispute, are expected to make factual contentions and point to the sources of evidence to sustain those contentions. On the other hand, the judge, who must determine the relevant facts in court, generally asks the first round of questions and has the right to ask for those documents, reports and records that he thinks are most pertinent to reach a decision.

These functional assignments correspond to systemic allocations of resources to perform these respective functions. Statutory regulation of lawyers' fees tends to keep overall fees low and requires counsel to concentrate their efforts on those aspects of the proceedings where their inputs can make the most difference. On the other hand, Germany is more generous with the provision of judicial resources than any other modern state. The large number of German judges represents an investment of public resources in the neutral decision makers in litigation. The judges have enough time per case to perform those case-analysis, steering and focusing functions most efficiently assigned to the person who will have to make the decision. It is not necessary to require the parties to address these functions inefficiently because of excessive case loads or a lack of judicial person-power.

This division of the work does not result in loss of party autonomy or contact with justice. A well educated independent judiciary supported by a large and prosperous private bar provide the best conditions under which adversarial civil justice can flourish. The large number of cases brought, presented, processed and decided each year in the various German courts speaks for the readiness with which Germans resort to their courts and the relish with which they litigate.

A feature of German civil justice worthy of further mention is the degree of direct interaction between judges and litigating parties which takes place at all stages of litigation. Parties are summoned to every important preliminary and plenary hearing. Judges speak directly with the parties both in the course of formal "hearing of the parties" (*Anhörung der Parteien*) at the outset of plenary proceedings and whenever it occurs to them (or sometimes to one of the parties themselves) at other points in a hearing or conference. In fact plenary proceedings in the local courts, the state district courts, and sometimes even the state appeals courts often more resemble four or five-way discussions among judge, counsel and parties than stylized presentations by opposing professional advocates.

From the standpoint of the parties this opportunity to interact directly with their judges tends to demystify justice and insure that they are in fact heard. In some respects this direct effectuation of the constitutional right to be heard may be one of the most important reasons why German civil justice enjoys wide public confidence and acceptance among the German people.

This does not mean that German civil justice does not have its limitations. The complementary assignment of responsibilities and roles among court and counsel described above results in rapid and efficient disposition of the great bulk of ordinary civil disputes. However this model may not suffice for larger and more complex cases which require investigation and analysis of complicated and relatively inaccessible fact material. Although larger amounts in controversy in such cases support somewhat more activity on the part of counsel, the statutory fee schedule can be a subtle limiting factor. And it is hard to expect that the publicly paid judge or judges will always have the time or incentive to dig into really difficult and recondite fact material to the extent needed to reach a really good decision. Some judges might tend to seek an "easy way out" of such cases. More purely partisan civil justice systems such as the American system might provide more thorough and objectively accurate resolutions of such complex cases, albeit at considerably higher overall cost.

The German system's strength within the realm of its intended activity, vindicating individual rights under existing law, may also not readily extend to cases which press the limits of the law and involve confrontations between major elements of the social economy. The effective limitations on lawyer compensation, the unavailability of a mechanism for collective litigation in most cases, and the relatively conservative culture of the career judiciary combine to discourage private litigation which may challenge the social or economic order. Issues of product safety, environmental pollution, discrimination, and professional negligence which affect large groups of potential claimants generally are addressed in Germany in legislative fora and to some extent in the administrative courts. Recently the Federal Constitutional Court and to some degree the Federal Supreme Court have played active and sometimes revolutionary roles in addressing some of these issues.

Finally, Germany's "loser pays" rule for costs and attorneys fees is designed to discourage frivolous litigation as well as provide full compensation to the party whose rights are vindicated. There may be some question whether this rule may also tend to deter some risk-averse litigants of moderate means from instituting potentially meritorious claims out of fear of the consequences of an adverse result. This effect may be mitigated to some extent by the availability of legal costs insurance.

The bottom line is that most Germans appear to be well satisfied, and even proud of the performance of German civil justice. Complaints about "litigation explosions," unpredictable and extreme verdicts, or excessive costs and delay of litigation so common in many modern societies are comparatively rare in Germany. Regardless of one's national background or legal perspective, the German system of civil justice is worth careful study and analysis. Comparative insights gained from such study can inform debate and reform in the context of almost any civil justice environment.

CHAPTER 2

History and Development of German Civil Justice

Germany has long known civil justice processes designed to enable private parties to seek law-based recourse against other private parties for vindication of harms suffered or enforcement of obligations. Over the centuries since Roman administrators built temples and baths in Cologne and Trier various forms of civil justice systems have developed, matured, and in turn have been reformed or supplanted in the territory now comprising the modern German state. The richness and continuity of this tradition of civil justice have contributed significantly to the institutions of civil justice as they are practiced in Germany today. Understanding of these modern institutions and how they work can be aided by some impression of where they came from and how they came to assume their present form. Without dwelling on the past, a brief glimpse of the background of German civil justice, may at least place German civil justice of today in some historical perspective.[1]

A. Germanic Civil Justice

German civil justice has its origins in the practices of the Germanic tribes which in late Roman times[2] inhabited the portions of western and central Europe encompassed by the borders of modern Germany. Germanic tribal society knew a process whereby a person injured through the wrongful act of another could appeal to the community for judgment of vindication. The injured party summoned the alleged wrongdoer before the assembled lord and "hun-

1. For a more complete history of German civil justice, see van Caeneghem, "History of European Civil Procedure", in: Cappelletti (ed.), *International Encyclopedia of Comparative Law*, Vol XVI, Ch. 2, pp. 55 ff.

2. Approximately 300–500 AD.

dred" (*Hundertschaft*),[3] the complaint was stated orally in prescribed form, and the answer followed in like form. If the facts were known and not disputed, the assembled community would then give judgment, which would usually be executed by the injured party. Such a process was in lieu of the injured party taking the law into his or her own hands even to the extent of waging war upon the opponent.

If there was a dispute of fact, the community would order that proof be had (proof judgment)[4] and declare the consequences if the facts be proved as alleged. Proof would be supplied by the parties. Conflicts in proof would be decided by party oath (*Rechtseid*) supported by "oath helpers" (*Eidhelfer*), or in some cases by "God's judgment" (*Gottesurteil*) through ordeal.

In later times judgment by the entire community yielded to proceedings before smaller groups of "judgment finders" (*Urteilsfinder*) or "law creators" (*Rechtschöpfer*, later *Schöffen*).[5] The role of the lord as presiding officer was formalistic and minor. The use of written documents and proof by witness developed only later. Oath and counter-oath made up the basis of the Germanic trial.

B. The Reception of Roman and Canon Law

Parts of Germany had known Roman law during centuries of Roman administration. In contrast to early Germanic civil justice, the later forms of Roman civil justice featured codified substantive and procedural law, prescribed forms of action, preparatory proceedings before a magistrate, followed, if necessary, by decision by a judge (*iudex*), and execution by a public official. Traces of Roman law and civil procedure remained in these areas even after the fall of Rome in the fifth century.

From the time of the fall of Rome to the Reformation the Church continued to develop a system of canon law which regulated many aspects of secular life such as marriage, family relationships and inheritance. This law was applied by canonical courts[6] which adopted both procedural and substantive

---

3. An ancient form of community organization among Germanic tribes; for the early Germanic procedure see Millar, *Civil Procedure of the Trial Court in Historical Perspective* (1952), pp. 12 ff.

4. Probably the earliest form of the "proof order" (*Beweisbeschluss*) in modern German procedure. See Ch. 8(C)(1) below.

5. Still the term used to refer to lay participants in criminal adjudication.

6. For the Romano-Canonical Procedure see van Caeneghem, in: *International Encyclopedia of Comparative Law*, Vol. XVI, Ch. 2, pp. 16 ff.

doctrine from both Roman law and the pre-existing Germanic customs. Civil proceedings before the canonical courts were largely conducted in writing. The court decided whether proof was necessary, and if so, ordered it. Proof was had by individual examination of witnesses rather than ordeals. The oath continued to play an important role. The factual and legal issues of a case were heard in logical sequence (*Reihenfolgeprinzip*), which led to prolonged proceedings with multiple hearings.

C. The Common German Civil Procedure

The widespread reception of Roman Law in Europe during the 13th–15th Centuries[7] brought a fusion of pre-existing Germanic civil justice and the Roman and canonical traditions into what became known as the "common German civil procedure" (*gemeine deutsche Zivilprozess*) of the Middle Ages and Renaissance. Compared to other European countries, adoption of Roman Law was rather late and slow in Germany.[8] One of the driving forces was the impact of academic legal education, which began with the foundation of the first universities in the second half of the fourteenth century. Despite these innovations in legal education, the German system of civil justice was dominated by the old Germanic system of oral proceeding before "law-finders" throughout the first half of the fifteenth century.

The rise of the modern territorial states led to the foundation of a system of central courts called "Hofgerichte" or "Kammergerichte", in which university educated judges (*Richter*) replaced the former "law-finders" (*Schöffen*). These academic lawyers rejected the traditional procedures and established procedural ordinances that specified the rules for litigating before the various courts. At the head of the new court system was the Imperial Supreme Court (*Reichskammergericht*) sitting in Frankfurt. This court assumed the role of appellate court for appeals from lower courts in many principalities.[9] The rules

---

7. For a discussion of the process by which Roman Law was "rediscovered" in the 11th century in northern Italy and with the aid of the university movement spread through Europe, see, e.g., Stein, *Roman Law in European History* (Cambridge 1999).

8. Van Caeneghem, in: *International Encyclopedia of Comparative Law,* Vol. XVI, Ch. 2, pp. 32 ff.

9. The Saxon Electors (*Kurfürsten*) did not generally acknowledge the jurisdiction of the Imperial Supreme Court, and maintained their own courts and procedure until the late 17th century. See van Caeneghem, in: *International Encyclopedia of Comparative Law,* Vol. XVI, Ch. 1, p. 59. The Saxon procedure required simultaneous assertion of all conceivable claims and defenses, and divided each proceeding into separate stages of assertion (*Sta-*

of procedure applied by this court have been subject to extensive research and are widely regarded as a milestone in the development of the modern system of German civil justice.[10]

German common civil procedure was largely in writing. Elaborate written pleadings were exchanged, and proof was had by examination of witnesses in the presence of the parties. Claims and defenses were considered *seriatim*, with argument and sometimes proof-taking at every stage. This resulted in a very prolonged form of litigation.

Imperial judicial reform in 1654 unified the previous procedural regime of the Imperial Supreme Court with that of the Saxon courts into a form of the German common procedure which endured until the mid-19th Century. Litigation was placed largely under the control of the parties, who structured the issues, asserted those facts they deemed helpful to their claims, and pointed to the sources of proof for the facts.[11] Pleading was in writing. The common German civil procedure took over from Saxon procedure the strict separation of the argument part of the proceeding from the reception of factual proof and also the requirement that parties assert all their claims and defenses at once on pain of preclusion from later assertion (*Eventualmaxime*).[12] Evidence was evaluated based on elaborate rules of proof (*Beweisregeln*), which specified what kind of proof was required to prove certain facts, and what weights could be given to various kinds of evidence. The German common civil procedure also included various forms of default judgment and a developed procedure for review of judgments by different kinds of appeal.

Looking back on the German common civil procedure of the 17th and 18th centuries, it must be acknowledged that for its time and circumstances it embodied notions of judicial fairness, accuracy and efficiency, which continue as

---

dium der Behauptung) and proof (*Stadium des Beweises*). The proof stage was introduced by a "proof judgment" subject to appeal.

10. See Sellert, *Prozessgrundsätze und Stilus Curiae am Reichshofrat im Vergleich mit den gesetzlichen Grundlagen des reichskammergerichtlichen Verfahrens* (1973); Smend, *Reichskammergericht* (1911); Diestelkamp (ed.), *Das Reichskammergericht in der deutschen Geschichte* (1990).

11. See van Caeneghem, in: *International Encyclopedia of Comparative Law*, Vol. XVI, Ch. 2, pp. 55 ff.; Wetzell, *System des ordentlichen Civilprocesses*, 3rd ed. (1878). Although the judges were permitted to direct the proceedings to a degree, the German common civil procedure embodied the principle of party control of litigation (*Verhandungsmaxime*) which remains fundamental to German civil justice today.

12. This principle is at tension with policy considerations favoring addressing claims and defenses in logical sequence in hopes of avoiding the need to address issues not ultimately necessary to decision of the case. See Ch. 7(K)(1) below.

the cornerstones of civil justice today, not only in Germany, but throughout the modern world. However as the 18th Century came to a close and the 19th Century dawned, it had come to be regarded as a cumbersome relic of earlier times. In the words of Goethe describing proceedings in the Imperial Supreme Court in *Poetry and Truth* (*Dichtung und Wahrheit*):

> "An unholy waste of files lay bloated and grew yearly, since the 17 judge-assessors were not at any one time able to keep up with the flow. Twenty thousand cases had heaped up, each year sixty could be disposed of, and double so many came in.... In addition, many abuses hindered the progress of justice."[13]

D. Civil Procedure Codes in the Age of Enlightenment

All over Europe, the Age of Enlightenment[14] brought a trend towards modernization of civil procedure.[15] At the center of the efforts was the idea of rationalizing litigation and making trials more efficient.

Criticism focused on the dominance of written litigation and the requirement that parties assert all their claims and defenses at once on pain of preclusion from later assertion (*Eventualmaxime*). The latter meant that the parties had to present every fact which was in some way connected with the trial.[16] Although these two rules of civil procedure had been regarded as important steps in modernization during the preceding centuries, they were later considered to be unduly cumbersome and obsolete. Another new principle brought by the Enlightenment was the notion that trials should be public, unless specific reasons should otherwise require.

---

13. *"Ein ungeheurer Wust von Akten lag aufgeschwollen und wuchs jährlich, da die siebzehn Assessoren nicht einmal imstande waren, das Laufende wegzuarbeiten. Zwanzigtausend Prozesse hatten sich aufgehäuft, jährlich konnten sechzig abgetan werden, und das Doppelte kam hinzu... Überdies hinderte so mancher Missbrauch den Gerichtsgang."* - Goethe, *Dichtung und Wahrheit*, 3rd part, 12th book, see *Goethes Werke* (Erich Trunz ed.), 13th ed. (1999), Vol. 9, p. 530, mn. 15–21.

14. Chronologically the late 17th and 18th Centuries.

15. Van Caeneghem, in: *International Encyclopedia of Comparative Law*, Vol. XVI, Ch. 2, pp. 87 ff.

16. Van Caeneghem, in: *International Encyclopedia of Comparative Law*, Vol. XVI, Ch. 2, p. 92.

The 18th and early 19th Centuries saw several of the German states enact procedural codes designed to reform and improve the pre-existing common civil procedure. One of the most remarkable examples was the civil procedure law introduced in Prussia under Frederick the Great. The first book of his collection of laws (*Corpus Juris Fridericianum*) was a new law on civil procedure, that reflects the enlightened despotism of his time. In the new law, the role of the judge as the representative of the state was redefined to be consistent with the Prussian concept of enlightened despotism. The judge was given the primary responsibility for the investigation of the facts (*Aufklärung des Sachverhalts*) by virtue of his office (*ex officio*), and the role of the litigating parties was marginalized.

The new law abandoned the principle of party control of litigation and required an "instructing judge" (*instruierender Richter*) to interact directly with the parties to structure the issues of the controversy. The issues were then reported in writing to a three-judge panel, which would then decide whether to receive evidence. All evidence was considered according to statutory rules of proof. Litigating lawyers were abolished and replaced by "justice commissioners" (*Justizkommissare*), state officials who assisted, but did not represent, litigants on a "cab-stand" basis.

This extreme form of judge-led procedure, which may be seen as the prototype as what today is called the 'inquisitorial procedure' did not endure because of lack of public confidence in the practically inquisitorial judge and assisting state officials.[17] Gradually the principle of party control of litigation was reinstated, and oral argument was reintroduced.[18]

The later Prussian procedure codes and 19th century civil procedure codes of other German states[19] show the influence of French civil procedure law. From France, where the *Code de Procédure Civile* had been adopted in 1806, came an extreme form of party control of litigation. The role of the lawyer (*Avocat*) expanded as that of the judge shrank.[20] Preliminary pleadings were

17. For the development of the Prussian civil procedure see Ebel, *200 Jahre preussischer Zivilprozess* (1972). It should be stressed that this extreme form of inquisitorial procedure bears little resemblance to the role of the judge today. The modern German system of civil procedure cannot be fairly characterized as an 'inquisitorial system'.

18. This took place pursuant to Prussian procedural reforms of 1833 and 1846. For an overview see Nörr, *Reinhard und die Revision der Allgemeinen Gerichts-Ordnung für die Preussischen Staaten* (1975).

19. See, e. g., the Bavarian Procedural Code of 1869.

20. See Pigeau, *La Procédure Civile des Tribunaux de France* (1807/1808); van Caeneghem, in: *International Encyclopedia of Comparative Law*, pp. 89 ff.; Rosenberg/Schwab/Gottwald, §4 (V)(2), p. 23. The judicial office was supposed to remain un-

exchanged only among lawyers. Claims could be presented in any order without risk of preclusion. The court became involved only when the parties deemed a claim ripe for decision. Party control of the litigation was somewhat tempered by the authority of the judge to disregard actions that he regarded as irrelevant or delayed.[21] Court sittings were public, and most argumentation by the parties and their lawyers was oral. There was no separate proof order; proof was taken as necessary on the issues to be decided. The *Code de Procédure Civile* was applied for some years in the territories on the left bank of the Rhine, and it was the model for several civil codes adopted in southern German states.[22]

During the course of the 19th Century, many of the German states enacted procedural codes embodying elements of the old common German procedure and procedural doctrine imported from France.[23] The once unitary German common civil procedure splintered into a number of local variations. These can roughly be divided into three groups: First, there were areas where the old system of German common procedure continued to prevail. Second, in Prussia a moderated version of the rules of Frederick the Great was applied. Third, in the territories on the left bank of the Rhine and in southern Germany, civil procedure was influenced by the French *Code de Procédure Civile.*[24]

E. The Unification of German Civil Justice

As Germany moved toward political unification during the latter half of the 19th Century, there was a corresponding movement toward unification of civil procedure law. In 1862 the German Confederation (*Bund*) had established a commission to develop a civil procedure law for the member states. The North German Confederation did the same in 1867. Various proposals based on the Hanoverian, the Prussian, and even the French procedural codes were circu-

---

tainted by participation in the litigation (*Prinzip der Reinerhaltung des richterlichen Amtes*).

21. Stein/Jonas, *Kommentar zur ZPO,* 19th ed. (1972), Vol. I, p. 35.

22. Lüke, in: *Münchner Kommentar zur ZPO,* 2nd ed. (2000), Vol. I, mn. 39.

23. Although comparative law was an active science in the 19th Century, and although German legal scholars were familiar with Anglo-American civil procedure law, there is little reflection of Anglo-American institutions in the various reforms and enactments of that time.

24. For an overview over the prevailing type of civil procedure in the different parts of Germany see van Caeneghem, in: *International Encyclopedia of Comparative Law,* Vol. XVI, Ch. 2, p. 93; Lüke, in: *Münchener Kommentar zur ZPO,* Vol. I, Einleitung, mn. 40.

lated, but none were adopted before the founding of the German Empire in 1871.[25]

The 1870s saw a succession of proposals for a procedural code as the new German Empire consolidated the judicial establishments of the various German states into a nationwide system of civil and criminal justice. An imperial commission published four different draft codes establishing and regulating civil justice throughout the Empire. A Reichstag commission made minor revisions, and the legislation was formally submitted for consideration by the national legislature on December 21, 1876.[26] During 1877 the Reichstag considered and published the Court Organization Law (*Gerichtsverfassungsgesetz*),[27] the Civil Procedure Code (*Zivilprozessordnung*),[28] the Criminal Procedure Code (*Strafprozessordnung*),[29] and Bankruptcy Code (*Konkursordnung*).[30] These new codes were ultimately adopted effective October 1, 1879. As amended from time to time over the years since their original adoption, these basic codes have formed the legal framework of the German civil and criminal justice system to the present day.

The Court Organization Law created a national system of courts for civil and criminal matters consisting of local courts (*Amtsgerichte*), district courts of general jurisdiction (*Landgerichte*), appeals courts (*Oberlandesgerichte*), and the Imperial Supreme Court (*Reichsgericht*) with its seat in Leipzig. The Civil Procedure Code created for the first time in German history a unified procedure for civil cases throughout the Empire. The new code embodied the principles of party control of litigation (*Dispositionsmaxime*) and orality (*Mündlichkeitsprinzip*). Although the new law invested the judge with some responsibility to see that justice was done between the parties in a fair and efficient manner, parties enjoyed great freedom in structuring their cases.

This reform is widely regarded as an expression of 19th century liberalism.[31] Reforms adopted in the following years tended to strengthen state control over civil procedure. Some of these reforms were sustained by the paternalistic idea

25. For a concise summary of these developments see Rosenberg/Schwab/Gottwald, §5(I)(1)–(3), p. 24.

26. For a documentation of the deliberations, see Schubert (ed.), *Entstehung und Quellen der Civilprozessordnung von 1877* (1987), 2 vol.

27. Published January 27, 1877.

28. Published January 30, 1877.

29. Published February 1, 1877.

30. Published February 10, 1877.

31. Stein/Jonas, *Kommentar zur ZPO*, 19th ed. (1972), Vol. I, p. 35; Sellert, "Die Reichsjustizgesetze von 1877 – ein gedenkwürdiges Ereignis?", 17 *JuS* 787 (1977).

that the judge as a representative of the state should guide the litigants. Other reforms were aimed at rationalizing civil procedure by preventing the parties from adopting inappropriate delay strategies.[32]

The core of the the Civil Procedure Code of 1877 has remained in effect to the present day. Despite a great number of changes its original basic principles remain cornerstones of the modern German civil justice system.

Over the years since 1879 there have been various amendments of the Civil Procedure Code. The adoption of the German Civil Code (*Bürgerliches Gesetzbuch*) and the German Commercial Code (*Handelsgesetzbuch*) in 1898 required a number of changes to the Civil Procedure Code to harmonize procedure with the new national substantive law.[33]

In 1924 the "Emminger reform" (*Emminger Novelle*) increased the authority of the judge with some compromise to the principle of party control of litigation. This reform was triggered by galloping monetary inflation at the time, which militated strongly in favor of expeditious proceedings.[34]

F. German Civil Justice in the 20th Century

Although Germany's civil justice system became implicated in the political catastrophes of the 20th century, its institutional structures survived these events outwardly unscathed. The worst of the legal and judicial crimes and abuses of National Socialism took place in the realm of criminal law.[35] Although substantive civil law and civil justice suffered serious and sometimes

---

32. Sellert, 17 *JuS* 787 (1977).

33. For an overview on early reforms Rosenberg/Schwab/Gottwald, §5 (II), p. 25.

34. The Emminger reform was named after the then Minister of Justice and became effective on February 13, 1924. Specific changes were the introduction of the principle favoring concentration of proceedings (*Konzentrationsmaxime*), a procedure for decision based on the state of the record (*Entscheidung nach Lage der Akten*), proceedings by consent before a single judge (*Einzelrichter*) of the district court of general jurisdiction, and reductions of the sizes of panels in the appeals courts (*Oberlandesgerichte*) and the Supreme Court (*Reichsgericht*) from 5 to 3 and 7 to 5 judges respectively. See Dannreuther, *Der Zivilprozess als Gegenstand der Rechtspolitik im Deutschen Reich 1871–1945* (1987), pp. 349 ff.; Rosenberg/Schwab/Gottwald, §5 (II)(2), p. 25.

35. See, e.g., Müller, *Furchtbare Juristen* (1987); translated as *Hitler's Justice* (Harvard University Press 1993); Gruchmann, *Justiz im Dritten Reich 1933–1940* (1988); Dreier/Sellert (ed.), *Recht und Justiz im 'Dritten Reich'* (1989).

shocking aberrations during 1933–1945,[36] the codified rules of civil procedure law emerged from the Nazi catastrophe more or less intact.[37]

When the Nazis initially came to power, they attacked the individualistic and liberal character of the system of civil justice and announced an intention to enact reforms. A comprehensive reform in 1933 replaced judicial oath-taking by parties with a legal obligation of truthfulness and proof through party examination.[38] The "Konzentrationsmaxime" was enhanced by giving the judge additional power to disregard claims and defenses asserted too late in the proceedings.[39]

The Nazis proclaimed the 1933 reforms as expressions of their ideology, especially its anti-individualism. For example, the statutory obligation of truthfulness (*Wahrheitspflicht*) was considered a consequence of the total subordination of the individual to the will of the people.[40] In fact, most parts of what became the 1933 reform were based on proposals that had been submitted in 1931. The original substance and basic ideas of the 1933 "Nazi" reforms were hardly a product of Nazi ideology. They have remained in the law on civil procedure to the present day.[41]

When the Federal Republic of Germany was established as the legal successor of the German Reich in 1949, the fundamental principal of "preservation of the unity of law" (*Wahrung der Rechtseinheit*)[42] as expressed in the Act on the Preservation of Unity of Law of September 12, 1950,[43] resulted in the placement of both substantive private law and civil procedure law in the realm of national or federal law (*Bundesrecht*). The German Procedural Code

36. Rüthers, *Die unbegrenzte Auslegung: Zum Wandel der Privatrechtsordnung im Nationalsozialismus*, 5th ed. (1997); Rüthers, "Recht als Waffe des Unrechts - Juristische Instrumente im Dienst des NS-Rassenwahns", 41 *NJW* 2825, 2828 (1988); Schröder, "*... aber im Zivilrecht sind die Richter standhaft geblieben*" (1988), pp. 14 ff.; Stürner, "Bemerkenswerte Entscheidungen aus 200 Jahren Rechtsprechung des Großherzoglichen Oberhofgerichts und des Oberlandesgerichts Karlsruhe in Zivilsachen", in: Münchbach (ed.), *200 Jahre Badisches Oberhofgericht - Oberlandesgericht Karlsruhe* (2003), pp. 25 ff., 36 ff., 45.

37. Lüke, in: *Münchener Kommentar zur ZPO*, Vol. I, mn. 51.

38. Law of October 27, 1933.

39. Dannreuther, *Der Zivilprozess als Gegenstand der Rechtspolitik* (1987), pp. 476 ff.

40. Dannreuther, *Der Zivilprozess als Gegenstand der Rechtspolitik* (1987), p. 477.

41. Lüke, in: *Münchener Kommentar zur ZPO*, Vol. I, mn. 50. Later legislation incorporated Nazi ideology into the system of civil justice, especially in family law procedure, but these changes were selective and did not affect the code on civil procedure as a whole.

42. See Articles 72 and 74 of the German Constitution (*Grundgesetz*).

43. *Gesetz zur Wiederherstellung der Rechtseinheit auf dem Gebiete der Gerichtsverfassung, der bürgerlichen Rechtspflege, des Strafverfahrens und des Kostenrechts*, BGBl. 1950 I, 455.

of 1879 was readopted as national law in the Federal Republic effective October 9, 1950. The Court Organization Law was also repromulgated with amendments corresponding to the federal structure of the postwar Federal Republic.[44]

The latter half of the 20th Century saw changes and reforms in German civil justice from time to time, the most important of which was the Law for the Simplification and Expedition of Court Proceedings of December 3, 1976, also known as the "Simplification Reform of 1976" (*Vereinfachungsnovelle von 1976*).[45] This law reinforced the principle of concentration of proceedings with the aim of limiting oral litigation in most cases to one day. Preliminary proceedings were expedited by authorizing case preparation in writing (*schriftliches Vorverfahren*). The reforms also enhanced the authority of the judge to disregard the delayed assertion of claims and defenses (*Zurückweisung verspäteten Vorbringens*).[46]

A further reform in 1990 introduced detailed regulations in such areas as expert testimony and witness examination in an effort to standardize civil procedure and make it simpler.[47]

The reunification of Germany in 1990 saw the extension of the civil justice system as well as the substantive civil law of the Federal Republic into the territory of the former German Democratic Republic.[48]

---

44. See Ch. 3(B)–(E) below for a description of the organization of the judicial system of the German Federal Republic.

45. *Gesetz zur Vereinfachung und Beschleunigung gerichtlicher Verfahren*, BGBl. 1976 I, 3281; see Putzo, "Die Vereinfachungsnovelle", 30 *NJW* 1 (1977). These reforms are often referred to as the "Stuttgart reforms" (*Stuttgarter Modell*) because they arose out of the work of judges in the district courts in Stuttgart. The initiative for these reforms was given by Fritz Baur, *Wege zu einer Konzentration der mündlichen Verhandlung im Prozess* (1966).

46. See Ch. 7 (K)(1) below on the procedural preclusions by delay.

47. The Simplification of Law Maintenance Act of December 17, 1990, BGBl. 1990 I, 2847. A 1993 reform expanded the jurisdiction of the local courts, restricted appeals, and encouraged resort to a single justice in ordinary cases in the state district courts. For a catalog of postwar legislative measures affecting civil procedure see Rosenberg/Schwab/Gottwald, §5 (II)(3), p. 26.

48. See the Treaty between the Federal Republic and the Democratic Republic concerning the Establishment of the Unity of Germany (*Vertrag zwischen der Bundesrepublik Deutschland und der Deutschen Demokratischen Republik über die Herstellung der Einheit Deutschlands*) of August 31, 1990. The unification treaty included special transitional arrangements for the court system in the new German states.

G. Contemporary Trends and Reforms

According to contemporary appraisals the modern German civil justice system functions well and enjoys a high degree of public confidence.[49] Nonetheless, in Germany, as elsewhere in the world, the civil justice system must always contend with the challenge to provide to the public rapid, high-quality and inexpensive judicial adjudication with limited financial and personnel resources. The process of re-examination and reform continues.

In 1998 the German rules on arbitration were subject to significant reform.[50] In the 1980's it became obvious that Germany had not maintained its appeal as a place for international commercial arbitration. The German rules on arbitration were perceived to be unresponsive to the needs of contemporary commercial enterprises. The 1998 reform adjusted the German rules to the UNCITRAL model.[51]

The most recent comprehensive reform of German civil justice was adopted in July 2001 and became effective for most purposes on January 1, 2002.[52] This reform was designed to strengthen the judgment of the court in the first instance by somewhat restricting review of first instance fact findings and access to other appellate remedies.[53] The effectiveness of this reform is subject to current debate.

Additional recent reforms concern electronic communication, service of process, hearings by video-conferences and the admission of lawyers to practice in all state courts without local restriction. International treaties[54] and di-

---

49. See, e.g., Zuckerman, "Civil Justice in Crisis: Comparative Dimensions of Civil Procedure", in: Zuckerman (ed.), *Civil Justice in Crisis* (1999), p. 3, 31. A more detailed critical and comparative analysis of German civil justice may be found in Ch. 13 below.

50. Berger (ed.), *Das neue Recht der Schiedsgerichtsbarkeit* (1998); Münch, in: *Münchener Kommentar zur Zivilprozessordnung*, 2nd ed. (2001), Vor § 1025, mn. 47 ff.

51. See Chapter 11(I) below.

52. See *Gesetz zur Reform des Zivilprozesses vom 27.7.2001* (*ZPO-RG*), BGBl I 2001, 1887 ff.

53. For an overview see Hartmann, "Zivilprozess 2001/2001: Hunderte wichtige Änderungen", 36 *NJW* 2577 ff. (2001); Greger, "Justizreform - und nun?", 57 *JZ* 1020 ff. (2002).

54. See Ch. 12(A)–(E) below on the new Brussels Regulation on Jurisdiction and Enforcement and on the effect of the Brussels and Lugano conventions on jurisdiction and enforcement of judgments within the European Union and the signatories of those conventions.

rectives of the European Union[55] have also resulted in and will continue to require conforming changes to German civil procedure as civil justice is "harmonized" within Europe, and eventually globally.[56]

55. For instance, Directive 98/27/EC of 19 May 1998, OJ L 166, 11/06/1998, p. 51, requires Member States to provide for the availability of judicial relief through collective forms of action in certain kinds of consumer cases. Implementation of this directive required amendment of the German law relating to interest group complaints (*Verbandsklage*). See Ch. 7(B)(5) below.

56. For European Harmonization see Grunsky/Stürner/Walter/Wolf (eds.), *Wege zu einem europäischen Zivilprozessrecht* (1992); Storme (ed.), *Approximation of Judiciary Law in the European Union* (1994); Hess, "Aktuelle Perspektiven der europäischen Prozessangleichung", 56 *JZ* 573 ff. (2001). For global harmonization see Hazard/Taruffo/Stürner/Gidi, *ALI/Unidroit Principles and Rules of Transnational Civil Procedure*, The American Law Institute, Discussion Draft No. 4, 2003; International Institute for the Unification of Private Law (ed.), "Harmonising Transnational Civil Procedure: The ALI/Unidroit Principles and Rules", *Uniform Law Review* 2001–4; Hazard/Taruffo/Stürner/Gidi, "Principles and Rules of Transnational Civil Procedure", 33 *NYU Journal of International Law and Politics* 769 ff. (2001); Stürner, "Some Remarks on a New Joint Project of the American Law Institute and UNIDROIT", 34 *The International Lawyer* 1071 ff. (2000).

CHAPTER 3

Organization and Structure of the German Judicial System

A. In General

German civil and criminal justice are dispensed through a nationwide system of mixed general-jurisdiction and specialized courts. Although the roles and jurisdictions of the various German courts differ, they all share certain common institutional features. Each German court is presided over by a professional judge.[1] All professional German judges have a complete legal education and training.[2] All professional judges hold salaried positions in the judiciary of the various German states or in the federal judiciary. Most German judges are full-time.[3] All professional judges are appointed for what becomes lifetime tenure[4] and are insulated from activities which would compromise

1. In some courts, the panel may also include one or more lay judges (*Laienrichter*) in addition to the professional judge.

2. See Ch. 3(G)(1) below. German legal training is based on the concept of the "complete jurist" (*Volljurist*), according to which all legal practitioners receive the same education and training required to serve as a judge. See Ch. 4(C) below on the education and training of lawyers and current proposals for change.

3. Some judges (e.g., certain law professors) serve part-time as judges, but in any event are full time public officials in their combined capacities. Some judges may be part-time members of more than one court, e.g. in some German states, the state constitutional courts may be staffed with part time judges who also serve on the state appeals courts.

4. A judge typically serves in a probationary capacity (*Richter auf Probe*) for the first three years of her career and thereafter has a lifetime appointment (*Richter auf Lebenszeit*). Judges of the Federal Constitutional Court serve single non-renewable terms of 12 years. See Ch. 3(E) below.

their judicial independence.[5] All German courts function according to the same basic procedural principles in civil cases. While the following description relates chiefly to the courts of general jurisdiction (*ordentliche Gerichte*)[6] in which most civil business is done, the workings and procedures of the specialized courts are in large part very similar.

An observer of the German justice system is immediately struck by the large number of judges employed in the dispensation of civil and criminal justice in Germany. In the entire world Germany is number one both in the absolute number of professional judges employed as well as the number of judges per capita. As of 1998 the official tally of German professional judges of all kinds was 20,969, or one judge per four thousand German citizens.[7]

This large number of public jurists speaks both to the high importance placed by German policy and culture on formal civil and criminal justice in the courts as well as the large role of the German judge in the processing and determination of civil and criminal litigation. While in other legal cultures the lawyer is considered the key figure in the administration of justice and the protection of legal rights, in Germany the judge takes on a central part

---

5. Judges' extracurricular activities are strictly regulated. They may write articles and books, teach and lecture at universities and other institutions of higher learning, and may, with the consent of both parties, serve as arbitrators in private arbitrations. See DRiG §§40–42.

6. The term "ordinary courts" comes from the fact that these courts were the earliest to develop as independent judicial organs and long predated the establishment of the specialized courts, which in some cases were outgrowths of governmental or administrative agencies.

7. See German Ministry of Justice *(Bundesministerium der Justiz, Referat für Presse- und Öffentlichkeitsarbeit), Zahlen aus der Justiz,* September 30, 2000. The significance of this number may be better appreciated by comparing it to the United States, with 10,539 full time professional state and federal judges in 1998 (9,065 in trial courts and 1,474 in appellate courts) (see *Bureau of Justice Statistics, State Court Organization 1998, June 2000; www.ojp.gov/bjs/pub/pdf/sco98.pdf*) resulting in a ratio of 1 judge per 27,000 citizens or 0.037 judges per 1000 in the population (based on a resident population of 281.4 million people, see *U.S. Census Bureau, USA statistics in brief, pp. IX, 7.18, www.census.gov/statab/www/poppart.html)* or the United Kingdom (numbers given for England and Wales), where in 2001, 2475 full time judges (not counting lay judges) dispensed justice (see *Lord Chancellor's Department, Judicial Statistics 2001, pp. 91, 99, www.lcd.gov.uk/judicial/jsar01/contents.html,)* to 52.9 million people (estimate for mid-2001, see *Office for National Statistics, 111 Population Trends (2002), p. 7)* at a ratio of 1 judge per 21,373 people or 0.047 per thousand. See also David S. Clark, "The Relative Importance of Judiciaries in Distinct Legal Traditions", in Nafziger and Symoniedes, Eds., *Law and Justice in a Multistate World: Essays in Honor of Arthur T. von Mehren,* (Transnational 2002) p. 609.

of this function. This results in a balance of private resources, represented by the parties and their lawyers, and public resources, represented by the judge and the court staff, that in Germany consists of a somewhat larger proportion of public and a somewhat smaller proportion of private resources than in some other systems.[8]

B. General and Specialized Court Jurisdictions

The legal workload of Germany's justice system is divided between a court system of general jurisdiction and several court systems of specialized jurisdiction. The court system of general jurisdiction (*ordentliche Gerichte*) exercises jurisdiction over all disputes cognizable by law, civil or criminal, which are not confided to the competence of one of the specialized courts.[9] The principal specialized court systems which exercise jurisdiction of a more or less "civil" nature[10] are the Labor Courts (*Arbeitsgerichte*), the Administrative Courts (*Verwaltungsgerichte*), the Social Welfare Courts (*Sozialgerichte*) and the Tax Courts (*Finanzgerichte*).[11]

An important component of the civil justice system in Germany is the Federal Constitutional Court (*Bundesverfassungsgericht*), which has the power to determine the constitutional validity of all German legislative enactments, court judgments, and administrative actions.[12] The particular role and function of the Federal Constitutional Court is discussed in greater detail below.

---

8. See Ch. 13(E) below for more comparative analysis on this issue.

9. See *Gerichtsverfassungsgesetz* (GVG) §13. See Bross, „Rechtswegprobleme zwischen den Zivil- und Verwaltungsgerichten", 79 *VerwArch* 97 (1988).

10. "Civil" is used here in the Anglo-American sense. In most continental-European systems court jurisdiction is divided in at least three conceptual categories, civil, criminal and administrative.

11. There are other specialized court systems such as the Patent Court (*Patentgericht*) in Munich, which handles appeals from non-issuances of patents and claims of patent invalidity, Attorneys Courts (*Anwaltsgerichte*) in the various states, which act on issues related to qualification or discipline of lawyers, military courts (*Wehrdienstgerichte*), and Civil Service Courts (*Disziplinargerichte*). Procedure before these courts is outside the scope of the present work.

12. In addition most, but not all of the German states have their own constitutional courts (*Landesverfassungsgerichte*) which adjudicate the constitutionality of state (*Land*) legislation and decide other disputes based on the constitutions of the individual states.

C. The Major Specialized Courts

Germany's four major specialized court systems exercise jurisdictions based on the natures of the issues being litigated. For instance, the Labor Courts have competence to decide issues arising from the employer-employee relationship, collective bargaining issues, and issues between management and workers' representatives. The Administrative Courts have jurisdiction over appeals from decisions of the state or federal administration or its administrative agencies as well as proceedings to review or compel action by a government administration or administrative agencies. The Social Welfare Courts are largely concerned with claims for various forms of government benefits. The jurisdiction of the Tax Courts can be rightly inferred from their name.

Each one of these basic specialized court systems operates a complete top-to-bottom judicial establishment with courts of first instance and appeals courts.[13] Each system is crowned by a Federal Supreme Court of last resort.[14] Proceedings in each of the specialized court systems is governed by a specialized procedure code for that court system supplemented by the German Civil Procedure Code (*Zivilprozessordnung* or *ZPO*) which governs to the extent that the specialized code does not otherwise provide.

Although the docket of all of the specialized courts taken together comprises only a fraction of all civil proceedings filed each year in Germany, the number of cases handled is not insignificant. For instance, in 1998 a total of 584,686 complaints were lodged in the various Labor Courts, and 201,543 were filed in Administrative Courts, compared with some 2.5 million in the courts of general jurisdiction.[15]

---

13. The Tax Court system has only two levels, a court of first instance (*Finanzgericht*) and the Federal Supreme Tax Court (*Bundesfinanzhof*).

14. These Federal Supreme Courts are not sited in the German federal capital (formerly Bonn, now Berlin), but are located in various principal cities in Germany. For instance, the Federal Supreme Labor Court sits in Erfurt, the Federal Supreme Social Welfare Court in Kassel. The Federal Tax Supreme Court has its seat in Munich. Both the Federal Supreme Court of general jurisdiction and the Federal Constitutional Court have been located in Karlsruhe since 1949. When Germany reunited in 1990–1992 the Federal Supreme Court declined an invitation to return to the traditional seat of the Supreme Court of the German Empire (*Reichsgericht*) in Leipzig. The elegant former Supreme Court building in Leipzig has been renovated to serve as the home of the Federal Supreme Administrative Court, which has been relocated there from its former seat in Berlin.

15. See German Ministry of Justice, *Zahlen aus der Justiz*, p. 9.

The focus of this work is primarily the function and procedures of the German courts of general jurisdiction. Space does not permit any detailed description of the procedural regimes of the various specialized courts. A few particulars on each will have to suffice.[16]

1. The Labor Courts

The labor court system, like all of the German court systems, operates as a decentralized system of Labor Courts (*Arbeitsgerichte*) of first instance, Labor Appeals Courts (*Landesarbeitsgerichte*) in the various German states (*Länder*),[17] and a Federal Supreme Labor Court (*Bundesarbeitsgericht*) exercising an appellate jurisdiction over all of the state labor courts.

Although there have been specialized tribunals in Germany for labor matters since 1926, the Labor Courts assumed their present form as a result of the Labor Courts Law (*Arbeitsgerichtsgesetz* or *ArbGG*), originally enacted in 1953, which as modified and amended from time to time governs their jurisdiction and activities to the present day.

The Labor Courts are vested with exclusive jurisdiction over all disputes relating to the employment relationship, including wages, terms and conditions of employment, collective bargaining, and termination of employment. Their jurisdiction also includes disputes between trade unions and employer associations and issues between worker representatives (*Betriebsrat*) and the employer's management.[18]

The first-instance Labor Courts are each staffed with a single professional judge and two lay judges, the latter being selected from lists provided by employers' and labor organizations respectively.[19]

The Labor Appeals Courts (*Landesarbeitsgerichte*) hear appeals on questions of fact and law (*Berufungen*) from decisions of the Labor Courts.[20] Their composition is the same as that of the Labor Courts, one professional judge and

---

16. Additional information on the various specialized courts and their role in the German justice system can be obtained from sources cited in the footnotes and in the bibliography.

17. There are currently 123 Labor Courts and 19 Labor Appeals Courts.

18. See ArbGG §§2 ff. A few claims are on the borderline between the jurisdiction of the labor courts and the courts of general jurisdiction. For instance, there is a split among the courts as to whether claims for restitution by forced workers during the Nazi regime are within the jurisdiction of the labor courts, or should be brought in courts of general jurisdiction. See Federal Supreme Labor Court, 53 *DB* 777 (2000).

19. See ArbGG §§16, 35, 41.

20. ArbGG §§33–39.

two lay judges, again equally from management and labor. Most of the German states have a single Labor Appeals Court which sits in several panels.

Appeals on questions of law or procedure only (*Revision*) from decisions of the Labor Appeals Courts go to the Federal Labor Supreme Court, which sits in Senates composed of three professional judges and two lay judges, the latter representing management and labor interests respectively.[21] A "Grand Senate" (*Grosser Senat*) of sixteen judges of the Federal Labor Supreme Court can be convened to resolve splits among Senates and clarify important legal principles.[22]

Parties need not be represented by counsel in most first-instance proceedings before the Labor Court.[23] Legal representation is required before the Labor Appeals Courts and the Federal Labor Supreme Court.[24]

The procedure in the labor courts is designed to be swift, simple, and relatively informal to foster the rapid and inexpensive determination of labor and employment issues. A characteristic feature of Labor Court procedure is that most proceedings start with an informal conciliation proceeding (*Gütetermin*) at which the professional judge meets with the parties and tries to assist them in reaching a compromise.[25] This process results in settlement of a large proportion of cases lodged in the Labor Court.[26]

---

21. Although the participation of lay judges in determinations of issues of law and procedure may seem anomalous, the participation of employer and employee representatives in proceedings to adjudicate labor issues may implement policies other than just the provision of specialized expertise to the determination of contested facts. At the appellate level, one of the functions of the lay judges may well be to keep the court "in touch" with the interests at stake, and to serve as a kind of link between the managers and workers on the one hand, and the court on the other. The participation of lay judges also facilitates a form of "mediation" approach, which has led to the development of a significant body of Labor Court case law regulating the collective bargaining relationship as well as strikes and other labor disputes.

22. ArbGG §45. This Grand Senate is composed of the court President, a judge from each regular senate, and 6 lay judges (equally representing management and labor) all appointed by the court presidium.

23. On the other hand, an employee party to a Labor Court case has the right to be accompanied and advised by a non-lawyer adviser, usually an official of the employee's union. ArbGG §11.

24. See ArbGG §11(2). See Koch, in: *Erfurter Kommentar zum Arbeitsrecht*, 3rd ed. (2003), ArbGG §11, mn. 12.

25. See Ch. 11(I) below on compromise settlements.

26. For instance, in 1998 about 41 per cent of cases filed in the Labor Courts were resolved by compromise settlement (of a total of 625,462 cases disposed of, 256,123 were resolved by settlement).

Another idiosyncrasy of Labor Court litigation is that in first instance proceedings both parties are required to pay their own attorneys fees and costs of suit regardless of the outcome.[27] On appeals the usual fee- and cost-shifting rules apply.[28]

The large number of cases filed each year[29] suggests that German employees and their employers and unions look to the Labor Court as the first line of resolution for the many disputes and frictions that are likely to arise in the employment relationship. The large proportion of such cases that are settled, and the small proportion of Labor Court judgments that are appealed to the Labor Appeals Court (5%)[30] can be seen as testimony to the effectiveness of the court in resolving these disputes and the confidence of the parties in the quality of the decisions rendered.[31]

2. The Administrative Courts

The Administrative Court system deals with issues of public law other than those sectors confided to specialized courts such as the Social Welfare Courts or the Tax Courts. Challenges to the actions of governmental officers or agencies, as well as all appeals from the decisions of administrative bodies go to the Administrative Courts (*Verwaltungsgerichte*), which are empowered to consider constitutional issues arising from public action or decisions so long as the constitutional validity of a post war legislative enactment is not in question. Administrative courts have existed in Germany since the late 19th century.[32] The present comprehensive framework dates from the adoption of the German Constitution (*Grundgesetz*) of 1949.[33]

---

27. ArbGG §12a(1). See German Constitutional Court, 24 *NJW* 2303 ff. (1971) for a discussion of the constitutionality of that provision.

28. ArbGG §12a(1), 64(6), 72(5). See Koch, in: *Erfurter Kommentar zum Arbeitsrecht*, ArbGG §12a, mn. 9.

29. In 1998, 584,696 cases were commenced in the German Labor Courts, see German Ministry of Justice, *Zahlen aus der Justiz*, p. 9.

30. This can be contrasted with the approx. 50 percent of judgments of the State District Court (*Landgericht*) which are appealed to the State Appeals Court (*Oberlandesgericht*). Rimmelspacher, in: *Münchener Kommentar zur Zivilprozessordnung*, 2nd ed. (2000 ff.), Vor § 511, mn. 9.

31. Only about 5% of the judgments of the Labor Appeals Courts are appealed on legal or procedural grounds to the Federal Labor Supreme Court.

32. The precursors of these courts in the form of review panels within the administration were established in the first half of the 19th Century. See Stürner, "Suing the Sovereign in Europe and Germany", 34 *George Washington International Law Review* (2003).

33. Forsthoff, *Lehrbuch des Verwaltungsrechts* I, 10th ed. (1973), §6.

The Administrative Court system consists of some fifty-two Administrative Courts (*Verwaltungsgerichte*) of first instance in the larger cities throughout Germany. Procedure before the Administrative Courts is governed by the Administrative Court Code (*Verwaltungsgerichtsordnung* or *VwGO*). The general Civil Procedure Code (*ZPO*) also governs in the absence of special rule The Administrative Courts generally sit in panels (*Kammern*) consisting of three professional judges and two lay judges (*ehrenamtliche Richter*).[34] The lay judges are appointed to four-year terms from lists of qualified candidates submitted by the localities of the Administrative Court districts and represent, in a general way, the interest of private citizens vis à vis the state.[35] An Administrative Court may act through a single professional judge (*Einzelrichter*) in any case which does not exhibit particular factual or legal difficulties and is not otherwise of fundamental significance.[36]

The Administrative Courts are the courts of first recourse for persons aggrieved by governmental action or administrative decision.[37] Second-instance appeals on both law and facts (*Berufungen*) from decisions of the Administrative Courts go to sixteen Administrative Appeals Courts (*Ober-* or *Landesverwaltungsgerichte*).[38] In most states these also sit in panels composed of three professional judges and two lay judges.[39]

The Federal Supreme Administrative Court (*Bundesverwaltungsgericht*) serves as the court of last resort within the Administrative Court system. That court sits in Senates generally composed of five professional judges and considers only review appeals on issues of law or procedure (*Revision*).[40] Review appeal to the Federal Supreme Administrative Court is only by permission of the lower court or the Supreme Administrative Court itself.

---

34. VwGO §5(3).

35. VwGO §§26(2), 28. See VwGO §§19–34 for provisions governing the selection and activities of lay judges.

36. VwGO §6.

37. See VwGO §45. Some cases go directly to the Administrative Appeals Courts or the Federal Administrative Supreme Court as the court of first instance. VwGO §§45, 47, 48 and 50.

38. The statute requires a single Administrative Appeals Court for each state, but permits each state some liberty in determining the composition of the court, even to the point of permitting states to share Administrative Appeals Courts or allocate cases among them. VwGO §3.

39. See VwGO §9(3). The composition of the appeals court can depend on particular state (*Land*) legislation and on the nature of the dispute.

40. VwGO §10. See Kopp/Schenke, *Verwaltungsgerichtsordnung*, 12th ed. (2000), §10, mn. 2 for a discussion of the consequence of an infringement of VwGO §10. For leave to appeal see VwGO §§132 ff.

In most cases a litigant cannot file a complaint in the Administrative Court without first lodging a formal objection (*Widerspruch*) to the administrative action or decision challenged. The purpose of this preliminary procedure is to attempt resolution of the dispute without formal court proceeding. Only after an unsuccessful attempt at this kind of informal resolution may a litigant resort to the Administrative Court.

Another special feature of the Administrative Court is the role of Senior Public Attorneys (*Oberbundesanwälte*) attached to the Federal Supreme Administrative Court, whose function is to represent the public interest in proceedings pending in that court.[41]

Much of the law with which the Administrative Courts are concerned is state public law, which can and does vary among the various German states (*Länder*). The role of the Federal Supreme Administrative Court thus includes the correct application and interpretation of both federal and state law in harmony with the Constitution and other basic principles underlying the legal systems of all the German states.

3. The Social Welfare Courts

Questions of entitlement to social welfare and insurance programs are decided by a system of Social Welfare Courts (*Sozialgerichte*). This system also consists of three layers, the Social Welfare Courts (*Sozialgerichte*) of the first instance, Social Welfare Appeals Courts (*Landessozialgerichte*) and a Federal Social Welfare Supreme Court (*Bundessozialgericht*). Procedure in the Social Welfare Courts is governed by the Social Welfare Courts Law (*Sozialgerichtsgesetz* or *SGG*) supplemented by the Civil Procedure Code (*ZPO*).

The sixty-nine Social Welfare Courts of the first instance sit in tribunals each consisting of one professional and two lay judges. The tribunals tend to be specialized according to the various principal programs of social welfare and insurance. Lay members of the tribunals are selected from various organizations depending on the subject matters of the tribunals' workloads. The background and experience of the lay judges often corresponds at least to some degree to the issues being determined by the tribunal.[42] Cases presenting only

41. See VwGO §35. In some states there are Public Attorneys who fulfil a similar function in the Administrative Appeals Courts. VwGO §36. See Kopp/Schenke, §36, mn. 2 for an enumeration of the respective states.

42. For instance, a panel deciding claims for disability benefits would often include a physician.

relatively simple factual and legal issues without fundamental significance may be referred to and decided by single professional judges.[43]

Second instance appeals on law and facts (*Berufungen*) from decisions of the Social Welfare Court are heard by regional Social Welfare Appeals Courts (*Landessozialgerichte*), which sit in panels of three professional judges and two lay judges. Review appeals on questions of law and procedure from decisions of the Appeals Courts are heard by the Federal Social Welfare Supreme Court, which also sits in panels of three professional and two lay judges.[44]

Representation by counsel is not required in first instance proceedings in the Social Welfare Court. However claimants are required to complete an informal threshold procedure in an effort to reach early resolution of the dispute before starting formal court proceedings.[45]

4. The Tax Courts

The Tax Courts (*Finanzgerichte*) hear appeals from administrative decisions of the authorities responsible for administration of all forms of taxation (including customs and import duties). First instance proceedings[46] are lodged in the Tax Courts, which sit in panels (*Kammern*) composed of three professional and two lay judges.[47] The Tax Court Law (*Finanzgerichtsordnung* or *FGO*), supplemented by the Civil Procedure Code (*ZPO*), governs procedure in the Tax Courts. Review appeals on questions of law or procedure from decisions of the Tax Courts are heard by five-judge panels of the Federal Supreme Tax Court (*Bundesfinanzhof*).[48]

---

43. SGG §202, ZPO §348a I Nr. 1.

44. Like the other Federal Supreme Courts, the Social Welfare Supreme Court can convene an Enlarged Senate (*Grosser Senat*) to resolve conflicts among panels and unify the law. SGG §41.

45. See SGG §78. This procedure is similar to the preliminary procedure in Administrative Court proceedings.

46. In almost all cases initiation of a complaint in the Tax Court must be preceded by administrative review proceedings within the agency. See FGO §44.

47. There are 19 Tax Courts located in major cities throughout Germany.

48. A review appeal is only by permission of the lower court or the Federal Supreme Tax Court, FGO §§36, 115. There is no second instance appeal on facts and law (*Berufung*) from a first-instance decision of a Tax Court.

D. Courts of General Jurisdiction

Germany's courts of general jurisdiction (*ordentliche Gerichte*) represent the bulk of its judicial establishment and are represented at some level in almost every locality in the country. All criminal prosecutions and all civil actions not within the jurisdiction of one of the specialized court systems are brought in one or the other of the courts of general jurisdiction.[49]

The courts of general jurisdiction are organized on four levels, the Local Courts (*Amtsgerichte*), the State District Courts (*Landgerichte*), the State Appeals Courts (*Oberlandesgerichte*) and the Federal Supreme Court (*Bundesgerichtshof*). Generally speaking, the Local Courts exercise civil jurisdiction in family and inheritance matters as well as other civil claims of relatively small amount. The State District Courts exercise a general civil jurisdiction over all civil cases not within the exclusive jurisdiction of the Local Courts and hear second instance appeals on facts and law (*Berufungen*) from decisions of the Local Courts in non-family cases. The State Appeals Courts have an exclusively appellate jurisdiction and determine second instance appeals on facts and law (*Berufungen*) from first-instance State District Court judgments and from Local Court judgments in family law cases. The Federal Supreme Court hears review appeals on law and procedure (*Revision*) from State Appeals Courts and from State District Courts acting as appellate courts. These review appeals are only by permission of the lower courts. If the lower court refuses to give permission, the party aggrieved may lodge a miscellaneous appeal from denial of permission with the Federal Supreme Court.

Each year Germany's courts of general jurisdiction hear and determine a truly impressive volume of civil litigation. For instance in 1998, some 2,080,928 civil actions were brought in various Local Courts throughout Germany.[50] In the same year a total of 505,187 cases (including 100,591 appeals from Local Court judgments) were filed in the State District Courts. In 1998 the State Appeals Courts received 69,600 appeals from State District Court judgments and another 26,056 appeals from Local Court judgments in family cases. In the same time period 6,096 cases were appealed to the Federal Supreme Court. These statistics[51] give a picture of a very busy court system in civil matters.

---

49. See GVG §13. See Thomas/Putzo/Hüsstege, *Zivilprozessordnung*, 24th ed. (2002), GVG §13, mn. 5.

50. German Ministry of Justice, *Zahlen aus der Justiz*, p. 4. Among these cases, 1,584,128 were ordinary civil cases and 496,800 were family cases.

51. German Ministry of Justice, *Zahlen aus der Justiz*, p. 5.

1. The Local Courts

The Local Courts (*Amtsgerichte*) are by far the most numerous of German judicial establishments. As of the end of 1998, there were 693 Local Courts established in all parts of Germany. Even the smallest town is likely to have a Local Court either within that town or in the neighboring locality. The ubiquitousness of these courts bespeaks their role in the German legal culture. These are truly the courts of the people.

a. Local Court Jurisdiction

The civil jurisdiction of the Local Courts tends to focus chiefly on legal matters of consequence to the common citizen, family law cases, non-contentious probate and inheritance matters, and smaller civil cases. Currently the Local Courts exercise an exclusive civil jurisdiction over most civil cases in which the amount in controversy does not exceed 5,000 Euro.[52] Also within the exclusive civil jurisdiction of the Local Courts are a variety of matters regardless of the amount in controversy. These include:

(1) All landlord - tenant matters involving residential real estate,[53]
(2) Claims arising between travelers and innkeepers, chauffeurs, boatmen, freighters and freight-forwarders,[54]
(3) Claims based on damage by wild animals,[55]
(4) Disputes arising from conveyances subject to life tenancies.[56]

The most significant category of cases within the jurisdiction of the Local Courts regardless of amount in controversy is composed of all sorts of family law cases such as divorce, annulment, child or spousal support, division of

---

52. GVG §23. The statute provides that the Local Courts shall have jurisdiction over any matters involving up to 5,000 Euro in controversy and which are not statutorily referred to the jurisdiction of the State District Courts without regard to amount in controversy. The jurisdictional amount was last revised in 2001.

53. GVG §23(2)(a). A mixed use is covered by this provision if the use as a residence is predominant. See Thomas/Putzo/Hüsstege, GVG §23, mn. 12.

54. GVG §23(2)(b). This provision does not apply to claims for compensation resulting from the cancellation of room reservations. See LG Frankfurt, 20 *BB* 268 (1965).

55. GVG §23(2)(d).

56. GVG §23(2)(g). These include a variety of arrangements in which real estate may be conveyed subject to defined obligations on the part of the grantee to provide to the grantor or grantors lifetime shelter, financial support, or a share in the revenues generated by the property. Such arrangements have been frequently utilized in Germany as a means to pass agricultural property from generation to generation.

marital property, and the like.[57] Most of these family law matters are confided to special sections of Local Courts designated as "Family Courts" (*Familiengerichte*).[58] There are special procedures applicable to Family Court matters which are discussed in Chapter 11(A) below.

The Local Courts also have substantial noncontentious civil jurisdiction (*freiwillige Gerichtsbarkeit*) in such matters as probate and inheritance and registration of legal title to real estate.[59] Although the court's role in such proceedings is often ex-parte and routine, serious disputes can arise in the context of both probate and real estate matters. The boundary between noncontentious jurisdiction and ordinary adversarial jurisdiction (*streitige Gerichtsbarkeit*) is not always very clear, and the principles governing whether a court decision issued in a non-contentious proceeding will govern a later adversary process with the same or overlapping subject matter are somewhat intricate.[60] Division of jurisdiction over adversarial disputes of all kinds, including those arising out of non-contentious probate and real estate matters initially within the exclusive jurisdiction of the Local Courts, is determined by the ordinary rules governing division of jurisdiction between the courts of first instance.[61]

b. Composition and Procedure of Local Courts

Civil matters within the jurisdiction of the Local Courts are heard by single judges.[62] Procedure in the Local Courts is governed by the Civil Proce-

---

57. GVG §23a. Thomas/Putzo/Hüsstege, GVG §23a, mn. 1 ff.

58. See GVG §23b. In the larger Local Courts, the Family Court section will be composed of one or more judges who are assigned, at least for a time, to handle family cases on a full time basis. In the smaller localities, a single Local Court judge sometimes sits both in ordinary Local Court matters and in Family Court cases. However the German states are authorized to consolidate family cases from several Local Court Districts into a single Family Court in the interest of maintaining consistency and unity in this important branch of the law. GVG §23c.

59. FGG §72, GBO §1. Bumiller/Winkler, *Freiwillige Gerichtsbarkeit*, 7th ed. (1999), §72, mn. 1 ff.

60. See Ch. 11(E)(1) below. See also Rosenberg/Schwab/Gottwald, *Zivilprozessrecht*, 15th ed. (1993), §11 for a discussion of the difference between noncontentious and adversarial jurisdiction and the boundary between them.

61. I.e., by subject matter and/or amount in controversy. See Ch. 5(B)(1) and (2) below.

62. GVG §22(1). However more serious criminal matters may be heard by panels of professional and lay judges (*Schöffengerichte*). GVG §§28 f., LwVG §2 provides for special sittings in agricultural land cases, where the confirmation of the agricultural land authority is required for the transfer of land. These cases are heard in the first instance by Local Court panels of one professional judge and two lay judges practicing as farmers. Second instance appeals go to State Appeals Court panels of three professional judges and two lay

dure Code,[63] which, however, contains several special provisions applicable only to Local Court proceedings. There are, for instance special procedural rules for family cases within the exclusive jurisdiction of the Local Courts.[64] There are also a number of provisions designed to simplify procedure in the Local Courts. For instance, the Local Court can exercise some discretion (*billiges Ermessen*) to specify the course of proceedings in cases where the amount in controversy does not exceed 600 Euro.[65] Local Court judgments (*Urteile*) in small claim disputes need not set forth detailed findings of fact (*Tatbestand*) and can dispense with written reasons when the judge's reasoning is reasonably disclosed by the minutes (*Protokolle*) of the proceedings.[66] There are also provisions facilitating the lodging of complaints and other pleadings orally with the court clerk and simplifying requirements of service and notification.[67]

The simplifications and shortcuts in Local Court procedure reflect not only the limited jurisdiction of Local Courts in most civil matters, but also the fact that parties in many Local Court proceedings are not represented by counsel. Although the presence of lawyers in Local Court has increased over the years, as of this writing, in 11.4 percent of the cases lodged in Local Courts in Germany both litigants proceeded without lawyers. In 43.9 percent of the cases, only the plaintiff employed a lawyer, whereas in the remaining 41.9 percent, both litigants were legally represented.[68] The system is designed to make it possible in many cases for a litigant to get a fair shake at justice in the Local Court without having to hire a lawyer.[69]

---

judges. Review appeals to the Federal Supreme Court are also heard by three professional judges and two lay judges.

63. ZPO §495. See Zöller/Herget, *Zivilprozessordnung*, 23rd ed. (2002), §495, mn. 3.

64. ZPO §§606–660 (Rules governing a variety of specified family law matters such as divorce, annulment, determination of custody and support of children, etc.). See Ch. 11(A) below for a brief description of this activity.

65. ZPO §495a. However the court must provide opportunity for oral argument (*mündliche Verhandlung*) if requested by a party.

66. See ZPO §§313a(1), 511(2); Thomas/Putzo/Reichold, §495a, mn. 3.

67. See ZPO §§496–499.

68. v. Mettenheim, in: *Münchener Kommentar zur Zivilprozessordnung*, 2nd ed. (2000 ff.), § 78, mn. 7. Numbers from West Germany in 1996. In most family matters and certain other designated kinds of cases representation by counsel is, however, required. ZPO §78(2).

69. This policy is effectuated by such provisions as those requiring the judge to advise an unrepresented litigant of any apparent lack of jurisdiction in order to avoid an unintended assumption of jurisdiction by consent. ZPO §504.

2. The State District Courts

The backbone of the German civil justice system is the State District Court (*Landgericht*) of general jurisdiction, of which there are now some 116 in the principal cities and towns throughout Germany. These courts serve as the courts of first instance for the great bulk of serious civil matters and also hear and decide appeals of law and facts (*Berufungen*) from most decisions of the Local Courts. It was for these courts that the Civil Procedure Code was written.

a. Jurisdiction of the District Courts

The District Courts exercise a general first-instance civil jurisdiction, regardless of amount in controversy over all matters which are not expressly consigned to the Local Courts.[70] This includes all contentious civil proceedings where the amount in controversy is in excess of 5,000 Euro other than family matters, residential landlord-tenant, and the other specialized kinds of cases within the exclusive jurisdiction of the Local Courts.[71]

The State District Courts also hear second instance appeals on facts and law from decisions of the Local Courts other than in Family Court matters.[72] Unlike the Local Courts, which exercise both adversarial and noncontentious jurisdiction, proceedings in the State District Courts are practically all adversarial.

b. Composition of the State District Courts

The State District Courts generally sit in panels (*Kammern*) of three judges for the more important and difficult cases. For ordinary civil cases, this means three professional judges. As discussed below, in commercial matters (*Handelssachen*) the District Court is composed on one professional judge and two lay judges (*ehrenamtliche Richter*). The Commercial Panels (*Handelskammern*)

---

70. GVG §71(1). The statute also gives the District Courts exclusive jurisdiction over certain claims nominally within the jurisdictional amount in controversy of the Local Courts. These include claims against the public treasury based on breach of duty by State Officials (*Beamte*) and claims against judges and officials for breach of official duty. GVG §71(2). Each German State is also given the power to confer exclusive jurisdiction on the District Courts within that State over various kinds of claims by citizens against that State. GVG §71(3).

71. See GVG §23 for an enumeration of the kinds of proceedings which are within the exclusive jurisdiction of the Local Courts regardless of amount in controversy.

72. GVG §72. If the amount in controversy does not exceed 600 Euro the Local Court must grant leave to appeal. ZPO §511.

are the only civil sittings of the District Court in which nonprofessional judges participate.[73]

A presiding judge (*vorsitzender Richter*) of each panel presides at the hearings and largely conducts the proceedings so far as the court is concerned. For most cases the presiding judge will designate one of the other members of the panel as reporting judge (*Berichterstatter*). The reporting judge is expected to become particularly familiar with the case record (*Akte*) and often will be delegated to write the judgment.[74]

The statute prescribing the composition of the District Court includes an important proviso. The State District Court is to consist of three judges, "insofar as a single judge is not to decide in place of the panel according to the provisions of procedural law."[75]

The provision encompasses several different circumstances. First, at various points the Civil Procedure Code expressly provides that a given court function may be performed by a single judge, in some cases the presiding judge, and in some cases a judge delegated by the presiding judge or the full court. In the past frequently conduct of State District Court preparatory hearings and conferences would be delegated to a single member of the panel (*vorbereitender Richter*), while the plenary hearings (*Hauptverhandlungen*) would take place before the full panel. The Stuttgart reforms of the 1970s sought to minimize preliminary oral proceedings in favor of a single, concentrated plenary hearing, and thus greatly reduced the number and kind of preliminary matters that could be delegated to a single panel member for separate hearing.

As of the present time, the role of a delegated or preparing judge is preserved in cases before Commercial Panels[76] and in proceedings on appeals from Local Court judgments.[77] Under some circumstances the presiding judge or the full court may delegate the taking of proof or some other judicial function to a single member of the panel (*beauftragten Richter*) or may

---

73. BauGB §220 provides for mixed panels of two State District Court judges and one judge assigned from the Administrative Court to hear and determine issues arising in connection with assembly of land for development.

74. See Ch. 8(B) below for a discussion of the roles of the various panel members during oral proceedings, and Ch. 9(B)(2) for a discussion on the role of the various judges during deliberations to reach a decision.

75. GVG §75 ("*soweit nicht nach den Vorschriften der Prozessgesetze an Stelle der Kammer der Einzelrichter zu entscheiden hat.*").

76. ZPO §349. See Ch. 3(D)(2)(c) below.

77. ZPO §527. See Ch. 10(D)(1) below on the activities of the single preparing judge on appeals.

request that it be done by a judge of another court (*ersuchten Richter*). One example is the assignment of a single member of the panel or even another judge to meet with the parties in an effort to reach settlement of the case.[78] The principle of immediacy (*Unmittelbarkeitsprinzip*) and the policy favoring concentrated proceedings (*Konzentrationsprinzip*) disfavor delegations beyond these. In most properly functioning panels such delegations are rare exceptions, not the rule.

The 1974 reform that reduced the preparatory role of the single judge also gave the parties the option to have the entire case referred to a single judge for all subsequent proceedings, including decision. Legislation adopted in 1993 enlarged the option of reference to a single judge to a presumption in many routine cases. Cases which disclosed "no particular legal or factual difficulties" and where the legal issue was of "no fundamental significance"[79] were to be assigned to a single judge as a matter of course, subject to remand to a full panel if the single judge was convinced that the decision was likely to be of "fundamental significance" after all.

By virtue of the 2002 reforms it is now the rule that a member of the panel hears and decides the case as an "original single judge" unless one of the statutory exceptions applies.[80] If a case assigned by statute to a single judge discloses legal or factual difficulties or has fundamental legal significance or if both parties so request, the single judge may refer the case to the full panel.[81] A case not automatically tried by a single judge must still be assigned to an "obligatory single judge," if the case discloses no difficulties or fundamental significance.[82] The panel can act without oral proceedings at any time after the filing of the complaint, provided that a case may not be assigned to a single judge after plenary oral argument before the panel.[83]

---

78. See ZPO §278(5). In this case, parties need not be represented by counsel. See ZPO §78(5) and Thomas/Putzo/Reichold, §278, mn. 6.

79. See ZPO §348 (pre-2002 version) (*"keine besondere Schwierigkeit tatsächlicher oder rechtlicher Art aufweist", "keine grundsätzliche Bedeutung"*).

80. (*originärer Einzelrichter*) ZPO §348(1) as amended effective January 1, 2002. Exceptions include media litigation, bank disputes, construction cases, liability of lawyers, medical malpractice cases, insurance cases, etc. See Ch. 7(E)(1) for a more complete discussion of the current rules on assignment of cases to single judges and to panels.

81. ZPO §348(3).

82. (*obligatorischer Einzelrichter*) The assignment is made by a non-appealable procedural order (*Beschluss*) issued by the entire panel. ZPO §348a(1) as amended effective January 1, 2002.

83. ZPO §348a(I)(3) (*"wenn bereits im Haupttermin vor der Zivilkammer zur Hauptsache verhandelt worden ist"*).

In order to facilitate early decision on assignment of cases to single judges the Civil Procedure Code requires a plaintiff to indicate in its complaint (*Klage*) whether there is any reason why the case should not be assigned to a single judge.[84] The defendant is required to make a similar representation in its answer (*Klageerwiderung*).[85] Unless one party or the other states a good reason for proceedings before the panel, review of the initial pleadings will usually result in prompt assignment of the case to a single judge.

Once a case has been assigned to a single judge, that judge becomes the court for the purpose of all further decisions. The single judge must fill all the roles. References to "presiding judge" (*vorsitzender Richter* or *Vorsitzender*), or to other members of the court all refer to the single judge. The decision of that single judge is the decision of the court.

The result of these reforms over the last thirty years has been a large increase in the proportion of District Court cases handled and decided by single judges. In 1984 some 24.3% of all District Court contested cases were referred to single judges. By 1998 this percentage had swollen to 37.7%.[86] This high proportion of single-judge first-instance proceedings in the District Court has led to new debate about the value of a multi-judge court in first-instance civil proceedings. The 2002 reforms, while retaining the three judge panel in name, have made single-judge proceedings the rule in District Court first instance proceedings.

c. Commercial Panels of the State District Courts

German civil justice retains specialized commercial panels (*Handelskammern*) within the State District Courts for the determination of disputes in commercial and business matters (*Handelssachen*).[87] Commercial and business matters within the competence of the commercial panels include:

---

84. ZPO §253(3). A complaint lacking such an indication cannot, however, be dismissed. See Thomas/Putzo/Reichold, §253, mn. 18; Zöller/Greger, §253, mn. 24.

85. ZPO §277(1).

86. See *Gegenäusserung der Bundesregierung, BT-Drucks.* 14/4722, pp. 146 ff. and Münchbach/Lotz, "Justizreform - Reform oder gut verkaufter Abbau des Rechtsschutzsystems?", 32 *ZRP* 379 (1999).

87. Doubtless this is a modern-day reflection of the mercantile courts which developed in several countries in Europe during the Middle Ages. The commercial panels can be more immediately traced to the French commercial courts (Tribunaux de Commerce), which developed during the 19th Century and were staffed entirely by merchant lay judges. The Court Organization Law provides that each state may, but is not required to, provide commercial panels of the State District Court to the extent deemed necessary. GVG §93. As of the present time each of the German states has elected to establish commercial panels.

(1) disputes arising out of dealings between merchants,[88]
(2) cases based on checks or bills of exchange,[89]
(3) disputes among members of a mercantile business,[90]
(4) cases based on trademarks or unfair competition,[91]
(5) certain admiralty cases,[92]

It should be noted that the provisions setting forth the competence of the commercial panels are not jurisdictional. A judgment rendered by an ordinary panel of the District Court in a matter cognizable by a commercial panel would not be void. Assignment of a case to a commercial panel is a matter of division of judicial business, not judicial power to decide.[93] By the same token, if a dispute is partly one cognizable by a commercial panel and partly one for an ordinary District Court panel, the entire dispute will be decided by the ordinary panel.[94]

Each commercial panel is staffed by a presiding judge (*Vorsitzender*), who is a professional State District Court judge, and two honorary judges (*ehrenamtliche Richter*).[95] The honorary judges are not legally trained, but are required to fulfil demanding professional qualifications within their spheres of commerce and industry. The statute requires that an honorary judge must be a German citizen at least 30 years old and a merchant or business-person with a residence or commercial seat in the district for which the commercial panel is responsible.[96] Honorary judges are appointed to four year renewable terms

---

88. GVG §95(1). But not most dealings between merchants and consumers. A party's status as a merchant is determined as of the commencement of the proceeding. See Schriever, „Die Kaufmannseigenschaft des Beklagten bei Klageerhebung", 31 *NJW* 1472 (1978).

89. GVG §95(2), (3). The decision may be based on a check proceeding pursuant to ZPO §602. See Zöller/Gummer, GVG §95, mn. 6 and Ch. 11(B)(1) below.

90. GVG §95(4)(a). See LG Osnabrück, 37 *MDR* 588 (1983).

91. GVG §95(4)(c), (5). See Thomas/Putzo/Hüsstege, *GVG* §95, mn. 6 for a discussion of cases based on unfair competition.

92. GVG §95(4)(f). See Baumbach/Lauterbach/Albers/Hartmann, *Zivilprozessordnung*, 61st ed. (2003), GVG §95, mn. 6 for an enumeration of the relevant statutes.

93. See, e.g., Rosenberg/Schwab/Gottwald, §33(II), pp. 168 ff.

94. Rosenberg/Schwab/Gottwald, §33(II)(1), pp. 168 f.

95. GVG §105. Lay judges cannot serve as single judges pursuant to ZPO §§348, 348a, but they may be assigned to discuss settlement of the case with the parties. Federal Supreme Court, 42 BGHZ 163, 175 (1965).

96. GVG §109. For additional qualifications and requirements for appointment as honorary judge, see Zöller/Gummer, GVG §109, mn. 3; Berger-Delhey, „Der Handelsrichter und sein Amt", 67 *DRiZ* 246, 248 (1989).

upon nomination by chambers of commerce and industry.[97] In most matters before the commercial panels the honorary judges have votes equal to those of the professional presiding judge.[98] The statute specifically authorizes the judges on commercial panels to make use of their own specialized knowledge in deciding issues requiring mercantile expertise or whether a mercantile custom or usage exists.[99] In the larger cities the State District Courts often have several commercial panels, each with its own field of expertise, so that a matter of commercial or business complexity will be adjudicated by persons with some depth of specialized knowledge.[100] Although the Local Courts do not have commercial panels, appeals from Local Court judgments which involve commercial or business issues will be referred to commercial panels in the State District Court.

Procedure before the commercial panels is governed by the Civil Procedure Code including some special provisions applicable only to matters before commercial panels.[101]

It should be noted that cases within the scope of competence of the commercial panels may also be delegated to the presiding judge as a single judge for all purposes, including final determination. If the matter is within the statutory scope of competence of the commercial panels, and hence one to which the expertise of the commercial panel judges might be relevant, reference to a single judge for decision requires the consent of the parties.[102]

Even in cases which are not delegated to a single judge for all purposes, a number of preliminary and preparatory tasks in a commercial panel case are performed by the presiding judge acting alone.[103] The idea is that the presiding judge has the responsibility to conduct the proceeding to the point that it

---

97. GVG §108. See Berger-Delhey, 67 *DRiZ* 246, 251 (1989).

98. GVG §105(2).

99. GVG §114. If one judge has specialized knowledge she can impart that knowledge to the others. See Federal Supreme Court, 12 BGHSt 18, 19 (1959).

100. Certain specialized matters such as those involving patents, trademarks, and claims of unfair competition can be referred to commercial panels in other districts if necessary to find suitably qualified panels. See, e.g., *Warenzeichengesetz*, §32(2); *Patentgesetz*, §143(2), and *Gesetz gegen den unlauteren Wettbewerb* §27; Rosenberg/Schwab/Gottwald, §22(II)(2), p. 108.

101. See, e.g., ZPO §349 (special role of Presiding Judge in matters before Commercial Panels), §§592–605 (check cases). These special rules are discussed in Ch. 11(B)(1) below.

102. ZPO §349(3). Such delegation occurs in an increasing percentage of cases cognizable by the commercial panels.

103. See, generally, ZPO §349. See Thomas/Putzo/Reichold, §349, mn. 5 ff.

can be disposed of in a single plenary proceeding before the panel.[104] This means that the presiding judge determines whether the case should be remanded from the commercial panel to the regular State District Court procedure, applications for continuances, withdrawals of claims, issues of prerequisites to suit, defaults, costs, legal aid, amount in controversy, attorneys fees and court costs, and the like.[105] The presiding judge is authorized to take evidence only when the subject matter is not one which would relate to the specific expertise of the honorary judges and when an immediate impression of the testimony is not necessary to evaluation of the evidence.[106] This division of function is designed to relieve the part-time honorary judges from frequent meetings and hearings on procedural details and to expedite the determination of the main issues.

Although the commercial panels hear only a small percentage of all civil cases filed in the State District Court,[107] often these cases are of great significance to the business community and hence the economy. While the efficacy of participation of honorary judges from the business and commercial community may be subject to debate, in the German legal culture they lend a degree of authenticity and credibility to civil justice that justifies their retention and continued use.[108]

3. The State Appeals Courts

Each of the German states (*Länder*) has at least one State Appeals Court (*Oberlandesgericht*) which exercises an almost exclusively appellate jurisdiction in civil and criminal cases. In each state (or appeals court district in states with more than one State Appeals Court) the Chief Judge (*Gerichtspräsident*) of the State Appeals Court also exercises some administrative and supervisory

---

104. ZPO §349(1) ("*... hat der Vorsitzende die Sache so weit zu fördern, dass sie in einer mündlichen Verhandlung vor der Kammer erledigt werden kann.*").

105. ZPO §349(2). That provision contains an enumeration which is not complete. See Zöller/Greger, §349, mn. 17; Bergerfurth, „Der ‚Einzelrichter' bei der Kammer für Handelssachen", 28 *NJW* 331, 334 (1975).

106. ZPO §349(1)(2). However, the presiding judge has to make a record of his taking of evidence. See Federal Supreme Court, 15 *NJW* 960 (1962).

107. In 1989 some 15% of the civil cases filed in District Courts within the Federal Republic of Germany as it then existed were assigned to commercial panels. Rosenberg/Schwab/Gottwald, §33(I)(1), p.167.

108. Berger-Delhey, 67 *DRiZ* 246, 247 (1989); Federal Constitutional Court, 34 *NJW* 912, 913 (1981); 48 BVerfGE 300, 316 ff. (1979).

jurisdiction over activities of certain court officials and other elements of the judicial system.[109]

The State Appeals Courts are busy. In 1998 some 85,600 civil appeals were filed in German State Appeals Courts.[110]

a. *State Appeals Court Jurisdiction*

The bulk of the State Appeals Courts' jurisdiction in civil matters consists of second instance appeals on facts and law (*Berufungen*) and various forms of miscellaneous appeals (*Beschwerden*) from judgments (*Urteile*) and other decisions and orders (*Beschlüsse, Entscheidungen*) of the State District Courts.[111] The State Appeals Courts also hear second instance and miscellaneous appeals from judgments and orders of the Local Courts in paternity cases and matters cognizable by the Family Court.[112] These latter bypass the District Courts and go directly to the State Appeals Courts.

Appeals to the State Appeals Courts are as of right, so long as the amount in controversy is more than 600 Euro. In other cases the court which issued the judgment must give permission to appeal.[113] For most civil cases, the State Appeals Court is the court of last resort.[114] Review appeal on questions of law and procedure to the Federal Supreme Court is available only on a discretionary basis for all but a few civil matters.[115]

b. *Composition and Procedure of the State Appeals Courts*

The State Appeals Courts usually sit in appellate panels or senates (*Senate*) each composed of three professional Appeals Court judges.[116] Each panel is

---

109. E.g. public notaries (*Notare*) and court executors (*Gerichtsvollzieher*). These responsibilities are often delegated to the chief judges of the various State District and Local Courts within each Appeals Court district.

110. The State Appeals Courts also hear appeals on law and procedure only in criminal cases, which comprise a smaller part of their caseload.

111. GVG §119(1)(2). See Thomas/Putzo/Hüsstege, GVG §119, mn. 3 ff.

112. GVG §119(1)(1).

113. ZPO §511(2). See also Ch. 10(D) below.

114. The State of Bavaria has availed itself of the option granted by Sections 8 and 10 of the Introductory Law to the Court Organization Code (*Einführungsgesetz zum Gerichtsverfassungsgesetz* or *EGGVG*) to establish a Bavarian State Supreme Court (*Bayerisches Oberstes Landesgericht*), which has the power to hear and decide appeals on law and procedure from Bavarian State Appeals Courts where an issue of Bavarian state law is raised.

115. See Ch. 3 (D)(4) below.

116. GVG §122.

under the chairmanship of a presiding judge, who conducts the oral proceedings. As in the State District Courts, the panels tend to be at least somewhat specialized, even within the overall realm of civil justice. In the larger states or appeals court districts (*Bezirke*) within a state, it is common for the Appeals Court to provide specialized panels for family law matters, for matters involving international litigation or foreign law, for real estate law, for construction law, for media law, for consumer law, and for matters involving business or commercial law.[117]

Procedure in civil appeals in the State Appeals Courts is governed by the Civil Procedure Code.[118] When a case is filed, the papers will be initially reviewed by the presiding judge of the panel to which it is assigned.[119] In a case of any complexity, the Presiding Judge will appoint a member of the panel as Reporting Judge (*Berichterstatter*) to become especially familiar with the record, and, if necessary, to write the court's judgment. The reporting judge will generally study the record and then write a bench memorandum (*Votum*) on the issues raised for consideration by the panel. The bench memorandum generally guides the course of further proceedings, and may well also outline the likely decision.

The presiding judge, or the reporting judge (if appointed) has the responsibility to take such measures as are needed to bring the appeal to a stage where it can be disposed of in a single plenary oral proceeding before the entire panel. If the taking of additional proof is deemed necessary, the proof-taking will generally be scheduled at the plenary hearing before the panel. The panel may also delegate the conduct of preparatory hearings and conferences and the taking of evidence to a single member of the panel. With the consent of the parties, this single judge can decide issues not specifically covered by the authorizing statute, including the merits of the appeal.[120]

The recent 2001/2002 reforms enlarge the role of the single judge at the appellate level. If a decision subject to appeal was rendered by a single judge, and if the case does not present special difficulties and has no fundamental sig-

---

117. A State is also authorized to provide that matters may be assigned to Appeals Courts panels in other Appeals Court Districts in order to obtain appropriate expertise, and to establish Appeals Court panels which, in effect, serve several Appeals Court districts, GVG §116.

118. See Ch. 10 below for a discussion of procedure on appeals.

119. If the appeal appears to be hopeless, the presiding judge may so advise counsel for the appellant and permit her to withdraw the appeal without incurring liability for full costs and attorneys fees.

120. ZPO §527. This has rarely occurred in recent decades. Only a relative handful of the cases decided by State Appeals Courts have been decisions by single judges with the consent of both parties.

nificance, the appellate court may refer the complete second instance appeal to be heard and decided by a single member of the panel.[121]

4. The Federal Supreme Court

The highest court in the German civil justice system is the Federal Supreme Court (*Bundesgerichtshof* or *BGH*), which sits in Karlsruhe. The Federal Supreme Court is the court of last resort for all criminal and civil matters.[122] Its judges are organized into civil and criminal senates (*Senate*). The senates are composed of 6–8 judges apiece, but sit in panels each of 5 judges, a Presiding Judge and four others. As of this writing the Federal Supreme Court consisted of 122 judges divided into 5 criminal senates (*Strafsenate*), 12 civil senates (*Zivilsenate*) and 4 senates dealing with specialized matters.[123] There is a considerable degree of specialization among the various senates. For instance, most family law appeals are referred to a senate specializing in that branch of the law. The same is true of cases involving business and commercial law, tort law, real estate law, media law, international and foreign law, and the like.

In cases posing issues where the decisions of the respective senates seem to diverge, a Grand Civil Senate (*Grosser Senat für Zivilsachen*) composed of judges representing the regular civil senates can be convened to resolve the difference and maintain the unity of the law (*Rechtseinheit*).[124]

The jurisdiction of the Federal Supreme Court is entirely appellate. The court has jurisdiction to hear review appeals on questions of law and procedure (*Revision*) from final judgments (*Urteile*) of the State Appeals Courts and as well miscellaneous appeals (*Rechtsbeschwerden*) from other Appeals Court decisions and orders.[125] The Federal Supreme Court may also entertain review appeals from final judgments of the State District Courts when the parties agree to appeal directly to the Federal Supreme Court (*Sprungrevision*) and

121. See ZPO §526 (effective January 1, 2002); for more details see Ch. 10(D)(1) below.

122. Subject to the jurisdiction of the Federal Constitutional Court (*Bundesverfassungsgericht*) for constitutional appeals. See Ch.10(H) below.

123. Such as antitrust matters, patent, supervision of the bar and patent agents, and the like.

124. GVG §132(1). A United Grand Senate (*Vereinigter Grosser Senat*) of judges from both civil and criminal senates can be convened to decide important questions common to both branches of the law. Procedure in matters before a Grand Senate is usually entirely in writing and addresses only important issues of law. See GVG §138.

125. GVG §133. This provision was revised by Act of July 7, 2001 (BGBl I, p. 1887). For a discussion of the old version, see Pfeiffer, „Der BGH - nur ein Gericht für das Grundsätzliche?", 52 *NJW* 2617 (1999).

omit any appeal on facts and law to the State Appeals Court. Finally, there are a few courts from which one can lodge a second-instance appeal (*Berufung*) to the Federal Supreme Court.[126]

Before the 2001 civil justice reforms, there were two significant thresholds which an appeal had to cross in order to reach the Federal Supreme Court. First of all, the case had to involve an amount in controversy of at least 60,000 DM.[127] Smaller cases could only be appealed to the Federal Supreme Court with the consent of the State Appeals Court.[128] Second, even if the case involved more than 60,000 DM, the Federal Supreme Court could reject the appeal if the senate was satisfied that "the legal issue is of no fundamental significance."[129]

As the caseload of appeals to the Federal Supreme Court burgeoned in recent years, more and more frequent use was made of this provision for discretionary rejection of appeals.[130] The preliminary stages of most appeals to the Federal Supreme Court came to resemble a kind of *certiorari* proceeding. In the preliminary proceedings (*Annahmeverfahren*) the appellant had to convince the senate to which the appeals papers had been referred that the appeal was of sufficient significance and had a sufficient likelihood of success as to warrant attention. The appeal went forward to the merits only if the Federal Supreme Court decided not to reject it.[131]

In 2001 following spirited discussion among bench, bar and public, reforms of the Civil Procedure Code designed to relieve the workload on Germany's

---

126. E.g. decisions of the German Patent Court (*Patentgericht*) in cases attacking the validity of patents. PatG §110.

127. The State Appeals Court was required to set forth the amount in controversy for purpose of application of this threshold (*Beschwer*) in its judgment. ZPO §546(2) (pre 2002 version).

128. ZPO §546 (pre 20002 version). The consent of the Appeals Court was based on the importance of the issue raised and whether the Appeals Court's judgment had differed on a point of law from a prior judgment of the Federal Supreme Court. The consent of the Appeals Court to a review appeal to the Federal Supreme Court ordinarily was set forth in its judgment.

129. ZPO §554b (pre 2002 version) ("*...wenn die Rechtssache keine grundsätzliche Bedeutung hat*"). The Federal Constitutional Court had ruled that this provision can be constitutionally applied only to cases which have little chance of success on the merits in order to protect parties with meritorious cases without fundamental legal significance from judicial arbitrariness.

130. In 1989 approximately 47% of the appeals subject to discretionary rejection were rejected and 53% accepted.

131. See ZPO §554b (pre-2002 version). Since rejection of the appeal required a vote of two-thirds of the Senate, as a practical matter two members of the Senate needed to be convinced of the substantial nature of the legal issue to secure acceptance of an appeal,

appellate courts passed the houses of Parliament. These reforms became effective January 1, 2002. Under the new reforms the Federal Supreme Court will now only hear appeals in cases where permission to appeal has been granted by state appellate courts or the Federal Supreme Court itself.[132]

For some time now the Federal Supreme Court has been a very busy court. In 1998 a total of 6067 civil appeals were lodged, of which 163 were by consent of State Appeals Courts and 4056 involved an amount in controversy in excess of the 60,000 DM jurisdictional minimum.[133] Of the latter, the court rendered judgment in 607, and rejected the rest as insubstantial under the previous version of ZPO §554b. This state of chronic overwork of the nation's highest civil and criminal appeals court has led to periodic calls for enlargement of the court or reform of its procedures, or both. As this book is written it is still not clear whether these most recent reforms will provide effective relief over time.

E. The Federal Constitutional Court

A description of Germany's civil justice system would not be complete without some mention of the Federal Constitutional Court (*Bundesverfassungsgericht*). Since the focus of this work is ordinary civil justice, and not constitutional law, such mention must be brief.[134]

The Constitutional Court has the unique role and power to review the constitutionality of legislation and governmental actions and policies, and, where appropriate, declare them unconstitutional. Established in its present form with the adoption of the German Constitution (*Grundgesetz*) in 1949, the Federal Constitutional Court is the highest institution in the judicial branch, coequal with the legislative and executive branches of the German government.[135] Jurisdiction, powers and procedure of the Federal Constitutional

---

132. See Ch. 10(E) below for a more detailed discussion of the procedure to obtain permission and of other features of the reforms.

133. See www.bundesgerichtshof.de/pics/statistik/stat_zivil_senate_1998.gif. The remaining 36 appeals were either leap-frog appeals (6) (*Sprungrevision*) or were allowable without limitations (30).

134. For additional discussion of the German Constitutional Court and its role in modern Germany, see Schlaich/Korioth, *Das Bundesverfassungsgericht*, 5th ed. (2001), mn. 1–50, pp. 1–40.

135. See GG Articles 20 and 92; German Constitutional Court, 7 BVerfGE 11, 14 (1961); 65 BVerfGE 152, 154 (1984); Jarass/Pieroth, *Grundgesetz*, 6th ed. (2002), Art. 93, mn. 2; Brohm, „Die Funktion des BVerfG - Oligarchie in der Demokratie?", 54 *NJW* 1

Court are set forth in the Constitution itself and in the Federal Constitutional Court Law (*Bundesverfassungsgerichtsgesetz* or *BVerfGG*).

The Federal Constitutional Court exercises a broad jurisdiction to construe and insure the primacy of the German Constitution and to adjust frictions and disputes between the various State and Federal branches of government.[136] Decisions of the Constitutional Court are binding on all branches of government and in appropriate cases are given the force of law.[137]

The Federal Constitutional Court is composed of two senates, each consisting of 8 judges. One senate hears mostly cases involving basic rights as guaranteed in Articles 1–20 of the Constitution. The other senate concentrates largely on matters involving the structure and function of politics and government under the Constitution.[138] In exceptional cases and in cases involving disputes and conflicts between branches of government and their agencies the two senates may together consider matters which override their respective areas of special focus.

Cases may be brought before the German Constitutional Court by individual and corporate private parties who claim that some law, public act, or even action by another private party is in violation of the German Constitution. They may also be brought by certain political organs or branches of government[139] to test the constitutional validity of legislation or of actions of the executive or judicial branch.

If a party raises an issue of the constitutionality of a statute in the course of ordinary civil litigation, and the court is of the view that the question is substantial, generally the litigation will be stayed in order to allow the matter to be submitted to and decided by the Federal Constitutional Court.[140] Or the judgment of a regular court might be seen as violating the Constitution. Such

(2001); Böckenförde, „Verfassungsgerichtsbarkeit: Struktur, Organisation, Legitimation", 52 *NJW* 9 (1999).

136. GG Article 93. See, e.g., Federal Constitutional Court, 13 BVerfGE 72 (1963).

137. BVerfGG §31. The rule of *stare decisis* does not formally apply to decisions of the other German courts, even the Federal Supreme Court. In practice, however, considerable deference is paid to prior court decisions of higher courts. See Ch. 10(E)(5) below.

138. These matters include, inter alia, determining whether a political party should be banned as in violation of the Constitution.

139. Such as a house of the German Parliament, a political party, the Federal or a state administration, or even a community. See BVerfGG §63.

140. See GG Article 100. If a court of ordinary jurisdiction is of the view that legislation material to its decision may be unconstitutional, it is required to raise the matter with the Constitutional Court on its own motion. The parties have the right to submit briefs to the Constitutional Court setting forth their respective positions on the constitutional issue referred. See Rosenberg/Schwab/Gottwald, §17(I)(2)(a), (II), p. 75 ff.

violation might arise from the law on which the decision is based, or from reasoning of the decision itself. In such a case an appeal to the Constitutional Court might be the only effective kind of appeal.

Appeal to the Constitutional Court (*Verfassungsbeschwerde*) from a judgment of one of the ordinary courts is really an independent Constitutional Court action in which the plaintiff alleges that the court judgment at issue is in violation of the Constitution 1) by virtue of the procedure with which the judgment was reached, 2) by reason of the law on which the judgment is based, or 3) by reason of some finding or reasoning of the judges in reaching the judgment. While court decisions other than final judgments are subject to constitutional appeal in rare cases of unusual significance, generally the Constitutional Court applies a doctrine of exhaustion of remedies. If there are non-constitutional grounds for appeal in addition to the constitutional claim, the Constitutional Court will require the parties first to present the non-constitutional issues to the ordinary courts in hopes that it will not be necessary to resort to the Constitutional Court.[141]

Judges of the Federal Constitutional Court are elected by the Federal Parliament (*Bundestag*), one-half by a committee of the House of Representatives (*Bundestag*) and one half by the Federal Senate (*Bundesrat*).[142] They come from the ranks of political life and from university faculties as well as from the professional federal judiciary.[143] Tenure of a judge on the Constitutional Court is for a single term of 12 years.[144]

Procedure in the Constitutional Court parallels in many respects the procedure in the ordinary courts, with some exceptions.[145] For instance, the judges reach a decision by majority vote of the senate,[146] but unlike judges of

---

141. Rosenberg/Schwab/Gottwald, §17(III)(4), p. 80.

142. Election of a judge of the Constitutional Court is by a two-thirds majority of the electing body in order to insure that all judges have the support and concurrence of more than one political party.

143. The statute requires that three members of each senate must be selected from members of the four Federal Supreme Courts. BVerfGG §2(3).

144. BVerfGG §4. See also Schefold, „Zur Problematik der beschränkten Amtszeit von Verfassungsrichtern", 43 *JZ* 291 (1988).

145. There are special procedural regulations for many of the specialized jurisdictions of the Constitutional Court such as election oversight, impeachment of federal judges, etc. See BVerfGG §§36–89.

146. See BVerfGG §30 for the procedure to be followed in reaching a decision. BVerfGG §15 requires a quorum of 6 judges. However in cases of special urgency a preliminary injunction requires a quorum of only 3 judges but a unanimous decision. See BVerfGG §32(6).

the ordinary courts, Constitutional Court judges who disagree with the majority opinion can, and do, file dissenting opinions.[147]

In recent years the workload of the Federal Constitutional Court has expanded beyond the capacity of that court to render prompt and efficient justice in every case. In 1999 the 16 judges of the Federal Constitutional Court were confronted by some 4885 new case filings. By necessity the Court has been compelled to exercise a kind of discretionary jurisdiction over the various kinds of constitutional appeals presented. Under the current practice of the court, three judges of a senate, acting unanimously, may summarily dismiss a straight constitutional appeal (*Verfassungsbeschwerde*) as unfounded or may similarly sustain the appeal and grant the relief requested.[148]

Most of the German states also have state constitutional courts which determine issues of the constitutionality of state legislation under state constitutions.[149] These courts generally have the power to adjudicate cases brought questioning the validity of state legislation or administrative practice under state constitutions. Some of them also review the constitutionality of judgments of the District Courts and State Appeals Courts to the extent that questions of state constitutional law are involved.[150] The workload of the state constitutional courts is relatively light. In 1999 the total number of cases filed in all of the German state constitutional courts was under 600.[151]

F. The European Court of Justice and the European Court of Human Rights

Because Germany is a Member State of the European Union and a signatory to the European Convention of Human Rights, its civil justice system is

147. BVerfGG §30(2). See Zierlein, „Erfahrungen mit dem Sondervotum beim Bundesverfassungsgericht", 34 *DÖV* 83 (1981), for a discussion of dissenting opinions.

148. See BVerfGG §§93a–93d. For a discussion of the constitutionality of that practice see Benda, „Aktuelle Probleme der Praxis des Bundesverfassungsgerichts", 33 *NJW* 2097 (1980); Schlink, „Zugangshürden im Verfassungsbeschwerdeverfahren", 37 *NJW* 89 (1984).

149. In the states which do not have their own Constitutional Courts claims of violation of the state constitution are referred to the Federal Constitutional Court. GG Article 99.

150. See Rosenberg/Schwab/Gottwald, §17(III)(8), p. 81.

151. German Ministry of Justice, *Zahlen aus der Justiz*, p. 4.

integrated with and subject to the European Court of Justice in Luxembourg and the European Court of Human Rights in Strasbourg, France.

The European Court of Justice (*Europäischer Gerichtshof* or *EuGH*) was established in 1957 as the judicial branch of the European Community to interpret the treaties and conventions establishing and governing the Community and to maintain unity and consistency of application of those treaties and the resulting European Community Law throughout the European Community. In 1989 the European Union created a Court of First Instance (*Gericht erster Instanz*) to hear cases involving certain disputes between individuals and organs of the European Union.[152]

The European Court of Justice functions as a constitutional court with respect to the treaties and conventions constituting the European Union, as an appeals court for the Court of First Instance, and as an authoritative instructing court for the national courts of the Member States in questions of European Union law. In civil litigation any German court can (at least in principle) certify (*vorlegen*) an unresolved question of European Union law material to the outcome of a pending case to the European Court of Justice for authoritative resolution.[153] The highest national appellate court to which appeal may be had as of right is required to certify unresolved questions of European Law material to the court's decision.[154] The decision of the European Court of Justice on matters of European Union law is binding on the courts of the Member States.[155]

Certification can be on motion of either party or on the court's own motion. In practice the lower courts, that is, the Local Courts and the District Courts, seldom certify questions to the European Court of Justice. Referrals from the State Appeals Courts and the Federal Supreme Court are more frequent. In 2001 some 85 questions of European law were certified to the European Court of Justice by German courts, four of them by the Federal

---

152. See *Rules of the European Court of First Instance* of May 2, 1991.

153. European Treaty, Art. 234(2). See Herdegen, *Europarecht,* 4th ed. (2002), mn. 219 ff. But see the exception of Art. 68(1) for visa, asylum, immigration and judicial cooperation in civil matters. European cases concerning these fields of law are subject to certification only by the highest appellate courts of the Member States.

154. European Treaty, Art. 234(3); Euratom, Art. 150(3). The procedure on certification (*Vorlage*) is regulated by the Interpretation Protocol of 1968 for original and new Member States.

155. See European Court of Justice, Case 69/85, *Wünsche/Deutschland,* 1986 ECR, 947, 953, mn. 15 (1995); European Court of Justice, Case 66/80, *International Chemical Corporation/Amministrazione delle Finanze dello Stato,* 1981 ECR 1191, 1215, mn. 13 (1981).

Supreme Court in civil matters.[156] An appellate court's refusal, without good reason, to certify a material question of European Law can be seen as a violation of the German Constitution cognizable by the Federal Constitutional Court.[157] A party aggrieved by such refusal could file a constitutional appeal (*Verfassungsbeschwerde*) with the Federal Constitutional Court, which could order that the matter be referred to the appropriate European court.

If there is doubt as to whether a question is within the jurisdiction of the European Court of Justice, the question of jurisdiction can be submitted to the European Court, which has ultimate jurisdiction to determine its own jurisdiction vis à vis the jurisdiction of the courts of the Member States.[158]

The European Court of Human Rights (*Europäischer Gerichtshof für Menschenrechte* or *EGMR*) exercises a kind of supranational quasi-appellate jurisdiction over matters involving human rights guaranteed by the European Convention on Human Rights (*Europäische Menschenrechtskonvention*). Signatories to this convention are not only the Member States of the European Union, but nearly all European countries including Russia and Turkey. A party asserting violation of a basic human right guaranteed by the Convention by either another private party or by some legislation, administrative action, or governmental organ of a signatory state, including judicial organs, practices, or decisions, must first exhaust all available administrative or judicial appeals in the signatory state, including in the case of Germany, resort to the Federal Constitutional Court.[159] Human rights litigants remaining unsatisfied can apply to the European Court of Human Rights in Strasbourg.[160] A decision by the European Court of Human Rights is binding on German parties, the German government and the German courts. The European Court of Human Rights

---

156. Annual Report of the Court of Justice of the European Community 2001 (2002), Table 17 and *Tätigkeitsbericht des Bundesgerichtshofs 2001,* http://www.bundesgerichtshof.de/bgh/statistik/taetigkeit2001.php

157. See Rosenberg/Schwab/Gottwald, §18(III)(2)(c), p. 85; Federal Constitutional Court, 41 *NJW* 2173 (1988).

158. See Rosenberg/Schwab/Gottwald, §18(II)(4), p. 84; European Treaty, Art. 234; Euratom, Art. 150.

159. See ECHR Art. 35(1); Frowein/Peukert, *Europäische Menschenrechtskonvention,* 2nd ed. (1996), Art. 26, mn. 25, 28.

160. For more information on the jurisdiction of the European Court of Human Rights and practice before that court, see Graf Vitzthum, *Völkerrecht,* 2nd ed. (2001), (III)(2)(b), mn. 274 ff.; Berger, *Rechtsprechung des Europäischen Gerichtshofs für Menschenrechte* (1987); Schlette, „Das neue Rechtsschutzsystem der Europäischen Menschenrechtskonvention", 56 *ZaöRV* 905 (1996); Stürner, "Suing the Sovereign in Europe and Germany", 34 *George Washington International Law Review* (2003).

may render a declaratory judgment which will then be implemented by national judicial relief or it may grant monetary compensation.

G. German Judges

The core element of the German system of justice is the German professional judge (*Berufsrichter*). The system requires and expects a high standard of energy, competence and integrity on the part of its judges. By the same token, German judges receive thorough training, enjoy strong civil service protection and full judicial independence, and can anticipate careers of esteemed public service in their roles as the main functionaries of Germany's justice system.

German judges hold salaried positions in the judicial branches of the various German states or the federal government. Following a probationary period at the beginning of their careers, they have lifetime tenure. The terms and conditions of their service and their performance are regulated by the German Judges Law (*Deutsches Richtergesetz* or *DRiG*). Ordinarily judges start in the lower branches of the justice system. They may apply for promotion to serve in the Appeals Courts and even the Federal Supreme Courts based on merit and seniority as determined by various appointment committees.[161]

1. Education and training

The German program for the education and training of judges and lawyers alike is based on the principle of the "complete jurist" (*Volljurist*). That is, every lawyer is given the same basic training required for a person to be appointed as a judge.[162] Although the educational facilities (universities) are administered and funded by the German States, the basic educational requirements to serve as a judge are specified by Federal law. The German Judges Law (*Deutsches Richtergesetz or DRiG*) requires that all future judges attend a German university for at least 3½ years, after which they must pass a First State Examination (*erstes Staatsexamen*). Following passage of the First State Examination, the judicial candidates are required to fulfil the requirements of a two-year internship (*Referendariat*) with various organs of justice including

---

161. See Ch. 3(G)(2) below for a discussion of the appointment and promotion process.

162. Indeed, the law provides that in order to be licensed as a lawyer (*Rechtsanwalt*) in Germany, one must fulfil the educational and training requirements to serve as a judge, *Bundesrechtsanwaltsordnung* (BRAO) §4. See Ch. 4(C) below.

the judiciary, the state attorney's office, an administrative agency, a private law office, and another justice-related enterprise of the candidate's choice (*Wahlstation*).[163] During the internship each candidate is paid a small monthly stipend by the state. Following this internship there is a Second State Examination (*zweites Staatsexamen*), which covers not only academic subjects but also the practical lessons from the internship. Successful passage of the Second State Examination is the final formal qualification for service in the German judiciary.

A law professor on any German law faculty is automatically qualified for appointment as a full-time or part-time judge regardless of completion of the internship or Second State Examination.[164] Some German law teachers, especially those specializing in procedural law, serve as part time judges on State Appeals Courts located near their universities.[165]

2. Appointment

Most German professional judges (*Berufsrichter*) serve courts maintained by the various German states, and practically all judges, except for some of the members of the Constitutional Court, start their judicial service on a state court.[166] Among the various German states there is some variation in the method of selecting and appointing judges. In some states, such as Hessen, Hamburg, Bremen and Berlin, appointment of new judges involves participation by judicial selection commissions combining elements of the state executive, legislative and judicial branches. In the others the state governmental administration (*Regierung*) or state ministry of justice is responsible for selection and appointment of judges.[167] Under either procedure, candidates apply for judicial vacancies and are evaluated on their merits. High scores on state exam-

---

163. See DRiG §§5–5b. See also Schmidt-Räntsch/Schmidt-Räntsch, *Deutsches Richtergesetz*, 5th ed. (1995), §5b, mn. 6 ff.

164. See DRiG §7. „*Ordentliche Professoren*" within the meaning of that provision are the traditional C4-professors appointed pursuant to the old BBesG §35(1). See Federal Constitutional Court, 37 *NJW* 912 (1984). See now BBesG §§32 ff.

165. For instance one of the co-authors of this text serves as part-time judge on a panel of the State Appeals Court of Baden-Württemberg which sits in Freiburg.

166. Although there is no legal impediment to appointment of a lawyer with some years experience to a judgeship on a state appeals court or even a Federal Supreme Court, as a matter of practice this is done very rarely.

167. When the state government makes the selection, the German Judges Law requires that input be received from the Presidential Council (*Präsidialrat*) of the state judiciary. DRiG §75. The Presidential Council is the elected representation of the judges.

inations and other indicia of intellectual ability, industriousness and judicial temperament such as published writings and strong recommendations from senior judges usually carry the most weight in such appointments. Political activity is usually not important in evaluating applicants for entry-level judgeships in the ordinary courts. Most entry-level judges are appointed at the completion of their legal educations soon after completing the second state examination. Occasionally a state's attorney with some years experience will enter the judiciary, much less frequently a jurist from private practice or the academy.

A young judicial candidate is initially appointed a probationary judge (*Richter auf Probe*) for a period not exceeding five years, during which she may be discharged for a simple failure of satisfactory performance.[168] Following successful service as a probationary judge for at least three years, the judge is appointed judge with life tenure (*Richter auf Lebenszeit*).[169] A judge is appointed to a particular court in a particular locality subject only to temporary assignment to service in a corresponding court at another location.[170]

Aside from professors who serve as part time judges, the great majority of German professional judges start and end their legal careers as judges. Normally there is little crossover into the judiciary from other branches of the legal profession, with the exception that sometimes senior public attorneys will become judges after several years of service. Judges very rarely leave the bench to enter private practice. Occasionally a judge may be called to serve as a senior public attorney or state attorney.

The German Constitution provides that a Federal Judicial Selection Committee (*Bundesrichterwahlausschuss*) composed of ministers from the respective states and an equal number of deputies of the German Parliament is responsible for electing judges to the Federal Supreme Courts.[171]

Judges of the Constitutional Court are often not professional judges before their selection, although judges from the Federal Supreme Courts are fre-

168. See DRiG §12. The procedure for appointment as a state's attorney (*Staatsanwalt*) is parallel. A person entering the judiciary after significant service in another organ of the justice system, e.g. as state attorney, can be appointed a judge by assignment (*Richter kraft Auftrags*) for a probationary period not to exceed two years. DRiG §16(1).

169. DRiG §10. See Baumbach/Lauterbach/Albers/Hartmann, *DRiG* §10, mn. 2.

170. See DRiG §37; Rosenberg/Schwab/Gottwald §24(II)(6), pp. 125 ff. The assignment may concern only a part of the judge's function. See Schmidt-Räntsch/Schmidt-Räntsch, §37, mn. 4c.

171. GG Art. 95(2). This system includes not only the Federal Supreme Court but also the four other specialized Federal Supreme Courts. Nominations of persons to serve as judges on these courts come from the various states, whose procedures for making the nominations vary. In each case there is provision for input from the state's judicial branch.

quently appointed.[172] The majority of appointees are individual jurists of high public or academic distinction, as befits a court which has the responsibility of safeguarding the constitutional structure of the entire country.[173] Constitutional Court judges are chosen by vote of the respective houses of the German Parliament. Political considerations play a major role in the selection and election of these judges.

3. Compensation, Evaluation and Promotion

German professional judges have a unique status as salaried members of the judicial branches of the states and federation and are entitled to various privileges and protections designed to safeguard their independence. Compensation is generally at a level of a senior academic civil servant or government official and is based largely on the particular judicial position and seniority in service.

German judicial service is hierarchical so far as responsibility, compensation and prestige are concerned. There are a number of levels and positions within the judiciary through which a judge can pass during an active judicial career. In general, compensation, responsibility and prestige are seen to increase with the level of court, starting at the bottom with the Local Courts[174] and leading to the Federal Supreme Courts at the top. Courts such as the State District Courts which sit in tribunals have designated presiding judges (*vorsitzende Richter*) who play larger roles in oral proceedings and enjoy slightly greater prestige and pay than the other sitting judges. Multi-judge Local and District Courts have chief judges (*Präsidenten*) and sometimes deputy chief judges (*Vizepräsidenten*). It is not uncommon that the compensation and prestige of such a position in a jurisdictionally "lower" court might exceed the compensation of an ordinary judge on a "higher" court.[175]

---

172. The Constitutional Court Organization Law requires that at least three judges in each of the two senates of the Constitutional Court have served on one of the Federal Supreme Courts. BVerfGG §2.

173. Currently the law requires that judges on the Constitutional Court possess the citizenship and educational qualifications for service as professional judges. BVerfGG §3(2). Additional qualifications are age of 40 years or more and eligibility for election to the German Parliament. BVerfGG §3(1).

174. And the corresponding lowest-tier courts in the specialized court systems.

175. So, for instance, the position of *Vizepräsident* of a busy Local Court would often be regarded as a promotion for a person serving as an ordinary or even presiding judge on a District Court.

Judges are evaluated for promotion to positions of leadership within a given court and for appointment to higher courts based on experience (seniority) and performance in office. There are also minimum requirements of age or judicial experience for some judgeships.[176] When a vacancy occurs, it is advertised and qualified persons invited to apply. There is no geographic limitation on judges within the system. A Local Court judge from Bavaria can apply for a vacant District Court judgeship in Baden-Württemberg or Berlin.[177] Although there is no formal barrier to movement between the various court systems, ordinary and specialized, movement of judges between court systems is not very common, at least after the several years of judicial activity.[178]

4. Independence

Judicial independence is a fundamental principle of the German Constitution and the framework of its legal system.[179] There are many features and institutions designed to enhance and safeguard the independence and impartiality of Germany's judiciary.

As noted above, German professional judges hold lifetime tenure. They can only be removed by statutorily prescribed judicial proceedings.[180]

German judges, although hierarchically organized, are not subject to orders from superior judges. They are not bound by prior decisions of higher courts other than decisions of the Federal Supreme Courts on remand of the same cases and decisions of the Constitutional Court in similar cases. Matters such as their duties, responsibilities and compensation are all defined as much as possible by statute. The idea is that a judge should be free to do her work without substantive control or interference by higher authority.

---

176. For instance, the minimum age requirement to be appointed as a judge of the Federal Supreme Court is 35. GVG §125(2).

177. In practice, however, local candidates tend to enjoy an advantage in state court appointments.

178. This is likely due to the importance of specialized knowledge to the workings of the specialized courts. There is some movement of judges between the labor courts and the courts of ordinary jurisdiction.

179. See GG Article 97; Federal Constitutional Court, 12 BVerfGE 81, 88 (1962); Papier, *„Die richterliche Unabhängigkeit und ihre Schranken“*, 54 *NJW* 1089 (2001); Jarass/Pieroth, Art. 97, mn. 1 ff.

180. DRiG §§30 ff. These provisions are exclusive. See German Constitutional Court, 17 *NJW* 1019 (1964).

H. Other Judicial Officers

Although judges play the dominant neutral role in German justice,[181] there are a number of other judicial officials who perform functions of some importance to the civil litigant. The most important of these are the court clerk (*Urkundsbeamter*), the magistrate (*Rechtspfleger*) and the court executor (*Gerichtsvollzieher*).

In a sense the principal of judicial independence extends even to these officials. Although their adjudicatory capacity is relatively minor, these officials derive their authority from statute law and perform their duties pursuant to statutory mandates. They are not formally subjected to the authority of the judges even though they work closely with them.

1. The Court Clerk

The German Court Organization Law specifies that each court is required to have a court office (*Geschäftsstelle*) staffed with an appropriate number of court clerks (*Urkundsbeamte*).[182] The statute also specifies the educational and experiential requirements for the position.[183] Court clerks are appointed by the Ministry of Justice, not the judges of the court they serve.[184]

The statutory duties of the court clerks include preparation of the minutes of hearings (*Sitzungsprotokolle*) and various other papers such as certificates of court costs, abstracts of judgments, and certified copies of court documents. The court clerks are responsible for maintenance of the case records (*Akten*) and calendars of court proceedings. They also attend to subpoenas to witnesses and requests by domestic and foreign courts for service of process or execution.[185]

---

181. The adversarial nature of the German civil justice system means that the role of the parties and their attorneys is at least as important as that of the judge. See Ch. 6 (B) below.

182. GVG §153(1).

183. Court clerks must have passed the examination for mid-level service in the Justice Department and have completed two years of preparatory service (*Vorbereitungsdienst*). GVG §153(2).

184. In practice, however, it is customary to obtain the approval of the chief judge (*Gerichtspräsident*) of the court to which the appointment is made.

185. See Rosenberg/Schwab/Gottwald, §26(I)(2), pp. 136 f., for a brief catalog of duties of court clerks.

The court clerk is an independent court functionary, not an assistant to the judges. A party may seek that a particular court clerk be excluded from acting in its case on same grounds as would disqualify a judge.[186]

2. The Magistrate

A number of minor judicial tasks are routinely performed by court magistrates or judicial officers (*Rechtspfleger*).[187] The magistrates are judicial officers in their own rights, not assistants to the professional judges. Their duties and jurisdiction are governed by their own statutory directives.[188]

The statute entrusts to the magistrate a number of judicial determinations otherwise within the province of a regular judge.[189] Some of these matters are delegated to the magistrate without reservation, which means that the magistrate decides the matter subject only to the prescribed appeals procedures.[190]

A large category of matters are statutorily assigned to the magistrate subject to reservation of certain issues for a judge. Many of these involve exercise of the Local Courts' noncontentious jurisdiction (*freiwillige Gerichtsbarkeit*). For instance the Magistrate's Law delegates guardianship matters, probate matters, bankruptcy matters and maintenance of the commercial register (*Handelsregister*) regulated by the Law on Noncontentious Jurisdiction (*Gesetz über die Angelegenheiten der freiwilligen Gerichtsbarkeit* or FGG) to the magistrate, subject to reservation of certain, usually contested, issues for the Local Court judge.[191]

With respect to matters delegated to the magistrate without reservation as well as those assigned subject to reservation of certain issues, the magistrate functions like a judge in her own right.[192] The magistrate attends to the dele-

---

186. ZPO §49. See also RPflG §10 concerning the disqualification of magistrates and Marx, „Ablehnung des Rechtspflegers wegen Besorgnis der Befangenheit", 107 *Rpfleger* 518, 520 (1999) for a discussion of grounds for disqualification.

187. The German term *Rechtspfleger* means literally "law curator". The function is most akin to that of a minor magistrate in American and English parlance, hence the use of that term in this text.

188. See Magistrates Act of November 5, 1969, BGBl I, p. 2065 (RPflG). By law every court is required to appoint a magistrate. Busy courts have a number of them.

189. See RPflG §3.

190. RPflG §3(1). Many of these matters involve the maintenance of court registers and the conduct of execution sales and partition proceedings.

191. RPflG §3(2). The specific issues reserved for the Local Court judge are set forth in RPflG §§14–19.

192. RPflG §9. See also Herbst, „Der Rechtspfleger - unabhängiges Rechtsprechungsorgan im vereinigten Deutschland", 102 *Rpfleger* 481 (1994).

gated matters in her own name and is required to seek judicial guidance only when the indicated action is outside the magistrate's competence[193] or when the matter entrusted to the magistrate is so closely connected with an issue under consideration by a judge that the entire matter should be handled by the judge.[194] Issues of the respective jurisdictions of judge and magistrate are decided by the judge.[195]

In ordinary civil litigation in the Local Court and the District Court magistrates are statutorily entrusted with a number of judicial functions[196] including:

a. Warning proceedings (*Mahnverfahren*);[197]
b. Public citation and forfeiture proceedings (*Aufgebotsverfahren*);[198]
c. Certain issues in connection with grant of legal aid;[199]
d. Certain formalized decisions in support cases;[200]
e. Taxation of court costs and attorneys fees;[201]

and a number of other discrete functions as described in Sections 20–24a of the Magistrates' Law.

A party aggrieved by a decision of a magistrate can file a miscellaneous appeal (*Beschwerde*) if the matter is one from which a miscellaneous appeal could have been taken had it been decided by a judge.[202] Otherwise the aggrieved party may file an objection (*Erinnerung*) with the magistrate. If the magistrate decides not to grant relief on the objection, she is required to refer the matter to a judge of the court to which the magistrate is assigned.[203] If the judge deems the objection well founded, the judge will issue a decision sustaining

---

193. RPflG §4. See also Uhlenbruck, „Die Zusammenarbeit von Richter und Rechtspfleger in einem künftigen Insolvenzverfahren", 105 *Rpfleger* 356, 359 (1997), for a discussion of the judge's right to handle matters delegated to the magistrate.

194. RPflG §6.

195. RPflG §7. See also Marquordt, „*Das Rechtspflegergesetz 1969*", 78 *Rpfleger* 1, 4 (1970).

196. See RPflG §3(3).

197. ZPO §§688 ff., RPflG §20(1). See also Hansens, "Zum Rechtspflege-Vereinfachungsgesetz", 99 *RPfleger* 133 (1991).

198. ZPO §§946 ff., RPflG §20(2).

199. RPflG §§20(4, 5), 24a. This includes both legal aid in connection with court proceedings (*Prozesskostenhilfe*) and legal aid out of court (*Beratungshilfe*).

200. RPflG §20(10)(c).

201. RPflG §21. See Dallmayer/Eickmann, *Rechtspflegergesetz*, 1st ed. (1996), §21, mn. 9 for an enumeration of the respective proceedings.

202. RPflG §11(1). See Ch.10(F) below on the procedure on a miscellaneous appeal.

203. RPflG §11(2). See GG Art. 19(4); Federal Constitutional Court, 16 *NJW-RR* 1077, 1078 (2001).

the objection. Otherwise the judge will dismiss the objection, without right of further appeal.

German magistrates must undergo a course of post-secondary study at a specialized vocational university of at least three years and pass a special magistrates examination (*Rechtspflegerprüfung*).[204] Persons who have satisfied the requirements for eligibility for judicial service are also qualified to serve as magistrates.[205] Legal interns (*Referendare*) can, in appropriate instances, perform the functions of magistrates during their internships.[206]

Magistrates are assigned their duties by the chief judge of the court in which they are employed. Upon satisfying the qualifications, they are entitled to civil service status and tenure (*Verbeamtung*) subject to special rules providing a form of judicial independence. In some courts individuals combine some of the duties of court clerks (*Urkundsbeamter*) and magistrates.[207]

German magistrates are important organs in the smooth and efficient working of the justice system and dispense a great deal of the justice, particularly in matters involving ordinary citizens. Typically the magistracy is a career in itself. Magistrates can be promoted to corresponding positions at larger and more prestigious courts, and greater seniority and competence can be reflected in the assignment of the various tasks within the magistrate's competence. However there is no possibility for a magistrate to be promoted to serve as a judge, at least not without undergoing the complete training required for judges.[208]

3. The Court Executor

The service of court papers at the behest of parties and the execution of court judgments are the statutory responsibilities of the court executor (*Gerichtsvollzieher*). Each court is required to be equipped with a court executor. The Federal and State Ministries of Justice appoint the court executors for the courts in their respective systems.[209]

---

204. See RPflG §2. The educational and experiential prerequisites are somewhat flexible and can include service in other branches of the justice system or study of law at a university. Some German States maintain specialized programs in specialized institutions of higher learning (*Fachhochschule*) for the training of magistrates. See, e.g., Bassenge/Herbst, *FGG/RPflG Kommentar*, 8th ed. (1999), §2.

205. RPflG §2(3).

206. RPflG §2(5).

207. This is likely to be the case in Local Courts in smaller localities. See RPflG §27(1).

208. See DRiG §5 and Ch. 3(G)(1) above.

209. GVG §154. See Federal Supreme Administrative Court, 36 *NJW* 896 (1983), for a discussion of the state's authority to issue directives.

The court executor is responsible for service of process at the instance of the parties[210] and all forms of execution which do not require the participation of the court itself.[211] The court executor operates as an independent public official, and is subject to substantive supervision by the court or the judges. The party seeking service of process (in the rare cases when personal service of process is still required) or the judgment creditor seeking execution will deal directly with the court executor in arranging these services.[212] The court executor is legally obligated to perform assignments punctually and in accord with the requirements of the law.[213] The court executor is required also to file a written report following each assignment, which is included in the case record (*Akte*) and has the status of a public document (*öffentliche Urkunde*). A party aggrieved by actions of the court executor in performance of execution can file an objection (*Erinnerung*) with the court in which the execution is taking place.[214] The court is also empowered to order the court executor to perform an execution if he unjustifiably fails or refuses to do so at the request of a party.[215]

I. Court Administration

The judicial branches of the German states and the federation are responsible for the administration of the German court systems and the allocation of judicial assignments among the various judges of the courts. Within the various state courts, matters such as assignments of judges to panels, senates, and localities are handled by governing boards (*Präsidien*) of the judges themselves. The number of judges on each court's governing board is specified in the Court Organization Law (*Gerichtsverfassungsgesetz*) based on the number

---

210. ZPO §192.

211. ZPO §753. See Baur/Stürner, *Zwangsvollstreckungs-, Konkurs- und Vergleichsrecht*, Vol. I, *Einzelvollstreckungsrecht*, 12th ed. (1995), §8(I), mn. 8.1, p. 98.

212. See Rosenberg/Schwab/Gottwald, §27(II), pp. 140 f.; Baur/Stürner, *Einzelvollstreckungsrecht*, §8(I)(2), mn. 8.5, p. 99. The state, however, is legally responsible for the consequences of breach of duty by court executors. See Federal Supreme Court, 52 *NJW* 2597, 2598 (1999).

213. The activities of court executors are partially governed by the Court Executor's Law (*Gerichtsvollzieherordnung* or GVO) as supplemented by regulations (*Geschäftsanweisung für Gerichtsvollzieher* or GVGA of April 1, 1980).

214. ZPO §766(1).

215. See ZPO §766(2); Baur/Stürner, *Einzelvollstreckungsrecht*, §43(II)(2), mn. 43.8, p. 499; Rosenberg/Schwab/Gottwald, §27(II)(2), p. 141.

of judicial positions in each court.[216] Other administrative matters are delegated to chief judges of specific courts at specific localities (such as, e.g., the Local Court (*Amtsgericht*) of Freiburg).

Although the courts' budgets are usually included within the budgets of the ministries of justice for the states as well as the federation, budgetary priorities are set by the various courts' governing boards and chief judges.

Although the courts have the power to attend to their own administrative functioning, they do not have the power to adopt procedural rules governing the conduct of litigation by litigants. All procedural and substantive regulation of civil and criminal justice is reserved to the legislature.

J. Court Facilities and Finances

German public policy and fiscal priorities place a premium on its justice system. Allocations of personnel and facilities, while never seen as over-abundant, appear to have kept pace with increasing needs. Reformers continue to strive to reduce cost and delay in civil proceedings. Yet the overall combination of facilities, personnel and procedures have managed to render a quality of civil justice which is seen as eminently satisfactory by most German citizens, and is the object of envy of many other civil justice systems.

1. Physical Facilities

The large size of the German judicial establishment requires significant public space dedicated to its use. Courtrooms, chambers and offices for support personnel are generally housed in public buildings owned by the German states or leased from cities, towns or other public entities. In some cases courts occupy leased space in private office buildings. Regardless of the shell in which the court facilities are housed, an effort is generally made to keep the court facilities separated from other government offices and to provide a level of privacy and security for court records.

The style and decor of court buildings and interiors varies greatly. Some courts are housed in traditional courthouse buildings and palaces of justice

216. See GVG §21a. For instance, a court with at least 40, but not more than 80 judicial positions would have a governing board consisting of the chief judge of the court and 8 other judges chosen by the active judges of the court.

(*Justizpaläste*) stemming from the 18th or 19th century.[217] Some of these structures have been restored after damage from war or natural deterioration. The courtrooms and interior appointments in such structures can range from restorations of the traditional to completely modern interiors within the historic shell.[218]

Many courts are housed in modern buildings or modern restorations of older structures. The style of court appointments in such structures tends to be more plain and utilitarian than in the traditional courthouses.[219]

Appeals courts occupy marginally more commodious and impressive facilities. However there is no attempt to impress through ostentation or ornament. The decor of the courtrooms and other facilities reflects a business-like and economical kind of judicial dignity. The facilities suggest that justice is serious business for court and litigants alike, without seeking to invoke any mystical awe on the part of the citizenry.

The facilities of the federal supreme courts are for the most part new and modern. Again, while the size of the courtrooms and the arrangement of the furniture bespeak to some extent the importance of the tribunal, the overall tenor is one of restraint rather than any form of physical opulence. Desks, woodwork and other appointments tend to be plain. Spaces are roomy, but not designed to awe by size or scale. What counts here is the quality of justice dispensed, not the impressive aura of the space in which it is done.

The quarters of the German Federal Constitutional Court in Karlsruhe are perhaps the most impressive judicial facilities in current use.[220] The striking design of the courthouse, which includes a glass wall in the main hearing room, is intended to project some of the values of transparency and public access embodied in the German Constitution.

---

217. For example, the State District Court in Munich is housed in the *Justizpalast*. The State Appeals Court in Hamburg is housed in a traditional but somewhat less ornate court building stemming from the late 19th century.

218. The District Court and the State Appeals Court in Freiburg are housed in what were originally 17th and 18th century townhouses. The exteriors maintain their original appearance, while the interiors have been remodeled in a modern and utilitarian style.

219. The Local Court in Munich is housed in a large modern structure stemming out of the 1970s. Interior appointments tend to be spare, modest and utilitarian.

220. The historic 18th Century courthouse of the Supreme Court of the German Empire (*Reichsgericht*) in Leipzig are being carefully restored and renovated to serve as the seat of the Federal Supreme Administrative Court. It can be anticipated that this facility, when open for business, will architecturally reflect some of the prestige and grandeur of the *Reichsgericht* of former times.

Within the courthouse physical facilities and accoutrements tend to be spare and functional. Until recently it could be said that the German courts have tended to lag in the use of information technology. In most courts, case files and records (*Akten*) still consist of bound sheaves of original papers clipped, stapled and tied together. Dockets and other court records are often kept in large books, with entries made by hand. Paper is still the dominant form of written communication, although the 2001 reforms have introduced the possibility of electronic pleading and other court documents.[221]

For some years judges have made routine use of dictating equipment to dictate minutes of hearings and conferences (*Protokolle*) and to write orders, judgments and correspondence. Most courts have computerized word processing for use by clerical staff. Actual use of computers in the courtroom by judges, clerical personnel, or lawyers, is currently very rare.

In 2002, the Civil Procedure code was amended to authorize hearings in all state courts by video-conference with the consent of the parties.[222] As of the writing of this text some courtrooms in each state are being equipped to test the potential of this technology.

Although some courts are equipped with their own libraries,[223] this is more the exception than the rule. There are just too many courts to expect that each judge will have immediate access to a law library right in the court building. Each judge is equipped with a small library of a few essential books for ready reference. More serious research must be done in a regional or university law library.

2. Staffing Levels

As indicated above, Germany has the highest proportion of judges per capita of any country in the world. And as the burden of litigation on its system has increased, the Federal and State governments have shown themselves ready to allocate the resources necessary to add additional judges to handle to load.[224]

221. See Chapter 6(D), 7(A)(1) below.

222. See ZPO §128a.

223. For instance, the Federal Supreme Court in Karlsruhe has an outstanding legal library.

224. For instance, in the State of Baden-Württemberg, the number of full-time Local Court judges was increased from 735 in 1992 to 761 in 2002 to meet growing demand for judicial services. In recent years budgetary constraints have tended to dampen further increases in judicial positions. In fact, the number of District Court judges decreased from 639 in 1992 to 569 in 2002 (information received from the Baden-Württemberg Ministry of Justice).

The reunification of Germany in the early 1990's brought a particular challenge to the German judicial system. The court system existing in the former German Democratic Republic was essentially scrapped, and that of the Federal Republic introduced in the former East German territory. The immediate need for well qualified judges and courthouse personnel was met by temporary assignment of judges from the former West German states and by a tremendous increase in new appointments. This created a shortage of judicial personnel for a time, but the ensuing decade saw the shortage fully remedied.

While it is rare for judicial resources and personnel to keep pace with growing demand in any system, in the German system the proof in the pudding can be found in the relative dispatch with which German civil litigation is handled and the apparent satisfaction with which Germans regard the performance of their system. As indicated below, a civil case in the local court reaches final judgment generally within 4.6–10.6 months of filing. A first instance judgment in a District Court case can be expected in 6.7 months. Cases in the State Appeals Courts are usually decided within 8.5 months of filing.[225]

These enviable statistics may tend to disguise the fact that in some cases proceedings can get protracted by either a succession of first instance hearings and proceedings or by a succession of interlocutory appeals. In a few instances this has led the European Court of Human Rights in Strasbourg to find violations of the right to a fair hearing based on excessive delay in disposition of civil cases in the German court system.[226]

3. Financial Support of the Civil Justice System

The bulk of the financial support for the German civil justice system comes from the budgets of the German states. Only the Federal Supreme Courts and the Federal Constitutional Court are directly supported by federal appropriations.[227]

The budget for the state supported judicial establishment is a portion of the budget of the state Ministry of Justice. The court system does not have an

225. See German Ministry of Justice, *Zahlen aus der Justiz*, p. 4 f.

226. See, e.g., most recently European Court of Human Rights, *Klein v. Germany*, 34 EHRR 16 (2002) with further references.

227. The various state-supported courts receive indirect federal support to the extent that all of the German States receive a portion of their budgets through a revenue-sharing arrangement with the Federal government.

independent budgetary capacity.[228] Officials of the Ministry of Justice responsible for coordination with the courts develop budgetary information with input from the courts themselves. The chief judges of the various state courts apply for financial allocations based on priorities set by the governing boards of the courts. The Ministry of Justice budgets are ultimately passed and approved by the state legislatures (*Landtage*) and the necessary funds appropriated.

German courts develop significant revenues from the exercise of their civil jurisdiction in the form of various fees and costs collected from civil litigants.[229] Depending on the amount in controversy, court fees for entertaining, processing, considering and resolving a single case can run to many thousand Euros. These revenues are paid to the state[230] through the respective courts and defray a significant part of the cost of providing public resources for civil justice. For instance, in the State of Baden-Württemberg court fees received can amount to more than 50 percent of the state costs included in the local courts' budget covering both civil and criminal cases.

K. Statistical Performance of the German Courts

The German court systems maintain detailed statistics on the volume and kinds of cases filed, considered and disposed of at each level. Even a quick cursory glance at this substantial volume of material conveys the impression that the system as a whole manages to hear, consider and dispose of a very large volume of civil business each year.

In 1998 the 693 Local Courts disposed of a total of some 1,584,128 non-family civil matters[231] and an additional 496,800 family court cases.[232] The average duration of a Local Court non-family civil proceeding in 1998 was 4.6 months, that of a family court proceeding was 10.6 months.[233] At least as of

---

228. An exception is the Federal Constitutional Court, which has its own budget and receives a direct appropriation from the German Parliament.

229. See Ch. 9(E) below. See also Ch. 13(E)(1)(b) for a comparison with the United States.

230. Court fees for cases in the Federal courts are paid to the Federal government.

231. These include only civil proceedings (*Zivilprozesssachen*) and not the many more or less ministerial matters within the Local Courts' non-contentious jurisdiction that never ripened into a civil dispute. See German Ministry of Justice, *Zahlen aus der Justiz*, p. 4.

232. German Ministry of Justice, *Zahlen aus der Justiz*, p. 4.

233. German Ministry of Justice, *Zahlen aus der Justiz*, p. 4.

1998 there continued to be disparities between the speed of dispositions between the "old" German states comprising the former Federal Republic of Germany (*BRD*) and the "new" states from the former German Democratic Republic (*DDR*).[234]

In the State District Courts some 404,496 first instance proceedings and 100,591 appeals were disposed of in 1998. The average time from filing to disposition was 6.7 months for first instance proceedings and 5.4 months for appeals.

The State Appeals Courts faced a caseload of some 69,600 appeals from the State District Courts and an additional 26,056 appeals from the Local Courts in family cases. The ordinary cases were disposed of in 8.5 months on average, the family appeals in 5.4 months.[235]

The civil docket of the Federal Supreme Court has continued to grow despite obvious strain and repeated calls for reform. In 1998 some 6,096 civil appeals[236] were filed in the Federal Supreme Court, which managed to dispose of 4,188 during the same time period. The court ultimately declined to hear 2,141 of the appeals. The 2,047 others received some sort of judicial disposition, ranging from 607 full final judgments to various forms of procedural dismissal or remand. The time from filing to judgment or other disposition of appeals in the Federal Supreme Court was less than 6 months in 30% of the cases and less than a year in 70% of the cases.[237]

---

234. See German Ministry of Justice, *Zahlen aus der Justiz*, p. 4. For instance, in 1998 the average duration of an ordinary civil case in the "old" German states was 4.5 months, in the "new" states, 5.3 months. The corresponding numbers for family cases are 9.9 months and 14.6 months.

235. German Ministry of Justice, *Zahlen aus der Justiz*, p. 5. The Local Court statistical discrepancy between the "old" and "new" German states in time to disposition is reversed in the state appeals courts. Cases on appeal took noticeably longer in the "old" German states than in the "new". For instance, the 1998 average time to disposition of ordinary appeals in the "old" states was 8.8 months, but only 7.1 months in the "new" states. This may reflect the fact that generally the number of appeals per judge is higher in the "old" states than in the "new".

236. Of these 4,255 were appeals on law and procedure (*Revision*). This number has steadily increased over the last two decades despite a 1991 increase in the minimum amount in controversy (*Streitwert*) to DM 60,000. 95.3% of the appeals on law and procedure were appeals as of right based on the DM 60,000 minimum amount in controversy. See Federal Supreme Court, *Angaben zur Arbeitsbelastung des Bundesgerichtshofs im Jahre 1998*, www.bundesgerichtshof.de/pics/statistik/stat_zivil_neueingaenge_1998.gif.

237. See Federal Supreme Court, *Übersicht über den Geschäftsgang bei den Zivilsenaten des Bundesgerichtshofes im Jahre 1998*, www.bundesgerichtshof.de/bgh/statistik/taetigkeit1998.php.

While even the Germans allow that there is room for improvement, it is clear that the German civil justice system operates at a high volume and level of efficiency in hearing and determining civil matters. It is no wonder that the general feeling among Germans is that they are well served by their justice system.[238]

---

238. See Gottwald, "Civil Justice Reform: Access, Costs and Expedition. The German Perspective", in: Zuckerman (ed.) *Civil Justice in Crisis* (1999), p. 207, 233.

CHAPTER 4

The German Bar and Access to Civil Justice

Lawyers play a crucial role in the German civil justice system as well as all aspects of German civil society. Germany has a large, powerful, well educated and well organized legal profession. The legal career is one which enjoys public respect and provides reasonable financial emoluments. Lawyers are held to high standards of competence and ethical behavior.

Although the German civil justice system places considerable reliance on the judge as the neutral representative of the state to dispense civil justice of high quality, the roles of lawyers as guardians and exponents of their clients' civil rights and liberties is well established. The lawyer's role is a vital complement to that of the judge at all stages of civil justice.[1]

Germany has a well developed and comparatively well financed system of legal aid, which is designed to insure that no meritorious case will fail of prosecution or defense for lack of the means to pay court costs or hire counsel.

A. History and Background of Lawyers in Germany

In the Middle Ages the development of law as a subject of university study led to the concept of the "jurist" (*Jurist*) or individual with university legal training. These persons tended to fill the various roles associated with civil justice, serving as judges, advocates, notaries, and officials associated with legal matters. Conceptually, and as a matter of legal tradition, those persons who practiced as advocates (*Anwälte*), were, and in a sense still are, members of a subset of legally educated "jurists" known as "complete jurists" (*Volljuris-*

1. For a more detailed discussion of the relative roles of lawyers and judges in the processing of civil cases, see Ch. 6(B)(4) and (C) below.

ten), namely those persons with the necessary legal education and training to serve any of the roles in the justice system.

Within this basic conceptual structure, the precise role and image of the advocate lawyer has undergone some transition over the years as notions of lawyers' roles in the body politic have evolved. For instance, for a time in late 18th century Prussia, parties to civil litigation were not represented by private advocates, but had the right to seek assistance from legally-trained "justice commissars" (*Justizkommissare*). The primary allegiance of these persons who were actually state officials (*Beamte*), was to the system of justice as a whole. They were charged with making sure that justice was done rather than merely zealously representing a party to the process. The number of "justice commissars" was limited and a very high standard of educational qualifications was required. Three quarters of the jurists who practiced in court were judges, and only one quarter served as advocates for parties.[2]

The era of the justice commissars was short, however. Even in Prussia, throughout most of the last several centuries, jurists practicing as advocate lawyers have filled roles similar to those they now fill, namely the representation of clients in civil disputes and criminal prosecutions before other jurists who serve as judges. Ease of entry into the profession and the number of advocates practicing at any one time has fluctuated over the years depending on legal philosophy and economics. Germany, as other countries, experienced its era of "free advocacy", when the barriers to law practice were significantly liberalized.[3] However until the turn of the twentieth century, the numbers of lawyers practicing as advocates was kept more or less in check by a combination of difficult entrance examinations, apprenticeship requirements and the cost of the required university education.

In Germany, as elsewhere in Europe the legal profession divided itself early on between lawyers who represented clients, generally in litigation (*Rechtsanwälte*), and lawyers who served as notaries (*Notare*) drafting contracts, conveyances and wills. Unlike advocate lawyers, notaries generally functioned as systemic neutrals, drafting documents for "the situation" when more than one party was involved. They were and are often public officials. In most of the German states the number of notaries is strictly regulated and a notarial practice is a highly coveted and lucrative position. Although notaries and their

---

2. See Blankenburg/Schultz, "German Advocates—A Highly Regulated Profession", in: Abel/Lewis (ed.), *Lawyers in Society—An Overview* (1995).

3. This occurred in the 1870's soon after unification of the German Empire. See Weissler, *Geschichte der Rechtsanwaltschaft* (1905), Section 6, Ch. 59, pp. 572 ff. See also, Gneist, *Freie Advocatur. Die erste Forderung aller Justizreform in Preussen*, 1867.

function are an important element of the German legal system, because they are not involved in any direct way with the system of civil justice in the courts, their activities will not be further discussed herein.

The twentieth century saw a tremendous increase in the number of advocate lawyers both absolutely and in relation to the rest of the population. In 1880, a point in time when many of the restrictions on access to the legal profession had been lifted, there were some 4,091 registered advocates, or about one for every 11,000 German citizens. By 1919 the number of lawyers had trebled to 12,032 and the ratio had become one lawyer per 5,260 citizens. These numbers and ratios held approximately steady until the early 1950's. However Germany's rebirth after World War II saw the beginning of a period of growth in its legal profession which has continued to the present day. Between 1950 and 1975 the number of lawyers as well as the ratio of lawyers to the rest of the population more than doubled to 26,854 lawyers each serving only 2,270 fellow citizens. By the end of the 20th Century, the number of lawyers had more than doubled once more, and the number of citizens served per lawyer had once more halved.[4]

During the nearly 50 years of existence of the German Democratic Republic, the legal profession, as such, was practically non-existent. Just prior to reunification in 1989 there were only 600 registered advocates in a country of 16 million people. During the last year before reunification the number of lawyers trebled to 1800, still a very modest number in comparison to the number of lawyers in the Federal Republic.

The Third Reich was a break not only in Germany's political and social culture, but also in the development of its bar and legal institutions. During the Nazi period the bar came under the domination of the National Socialist party and government. Jewish lawyers and lawyers belonging to other groups persecuted by the Nazis were excluded from the practice of their professions. Many were murdered, others emigrated to foreign states. Only a few survived in Germany. A small number of the emigrants returned after World War II.

Although there was some resistance to the Nazi measures by individual German lawyers, in the main the bar and its membership sought to adapt to the new realities of power.[5] The notorious crimes and excesses of the Peoples Court (*Volksgerichtshof*) and its judicial progeny represent an extreme break-

4. In 1995 there were 70,438 lawyers or one lawyer per 1080 persons in the population. See Blankenburg/Schultz, in: *Lawyers in Society—An Overview*, Table 1 and sources cited.

5. See Ostler, „Rechtsanwälte in der NS-Zeit", 33 *AnwBl* 50, 59 (1983); Knobloch, „Deutsch das Recht und deutsch auch die Juristen", 40 *AnwBl* 483, 486 (1990); see also Wassermann, „Juristen im Widerstand gegen das NS-Regime", 55 *NJW* 1018 (2002).

down of German legal culture. It can safely be assumed that the influence of National Socialism was also felt in many of the more mundane functions of the German criminal justice system and even in some civil cases. In general the lawyers were co-opted into the system. No lawyer could be admitted to practice without being a member of Nazi-dominated professional organizations.[6] Nor was the bar more deeply engaged in resistance activities than other segments of German society.

Lawyers have, however, played a prominent role in the rebuilding of the German justice system and legal culture following World War II. The adoption of the German Constitution (*Grundgesetz*) and the establishment of the Federal Constitutional Court (*Bundesverfassungsgericht*) have reestablished the rule of law in Germany at the core of the German state. It is not surprising that Germany should offer a great deal of work for lawyers.

B. Current Status, Role and Function of the German Legal Profession

As of this writing it can be said that the German legal profession is at a high point of public esteem and economic success. Lawyers in practice generally enjoy satisfactory incomes and working conditions. More important, they are perceived as being important and effective elements of the system of justice and maintenance of a democratic society. The first section of the German Attorneys Law declares that "the German attorney is an independent organ of the administration of justice."[7] The independence and freedom of the legal profession is seen as a material element in the effort to set boundaries on the power of the state as contemplated by the German constitution.[8] German law also declares and protects the right of members of the legal profession to provide legal advice and represent others in legal matters of all kinds as well as

6. For the "NS-Rechtswahrerbund" see Willoweit, *Deutsche Verfassungsgeschichte*, 4th ed. (2001), §40(II)(2), p. 352; Rüthers, *Entartetes Recht* (1988), p. 53; for the forced integration of the German Lawyers' Association (*Deutscher Anwaltsverein*) into the League of NS-German Jurists (*Bund Nationalsozialistischer Deutscher Juristen*) see Rüthers, p. 50.

7. BRAO §1 ("Der Rechtsanwalt ist ein unabhängiges Organ der Rechtspflege"). This is reinforced by the following section of the Attorneys Law which states that the attorney "practices a free profession" (*übt einen freien Beruf aus*) and that his activity is not a trade (*Gewerbe*).

8. Kleine-Cosack, *Bundesrechtsanwaltsordnung*, 3rd ed. (1997), §1, mn. 6.

every person's "right to be advised by an attorney of choice in all legal matters and to be represented before all courts, arbitration tribunals or administrative agencies."[9]

As is the case in many countries, the relatively free entry and consequent explosive growth of the profession have led to a perception of overcrowding. And the growth of the international mega-firms may result in some loss of independence for those lawyers from German firms which have merged with or been taken over by the international giants.[10]

It should be noted that only a fraction of those persons who receive a German legal education enter the practice of advocacy. In 1990 only about 35% of German jurists were in private law practice. Of the others, some 14% were serving as judges or public attorneys, 25% held positions in government service, and 26% worked in various capacities in private employment, some as in-house counsel and some in non-legal management positions.[11] As the number of jurists continues to grow, it can be anticipated that a shrinking fraction of the total will find employment in the traditional role of advocates representing clients in court.

C. Education and Training of German Lawyers

Although access to the German legal profession has been liberalized over the last several decades, its educational prerequisites and internship requirements continue to be some of the most rigorous in the world. Basically, in order to practice as an advocate lawyer (*Rechtsanwalt*), one must complete the same program of education and training required for service as a judge or public attorney.[12] This includes, first, a university education of at least 3½ years, second, a comprehensive state examination, third, a two-year series of

---

9. BRAO §3 ("... *das Recht, sich in Rechtsangelegenheiten aller Art durch einen Rechtsanwalt seiner Wahl beraten und vor Gerichten, Schiedsgerichten oder Behörden vertreten zu lassen*").

10. See Ch. 4(G)(1) below on organization of German lawyers into firms.

11. Blankenburg/Schultz, in: *Lawyers in Society—An Overview*, Table 2 and sources cited.

12. The Federal Attorneys Law (*Bundesrechtsanwaltsordnung*) provides that only persons "who have achieved the prerequisites to service as a judge under the German Judges Law" ("*Befähigung zum Richteramt nach dem Deutschen Richtergesetz*") may be admitted to practice as advocate attorneys.

evaluated internships and fourth, a second comprehensive state examination. The length and rigor of this program tend to screen out at least some of the many persons who enroll in the law faculties of Germany's public universities. At the same time, the long duration of this program means that German lawyers start their practices somewhat later than their counterparts in other European countries. The expense and complexity of this program have been frequently questioned and are currently again under critical examination by reformers who debate whether the concept of the "complete jurist" (*Volljurist*) is of continuing validity under current conditions.[13] Despite this criticism, the "complete jurist" survived the most recent reforms of legal education in 2001–2002.

The basic requirements for admission to law practice as well as most statutory provisions regulating law practice are found in German federal law.[14] On the other hand, the educational institutions preparing persons for law practice are operated by the various states, the examinations to test legal competence are administered by the various states, the internship programs are state-run, and actual admission to law practice is on a state by state, and sometimes court-by-court basis. This division of responsibility pursuant to German federalism produces some local variation in lawyer education and training within an overall uniform framework.

1. Formal Legal Education

The core of a German lawyer's preparation for practice is a university education of at least three and one half years. In practice, must German law students spend at least four to five years in their university studies. University courses of study spanning more than five years are rare, but not unheard of. A person is eligible for university study after a preparatory study of 13 years, culminating passage of the final secondary-school examination (*Abitur*). Most persons who take the final secondary school examination do so following study at a university preparatory school (*Gymnasium*).

As of the present time, admission to the law faculty of a German university is free to all secondary school graduates who have passed the final examination, although at various times in the past overcrowding at specific universities has led to the adoption of entrance thresholds (*Numerus clausus*)

13. See v. Münch, „Juristenausbildung", 51 *NJW* 2324 (1998); Stolleis, „Gesucht: Ein Leitbild der Juristenausbildung", 54 *NJW* 200 (2001) for a discussion of potential reforms.

14. See Ch. 3(G)(1) above and Ch. 4(E) below on regulation of the legal profession.

based mainly on scores on the final secondary school examinations. The policy of free admission to university study in general[15] and to law studies in particular has led to very large numbers of person studying law in German universities.[16] The perceived over-taxing of public educational resources in the overproduction of jurists has led to discussion of competitive entrance requirements and even tuition as prerequisites for the university study of law.[17]

Although there is no statutorily prescribed curriculum for law study at a German university,[18] tradition and the subject matter of the state examinations combine to produce a course of university study focused primarily on explication and application of the doctrine of substantive and procedural law, with relatively little exposure to practice skills. Most basic courses are presented as large lectures to audiences of 100–400 students.[19] Smaller "workgroups" (*Arbeitsgruppe*) of beginning students work with academic assistants (*Assistenten*)[20] on solving actual or hypothetical cases and problems to learn the process of relating facts to statute and codified law, to hone other skills of legal reasoning and to deepen understanding of doctrine.

There are few regular examinations at the end of courses or semesters. Students are sometimes required to take final examinations in certain basic jurisprudential courses such as history of law, legal theory, philosophy of law and the like. Each law student must pass case-solution examinations in cer-

15. As construed by the Federal Constitutional Court (33 BVerfGE 303, 329 ff. (1972); 85 BVerfGE 36, 54 ff. (1991)) the German Constitution guarantees every German citizen a free choice of institution of higher learning (*Ausbildungsstätte*). GG Art. 12(1); for a survey see Stein/Frank, *Staatsrecht*, 18th ed. (2002), §56(I)(4)(a), pp. 431 f.

16. For instance, as of 1999, a total of 120,000 students were enrolled in law faculties of public universities in Germany. See Schlosser, „Anwaltsausbildung in Europa", 52 *NJW* 3003, 3004 (1999); the number of law students has increased from 79,000 in 1990 to 110,000 in 1996, see Redeker, „Neue Anläufe zu einer Reform der Juristenausbildung", 48 *AnwBl* 225 (1998).

17. See Münch, „Juristenausbildung", 51 *NJW* 2324, 2326 (1998); Schmoll, „Alter Wein in neuen Schläuchen", *Frankfurter Allgemeine Zeitung* of July 15, 2002, p. 10.

18. Section 5a of the German Judges Law (DRiG) sets forth as obligatory subjects civil law, criminal law, public law and procedural law, as well as methods of legal reasoning and the philosophical, historical and social foundations of law.

19. German university students are not required to attend lectures, so that the actual number of attendees in any course may vary over time and with the popularity of the lecturer or the students' interest in the subject matter.

20. An academic assistant is a young academic working under the supervision of a faculty member, generally preparing for eligibility for appointment as a professor. Senior academic assistants are of rank equivalent to assistant professors in Anglo-American institutions of higher learning.

tain basic subjects after the first two or three semesters of study.[21] In later semesters students are expected to pass similar examinations for advanced students and to participate in seminars and write seminar papers.[22] Most universities also offer courses to improve depth of understanding (*Vertiefungskurse*) and courses focused on preparation for the state examination. The latter frequently include practice exams.

Traditionally German university students have followed a "free course of study" (*freies Studium*) without unduly strict course requirements. Theoretically a German law student can visit those courses and lectures she deems of interest or value and otherwise prepare for the state examination by individual reading and study. There is also no hard and fast time requirement. A student can take the time he needs to be prepared for the first state examination, be it four, five or even six years.[23]

The courses offered at all German universities are generally calculated to provide an all-around theoretical exposure to German law and legal thinking. However, the first state examination emphasizes practical application of law by solution of cases. In the opinion of many academics and practitioners the university education focuses primarily on developing these practical skills. Although all universities offer courses and exercises in preparation for the state examination, many, if not most, German law students supplement their university studies with intensive "examination coaching" (*Repetitorium*) by private teachers or coaches. Unlike the university courses, these programs are not free, but are offered on a proprietary basis by individuals and proprietary educational enterprises in the environs of all German universities. The programs focus exclusively on preparing the students to pass the examinations. They include not only supplementary lecture and exercises on the "black letter" legal doctrine, but also additional practice examinations. The ubiquity and im-

---

21. The exact composition of these examinations varies by state and university. At the University of Freiburg, in Baden-Württemberg, law students are required to pass a small test (*kleiner Schein*) as well as a more major test (*grosser Schein*) in criminal, civil and administrative law. These tests are typically graded by academic assistants under the supervision of professors.

22. Sometimes a basic jurisprudential course with an examination can be substituted for a seminar with paper.

23. There has been some effort to encourage students to complete their university educations more expeditiously. For instance, in Baden-Württemberg, if a law student takes the first state examination within four years of commencement of university study, an unsatisfactory result on the first examination will not count against the student on a later try. This "free shot" (*Freischuss*) is designed to encourage students to take the first state examination as early as possible.

portance of these examinations preparations courses have long led some to question the relevance of the German university curriculum or of the state examinations or both. As of the present time they are facts of life in German legal education.[24]

2. The First State Examination

The culmination of the university legal education and the gate to further training to become a lawyer is the first state examination (*Erste Staatsprüfung*). Each German state develops and administers its own examination. Questions are suggested by law professors, but each state's examination is designed and compiled by its ministry of justice. The questions consist largely of "case solving" (*Falllösung*) in specified basic areas of doctrine such as civil law, criminal law, public law, and procedure. In addition each student may choose a specified number of additional questions from legal subjects of choice (*Wahlfächer*).

The first state examination consists of a written and an oral part. A person can take the oral part of the examination only upon achieving a passing grade in the written part. The two parts are separated by the several months required in order to correct the written examinations.

The examinations are graded by professors, supplemented by a cadre of public attorneys and judges. Each examination is graded twice, and the results

---

24. The gap between academic scholarship and the more practical requirements of the First State Examination is a long established feature of German legal education. See *Dichtung und Wahrheit*, 2nd Part, 9th Book, where Goethe reports on being coached by a private teacher ("*Repetent*") during his law studies in the 18th century, first in Leipzig and then in Strassburg. The *Repetent* argues:

> You will not be asked how and where law was created and what was its inner or external origin..., how time and tradition changed a law.... With such research many scholars spent their whole life; but we ask for that which exists at present, this should be imprinted firmly in our memory, so that we will be aware of it when we need it for the protection of our clients. So we equip our young people with the necessities of their present lifetime, and all the other will develop according to their gifts and activities....

Goethes Werke (Erich Trunz ed.), 13th ed. (1999), Vol. 9, p. 360, mn. 25–35 (*Es wird nicht nachgefragt, wie und wo ein Gesetz entsprungen, was die innere oder äussere Veranlassung dazu gegeben..., wie es durch Zeit und Gewohnheit abgeändert.... In solchen Forschungen bringen gelehrte Männer ganz ihr eigenes Leben zu; wir aber fragen nach dem, was gegenwärtig besteht, dies prägen wir unserem Gedächtnis fest ein, dass es uns stets gegenwärtig sei, wenn wir uns dessen zum Schutz unserer Klienten bedienen wollen. So statten wir unsre jungen Leute fürs nächste Leben aus, und das weitere findet sich nach Verhältnis ihrer Talente und ihrer Tätigkeit...).*

are averaged for the final grade. In most states grading is done on a state-wide basis, so that practitioners from a given locality within a state may be grading examinations of students from other regions. Professors grade only examinations from their own universities. Grading of the written examinations is blind in that the identities of the students are not known to the graders.

The oral examinations are administered by panels of four or five examiners depending upon the state. The examiners are professors, states attorneys and judges. The oral examination score is the average of the scores awarded for the different legal subjects which are examined.

A person's score on her state examinations is an important professional qualification and is considered in subsequent appointment and employment decisions. For this reason all of the German states use the same 18-point scale for examination grading. On this scale 4 is the minimum passing grade.[25] Although the distribution varies to some extent from state to state, in the main grades over 11 or 12 are uncommon and grades in the 14–18 range are exceedingly rare.

The first state examination is an important screen for the legal profession. It is estimated that about 60–70% of those persons who enroll in a university law faculty ultimately take the first state examination in law. Of those who take the examination, about 80% per cent ultimately pass, 60–70% on the first attempt.[26] If one does not pass on the first attempt, one may try again. If one does not pass the examination in two attempts, one may not take the examination again without specific permission from the ministry of justice.[27] A recent reform provides that examinations in the optional subjects (*Wahlfächer*) will be prepared and graded by each university rather than on a statewide basis, and that such individual university examinations will be included as part of the first state examination, but weighed somewhat less than the uniform statewide portion.[28]

---

25. Further gradations are 4–6, "sufficient" (*ausreichend*); 7–9, "satisfactory" (*befriedigend*); 10–12, "completely satisfactory" (*vollbefriedigend*); 13–15, "good" (*gut*); and 16–18, "very good" (*sehr gut*). In the final grades based on an average of the written examination and the oral examination the "good" category starts at 11.5 and the "very good" starts at 14.

26. See „Berichte und Dokumente", 41 *JuS* 930 (2001).

27. In some states, such as Baden-Württemberg, a "free shot" (*Freischuss*) taken within four years of starting legal studies is not counted against this maximum. A student who takes a free shot may try again regardless of the results. If the result on the second try is better than the first, that result governs. Otherwise it may be disregarded.

28. See *Gesetz zur Reform der Juristenausbildung* of July 11, 2002, BGBl I, p. 2592; DRiG §§5(1), 5a(2).

3. Post-University Professional Training

Following the first state examination, a person desiring to serve as a judge or practice as a lawyer must complete a two-year internship (*Referendariat*) consisting of successive placements in various branches of the justice establishment. The structure and ingredients of this program are spelled out by statute.[29] The idea is that all judges and lawyers should be "complete jurists" (*Volljuristen*) and possess some familiarity with all aspects of the rendition of justice.

Each young jurist is required to complete a 3–9 month internship with each of

a. A civil court,
b. A criminal court or state's attorneys office,
c. An administrative agency, and
d. A private law office.[30]

In addition, each intern can choose a fifth internship either with one of the foregoing institutions or at another place of legal activity such as a legislature, a specialized court, a notary's office, a legal department of a business enterprise, a non-profit enterprise, a labor union, or even a law office in a foreign country. Interns are not paid by the law offices or agencies in which they are interned, but receive internship stipends from the ministry of justice of the German state in which they are interning during the time they are actively serving. Each intern receives a graded evaluation for each internship. Satisfactory completion of the four obligatory internships and one qualifying internship of choice is a prerequisite to taking the second state examination and qualification to practice.

The internship system provides German jurists with an important transition to the world of law practice. It is a vital complement to the academic and theoretical legal education which they obtain at the university. The internships give the young lawyers some opportunity to become acquainted with the skills of law practice in its various forms which they do not encounter in the academic environment. Often experience during the internships helps young jurists decide on which branch of the legal profession they will follow for the rest of their careers.

---

29. DRiG § 5b.

30. The recent reform provides for 9 months of mandatory internship in a private law office in most cases. See *Gesetz zur Juristenausbildung* of July 11, 2002, BGBl I, p. 2592; DRiG § 5b(4). This change reflects the fact that most young jurists will become private lawyers after their second state examination.

On the other hand, there continues to be debate about whether a lawyer who will work within a corporation, or in a corporate law practice in a large firm, needs to acquire experience in the operation of a criminal court or state's attorneys office, or whether a future judge needs to spend time in an administrative agency or private law office.[31] Critics of the "complete jurist" philosophy and the 2-year internship system point to its large cost in terms not only of money but also of postponing entry into active law practice. Currently the large numbers of young lawyers who have passed their first examination have resulted in shortages of available internship positions and delays of several months between receipt of results of the first state examination and commencement of internship in many of the German states.

That having been said, recent proposals to reduce the length of the internship period and number of different internship stations have not been successful. The only result has been some increased specialization within the traditional internship structure.

4. Further Academic Training

The successful completion of the first state examination marks the conclusion of most German lawyers' academic educations. Some jurists, however, continue in order to obtain their doctoral degrees. The usual requirements involve the writing of a doctoral dissertation[32] under the supervision of a faculty member and the participation in one or more doctoral seminars. A lawyer who has achieved the doctoral distinction (*Doktorwürde*) is addressed both in writing and in formal spoken conversation as "Doctor..." (*Herr or Frau Doktor....*). In recent years it has become commonplace for top-class German jurists to spend an additional year in the U.S., Great Britain, France or Italy studying for a foreign degree like the LL.M. or the French *licence er droit* or *maîtrise*. Those additional qualifications are important when applying for positions in international law firms, law faculties or the administration of the European Union.

---

31. See the proposals of the Federal Bar Association (*Bundesrechtsanwaltskammer*) and the German Bar Union (*Deutscher Anwaltsverein*), 47 *AnwBl* 102 (1997); Redeker, *48 AnwBl* 225, 228 (1998); Hoffmann-Riem/Willand, „Forum - Neue Perspektiven der Juristenausbildung", 38 *JuS* 106, 109 (1998).

32. The doctoral dissertation must be reviewed by a panel of two or three professors, who also administer the oral doctoral examination. All doctoral dissertations are published, usually at the expense of the doctoral candidates.

5. The Second State Examination

Following the satisfactory completion of the internship period (*Referendariat*), the young jurist is eligible to take the second state examination. These are also administered by each state, although the requirement is a national one.[33] The second state examination, like the first, consists of two parts. The written part addresses the practical education received during the obligatory internships.[34] If the young lawyer passes the written part, she undergoes an oral examination by public attorneys, judges and private practitioners designed to assess the examinee's "entire legal education and training."[35] Successful passage of this second state examination, which is graded on the same 18-point scale as the first, is the final qualification for a young jurist to serve as a judge or to be admitted to the bar as an advocate attorney (*Rechtsanwalt*).

D. Admission to Practice

1. Admission as an Attorney

Although the basic qualifications for admission to the bar are set forth in federal law,[36] admission to the bar of the various courts is administered by the states. A federal statute specifies the exclusive grounds on which admission can be denied.[37] They include forfeiture of constitutional rights by decision of the Federal Constitutional Court, conviction of certain crimes, prior disbarment within 8 years, pendency of disciplinary proceedings (against a former judge), mental or physical incapacity, bankruptcy or financial insolvency, simultaneous practice of an inconsistent profession such as judge, soldier, or government official, criminal attacks on free and democratic legal institutions, and conduct "which makes him appear unworthy to practice the profession of a lawyer."[38]

---

33. See DRiG §5(1).

34. DRiG §5d(3). This can be taken at the conclusion of the 4 obligatory internships and can consist in part "take-home" case solutions (*Falllösungen*).

35. DRiG §5d(3) ("*gesamte Ausbildung*").

36. See BRAO §4; DRiG §5.

37. BRAO §7.

38. BRAO §7 ("*...das ihn unwürdig erscheinen lässt, den Beruf eines Rechtsanwalts auszuüben*"). For a discussion of these various grounds for denial of admission and citations to case law, see Kleine-Cosack, §7.

Application must be filed with the ministry of justice in the state in which admission is sought. The state ministry of justice in turn refers the application to the bar association (*Rechtsanwaltskammer*)[39] in the judicial district in which the applicant intends to practice. The bar association is required to investigate the application to determine whether any of the statutory grounds for denial of admission exist and file an official report with the ministry of justice within two months of receiving the request.[40] If the bar association reports that there is no statutory ground for denial of admission, the state ministry of justice issues a certificate of admission (*Urkunde*). On issuance of the certificate of admission, the applicant is entitled to the use of the title "Attorney" (*Rechtsanwalt*) and to be admitted to practice before the courts.[41]

If the bar association's report identifies a statutory ground for denial, the state ministry of justice suspends further action on the application and furnishes a certified copy of the report to the applicant. Within one month of receipt of the adverse report the applicant may file an "application for judicial decision" *(Antrag auf gerichtliche Entscheidung)* in the attorneys court (*Anwaltsgerichtshof*)[42] for the state appeals court district in which she intends to practice.[43] If the attorneys court determines that grounds for denial exist, the application is denied. If the attorneys court finds no ground for denial, the application is deemed granted and the ministry of justice must issue the certificate. If no appeal is filed the application is deemed withdrawn.[44]

2. Admission to Practice in Court

Every German advocate attorney must be admitted to practice by at least one court of ordinary jurisdiction, either a local court, a state district court, or a state court of appeals. Upon admission to practice, each lawyer automatically becomes a member of the bar association of the state appeals court district in which his office is located.

---

39. BRAO §§6 ff., 19 ff. For a discussion of the legal status and role of the bar associations in the regulation of the bar see Ch. 4(E)(2) and (3) below.

40. This time can be extended if the bar association requests within the two months time and gives reasons.

41. BRAO §12.

42. For a discussion of the constitution of the attorneys courts and their role in the regulation of the bar see Ch. 4(E)(3) and (4) below.

43. BRAO §9(2). The attorneys court must commission an additional report. See German Federal Supreme Court, 25 *BRAK-Mitt.* 236 (1994).

44. BRAO §9(3).

Traditionally a lawyer was permitted to appear in civil matters only before courts to which she had been admitted. A lawyer admitted in any local or state district court could appear in any local court in a case in which counsel was required. A lawyer admitted in any state district court could appear in all local courts in Germany regardless of whether counsel was mandatory. Traditionally a lawyer could be admitted to practice before only one state district court.[45] There was also a separation of the bars of the state district courts and local courts on the one hand and the state appeals courts on the other.[46]

Recent developments in the European Union[47] have spurred liberalization of bar admission requirements within Germany. Effective January 1, 2000 the traditional "localized admission" (*lokalisierte Postulationsfähigkeit*) was abolished so that now a lawyer admitted to practice before a single German district court can appear in district courts and local courts nationwide.[48] On December 13, 2000 the German Federal Constitutional Court ruled that the traditional ban on simultaneous practice before state district or local courts on the one hand and state appeals courts on the other violated Article 12 of the German Constitution guaranteeing citizens the right to work and practice professions untrammeled by unreasonable government strictures.[49] The result of these developments is that a German lawyer admitted to the bar of any of the ordinary state local, district or appeals courts has the right to appear before all of them.

3. Specialized Courts

The code governing procedure in each of the main specialized courts prescribes the qualifications of persons authorized to appear for or with others before such courts. In some cases litigants may be represented or advised by persons who are not lawyers. For instance a union representative may provide assistance to a worker in first-instance and appellate proceedings before the

45. BRAO § 18, ZPO § 78.

46. See BRAO, § 25. For a discussion of the rationale of this rule, see Henssler/Prütting, *Bundesrechtsanwaltsordnung* (1997), § 25, mn. 3.

47. See Ch. 4(D)(4) below.

48. *Gesetz zur Neuordnung des Berufsrechts der Rechtsanwälte und der Patentanwälte in Deutschland*, BGBl I, 1999, 2448; Kirchberg, „Einheitliche Postulationsfähigkeit ab dem 1.1.2000", 53 *NJW* 486 (2000).

49. German Federal Constitutional Court, BvR 335/97, *103 BVerfGE 1 (2000)*. The statutory ban on simultaneous practice before state appeals courts has also been recently abolished, see *Gesetz zur Änderung des Rechts der Vertretung durch Rechtsanwälte vor den Oberlandesgerichten* of July 23, 2002, BGBl. I, p. 2850.

Labor Court.[50] Accountants and management consultants may appear for certain clients at first and second instance in the Administrative Court.[51]

There is no special admission requirement for lawyers to practice before the specialized courts. A lawyer authorized to practice before the ordinary courts may also appear in any of the specialized courts.[52]

A few courts, such as the German Patent Court, have their own specialized bars with special requirements for admission.[53]

4. Foreign Attorneys

Traditionally admission to the German bar and to practice before the German courts was limited to lawyers who had received their full education and training in Germany. However in recent years this tradition has yielded to developments within the EU so that now lawyers from other EU nations have broad access to practice in Germany.

A 1998 European Union Directive requires member states to permit lawyers educated and qualified in other member states to practice under their home state designations in all EU member states.[54] Pursuant to that directive, Germany enacted the Law for the Implementation of the EU Directive on the Law of the Legal Profession (*Gesetz zur Umsetzung von Richtlinien der Europäischen Gemeinschaft auf dem Gebiet des Berufsrechts der Rechtsanwälte*).[55] Now, a lawyer licensed under the laws of another member state[56] can practice in Germany as a "European lawyer" (*europäischer Rechtsanwalt*), but only under the official designation of his home state. Thus, a French lawyer may appear in Germany not as a "*Rechtsanwalt*" but as an "Avocat".[57] However, after three years' continuous practice in Germany, a European lawyer is entitled to auto-

50. See ArbGG § 11. Parties must be represented by lawyers in the Federal Supreme Labor Court.

51. See VwGO § 67(1) and (2). A lawyer is mandatory for most cases in the State Administrative Appeals Courts and for all cases in the Federal Supreme Administrative Court. See Kopp/Schenke, *Verwaltungsgerichtsordnung*, 12th ed. (2000), § 67, mn. 4, 6b.

52. See, e.g., ArbGG § 11; VwGO § 67.

53. See *Patentanwaltsordnung* (PatAnwO) §§ 5–32; Feuerich, *Patentanwaltsordnung* (1997).

54. European Parliament and Council Directive 98/5/EC of February 16 1998, OJ L 77, 14/03/1998, p. 36.

55. Law of March 9, 2000, BGBl I, p. 182 (hereinafter European Attorneys Law).

56. Or of states which are members of the European Free Trade Association, namely Norway, Iceland, Liechtenstein, and Switzerland, see European Attorneys Law, § 1.

57. European Attorneys Law, § 2.

matic admission to the German bar and to practice as a German lawyer under the usual designation of "*Rechtsanwalt*".[58]

Locally qualified lawyers from other member states may also obtain immediate admission to the German bar by taking a modified entry examination (*Eignungsprüfung*) offered by one of the various German states. The examination is designed to measure "the applicant's professional knowledge and his competence to practice in the profession of an advocate lawyer in Germany".[59] The applicant is examined on civil law and the law regulating the legal profession plus one subject of choice (*Wahlfach*) from each of two choice groups.[60] Successful examinees may obtain immediate admission to practice in Germany on the same basis as German-educated lawyers.

European lawyers who have not established offices in Germany may appear in German courts in behalf of their own clients so long as they are associated with lawyers regularly admitted to practice before German courts.[61]

Lawyers from jurisdictions which are not members of the EU and the European Free Trade Association but are members of the World Trade Organization may practice in Germany as foreign attorneys under the appropriate designation for their home jurisdictions.[62] Their practices, however must be limited to matters involving the law of their home jurisdictions, and international law (*Völkerrecht*). They may participate as "foreign attorney" members of the local bar associations (*Anwaltskammer*) but may not appear before German courts.

5. The Bar of the Federal Supreme Court

The Federal Supreme Court has its own exclusive bar of specially admitted appellate advocates.[63] Any person with a civil case before the Federal Supreme Court must be represented by a member of the bar of that court.[64]

58. European Attorneys Law, § 11. The lawyer must be able to prove active practice as a European lawyer in Germany for the minimum three-year period.

59. European Attorneys Law, § 17 ("*die beruflichen Kenntnisse des Antragstellers... und... seine Fähigkeit, den Beruf eines Rechtsanwalts in der Bundesrepublik Deutschland auszuüben*").

60. European Attorneys Law, § 20. One group consists of either Criminal Law or Public Law. The other consists of Commercial Law, Labor Law, other areas of civil law not included in the mandatory portion of the exam, as well as Public Law and Criminal Law.

61. European Attorneys Law, §§ 25 ff.

62. See BRAO § 206 (as amended by European Attorneys Law, Article 2, § 4).

63. See BRAO §§ 164–174 for provisions regulating the practice of law before the Federal Court of Justice.

64. See ZPO § 78(1)(4). A criminal defendant may be represented in the Federal Court of Justice by a lawyer admitted to any German court.

Candidates for admission to practice before the Federal Supreme Court are proposed by the Federal Bar Association (*Bundesrechtsanwaltskammer*) and the Bar Association of the Federal Supreme Court *(Rechtsanwaltskammer bei dem Bundesgerichtshof)*.[65] The proposals are considered by a special selection committee consisting of the chief justices of the civil senates of the court and members of the governing boards of the Federal Bar Association and the Bar Association of the Federal Supreme Court.[66] The committee in turn proposes to the Federal Ministry of Justice twice the number of candidates it considers appropriate for admission. The Federal Ministry of Justice makes the final selection from this list.[67]

An attorney admitted to practice before the Federal Supreme Court cannot be admitted to practice before any other court.[68] The result of this regime is that the bar of the Federal Court of Justice consists of a small number of elite appellate advocates.[69] As a matter of policy, the value of high quality professional advocacy at the highest appellate level provided by such a restrictive structure must be weighed against the value of new and diverse advocate perspectives which one might expect to find in a more open system.

E. Regulation of the German Bar

Regulation of the German bar is mainly a matter of statutory law. Neither the courts nor the local bar associations are given the authority to adopt regulatory norms of general application. Only the German Federal Bar Association has the authority to enact a Code of Ethics, which implements a framework of state legislation. The local bar associations and courts are involved with the interpretation, application and enforcement of the legal requirements and the requirements of the Code of Ethics.

---

65. BRAO §166. A candidate must be at least 35 years old and have practiced as an attorney for at least 5 years.

66. BRAO § 165.

67. BRAO § 170. Applicants who are not selected for admission may file an application for judicial decision in the German Federal Supreme Court, see Kleine-Cosack, § 170, mn. 3.

68. BRAO § 171. Recently, the German Federal Supreme Court held that this provision did not violate GG Articles 3, 12, see decision of March 4, 2002, AnwZ 1/01; 150 BGHZ 70 (2002).

69. As of 1999, the membership of the bar of the Federal Court of Justice consisted of 30 attorneys.

1. The Federal Attorneys Law and the Code of Ethics

The Federal Attorneys Law (*Bundesrechtsanwaltsordnung* or BRAO) is the basic code of conduct for German lawyers. Prior to 1987 the statute was supplemented by various ethics guidelines adopted by the Federal Bar Association as well as local bar associations. These guidelines regulated attorney advertising, practice with non lawyers, and formation of firms and other combinations, particularly across judicial district lines.

In 1987 the Federal Constitutional Court ruled that the bar associations did not have authority to adopt mandatory guidelines without a clear statutory basis. The Constitutional Court held that many of the guidelines were impermissible infringements of the constitutionally guaranteed (GG Article 12) right of free choice and practice of a profession, which can only be restricted by law, regulations, or codes of ethics enacted within a more specific statutory framework.[70] This led to an expansion of the regulatory statute on the one hand, but a general liberalization of control in the areas formerly covered by the guidelines of ethics on the other.

In 2001, the Federal Bar Association adopted a new Code of Ethics (*Berufsordnung für Rechtsanwälte* or BORA) which meets, in principle, the requirements of the decision of the German Constitutional Court, though some rules of this code are still seriously disputed.[71] A code of guidelines of the Association of European Attorneys supplements national law but is not, strictly speaking, legally binding.[72] This code may influence the interpretation of national law and further the harmonization of the different rules of ethics in Europe and worldwide.

Other legal norms of importance to the lawyer-client relationship and the practice of law come from the general Civil Code (*Bürgerliches Gesetzbuch* or BGB) contract and tort law, various laws granting consumer rights and regulating the conduct of businesses and the Attorneys Fee Code (*Bundesgebührenordnung für Rechtsanwälte* or BRAGO). Certain kinds of attorney mis-

---

70. See Federal Constitutional Court, 76 BVerfGE 171 (1987), 41 *NJW* 191 (1988). See also Kleine-Cosack, Einleitung, mn.12.

71. See Berufsordnung für Rechtsanwälte of November 1, 2001, 33 *BRAK-Mitt.* 219 (2002). BORA §13, which contained the requirement of a special hint to the opponent's attorney before applying for a default judgment, was declared unconstitutional by the German Constitutional Court, 101 BVerfGE 312 (1999) before the new code was formally enacted.

72. See Professional Ethics for the Attorneys of the European Union, November 28th 1998, in: Schönfelder, *Deutsche Gesetze*, Ergänzungsband (Supplementary Volume), No. 98/1.

conduct such as misappropriation of client funds, representation of parties with conflicting interests, and disclosure of client secrets are also regulated by the Criminal Code.[73] Legislative regulation of attorneys and their conduct is almost entirely a matter of federal law. There is very little room for state law regulation.

The basic duty of the lawyer is set forth in Section 43 of the Attorneys Code:

> "The attorney must practice his profession conscientiously. He must show himself, within and without the profession, as worthy of the esteem and the confidence which the position of the attorney commands".[74]

This basic provision has been construed, for instance, to prohibit attorneys from extravagant advertising to attract clients,[75] to require an attorney to exercise collegial courtesy in dealing with opposing counsel, to forbid conflicts of interest, and to require attorney confidentiality, even though some of these areas are regulated by other civil and criminal statutes.[76]

Further provisions of the BRAO set forth rules on conflicts of interest,[77] mandatory representation of clients in certain situations,[78] and possession of client files.[79] The code also contains a special three-year statute of limitations for breach of contract claims by clients against their attorneys.[80] There are pro-

73. See StGB § 203, penalizing unauthorized breaches of client confidences. See Luban, „The Sources of Legal Ethics", 48 *Rabels Zeitschrift* 245 (1984) for a comparison of German and American views on confidentiality. See also StGB § 266 (misappropriation) and StGB § 356 (representation of parties with conflicting interests).

74. BRAO § 43: *"Der Rechtsanwalt hat seinen Beruf gewissenhaft auszuüben. Er hat sich innerhalb und ausserhalb des Berufes der Achtung und des Vertrauens, welche die Stellung des Rechtsanwalts erfordert, würdig zu erweisen".*

75. See Kleine-Cosack, § 43, mn. 20. An outright ban on advertising was struck down by the German Constitutional Court as an unwarranted infringement on the right of free practice of the profession guaranteed by Article 12 of the German Constitution. Decision of April 17, 2000, 1 BvR 721/99, 53 *NJW* 3195 (2000). See BORA §§ 6, 7.

76. See Kleine-Cosack, § 43, mn. 44–57.

77. BRAO §§ 45–47. While in-house lawyers may combine private law practice with employment by a business enterprise, see Federal Constitutional Court, 46 *NJW* 317 (1993), they are precluded from representing clients in a matter in which they have acted as in-house lawyer, see BRAO § 46(2), (3).

78. BRAO §§ 48, 49.

79. BRAO § 50. See Kleine-Cosack, § 50, mn. 5 ff. for a discussion of the lawyer's lien.

80. BRAO § 51b. This provision does not apply to non-contract claims, such as claims based on intentional or non-intentional tort. See Kleine-Cosack, § 51, mn. 3 and BGB § 199(3).

visions regulating the delegation of client representation to other lawyers and for continued representation of clients and the winding up of a law practice on a lawyer's death.[81]

The Federal Constitutional Court decision invalidating many of the provisions of the former ethics guidelines has resulted in an amendment of the BRAO which specifies in more detail many areas of lawyer activity. The new Code of Ethics of the Federal Bar Association[82] contains further implementations and supplementary rules of professional ethics. The regulations of the BRAO as amended and of the new Code of Ethics cover the basic duties and obligations of the profession such as independence, confidentiality, avoidance of conflicts of interest, maintenance of an office, professional corporations or companies, limited professional liability, obligatory insurance, financial cooperation with non-lawyers, advertising, legal aid, records keeping, obligations vis a vis the courts, handling of court papers, service of process, lawyers' garb,[83] lawyers' special obligations in foreign cases and the like. The BRAO regulates special duties in connection with specialized practice, while requirements for designation as a specialist (attorney of administrative law, tax law, etc.) are regulated by the Federal Law on the Specialization of Attorneys (*Fachanwaltsordnung*).

2. Bar Associations

A major portion of the Attorneys Code is devoted to the establishment of bar associations (*Anwaltskammer*)[84] and to spelling out the procedures for attorney discipline and disbarment. The statute establishes a bar association in each state appeals court judicial district consisting of all of the attorneys admitted to practice within the district.[85] The bar associations are considered

81. See BRAO §§53–55.

82. See BRAO §59b, which is the statutory basis of the Federal Bar Association's authority to enact a new code of ethics.

83. When a lawyer is expected to wear a robe for a court appearance. For a discussion of that obligation see Braun, „Amtstracht oder Robe", 27 *BRAK-Mitt.* 181 (1996); see BORA §20.

84. The term "*Anwaltskammer*" is literally translated as "attorneys' chamber". Functionally it fulfills the role both of a local professional association and a public administrative agency regulating the legal profession. It is translated here as "bar association" in the sense of the "unified bar associations", which combine the same functions in several American states. There are also purely voluntary bar associations which have no regulatory function. See Ch. 4(F) below.

85. BRAO §60. Attorneys are automatically members of a bar association by force of law. With the liberalization of admissions, this may have been changed to include all of the attorneys with their offices in the district.

entities of public law and function under the public oversight of the ministry of justice in each state.[86] Each bar association has a governing board (*Vorstand*) consisting of 7 members elected by the membership at large. The governing board's responsibilities include education of members of the association in legal ethics (*Berufspflichten*), resolution of disputes among the members, oversight of members' professional conduct, nomination of members to the attorneys court, preparation of reports on bar applications or investigations for the ministry of justice, and supervision of internships.[87] It elects its own president, vice president, secretary and treasurer. The Federal Bar Association is, in a sense, the parent organization of the local bar associations. Its significance has been increased by its new authority to draft and enact rules of ethics which implement the framework legislation of the BRAO.[88]

3. Attorney Discipline

An important role of the bar associations and their governing boards is the handling of complaints and charges of attorney misconduct. Minor attorney-client disputes and complaints are usually handled informally by the governing board of the bar association dealing directly with the parties. The governing board has the authority to issue reprimands (*Rügen*) to attorneys who have committed minor breaches of ethical standards.[89]

More serious complaints are referred to the office of the state attorney general (*Staatsanwaltschaft*), who has the authority to institute proceedings before an attorneys court (*Anwaltsgericht*). There is at least one attorneys court in each state appeals court district. The judges of the attorney courts are members of the district bar association as selected by the state ministry of justice from lists of nominees submitted by the bar association.[90] These "honorary judges" (*ehrenamtliche Richter*) are appointed for 4-year terms of part-time service.[91] When they are sitting on pending cases they are subject to the same kinds of duties, obligations and regulation as a professional judge (*Berufsrichter*).[92]

---

86. BRAO § 62.
87. BRAO § 73. See Henssler/Prütting/Hartung, § 73, mn. 5–9.
88. See BRAO §§ 175 ff., 191a ff. and § 59b.
89. BRAO § 74.
90. BRAO § 94.
91. Lawyers who serve as honorary judges on an attorneys court are entitled to add the designation "honorary judge" (*ehrenamtlicher Richter*) to their professional titles
92. BRAO § 95. See Henssler/Prütting/Dittmann, § 95, mn. 6 ff.

Each attorneys court is organized into as many 3-judge panels (*Kammern*) as the amount of business warrants. Each panel includes a presiding judge (*Vorsitzender*) and two others. Clerical facilities for the attorneys courts are generally provided by the bar associations.

An attorneys court has the power to impose various sanctions on delinquent attorneys including warning (*Warnung*), fine (*Geldbusse*), censure (*Verweis*), limitation of practice, suspension, and disbarment (*Ausschliessung aus der Rechtsanwaltschaft*).[93]

Procedure before the attorneys courts is regulated by several sections of the Attorneys Law[94] as supplemented by the Criminal Procedure Code and the Court Organization Law.[95] The procedural provisions attempt to strike a balance between protection of the public from incompetent, unethical or dishonest practitioners on the one hand and protection of the right of the accused lawyer to a fair hearing and procedure at all stages of the proceeding on the other.[96]

4. Appeals in Disciplinary Matters

Either the state attorney general or the accused attorney may appeal judgments and decisions of attorneys courts to the attorneys appeals court (*Anwaltsgerichtshof*) having jurisdiction for that state. There is an attorneys appeals court for each German state or state appeals court district. The statute also authorizes more than one state to share a single attorneys appeals court.[97]

Like the attorneys court, the attorneys appeals court utilizes lawyers as part-time honorary judges (*ehrenamtliche Richter*). However a strong minority of the judges on the attorneys appeals courts are professional state appeals court judges assigned to this duty on a part-time basis.[98]

The attorneys appeals courts are organized into five-judge senates composed of a presiding judge (who must be an attorney honorary judge), two professional judges, and two other honorary judges.[99]

---

93. BRAO § 114. See also Görl, „Berufsverbot nach der BRAO und dem StGB", 18 *BRAK-Mitt.* 54 (1987).

94. See BRAO §§ 116–161.

95. BRAO § 116.

96. So, for example, an attorneys court can issue what amounts to a preliminary injunction, pendente lite, prohibiting an attorney's practice, if pressing circumstances (*dringende Gründe*) so require. BRAO § 150. On the other hand, such drastic temporary measures can only be taken after notice, hearing and with right of expedited appeal. See BRAO §§ 150a–157.

97. BRAO § 100(4).

98. See BRAO § 102.

99. See BRAO §§ 101(3), 104.

The attorneys appeals court hears procedural appeals as well as second-instance appeals from decisions and judgments of the attorneys courts.[100] Decisions of the attorneys appeals court are subject to revision appeal (*Revision*) to the Federal Supreme Court if the remedy either granted or withheld was suspension or disbarment, or if the decision of the attorneys appeals court authorized further appeal in a case of fundamental legal or regulatory significance.[101] In the Federal Supreme Court such appeals are heard by a special senate consisting of the Chief Justice of the court, three other judges of the Federal Supreme Court and three attorneys. The Chief Justice, or in his absence, one of the other Federal Supreme Court judges serves as presiding judge in proceedings before this special senate. The attorney members of the senate are appointed to four-year terms by the Federal Ministry of Justice from a list of nominees provided by the Federal Bar Association (*Bundesrechtsanwaltskammer*) and developed in turn from lists of names submitted by the bar associations in the various states.

This elaborate apparatus for the handling of grievances and complaints against attorneys is used relatively seldom, although in recent years there has been some increase in formal charges of attorney misconduct.[102] So, for instance, in 1992 the total caseload of all of the attorneys courts in Germany amounted to less than 500 cases.[103] Decisions of attorneys courts and the relatively rare decisions of attorneys appeals courts are printed in the attorneys journals and are widely read by members of the bar. But most disputes between clients and lawyers as well as between lawyers and lawyers continue to be handled informally within the bar associations and rarely involve the official apparatus.

F. Lawyers' Organizations

The mandatory bar associations perform not only public regulatory functions, they also serve as professional associations representing the interests of the bar in general. Among other functions the local bar associations disseminate information on law reforms to their members and solicit their perspectives, assist individual members with guidance and advice, and conduct local programs of continuing legal education.

---

100. BRAO §§ 142, 143.

101. BRAO § 145.

102. Blankenburg/Schultz, in: *Lawyers in Society—An Overview*, p. 108.

103. Most of these were relatively innocuous disputes concerning such matters as an attorney's desire to combine private law practice with employment by a business enterprise as an in-house lawyer. See Blankenburg/Schultz, in: *Lawyers in Society—An Overview*, p. 108.

In addition to the local bar associations, there are a number of voluntary bar organizations, the largest of which is the German Lawyers Association (*Deutsche Anwaltsverein*) with a membership in 1990 of some 60,000 attorneys.[104] The German Lawyers association publishes a lawyers journal (*Anwaltsblatt*), holds biennial national meetings, represents the interests of practicing lawyers with respect to proposed and pending legislation, and sponsors programs of continuing legal education. There are also a few voluntary organizations for specialists such as criminal defense lawyers.

The Conference of German Jurists (*Deutscher Juristentag*) takes place every two years and includes not only practicing lawyers but also judges and academics.[105] These conferences typically attract two to three thousand jurists who gather to hear addresses by distinguished colleagues and to discuss important issues of law reform and policy. The Conference of German Jurists can exercise considerable influence on both form and content of pending legislation.

G. German Civil Law Practice

From tradition and training, most German lawyers are fundamentally advocates for their clients in litigated proceedings. Traditionally practically all German advocate lawyers regularly conducted civil cases for their clients as a significant, if not the major part of their professional activity. In the past the role of the lawyer as planner, out of court adviser, and organizer was seen as subsidiary to the lawyer's primary role as advocate. Much of what in other systems is considered "office law practice" such as conveyancing, corporate law, and drafting of wills and trusts, was traditionally performed by notaries.

In recent years the balance of practice activity of many German advocate lawyers has shifted. In large firms in metropolitan areas there has been tremendous growth in non-litigation legal work for lawyers. Lawyer advocates spend

104. This consisted of about two-thirds of the registered attorneys in Germany at that time. Blankenburg/Schultz, in: *Lawyers in Society—An Overview*, p. 108.

105. Conferences of German Jurists have been taking place on a biennial basis (with some interruptions) since the first such conference was held in Berlin in 1860. During the Third Reich the Conference of German Jurists dissolved itself in 1933 rather than come under the domination of the Nazis. For an overview on the history of this organization see Conrad/Dilcher/Kurland, *Der Deutsche Juristentag 1860–1994* (1997); for its history during the Third Reich especially Conrad, p. 19–21.

more time advising clients and representing them in negotiations and other structured activity outside actual litigation. Although some key corporate documents, land conveyances, contracts, and wills require at least the blessing of a notary, advocate lawyers now negotiate and draft many legal documents, reports and memoranda for their clients, and represent their clients in working with notaries to create key corporate documents such as joint-venture agreements. Lawyers are active in the growing areas of corporate merger and takeover activity, both outside and in litigation.

Traditionally there was no such thing as a litigation specialist. All lawyers conducted litigation and went to court as necessary to represent their clients. More recently there has become a discernable trend toward some specialization within litigation as individual attorneys or firms concentrate their practices and generate reputations within such areas as family law, criminal law, corporate law, media law, building law, antitrust law and the like. And there is a growing number of advocate lawyers who consider themselves as non-litigators and leave the court work to others.

The German Attorneys Law provides for the accreditation of specialist lawyers in several specific areas of the law and authorizes a lawyer who has been certified to utilize the designation "specialist attorney" (*Fachanwalt*) in connection with the areas certified.[106] As of the present time, specialist accreditation is available for labor law, tax law, social benefits law, administrative law, family law, criminal law and insolvency law.[107] The accreditation process is conducted by the bar associations, which maintain credentials committees in each of the designated areas. As of January 1, 2000 approximately 11% of the lawyers admitted to practice in Germany were accredited as specialists in one or more fields.[108]

Up until very recently German lawyers traditionally practiced primarily as solo practitioners or members of very small partnerships. As indicated above, a significant number of advocate lawyers and other jurists not admitted to

---

106. See BRAO § 43c and The Federal Law on the Specialization of Attorneys (*Fachanwaltsordnung* or FAO); further Ch. 4(E)(1) and Hartung/Holl, *Berufsordnung*, 2nd ed. (2001), Einführung zur Fachanwaltsordnung.

107. See BRAO § 43c(1)(2) and FAO §§ 1 and 5.

108. See Kilian, "Developments in the German legal profession in 2000", *Documentation Centre for the Law of the Legal Profession in Europe*, www.uni-koeln.de/jur-fak/dzeuamwe/developmentsgermanlegalprofession2000.pdf. The statute permits accreditation as a specialist in no more than two fields of law, BRAO § 43c(1)(3). See also Kirchberg, „15 Jahre Fachanwaltschaften - eine kritische Rechtsprechungsbilanz", 55 *NJW* 1386 (2002) for a discussion of important provisions.

practice as advocates traditionally have been and still are employed as civil servants or as in-house lawyers of business enterprises.[109]

In the last several decades, German law practice has seen tremendous growth in larger partnerships and law firms. Now partnerships of 50 or more lawyers are common in most cities of any size, and law firms of over 100 lawyers are to be found in all the major cities. Many of the larger partnerships and firms have branch offices in several German cities.

Traditionally German lawyers were permitted to practice only as solo proprietors or in partnership with other lawyers. However in 1994 the Bavarian Supreme Court (*Bayerisches Oberstes Landesgericht*) ruled that lawyers could form limited liability companies so long as each lawyer remained personally liable for work in which he had personally participated.[110] This decision was followed by another decision by the same court ruling that lawyers could form stock corporations (*Aktiengesellschaften*) provided that all the shareholders and directors are lawyers or professionals with whom lawyers are permitted to conduct a multi-disciplinary practice.[111] These decisions have been reflected in liberalizing amendments to the German Attorneys Law.[112]

A very recent phenomenon is the appearance of the "international law firm" with branches or major offices in several countries in Europe, North America and East Asia. Such firms, frequently outgrowths of large English solicitors' firms and American law firms headquartered in London, New York and Washington, can have as many as 2,000–5,000 lawyers, and often include by merger or "takeover" what were formerly major firms in Germany and other continental-European countries.

Another recent development is the growing activity of international accounting firms in the provision of legal services. Traditionally German law forbade many areas of law practice to non-lawyers or enterprises operated and controlled by non-lawyers. However a 1994 amendment to the German Attorneys Law eliminated many of these barriers, so that now international accounting firms can and do become involved with many of the most lucrative areas of private law practice.[113]

---

109. It is in dispute whether in-house attorneys, who have, in effect, only one client, may be admitted to represent that client in court. See German Federal Supreme Court, 52 *NJW* 1715, 1716 (1999); German Constitutional Court 87 BVerfGE 287, 329 (1998).

110. Decision of November 24, 1994, 3 Z BR 115/94, 15 *ZIP* 1868 (1994).

111. Decision of March 27, 2000, 3 Z BR 331/9, 50 *AnwBl* 368 (2000).

112. See BRAO §§ 59c–59o.

113. BRAO § 59a. For discussions of issues of multi-disciplinary practice, see Michalski/Römermann, „Interprofessionelle Zusammenarbeit von Rechtsanwälten", 47 *NJW* 3233

The emergence of international law and accounting firms as major elements in German law practice has raised concerns among some German practitioners and academics about preservation of the independence of the German legal profession and the legal traditions of German law practice.[114]

H. Lawyers Fees and Compensation

In litigated matters German lawyers' fees and compensation are in principle determined by a comprehensive statute prescribing a fixed attorneys fee based on the amount in controversy for every stage of a litigated case. The Federal Attorneys Fee Law (*Bundesgebührenordnung für Rechtsanwälte*) provides:

> "The compensation (fees and expenses) of an attorney for his professional activity shall be measured according to this law."[115]

The law goes on to set forth in detail the circumstances under which attorneys are to be compensated and the amount of compensation for each kind of professional service rendered.

The compensation scheme of the Attorneys Fee Law is built around the concept of a "fee" (*Gebühr*) for a unit of professional service. A number of statutory sections associate described litigation activities with a specified number of fee units. For instance, the preparation and filing of an ordinary civil case is associated with one fee unit.[116] However if the matter proceeds to oral argument (*Hauptverhandlung*) or the taking of evidence additional units of fees become payable. In an effort to encourage settlements, a lawyer is authorized to charge a special extra fee unit on effecting a settlement.[117] The Attorneys Fee Law also regulates charges for various kinds of costs and dis-

---

(1996); Ewer, „Interprofessionelle und intraprofessionelle Kooperation unter Beteiligung der Anwaltschaft", 50 *AnwBl Sonderheft II* 71 (2000); Henssler, „Die interprofessionelle Zusammenarbeit in der Sozietät", 50 *AnwBl Sonderheft II* 77 (2000). In 1999 the German Federal Supreme Court, 53 *NJW* 1333 (2000), held that the principle of joint liability of the members of a partnership did not apply to non-lawyer members of an interdisciplinary firm in cases involving only legal matters.

114. See especially Ahrens, Henssler and de Lousanoff, "Der europäische Rechtsanwalt zwischen Rechtspflege und Dienstleistung", 115 *ZZP* 281, 321, 357 (2002).

115. BRAGO § 1 ("*Die Vergütung (Gebühren und Auslagen) des Rechtsanwalts für seine Berufstätigkeit bemisst sich nach diesem Gesetz.*"). For proposed reforms see Ch. 9(E)(2) below.

116. BRAGO § 31.

117. BRAGO §§ 23, 31(1)(4). This applies if the settlement was reached outside or in the course of litigation, although the amount of the fee will usually be lower in case of in-court settlements.

bursements incurred and made by the lawyer such as charges for travel time and expenses, postage and telephone charges, photocopies, and the like.[118]

The amount associated with each fee unit varies depending on the value of the subject matter with respect to which the legal services were employed *(Gegenstandswert)*.[119] In litigated cases this is generally the same as the amount in controversy (*Streitwert*) and is determined according to the rules set forth in the Court Costs Law (*Gerichtskostengesetz* or GKG).[120] If there is a dispute about the amount in controversy it is decided by the court in which the action is pending.[121] The fee schedule of the Attorneys Fee Law also applies to non-litigated matters of the kind that could have been the subject matter of litigation. In the absence of a court-determined amount in controversy, the value of the subject matter is determined according to the lawyer's sound discretion, subject to some guidelines in the law.[122]

The Attorneys Fee Law specifies in tabular form the amount per fee unit at each level of value of the subject matter. For instance, for an amount in controversy of 50.000 Euros, each full unit of fee would be worth 1.046 Euros.[123] The levels of fees associated with the respective amounts in controversy are periodically reviewed and in recent years have been regularly increased to meet changing economic conditions.[124]

The Attorneys Fee Law permits clients and their lawyers to enter into agreements providing for payment of compensation to the lawyer at rates and amounts different from those provided in the statutory schedule.[125] A lawyer can collect from the client compensation higher than that provided by the

---

118. See BRAGO §§25–28.

119. BRAGO §7, "Insofar as this law does not otherwise prescribe, the fees will be computed according to the value of the subject matter of the lawyer's activity (value of the subject matter)." ("*Die Gebühren werden, soweit dieses Gesetz nichts anderes bestimmt, nach dem Wert berechnet, den der Gegenstand der anwaltlichen Tätigkeit hat (Gegenstandswert).*").

120. BRAGO §8(1).

121. BRAGO §9; see Ch. 9(E) below on determination and taxation of court costs and attorneys fees for further information on fixing the amount in controversy.

122. BRAGO §8(2). In matters not involving money or property where it is difficult to assess the value of the subject matter of the legal services, the starting point is a more or less arbitrary 4.000 Euros, which is subject to upward or downward adjustment "according to the state of the case" (*nach Lage des Falles*).

123. BRAGO §11, Attachment 1.

124. The last general increase was in 1994. See Law on the Alteration of Cost Rules (*Kostenrechtsänderungsgesetz*) of June 24, 1994, BGBl. I, p. 1325. A new increase is now being discussed.

125. BRAGO §3. However in a litigated matter a lawyer cannot agree to accept a fee lower than that provided by the Attorneys Fee Law. See BRAGO §3(1) and (5).

statute only if the client has signed a written agreement providing for such compensation.[126] Such agreements can specify fees based on hourly rates (*Stundengebühren*), as well as flat fees (*Pauschalgebühren*) for the performance of described legal services, and even for determination of the actual amount of the fee by the governing board of the bar association in case of dispute.[127]

A lawyer and client may not agree on increased compensation based on a favorable outcome (*Erfolgshonorar*). By the same token, compensation computed as a percentage of the recovery or the amount in controversy is not permitted. Nor may a lawyer agree to accept no compensation or compensation at a rate lower than that prescribed by statute in the event of an unfavorable outcome. These restrictions are designed to prevent extreme price competition among attorneys in litigated matters.[128]

Traditionally, and even now among smaller firms and sole practitioners, fees for out of court consultation and advice have been determined according to the fee schedule and rules for fees in litigated matters. In large firm practice, however, fees are usually determined by contract, frequently on an hourly basis. Early in the engagement the lawyer and the client sign a fee agreement specifying the basis and amount of compensation as well as how and when it is to be paid.[129]

Fees for litigation services have traditionally followed the statutory formula. This is because only the statutory fees may be taxed by the court to the unsuccessful party. Traditionally German lawyers have been reluctant to demand (and their clients have been equally reluctant to agree to) fees which could not be recovered from the other side.

In recent years some lawyers, particularly those in large metropolitan and international firms, have begun to enter into agreements with their clients providing for litigation fees greater than those authorized by the statutory schedule. Sometimes such agreements even provide for compensation to the lawyer

---

126. BRAGO § 3(1). If the fee is unreasonably high, on complaint of the client the court can reduce it to the level provided by the Attorneys Fee Law, BRAGO § 3(3).

127. BRAGO § 3(2).

128. See BRAO § 49b(2); Bruns, „Das Verbot der quota litis und die erfolgshonorierte Prozessfinanzierung", 55 *JZ* 232, 236 ff. (2000); Kleine-Cosack, § 49b, mn. 6 ff.; Henssler/Prütting/Dittmann, § 49b, mn. 15.

129. See BRAO § 49b(1) and BRAGO § 3(5). In non-litigated matters client and lawyer may agree on a fee structure lower than that prescribed by the statute for corresponding litigated cases. Some clients enter into retainer agreements (*Dauerberatungsverträge*) with their lawyers under which the lawyers agree to provide all of the legal services required by the client (other than litigation) over a specified period for a specified lump-sum or hourly fee. There is substantial price competition among major law firms for the largest and most lucrative legal matters.

on an hourly basis. However if such a lawyer is successful in court, the only attorneys fee that may be taxed against the opposing party is what the statute would provide, regardless of what the client actually paid. The principle that the successful litigant should be entitled to full recovery of its attorneys fees is becoming compromised by such arrangements ever more frequently.[130]

If the parties have not otherwise agreed, the lawyer's fees are due and payable at the conclusion of the matter for which the lawyer was retained.[131] However it is both permitted and customary for lawyers to require advance payment (*Vorschuss*) of an amount deemed appropriate to cover anticipated fees and costs of a contemplated litigated matter.[132]

If there is some potential dispute as to the amount of a lawyer's fee (either between the lawyer and the client or between the lawyer and the other (losing) side which will ultimately be responsible for payment of the fee), the court in which the case is pending will determine the proper fee upon application of either lawyer or client.[133] In the ordinary courts this is done by a magistrate (*Rechtspfleger*) and follows the form of the procedure for taxation of court costs.[134]

This system of fee regulation has traditionally had the effect of seriously limiting the incomes of German litigating lawyers and discouraging the development of a litigation specialty. Although lawyers can obtain some relief from the strictures of the Attorneys Fee Law by contracting with their clients, the fact that charges in excess of those permitted by the statute cannot be shifted to a losing opponent has limited the usefulness of this option in many situations. The fact that the statute bases charges not on actual effort expended, measured by time or otherwise, but on the stage of litigation reached tends also to limit lawyers' activity in individual cases to an amount of activity which can be reasonably compensated by the statutory fee. These economic circumstances complement the conceptual structure of the German civil justice system in its dependence on the judge to do a lot of the "heavy lifting" in civil case resolution.[135]

---

130. On the other hand it can be said that it is sometimes impossible to provide aggressive representation in difficult or complex cases for the kind of compensation provided in the Attorneys Fee Statute.

131. BRAGO § 16. The lawyer must provide the client with a detailed itemized written and signed bill as a precondition to demanding payment. BRAGO § 17.

132. BRAGO § 17.

133. See BRAGO § 19 and ZPO §§ 103 ff.; Ch. 9(E)(5).

134. If the amount in controversy is at issue, this must be determined by the judge or panel before which the case was pending. See BRAGO § 19(4); Ch. 4(H) above and Ch. 9(E) below.

135. See Ch. 13(D) and (E) below for a more extended comparative discussion of this issue.

I. Legal Aid and Access to Justice in Modern Germany

Germany is a world leader in affording its citizens, regardless of economic circumstances, reasonable access to its civil justice system. As early as 1879 Germany had a "poor persons law" (*Armenrecht*) providing for appointment of lawyers to represent poor litigants in court proceedings.[136] The German Constitution has been repeatedly construed by the Federal Constitutional Court to require legal assistance in a number of litigation situations as a basic right stemming from the principle of the rule of law (*Rechtsstaat*).[137] The European Court of Human Rights has ruled that at least in family law cases the right to a fair hearing guaranteed by Article 6, section 1 of the European Convention on Human Rights requires appointment of counsel for indigent litigants.[138] The current manifestation of this tradition and constitutional guarantee are federal statutes providing frameworks for legal aid in both non-litigation contexts and in litigation.

1. Out of Court Legal Assistance

The Legal Advice Assistance Act (*Beratungshilfegesetz*), was enacted in January 1980 and requires the various German states to provide non-litigation legal assistance to indigent persons in certain designated areas.[139] Under this law the states are given some latitude on how to provide the legal assistance, whether through "legal advice centers" (*öffentliche Rechtsberatung*) or reimbursement of private attorneys, and the scope of matters covered in addition to those required by the federal legislation. As of the present time most states have adopted programs under which indigent persons seeking legal advice assistance apply to the local court for authorization. Authorization is granted based on a means test and some screening on the significance of the legal issue on which help is sought. Assistance is rendered on a sliding scale dependent on income and property. In most states all lawyers registered to practice are required or encouraged to take part in this program.

---

136. The German tradition of legal aid for the indigent was exported to the New World during the 19th century. What is now the New York Legal Aid Society was originally organized in 1876 as the German Legal Aid Society (*Der Deutsche Rechtsschutzverein*) by German-Americans to provide free legal assistance to indigent German-American immigrants. See Bath/Nessen, "The History of the New York Legal Aid Society", 6 *ZZPInt* 239 (2001).

137. See, e.g., 9 BVerfGE 124, 131 (1959); 81 BVerfGE 347, 356 f. (1990).

138. *Airey v. Ireland*, 2 Eur. Ct. HR Rep. 305 (1979).

139. This act was amended in 1994. See BGBl I, p. 2954 for the current version.

2. Legal Aid in Civil Litigation

Legal aid in litigation is regulated by federal law,[140] the chief terms of which are incorporated into the Civil Procedure Code and the Attorneys Fee Law.[141] The underlying principle is set forth in the following terms:

> A party, whose personal and economic circumstances are such that he or she cannot in whole or in part afford the costs of conducting litigation will receive legal assistance on application, if the intended prosecution or defense of litigation offers reasonable prospects of success and appears not to be capricious.[142]

Legal aid is available in all legal proceedings, with the exception of arbitrations and the legal aid application procedure itself. In practice the great bulk of legal aid is rendered in various family court proceedings and to a lesser extent in consumer, landlord tenant, and personal injury cases.

The procedure for the legal aid application is spelled out in some detail in the Civil Procedure Code.[143] An indigent person who wishes to initiate litigation or defend a case brought against him can either apply to the court directly for legal assistance or, as is more often the case, go to a lawyer for help in the application process.[144] All lawyers are eligible and expected to participate in representation of legal aid clients, there is no panel or list. Most lawyers will agree to assist an indigent litigant in the application process if there is some reasonable chance of eligibility and if they would be willing to take on the case if legal aid is granted.

Legal aid is granted only on an instance-by-instance basis.[145] If legal aid is sought and received by a defendant in a state district court case, and there is

---

140. The most recent comprehensive reform of this system took place in 1980 at the same time as legal advice assistance was introduced. See BGBl I, p. 689 as amended by the Law for the Alteration of the Legal Aid Law of 1994, BGBl I, p. 2954.

141. See ZPO §§ 114–127a; BRAGO § 121–130.

142. ZPO § 114 ("*Eine Partei, die nach ihren persönlichen und wirtschaftlichen Verhältnissen die Kosten der Prozessführung nicht, nur zum Teil oder nur in Raten aufbringen kann, erhält auf Antrag Prozesskostenhilfe, wenn die beabsichtigte Rechtsverfolgung oder Rechtsverteidigung hinreichende Aussicht auf Erfolg bietet und nicht mutwillig erscheint.*").

143. See ZPO §§ 114–127a.

144. For an article describing the legal aid application process see Friedrich, "Wie erhalte ich Kostenhilfe?", 48 *NJW* 617 (1995). The Federal Ministry of Justice maintains an informational web site, with a downloadable explanatory brochure at http://www.bmj.bund.de/.

145. ZPO § 119(1)(1). See Thomas/Putzo/Reichold, *Zivilprozessordnung*, 25th ed. (2003), § 119, mn. 8–12.

an appeal by either party to the state appeals court, the indigent party must apply for legal aid anew in the state appeals court. However if the party appealing is the opponent of the party seeking legal aid, the court grants legal aid based solely on financial eligibility and does not apply any threshold based on prospect of success or non-capriciousness.[146] Proceedings in execution of judgment are considered separate proceedings for the purposes of legal aid, which must be separately sought for different forms of execution or for executions in different court districts.[147]

a. Procedure on Legal Aid Applications

The application for legal aid in a litigated matter is filed in the court in which the subject case is pending or will be filed *(Prozessgericht)*.[148] Legal aid is available not only in the ordinary courts, but also the specialized court systems, under substantially the same terms.

The application for legal aid requires the applicant to provide financial information in some detail and to set forth with some particularity the nature of the claim or defense for which the legal assistance is sought. In some cases a draft of the proposed complaint (*Klage*) will be attached to the legal aid application. The purpose of this showing is to enable the court to determine whether the litigant's legal position has some reasonable prospect of success and is not capricious.[149]

If, as is usually the case, there is an identified opposing party to the proceeding or expected proceeding, that party will be given notice of the application and the opportunity to submit a written response or comments.[150] The response can address either financial eligibility or possibility of success, or both.[151] Some defendants use this opportunity to try to head off what they perceive as a frivolous claim. If the state of the papers suggests a possibility of compromise settlement of the claim in chief, the court can invite the parties

146. ZPO § 119(1)(2).

147. See ZPO 119(2) and Thomas/Putzo/Reichold, § 119, mn. 10.

148. An application for legal aid tolls, in principle, the statute of limitations on the underlying claim. See BGB § 204(1)(14) as enacted in 2001 and Rosenberg/Schwab/Gottwald, § 90(IV)(2), p. 497.

149. See ZPO § 114.

150. ZPO § 118(1)(2). This notice can be waived if the court deems it to serve no purpose (*unzweckmässig*).

151. However confidential information about a legal aid applicant's financial condition will only be made available to the opponent with the consent of the applicant, ZPO § 117(2).

to a conference to explore settlement, and to enter any settlement reached in the record.[152]

In determining whether to award legal aid to an applicant, the court must decide three issues: (1) Is the party financially eligible according to the requirements of the statute? (2) Does the party's position offer reasonable prospects of success? (3) Is the action non-capricious?[153] An affirmative finding on these issues requires the grant of legal aid.

Financial eligibility is based on an elaborate statutory income and property test.[154] From the aggregate of all income and receipts of a party, including monetary support by a spouse, certain amounts are deducted for ongoing shelter and support to determine the total amount that the person can be expected to pay for legal services on a monthly basis. For instance, if the allocable income after deductions (*einzusetzendes Einkommen*) is 500 Euros, the party would be expected to be able to pay monthly installments of 175 Euros toward litigation costs.[155]

In addition, a party's net property (after exemptions provided in the Social Welfare Law) is also chargeable in full in computing eligibility for legal aid. The court compares the anticipated costs of the litigation, both court costs and attorneys fees, to the litigant's available property and the amount that can be expected to be paid in monthly installments. If the anticipated fee does not exceed the total of the available property plus what could be realized from no more than 4 monthly installments at the rate chargeable to the party according to the statutory table, the party is ineligible for legal aid. When the anticipated costs exceed this formula amount, legal aid is granted.[156] A party's obligation to pay monthly installments is in each case limited to 48 payments.[157]

In order to protect the lawyer, the state treasury will pay the legal aid fee to the party's lawyer in full and look to the party to reimburse it in installments as provided in the order granting legal aid.[158] The order granting legal aid sets the monthly amount the party is required to pay and how it is to be paid.

---

152. ZPO § 118(1)(3). This informal conference is not to take the place of oral argument (*mündliche Verhandlung*) in the case in chief. See Rosenberg/Schwab/Gottwald, § 90(IV)(3)(c), p. 498.

153. ZPO § 114; see Thomas/Putzo/Reichold, § 114, mn. 2–8.

154. ZPO § 115.

155. ZPO § 115(1).

156. See ZPO § 115(2)–(3) and Thomas/Putzo/Reichold, § 115, mn. 17 ff.

157. See ZPO § 115(1)(4).

158. ZPO § 122(1)(4); BRAGO §§ 121 ff.

The most problematical of the required findings is the required prospect of success on the merits. The Federal Constitutional Court has stressed that this threshold should not be set too high.[159] If the claim raises a reasonable possibility that relief could be granted legal aid should be allowed, even if there appears to be an equal possibility that the claim would fail.[160]

> A reasonable prospect of success such that a party capable of paying the costs would take on the case is sufficient. The preliminary evaluation of prospect of success is not to lead to the result that proceedings on the legal aid application become a substitute for a proper case in chief. If there are difficult and unclarified legal questions to be decided, the necessary prospect of success should be found. Sufficient prospects of success can exist for both parties to the case so that each of them should receive legal aid.[161]

The court's determination of likelihood of success is to be made on the representations of the party seeking legal aid in the application, any attached pleadings or documents and the comments of the opponent (if any).[162] Although the court may request further information and even receive documentary evidence in support of the application, the court is authorized to receive witness testimony only in extraordinary circumstances.[163] The court is not supposed to make fact findings based on disputed evidence.

In family court matters the "reasonable prospect of success" (*hinreichende Aussicht auf Erfolg*) standard is modified by the strong policy in favor of legal representation of affected parties in family court litigation. If a party seeks to contest any part of a family court proceeding, ordinarily that party will be granted legal aid for the employment of counsel, regardless of the prospect of success of the party's position.[164]

---

159. See 67 BVerfGE 245 and 251 (1984); 81 BVerfGE 347, 357 (1990); 45 *NJW* 889 (1992).

160. See Thomas/Putzo/Reichold, § 114, mn. 3.

161. Rosenberg/Schwab/Gottwald, § 90(III)(1), p. 495 ("*Es genügt eine hinreichende Erfolgsaussicht, bei der auch eine zahlungsfähige Partei den Prozess auf sich nehmen würde. Die Vorprüfung der Erfolgsaussicht darf daher nicht dazu führen, dass das PKH-Verfahren anstelle eines sinnvollen Hauptsacheverfahrens tritt. Sind schwierige, ungeklärte Rechtsfragen zu entscheiden, so ist daher die nötige Erfolgsaussicht zu bejahen. Die Erfolgsaussicht kann für beide Parteien des Prozesses bestehen, so dass jeder von ihnen Prozesskostenhilfe zu gewähren ist.*").

162. ZPO § 118(1).

163. ZPO § 118(2). See Thomas/Putzo/Reichold, § 118, mn. 9.

164. See Thomas/Putzo/Reichold, § 114, mn. 6 and cases therein cited.

The third criterion, absence of capriciousness (*Mutwilligkeit*), is designed to screen out cases that, although perhaps technically meritorious, would not be pursued by a person with the money to pay the cost of litigation. This includes suits where the opposing party has already agreed to render performance voluntarily, repeated filing and withdrawal of a complaint for the ostensible purpose of harassment, and family court proceedings designed to harass the opposing party.[165]

Once the court has determined that a litigant has met the statutory criteria, legal aid is granted for all proceedings before that particular court in that instance of the proceeding.[166] The recipient of legal aid is also relieved of the obligation to advance court costs, expert witness fees, and the like.[167] The court's decision is ordinarily reached without oral argument. If the application is denied, the decision must be supported by reasons.[168] There is no taxation of costs in proceedings on applications for legal aid.[169]

A party denied legal aid in a first-instance proceeding in the local court or the state district court may lodge a procedural appeal (*Beschwerde*) in the state district court or state appeals court as the case may be.[170] A denial of legal aid in a case on appeal is subject to revision appeal only, which requires the permission of the court which denied the application.[171] An order granting legal aid may not be appealed by the opposing party, but may in very limited circumstances be appealed by the state treasury.[172]

Once legal aid is granted for a legal proceeding, the order granting legal aid remains in effect for that instance regardless of changes in the apparent prospects of success as the litigation unfolds. Legal aid can be cancelled during the proceeding only if it appears that it was obtained fraudulently or by gross neglect in the completion of the application forms and disclosures of financial condition or in representations relevant to the determination of prospects of success.[173] Awards of legal aid and the installments payable by the

165. See Rosenberg/Schwab/Gottwald, § 90(III)(2), p. 495 and cases cited.

166. The application for legal aid lapses with the conclusion of the proceeding in which it is filed.

167. ZPO § 122(1).

168. This requirement may explain why German courts tend to grant legal aid in close cases.

169. ZPO § 118(1)(4) and (5).

170. ZPO § 127(2).

171. ZPO § 574(1)(2).

172. ZPO § 127(3). Such appeals generally relate to the manner of calculating financial eligibility and required payment of installments.

173. ZPO § 124.

legal aid recipient may be altered based on an alteration of financial circumstances at any time during the 4-year period for payment of installments.[174] If the recipient's financial condition deteriorates during this time the amount repayable may be reduced. If there is unexpected improvement in financial ability, the remaining installments payable may be increased.

b. Fee Schedule in Legal Aid Cases

The grant of an application for legal aid in litigation entitles the recipient to representation of a willing attorney of her choice (*zur Vertretung bereiter Rechtsanwalt ihrer Wahl*). There is no requirement that the party pick from a particular list of lawyers. All lawyers admitted to practice where the case is pending are eligible.[175]

The lawyer who undertakes a legal aid case has a claim to compensation only from the state treasury (*Landeskasse*) and relinquishes any claim for compensation from the client.[176] Compensation is calculated based on stage of proceeding and amount in controversy according to the same rules as for any ordinary case. However the Federal Attorneys Law prescribes a different and lower fee schedule for services in legal aid cases.[177] Although the fee schedule is the same for the smallest case, for cases with a subject matter value of 3,500 Euros and more, the legal aid fee schedule tapers progressively with increasing subject matter values to a level of half the amounts set forth on the regular fee table for subject matter values of 16,000 Euros and above. The statutory fee is paid by the state treasury upon completion of the stage of proceedings for which the legal aid was authorized by judgment, documented settlement or other final disposition.

c. Taxation of Costs in Legal Aid Cases

Legal aid funds are made available only to pay the recipient's own attorney. There are no funds to satisfy the obligations of an indigent person who loses a case and is taxed with the opponent's attorney's fees. The winning opponent is left to collect such funds as best it may.[178]

---

174. ZPO § 120(4). See Thomas/Putzo/Reichold, § 120, mn. 9 ff.

175. ZPO § 121. A lawyer not admitted to practice before the court deciding the case can be employed only if the employment will not increase the cost of representation.

176. ZPO § 122(1)(3).

177. BRAGO § 123.

178. The risk of being compelled to pay the opponent's attorney's fees can operate to deter an indigent party from initiating litigation even if legal aid is available to defray the fees and expenses of his own counsel. However a client who receives full legal aid would

With the grant of legal aid, the attorney's claim for compensation is transferred to the state, which also succeeds to the legal aid recipient's claim for reimbursement of attorneys fees taxed against a losing opponent.[179] If a legal aid recipient wins the proceeding for which legal aid was granted and costs are taxed against the losing party,[180] the state treasury is entitled to have costs and attorneys fees taxed at the level provided by the Attorneys Fee Act for paying clients. This is true regardless of whether the opponent is also receiving Legal Aid. Any money received is first used to reimburse the state for its outlays for court costs and legal aid fees for the winning recipient's attorney. To the extent that the actual amount collected by the state treasury on account of such costs exceeds the amount of attorneys fees paid to the recipient's lawyer according to the legal aid reduced fee schedule, the state treasury is to pay over the difference to the winning recipient's lawyer up to the full fee otherwise payable.[181]

3. Magnitude and Burden of Legal Aid

Since legal aid is a responsibility of the various German states, there are no statistics kept on a national basis. However it is clear that since the law was modernized in 1980, the trend has been one of continuous increase in both number of cases and amount of expenditure. As of April 1999, a respected German commentator estimated the overall cost of legal aid in Germany at $286 Million annually, up from about $200 Million a decade before.[182] The great bulk of aid continues to be rendered in family law cases. Most is rendered without any contribution of installment payments by the recipients.[183]

J. Legal Cost Insurance

It is possible for Germans to protect themselves against the financial impact of having to hire counsel or pay an opponent's lawyers' fees by the pur-

---

also likely be exempt from execution of such an award if made. See Ch. 11(F)(1)(a) and (d) below on executions

179. BRAGO § 130.

180. See Ch. 9(E) below for the procedure on taxation of costs and attorneys fees.

181. BRAGO § 124. Needless to say, this additional payment cannot bring the total amount received by the lawyer to a level in excess of the normal fee schedule.

182. Gottwald, "Civil Justice Reform: Access, Cost, and Expedition. The German Perspective", in: Zuckerman (ed.), *Civil Justice in Crisis* (1999), p. 207, 223 f.

183. Gottwald, in: *Civil Justice in Crisis*, p. 224.

chase of legal cost insurance offered by private insurance companies. Some policies are limited to litigation costs arising from particular circumstances or relationships, such as legal costs arising out of automobile accidents. Others are more general in scope. The typical legal cost insurance policy reimburses the policy-holder's costs for attorneys fees of his own attorney as well as the obligation to pay court costs and the opponent's costs for legal representation in case of defeat.

A large percentage of ordinary German citizens hold some kind of legal cost insurance policy.[184] Between 1975 and 1990 the gross amount of annual premiums paid by Germans for legal cost insurance trebled to a total of over 1.5 billion Euros.[185]

Some judges and commentators have assailed legal cost insurance as the cause of a "litigation explosion" in frivolous civil claims.[186] More recent research has found that while insured litigants may be a bit more contentious on the fringes, except in small traffic civil and criminal matters, legal insurance has not resulted in a significant number of claims or defenses that can be termed "frivolous".[187]

As discussed above in Germany agreed compensation based on favorable outcome and contingency fees are not permitted. Uninsured German plaintiffs not eligible for legal aid are often required to advance litigation costs and attorneys fees. Depending on the amount in controversy, these costs and fees can be significant and can constitute a barrier even for well-to-do plaintiffs.

In recent years commercial finance firms have entered the market of underwriting the assertion of plaintiffs' personal injury and other claims in liti-

---

184. In 1979 40% of households were estimated to have some form of legal cost insurance. About one third of these were for automobile related matters only, the rest had more general coverage, Blankenburg/Schultz, in: Abel/Lewis (ed.) *Lawyers in Society - An Overview*, p. 26.

185. See Jagodzinski et al., "Rechtsschutzversicherung und Streitverhalten", 46 *NJW* 2769 (1993). In 2001, a total of 2,7 billion Euros of premiums was paid, see *Gesamtverband der deutschen Versicherungswirtschaft*, www.gdv.de/fachservice/index.html (January 1, 2003).

186. See, e.g., van Büren, „Rechtsschutz-Versicherung—Partner der Anwaltschaft?", 41 *AnwBl* 501 (1991); Blankenburg/Fiedler, *Die Rechtsschutzversicherungen und der steigende Geschäftsanfall der Gerichte* (1981).

187. Jagodzinski et al., "Rechtsschutzversicherung und Streitverhalten", 46 *NJW* 2769, 2771 ff. (1993). Insured parties were found to be 5–10% more likely to institute or defend litigation than uninsured litigants, resulting in an increased burden on the courts of between 4 and 8%. However most of the additional claims had at least some merit. Only in the area of small traffic cases did the study find a significant increase in trivial or frivolous cases associated with insurance. The authors suggest a deductible or co-insurance as possible brakes on nonmeritorious small traffic claims and defenses.

gation. The finance firm contracts to pay all the costs required to be advanced by the claimant, as well as the opponent's costs and fees if the claimant loses. In return the plaintiff assigns to the finance company a portion of the claim on which suit is to be brought. The finance company's share is usually expressed as a percentage of the recovery, generally between 30 and 50 percent.[188] Because the finance company is not a lawyer it is not subject to the prohibition against contingent percentage compensation which prevents lawyer's from charging contingent fees themselves. A party who utilizes this form of financing may choose its own attorney, but the finance contract will require that some litigation decision, such as settlement, may be reached only with consent of the finance company.

Although this form of litigation finance and support is a new phenomenon in Germany, the finance companies advertise aggressively for business and even feature their services on interactive web sites.[189] The entities offering this service have maintained that it is not an insurance contract, but merely a means of finance secured by the claim to be pursued. Commentators are not so sure.[190]

Some have criticized this new form of litigation as a circumvention of the prohibition against contingent compensation, and on the ground that it changes the balance between the parties, since there are no such contracts available to potential defendants.[191] On the other hand it has also been argued that the three-cornered finance company-client-lawyer relationship is not subject to some of the theoretical and practical disadvantages of the direct contingency fee arrangement and that it does provide access to justice for some litigants who would not otherwise be able to get into court.[192]

---

188. See Dethloff, "Verträge zur Prozessfinanzierung gegen Erfolgsbeteiligung", 53 *NJW* 2225 (2000) for a more complete description of this form of litigation finance.

189. See, e.g., www.foris.de (Foris AG); www.juragent.de (Juragent AG - for claims starting at 100,000 DM); www.das-profi.de (D.A.S.ProFi AG - advertising that 70–80% of the proceeds remains the claimant's); www.acivo.com (Acivo Prozessfinanzierung - for claims starting at 10,000 Euros).

190. E.g. Fritzsche/Schmidt, "Eine Neue Form der Versicherung", 52 *NJW* 2998, 2999 ff. (1999), where the authors argue that the FORIS litigation finance contract should be regulated as an insurance contract.

191. E.g. Bruns, 55 *JZ* 232 (2000).

192. Dethloff, 53 *NJW* 2225, 2230 (2000).

CHAPTER 5

Subject Matter Jurisdiction and Venue in Civil Cases

German law sets a number of different bounds on the power of its courts to act in civil cases which can be considered under the rubric of "jurisdiction". The various specialized court systems have defined kinds of cases which they are empowered to consider. Within the ordinary court system, there is a division of subject matter jurisdiction between the local courts and the state district courts. Within each court system there is a territorial allocation of jurisdiction of the respective courts in the various German states as well as legal limits to the extent to which German courts can adjudicate cases involving parties outside the territory of Germany.

The various concepts of court competence referred to by the term "jurisdiction" (*Zuständigkeit*) are not precisely the same in German and in Anglo-American legal parlance. One must therefore be careful in the use of terminology. In this text choice of the correct specialized German court system will be referred to using the German terminology of "choice of legal path" (*Rechtsweg*). Issues of choice of the correct court of first instance within the ordinary court system will be considered as issues of "subject matter jurisdiction" (*sachliche Zuständigkeit*). The geographic division of jurisdiction of the various courts over matters within Germany will be discussed under the heading of "venue" (*örtliche Zuständigkeit*). Issues of the competence of German courts in international matters (*internationale Zuständigkeit*) will be discussed in Ch. 12 below.

A. Division of Jurisdiction among the Specialized German Court Systems

Each of the specialized German court systems has its own statutorily defined area of judicial competence. For instance the Labor Court (*Arbeitsgericht*) is vested with exclusive jurisdiction over a number of defined categories of civil legal disputes (*bürgerliche Rechtsstreitigkeiten*) arising from the employment relationship, collective bargaining, and similar matters.[1] Similar areas of exclusive competence have been provided for the Administrative Court, the Social Welfare Court, and the Tax Court in their respective areas of responsibility.[2] Questions of the respective competence of these courts to hear civil disputes involve the choice of the proper "legal path" (*Rechtsweg*) to relief rather than simple division of subject matter jurisdiction (*sachliche Zuständigkeit*) within a unitary legal system.

Sometimes the question of whether a particular dispute belongs properly in, say, the Labor Court or the Administrative Court on the one hand, or the ordinary courts on the other is a close one. If the case was originally brought in the specialized court, that court has jurisdiction to determine whether the proper legal path was chosen. The same is true if the case was originally brought in the ordinary courts.[3]

The issue of the jurisdiction of the court system in which a case is brought is a "prerequisite to suit" (*Prozessvoraussetzung*) which is considered by the judge on her own motion when initially examining the complaint, and which may be raised by either party or by the court on its own motion at almost any stage of the proceedings.[4]

The court starts with the claims and fact assertions of the plaintiff's complaint. If there are multiple causes of action asserted in support of a single claim for relief (*Antrag*), it usually suffices if one of the causes of action is within the area of responsibility of the court in which the case was brought.[5] If fact findings are necessary to determine the jurisdictional issue, the court can take evidence in a preliminary phase of the proceeding. If a court finds that the plaintiff has chosen the wrong legal path, the court is to refer the complaint directly to the court system in which it should have been originally brought.[6]

---

1. See ArbGG § 2(1). See Koch, in: *Erfurter Kommentar zum Arbeitsrecht*, 3rd ed. (2003), ArbGG § 2, mn. 4 ff. for a discussion of the different categories.

2. VwGO § 40(1) (Administrative Court), SGG § 51(1) (Social Welfare Court), and FGO § 33 (Tax Court). See Rosenberg/Schwab/Gottwald, *Zivilprozessrecht*, 15th ed. (1993), §§ 13–16. See Ch. 1(B)(1) and Ch. 3(B) and (C).

3. GVG § 17a. See Thomas/Putzo/Hüsstege, *Kommentar zur Zivilprozessordnung*, 25th ed. (2003), GVG § 17a, mn. 6 ff.

4. See Thomas/Putzo/Reichold, vor § 253, mn. 10 ff.; Zöller/Greger, *Kommentar zur Zivilprozessordnung*, 23rd ed. (2002), vor § 253, mn. 9.

5. Rosenberg/Schwab/Gottwald, § 9(III)(2), (IV), pp. 46 ff.; GVG § 17(2).

6. GVG § 17a(2).

A decision to refer or not refer a case to another court system is appealable.[7] However such decision once taken, binds all courts.[8] If choice of the correct legal path has not been made the subject of a separate decision, a final judgment on the merits entitled to *res adjudicata* effect cannot be attacked on the ground that it was issued by the wrong court system.[9]

Of course any case which directly seeks invalidation of a statute on the ground that it offends the German Constitution belongs to the exclusive jurisdiction of the Federal Constitutional Court and would be subject to dismissal if it were brought in any of the other courts. If a case raising a constitutional issue is brought in one of the other courts and the constitutional issue is one of several issues which might be dispositive of the case, the court usually retains the case to hear and decide the other issues. If the case cannot be decided on some non-constitutional basis, the court is required to refer (*vorlegen*) the constitutional question to the Constitutional Court.[10]

There are also some matters which fall within the exclusive jurisdiction of specialized courts outside the major specialized court systems. For instance, claims of invalidity of a patent as well as appeals from German Patent Office decisions must be brought in the German Patent Court (*Patentgericht*).[11] There are also specialized courts which have exclusive jurisdiction to hear cases involving river navigation (*Schifffahrtsgericht*),[12] and the Attorneys Courts (*Anwaltsgerichte* and *Anwaltsgerichtshöfe*) in the various states which have exclusive jurisdiction over certain issues relating to the licensing and discipline of attorneys.[13]

---

7. See GVG § 17a(4) and Ch. 10(F) below on the procedure for such appeals.

8. GVG § 17a(1) and (2)(3). See Rosenberg/Schwab/Gottwald, § 9(III)(6), p. 48. The decision to refer a case binds all courts with respect to the choice of legal path but not with respect to subject matter jurisdiction or venue. See German Federal Supreme Labor Court, 49 *NJW* 742 (1996). As a matter of principle unlawful or wrong decisions are binding (see German Federal Supreme Court, 53 *NJW* 1343 (2000)) except in cases of clear arbitrariness. Federal Supreme Court, 55 *NJW* 2474 (2002).

9. See GVG § 17a(5) and Zöller/Gummer, GVG § 17a, mn. 2; Thomas/Putzo/Hüsstege, GVG § 17a, mn. 5.

10. See Ch. 3(E) above, Law on the German Constitutional Court (*Gesetz über das Bundesverfassungsgericht* or *BVerfGG*) § 80.

11. See *Patentgesetz* (PatG) § 65.

12. See GVG § 14.

13. See Ch. 4(E)(3) and (4) above on the function of these courts.

B. Division of Subject Matter Jurisdiction within the Ordinary Court System

Once it has been determined that a particular civil dispute does not belong to the exclusive jurisdiction of one of the specialized courts, it automatically becomes subject to the jurisdiction of the ordinary courts (*ordentliche Gerichte*). These courts exercise a general residual jurisdiction over civil disputes not within the jurisdiction of the specialized courts.

> "All civil legal disputes and criminal prosecutions, which are neither within the jurisdiction of administrative agencies or courts nor referred to special courts by federal law, belong before the ordinary courts."[14]

Within the ordinary court system cases are allocated to the subject matter jurisdiction (*sachliche Zuständigkeit*) of either the local courts (*Amtsgerichte*) or the state district courts (*Landgerichte*). The statute provides that "all civil legal disputes which are not referred to the local courts belong before the civil panels, including the commercial panels" of the state district court.[15] The state district court is therefore the court of general residuary jurisdiction for ordinary civil disputes. There is no overlap of subject matter jurisdiction between the local courts and the state district courts, every civil case belongs in one court or the other.[16]

1. Subject Matter Jurisdiction Based on Amount in Controversy

The local courts have exclusive subject matter jurisdiction of all civil cases not specifically confided to the jurisdiction of the state district courts, regardless of the form of the relief requested, in which the value of the object of the

14. GVG § 13 ("*Vor die ordentlichen Gerichte gehören alle bürgerlichen Rechtsstreitigkeiten und Strafsachen, für die nicht entweder die Zuständigkeit von Verwaltungsbehörden oder Verwaltungsgerichten begründet ist oder auf Grund von Vorschriften des Bundesrechts besondere Gerichte bestellt oder zugelassen sind.*").

15. GVG § 71(1) ("*Vor die Zivilkammern, einschliesslich der Kammern für Handelssachen, gehören alle bürgerlichen Rechtsstreitigkeiten, die nicht den Amtsgerichten zugewiesen sind.*").

16. In some cases, however, parties may consent to jurisdiction of a court which does not have subject matter jurisdiction (ZPO §§ 39, 40) and objections to subject matter jurisdiction may be waived. See Ch. 5(D) and (F) below.

controversy (*Streitgegenstand*) does not exceed 5,000 Euros.[17] All claims which are economically based (*vermögensrechtlich*) are subject to this jurisdictional test. Jurisdiction over non-economic claims, such as claims for declaratory judgment of non-economic relationships, must be based on other statutory provisions.[18]

The amount in controversy for the purpose of subject matter jurisdiction is usually determined on the basis of the claims set forth in the plaintiff's complaint. The idea is to estimate the economic interest of the claimant in the matter placed before the court for legal decision. Claims for declaratory judgment establishing or denying economic relationships are similarly valued, although a claim for a positive declaratory judgment (*positive Feststellungsklage*) is usually valued at between 20% and 80% of the value of a corresponding claim for performance.[19] If a plaintiff asserts a partial claim (*Teilklage*), it is the amount which is placed in suit, not the overall amount of the obligation, that counts.[20]

For jurisdictional purposes, the amount in controversy is determined at the time of filing of the complaint.[21] As long as the subject matter in dispute remains the same, later alterations of the amount in controversy by amendment of the pleadings or otherwise does not deprive the court of jurisdiction to continue to hear and determine the case.[22] A partial withdrawal or amendment of a claim which reduces a state district court claim to 5,000 Euros or less will not affect the jurisdiction of the court in which it was originally commenced. The same is true if a claim properly commenced in the local court is later determined to be worth more than 5,000 Euros. If, however, during the course of litigation a local court plaintiff's claim is amended and thereafter appears to be worth more than 5,000 Euros, or a local court defendant asserts a coun-

---

17. GVG §23(1).

18. See Rosenberg/Schwab/Gottwald, §32(I)(2), p. 158. For instance, family cases are within the exclusive jurisdiction of the local courts regardless of amount in controversy. See Ch. 11(A) below.

19. See Rosenberg/Schwab/Gottwald, §32(IV)(1), p. 162; German Federal Supreme Court, 23 *NJW* 2025 (1970).

20. However if the plaintiff simultaneously files a series of partial claims based on the same underlying obligation in order to remain within the jurisdiction of the local courts, the court is obliged to consider them as a group and either dismiss them as not allowable (*unzulässig*) or, on motion of the plaintiff, transfer them to the district court. Rosenberg/Schwab/Gottwald, §32(II)(1), p. 159; OLG Hamm, 22 *OLGZ* 337 (1987); Zöller/Vollkommer, §1, mn. 23.

21. ZPO §4(1); see Ch. 5(F) below.

22. Supreme Court of the German Empire, 98 RGZ 86 (1920); Rosenberg/Schwab/Gottwald, §32 (IV)(2), p. 162 f.

terclaim of more than 5,000 Euros, either party can request that the matter be transferred to the appropriate state district court.[23]

If a party joins several claims in a single complaint, the amount in controversy is generally determined based on the arithmetic total of the claims presented.[24] Multiple restatements of the same claim for relief based on several causes of action, however, are not cumulated.[25] If several local court claims are consolidated after filing, the fact that the total of the consolidated claims exceed the local court jurisdictional maximum does not affect the jurisdiction of the local court. On the other hand, a lack of subject matter jurisdiction of the district court can be cured by consolidating pending claims between the parties so that the total amount claimed exceeds 5,000 Euros.[26]

In cases in which the complaint does not set forth an amount in controversy in money or monetary value the court has to determine the amount in controversy based on its sound discretion (*nach freiem Ermessen*)[27] subject to certain rules.[28] For instance, if the matter in controversy is the existence or duration of a tenancy of non-residential real estate, the amount in controversy is defined as the total amount of rent for the time period in controversy subject to a maximum of 25 times the yearly rent.[29] In inheritance disputes, a claim for an inheritance is valued at what the plaintiff would receive if successful, while a claim to deny an inheritance to another is assessed at the amount which the defendant would be deprived of, not what the plaintiff would gain, if anything.[30] If the complaint does not set forth a definite amount

---

23. ZPO §506. If this occurs before the state district court as an appellate court, the matter may be transferred to the first instance section of the district court. For disputed details see Thomas/Putzo/Reichold, §506, mn. 5.

24. ZPO §5. However claims of the plaintiff's complaint and of any counterclaim are not cumulated for purposes of determination of amount in controversy. Thus a complaint for 5,000 Euros and a counterclaim in same amount would be within the jurisdiction of the local court. German Federal Supreme Court, 59 BGHZ 17 (1973).

25. Rosenberg/Schwab/Gottwald, §32 (IV)(3), p. 163 ff.

26. See ZPO §147; Stein/Jonas/Leipold, *Kommentar zur Zivilprozessordnung*, 21st ed. (1994), §147, mn. 26.

27. ZPO §3. See Thomas/Putzo, §3, mn. 4 ff. for a discussion of various matters in controversy.

28. See ZPO §§6–9.

29. ZPO §8. This applies only to non-residential real estate. Disputes concerning tenancy of residential real estate are within the exclusive jurisdiction of the local courts regardless of amount in controversy. GVG §23(2)(a). See Ch. 5 (B)(2) below.

30. Compare German Federal Supreme Court, 28 *NJW* 1415 (1975) with German Federal Supreme Court, 23 *NJW* 197 (1970); see Rosenberg/Schwab/Gottwald, §32(IV)(5), pp. 165 ff.

in numbers, the court has to determine the monetary value of a finding in the plaintiff's favor.[31]

If subject matter jurisdiction is contested based on amount in controversy, the court can address the matter in a preliminary phase of the case before addressing the merits.[32] The court can take also evidence to assist it in reaching a determination of the amount in controversy for jurisdictional purposes.

2. Subject Matter Jurisdiction Regardless of Amount in Controversy

There are a number of statutory provisions which specify the subject matter jurisdiction of certain kinds of disputes regardless of the amount in controversy.

The largest categories of matters statutorily confided to the exclusive jurisdiction of the local courts are:

a. Landlord-tenant matters involving residential real estate (*Wohnräume*),[33]
b. Divorce and other matrimonial actions (*Ehesachen*),[34]
c. Matters concerning child support, custody and protection.[35]

Landlord tenant matters within the local court jurisdiction include claims which frequently far exceed the local court's jurisdictional maximum for ordinary civil cases. For instance, the amount in controversy for an eviction case could be considered as equal to the total amount of rent due for up to 25 years.[36] Eviction of a tenant from a house or apartment renting at 1,000 Euros per month could result in an actual amount in controversy of some 12,000 Euros or even more.

---

31. Rosenberg/Schwab/Gottwald, §32(IV)(5), pp. 165 ff. For instance, in cases seeking the turnover of documents, it is frequently very difficult to determine the value in controversy. A case seeking a savings passbook or a check would be valued at the amount of the plaintiff's money that would be subject to diversion by the defendant on retention of the passbook or check.

32. ZPO §§11, 280.

33. GVG §23(2)(a). A mixed use is covered by this provision if the residential use is predominant, see Thomas/Putzo/Hüsstege, GVG §23, mn. 12.

34. GVG §23a. See Ch. 11(A) below on special procedures in marital and family cases.

35. GVG §23a.

36. See ZPO §8 and GVG §23(2)(a). However for purposes of computing court costs and attorneys fees the amount in controversy in a landlord-tenant case involving residential real estate is pegged at 12 times the monthly rent, GKG §61. See Ch. 9(E) below (judgments for costs and attorneys fees).

An even larger and more significant category of local court jurisdiction is marriage and family cases. The local court is exclusively charged with adjudicating virtually all aspects of marriage claims and all matters concerning the care, support and protection of children. It exercises this jurisdiction mainly through a special division of the local court known as the "family court" (*Familiengericht*),[37] which has its own specialized procedures.[38] In this capacity local court judges adjudicate matters, such as alimony and division of marital pensions and property, with economic values far in excess of the jurisdictional maximum applicable to other kinds of civil cases. A third category of cases within the exclusive jurisdiction of the local courts regardless of amount in controversy are bankruptcy proceedings[39] (*Insolvenzverfahren*).[40]

The local courts are statutorily vested with jurisdiction over a variety of minor actions such as claims arising from transfers of possession of real estate subject to obligation of term or lifetime support or monetary payments to a retiring farmer (*Leibgeding*),[41] claims between innkeepers and other travel facilitators on the one hand and travelers on the other,[42] claims for damage by wild animals,[43] and certain proceedings whereby a debtor calls upon all its creditors to state their claims upon pain of preclusion (*Aufgebotsverfahren*).[44]

Finally, the local court retains jurisdiction regardless of amount in controversy over certain matters which are ancillary to its principal subject matter jurisdiction such as claims of attorneys and court executors for statutory fees,[45] claims by intervenors,[46] and claims for provisional measures (*einstweilige Verfügungen*) in special cases where expeditious action is required.[47]

---

37. For further information on the organization and operation of the family court see Ch. 3(D)(1)(a) above, Ch. 11(A) below.

38. See ZPO §§606–661, Ch. 11(A) below.

39. See InsO §2.

40. See InsO §2 and Ch. 11(G) below for a description of bankruptcy procedure.

41. GVG §23(2)(g).

42. GVG §23(2)(b).

43. GVG §23(2)(d).

44. GVG §23(2)(h). In general, these cases are delegated to magistrates. See *Rechtspflegergesetz* (RPflG) §20(2) and Ch. 3(H)(2). In special cases another court may be specified by state law. See *Gesetz betreffend die Einführung der Zivilprozessordnung* (EGZPO) §11. For the *Aufgebotsverfahren* see ZPO §§946 ff.

45. ZPO §34. However, the Federal Supreme Labor Court held that disputes over fees arising from proceedings in the Labor Courts belong to the jurisdiction of the ordinary courts. See German Federal Supreme Labor Court, 51 *NJW* 1092 (1998).

46. See ZPO §64. This provision establishes exclusive subject matter jurisdiction and venue. See Zöller/Vollkommer, §64, mn. 4.

47. ZPO §§919, 937, 942. For a discussion of provisional measures, see Ch. 11(D) below.

On the other hand, there are a few kinds of cases which are statutorily placed within the exclusive jurisdiction of the state district courts regardless of the amount in controversy. These include,

1. Civil claims based on dereliction of duty against judges, state officials, and (at the option of the respective German states) against the state or federal governments,[48]
2. Actions and claims as created or authorized by a number of specific federal statutes, such as patent infringement cases,[49] claims based on anti-trust law,[50] and various corporate governance claims.[51]

As is the case with the local courts, the state district courts also possess subject matter jurisdiction, regardless of the amount in controversy, to determine all issues and claims ancillary to matters within their primary jurisdiction.

3. Jurisdiction of the Commercial Panels of the State District Courts

Within the subject matter jurisdiction of the state district courts, there is a specialized jurisdiction of the "commercial panels" (*Kammer für Handelssachen*) in certain commercial and business cases. The commercial panels, which include lay "honorary judges" (*ehrenamtliche Richter*)[52] are given subject matter jurisdiction over a variety of "commercial matters" (*Handelssachen*), including:

a. claims against a merchant which are commercial matters for both parties,[53]

48. GVG §71(2).

49. PatG §143(1). This includes claims for non-economic relief, see German Federal Supreme Court, 14 BGHZ 72, 81 (1954).

50. GWB §87(1). The dispute may involve related claims based on the same factual or similar legal grounds. See GWB §88 and Winterfeld, „Zur Zuständigkeitsverteilung zwischen allgemeinen Zivilgerichten und Kartellgerichten", 38 *NJW* 1816 (1985).

51. See Rosenberg/Schwab/Gottwald, §32(III)(2)(b), p. 159, for a partial listing of these claims and others within the statutory jurisdiction of the state district courts.

52. See GVG §§93, 94, 105 ff. and Ch. 3(D)(2)(b), (c) above for a discussion of the organization and staffing of the commercial panels.

53. GVG §95(1)(1). This jurisdiction does not, however, extend to claims between a merchant and a consumer.

b. claims based on checks and bills of exchange,[54]
c. claims arising out of various forms of business organization,[55]
d. claims for unfair competition,[56] and
e. various business related claims relegated to the state district courts by the capital market, the stock company and corporate reorganization laws.[57]

Although the law and commentary refer to the "jurisdiction" (*Zuständigkeit*) of the commercial panels, the assignment of cases to commercial panels is more a matter of efficient conduct of judicial business rather than a matter of underlying competence to decide. Cases within the jurisdiction of the commercial panels are filed like any other state district court cases. Upon application of either party (but not on the court's own motion) they may be referred to a commercial panel if all the claims are within the commercial panels' described realm of responsibility.[58] If it later appears that the case does not belong to the commercial panel or if a counterclaim or amendment presents a claim not belonging to the commercial panels the case or claim can be remanded to a civil panel of the state district court.[59] Decisions to refer a case to a commercial panel or to remand it to an ordinary civil panel are ordinarily not appealable. The fact that a matter is a commercial matter within the jurisdiction of a commercial panel does not affect the validity of a decision of an ordinary civil panel of the state district court.[60]

---

54. GVG §95(1)(2), (3). See Ch. 11(B) below for a description of an optional expedited procedure for cases brought on checks and bills of exchange.

55. GVG §95(1)(4).

56. GVG §95(1)(5).

57. GVG §95(1)(6) and (2). See Rosenberg/Schwab/Gottwald, §33(I), pp. 167 f. for a discussion of the jurisdiction of the commercial panels.

58. GVG §§96(1), 98(1). A commercial panel may sever claims which are not within the jurisdiction of the commercial panels according to ZPO §145(1) and determine only the "commercial part" of the case, leaving the rest to be transferred to a normal civil panel. See Gaul, „Das Zuständigkeitsverhältnis der Zivilkammer zur Kammer für Handelssachen", 39 *JZ* 57, 61 (1984); Zöller/Gummer, GVG §95, mn. 1. However, a claim within the jurisdiction of a commercial panel may be supported by legal grounds of both commercial and non-commercial character. See Thomas/Putzo/Hüsstege, GVG §95, mn. 1; Brandi-Dohrn, „Die Zuständigkeit der Kammer für Handelssachen bei mehrfacher Klagebegründung", 34 *NJW* 2453 (1981).

59. See GVG §§97, 99, 101.

60. See Thomas/Putzo, §§93–95, mn. 1; Zöller/Gummer, GVG §94, mn. 3. However, the constitutional right to a "legal" or statutory judge (GG Art. 101, GVG §§16, 21e) should not be violated. Thus, a panel must not arbitrarily assert jurisdiction.

4. Functional Jurisdiction

German civil procedure also includes the concept of "functional jurisdiction" (*funktionelle Zuständigkeit*) to describe the allocation of the various functions relating to the processing of civil cases among the organs of the justice system. These functions include first instance proceedings, second instance appeals on fact and law, revision appeals on law and procedure, and execution. The functional jurisdiction of the various court organs within the ordinary court system sometimes varies with the subject matter jurisdiction of the courts of first instance. For instance, the state district courts exercise a functional jurisdiction entertaining second instance appeals in ordinary civil cases commenced in the local courts. However in family cases this second instance functional jurisdiction is exercised by the state appeals courts.[61] The local courts exercise the functional jurisdiction of execution for cases arising in all of the courts.[62]

C. Venue

In Germany the term "territorial jurisdiction" (*örtliche Zuständigkeit*) is synonymous with the term "venue" (*Gerichtsstand*) and refers to the court location within Germany in which a civil action must be brought. The following discussion will be confined to venue for civil actions.

The German federation, including its judicial system, is organized by states. Each state is in turn divided into judicial districts for the state district court (*Landgerichtsbezirke*) and (smaller) local court districts (*Amtsgerichtsbezirke*) for the local courts.[63] The states are authorized to consolidate judicial districts for various purposes, such as to provide more specialized commercial panels[64] and to provide a single family court to exercise jurisdiction in multiple local court districts.[65]

---

61. For a discussion of procedure on second instance appeals see Ch. 10(D)(1) below.

62. See Ch. 11(F) below for a discussion of procedures on execution of civil judgments. See Rosenberg/Schwab/Gottwald, §31, pp. 154 ff. for a discussion of the concept of functional jurisdiction.

63. The delineation of judicial districts and local court districts is a matter of state law.

64. See Rosenberg/Schwab/Gottwald, §34(I)(2), p. 171.

65. GVG §23c. See Zöller/Gummer, GVG §23c, mn. 2, 6 for an enumeration of the states which have made use of this authorization.

1. Venue Based on Residence of the Defendant

The basic rule of venue (which is subject to many exceptions) is that a civil case must be brought in the judicial district in which the defendant has its residence (*Wohnsitz*).[66] If a party does not have a current residence in Germany, the party may be sued in any district in Germany of temporary sojourn (*Aufenthalt*), or if such a place is not known, in the district of last known residence.[67]

A corporate party or a fiduciary of property is deemed to have its residence in the district of its "seat" (*Sitz*). Generally the seat of a corporation is designated in its corporate charter. Otherwise it may be considered as the place where the corporate administration takes place.[68]

A public official is subject to suit in the district of her official office (*Amtssitz*).[69] The public treasury can be sued in the district in which are located the officials designated to represent the public treasury in the dispute.[70] A trustee in bankruptcy is subject to suit in the judicial district of the bankruptcy court.[71]

2. Special Venues

In addition to the general venue based on the residence of the defendant, the Civil Procedure Code provides for a number of special venues for special circumstances or specified kinds of claims. Some of these special venues are exclusive, some are supplementary to the general residence-based venue provisions.

Persons such as students, workers, household helpers, and employed persons who are sojourning at a place for a significant period of time (*von längerer Dauer*) although not formally residents of that place, may be sued for any economically-based (*vermögensrechtlichen*) claim in the place of sojourn.[72]

---

66. ZPO §§ 12, 13. BGB §§ 7–11 define the prerequisite "residence", see Zöller/Vollkommer, § 13, mn. 3; German Federal Supreme Court, 3 *NJW-RR* 387 (1988).

67. ZPO § 16.

68. ZPO § 17(1). See Zöller/Vollkommer, § 17, mn. 9 ff.

69. ZPO § 17(2).

70. ZPO § 18. If this location spans more than one district, the state or federal government as the case may be can specify the official location by regulation. ZPO § 19.

71. ZPO § 19a.

72. ZPO § 20. This applies not only to persons who do not have a residence elsewhere in Germany, but also to persons who do. This provision does not apply to non-economic claims such as claims for divorce or other declarations of personal status.

A business enterprise which has places of business (*Niederlassungen*) in more than one judicial district is subject to suit in any judicial district in which it has a place of business but only for matters arising out of the conduct of business by that place of business.[73] Major enterprises, such as banks, insurance companies and industrial concerns, are thus locally accessible to creditors and others doing business with the local branch.[74]

Economic and proprietary (*vermögensrechtliche*) claims against persons who have no residence in Germany can be asserted in the district in which property of the defendant or property involved in the claim at issue in the lawsuit is located.[75] When the property in question is a debt or a claim against a third person, the location of the property is the residence of the third-party debtor or obligor.[76] There is no requirement that the property equal or exceed in value the amount of the claim, and the validity of any judgment rendered is not limited to the value of the property located in the district.[77]

Claims against a shipowner or operator can be brought in the district of the home port of the vessel (*Heimathafen*) regardless of the location of the owner or operator.[78]

Claims based on contracts may be brought in the place in which the contract was to be fulfilled (*Erfüllungsort*).[79] The place of fulfillment is to be de-

---

73. ZPO §21(1). This venue supplements the general residence-based venue provisions (ZPO §§13, 17). See German Federal Supreme Court, 88 BGHZ 331, 336 (1984).

74. See the similar provision of Article 5 No. 5 of the European Union Regulation No. 44/2001 of December 22, 2000 on Jurisdiction and the Recognition and Enforcement of Judgments in Civil and Commercial Matters, OJ L 12, 16/01/2001, p. 1 (hereinafter referred to as the "Brussels Regulation" or BRJE). In principle, that regulation only applies in international matters within the European Community, see Thomas/Putzo/Hüsstege, EuGVVO Vorbem., mn. 9, 11 and Ch. 12(A) and (B)(2)(a) below.

75. ZPO §23. According to Article 3 of the Brussels Convention of 1968, now enacted as Article 3 of the Brussels Regulation, this provision cannot be applied to any person who is resident in any member state of the European Union. See Ch. 12(B)(2)(c) below.

76. ZPO §23(2). When the claim is a secured claim, venue is also proper in the district in which the collateral is located.

77. German Federal Supreme Court, 42 *NJW* 1431 (1989); 43 *NJW* 990–992 (1990); Rosenberg/Schwab/Gottwald, §36(I)(3), pp. 174 f. In international matters this jurisdiction is limited to disputes that bear some minimal relationship to Germany. German Federal Supreme Court, 115 BGHZ 90 (1992). This limitation does not apply to purely domestic cases, see OLG Stuttgart, 36 *RIW* 831 (1990); Zöller/Vollkommer, §23, mn. 1; Ch. 12(B)(2)(c) below.

78. HGB §488; Law on Domestic Navigation (*Binnenschifffahrtsgesetz* or *BinnSchiffG*) §6.

79. ZPO §29.

termined according to the provisions of the Civil Code[80] and may vary for the parties to the contract.[81] The place of fulfillment which counts is that of the obligation involved in the suit, whether for specific performance of an obligation or for damages based on breach of obligation.[82] Mercantile parties (*Kaufleute*) or public entities may agree on the place of fulfillment for purposes of venue.[83] However contract claims based on door-to-door solicitation may only be brought in the district in which the customer (*Kunde*) is resident or at least has an ongoing sojourn (*dauernden Aufenthalt*).[84] Claims brought pursuant to the special "warning process" (*Mahnverfahren*) must be brought in the district of residence of the applicant (*Antragsteller*).[85]

The exclusive venue for landlord-tenant cases is the local court district in which the rented property is located.[86] Traditionally this exclusive venue applied only to residential property. However a 1993 reform made it applicable to business premises as well.[87]

Tort claims may be brought in the district in which the tortious conduct (*unerlaubte Handlung*) took place.[88] This includes not only personal injury cases, such as automobile accident claims, but also business tort claims. When a claim is based on tortious conduct which took place in more than one district, venue

80. See BGB §§269, 270 and various special provisions; Zöller/Vollkommer, §29, mn. 24.

81. For instance, if goods are to be manufactured by one party in one district in return for payment to be made by the other party in another, under German law the place of fulfillment of the obligation of payment is the residence of the debtor. BGB §§269, 270; but see for international contracts CISG Art. 57. The German law on place of fulfillment can be compared to the current European law which defines the place of fulfillment for all obligations of a contract as that place where the most characteristic obligation of the contract must be fulfilled. For example, in a contract for sale of goods, the place of delivery of the goods would be considered the place of fulfillment of the contract and hence the correct venue for claims based on both the obligation to deliver the goods and the obligation to make payment. See Article 5 No. 1(b) of the Brussels Regulation and Ch.12(B)(2)(3) below.

82. Supreme Court of the German Empire, 40 RGZ 408 (1898); OLG Saarbrücken 53 *NJW* 670, 671 (2000).

83. ZPO §29(2). Such agreements may not be inferred from terms printed on bills and similar one-sided documents, but may be contained in order confirmations and invoices which complete the conclusion of a contract. See Rosenberg/Schwab/Gottwald, §36(II)(1), pp. 175 f.

84. ZPO §29c.

85. ZPO §689. See Ch. 11(C) below for a discussion of warning process.

86. ZPO §29a. This includes cases for eviction when there has existed a rental relationship.

87. See *Gesetz zur Entlastung der Rechtspfleger* of January 11, 1993, BGBl I, p. 50.

88. ZPO §32. See, in general, Rosenberg/Schwab/Gottwald, §36(II)(8), p. 177.

can be properly laid in any district in which some of the tortious conduct took place.[89] When the tortious conduct is not complete without an actual intention to cause damage, the place in which the damages were sustained can also be a proper venue.[90] However this does not extend venue to a district having no connection to the tort other than the later suffering of the victim.[91] Nor does it authorize suit where the claimant is located if that place has no connection with the tort other than as a place in which not-intended damages were sustained.[92]

Strict liability claims for injury from environmental pollution (*durch Umwelteinwirkung verursachten Schaden*) from specially identified hazardous activities must be brought in the district where the polluting facility (*Anlage*) is located.[93]

Claims relating to the title, ownership, possession, or division of real estate or the establishment or discharge of liens against real estate must be brought in the district in which the real estate is located.[94] If the real property lies in more than one district and there is dispute over which is the proper district for purposes of venue, the next highest court will determine the one district in which venue is proper.[95] This venue will also support related claims against the defendant in the real property claim, such as claims for personal liability under a mortgage, or for damage to the real estate at issue.[96]

---

89. Supreme Court of the German Empire, 72 RGZ 41 (1910). For instance, a claim for libel against a newspaper can be brought not only in the district in which the newspaper is published, but in any district in which the newspaper circulates. German Federal Supreme Court, 30 *NJW* 1590 (1977).

90. German Federal Supreme Court, 33 *NJW* 1224, 1225 (1980); 49 *NJW* 1411, 1413 (1996). If, for example, the plaintiff suffers financial loss because of an intentional disregard of the plaintiff's legitimate interests (see BGB § 826) venue is laid in the district of the plaintiff's residence. See OLG Koblenz 43 *WM* 622, 623 (1989).

91. German Federal Supreme Court, 33 *NJW* 1224, 1225 (1980). Compare Article 5 No. 3 of the Brussels Regulation, Ch.12(B)(2)(d).

92. This jurisdictional construct reflects the structure of German tort law which permits tort actions only for infringement of special legally protected interests (*Rechtsgut*) and for intentionally caused harm. See BGB §§ 826, 823 ff.

93. ZPO § 32a. The activities covered are set forth in the Standards on Liability for Environmental Pollution (*Umwelthaftungsgesetz* or UHG). This does not apply when the facility is located outside Germany.

94. ZPO § 24. In cases involving equitable servitudes, venue is laid in the district of the burdened land. ZPO § 24(2).

95. See ZPO § 36(1)(4). For local court cases the state district court makes this determination. The state appeals court would similarly determine the proper venue for cases brought in the state district court.

96. ZPO §§ 25, 26. The venue for ancillary personal claims is not exclusive and such claims can be brought according to the general venue rules.

The provisions for venue in family law cases are intricate. Venue in marital cases is based on a series of layered provisions designed to provide a single exclusive venue in all situations.[97] First of all, the local court in the district in which a married couple has its "usual common sojourn" (*gemeinsamen gewöhnlichen Aufenthalt*) is the exclusive venue for any case brought to determine the existence or validity of a marriage or for divorce.[98] If, at the time of commencement of the action there is no such location within Germany, the exclusive venue is in the district in which a spouse has usual sojourn with one or more minor children. If there is no such district, then venue falls to the district in which the spouses last had usual common sojourn so long as one of the spouses continues to sojourn within the district.[99] Next in line is the district of the usual sojourn of the defendant, and if there is no such district in Germany, then the district of usual sojourn of the plaintiff.[100] If all else fails, venue is laid in the local court for Schöneberg, Berlin.[101] For the purposes of the family law venue statute, "place of usual sojourn" is the place where a person generally, if not without interruption, sojourns. A temporary absence will not vitiate usual sojourn, and a temporary presence will not establish it.[102] If a divorce or other matrimonial case is pending, the proper venue for other family law matters such as marital support and custody and support and visitation of children of the marriage is the district in which the matrimonial case is pending.[103] Otherwise the usual rules of venue apply.[104]

Claims for marital support (*Unterhaltssachen*) other than incident to a claim affecting the marriage status must be brought in the district of residence of the defendant if the defendant is a resident of Germany. However if the defendant has no residence in Germany, such claims can be brought in the district of the plaintiff's residence.[105] A claim for collection of support or estab-

---

97. ZPO §606. For the jurisdiction of the German courts in European marital and family cases, see Ch. 12(A) below.

98. ZPO §606(1).

99. ZPO §606(2).

100. If both parties bring suit based on this venue, the district in which suit first becomes pending (*rechtshängig*) becomes the proper venue for both claims, ZPO §606(2).

101. ZPO §606(3).

102. Rosenberg/Schwab/Gottwald, §36(IV)(3), p. 180.

103. ZPO §621(2). See Zöller/Philippi, §621, mn. 85 ff.

104. ZPO §621(2).

105. ZPO §23a. This includes claims for establishment, increase, or collection of support, either by operation of law or by contract, as well as declaratory judgment claims by the person likely to be charged with the obligation. See Rosenberg/Schwab/Gottwald, §36(IV)(1), p. 179.

lishment of increased support in behalf of a child against a father, a mother, or both parents may be brought, depending on the circumstances of the case, in the district in which the child or either parent resides.[106]

The proper venue for a probate matter, including probate of a will, a will contest, and various claims for inheritances, intestate succession, and the like is the district of residence of the decedent at the time of death.[107] For German decedents not resident in Germany at the time of death venue is laid at the place of the decedent's last residence in Germany, and in default thereof, at the seat of the German federal government.[108]

The foregoing provisions for venue are only some of the most important and common ones. There are many special venues for particular kinds of claims.[109] Careful German lawyers always check for proper venue before filing suit.

3. Venue by Connection

If a matter has a factual connection (*Sachzusammenhang*) to a case already in suit, venue of the connected matter can be laid in the court in which the related case is pending. This is true of a counterclaim factually or legally related to a pending claim.[110] According to the prevailing view, when a single claim for relief is supported by multiple causes of action with different venues, the causes of action can be asserted in a single proceeding under the theory of venue by connection. [111]

Joinder of claims of multiple claimants or against multiple defendants which have multiple statutory venues requires a special decision of the next higher court fixing the proper venue for the joined proceeding.[112]

---

106. See ZPO §35a. See also ZPO §642(1)(1) providing exclusive venues for special cases. If, however, a matrimonial case is pending in another court, the proper venue is the district of that court (ZPO §§642(2)(1)). See Zöller/Vollkommer, §35a, mn. 2.

107. ZPO §27(1).

108. ZPO §27(2).

109. See, e.g., UWG §24 (cases of unfair competition); AMG §94a (cases asserting strict liability of manufacturers of drugs).

110. ZPO §33. This does not apply to counterclaims having exclusive statutory venues.

111. See Rosenberg/Schwab/Gottwald, §36(VI), p. 181. Venue by connection parallels provisions for choice of specialized court under which a specialized court may adjudicate a claim based on causes of action both within and without the specialized court's statutory competence. See Ch. 5(A) above; GVG §17(2)(1).

112. See Ch. 5 (E) below. European law provides specific rules of venue for case joining multiple parties without the need for a special court determination in each case. See Article 6 No. 1 of the Brussels Regulation and Ch. 12(B)(2) below.

D. Subject Matter Jurisdiction and Venue by Agreement

In some cases the parties to a law suit may agree on both subject matter jurisdiction and venue for suits based on a particular described agreement or relationship.[113] Although historically there was great freedom for parties to reach such agreements, in recent years subject matter jurisdiction and venue by agreement have been severely restricted and regulated.[114]

Subject matter jurisdiction and venue may not be varied by agreement in cases seeking non-economic relief (*nicht-vermögensrechtliche Streitigkeiten*) such as divorce cases and other cases seeking declarations of non-economic status, or where the statute provides for an exclusive subject matter jurisdiction or venue.[115] This latter limitation excludes contractual specification of jurisdiction or venue in a large number of cases, such as landlord-tenant cases, family law matters, cases involving real estate, and the like, all of which have exclusive statutory subject matter jurisdiction or venue, or both.

Within these constraints merchants, corporate entities, and public bodies may agree in advance on the jurisdiction and venue for cases arising out of a specified legal relationship or circumstances.[116] Such agreements need not be in writing or fulfil any particular formalities,[117] and may be inferred from silence in appropriate circumstances.[118]

An agreement for a special subject matter jurisdiction or venue is not valid if the charged party is an individual or party not in one of the categories specifically referred to in the statute. If one party to a legal transaction or relationship does not have a residence in Germany, the parties may agree in ad-

113. This is not true, however, for choice of the proper court system within the judicial branch or "functional jurisdiction" of the various courts within a court system.

114. See *Gesetz zur Änderung der Zivilprozessordnung* of March 21, 1974, BGBl I, p. 753.

115. ZPO §40(2). If the statute provides for exclusive subject matter jurisdiction, but not an exclusive venue, then only the latter would be subject to variance by agreement.

116. The agreement must name a particular court and may not leave free choice of court to one of the parties. OLG Karlsruhe, 8 *OLGZ* 479 (1973). If the agreement names a number of specified courts, ZPO §35 will apply.

117. Between merchants such agreements can be, and often are contained in "general conditions of doing business" (*allgemeine Geschäftsbedingungen*) printed on order forms, invoices, and the like.

118. ZPO §38(1). There is some dispute about the legal nature (*Rechtsnatur*) of such agreements, substantive or procedural. In any event, it is generally agreed that the court referred to in the agreement has jurisdiction to interpret the agreement. See Rosenberg/Schwab/Gottwald, §37(I)(1), pp. 182 f.; Lüke, *Zivilprozessrecht*, 8th ed. (2003), mn. 89.

vance in writing on jurisdiction and venue in a specified German court for disputes arising between them.[119]

After a dispute has arisen, but still subject to the general limitations mentioned above, practically any parties may agree on subject matter jurisdiction and venue for resolution of their dispute. Such agreements must be in writing and expressly refer to the dispute in question.[120]

If a defendant fails to object to the jurisdiction or venue of the court at or before the beginning of the plenary proceedings (*Hauptverhandlung*),[121] such a failure to object is treated as an implied consent and is valid in cases for which the parties would have otherwise been permitted to agree on jurisdiction or venue.[122]

E. Jurisdiction and Venue by Judicial Specification

In some cases it is difficult to determine from the statute the proper subject matter jurisdiction or venue for the particular parties or case presented. For instance, if claims against a number of defendants resident in different judicial districts are joined in a single complaint, or if claims with conflicting statutory jurisdictions or venues are joined in a single case, or if a real estate action addresses land located in more than one district, it is necessary to determine which court has subject matter jurisdiction and venue of the action. This function is performed by the next higher court in the system, which will, upon application, specify which court will have jurisdiction and where venue will lie.[123] An application can be filed either before or after the filing of the

119. ZPO §38(2). However if one of the parties is a German resident, the venue chosen must be the district of residence of the party or a statutory special venue.

120. ZPO §38(3). Such an agreement may also be concluded if the defendant has moved his residence outside of Germany after conclusion of the contract at issue, or if the defendant's residence is not known as of the time the complaint is filed.

121. See Ch. 8(B)(1) and (2) below on procedures during the plenary proceedings. For purpose of this rule the beginning of the plenary hearing can be either the parties formal statement of claims (*Stellung der Anträge*) or the conduct of argument on the merits without raising objection to the court's jurisdiction or venue.

122. ZPO §39. In the local courts, where the parties need not be represented by counsel, this is the case only if the court has previously called this issue to the defendant's attention and warned him of the consequences of failure to object. See ZPO §504.

123. ZPO §36(2)–(4). This procedure is also utilized if the court with apparent jurisdiction and venue is unable to entertain the claim because of death or disability of a judge.

complaint.[124] The court decides the application without oral proceedings and its decision specifying the court which will entertain the proceedings is final.[125]

F. Objections to Subject Matter Jurisdiction and Venue and Consequences of Lack of Subject Matter Jurisdiction or Venue

Both subject matter jurisdiction and the venue of the court in which a case is filed are considered "prerequisites to suit" (*Prozessvoraussetzungen*) which the court is required to check on its own motion following the filing of any complaint or counterclaim. The defendant's answer can also contest subject matter jurisdiction and venue and request dismissal for failure of either. Issues of subject matter jurisdiction and venue may be raised even in the plenary proceedings.[126]

The court first considers the allegations of the complaint to determine whether there is subject matter jurisdiction and proper venue for the claims stated. For many cases what counts is the facts asserted with particularity.[127] If they are disputed, the court may found its determination of jurisdiction on the plaintiff's well pleaded assertions of fact despite assertions by the defendant to the contrary.[128] The fact that the court may ultimately find that the plaintiff's claim is unfounded or that the amount owed is below the jurisdictional minimum does not mean that the court is deprived of subject matter jurisdiction.

There are some situations in which the determination of jurisdiction or venue may require the resolution of factual disputes and even the taking of

124. See Rosenberg/Schwab/Gottwald, § 38, for a discussion of proceedings on such applications.

125. ZPO § 37.

126. Subject, however, to the provisions of ZPO § 39, which provides that participation in plenary argument without previous objection to jurisdiction or venue has the effect of agreement to jurisdiction or venue for those cases where jurisdiction or venue can be changed by agreement. See Ch. 5(D) above.

127. The plaintiff's characterization of the legal nature of the claim is not conclusive. See Rosenberg/Schwab/Gottwald, § 39(I)(2), pp. 190 f.

128. So, if the plaintiff asserted that the defendant owed her a debt of 6,000 Euros, the judge would be entitled to find subject matter jurisdiction in the state district court even if the defendant disputed the amount of the debt and contended that the amount owed was only 1,000 Euros. Where there is dispute about the value of the subject matter of the controversy, the court is free to make its own evaluation and is not bound by the assertions of either party.

proof. For instance, if the plaintiff asserts that the parties have agreed on a particular subject matter jurisdiction or venue and the defendant denies such agreement, the court will have to determine the existence or non-existence of the agreement in order to decide the prerequisites of suit. The same is true if the plaintiff asserts that the defendant lives in a particular judicial district for the purpose of venue and the defendant contests this fact. In these cases, if the parties are unable to agree on the court's jurisdiction or venue, the court must make a preliminary determination based on hearing and, if necessary, proof. If a question of jurisdiction or venue is present, that question ordinarily will be decided before the court addresses the merits of the controversy.[129]

Strictly speaking, jurisdiction and venue must exist as of the time of the final oral arguments before decision, since the issuance of a judgment must be supported by the prerequisites to suit.[130] However a special provision of the Civil Procedure Code provides that during the pendency of a lawsuit, "the jurisdiction of the court will not be affected by a change in the circumstances on which jurisdiction is based."[131] This has been interpreted to support ongoing subject matter jurisdiction and venue of a court if the circumstances satisfied the statutory requirements at any time during the proceedings.[132] To the extent that jurisdiction is based on amount in controversy, so long as the claims for relief are not expanded or contracted, the amount in controversy is determined at the outset of the proceeding and governs, unless amended, for the entire instance.[133]

If, on its own motion or on motion of a party, the court determines that it lacks either subject matter jurisdiction or proper venue, the court cannot further address the merits, but must dismiss the action as "non-justiciable" (*unzulässig*). Such a dismissal is a procedural dismissal (*Prozessabweisung*), and is generally without prejudice to maintenance of the action in a court having jurisdiction or in the proper venue.[134]

---

129. See Rosenberg/Schwab/Gottwald, §39(I)(4), p. 192. The court may defer decision of the issue and rule on any issues of jurisdiction or venue in its final judgment.

130. Supreme Court of the German Empire, 52 RGZ 136 (1903); Rosenberg/Schwab/Gottwald, §39(I)(5), pp. 192 f.

131. ZPO §261(3)(2) ("...*die Zuständigkeit des Prozessgerichts wird durch eine Veränderung der sie begründenden Umstände nicht berührt.*").

132. Rosenberg/Schwab/Gottwald, §39(I)(5), pp. 192 f.

133. ZPO §4(1). See Ch. 5 (B)(1) above. A new amount in controversy is fixed at each level of appeal.

134. The plaintiff would, however, bear responsibility for costs and attorneys fees by virtue of such a dismissal. See Ch. 9(E)(3) below on court costs and attorneys fees.

If the court proposes to dismiss an action for lack of subject matter jurisdiction or improper venue, but there is another court in Germany which has subject matter jurisdiction and venue, the plaintiff may apply to have the case transferred to the proper court in lieu of dismissal.[135] Transfer is also available if subject matter jurisdiction or venue has been destroyed by amendment of the complaint or by a counterclaim.[136] The case can be transferred at any stage of the proceedings if the right to object to jurisdiction or venue has not been waived or lost by implied consent.[137] If there are more than one other court with subject matter jurisdiction and proper venue, the plaintiff may choose the court to which the case will be transferred.[138]

A plaintiff's application for transfer can be made at the clerks office (*Geschäftsstelle*) and does not require a lawyer, even in the state district court. After the defendant has been given opportunity for comment (*Stellungnahme*), the court can decide the issue by simple order (*Beschluss*) without the need for oral argument.[139] If the statutory preconditions are satisfied, transfer to the appropriate court is mandatory. An order of transfer is noncancellable by the transferring court and is binding on the court to which the case is transferred.[140] The case becomes pending in that court on receipt of the case record.[141] An order transferring a case, or refusing to transfer a case (because of the lack of another German court having subject matter jurisdiction and proper venue) is final and not subject to appeal.[142]

There is some controversy over whether after a case has been transferred the parties may agree on jurisdiction and venue in the court from which the

---

135. ZPO §281. See Thomas/Putzo/Reichold, §281, mn. 1.

136. ZPO §§33, 506; see Ch. 5(B)(1) above.

137. See Ch. 5(D) above. The case can be simply sent to the proper court without further formality if pendency (*Rechtshängigkeit*) has not occurred. German Federal Supreme Court, 36 *NJW* 1062 (1983) and Ch. 7(F) and (G) below.

138. ZPO §281(1). Such transfers occur relatively frequently, in 1989 in 7.3% of the cases originally filed in the local courts and 6.9% of the cases filed in the state district courts. Rosenberg/Schwab/Gottwald, §39(II)(2), p. 193.

139. ZPO §281(2). In difficult cases the court can order oral argument.

140. However the transferee court is free to dismiss for another reason or to retransfer the case by agreement to a court other than the court from which it came. If, for example, a local court transferred a case to another local court based on improper venue in the first court, the transferee court would be free to transfer the case to the state district court based on lack of subject matter jurisdiction.

141. ZPO §281(2)(3). For the purposes of costs and statute of limitations, the transferred proceeding is a single unitary proceeding, albeit in two separate courts.

142. ZPO §§281(2)(2), 506(2).

case was transferred or in a third court.[143] The current state of the case law tends to deny effect to such agreements based on the provisions of ZPO §261(3) providing that circumstances occurring after a court has subject matter jurisdiction and venue of a case do not affect jurisdiction and venue.[144]

A judgment dismissing a case for lack of jurisdiction or venue is subject to appeal.[145] If lack of jurisdiction or venue is raised by the defendant, and the court decides that it does have jurisdiction or that venue is proper, the bases for the decision must be explained in an interlocutory judgment (*Zwischenurteil*), or in the final judgment on the merits (*Endurteil*). The defendant may not appeal the judgment on that basis.[146] A decision by a court that it does not have subject matter jurisdiction over a particular case is binding on any other court in which the case is later filed.[147]

Final judgments are not generally subject to collateral attack on the ground of lack of subject matter jurisdiction or improper venue. The result of this regimen is that a party subject to the German justice system who is sued in a court which may lack either subject matter jurisdiction or proper venue cannot sit back and assume that the resulting judgment will not be enforceable but must raise these matters in a timely fashion within the litigation.[148]

---

143. Rosenberg/Schwab/Gottwald, §39(II)(2)(g), pp. 196 f.

144. See German Federal Supreme Court, 17 *NJW* 585, 586 (1963).

145. See ZPO §511(1); Thomas/Putzo/Reichold, §511, mn. 2 and §280, mn. 4.

146. ZPO §513(2). This section does not apply if the court decides that it does have international jurisdiction. See German Federal Supreme Court, 57 *NJW* 426 (2003) and CH. 12(B)(5) below.

147. ZPO §11. However this does not extend to a declaration that another court does have jurisdiction.

148. See Ch. 12(B)(5) below for binding effect of judgments of German courts involving issues of international jurisdiction.

CHAPTER 6

Fundamental Principles of German Civil Justice

A brief discussion of some of the key principles underlying the German civil justice system and its function can help observers and practitioners from other backgrounds reach a better understanding of why German civil justice is the way it is.

The German civil justice system is based on a particular conception of the nature and purpose of civil litigation and the role of civil justice in society as a whole. The configuration of public and private institutions and the roles of participants are calculated to achieve these purposes with effect and efficiency.

The system is also structured around a number of abstract principles which are either associated with the avowed purposes of civil litigation, or which are intended to implement other fundamental social and human rights and values in the litigation context. Although some of these principles are more or less expressly stated in the German Constitution or the European Convention on Human Rights, many others are not set forth *in haec verba* anywhere, but find expression more indirectly in specific statutory provisions or in case law. Many statutory provisions are justified and construed as implementations of one or more of these fundamental abstract principles. Courts frequently cite these principles in support of judicial decisions establishing or enforcing procedural norms. German text writers generally identify and discuss these principles both in the abstract and in connection with specific provisions of the civil procedure code and specific decisions.[1]

---

1. See, e.g., Rosenberg/Schwab/Gottwald, *Zivilprozessrecht*, 15th ed. (1993), §§77–85, pp. 422 ff. consisting of a catalog and discussion of the salient abstract principles underlying German civil procedure; Lüke, *Zivilprozessrecht*, 8th ed. (2003), §2, mn 5 ff., a short version of the same, and Jauernig, *Zivilprozessrecht*, 27th ed. (2002), §§24–31, pp. 80 ff.

The importance of these abstract and institutional features of German civil justice to an understanding of the specific functions of the system suggests some treatment of these subjects before further detailed consideration of German civil procedure law and litigation practice.

A. Nature and Purpose of a Civil Law Suit

Contrary to many preconceptions and in contrast to criminal proceedings, German law conceives of a civil law suit between private parties primarily as a means to effectuate the parties' individual rights.[2] "The purpose of civil litigation consists of the determination and effectuation of subjective rights."[3] A civil law suit is fundamentally a dispute between parties which the State has been requested to resolve according to principles of law. In that sense, it is a substitute for or successor to the primitive individual's ability to protect his or her rights by "self help" (*Selbsthilfe*) which the state now forbids in the interest of preserving public peace and order.[4] The development of the modern social economy has led to replacement of the somewhat unreliable and disorderly self help with the more scientific processes of civil justice so that members of the social unit can obtain protection and redress of their individual rights peacefully and regardless of individual physical or economic strength.

> "The state can only forbid the use of self help if the state itself guarantees the parties legal protection through its own institutions, and it does this through civil justice. The state fulfills thereby one of its

---

2. See, e.g., Koetz, "Civil Litigation and the Public Interest", 1 *Civil Justice Quarterly* 237 (1992); Jauernig, §1. German civil procedure law (*Zivilprozessrecht*) is classified as public law (*öffentliches Recht*) because it effectuates constitutional rights (fair and effective trial, right to be heard, access to justice) and the rule of law (*Rechtsstaat*) requiring that disputes between private parties be resolved by the courts and their judges according to law. See German Constitution (*Grundgesetz*) Articles 1, 19(4), 20, 92, 101, 103; European Convention on Human Rights Art. 6; Rosenberg/Schwab/Gottwald, §§1(VI), (VII), 3(I), pp. 5 ff., 13 ff.; Federal Constitutional Court, 57 BVerfGE 250, 275 (1981).

3. Rosenberg/Schwab/Gottwald, §1(III)(1), p. 3 ("*Der Zweck des Zivilprozesses besteht also in der Feststellung und Verwirklichung subjektiver Rechte.*"). See also Lüke, §1, mn. 1, pp. 2 f.; Jauernig, §1(II)(1) stating the central purpose of civil justice in precisely the same terms; for a more detailed discussion Stürner, *Die Aufklärungspflicht der Parteien des Zivilprozesses* (1976), §5(III), pp. 48 ff.

4. See, e.g., Lüke, §1, mn. 1.

most important assignments, a cultural assignment in the true sense of the word. The purpose of civil justice consists, therefore, in the determination and realization of subjective rights."[5]

The peaceful resolution of disputes is of course an important goal of civil justice. But the core function of civil justice is to vindicate individual rights. The system must resolve those disputes according to the standards and procedures provided by the law. It is not enough for a judgment to provide a peaceful resolution of the parties' dispute. The judgment must be correct as a matter of material law.[5]

Of course the determination and enforcement of private rights leads to the ongoing development and improvement of the law itself. However the prevailing view is that improvement of the law is more a by-product than the driving purpose of civil justice.[7]

The civil justice system has been described as the state's response to the individual citizen's inherent "claim to justice" (*Justizanspruch or Justizgewährungsanspruch*) which is rooted in the concept of a state ruled by law (*Rechtsstaat*).[8] The claim to justice does not entitle the citizen to a correct decision in every case. Rather the claim to justice encompasses access to a competent and independent judge who will decide the case according to a fair procedure applying the norms of law. The courts have the duty to accept civil complaints, process the complaints according to a reasonable procedure, examine the relevant facts and applicable law, and, when the matter is ripe, ren-

5. Rosenberg/Schwab/Gottwald, §1(III)(1), pp. 2 f. ("*Der Staat kann aber die Selbsthilfe nur verbieten, wenn er selber durch seine Organe den Parteien Rechtsschutz gewährt, und er tut es durch den Zivilprozess. Der Staat erfüllt damit eine seiner wichtigsten Aufgaben, eine Kulturaufgabe im wahren Sinne des Wortes. Der Zweck des Zivilprozesses besteht also in der Feststellung und Verwirklichung subjektiver Rechte.*")

6. E.g. Rosenberg/Schwab/Gottwald, §1(III)(3–5), p. 3.

7. Rosenberg/Schwab/Gottwald, §1(III)(3), p. 3. "As civil justice enables the parties to vindicate their rights, it also promotes the development of the law and the preservation of objective legal norms. This is, however, not an independent purpose of civil justice in addition to the protection of subjective legal rights, as is asserted by many authors." ("*Indem der Zivilprozess den Parteien zur Durchsetzung ihrer Rechte verhilft, dient er auch bei der Rechtsfortbildung zugleich der Bewährung des objektiven Rechts. Dies ist aber kein selbständiger Prozesszweck neben dem Schutz der subjektiven Rechte, wie es von manchen Autoren behauptet wird.*")

8. See Jauernig, §36(I) (differentiating the constitutional claim to justice from the disputed right to a correct decision in an individual case (*Rechtsschutzanspruch*)); Rosenberg/Schwab/Gottwald, §3, pp.13 ff. (to the same effect); Stürner, *Aufklärungspflicht der Parteien*, §5(II), pp. 31 ff.

der a judicial decision. The right to justice also includes the ability to obtain effective enforcement of the decisions rendered.[9]

The citizen's claim to justice finds reflection in several provisions of the modern German Constitution. For instance, Article 97 of the Constitution guarantees the independence of all German judges. Article 101 gives every citizen a right to a "lawful judge" (*gesetzlicher Richter*), whose jurisdiction, powers and case assignments are prescribed by law of general applicability. The "right to be heard" (*rechtliches Gehör*), encompassing several aspects of procedural fairness, is guaranteed by Article 103.

More general provisions of the Constitution have been applied to vouchsafe and reinforce the German citizen's right to justice. For instance, the basic guarantee that "All persons are equal before the law" set forth in Article 3 of the Constitution[10] has been interpreted to require that parties have equal chances (*Waffengleichheit*) in civil proceedings,[11] including access to legal aid where necessary. Even the basic principle that litigation is under the control of the parties (*Dispositionsmaxime*) finds support in Article 2 of the Constitution, which guarantees citizens the maximum scope of personal freedom consistent with an ordered society.[12]

In several extreme cases the German Federal Constitutional Court has even set aside manifestly wrong decisions of civil courts as denials of a party's constitutional claim to justice. This degree of judicial activism has resulted in some criticism and the observation that the Federal Constitutional Court may be attempting to function as a "supreme civil court" (*oberstes Zivilgericht*) in constitutional guise.[13]

---

9. See, in general, Rosenberg/Schwab/Gottwald, §3(II), p. 13 f. and Rosenberg/Gaul/Schilken, *Zwangsvollstreckungsrecht*, 11th ed. (1997), §1(III)(1), p. 6; Baur/Stürner, *Zwangsvollstreckungs-, Konkurs- und Vergleichsrecht*, Vol. I: *Einzelvollstreckungsrecht*, 12th ed. (1995), §7(I), mn. 7.1, p. 81.

10. German Constitution, Article 3(1)(*Alle Menschen sind vor dem Gesetz gleich*).

11. On equal chances of the parties see German Constitutional Court, 32 *NJW* 1925, 1927 (1979); Vollkommer, "Der Grundsatz der Waffengleichheit im Zivilprozess - eine neue Prozessmaxime?", in: Gottwald et al. (ed.), *Festschrift für Karl Heinz Schwab* (1990), p. 503; Stürner, "Die Einwirkungen der Verfassung auf das Zivilrecht und den Zivilprozess", 32 *NJW* 2334, 2337 (1979).

12. See, e.g., Stürner, "Verfahrensgrundsätze des Zivilprozesses und Verfassung", in: Grunsky et al. (ed.), *Festschrift für Fritz Baur* (1981), p. 647, 650. The principle of party control of litigation is discussed in Ch. 6(B)(2) below.

13. See Ch. 3(E) above and Ch. 10(H) below on constitutional appeals; Diederichsen, "Das Bundesverfassungsgericht als oberstes Zivilgericht - ein Lehrstück der juristischen Methodenlehre", 198 *Archiv für die civilistische Praxis* 171 (1998).

As in every legal system, some disputes involve more explicit public policies than others. Of course in every case there is a strong public policy in conforming reality to the rule of law.[14] Private civil litigation can also, and does in some cases, involve the invocation and enforcement of public policies as embodied in specific laws.[15] Regardless, however, of the kind or degree of public interest involved in maintenance of the suit, the principle that the overall control of the initiation, termination, and scope of a lawsuit remains with the parties (*Dispositionsmaxime*) is central to German civil justice.

That being said, once the parties have invoked its assistance, and within the scope of the dispute confided to it, the State, in the form of the court, assumes a degree of positive responsibility to resolve the dispute according to the requirements and standards of law. The principle that a state has a responsibility to resolve civil disputes by fair application of uniform standards of law underlies every system of civil justice. What differs between systems is how much activity the neutral participants are expected to undertake in the course of the proceedings to ensure that the result is of high quality and fairly reached. The German system gives the judge the responsibility to undertake a certain amount of positive activity during the proceedings in the interest of insuring a fair and just outcome. It is the judge's exercise of this positive responsibility, carefully bounded and defined by the ZPO, that leads observers from common law traditions to mischaracterize German civil procedure as "inquisitorial" or "judge centered."[16] In fact, German civil proceedings involve a sophisticated balance and coordination of activity and responsibility between

---

14. See Rosenberg/Schwab/Gottwald, §1(III)(3), p. 3; Jauernig, §1(II)(3).

15. For example, when established interest groups (*Verbände*) sue to enforce environmental protection or unfair competition laws. See Ch. 7(B)(5) below. The private enforcement of public policies has been referred to as a "second purpose" of civil justice. In a sense, the plaintiff is functioning on behalf of the collective legal order (*Funktionär der Gesamtrechtsordnung*). Jauernig, §1(II)(2); Rosenberg/Schwab/Gottwald, §§1(III)(2), 47, pp. 3, 243 f.

16. Procedural regimes in which the judge plays an active role have been associated with the countries of continental Europe. In many of these countries the establishment of an independent judiciary preceded the development of a powerful elected legislature. In the early years of the modern era European judges may have played greater roles in protection and vindication of citizens' rights than did the courts in countries such as England and the United States, where there were strong legislatures and a large and well established Bar to fulfil the same function. See Würtenberger, "Verfassungsrechtliche Streitigkeiten in der zweiten Hälfte des 18.Jahrhunderts", in: Klein et al. (ed.), *Festschrift für Ernst Benda* (1995), pp. 443, 450 ff.; Neugebauer-Wölk, *Reichsjustiz und Aufklärung* (1993); Klein, *Freyheit und Eigenthum* (1790), p. 164 ("He who lives in a monarchy which provides for freedom of its citizens is not keen on becoming a republican.")

parties, their counsel and the court designed to promote fair and just outcomes of civil disputes efficiently and at reasonable cost.

B. Roles of Parties and Counsel

In most cases, the scope and conduct of German civil proceedings are fundamentally determined by the parties. "The parties can decide individually or together the "whether" and the "concerning what?" of the proceeding."[17] According to the principle of party control of the cause of action (*Dispositionsmaxime*) the parties determine the subject matter and scope of the issues of the proceeding, if and when it is initiated, and if it is to be voluntarily terminated. Within the proceeding itself, the parties, not the court, decide the source of factual proof in most instances.[18] Even in areas where German judges are traditionally seen as relatively active, such as taking of factual proof by examination of witnesses, the parties have overlapping responsibilities which can importantly contribute to outcomes in individual cases. German civil litigation is thus truly adversarial.[19]

1. Party Control over the Scope and Nature of the Proceedings

The principle that the parties have control over the nature and scope of civil litigation (*Dispositionsmaxime*) is a fundamental guiding principle of German civil justice and finds expression in statutes and court rules as well as in tradition and practice.[20] Most civil cases can only be initiated by a complaint of a private party.[21] The scope of the proceeding in terms of the issues presented and relief requested is governed by the formal claims for relief (*Anträge*) of

17. Stürner, *Die richterliche Aufklärung im Zivilprozess* (1982), Ch.(I), mn.1.

18. The principle that the parties are responsible for the identification and nomination of sources of factual proof in civil proceedings is referred to as the *Verhandlungsmaxime* or *Beibringungsgrundsatz.* See generally Rosenberg/Schwab/Gottwald, §78, pp. 421 ff.

19. Although misconceptions persist, German civil procedure has been recognized as fundamentally adversarial by observers and commentators on both sides of the Atlantic. See Stürner, *Richterliche Aufklärung*, Ch.(II)(2), mn. 11; Rosenberg/Schwab/Gottwald, §78(I)(3), (4), p. 425; Langbein, "The German Advantage in Civil Procedure," 52 *Chicago Law Review* 823 (1985).

20. Also referred to as the "Parteiprinzip".

21. Including not for profit corporations and authorized private interest groups (*Verbände*). Rosenberg/Schwab/Gottwald, §47, pp. 243 f.; see Ch. 7(B)(5) below.

the parties.[22] The parties have the right to withdraw proceedings, to vary their form by agreement, and to terminate them by settlement. Absent a request for relief initiated by a party in most cases a German court has no power to commence a civil proceeding.

Exceptions to this rule of strict party control of the scope and nature of civil proceedings are partially "non-contentious" proceedings such as guardianships, adoptions, probate, land registration proceedings and the like (*freiwillige Gerichtsbarkeit*).[23] In such proceedings the court can exercise greater control over the scope of the issues and the initiation or termination of the proceeding than in traditional adversarial (*streitig*) cases between contending parties. Of course even so-called "noncontentious" proceedings often involve serious disputed issues between private parties.[24] In such cases the contending parties may exercise some control over the scope of the issues directly involving their respective interests, while the court may nevertheless exercise an overriding control over those issues directly confided to it.[25] The line between adversarial (*streitige*) proceedings in which the principle of party control of litigation (*Dispositionsmaxime*) prevails and noncontentious proceedings (*freiwillige Gerichtsbarkeit*) is not always clear.[26] Another area in which the principle of strict party control of proceedings may be relaxed to a certain extent is family cases involving the rights and welfare of third parties such as minor children.[27]

In the ordinary civil case a party has the right to choose which legal claims arising out of a particular relationship, transaction or occurrence will be sub-

---

22. This is important because the legal effect of a judgment on future claims between the parties depends in large part on the specific claims for relief which were placed before the court which rendered the judgment. See Ch. 9(F) below.

23. See Baur/Wolf, *Grundbegriffe des Rechts der freiwilligen Gerichtsbarkeit*, 2nd ed. (1980), Ch. 3(I), pp. 57 ff.; Brehm, *Freiwillige Gerichtsbarkeit*, 2nd ed. (1993), § 14(I), pp. 133 ff. These cases are considered "noncontentious" because they are initiated in part by the court or a public office or they involve public interests other than those of the immediate parties. However private parties affected by these proceedings have the constitutional right to be heard (*rechtliches Gehör*), and they can become very adversarial. See Ch. 11(E) below for a discussion of exercise of non-contentious jurisdiction.

24. For instance disputes between claimants to an estate or between parents in a child protective matter.

25. These are generally issues involving some aspect of the public interest not likely to be advanced by an affected party, such as the welfare of a child in a child protective proceeding, or the public interest implemented by laws requiring public approval of certain agricultural land transfers. See BGB §1666 (child protective proceeding); Baur/Stürner, *Sachenrecht*, 17th ed. (1999), §27(II)(1), pp. 306 f. (agricultural courts).

26. See, e.g., Jauernig, §3(IV); Rosenberg/Schwab/Gottwald, §11(II), pp. 54 f.

27. See Ch. 11(A) below for a brief discussion of family court proceedings.

mitted to the court for determination or enforcement. A plaintiff can choose to submit less than all of a single or group of related claims against a single defendant or group of related defendants. The court cannot interfere with this choice or bar later submission of the withheld or omitted claims, even if efficiency would favor submission and determination of all claims as a group.[28] This is true for both parties. There is no rule requiring the submission of counterclaims by the opposing party.[29] The court can and does require the parties to clarify their claims and positions, but the basic right to choose and define the claim being submitted to the court for decision remains with the parties.[30]

2. Party control over proof of facts

The parties' control over their own cases extends to delineating the sources of factual proof for the contentions at issue. A party has the responsibility to describe to the court the factual proof for each contested factual allegation of its claim or defense and to identify the source of that proof.[31] By the same token, in deciding the case, the court is required to confine its consideration to facts from those sources which have been brought forward or identified by the parties.[32]

This allocation of responsibility for fact development between parties and court is referred to as the principle of party control of facts and the means of

28. German courts are authorized to transfer, consolidate, and sever claims in cases once they have been brought. However such devices as the class action, as well as special representative actions, in which the court purports to adjudicate the rights of persons not formal parties to the proceeding may be consistent with the legal concept and role of parties in German civil procedure only under very limited and special circumstances. See Ch. 7(B) below.

29. Of course later assertion of opposing claims logically within the scope of the plaintiff's claims (*Anträge*) could be governed by the court's judgment on those claims. See Ch. 9(F) below on the res adjudicata effect of German civil judgments.

30. In Germany the scope of the doctrine of *res adjudicata* does not generally extend to "causes of action" or matters which "could have been determined" in a prior judgment, but only to the particular claims for relief (*Anträge*) which were in fact presented and adjudicated. It has been argued that in some cases a judgment on a partial claim originally asserted without disclosure that it is part of a larger claim (*verdeckte Teilklage*) may bar assertion of the undisclosed remainder of the claim later on. See Ch. 9(F)(2)(a) below.

31. See 67 BVerfGE 39, 42 (1984) for a recognition of the *Verhandlungsmaxime* by the German Federal Constitutional Court.

32. When significant facts not previously mentioned by one of the parties come up in the course of a hearing, the court is required to give the parties a chance to comment on the new facts before relying on them in a decision. ZPO § 139(2), Ch. 8(B)(3) below.

proof (*Verhandlungsmaxime*)[33] and lies at the core of German civil procedure.[34] This principle is not set forth in a single statutory provision, but suffuses the ZPO.[35] Often it is to be inferred from the negative. The ZPO specifies the exceptions and assumes the applicability of the principle in the ordinary course.[36] It is to be contrasted to the principle of investigation by the court (*Untersuchungsmaxime*), according to which the judge undertakes a positive responsibility to ascertain and clarify the facts related to a particular event or circumstance and which generally prevails in German criminal procedure. Much has been written about the *Verhandlungsmaxime* and its consequences for the conduct of civil litigation in Germany.[37]

An important corollary of the *Verhandlungsmaxime* is that the court must accept as true facts which are not disputed by the parties without requiring that proof be provided.[38] By their respective pleadings or by stipulation the parties can agree on the facts governing the proceeding. "The court may only examine the truth of a fact within the borders set for the court by the parties."[39]

The Civil Procedure Code sets forth the parties' responsibilities with respect to each other's factual assertions with great specificity. According to ZPO §138,

> (1) The parties are to give their declarations concerning factual circumstances completely and truthfully.
>
> (2) Each party must declare its position with respect to the facts asserted by its opponent.

---

33. Also sometimes referred to as *Beibringungsgrundsatz.*

34. See Jauernig, §25; Rosenberg/Schwab/Gottwald, §78, pp. 424 ff.

35. Many ZPO sections embody aspects of this principle. For instance, see §§130(3), 138(I)–(III), 282(I), 288(I), 331(I), 359(3), 371, 373, 420, 424, 445, 592.

36. See, e.g., ZPO §616(I) which specially authorizes the court in matrimonial cases to hear and consider facts which were not brought forward by the parties.

37. A brief discussion of the *Verhandlungsmaxime* is contained in every treatise on German civil procedure. See, e.g., Rosenberg/Schwab/Gottwald, §78, pp. 242 ff.; Jauernig, §25, pp. 72–84; Lüke, §2(II), mn. 13–24. For more explicit and detailed discussions of the *Verhandlungsmaxime*, see Wassermann, *Der Soziale Zivilprozess* (1978); Leipold, "Zivilprozessrecht und Ideologie", *37 JZ* 441 (1982).

38. Whether this principle is one of basic procedure (*Verhandlung*) or should be considered as a rule of proof (*Beweisregel*) is open to dispute. See Endemann, *Der Deutsche Civilprozess* (1868), §197, pp. 762–765; Prütting, in: *Münchener Kommentar zur Zivilprozessordnung*, 2nd ed. (2000 ff.), §288, mn. 3; Rüssmann, in: Ankermann/Wassermann (ed.), *Kommentar zur Zivilprozessordnung* (1987), vor §288, mn. 1 ff.

39. Jauernig, §25(IV)(2) ("*Das Gericht darf also die Wahrheit einer Tatsache nur in den Grenzen nachprüfen, die ihm von den Parteien gesetzt sind.*").

(3) Facts which are not expressly contested are to be treated as admitted, unless the intention to contest them appears from the parties declarations.

(4) A declaration of lack of knowledge is allowable only with respect to facts which were neither the party's own actions nor the subject of its own observations.[40]

These provisions make it clear that parties to German litigation cannot get away with vague allegations of fact in their own pleadings or with general denials of their opponents' factual contentions. The parties must engage with the facts early on and play a constructive role in the clarification and refinement of factual disputes even at the pleading stage of the litigation. To the extent that the pleadings are unclear, if the parties do not clear up ambiguities in their own submissions, the court will order them to do so during the course of preparatory proceedings so that the exact nature and scope of factual disputes will be clear to all by the beginning of the plenary phase of the litigation.[41]

3. Division of responsibility for assertion and proof of facts between parties and court

The responsibility of a party to assert specific facts sufficient to sustain a claim or defense starts with the initial pleading, whether complaint or answer. A party must also be prepared to identify a plausible source of proof of facts alleged in the event that they are contested. The judge looks at each pleading at the time it is filed to see whether the party has alleged facts and identified credible sources of proof of such facts sufficient to establish the legal elements of the claim or defense. If such facts are lacking, and the party fails to correct

40. *(1) Die Parteien haben ihre Erklärungen über tatsächliche Umstände vollständig und der Wahrheit gemäss abzugeben.*
(2) Jede Partei hat sich über die von dem Gegner behaupteten Tatsachen zu erklären.
(3) Tatsachen, die nicht ausdrücklich bestritten werden, sind als zugestanden anzusehen, wenn nicht die Absicht, sie bestreiten zu wollen, aus den übrigen Erklärungen der Partei hervorgeht.
(4) Eine Erklärung mit Nichtwissen ist nur über Tatsachen zulässig, die weder eigene Handlungen der Partei noch Gegenstand ihrer eigenen Wahrnehmung gewesen sind.

41. Preparatory proceedings are discussed in Ch. 7 below. Plenary and evidentiary proceedings are the subject matter of Ch. 8.

the defect after the court has brought it to its attention, the claim may be dismissed or the defense struck as insufficient.[42]

Once a party has brought forward or identified the evidence, the responsibility for eliciting and evaluating that evidence shifts to the court. The court is obligated, however, to receive and consider all proof proffered by a party on a given proposition or issue. So, for example, if a witness identified by a party as supporting its position on a particular issue in the case also has information favoring the opponent on that or some other issue, the judge is entirely free to consider the information for whatever inferences it will support.[43]

As will be seen below, a party's basic responsibility to found all of its contentions with credible facts is somewhat mitigated by the judge's obligation to give the parties a chance to clarify unclear facts and factual assertions. The *Verhandlungsmaxime* does not prevent the court from assisting both parties by suggesting that they clarify their assertions, supply omitted details, or take account of the court's tentative conclusions of fact or law in fulfilling their roles in the proceeding.[44]

4. The Role of Counsel in German Litigation

German civil justice assigns very important roles to professional lawyers in the preparation and argument of civil cases. In all of the ordinary civil courts other than the local courts representation by counsel is mandatory, and a case will be dismissed or a pleading will be returned if it is not signed by an attorney qualified to practice in German courts.[45] Even in those local court cases where representation by counsel is not required, many litigants hire lawyers to conduct their litigation.

On the other hand in smaller cases in the local courts, counsel fees can increase the cost of litigation to the point where access to justice may be impaired. The German system thus permits parties in local court cases other than family cases to litigate pro se, or with the help of a non-lawyer representative

42. See, in general, Jauernig, §25(V). For a discussion of the court's obligation to advise parties of apparent defects in pleadings and other submissions see Ch. 6(C)(2) below.

43. This includes all items of proof identified or incorporated in the case record (*Akte*). See Ch. 8 below for a more detailed discussion of the roles of court and parties in the reception and evaluation of proof.

44. See Ch. 6(C)(2) below on the judge's duty to give the parties hints and feedback (*Hinweispflicht*).

45. See Ch. 4(C) and (D) above on qualifications of persons to practice as attorneys in Germany.

or helper, in the interest of reducing unnecessary cost and expense. In all cases German judges interact not only with the lawyers, but also directly with the parties throughout the proceeding.

a. Representation by counsel

All parties to civil litigation are entitled to be represented by counsel of their own choosing and at their own expense at all stages of the proceedings. This right to legal assistance and representation is considered as a fundamental human right protected by the German Constitution. Although counsel are not required in non-family cases in the local courts, a litigant who is not able to afford to hire counsel can be granted legal aid if the local court judge is convinced that the case is sufficiently complex to warrant assistance of counsel.[46]

In most civil cases in German courts there is compulsory representation by counsel (*Anwaltszwang*). ZPO §78 requires each party to civil litigation in the state district courts, in the state appeals courts, and in family cases in the local courts to be represented by a lawyer admitted to practice before a German court.[47] Attorneys are required to obtain written litigation powers of attorney (*schriftliche Prozessvollmacht*) from their clients and to file these powers of attorney with the court in which the litigation is pending.[48] In the event that a party to litigation in a court where counsel is compulsory is unable to find a lawyer, the court can appoint a counsel (*Notanwalt*) to represent the otherwise unrepresented party for that particular instance of the case.[49]

If a party is represented by counsel in a case, pleadings and briefs are submitted and signed solely by counsel, service on an attorney counts as service on the represented party, and parties are generally held to the strategic and tactical decisions made in their behalf by their lawyers, even if those decisions turn out to be mistaken.[50] It is generally agreed that the court's duty to give hints and feedback on certain basic matters is somewhat relaxed if a party is represented.[51]

---

46. See ZPO §§114, 121(2); Musielak/Fischer, *Kommentar zur Zivilprozessordnung*, 3rd ed. (2002), §121, mn. 10 f.; Zöller/Philippi, *Zivilprozessordnung*, 23rd ed. (2002), §121, mn. 4. For additional discussion of access to justice and legal aid see Ch. 4(I) above.

47. See Ch. 4(D) above on admission to practice of German and now European lawyers.

48. ZPO §80. See Zöller/Vollkommer, §80, mn. 8–11 for a discussion of the form of the power of attorney.

49. ZPO §78b.

50. See ZPO §85. For a discussion of the scope of a litigation power of attorney see Rosenberg/Schwab/Gottwald, §55(II)(6)(f), pp. 294 ff.

51. See Ch. 6(C)(2) below.

Even in cases in which the parties are required to be represented by attorneys, German judges are authorized and required to interact directly with the parties themselves, without intermediation by a lawyer, at all oral hearings. The judges speak directly with the parties in such vital matters as the statement of the parties claims and contentions (*Anhörung der Parteien*), in settlement discussions (*Güteverhandlungen*), and to make sure that not only the lawyers, but the parties themselves are enlightened by the court's "hints and feedback" during the proceedings.

b. Litigating Pro Se

In local court cases other than family cases, litigants frequently appear without counsel. The rules and procedures in the local courts are designed to facilitate access to those courts by persons without lawyers. For instance, in smaller cases a party may lodge an oral complaint with the clerk of courts (*Urkundsbeamter*) at the clerk's office of the court. That official will reduce the complaint as orally recited by the plaintiff to writing for consideration by the court and further proceedings. The same is true of a defendant's answer.[52]

The relative informality of pleadings in German cases in general lends itself to party self-representation.[53] Some of the simplified procedures, such as the warning procedure (*Mahnverfahren*) are designed to be conducted by the parties themselves, sometimes using pre-printed forms.[54] If a party does not have counsel, all communications must be served on the party itself, and there is no simplified "lawyer to lawyer" service available.[55]

In cases where representation by a lawyer is not required a party may give a power of attorney (*Vollmacht*) to any person, who can then represent the party, with or without compensation.[56] Such non-lawyer legal representatives may not provide representation in litigation as a regular business without obtaining a license (*Erlaubnis*) from the state ministry of justice.[57]

---

52. ZPO §496.
53. See Ch. 7(A) below on form of complaints and other pleadings and briefs.
54. For discussion of these particular forms of civil proceeding see Ch. 11(C)(2) below.
55. See Ch. 7(F) below on the various means of service of court papers.
56. ZPO §79.
57. ZPO §157(1), (3). See Zöller/Vollkommer, §78, mn. 9 ff. for a discussion of various categories of professionals with status as licensed legal consultant (*Rechtsbeistand mit Erlaubnis*) for court proceedings in the areas of their respective professional expertises. For the constitutionality of this limitation of the right of free choice and practice of profession (GG Art. 12) see German Constitutional Court, 29 *NJW* 1349 (1976).

In courts in which a lawyer is not required a party may also enlist the aid of a non lawyer consultant (*Beistand*) to assist in the litigation.[58] The consultant does not represent the party, but works with the party. A party can be bound by his consultant's assertions of fact or positions taken if the party is aware of the assertions and does not promptly contradict them.[59] Representation and assistance by non-lawyer representatives and consultants is more common in the specialized courts than in the ordinary courts.

If a party does not have a lawyer, the judge must be especially mindful of the obligation to give the party hints and feedback. There are several points at which the court is required to give specific hints and feedback if a party is *pro se*, or if the case is of a kind for which representation by counsel is not required.[60]

C. Role of the Judge

In German civil litigation the judge has a positive responsibility to conduct the case as presented by the parties in a manner to reach a prompt, economical and just resolution of the dispute. The principal areas in which the judge exercises this responsibility are:

- The review of complaints and certain other party submissions to determine whether prerequisites to suit (*Prozessvoraussetzungen*) have been satisfied,
- The ordering of the legal and factual issues raised by the parties to facilitate efficient determination of the controversy,
- The examination of witnesses and other means of proof proffered by the parties,
- The appointment of expert witnesses on fact issues involving expertise,[61]
- The provision of "hints and feedback" (*Hinweise*) to the parties and their counsel on issues of law and fact as well as the judge's tentative processes of decision in order to forestall surprise or cure inadvertence.

It must be emphasized that the area of "judicial activism" for German judges is fairly restricted and relatively well defined. The judicial activities

58. ZPO §90(1).

59. ZPO §90(2). See generally Zöller/Vollkommer, §90, mn. 1–4; Rosenberg/Schwab/Gottwald, §57, pp. 303 f.

60. See Ch. 6(C)(2) below; Zöller/Greger, §139, mn. 15 ff.

61. If the parties agree on a particular expert, the court is bound to accept their choice. ZPO §404(4).

listed above do not relieve the parties of their essential control or responsibility for the proceeding, nor do they clothe the judge in the mantle of an inquisitor. Overall they have been referred to as part of the judges "duty to provide clarification" (*Aufklärungspflicht*) in the processing of the parties' case.[62] Most of these individual judicial functions listed above will be discussed in greater detail in those sections of this work which deal with the phases of the proceedings to which they relate. However the duty to structure the proceeding to reach an efficient and fair termination and the duty to provide feedback or hints to the parties and counsel find application throughout all civil proceedings and should be discussed here.

1. The Judge's Duty to Structure the Proceedings

The structuring of the proceeding is a function shared by the court and by the parties. On the one hand, the parties determine the scope of the lawsuit by the claims for relief (*Anträge*) in their pleadings (*Dispositionsmaxime*) as well as the means of factual proof to be adduced in determination of the case (*Verhandlungsprinzip*). As described above, the scope of controversy and the fact sources to be exploited are the responsibility of the parties.[63]

On the other hand, once the case has been brought before the court, the responsibility for how and in what order the controversy will be resolved belongs largely to the court.

> "The court has the duty to conduct the proceedings in accord with law and in a manner appropriate to their purpose, in order to address the legal dispute thoroughly and at the same time expeditiously and to bring it via the shortest way to an end."[64]

The court determines whether the case will be prepared for plenary hearing and determination by a preliminary hearing or by written proceedings.[65] The

---

62. For an overall discussion of the judge's duty to promote clarification, with particular reference to the *Hinweispflicht*, see, e.g., Stürner, *Die richterliche Aufklärung im Zivilprozess* (1982); Peters, *Richterliche Hinweispflichten und Beweisinitiativen im Zivilprozess* (1983); Rosenberg/Schwab/Gottwald, §78(III), pp. 424 ff.

63. The principle that the parties retain overall control of the judicial proceeding is also referred to as the "party-principle" (*Parteiprinzip*).

64. Rosenberg/Schwab/Gottwald, §79(I), p. 435 ("*Das Gericht ist verpflichtet, das Verfahren gesetzmässig und zweckentsprechend abzuwickeln, den Rechtsstreit zugleich erschöpfend und doch schleunig zu verhandeln und auf kürzestem Wege zu beenden.*"). See ZPO §§272(1), 273.

65. ZPO §272(2). See Ch. 7(E)(2) below.

court also decides in what order the legal and factual issues will be addressed.[66] The court acts on its own motion to set dates and times for hearings and deadlines for submission of briefs and other papers by the parties.[67] The court has the power to raise additional legal issues which relate to the claims placed in issue by the parties.[68] The court may on its own motion (or at the request of a party) require the personal appearance of the parties at a hearing and the production of documents or other objects, or may decline to do so.[69] The court has the power to initiate and mediate settlement discussions and even propose settlements.[70] The exercise of these powers in an efficient and fair manner is an important function of German presiding judges.

2. The Judge's Responsibility to Give Hints and Feedback

The court's responsibility for ordering and managing the processing and decision of the case can be regarded mainly as a matter of efficient judicial management. The German court's obligation to give hints and feedback to the parties to avoid surprise and promote the fair and just determination of the suit (*Hinweispflicht*) goes one step further.[71] The degree to which a German judge is expected to expose her thinking processes to the parties to protect them from surprise and prevent injustice in the individual case is an important feature of German civil justice.

The nature of the judge's obligation to provide hints and feedback to the parties in a civil law suit and how it should be exercised have been the subject

66. See ZPO §§136(3), 139, 272, 273, 278 ff. The court is abjured to address the issues in a manner so as to lead to a prompt decision of the underlying controversy with a minimum of judicial proceedings. Thus dispositive legal issues ordinarily should be taken up before factual disputes requiring proof. See, e.g., Schellhammer, *Die Arbeitsmethode des Zivilrichters*, 14th ed. (2002), Part 2, Ch. 7, mn. 38–45.

67. See ZPO §§214 ff., 274 ff., 283, 296, 358a. This is a relatively new development as German courts have sought to expedite litigation and reduce delay. Historically dates and deadlines were set at the instance of parties so that unless a party chose to "push" a suit, it would not move forward on its own. Rosenberg/Schwab/Gottwald, § 84(I), p. 451 f.

68. However when the court raises a legal issue which the parties have not addressed, the court is obliged to bring it to the attention of the parties before using it as a grounds for decision. ZPO § 139(2).

69. ZPO §§ 273(2)(3), 141 ff. See Ch. 7(L) and 8(B) and (C) below.

70. ZPO §278. See Ch. 7(M) and 8(B)(4) below.

71. This duty to give hints and feedback is an aspect of the judicial duty of clarification (*richterliche Aufklärungspflicht*).

matter of considerable case law and text-writing ever since the obligation was extended to Germany as a whole by the Civil Procedure Law of 1877.[72] The judge's failure properly to exercise this role is often utilized as a procedural ground for a review appeal (*Revision*).[73] Both the German Constitutional Court (*Bundesverfassungsgericht*) and the German Federal Supreme Court (*Bundesgerichtshof*) have repeatedly attempted to describe the obligation in the context of the circumstances presented by specific cases.[74]

It is important not to confuse the judge's obligation to give hints and feedback as an expression of inquisitorial responsibility for determining the truth of the case at hand. It is more aptly characterized as requiring the judge to advise and assist the parties in resolving their dispute according to law.[75]

Most recently the Civil Code provisions which define the duty to give hints and feedback were amended to make the judge's obligations even more clear and explicit than had past formulations.

ZPO §139 now provides:

> (1) The court is to discuss with the parties the relevant facts and issues in dispute from a factual and legal perspective to the extent reasonable and to raise questions. It is to cause the parties timely and completely to declare their positions concerning all material facts, especially to supplement insufficient references to the relevant facts, to designate the means of proof, and to set forth claims based on the facts asserted.
>
> (2) The court may base its decision on a claim, other than a minor auxiliary claim, on a point of fact or law which a party has apparently overlooked or considered insignificant only if the court has called the

72. For a current overview see Piekenbrock, "Umfang und Bedeutung der richterlichen Hinweispflicht", 52 *NJW* 1360 (1999). For a more detailed description of the history of the judge's obligations of clarification in German Civil procedure law see Stürner, *Richterliche Aufklärung*, Ch.(I) and (II), mn. 2–5; Peters, *Richterliche Hinweispflichten*, §§2–25, pp. 4–103.

73. In civil cases review appeals after second instance appeals are limited to questions of law and procedure. See Ch. 10(E) below.

74. For example see Federal Constitutional Court, 29 *NJW* 1391 (1976); 32 *NJW* 1925, 1928 (1979); 44 *NJW* 2823 (1991); 45 *NJW* 678, 679 (1992); 49 *NJW* 3202 (1996) (constitutional right to a fair trial and the court's obligation to provide hints and feedback); Federal Supreme Court, 42 *NJW* 2756 (1989); 8 *NJW-RR* 569, 570 (1993) (lack of factual assertions); 38 *NJW* 3078 (1985); 42 *NJW* 2756 (1989) (lack of evidence).

75. See Stürner, *Richterliche Aufklärung*, Ch. (II), mn. 13–14; Peters, *Richterliche Hinweispflichten*, §27, p. 107.

> parties' attention to the point and given opportunity for comment on it. The same provision applies if the court's understanding of a point of fact or law differs from the understanding of both parties.
>
> (3) The court is to call attention to the court's inclinations which exist with respect to those points which may be noticed on the court's own motion.
>
> (4) Hints and feedback according to this requirement are to be communicated and documented in the record as early as possible. Their rendition can only be proven through the content of the record. Only evidence of forgery of the record can be received to contradict its contents.
>
> (5) If a party is not prepared to respond immediately to a judicial request for clarification the court on the motion of the party may set a time limit for further clarification by written argument.[76]

The current version of ZPO §139 represents an effort to set forth in one place some of the key elements of the judicial duty to give hints and feedback and avoid surprise as previously found in several places in the Civil Procedure Code and elaborated in case law. This section by no means exhausts the court's

---

76. *(1) Das Gericht hat das Sach- und Streitverhältnis, soweit erforderlich, mit den Parteien nach der tatsächlichen und rechlichen Seite zu erörtern und Fragen zu stellen. Es hat dahin zu wirken, dass die Parteien sich rechtzeitig und vollständig über alle erheblichen Tatsachen erklären, insbesondere ungenügende Angaben zu den geltend gemachten Tatsachen ergänzen, die Beweismittel bezeichnen und die sachdienlichen Anträge stellen.*
(2) Auf einen Gesichtspunkt, den eine Partei erkennbar übersehen oder für unerheblich gehalten hat, darf das Gericht, soweit nicht nur eine Nebenforderung betroffen ist, seine Entscheidung nur stützen, wenn es darauf hingewiesen und Gelegenheit zur Äusserung dazu gegeben hat. Dasselbe gilt für einen Gesichtspunkt, den das Gericht anders beurteilt als beide Parteien.
(3) Das Gericht hat auf die Bedenken aufmerksam zu machen, die hinsichtlich der von Amts wegen zu berücksichtigenden Punkte bestehen.
(4) Hinweise nach dieser Vorschrift sind so früh wie möglich zu erteilen und aktenkundig zu machen. Ihre Erteilung kann nur durch den Inhalt der Akten bewiesen werden. Gegen den Inhalt der Akten ist nur der Nachweis der Fälschung zulässig.
(5) Ist einer Partei eine sofortige Erklärung zu einem gerichtlichen Hinweis nicht möglich, so soll auf ihren Antrag das Gericht eine Frist bestimmen, in der sie die Erklärung in einem Schriftsatz nachbringen kann.

obligation to engage with the parties on issues of fact and law. For instance ZPO §§279(3), 285 make specific reference to the court's obligation to discuss the results of reception of evidence and the conclusions to be drawn therefrom with the parties before rendering any decision. Such discussions involve the same judicial obligation to give hints and feedback.[77]

It is safe to say that regardless of whether explicitly delineated in ZPO §139, the judicial duty to promote clarification is pervasive and relates to all judicial action.[78] Although some of the cases on hints and feedback currently on the books may be construing obsolete statutory language, the essence of the duty to provide hints and feedback has not really been fundamentally changed by the recent changes in statutory language.[79] In this sense the statutory change is more a matter of convenience and refinement than creation of any new procedural right or obligation.

a. Discussion of the Issues in the Case

ZPO §139(1) affirmatively requires the judge to initiate a discussion of the factual and legal issues of the case with the parties (and their lawyers) and to place questions to them designed to clarify unclear or missing fact assertions and simplify the issues.[80] The judge is required to so indicate where the parties have suggested the existence of relevant facts, but have not particularized them. Apparent contradictions in factual assertions must be called to the attention of the parties. The judge is expected to point out those factual assertions which are ambiguous or unclear before finding them insufficient on account of ambiguity or lack of clarity. On the other hand, the judge is not required repeatedly to mention the same omission or lack of clarity.[81] Nor need the judge mention defects in pleadings or oral assertions which have been already raised by the opposing party, at least in cases where the parties are represented by counsel.[82] Ultimately it is not the job of the judge to relieve the

---

77. See Ch. 8(D)(2) below for a discussion of this dialogue in plenary and evidentiary proceedings.

78. See, e.g., Musielak/Stadler, §139, mn. 3.

79. See Musielak/Stadler, §139, mn.2; Zöller/Greger, §139, mn. 1.

80. See, generally Zöller/Greger, §139, mn. 3–4.

81. See, e.g., Musielak/Stadler, §139, mn. 7; Federal Supreme Court, 33 *NJW* 2522, 2523 (1980). For further examples see Piekenbrock, 52 *NJW* 1360, 1362 (1999).

82. See, e.g., Federal Supreme Court, 37 *NJW* 310, 311 (1984). Since the 2001 reforms some commentators suggest that the judge should give a hint in these circumstances. See, e.g., Zöller/Greger, §139, mn. 3; Thomas/Putzo/Reichold, *Zivilprozessordnung*, 24th ed. (2002), §139, mn. 12.

parties of the consequences of gross and persistent negligence or lack of competence of their counsel.[83] This requirement that the judge initiate discussion with the parties on unclear fact assertions continues throughout the proceedings, and even on second-instance appeal.

b. Calling Attention to Dispositive Issues of Law or Fact

The second paragraph of ZPO §139 explicitly codifies a duty that previously had found reflection at various points in the Code. If a party seems to have overlooked or discounted the materiality of a point of view (*Gesichtspunkt*) the judge has to call this point of view to the party's attention before relying on it in a decision of consequence to the outcome of the case. The idea is to avoid a party being taken by surprise by the court's fact finding or reasoning without having a chance to address the issue before it is too late.[84] Even if the parties agree with each other on an issue, if the court has another point of view, it is obliged to call this to the parties' attention and give them a chance to address it.[85]

The court is under no obligation to give prior disclosure of an intended basis for decision if it has been mentioned in the pleadings or briefs of at least one of the parties, or if the basis for the decision is one of the common everyday bases that one should expect to address in a case of the kind before the court. On the other hand, if the court proposes to rely on a recent higher court decision not mentioned by either party, or if the court views the case entirely differently than the parties have presented it, the court must call its proposed reasoning to the parties' attention before proceeding further.[86]

While the court's obligation to give hints and feedback seems largely to be founded in considerations of fairness to the parties and preservation of their right to be heard, it can be argued that intelligent dialogue between the court and counsel leads to a better quality of judicial product overall. Sometimes

83. Federal Supreme Court, 37 *NJW* 310 (1984); 13 *NJW-RR* 16 (1998); Musielak/Stadler, §139, mn. 6 Stürner, *Richterliche Aufklärung*, Ch.(II)(3), mn. 16 and Ch.(III)(3), mn. 62; dissenting see, e.g., Peters, in: *Münchener Kommentar zur Zivilprozessordnung*, 2nd ed. (2002), §139, mn. 14. But the judge is obliged to initiate clarification if counsel simply misunderstood the law or a preceding hint of the court. See Federal Supreme Court, 127 BGHZ 254, 260 (1994); 52 *NJW* 1264 (1999).

84. See Zöller/Greger, §139, mn. 5–8; Musielak/Stadler, § 139, mn. 17 ff.; Thomas/Putzo/Reichold, §139, mn. 15 ff.

85. §139(2)(2).

86. See, e.g., Federal Constitutional Court, 9 NJW-RR 188 (1994); Federal Supreme Court, 46 NJW 667 (1993); Thomas/Putzo/Reichold, § 139, mn. 23; Stürner, *Richterliche Aufklärung*, Ch.(III)(6), mn. 85.

the court can get the wrong slant on a case because it has mis-perceived or ignored some important fact or inference. Alerting the parties and their lawyers to the court's direction of reasoning gives them a chance to disabuse the court of misconceptions before they become erroneous judicial decisions.

c. Concerns about Matters Subject to the Court's Own Motion

Although the parties mainly control the claims and defenses that may be considered in a civil case, certain matters such as prerequisites to suit (*Prozessvoraussetzungen*), may be raised by the court on its own motion. If the court is entertaining concerns about one of these issues, the court is obliged to let the parties know.[87] Sometimes the defect can be mended or the missing prerequisite may be supplied so that a potentially unnecessary procedural dismissal (*Prozessabweisung*) and re-institution of the action can be avoided.

d. Timing of Hints and Feedback

Although ZPO §139(4)(1) does not set forth a particular timing for hints and feedback, the idea is that the hints and feedback should be given promptly enough so that affected parties can effectively address the issue in oral argument, written comments, and, when appropriate, by additional assertions of fact and proffers of evidence. Failure to afford parties and their counsel fair opportunity to react to hints and feedback can be a denial of the right to be heard (*rechtliches Gehör*). In simple cases it may be reasonable to expect a more or less immediate response from the parties. In more complex situations a reasonable opportunity may require a continuance of a plenary hearing for this purpose or at least fair opportunity for further written response (ZPO § 139(5)).[88]

e. Hints and Feedback—Particular Issues

The circumstances where the judge is expected to provide the parties some feedback or a hint of where the judge is going are numerous. For instance, when a party would be threatened by a preclusion for failure to bring forward a factual or legal assertion, or failure to designate the means of proof,[89] the judge is be expected to call this failure to the party's attention and give an op-

---

87. See ZPO §139(3); Zöller/Greger, §139, mn. 9 and Ch. 6(C)(2)(e) below.

88. See Zöller/Greger, §139, mn. 14; Thomas/Putzo/Reichold, §139, mn. 32 f.; Federal Supreme Court, 52 *NJW* 2123 (1999).

89. Zöller/Greger, § 296, mn. 32. See Ch. 7(K) and 8(A)(2) below for a discussion of the role of preclusions in German procedure.

portunity to cure the deficit before invoking the preclusion.[90] In this situation the judge's obligation to give an opportunity to make an omitted assertion or proffer makes it possible for a lawyer to concentrate initially on the defenses and issues which seem most important at the time without having to put forward every conceivable contingent claim or defense for fear of preclusion.[91]

The court is expected to so indicate if it has concerns about the basic prerequisites to suit (*Prozessvoraussetzungen*) in hopes of timely clarification.[92] As the case goes along and the parties assert their claims and defenses and designate the proof for the same, the court is expected to provide timely hints and feedback to promote clarification and prevent unintentional slips or ambiguities. Thus if the plaintiff has chosen the wrong formulation of his claims, the court should suggest the possibility of a change.[93]

On the other hand, the obligation to give hints and feedback does not permit the court to suggest that a party enlarge his demand or add another claim or element to enlarge the subject matter or change the "goal of the case" (*Prozessziel*).[94] Nor may the judge warn a party about the consequences of an impending bar of the statute of limitations (*Verjährung*).[95] Sometimes the boundary is not entirely clear. For instance, does the judge overstep his bounds to suggest to a party that an unpromising complaint to forestall execution should be transformed into a more likely complaint for declaratory judgment?[96]

---

90. Precluding a party from raising an omitted legal or factual assertion without specific prior judicial warning can invalidate the preclusion on appeal. See Stürner, *Richterliche Aufklärung*, Ch.(II)(5), mn. 33 f.

91. Federal Constitutional Court, 51 *NJW* 2044 (1998); Stürner, *Richterliche Aufklärung*, Ch.(II)(5), mn. 34. See on this problem also Lüke, §17(IV), mn. 194.

92. ZPO § 139(3). Zöller/Greger, §139, mn. 9; Stürner, *Richterliche Aufklärung*, Ch.(III)(1), mn. 53.

93. For instance, if the plaintiff has improperly pled a claim for declaratory judgment (*Feststellungsklage*) in the form of a claim for present performance (*Leistungsklage*), the court should suggest the proper formulation. See Stürner, *Richterliche Aufklärung*, Ch.(III)(2), mn. 55; Peters, *Richterliche Hinweispflichten*, §30(I), pp.122 f.

94. Musielak/Stadler, §139, mn. 5; Rosenberg/Schwab/Gottwald, §78(III)(1)(b), p. 429; Stürner, *Richterliche Aufklärung*, Ch.(III)(2), mn. 56.

95. Musielak/Stadler, §139, mn. 9; Stein/Jonas/Leipold, *Kommentar zur Zivilprozessordnung*, 21st ed. (1994), §139, mn. 24; Stürner, *Richterliche Aufklärung*, Ch.(III)(2), mn. 60. But see Federal Supreme Court, 51 *NJW* 612 (1998) (settlement negotiations and warning about the consequences of the statute of limitations).

96. In 1957 the Federal Supreme Court was of the view that such a suggestion would go beyond the judicial obligation of clarification. 24 BGHZ 269, 278 (1957). But see, Stürner, *Richterliche Aufklärung*, Ch.(III)(2), mn. 57.

The obligation of the court to provide hints and feedback in order to promote clarification extends through the proof designation and proof taking (*Beweisaufnahme*) phases of the proceeding. So where a party fails to request the taking of proof on a disputed factual issue, or to name a source of proof, the judge is expected to step in and bring the omission to the attention of the party or its lawyer. The same is true if the party offers a means of proof which is legally insufficient to establish the proposition to be proved.[97] Again, the judge is not required to protect parties against serious neglect or incompetence of their lawyers.[98]

Once the proof originally designated by the parties has been heard, the court will share with the parties its reaction to the proof, and indicate those areas in which there is still uncertainty.[99] Whether the judge is required to suggest to the parties potential avenues or sources of additional proof on points not clearly established is somewhat disputed. On the one hand, the judge would be expected to call the parties attention to items of proof which the court could request on its own motion if it wished to do so.[100] On the other hand, where the case record (*Akte*) does not point clearly to further sources of proof, or where an additional witness is mentioned in the case record but has not been expressly requested by one of the parties, the judge is not required to step in and suggest a new avenue of proof or potential witness.[101] The judge could, however, ask one of the parties why that party had not requested the testimony of a particular identified witness, which might have the same effect as suggesting that the witness be called.[102] By the same token, if the judge evaluates the evidence in a surprising manner, the judge should advise the parties and give them opportunity to react.[103]

---

97. See Zöller/Greger, §139, mn. 16; Stürner, *Richterliche Aufklärung*, Ch.(III)(4), mn. 69–73

98. Federal Constitutional Court, 32 *NJW* 1925, 1928 (1979); Federal Supreme Court, 46 *NJW* 2531, 2533 (1993); Stürner, *Richterliche Aufklärung*, Ch.(III)(4), mn. 70; Musielak/Stadler, § 139, mn. 14.

99. ZPO §§279(3), 285(1). See Ch. 8(B)(3) below.

100. See ZPO §§139(1)(2); 141–144, 273(2). These rules include all items of factual proof (other than witnesses) identified or referred to in the case record. See Stürner, *Richterliche Aufklärung*, Ch.(III)(4), mn. 72; Federal Supreme Court, 24 BGHZ 308, 315 (1957).

101. Stürner, *Richterliche Aufklärung*, Ch.(III)(4), mn. 72; Musielak/Stadler, §139, mn. 14.

102. Stürner, *Richterliche Aufklärung*, Ch.(III)(4), mn. 72.

103. See Ch. 8(B)(3) below; Federal Constitutional Court, 45 *NJW* 678, 679 (1992); Federal Supreme Court, 41 *NJW* 2756 (1989), Thomas/Putzo, §139, mn. 8; Stürner, *Richterliche Aufklärung*, Ch.(III)(4), mn. 74.

f. Form and Circumstances of Hints and Feedback

The court can exercise its obligation to give hints and feedback in various forms. A simple statement by the court of its current inclination during an oral hearing, or a question to a party or counsel is common.[104] A court may also provide hints and feedback in the various procedural orders issued from time to time to request and set deadlines for briefs or schedule hearings.[105] If a court intends to decide the case in a manner which would implicate ZPO §139(2), the court might provide the parties with a summary of the significant reasons for a proposed decision and invite their comments or proposals.

On the other hand, it is not appropriate for the judge to provide feedback or hints to a party or the party's counsel through *ex parte* communications in writing or by telephone. The court must be careful that a telephone conversation for the purpose of scheduling a hearing or requesting that a document be brought to the hearing does not involve discussion of the case in a way that will give the impression of partiality.[106] The judge's obligation to promote clarification should be exercised in the presence of both parties.[107]

The new version of ZPO §139(4) codifies a requirement that had developed earlier in case law, namely that the giving of required hints and feedback should be documented in the case record (*Akte*). The statute provides that the giving of hints and feedback can be proved only through the contents of the record, not by later recollection of the judges or participants. Hints and feedback can be made of record in a procedural order (*Beschluss* or *Verfügung*) or other written communication from the court to the parties or their lawyers, by inclusion in the minutes of an oral hearing or conference, and even by mention in the factual recitals of a judgment.[108]

---

104. The court is often well advised to make sure that the hint is included in the minutes (*Protokolle*) of the hearing. See ZPO §139(4); Musielak/Stadler, §139, mn. 26.

105. See, e.g., Schellhammer, Part 7, Ch. 3, mn. 468 for a form of "order for clarification" (*Aufklärungsbeschluss*) in which the judge orders a party to clarify a particular factual assertion within a set time limit.

106. It is common practice for German judges to telephone counsel to request that a particular document mentioned in the case record be brought to an upcoming hearing. Some appellate judges will also telephone counsel to recommend that an improvident appeal be withdrawn before the obligation to pay costs is incurred. See Ch. 10(D)(1) below.

107. State Appeals Court of Oldenburg, 16 *NJW* 451 (1963); Zöller/Greger, §139, mn. 4; Stürner, *Richterliche Aufklärung*, Ch.(II)(4), mn. 32.

108. Zöller/Greger, §139, mn. 13. Frequently hints and feedback are contained in procedural orders issued pursuant to ZPO §273 in preparation for a preliminary or plenary hearing.

Another context which may be said to involve the judge's obligation to provide hints and feedback is the judge's duty to promote settlement negotiations. The role of the judge in suggesting and mediating settlement negotiations and promoting and effectuating settlements is discussed below.[109]

It is safe to say that the judge's obligation to promote clarification and give the parties hints and feedback is more stringent when the parties are unrepresented by counsel, as is the case frequently in the local courts (*Amtsgericht*) and occasionally in the other courts.[110] Where the parties have counsel, the court's burden in this respect may be lighter.[111] However even when the parties are represented by counsel, the court should provide hints and feedback in order to avoid serious miscarriages of justice.[112] The court's obligation to provide hints and feedback is not intended to protect parties from negligent and incompetent counsel, but rather to support the activities of parties or counsel as the case may be in the interest of a just, fair and expeditious conclusion of the litigation.[113]

g. Consequences of Failure to Provide Hints and Feedback

The failure of the court to give an appropriate hint before exercising a preclusion, dismissing a complaint for lack of factual support, or grounding a decision on a point imperfectly addressed by the parties may be grounds for reversal or remand of the decision on appeal. Noncompliance with the provisions now contained in ZPO §139 or §279(3) is frequently included with other grounds in both second instance appeals (*Berufungen*) as well as review

---

109. See Ch. 7(M) and 11(I). ZPO §278, ArbGG §§54, 57 require German judges actively to promote settlement of civil and labor cases before them. There is some question whether remarks and feedback about the likely outcome of the lawsuit made by the judge's during settlement negotiations stem from the general obligation of clarification or whether they are a product of the judge's specific responsibility to promote settlement. See Stürner, *Richterliche Aufklärung*, Ch.(IV)(2), mn. 102–103.

110. In most cases in the state district courts parties must be represented by counsel. In the labor court (*Arbeitsgericht*) and the administrative court (*Verwaltungsgericht*) self-representation is permitted and occurs with some frequency. See ZPO §78(1); ArbGG §11(1); VwGO §67.

111. See, e.g., Federal Constitutional Court, 32 *NJW* 1925, 1928 (1979); Federal Supreme Court, 33 *NJW* 223, 224 (1980); 37 *NJW* 310 (1984); 13 *NJW-RR* 16 (1998); Musielak/Stadler, §139, mn. 6; Stürner, *Richterliche Aufklärung*, Ch.(II)(3), mn. 14–18, Ch.(III)(3), mn. 62; Piekenbrock, 52 *NJW* 1360, 1362 (1999); dissenting, Peters, *Richterliche Hinweispflichten*, §31(VI), pp. 143 f.; Peters, in: *Münchener Kommentar zur ZPO*, §139, mn. 11 ff.

112. See, e.g., Federal Supreme Court, 48 *NJW* 399, 401 (1995).

113. Stürner, *Richterliche Aufklärung*, Ch.(II)(3), mn. 14–18; Musielak/Stadler, §139, mn. 6.

appeals (*Revisionen*) to the Federal Supreme Court.[114] In a second-instance appeal sometimes the appellate court can correct an erroneous omission of a required judicial hint and feedback by allowing the affected party an opportunity to address the issue in question at that level.[115] A remand will be only ordered if requested by a party and if the lower court's failure to give proper hints and feedback caused the entire inquiry to go awry.[116]

Failure to provide hints and feedback is a procedural error cognizable on review appeals on questions of law and procedure (*Revision*).[117] The appellant must be prepared to show the appellate court what procedural steps it would have taken had the lower court given appropriate hints and feedback in compliance with ZPO §139, and the likely effect of such steps on the outcome of the case.[118] Ordinarily the relief granted on such an appeal would be a vacating of the decision and remand to the lower court for further proceedings to provide the missing hints and feedback and permit the appellant to address the point in question.[119]

h. Judicial Assistance versus Judicial Impartiality

The German court's statutory obligation to provide hints and feedback during the course of civil proceedings requires the court to steer a careful course between too little and too much judicial engagement with the preparation and presentation of the parties' cases. A judge who over-exercises the obligation to provide hints and feedback may appear to be partial to the party who appears to benefit from this judicial assistance.[120] A judge who functions only as an umpire and holds back on hints and feedback to parties and counsel may be failing to comply with the requirements of ZPO §§139 or 279.

The judge's role has been likened to that of a chess player playing against himself.[121] Or, more aptly, he must advise each player on the best available

114. See, e.g., Federal Supreme Court, 6 *NJW-RR* 256 (1991); 3 *NJW-RR* 208, 209 (1988); Zöller/Greger, §139, mn 20; Musielak/Stadler, §139, mn. 4; Stürner, *Richterliche Aufklärung*, Ch.(V), mn. 108f.

115. See Ch. 10(D)(2) below on proceedings in second instance appeals.

116. See ZPO §538(2)(1) as in force since 2002; Ch. 10(D)(4) below; Stürner, *Richterliche Aufklärung*, Ch.(V), mn. 109; Federal Supreme Court, 6 *NJW-RR* 256 (1991), Zöller/Greger, §139, mn. 20; Musielak/Stadler, § 139, mn. 4.

117. See Ch. 10(E) below on proceedings on review appeals.

118. See, e.g., Federal Supreme Court, 3 *NJW-RR* 208, 209 (1988); Zöller/Greger, §139, mn. 20; Musielak/Stadler, § 139, mn. 4; Stürner, *Richterliche Aufklärung*, Ch.(V), mn. 108.

119. See ZPO §§562(2), 563.

120. See ZPO §§42 ff. for the grounds and procedure for disqualification of a judge on grounds of partiality.

121. Wassermann, *Der soziale Zivilprozess* (1978), p. 176.

move.[122] It is very hard to play this role effectively without overstepping the bounds one way or the other. An easy solution would be to withdraw the judge entirely from the fray and adopt a rule requiring the judge to observe the kind of detached judicial neutrality customarily found in England or America. However such an approach would be inconsistent with the German concept of the state's social responsibility to provide substantial justice[123]—"the truly neutral judge is the one whose activity results in material justice between the parties".[124]

How far should the judge go to support the apparently weaker party or to find a just outcome regardless of the presentations of the parties? To what extent should the judge ignore form in favor of substantial justice? These issues are debated in the literature and to a lesser extent in the decisions.[125]

The right road undoubtedly lies somewhere in the middle. Clearly the judge must maintain and follow the formal structures of the legal system and hold the parties to its requirements. On the other hand, the judge must also keep in mind the overall purpose of the system to provide material justice and must strive to make it do so in the individual case. The judge can interpret the parties' positions, but should not incite them to fundamentally new activities. Such a middle ground respects the parties roles and autonomy in the proceedings, but also furthers material justice within those bounds.[126]

D. The Role of the Case Record

The principal of orality (*Mündlichkeitsprinzip*) in German civil justice is complemented by a principle that court proceedings must take place within a

122. Stürner, *Richterliche Aufklärung*, Ch.(II)(4), mn. 19.

123. This responsibility was described by the influential Austrian proceduralist Franz Klein. See Klein, *Pro futuro. Betrachtungen über Probleme der Civilprozessrechtreform in Österreich* (1891), pp. 19 ff.; see ZPO Austria §§182, 183.

124. Stürner, *Richterliche Aufklärung*, Ch.(II)(4), mn. 21 ff. ("...*vielmehr ist neutral nur der Richter, der durch seine Aktivitäten materielle Gerechtigkeit schafft.*") describing the position of the German Federal Constitutional Court, 29 *NJW* 1391 (1976), but not without critical comments.

125. See, e.g., Federal Constitutional Court, 29 *NJW* 1391 (1976); 32 *NJW* 1925, 1928 (1979).

126. For a discussion of this issue see Stürner, *Richterliche Aufklärung*, Ch.(II)(4), mn. 19–29; Peters, *Richterliche Hinweispflichten* §27, pp.106 ff.; Riedel, *Das Postulat der Unparteilichkeit des Richters* (1980); Nörr, *Zur Stellung des Richters im gelehrten Prozess der Frühzeit: Iudex secundum allegata non secundum conscientiam judicat* (1967).

written framework (*Schriftlichkeitsprinzip*).[127] Within this context the case record (*Akte*) plays an important role in the regularity and reviewability of German civil justice. Every civil proceeding in a German court is painstakingly documented in a comprehensive case record. The case record includes all pleadings and letters of the parties and their counsel, all orders, forms and other dispositions of the court, any documentary evidence, minutes (*Protokolle*) of oral conferences and hearings and summaries of any witness testimony or party proof taken by the court at any stage of the case. All decisions of the court are taken with reference to the record of the case and must be based on facts, contentions and claims for relief documented in the case record. A single case record is maintained for a civil proceeding from its initiation by filing of a complaint until issuance of final judgment, and is transmitted to the appeals court in case of appeal.

Currently a case record generally consists of a bound sheaf of original papers, carefully clipped together between flimsy paper covers. Recent amendments to the Code of Civil Procedure authorize widespread use of electronic documents and even e-mail for pleadings, briefs and other court communications. It seems likely that case records will be created and maintained in electronic digital form in the relatively near future.[128]

When not in use by the court for hearings or for deliberations the case record is ordinarily kept on file in the offices of the clerk of the court in which the case originated. If a judgment or order in the case is appealed to another court, the original record is transmitted to the appellate court and is generally returned to the originating court after the appeal is decided.

The case record is the cumulative history of proceedings and documentation of factual material elicited in a case. The case record represents the unitary nature of the civil case, and brings together all the written and significant oral assertions and arguments of counsel and all proof received in a single, continually evolving and developing form. Courts, counsel and parties can refer to the record at any stage of the proceedings to support fact contentions and legal arguments.

---

127. See generally Rosenberg/Schwab/Gottwald, §§80, 106(IV), pp. 440 ff., 605 f.; Lüke, §2(III), mn. 52 ff.

128. See, e.g., ZPO §130a, authorizing the various German states to provide for electronic filings of litigation documents such as briefs (*Schriftsätze*), motions or applications (*Anträge*), expert witness testimony (*Gutachten*) in civil actions subject to the Civil Procedure Code. This provision was introduced by the Law for the Adaptation of the Formal Requirements of Private Law to Modern Forms of Legal Communications of July 13, 2001, BGBl 2001, I, 1542. See also Stadler and Kodek, "Der Zivilprozess und neue Formen der Informationstechnik", 115 *ZZP* 413 and 445 (2002); Zöller/Greger, §130a, mn. 1 and Musielak/Stadler, §30a, mn. 1 ff. Electronic filing is also discussed in Ch. 7(A)(1) below.

1. Minutes of Hearings and Conferences

Important components of the case record are the minutes (*Protokolle*) of oral hearings and conferences with parties and counsel (*Verhandlungen*) and of hearings for the reception of evidence (*Beweisaufnahme*). The Civil Procedure Code requires that "minutes are to be made of oral arguments and every reception of evidence."[129] The contents of the minutes are also statutorily prescribed. They must include both formal matters such as caption of the case, identification of the judges, lawyers and parties present, and time and place of the proceedings and the substantive content of the proceedings which took place. The minutes must specifically document such matters as any applications, claims or motions (*Anträge*) made or clarified at the hearing or conference, any party admissions and other clarifications of position, statements and testimony by witnesses, results of a view of evidence (*Augenschein*) and any decisions, procedural orders (*Verfügungen*), or hints and feedback (*Hinweise*) reached or communicated during the hearing. Such matters as withdrawal of claims or waivers of appeals, as well as the results of efforts to promote settlement must also be minuted.[130]

These minutes are not verbatim transcripts or recordings of all that was said, but are verbal summaries of the key elements of the proceedings or evidence.[131] They are created by the presiding judge or clerk of courts usually on the spot and in the presence of the parties and counsel. Written documents discussed or presented at the hearing may be incorporated in the minutes by reference.

If the minutes are being kept by the clerk, that official is responsible for determining the contents, but the presiding judge may dictate key portions, such as a summary of the testimony of a key witness, or a restatement of a party's assertions of complex fact. If the presiding judge is keeping the minutes the proceeding usually pauses from time to time to allow him to perform this task. Typically, at the beginning, at the end and at various points during the hear-

129. ZPO §159(1)("... *über die Verhandlung und jede Beweisaufnahme ist ein Protokoll aufzunehmen.*"). The clerk of courts (*Urkundsbeamter*) is responsible for preparing the minutes unless the presiding judge otherwise orders.

130. See ZPO §160(1) and (3) for the required content of judicial minutes.

131. See §§159(1), 160(2). Apparently the practice of making summaries of oral proceedings and testimony instead of verbatim transcriptions was originally an economy measure. See Rosenberg/Schwab/Gottwald §80(I), p. 440. In the modern age of electronic recording, actual contemporaneous recording of court proceedings and testimony (as opposed to dictated summaries) remains more the exception than the rule. Even the recent reforms authorizing the conduct of hearings and conferences by interactive video conference provide also for recording in traditional form. See ZPO §128a(3)(1).

ing or testimony the presiding judge interrupts the discussion to minute a segment of the hearing or proof. In the past the judge would dictate to a clerical person in the courtroom. Currently many judges dictate the minutes into a dictating machine to be transcribed later on.[132]

The minutes of hearings and conferences are particularly important because of the tradition and principle of orality (*Mündlichkeitsprinzip*) in German civil justice. Parties' written contentions, claims and admissions can be modified, supplemented and contradicted by statements made during oral hearings and conferences. According to the principle of orality, such oral statements generally prevail over prior written ones.[133] Thus it is very important that these oral statements be accurately recorded when they are made. Frequently the minutes of a hearing or conference will have the practical effect of pleadings and preliminary dispositions in defining the scope and direction of a civil case.

The process of summarizing the proceedings and proof as the case goes along requires the judge to be engaged with the parties' contentions or proof, as the case may be, and to think about what is being presented or heard. The summary includes only information relevant to the case as then perceived by the parties and court.[134] Extraneous material is weeded out in the process of dictating the minutes. Thus the very process of creating the minutes is part and parcel of the process of deciding the case.

Although the minutes are made by the clerk of courts or dictated by the judge the parties and their counsel have an important role in reviewing the minutes to insure accuracy and completeness from their points of view. The statute requires the judge to share the contents of the minutes with the parties as promptly as possible, preferably as the minutes are being made, and secure their assent to their accuracy and completeness.[135] If the minutes have

---

132. ZPO §160a prescribes the procedure for contemporaneous recording of minutes of a conference or hearing with a tape recorder or dictaphone. If the minutes are recorded in this manner, they are to be transcribed promptly following the hearing. The tapes must be maintained for a month after the transcription has been delivered to the court and parties or until conclusion of the proceedings. See ZPO §160a(1) and (2)(1) and (3). Contemporaneous recordings of witness testimony need only be transcribed on application of a party or on request of an appellate court. See ZPO §160a(2)(2) and (3).

133. See Ch. 6(E)(1) and Ch. 8(B)(3) below.

134. This can mean that information that might become relevant to the case at a later stage of fact or legal development may not be picked up in the minutes of an earlier conference or hearing. In such a case if a party realizes the relevance of information presented at an earlier hearing and not then deemed significant, the party must refer to the information again in the current context, either orally or in writing.

135. ZPO §162.

been kept by the clerk of courts generally the judge will read them aloud, making his own corrections in the process. If the judge created the minutes by dictation during the hearing, the judge can secure the parties' assent by playing the minutes as dictated on tape back for them or by dictating the minutes in the presence of the parties and their counsel.[136] Minutes created after the hearing from a tape-recording of the hearing or the testimony can be sent to counsel with a request for corrections or additions within a specified time.

Judges who create their own minutes frequently have the parties and their counsel present as the minutes are being dictated. At intervals during the dictation the judge pauses to give the parties opportunity to state objections. If the judge states a fact or contention in a manner that does not fairly reflect a party's understanding of the fact or contention, the party may raise the point with the judge and propose that the fact or contention in question be restated in the minutes. If the judge disagrees, the party can request that the disagreement be noted in the minutes, but ordinarily may not appeal the judge's ruling on the matter at that time.[137]

A party also has the right to request that any fact relating to the propriety of a judge's decision be made of record either by written submission or in the minutes of a hearing or conference. Offers of proof, issues of a judge's impartiality, or facts relating to procedural dispositions and orders all must be made of record if a party or counsel so requests in order to protect the party's right to appellate review or reconsideration.

Errors in minutes of judicial proceedings are subject to correction at any stage of the proceedings. After hearing both parties the judge who originally made the minutes can make the correction on the original minutes or attach a supplemental document.[138] Finally the minutes of each hearing or conference must be signed by the presiding judge and the clerk of courts (*Urkundsbeamter*). The clerk also certifies to the accuracy of transcription of any portion of the minutes which were dictated or electronically recorded.[139]

---

136. ZPO §162. This requirement can be waived by the parties. See Seitz/Büchel/Dresenkamp, §A(XI), mn. 40–42 for a description of the process of creating and securing party assent to minutes of a hearing for taking of evidence. In any event the fact that the parties and counsel have either reviewed and approved the minutes, or waived the opportunity to do so must itself be noted in the minutes.

137. ZPO §160(4). However improper minuting of a party's contention or a witness's testimony can support a later appeal from the final judgment. See Ch.10(E)(2) below.

138. ZPO §164. See Zöller/Stöber, §164, mn. 2 ff. and Musielak/Stadler, §164, mn. 3 for a discussion of the process of correcting the minutes of a hearing.

139. ZPO §163(1)(1).

The minutes are the official record of what takes place at any hearing or conference. Proof of the observance or omission of any required formal or procedural step can only be had from the minutes, which can be collaterally attacked only on grounds of forgery (*Verfälschung*).[140]

2. Use of the Case Record by the Court

Much of a judge's work in civil litigation is review of case records, early on to determine the existence of the prerequisites to suit, later to identify the parties' respective claims for relief, factual assertions, and legal theories, and ultimately to make factual determinations and reach decisions.[141] It is common for judges to make abstracts of bulky case records (*Aktenauszüge*) in order to keep track of the parties' respective claims and contentions as they may develop during the course of the proceedings. At the point of reaching a fact determination, the reporting judge (*Berichterstatter*) of a panel will often be expected to develop from the case record a complete fact statement (*Sachbericht*) as a component of a proposed decision (*Votum*).[142] This fact statement is then used by the panel in its deliberations. A shortened version may become the factual findings (*Tatbestand*) for the judgment.

3. Access to Case Records

Case records in civil cases in Germany are not open to the public either before or after judgment. The parties and their counsel are entitled to free access to the official records of their cases,[143] but others may look at case records only with the consent of the parties involved or by order of the chief judge of the court upon a showing of some legitimate interest in so doing.[144] Judges'

---

140. ZPO §165.

141. This does not mean that many cases are decided based solely on a review of the case record without hearing the parties orally. In almost all contested cases the ultimate decision will be preceded by at least one oral hearing. Exceptions are, e.g., orders transferring the case to the proper court (ZPO §§281(2)(2), 128(4), see Ch. 5(F) above), judgments by default in cases lacking any statement of defence (ZPO §331(3), see Ch. 9(A)(1)) or decisions based on the state of the record (*Entscheidungen nach Lage der Akten*, ZPO §331a. See Ch. 9(C) below).

142. The first drafts of such fact statements are often delegated to legal interns (*Referendare*). See Schellhammer, Part 3, Ch. 10, mn. 105.

143. ZPO §299(1).

144. ZPO §299(2). The question of whether research use by a legal academic is a legitimate ground for granting access to case records seems not to be definitively resolved

notes, summaries, proposed decisions and similar papers are maintained separately from the case records and are generally not subject to disclosure to anyone.[145]

Transmittal of information from case records concerning the parties or other participants in civil litigation to other public authorities is subject to comprehensive statutory regulation as a part of the Introduction to the Court Organization Law.[146] Disclosure of personal data by civil courts and their agencies is only permitted for clearly specified purposes and in accord with the statutory requirements.[147]

E. General Principles Applicable to Civil Proceedings

German civil litigation is organized around several more or less abstract principles or "axioms" which underly the more specific requirements of the ZPO and govern and inform decision-making and practice by judges and lawyers. Some of these principles are set forth in statutory provisions of general applicability. Others find their origin or reflection in provisions of the German Constitution. Still others have been identified and abstracted by scholars and in judicial decisions as implicit in German justice. Literature and learning about German civil justice and its procedures is often organized around these principles. Many textbooks list and summarize the "basic principles" early on and then make reference to them as they are applicable to particular issues.

Some of these basic principles, such as the principle of party control of the scope and nature of civil proceedings (*Dispositionsmaxime*), the principle of party control of the facts and means of proof (*Verhandlungsmaxime, Beibringungsgrundssatz*) and the obligation of the court to promote clarification (*Aufklärungspflicht*) have already been discussed in some detail.[148] Other fre-

---

and may depend on the judge who is asked for such access. See, e.g., Musielak/Huber, §299, mn. 3.

145. ZPO §299(4).

146. *Einführungsgesetz zum Gerichtsverfassungsgesetz* or *EGGVG* §§12–22.

147. Some of the purposes for which data may be transmitted to public agencies include entry of information relative to title to real estate in real estate registers, apprehension of suspected criminals, disclosures required for national security or international treaty obligations, and under circumstances when disclosure is required "to prevent the most serious impositions on the rights of another person." ("...*zur Abwehr einer schwerwiegenden Beeinträchtigung der Rechte einer anderen Person*..."). EGGVG §§15, 16, 17.

148. See Ch. 6(B) and (C) above.

quently cited principles on which German civil proceedings proceed include the principle of orality (*Mündlichkeitsprinzip*), the principle of publicity (*Öffentlichkeitsprinzip*), the principle of immediacy (*Unmittelbarkeitsprinzip*), the principle favoring concentration of proceedings (*Konzentrationsmazime*), the principle of free evaluation of evidence (*freie Beweiswürdigung*), and the constitutional right to be heard (*rechtliches Gehör*).

The principles of orality and publicity, and the right to a legal hearing relate to all or most phases of German civil litigation, and will be discussed here. The principle favoring concentration of proceedings is mentioned at several points in this text in connection with structuring preparatory and plenary proceedings to avoid excessive protraction and multiplication of hearings.[149] The principles of immediacy and of free evaluation of evidence find application largely in the evidentiary phases of the proceedings and will be discussed in connection with those phases.[150]

1. The Principle of Orality

Traditional German civil justice is founded on the principle that the parties' assertions, arguments and proof are to be presented in person and orally to the court, that discussion of the legal and factual issues between parties, counsel and the court will be oral, and that the court's decision will be announced orally at a hearing at which the parties and their counsel have the right to be present. The kernel of this principle of orality (*Mündlichkeitsprinzip*) is that court decisions will be founded only on that which has been orally set forth or referred to in open court. The primacy of oral proceedings in German civil litigation was the result of 19th Century reforms designed to bring immediacy and dispatch to civil litigation.[151] Prior to that time, the tendency was to require that everything of consequence in a civil proceeding be in writing (*Schriftlichkeitsprinzip*).[152] In recent years the emphasis on orality

149. See Ch. 7(K), Ch. 8(A)(2) below. This principle appears to be a kind of corollary to the policy in favor of expediting civil litigations (*Beschleunigungsmaxime*).

150. See Ch. 8(C) and (D) below.

151. The formal introduction of the principle of orality into the ZPO took place in 1879. See, e.g., Lüke, §2(III), mn. 25. Precursors to the orality principle can be found in procedural regulations in various German states from shortly after the French Revolution. See, e.g., Rosenberg/Schwab/Gottwald, §§4(V), 80(I), pp. 22 ff., 440.

152. See Ch. 2(B)–(D); Rosenberg/Schwab/Gottwald, §4(III), pp. 19 f. This principle, which still applies to a certain degree in some civil law procedural systems, is expressed in Latin as "*quod non est in actis, non est in mundo.*" (What is not in the court record, does not exist.)

has become less pronounced. Modern civil justice consists of a mixture of written and oral procedures. Each mode is employed when fairness, efficiency and economy would so indicate.[153]

According to the principle of orality, "the parties argue the legal issues in dispute orally before the court."[154] Strictly speaking, written pleadings, briefs, and similar exchanges between the parties are only means of preparation for the oral hearing, where the parties' contentions, assertions and arguments are to be stated orally to the court.[155] Up until quite recently it was customary for many lawyers to read or at least summarize their written pleadings at the outset of an oral session of the court. Now it is more common for the judge to incorporate the assertions of the pleadings and briefs into the oral discussion by reference.

It should be noted that only decisions which result in judgments (*Urteile*) require oral proceedings.[156] There is no general requirement of orality for decisions other than judgments, nor are oral proceedings required for judgments assessing and allocating costs and attorneys fees.[157] Miscellaneous appeals (*Beschwerde*), warning proceedings, and various other kinds of expedited or specialized proceedings also frequently take place without oral hearings.[158]

A recent reform has sought to introduce the possibility of proceedings in writing in cases where the parties agree to dispense with oral proceedings, and

153. See Rosenberg/Schwab/Gottwald, §80(III), p. 441 discussing the comparative advantages of oral and written procedures for various phases of civil litigation. A degree of orality in civil judicial proceedings may be guaranteed by the European Convention on Human Rights Art. 6(1) and the German Constitution Art. 1(1), 2(1). For a detailed discussion see Stürner, "Verfahrensgrundsätze des Zivilprozesses und Verfassung", in: Grunsky et al. (ed.), *Festschrift für Fritz Baur* (1981), pp. 647 ff., 661 ff.

154. ZPO §128(1) (*Die Parteien verhandeln über den Rechtstreit vor dem erkennenden Gericht mündlich*).

155. Indeed, the original concept was that the parties should appear before a completely impartial court, so that written preparatory submissions were not required or favored. See, e.g., Lüke, §2(III)(1), mn. 26.

156. ZPO §128(4). These are usually dispositional decisions on the merits.

157. Many judicial decisions result in simple orders (*Beschlüsse*) or procedural orders (*Verfügungen*) and do not require oral proceedings. In many cases the constitutional right to be heard (*rechtliches Gehör*) may require that the court give the parties notice and opportunity to comment in writing, even if no oral proceedings are called for. See Ch. 6(E)(3) below.

158. For a more detailed discussion of which kinds of proceedings are subject to the requirements of the orality principle and why, see Rosenberg/Schwab/Gottwald, §81(II), pp. 442 f.

under very limited circumstances, when ordered by the court.[159] In a case in which at least one oral hearing has been held, if both parties fail to appear for a subsequent oral hearing, the court is authorized to enter judgment based on the state of the record (*Entscheidung nach Lage der Akten*).[160] As of the present this partial reintroduction of purely written civil litigation seems to be met with an unenthusiastic reaction among German textwriters at least.[161]

A corollary of the principle of orality is that the plenary oral proceeding is a single, continuous hearing, even when under exceptional circumstances it may be divided into various sessions for purposes or legal argument, proof taking and announcement of decision.[162] Various hearings are therefore cumulative, and assertions made or proof taken at a prior session will govern subsequent proceedings unless otherwise ordered by the court. Although it is theoretically possible for a case to consist of a lengthy string of conferences and hearings, in recent years the tendency has been to concentrate oral proceedings into one or two concentrated sessions.[163] Nowadays most cases are disposed of with no more than two or three hearings or in person conferences with the court.

2. The Principle of Publicity

German civil justice is public justice. In principle, all plenary proceedings are open to the public.[164] This includes hearings for the rendition of the final judgment and any other important decisions along the way.[165] Courtrooms and courthouses are easily accessible to the public.[166]

Proceedings can be closed to the public only under limited circumstances. For instance, proceedings in family cases (*Familien- und Kindschaftssachen*) are, as a rule, closed to the public.[167] Part or all of a civil proceeding may be

---

159. ZPO §128(2).

160. ZPO §251a.

161. See, e.g., Jauernig, §28(V).

162. See Ch. 8(B) below; Rosenberg/Schwab/Gottwald, §81(V), pp. 446 f.

163. Procedural reforms were enacted in 1976 with the aim of concentrating oral proceedings into a single session in many cases, the so-called "Stuttgart model" (*Stuttgarter Modell*). See ZPO §272 and Ch. 2(F). The effect of this reform is discussed in greater detail in Ch. 7(E)(2) below.

164. *Gerichtsverfassungsgesetz* (GVG) §169.

165. GVG §173.

166. While civil proceedings are often of interest only to the concerned parties, frequently lawyers and clients awaiting their own hearings or conferences will compose the courtroom audiences for prior hearings or takings of evidence.

167. GVG §170.

closed to the public if the subject matter of the proceeding is likely to damage the personal or family interests of a party or witness.[168] Under a limited number of circumstances, proceedings may be closed to safeguard security of parties or witnesses, to protect important trade secrets or secrets of state, to protect against public dissemination of privileged material required to be revealed in court, and when a witness younger than 16 years of age will be interrogated.[169]

While the press is welcome at any public court hearing or proceedings, audio-recording, videotaping, and filming of court proceedings for public showing or broadcast is not permitted.[170]

The principle of publicity is somewhat compromised with respect to the written records and documents in the proceeding. The case record (*Akte*) is confidential and access to the record and documents on file is limited to the court and the parties and their counsel, unless the court allows access to others for good cause shown.[171] Once a final judgment or decision has been rendered, the judgment or decision itself is public and any person having a good reason to see it may demand a copy.[172] Even following final judgment, German courts may not disseminate information from their files about private parties to other government agencies or other persons except under statutorily prescribed circumstances.[173]

---

168. GVG §171(b). The court is empowered to close a proceeding if the threatened damage to personal interests of a party or witness outweighs the interest in public disclosure.

169. GVG §172.

170. GVG §169(2). An important and recent exception to this rule permits televising of the public rendition of judgments by the Federal Constitutional Court. See *Bundesverfassungsgerichtsgesetz (BVerfGG)* §17a. For a discussion of the constitutional right to a public hearing, freedom of press and information and the constitutionality of GVG §169(2) see Federal Constitutional Court, 54 *NJW* 1633 (2001) and Stürner, "Gerichtsöffentlichkeit und Medienöffentlichkeit in der Informationsgesellschaft", 56 *JZ* 699 (2001). As a matter of principle the European Convention on Human Rights Art. 6(1) and the German Constitution guarantee public hearings in courts. See Stürner, in: *Festschrift für Fritz Baur*, pp. 659 ff.

171. ZPO §299 gives the parties the right to review the case record and to make copies of materials contained therein. Judges' notes, drafts of decisions and orders, votes, and similar judicial work product is maintained confidential within the court. ZPO §299(4). See Ch. 6(D)(3) above.

172. Zöller/Greger, §299, mn. 7; Federal Administrative Court 52 *NJW* 2694 (1997). Ordinarily the identity of the parties and any personal data will be excised unless these are already matters of public knowledge.

173. See *Einführungsgesetz zum Gerichtsverfassungsgesetz* (EGGVG) §§12–22.

Parties, of course, have the right to participate in all hearings and oral proceedings in their cases, and to be notified of the time and place of all oral hearings and evidentiary proceedings. Parties have the right to receive copies of all written submissions made to the court by an opposing party. This guarantee of party access to the record and party participation in all hearings is sometimes referred to as the principle of party publicity (*Parteiöffentlichkeit*).[174]

3. The Constitutional Right to Be Heard

The German constitutional right to be heard (*Recht auf rechtliches Gehör*) is founded not only on the German Constitution,[175] but also on the European Convention on Human Rights.[176] "The right to be heard seeks to guarantee a fair proceeding between the parties."[177] Although enshrined in the German constitution for the first time in 1949, the right to be heard has long been a fundamental principle in German civil justice and underlies many of the requirements of the ZPO.

As applied to civil litigation between parties, the right to be heard guarantees a litigant, as well as a third party whose interests are directly affected by the outcome of a law suit, an opportunity to address the court in support of its own claims and proof and in opposition to the assertions and proof of the opponent.[178] The court may not grant relief on a claim unless the defendant has had the opportunity to appear and defend. The court may not base a decision on a legal or factual proposition which the affected parties have not had the opportunity to address.[179]

By the same token, the right to be heard requires the court to consider and address each significant contention of fact and law put forward by a party.[180]

---

174. See ZPO §357 for the taking of evidence and, e. g., Lüke, §2(V), mn. 34.

175. German Constitution (*Grundgesetz*), Article 103(I).

176. European Convention on Human Rights, Article 6(I).

177. *"Das Recht auf rechtliches Gehör will den Parteien ein faires Verfahren garantieren."* See Jauernig, §29(II).

178. See, e. g., Rosenberg/Schwab/Gottwald, §85(III), pp. 456 ff.; Jauernig, §29(II); Lüke, §2(VI), mn. 35. See especially ZPO §§130 ff., 253(1), (5), 270 f., 274 ff., 279(3), 282(2), 285(1), 357, 364, 404a(4)(5), etc.

179. See. e. g., Lüke, §2(VI), mn. 36. The right to be heard does not require that the parties actually be heard on every potential issue. It suffices if the parties have reasonable opportunity to take a position on the significant factual or legal propositions, either orally or writing, before they are used as the basis for a judicial decision.

180. See, e.g., Federal Constitutional Court, 43 *NJW* 3191, 3192 (1990); Rosenberg/Schwab/Gottwald, §85(III), p. 457.

A judgment which fails to address a significant legal or factual contention raised by a party is constitutionally, as well as legally, defective.

The right to be heard drives many of the requirements of notice and opportunity to comment set forth throughout the ZPO. For instance, even in the course of entering a judgment by default against a party which has failed to defend, the court may not consider factual or legal assertions as to which the defaulting party has not had prior notice and realistic opportunity to comment.[181] The right to be heard must be an effective right to be heard. Such discretionary judicial actions as refusing to grant a party's request for a continuance to enable an informed response to a new contention of the opponent or a new approach by the court can implicate this constitutional right.[182]

The judge's obligation to give hints and feedback can involve the constitutional right to be heard. The court may not constitutionally preclude a party from bringing forward factual or legal assertions to meet a particular concern or approach of the court unless the court has given the party reasonable hints and feedback.[183] On the other hand, the right to be heard is not necessarily greater than the requirements of ZPO §139 (requiring the court to provide hints and feedback).[184] Thus, the right to be heard does not require the judge to share with the parties her anticipated decision if the issues have already been addressed by one or the other of the parties or if they are the everyday issues to be anticipated in cases of the type.[185]

The constitutional right to be heard operates in connection with other specific constitutional rights as a kind of right to due process of law on a national scale.[186] It also finds application in international jurisprudence. The European

181. See, e. g. Lüke, §2(VI), mn. 35, also ZPO §335(1)(2)–(4) and Ch. 9(A)(1) below (on default judgment).

182. See, e.g., Lüke, §2(VI), mn. 36 for a number of examples of procedural measures which can implicate the right to be heard.

183. The otherwise applicable preclusion under ZPO §296 is constitutionally blocked. See Federal Constitutional Court, 60 BVerfGE 1 (1982); 40 *NJW* 2003 (1987); Rosenberg/Schwab/Gottwald, §85(III)(1)(4), p. 457; Ch. (C)(2) above.

184. The existence and extent of a constitutional right to a legal dialogue is referred to in the literature as "disputed" (*umstritten*). See, e.g., Jauernig, §29(IV); Lüke, §2(VI), mn. 37.

185. On the other hand, if the basis for decision is a surprising one, the judge is required to advise the parties and give opportunity for comment before rendering the decision. ZPO §139(2). See Federal Constitutional Court, 78 BVerfGE 123, 126 f. (1988) and Ch. 6(C)(2)(b) above.

186. See German Constitution (*Grundgesetz*) Art. 1, 19(4), 20, 92, 101, 103 and, e.g., Federal Constitutional Court, 57 BVerfGE 250, 275 (1981). See also Ch. 6(A) above and Stürner, in: *Festschrift für Fritz Baur* (1981), pp. 648 ff.

Court of Human Rights has repeatedly held that excessive delay in the determination of a civil proceeding violates the parties right to be heard within a reasonable time as guaranteed by the European Convention on Human Rights.[187]

The constitutional status of the right to be heard means that a decision or action by the court which violates the right to be heard may be subject to constitutional appeal (*Verfassungsbeschwerde*) to the German Constitutional Court (*Bundesverfassungsgericht*). Since most violations of the constitutional right to be heard are also violations of requirements of the ZPO, an assertion of a violation of the right to be heard can give a litigant "two [successive] bites at the apple" on the issue.

187. See European Convention on Human Rights, Article 6(I); European Court of Human Rights, *Pammel v. Germany,* 26 EHRR 100 (1998); *Ruiz-Mateos v. Spain,* 16 EHRR 505 (1993); *Süssmann v. Germany,* 25 EHRR 64 (1998). See Ch. 3(F) and (I)(2).

CHAPTER 7

Preparatory Stages of a Law Suit

A modern German civil law suit has two main phases, the initial preparatory phase (*Vorbereitungsphase*) and the plenary phase of the main oral argument (*Hauptverhandlung*). The preparatory phase includes the filing of the complaint in court, the initial examination of the complaint by a judge, service of the complaint, filing and service of responsive pleadings, and any preliminary preparatory hearings or conferences required to prepare the case for the parties to address with the court on the merits. Although the focus of the preparatory proceedings is the preparation of the case for plenary disposition in the second phase, in actuality many cases are disposed of either by procedural dismissal (*Prozessabweisung*) or by settlement (*Vergleich*) during the preparatory phases and never reach plenary oral argument.

Traditionally these various preliminary steps could lead to protracted preparatory proceedings in some cases. However over the last few decades the German legislature and courts have applied the principle of concentration of proceedings (*Konzentrationsmaxime*) ever more rigorously. Now relatively strict time limits, evidentiary and issue preclusions and the use of written preparatory process have shortened the preparatory phase and in most cases concentrated the plenary proceedings into a single main oral hearing.

A. The Complaint

A civil law suit in most German courts commences with the institution of a complaint (*Klageerhebung*). A complaint is formally instituted when a written complaint is filed in the administrative office of the court and served on the defendant.[1] The complaint becomes pending (*anhängig*) for purposes of

1. ZPO §253(1); See, e.g., Jauernig, *Zivilprozessrecht*, 28th ed. (2003), §40, p. 161; Zöller/Greger, *Zivilprozessordnung*, 23rd ed. (2002), §253, mn. 5; Lüke, *Zivilprozessrecht*, 8th ed. (2003), §12(I), mn. 138.

the statute of limitations and other time limits upon receipt of the complaint at the administrative office of the court.[2] However it does not become legally pending (*rechtshängig*), with the various procedural consequences of that status until served.[3]

In most courts the complaint must be in writing (*Klageschrift*).[4] The complaint must be signed by the plaintiff or the plaintiff's attorney.[5] A complaint filed in a court where representation by counsel is required must be signed by an attorney admitted to practice in a German court.[6] The filing of the complaint must be accompanied by a prepayment of the initial filing fee based on the amount in controversy (*Streitwert*) specified in the complaint.[7]

1. Form of the Complaint

German practice is liberal on the form of complaints and other pleadings. Although such documents usually are captioned with the names of the parties to the suit and the docket number of the proceeding, there is no prescribed standard form for written pleadings, or other written submissions.

---

2. ZPO §167.

3. ZPO §§261, 253. See Ch. 7(F)(5) below on service of the complaint.

4. Certain proceedings before the local court or the labor court may be initiated orally. In such cases the complaining party appears at the administrative office of the court and the gist of the claim is converted into a written complaint by a court clerk (*Urkundsbeamter*). See ZPO §496; Zöller/Herget, §496, mn. 3; Ch. 6(B)(4)(b).

5. Common Senate of the Federal Supreme Courts, 33 *NJW* 182, 174 (1980); see Ch. 3(B). In the local courts if the plaintiff is not represented by counsel the complaint must be signed by the plaintiff. See, e.g., Stein/Jonas/Leipold, *Kommentar zur Zivilprozessordnung,* 21st ed. (1996 ff.), §129, mn. 8; German Federal Supreme Court, 33 *NJW* 291 (1980).

6. Representation by counsel is required in all cases in the state district courts and state appeals courts and in family cases in the local courts. ZPO §78. The rules of admission to practice before German courts of first instance have been liberalized to permit attorneys admitted to appear before any court of any one German state (*Land*) to appear generally in courts throughout Germany. See Jauernig, §21(III)(3), p. 65; Zöller/Vollkommer, §78 mn. 1. More recently Germany has further liberalized its bar admission rules to permit appearances of attorneys admitted to practice before courts of other EU nations to appear in German local courts (*Amtsgerichte*) and state district courts (*Landgerichte*). See *Gesetz über die Tätigkeit europäischer Rechtsanwälte in Deutschland* of March 13, 2000, BGBl. I 182. See Ch. 4(D) above for a more detailed discussion of admission to practice in court.

7. German civil court costs are paid in installments based on the stage the proceeding has reached. See *Gerichtskostengesetz* (GKG) §§65, 68; ZPO §379. See Ch. 9(E) below on the computation, payment and reimbursement of court costs.

They are frequently typed or printed on the letterheads of the attorneys who file them.

In some kinds of cases it is common to use pre-printed form complaints prepared by the courts. For instance, in warning proceedings *(Mahnverfahren)* the use of pre-printed forms is encouraged in the interest of easy processing of these repetitive and numerous proceedings.[8]

In July 2001 the German Parliament authorized the use of electronic versions of litigation documents required to be in writing as and when prescribed by the Federal and State Ministries of Justice for their respective courts.[9] Documents submitted in electronic form are to be authenticated with signatures complying with the Electronic Signature Act (*Signaturgesetz*).[10] An electronic document is deemed filed with the court as soon as it has registered on the facilities provided by the court for reception of such submissions.[11]

The text of the new law authorizes electronic documents "to the extent that the written form is prescribed for preparatory briefs and attachments, for applications and explanations of the parties, as well as for statements, declarations, expert opinions, and explanations of third parties."[12] Although the specific statutory provision authorizing electronic documents does not specifically mention complaints, it appears clear from the statutory language as a whole that complaints can also be in electronic form.[13]

The recent law authorizing electronic service of documents appears to permit electronic service of a complaint on a party represented by a lawyer who

---

8. See ZPO §§689, 702, 703c. See Ch. 11(C) below for a discussion of the warning proceeding. In fact, it is common for applications for a warning notice (*Mahnbescheid*) to be submitted in electronic form.

9. Law on the Adaptation of the Requirements of Form of Private Law and other Requirements to Modern Legal Commerce (*Gesetz zur Anpassung der Formvorschriften des Privatrechts und anderer Vorschriften an den modernen Rechtsgeschäftsverkehr*) of July 13, 2001, effective August 1, 2001, now ZPO §130a. See Stadler and Kodek, "Der Zivilprozess und neue Formen der Informationstechnik", 115 *ZZP* 413 and 445 (2002); Ch. 6(D) above.

10. *Gesetz über Rahmenbedingungen für elektronische Signaturen* of May 16, 2001, BGBl. I, 876, effective May 22, 2001.

11. ZPO §130a(3).

12. ZPO §130a *(Soweit für vorbereitende Schriftsätze und deren Anlagen, für Anträge und Erklärungen der Parteien sowie für Auskünfte, Aussagen, Gutachten und Erklärungen Dritter die Schriftform vorgesehen ist...)*.

13. ZPO §§130a, 253(4). Presumably the scope of authorization for electronic filing will be made clearer in the anticipated implementing regulations to be issued by the Federal and State Ministries of Justice. To date no such regulations have appeared.

has expressed a willingness to accept electronic service.[14] Since complaints must be served under the auspices of the court, such service is unlikely to take place unless and until electronic filing of complaints in court is permitted.[15] At least two leading commentators have opined that the new law permits electronic filing of complaints.[16]

2. Content of the Complaint

The requirements as to content of complaints, on the other hand, are considerably more rigorous. It is said that the complaint is first directed at the court, and secondly to the opposing party. The complaint must set forth a particularized request for the aid of the court in the form of a judgment (*bestimmter Klageantrag*). The complaint must also suffice to give the opposing party notice that the plaintiff has invoked the aid of the court and the nature of the relief requested.[17]

A good part of the contents of the complaint are statutorily specified. For instance, ZPO §§130, 253 require that the complaint contain the name of the court and the names of all parties to the suit, definite and particularized claims for relief (*Anträge*), as well as a definite statement of the factual subject matter of the proceeding (*Klagegegenstand*). The complaint may also contain an explanation of the legal basis for the claim (*Rechtsgrundlage*) but is not expressly required to do so.

The particularized claim for relief is an important part of the complaint because of its role in determining the scope of claims preclusion (*Umfang der Rechtskraft*) for purposes of applying the doctrine of *res adjudicata*.[18] It is said that the complaint should set forth a request for relief with enough completeness and particularity that execution of the judgment requested could be taken directly from the complaint.[19]

---

14. See Law for the Reform of Service of Process in Court Proceedings (*Gesetz zur Reform des Vefahrens bei Zustellungen im gerichtlichen Verfahren* or *ZustRG*) of June 25, 2001, BGBl 2001 I, No. 29; ZPO §174(3)(3).

15. See ZPO §166(2); Ch. 7(F) below on service of process.

16. Zöller/Greger, §130a, mn. 3; Musielak/Stadler, *Kommentar zur Zivilprozessordnung*, 3rd ed. (2002), §130a, mn. 2.

17. See Jauernig, §39(II); Stein/Jonas/Schumann, §253, mn. 25 ff. for a detailed description of the content of the complaint.

18. See Ch. 9(F) below for a discussion of the binding effect of German civil judgments.

19. See Jauernig, §39(II)(2), p. 158 and Baur/Stürner, *Zwangsvollstreckungs-, Konkurs, - und Vergleichsrecht*, 12th ed. (1995), vol. I, *Einzelvollstreckungsrecht*, mn. 13.2, 13.3. for the particularity needed to obtain execution. So, for example, if the complaint sought re-

This requirement can be satisfied easily in some kinds of cases seeking return of specific property or narrowly described specific performance. On the other hand, it can be difficult in some kinds of cases, such as actions for damages for personal injuries or unjust enrichment, to specify the exact amount of damages sought at the time the complaint is filed. This is also true in antitrust cases and cases of unfair competition in which injunctive relief may be sought. In some cases seeking damages the statutory requirements for specificity have been judicially interpreted to permit either a complaint without any definite enumerated money demand, or with a demand expressed merely in terms of order of magnitude.[20] If a plaintiff fails to set forth its claims for relief and the subject matter of the suit with sufficient particularity, the court's responsibility to promote clarification requires the court to point out the deficiency and give the plaintiff an opportunity to cure it.[21]

3. Classification of Complaints

Claims for relief that may be included in civil complaints are classified in three groups, claims for affirmative relief (including payment of damages) (*Leistungsklagen*), claims for declaratory judgment (*Feststellungsklagen*), and claims for the alteration of legal rights or relationships (*Gestaltungsklagen*). It is possible to include claims of more than one class in a single complaint.[22]

A complaint for affirmative relief need merely set forth the nature of the claim and the fact that performance or payment is due and has not been rendered.[23] The demand can be either for payment of money due, for payment of money damages or for specific performance of a legal or contractual obligation to the extent authorized by substantive law.[24]

---

possession of an automobile, the complaint should set forth the serial number or other identifying number so that the automobile could be identified for purposes of execution.

20. See, e.g., Jauernig, §39(II)(2), p. 158; Zöller/Greger, §253, mn. 14, 14a; Stein/Jonas/Schumann, §253, mn. 81 ff.; German Federal Supreme Court, 132 BGHZ 341, 350 (1997). The most common cases are personal injury cases which include claims for pain and suffering.

21. See Ch. 6(C) above on the judge's duty to promote clarification.

22. ZPO §260. See Rosenberg/Schwab/Gottwald, §99(I), p. 560 ("*objektive Klagehäufung*"). See also Ch. 7(A)(5) below on joinder of claims.

23. If it turns out during the proceedings that performance is not yet due, in most cases the complaint will be dismissed as premature, usually with leave to refile later on if performance is not rendered when due. See, Zöller/Vollkommer, Vor §322, mn. 57; Rosenberg/Schwab/Gottwald, §92(II), pp. 512–514.

24. Under German law specific performance of contractual and other legal obligations is freely available and is generally awarded before resort to damages. See, e.g., Medicus,

A complaint for declaratory judgment seeks a declaration of the existence (*positive Feststellungsklage*) or non-existence (*negative Feststellungsklage*) of a legal relationship or obligation. It does not seek affirmative relief in terms of payment or performance, but has a declaratory effect. There is no execution on such judgments except for costs. The plaintiff must set forth in the complaint not only the legal relationship (*Rechtsverhältnis*) at stake, but also the circumstances making declaratory judgment necessary and the unavailability of simple affirmative relief. While ordinarily claims for declaratory judgment and claims for affirmative relief are seen as mutually exclusive, there are a number of statutory and practical exceptions tied to specific circumstances.[25]

A complaint for alteration of a legal relationship seeks a change in an existing legal relationship such as a marriage. Thus, claims for annulment of marriage or divorce as well as a smaller group of claims to revise existing private law relationships (e.g., landlord-tenant issues over the terms of the tenancy but not eviction, cases seeking dissolution or exclusion of a member of a business association), are considered complaints for alteration of legal relationships.[26] Sometimes, such as in divorce and other family matters, claims for alteration of legal relationship are not completely adversarial, and partake of the character of noncontentious jurisdiction (*freiwillige Gerichtsbarkeit*) in which the principle of party control of litigation (*Verhandlungsmaxime, Dispositionsmaxime*) is somewhat relaxed.[27]

Schuldrecht - Allgemeiner Teil, 14th ed. (2003), §3(I), mn. 18; Baur/Stürner, *Einzelvollstreckungsrecht,* §6(IV)(2), mn. 6.45. The most recently reformed German law of obligations authorizes suits for damages only if the claimant has set a final deadline for execution of the obligation and performance has not been rendered, BGB §281. For a survey on the reform of the law of obligations (*Schuldrechtsreform*) see, e.g., Lorenz/Riehm, *Lehrbuch zum Neuen Schuldrecht* (2002).

25. See generally Zöller/Greger, §256, mn. 7a; Rosenberg/Schwab/Gottwald, §93(III), pp. 521–523; German Federal Supreme Court, 49 *NJW* 2725, 2726 (1996); 71 BGHZ 306 (1978). So, for example, it is possible to make use of declaratory judgment in a personal injury case when the amount of damages is not fully known but the statute of limitations is about to expire.

26. Before initiating a proceeding seeking a declaratory judgment of invalidity of a contractual relationship because of fraud or mistake, a party must normally serve the opponent with a timely written declaration of rescission. See BGB §§119–124.

27. For a description of noncontentious jurisdiction, see Ch. 11(E) below. The principle of party control of litigation is discussed in Ch. 6(B) above.

4. Additional Elements of a Complaint

In addition to the minimum mandatory requirements set forth in ZPO §253(1) and (2), there are additional elements which "should" be included in a complaint as a matter of statutory law, and which are included in almost every complaint as a matter of practice. The same section of the ZPO which sets forth the minimum requirements for the complaint also provides that the complaint "should" set forth the amount in controversy (in the event that the relief requested is in form other than a money judgment) and should also set forth any reasons that may mitigate against referral of the complaint to a single judge (*Einzelrichter*).[28] The specification of the amount in controversy is important for the determination of the court fees as well as counsel fees for both parties. Most routine civil cases are now expected to be referred to single judges. Since German judges become involved with the complaint at a very early stage of the proceedings, it is administratively helpful to know if there are reasons why this kind of referral should not be made at the earliest possible time.

Complaints are also expected to conform to the general requirements for written pleadings and briefs (*Schriftsätze*). Included among these is the requirement of designation of the means of proof which would serve to prove the factual assertions in the pleading.[29] Usually the plaintiff will comply with this recommendation by appending to each significant factual assertion in the complaint a kind of citation to the kind and source of proof which the plaintiff expects will factually back up the assertion. Where the anticipated means of proof is a document and the document is in the possession of the pleader, the original or a copy of the relevant portions are to be physically attached to the complaint.[30] Where the expected source of the proof is witness testimony,

---

28. ZPO §253(3). In the state district courts (*Landgerichte*) cases can be heard by single judges or by three-judge panels. The May 2001 reform to the Civil Procedure Code provided that most ordinary cases will be heard by single judges, and that three-judge panels will be reserved for cases of more than ordinary difficulty or significance. ZPO §§348, 348a. See Ch. 3(D)(2)(b) above on the organization of the German civil court system, Ch. 7(E)(1) below on the process of determining whether a case will be heard by one judge or three.

29. See ZPO §130. Pleadings subsequent to the complaint should also include statements of the pleader's position with respect to assertions of fact and law in a prior pleading from the opponent, and designation of sources of proof controverting the opponent's assertions. See Ch. 8 below.

30. ZPO §131. If the document is believed to be in the possession of the opposing party or a third party, it need merely be described as specifically as possible.

the citation should include the names and addresses of the witnesses expected to testify to the facts asserted.

It is important for fact allegations in the complaint to be as specific and accurate as the pleader can make them. German civil procedure requires specific fact pleading and does not permit mere notice pleading. The legal requirement of specificity is complemented by the practical incentive for the pleader to avoid creating unnecessary issues of fact by overbroad assertions. Overbroad fact assertions which are not backed up by credible proof can be penalized by assessment of costs regardless of the overall outcome of the case.[31] Moreover, it is important that the court's first impression of the claim gained from reading the complaint be a credible one.

The result of these statutory requirements and practical incentives is that civil complaints in Germany are likely to be fairly lengthy recitations of facts deemed relevant to support the claim in a good deal of detail, names and addresses of witnesses, and designations or actual copies of relevant reports, documents, etc. From such a complaint the judge should be able to determine exactly what the plaintiff says happened and how the plaintiff proposes to prove it.

So, for instance, in a simple negligence case seeking damages for personal injuries and property damage from an automobile accident, the plaintiff's complaint would typically include in support of its prayers for relief (*Anträge*):

1. specific allegations of precisely how and why the accident occurred,
2. an identified source of proof for each allegation,
3. the amounts of damage set forth with precision,
4. attached copies of bills, police and medical reports, and even photographs to support the allegations.[32]

Such a pleading gives the judge (as well as the opposing party) a rather exact and complete picture of the facts deemed important by the plaintiff and of the potential problems of proof that might be expected.

5. Joinder of and Splitting of Claims

A plaintiff may join as many claims for relief as he has against the named defendant. There is no requirement that the claims be factually or legally re-

31. ZPO §96; Zöller/Herget, §96, mn. 1. In practice German courts rarely make use of this authority.

32. For an example of a typical complaint in an automobile accident case see Schellhammer, *Die Arbeitsmethode des Zivilrichters*, 14th ed. (2002), pp. 59–63.

lated so long as the subject matter jurisdiction and venue of the court are correct for each claim and so long as the form of procedure is the same for all claims.[33] Mere assertion of alternative factual or legal grounds for the same relief requested are not considered separate claims. The court is free to address factually or legally separate claims in separate hearings and is not required to hear everything at once.[34]

By the same token, the plaintiff is permitted to assert less than all of its claims, even claims based on the same facts, occurrence or document, against the defendant. For instance, if the defendant had given the plaintiff a promissory note for 100,000 Euros, and the note had come due, the plaintiff would not be required to sue for the entire 100,000 Euros at once, but could sue for any part of the entire sum without prejudicing his right to sue for the balance at a later time. A partial complaint can permit the plaintiff to test the legal and factual sufficiency of a claim without being exposed to costs based on a large amount in controversy in the event of an adverse decision.

A complaint which discloses that the particular sum sued for is part of a larger legal claim is referred to as an "open partial complaint" (*offene Teilklage*). However if the plaintiff sues for a sum or other relief that is only part of what he is entitled to without specifying the partial nature of the claim, the complaint is a "hidden partial complaint" (*verdeckte Teilklage*). Both are permissible, although there has been dispute as to the extent of binding effect of a judgment on a hidden partial complaint.[35] This right of the plaintiff to determine the extent of his legal rights that he will assert in any one case is based on the principle of party control of litigation (*Dispositionsmaxime*).[36]

A plaintiff can also assert claims in the alternative, with the subordinate claim (*Hilfsantrag*) only to be decided in the event that relief is not available on the claim in chief (*Hauptantrag*). For instance, the plaintiff could seek a judgment of specific performance requiring the defendant contractor to rem-

---

33. ZPO §260. For instance a claim subject to the documentary or check process (see Ch. 11(B) below) could not be joined with a claim subject to the ordinary process.

34. ZPO §145.

35. See Jauernig, §63(III), p. 244. In the case of an open partial complaint, it is clear that a judgment relates only to the amount sued for and does not bind the parties or the court with respect to future suits for balances of the overall claim. The prevailing view today is that even a hidden partial complaint does not prevent a plaintiff from suing for any additional balance of the overall claim. Zöller/Vollkommer, Vor §322, mn. 47, 48; Gottwald, in: *Münchener Kommentar zur Zivilprozessordnung*, 2nd ed. (2000 ff.) §322, mn. 119; German Federal Supreme Court,135 BGHZ 181 (1998). See Ch. 9(F) below on the binding effect of judgments.

36. See Ch. 6(B) above for a discussion of this basic principle of German civil justice.

edy specified defects in a building constructed for the plaintiff, and in the alternative, could seek damages for the defects in the event that the court deemed the specific remedy impractical.[37]

B. Joinder of Parties

The classic conception of civil litigation in Germany involves two parties, Plaintiff (*Kläger*) and Defendant (*Beklagter*). Multiple persons or entities may join or be joined in these roles when the claims asserted by or against them are legally or factually related. Such persons are referred to as comprising a "suit group" (*Streitgenossenschaft*).[38] Persons with completely unrelated claims generally cannot assert them in the same suit.

1. Joinder of Claimants

Parties asserting legal claims may join their claims in a single suit (*Klagehäufung*) under a number of circumstances specified by the Civil Procedure Code. Persons asserting a single joint legal right, e.g. joint owners of real or personal property, may constitute an "active suit group" (*aktive Streitgenossenschaft*) and join together as plaintiffs to assert or enforce their joint right. The same is true of persons whose claim against the defendant is based on the same factual or legal grounds, such as several persons injured in the same accident or several claimants under the same contract.[39]

Persons may also join together as an active suit group if the subject matters of their claims are similar (*gleichartig*) as a matter of fact or law.[40] For instance, claims by several plaintiffs against the same defendant arising out of accidents occurring on the same premises or involving the same product would likely contain enough common elements of fact or law to support an active suit group.

If the court deems that the claims are not sufficiently related to constitute an active suit group, the court will sever them but will not dismiss them.[41] By

---

37. See Jauernig, §88(III), p. 329; Zöller/Greger, §260, mn. 4.

38. See in general Lüke, *Die Beteiligung Dritter im Zivilprozess,* 1st ed. (1993); Lindacher, "Die Streitgenossenschaft", 26 *JuS* 379 and 540 (1986).

39. ZPO §59. Another example is of a number of heirs bringing suit against a third party based on a claim of a testator who died before the suit was brought.

40. ZPO §60.

41. ZPO §145. See Jauernig, §81(I)(3), p. 313; Zöller/Vollkommer §60, mn. 8; Lüke, *Zivilprozessrecht,* §40(I), mn. 444. According to prevailing opinion, if neither party raises an issue over the propriety of a suit group, the court is not required to not raise the mat-

the same token, the court can also consolidate separately brought cases for the purpose of joint hearings or other proceedings when the claims "are legally connected or could have been asserted in a single complaint."[42]

2. Joinder of Defendants

The same provisions which permit different parties to join the same suit as plaintiffs also permit claims to be asserted against multiple defendants in the same suit if the same prerequisites of commonality are satisfied.[43] So, for instance, an insurance company can bring a single suit against a number of policy holders for unpaid premiums, or a landlord can proceed against several tenants on the same ground in a single eviction action.[44] Joinder of multiple defendants by one or more plaintiff constitutes a "passive suit group" (*passive Streitgenossenschaft*).

3. Proceedings upon Joinder of Parties

Parties joined as either plaintiffs or defendants generally retain considerable freedom of action and individual control over their own claims.[45] Joinder of the claims for the purposes of suit does not constitute a legal fusion of the claims. Each claim must be individually examined for prerequisites to suit (*Prozessvoraussetzungen*), default by a single claimant results in a default judgment only so far as his claim is concerned, and the court's decision can deal with the claims individually and differently as the law and facts may indicate.[46] By the same token, the Civil Procedure Code specifically provides that joined parties retain the right individually to control the assertion or defense of their claims and that all parties joined as either plaintiffs or defendants are to be individually notified of court activities and individually summoned to conferences and hearings.[47] Joined parties are treated as individuals, and no party

---

ter on its own motion. See Thomas/Putzo, *Zivilprozessordnung*, 25th ed. (2003), §60, mn. 7; Stein/Jonas/Bork, vor §59, mn. 9.

42. ZPO §147 ("*... in rechtlichem Zusammenhang stehen oder in einer Klage hätten geltend gemacht werden können.*").

43. ZPO §§59, 60.

44. See Jauernig, §81(I)(3); Zöller/Vollkommer, §60, mn. 7.

45. The exception is for parties to a "necessary suit group" (*notwendige Streitgenossenschaft*), where a unitary decision binding all parties is required. See Ch. 7(B)(4) below.

46. Jauernig, §81(III); Zöller/Vollkommer, §61, mn. 8.

47. ZPO §63. A party can nominate another joined party as a witness rather than be relegated to party interrogation, since the joined cases are legally separate. See Jauernig, §81(III). To the extent that joined parties request party interrogation, the court can deter-

can be legally advantaged or disadvantaged by the success or failure of another member of the suit group.[48]

This solicitude for the integrity of each individual's factual and legal position does not mean that joined parties are not affected by the overall result of consolidated proceedings for oral argument and the reception of evidence. It would be unusual for a court to find a single contested fact scenario differently for different affected joined parties. Common legal principles would likely be applied in a consistent manner regardless of variations in individual parties' assertions.[49]

4. Required Joinder of Parties

Joinder of either plaintiffs or defendants is required "if the disputed legal relationship of all members of the suit group can only be determined on a unitary basis, or if the suit group is a necessary one for another reason."[50] The requirement for a single decision binding multiple claimants or defendants can arise out of procedural law or substantive law. Joinder can be required, for instance, if claimants who can act only jointly seek to assert a joint claim, or if certain kinds of collective liability are asserted against a group of defendants.[51] Required joinder is frequently encountered in claims asserted *in rem* in behalf of or against real estate owned in condominium or, in real estate matters, in behalf of or against a group of heirs of one or more testators.[52]

The Civil Procedure Code is silent as to the consequences of failure to join a necessary party. Logically it would seem that if joinder is in fact legally necessary, inclusion of the necessary parties would be a prerequisite to suit

---

mine whether to examine all or merely some of them in the interest of avoiding unnecessary repetition and waste of time. ZPO §449.

48. ZPO §61. A party who defaults or assents to judgment by acknowledgment in effect drops out of the suit group, as does a party who accepts a first instance judgment and fails to continue with an appeal. See Jauernig, §81(III).

49. See Jauernig, §81(III); Lüke, *Zivilprozessrecht*, §40(I), mn. 445; Lüke, *Die Beteiligung Dritter im Zivilprozess*, pp. 273 ff.

50. ZPO §62 (*"Kann das streitige Rechtsverhältnis allen Streitgenossen gegenüber nur einheitlich festgestellt werden oder ist die Streitgenossenschaft aus einem sonstigen Grunde eine notwendige,..."*).

51. See, e.g., Jauernig, §82, p. 315; Zöller/Vollkommer, §62, mn. 17, 18; Lüke, *Zivilprozessrecht*, §40(II), mn. 446–448. Joinder is not required if the obligors are alleged to be jointly and severally liable.

52. See Jauernig, §82(I) and (II), pp. 315, 316; Musielak/Weth, §62 mn. 3–12, for a discussion of the somewhat intricate law of required joinder of various kinds of claims.

(*Prozessvoraussetzung*), and failure to include all necessary parties would lead to procedural dismissal without prejudice (*Prozessabweisung*). Although the claim may be legally allowable, if the substantive law requires that the right in question be asserted by the entire group, the complaint will be considered unfounded (*unbegründet*). On the other hand, it is clear that once the necessary parties have been joined, a party's later failure to participate in the proceeding will not result in an individual adverse judgment. Contrary to the usual rule, a defaulting necessary party is bound by the actions taken by the active members of the suit group, who are said to "represent" (*vertreten*) the absent party for such purposes.[53]

5. Collective Litigation

Although it is possible for large numbers of persons to be joined as plaintiffs or defendants in single proceedings where circumstances warrant, German law has traditionally been reluctant to adopt institutions of mass litigation. Outside of limited circumstances under which served, but non-participating parties in necessary suit groups are "represented" by their participating co-parties, the principle that litigants must individually come before the court in order to benefit from or be bound by civil litigation is fundamental to German civil justice. For this reason the Anglo-American style of "class action" or "group action" is not known in Germany.

This does not mean that Germans cannot be indirectly affected by litigation that addresses their interests or even their rights. Constitutional litigation brought by a single party can invalidate a statute or doctrine that affects many persons other than the parties to the case. Even ordinary civil litigation (e.g. environmental cases) can result in injunctions that may bring relief or benefit to persons other than those who were active parties in the case.[54] However traditionally a monetary judgment in favor of persons not named as parties to the case was unknown.

In recent decades German civil procedure has seen the introduction of collective litigation in the form of "interest-group complaints" (*Verbandsklagen*) asserted by recognized consumer and environmental "interest groups" (*Verbände*) on behalf of their members and the common interests with which they

53. ZPO §62, Jauernig, §82(IV), p. 317.

54. Such litigation can also bring indirect burdens to non-parties as well. For instance an enterprise enjoined from polluting may have to shut down to the detriment of persons employed there.

are associated. Regulatory laws protecting competition and consumer interests have authorized voluntary associations focused on these aspects of the public interest to seek injunctive relief against defendants violating these statutes.[55] An adverse decision on an interest group complaint does not bind any individual claimant, whether or not a member of the interest group, with respect to any individual claim for injunctive relief or damages. On the other hand, a decision in favor of the interest group can be binding on the defendant in later suits by individual claimants raising the same issue.[56] In any event, such groups are frequently able to muster greater litigation resources than can individual litigants joined in a particular suit on an *ad hoc* basis.

Interest group claims in Germany and throughout Europe received a significant impetus with the issuance of European Union Directive 98/27 of May 19, 1998 requiring that Member States authorize interest group complaints in consumer matters seeking injunctive relief and authorizing the Member States to include in such collective remedies some form of mass monetary compensation to injured parties. Following an extensive comparative study by the Max-Planck Institute on International and Comparative Private Law in Hamburg,[57] Germany adopted a new Law on Injunctive Relief (*Unterlassungsklagengesetz or UKlaG)* in consumer matters. The new law authorizes qualified consumer interest groups and chambers of commerce to request injunctive relief against the use of unfair standard contract terms (*allgemeine Geschäftsbedingungen*) as well as against violations of other consumer protective provisions.[58] The recently amended Environmental Protection Law also permits qualified environmental interest groups to bring complaints in the administrative courts to enforce environmental standards and regulations without hav-

---

55. See, e.g., Law against Unfair Competition *(Gesetz gegen den unlauteren Wettbewerb* or *UWG*) of June 7, 1909, RGBl. I, 499, §13(2) and §8(3) of the *Regierungsentwurf* (legislative proposal of the federal government) on reform of the *UWG* of May 7, 2003, which is likely to be adopted by the German parliament; Law Authorizing Suits for Injunctive Relief in Consumer Protection and other Matters (*Gesetz über Unterlassungsklagen bei Verbraucherrechts- und anderen Verstössen* or *UKlaG*) of November 26, 2001, effective January 1, 2002, BGBl. I, 3173, §§1, 2.

56. See, e.g., UKlaG §11. In subsequent proceedings individual claimants must refer to the favorable outcome of the interest group case.

57. See Basedow/Hopt/Baetge, *Die Bündelung gleichgerichteter Interessen im Prozess: Verbandsklage und Gruppenklage* (1999); Greger, "Verbandsklage und Prozessrechtsdogmatik", 113 *ZZP* 399 (2000); Koch, "Die Verbandsklage in Europa", 113 *ZZP* 413 (2000).

58. UKlaG §§1, 2. A similar right had previously existed under the Law Regulating the Use of Standard Contract Terms *(Gesetz zur Regelung der Allgemeinen Geschäftsbedingungen*), which has since been repealed.

ing to assert an injury to their own proprietary interests.[59] As of the present time Germany has not accepted the EU's invitation to add claims for monetary compensation to consumer interest group complaints, but discussion of further reform proposals along these lines is ongoing.

Under German corporation law the court may appoint a shareholder representative to assert claims against corporate entities for compensation for economic losses sustained by shareholders in connection with formation or restructuring of corporations, trusts or other similar entities.[60] Similar solutions are now being considered for claims against corporations, directors, and others in securities litigation.

While these developments are considered by many as significant enlargements of the role of collective litigation in Germany, no development of a real American-style class action culture is anticipated. One reason is that the German social insurance and welfare system, which is funded in part by industry, fulfils in many cases the restitutory role left to class litigation in the United States.

C. Intervention

German law recognizes two forms of intervention in civil actions by persons not originally parties. Principal intervention *(Hauptintervention)* is relatively rare. Auxiliary intervention (*Nebenintervention*), whether voluntarily or as a result of notice of pending claim (*Streitverkündung*) is relatively common. In ordinary civil proceedings in courts other than the Federal Constitutional Court there is no provision for the participation of non-parties to represent the public interest or special interests as *amici curiae*.[61]

1. Principal Intervention

The Civil Procedure Code authorizes a person not party to a pending case, "who in whole or in part claims a thing or a right about which litigation between other persons is pending" to assert his claim in a suit against both par-

59. *Naturschutzgesetz* (BNatSchG) of March 25, 2002, effective April 4, 2002, BGBl. I 1193, §61.

60. *Aktiengesetz* (AktG) §306(4); *Umwandlungsgesetz* §§307–308.

61. See Rosenberg/Schwab/Gottwald, §51(VI)(4), p. 278. The Federal Constitutional Court is frequently required to receive comments on particular kinds of issues from a variety of public bodies and other persons affected. See e.g. BVerfGG §77.

ties.[62] The intervenor's complaint must be filed in the first-instance court of the pending suit before judgment is final. For instance a person claiming status as assignee of a claim in litigation could file a complaint in the court in which the suit was pending as a principal intervenor and simultaneously assert the assignment against the plaintiff and the underlying claim against the defendant.[63] The statute authorizes the court upon request of a party to stay the underlying action in order first to determine the status of the intervenor.[64]

If the defendant in the underlying action is not contesting the existence of the obligation, but only to whom it is owed, the defendant can give third party notice (*Streitverkündung*) to the alternate claimant, who can then appear as principal intervenor. This transforms the case into one of interpleader (*Prätendentenstreit*). If the defendant wishes to save further time and effort by dropping out of the case, it can pay the amount due into court and leave it to the competing creditors to litigate their respective entitlements.[65]

2. Auxiliary Intervention

A more common form of intervention is "auxiliary intervention" (*Nebenintervention*) under which a person not originally a party to a suit may intervene to support the position of a party whose victory or defeat will legally affect the interests of the intervenor (*Nebenintervenient*).[66] The role of the intervenor is not to assert its own claim in the action, but to assist an existing party to assert or defend an existing claim.[67]

A person may seek leave to appear as an auxiliary intervenor at any stage of a pending civil proceeding right up to the various levels of appeal. The prospective intervenor must file a pleading (*Schriftsatz*) with the court in which the case is pending requesting leave to intervene and explaining the nature of the intervenor's interest that will be legally affected by the outcome of

---

62. ZPO §64 ("*Wer die Sache oder das Recht, worüber zwischen anderen Personen ein Rechtstreit anhängig geworden ist, ganz oder teilweise für sich in Anspruch nimmt...*"). For a discussion of problems of principal intervention see Koussoulis, "Aktuelle Probleme der Hauptintervention", 100 *ZZP* 211 (1987).

63. See Jauernig, §85 (I), p. 323.

64. ZPO §65.

65. ZPO §75. Also referred to as "creditor suit" (*Gläubigerstreit*). See Jauernig, §85(II), p. 323.

66. ZPO §66.

67. Hence the alternate designation "suit helper" (*Streithelfer*). See Jauernig, §83(I), p. 318.

the case.[68] Auxiliary intervention is generally allowed unless either party objects, in which case the court must decide the status of the auxiliary intervenor by interlocutory judgment after oral hearing.[69]

Although the auxiliary intervenor does not become a party to the proceeding in its own right, it can act in the interest of the supported party by making assertions of fact and law, nominating witnesses, and appearing at and conducting oral argument and taking of evidence. With the consent of the party whose position it is supporting, an intervenor can take over the presentation of that position, so that the supported party need not further actively participate in the case.[70]

At the same time, the auxiliary intervenor takes the case as it finds it, and cannot contradict a position already taken by the assisted party.[71] Nor can an intervenor bring forward assertions, means of defense (*Verteidigungsmittel*) or proof which the assisted party would be precluded from utilizing by ZPO §296 or other preclusive provisions.[72] An intervenor is not authorized to lodge an appeal if the assisted party refuses to do so.[73]

Since an auxiliary intervenor is not technically a party to the case, an adverse final judgment does not entitle the opposing party to obtain execution against the intervenor.[74] On the other hand, the intervenor's ability to challenge the judgment in a later suit between him and the party assisted is materially reduced. The intervenor cannot challenge the legal or factual basis for the prior judgment or the adequacy of the assisted party's prosecution or defense of the underlying matter.[75] In order to avoid being bound by the result

---

68. ZPO §70. In the local court a person can file an oral intervention which is minuted at the clerk's office. ZPO §496.

69. ZPO §71. An interlocutory judgment allowing or denying auxiliary intervention is subject to miscellaneous appeal by any aggrieved party or the intervenor.

70. See ZPO §67; Rosenberg/Schwab/Gottwald, §50(IV)(2), p. 265; Jauernig, §83(IV), p. 320.

71. ZPO §67. This can be particularly important if the intervention takes place at the appellate level. See Federal Supreme Court, 50 *NJW* 2385, 2386 (1997); Jauernig §83 (IV), p. 320.

72. Zöller/Vollkommer, §67, mn. 4. See Ch. 7(K)(1) below on preclusion of late-designated facts and proof.

73. Zöller/Vollkommer, §67, mn. 9. However refusal of an assisted party to consent to an appeal may vitiate the validity of the judgment as between the assisted party and the intervenor. See ZPO §68.

74. Rosenberg/Schwab/Gottwald, §50(IV)(5)(a), p. 267. Nor is the judgment routinely served on the intervenor.

75. This is a rare example of issue preclusion in German procedural law.

in the underlying case the intervenor must show that the assisted party hindered the intervenor's ability to bring forward assertions or evidence 1) by its conduct of the matter prior to intervention, 2) by specific declarations or actions thereafter, or 3) by intentional or grossly negligent failure to bring forward means of proof which were not known to the intervenor.[76]

D. Notice of Pending Suit to Third Parties

German civil procedure does not allow a defendant who has a claim for reimbursement, contribution or indemnity against a third party simply to add the third party to the suit.[77] In such a case the defendant must defend the suit as best it can and then proceed separately against the third party in the event of an unfavorable outcome.

A defendant in such a position can, however, obviate potential objections by the third party based on inadequate defense of the claim by filing and serving the third party with a "notice of pending suit" (*Streitverkündung*) and inviting the third party to participate as an auxiliary intervenor.[78] Once the notice has been given, the third party will be bound by the outcome between the original parties to the same extent as if it had intervened on its own.

A notice of pending claim can be filed and served at any time during the pendency of the suit. It consists of a simple pleading describing the suit and setting forth the reason for notifying the third party.[79] It can be directed to any person against whom the defendant (or the plaintiff on a counterclaim) has "a claim for reimbursement or indemnity" in the event of unfavorable outcome of the suit.[80] The recipient of the notice has the right to appear as auxiliary intervenor and to assist in defending the suit. If the party notified does not appear, the suit proceeds regardless. If the suit is lost, the third party is bound by the result to the same extent as if it had intervened voluntarily, ex-

---

76. ZPO §68; Rosenberg/Schwab/Gottwald, §50(V), p. 268; Jauernig, §83(V), p. 321.

77. See Rosenberg/Schwab/Gottwald, §51(V), p. 277. Note, however, that German domiciliaries may be joined as third-party defendants in suits pending in those EU Member States which permit such joinder, BRJE Articles 6(2) and 65. See Ch. 12(B)(2)(h) below.

78. ZPO §72. See, in general, Jauernig, §84, p. 322; Lüke, *Zivilprozessrecht*, §42, mn. 455 ff.; Rosenberg/Schwab/ Gottwald, §51, p. 272.

79. ZPO §73.

80. ZPO §72 *(Anspruch auf Gewährleistung oder Schadloshaltung)*. A recipient of a notice of pending suit which has its own claim for reimbursement or indemnity against a fourth party can file and serve its own notice of pending claim against the potentially liable fourth party. ZPO §72(2).

cept that the relevant time is the time the third party received notice and could act on it rather than the time of actual intervention.[81] Basically, the third party would be precluded from questioning the factual or legal basis of the court's decision or the adequacy of the defendant's conduct of the suit based on proceedings occurring after service of the notice of pending suit.[82]

German law even recognizes the validity of notices of foreign suits directed to German domiciliaries, provided that the notice complies with the terms of the EU Regulation on Service of Process or the Hague Convention on Service of Process Abroad and is given at a time and in a manner so as to provide actual notice and a reasonable opportunity to participate in the defense.[83]

While the court in which the case is pending will not decide any issues between the defendant and the third party, the preclusive effect of the notice of pending claim-intervention rules has the effect of eliminating many such issues and simplifying and speeding resolution of those indemnity claims that are brought. For this reason such notices are commonplace in many forms of civil litigation such as building construction cases and even cases arising from automobile accidents which involve a number of parties.

E. Preliminary Examination of the Complaint

Upon filing with the court, the complaint and its attachments are promptly assigned and delivered to a judge or chamber of the court for further proceedings. At this point the single judge or panel to whom or to which the complaint has been assigned[84] will briefly review the complaint in order to deter-

81. ZPO §74. As is the case with voluntary intervention, a recipient of a notice of pending claim is not bound in its own relationship with the opposing party.

82. See Ch. 7(C)(2) above.

83. Rosenberg/Schwab/Gottwald, §51(II)(1), p. 273; Schack, *Internationales Zivilverfahrensrecht*, 3rd ed. (2002), §17(VI)(3), mn. 923. The preclusive effect of the notice of pending suit will depend on whether German courts will recognize the foreign judgment. See Ch. 12(C)(2)(a) and (E) below for a discussion of the EU Service Regulation and the Hague Service Convention. There is some dispute as to whether the requirements for service of a notice of pending suit are the same as for service of a complaint, but the careful lawyer will be sure to comply with the latter in order to be sure to obtain the benefit of this legal doctrine. See Zöller/Vollkommer, §73, mn. 1; Hess, "Der Binnenmarktprozess", 53 *JZ* 1021, 1029 (1998).

84. Within multi-judge or multi-panel courts assignment of incoming cases is based on an "assignment plan" (*Geschäftsverteilung*) adopted by the court's elected "Presiding

mine 1) (in the state district courts) whether the case will be handled by a single judge or by a three-judge panel, and 2) whether preliminary proceedings preparatory to the plenary hearing (*Haupttermin* or *Hauptverhandlung*) should be conducted by early preliminary hearing (*früher erster Termin*) or by exchange of written pleadings and briefs (*schriftliches Vorverfahren*).

If, during the course of this initial cursory review, the judge were to notice patent defects in the alleged jurisdiction of the court,[85] the capacity and representation of the parties,[86] or other of the prerequisites to suit (*Prozessvoraussetzungen*) which the court may consider on its own motion (*von Amts wegen*),[87] the court is supposed to call these to the attention of the plaintiff or the plaintiff's lawyer, in order that the defects might be corrected at the earliest possible time.[88] If the defects appear to be ones which can not be corrected, or if the plaintiff fails to do so as a result of the court's hint and feedback, the court will dismiss the case. Usually such a dismissal is a procedural dismissal (*Prozessabweisung*) without prejudice to the merits of the case. The plaintiff thus could reinitiate the case in the same or another court once the prerequisite to justiciability had been satisfied.[89]

1. One Judge or Three?

Traditionally cases in the state district courts were heard by three-judge panels unless the parties consented to disposition by a single judge or unless the panel decided that the case did not "exhibit particular difficulties of a legal or factual nature or have fundamental significance" and referred the case to a

---

Committee" (*Präsidium*) at the beginning of each judicial year. See GVG §21(e)(1). Within a panel the cases are distributed on the basis of an internal "assignment plan" adopted by the members of the panel (GVG §21g(1)). Such plans often provide that cases with specialized subject matters will be assigned to specified judges or groups of judges (*Spruchkörper*) or chambers "specializing" in those particular subject matters. See Ch. 3(D) above.

85. This could be either subject matter jurisdiction (*sachliche Zuständigkeit*) or venue (*örtliche Zuständigkeit*) of the court. See Chapter 5(B) and (C) above for a discussion of subject matter jurisdiction and venue.

86. For instance, in the court of general jurisdiction, the lack of a signature of an attorney.

87. See Rimmelspacher, *Zur Prüfung von Amts wegen im Zivilprozess* (1966); Zöller/Greger, §253, mn. 9–21; Lüke, *Zivilprozessrecht,* §13(I) and (II), mn. 149–152; Rosenberg/Schwab/Gottwald, §96, p. 534. In principle such prerequisites to suit may be noticed by the court at any stage of the proceeding.

88. ZPO §139(3). This is an example of the judge's duty to give hints and feedback. See Ch. 6(C)(2)(e) above.

89. Rosenberg/Schwab/Gottwald, §96(V), p. 538; Jauernig §33(V), p. 128.

single judge for plenary proceedings and disposition.[90] The July 2001 Civil Procedure Reform Law,[91] which came into force on January 1, 2002, attempts to make single-judge dispositions the rule rather than the exception in the state district court.

Every case is now automatically assigned to a single judge unless the case belongs to a number of specified categories or unless the single judge who would otherwise receive the assignment is a "probationary judge" (*Richter auf Probe*)[92] and does not have at least one year's experience in civil adjudication.[93] The categories of cases presumptively reserved for three-judge panels (*Kammern*) include media litigation, bank disputes, construction cases, cases involving issues of the competence of lawyers, engineers, accountants and similar professionals,[94] health care malpractice cases, commercial cases within the jurisdiction of commercial panels (*Handelskammern*) of the state district courts, freight and transportation cases, insurance cases, copyright cases, telecommunications and information technologies matters, patent and copyright cases, and cases which are relegated to the jurisdiction of the state district courts regardless of amount in controversy.[95]

A case in one of the categories not automatically assigned to a single judge must nonetheless be referred to a single judge if the panel to which it is assigned is of the view that the case does not present particular difficulties of a legal or factual nature and is not of fundamental significance, provided that the plenary proceeding (*Haupttermin*) has not already commenced before the

---

90. See Ch. 3(D)(2)(b) above and ZPO §348 (pre-July 2001 version) ("... *besondere Schwierigkeiten tatsächlicher oder rechtlicher Art aufweist oder grundsätzliche Bedeutung hat*"). Prior to the 1976 "Stuttgart reforms" the role of a single judge in both the state appeals courts and the state district courts had been limited to preparatory proceedings in anticipation of a plenary hearing and decision by the panel. The 1976 reforms authorized referral of first-instance non-commercial cases to a single judge for decision based either on consent of the parties or a finding that the case exhibited no particular difficulties, etc. The 1993 reform made such a referral presumptive and placed the burden on the parties to demonstrate why the case should not be referred. See Deubner, in: *Münchener Kommentar zur Zivilprozessordnung,* 2nd ed. (2000 ff.), §348, mn. 1 ff., 20 ff.

91. *Gesetz zur Reform des Zivilprozesses* of July 27, 2001 or ZPO-RG, BGBl. I 1887 ff. See Ch. 3(D)(2)(b) above.

92. See Ch. 3(G) above on the training and promotion of judges.

93. ZPO §348(1).

94. Including both compensation claims asserted by such professionals and claims for professional negligence against them. See Musielak/Wittschier, §348, mn. 10.

95. ZPO §348(1)(a)–(k). See Ch. 3(D)(2)(a) and Ch. 5(B)(2) above for a brief description of cases relegated to the jurisdiction of the state district courts regardless of amount in controversy.

panel.[96] The decision to make such a referral is made by the panel after giving both parties opportunity for comment. Usually the plaintiff will state its position in the complaint.[97] The defendant is required to take a position on the issue in its answer (*Klageerwiderung*).[98] The panel's order referring the case or refusing to refer the case is not appealable.[99]

On the other hand, a single judge to whom a case is automatically assigned ordinarily should request that the case be handled by the panel "if the case exhibits particular difficulties of a legal or factual nature" or "the legal issue has fundamental significance" or if the parties unanimously so request.[100] A single judge should also request that the panel take up a case originally assigned to her by panel decision when, as a result of "a material change in circumstances," the same criteria apply.[101] In either case the panel has to decide whether to accept the referral.[102] Its decision is rendered after hearing from the parties by a simple order and is not appealable.[103]

Before the 2001 reforms practice with respect to division of cases among single judges and three-judge panels varied widely among the various German states and appeals court districts. It is too soon to tell whether the more specific single-judge-oriented provisions of the current law will lead to greater and more consistent use of single judges throughout Germany.

2. Preparation by Oral Hearing or Written Briefs?

Traditionally cases were prepared for oral argument and decision by a preliminary hearing at which the court would discuss the issues with the parties and counsel and shape the ongoing proceedings for efficient argument, taking of evidence and decision. In recent years growing caseloads and pressure

96. ZPO §348a(1).

97. See ZPO §253(3).

98. ZPO §277(1)(2); see Ch. 7(J) below.

99. ZPO §348a(3). See Musielak/Wittschier, §348a, mn. 21 ff.

100. ZPO §348(3) ("...*wenn die Sache besondere Schwierigkeiten tatsächlicher oder rechtlicher Art aufweist... die Rechtssache grundsätzliche Bedeutung hat...*").

101. ZPO §348a(2) ("...*aus einer wesentlichen Änderung der Prozesslage...*").

102. The panel is obliged to accept the re-referral if the panel finds that changed circumstances have indeed made the matter one of particular difficulty or fundamental significance. If the re-referral is based on unanimous request of the parties, the panel may, but is not required to accept the case. See Musielak/Wittschier, §348a, mn. 6, 18.

103. ZPO §§348(3)(3) and (4), 348a(2)(3) and (3). See Musielak/Wittschier, §348, mn. 19 and §348a, mn. 17 ff. Once a case has been re-referred to and accepted by the panel it remains there and cannot be sent back to the single judge.

for greater judicial "efficiency" have led to a greater use of written preparatory proceedings.[104]

Whether a case will be prepared by oral hearing or exchange of written briefs is decided by the presiding judge based on her initial review of the complaint.[105] The determination is a pragmatic one, based on the presiding judge's view of which form of preliminary procedure would most efficiently shape the legal and factual issues for clarification and decision in a single principal hearing.[106] The judge might choose an early preliminary hearing if the review of the complaint suggests that the early hearing might lead to final disposition of the matter, either by judgment or settlement. On the other hand, if the judge suspects that the defendant may elect not to defend, the written procedure could lead to a default judgment without the need to schedule any hearing at all.[107]

The judge's determination is not incorporated in any kind of formal order or decision, but merely forms the basis for further orders and dispositions in handling the case. If either party is dissatisfied with the method of preparation chosen, the party is free to request that the court schedule (or dispense with) an oral preliminary hearing as the case may be, and support its request with a statement of why the other procedure would be a more efficient means of preparing the case.

F. Service of Process

Service of process is governed by §§166–213 of the ZPO, which specify in some detail how various forms of service of process are to be accomplished.[108] The basic purpose of service is to insure that the addressee is given the op-

104. Preparation of cases by filing and exchange of written briefs (*Schriftsätze*) was introduced in the 1976 "Stuttgart reforms" aimed at concentrating the oral portions of the proceedings. See Ch. 2(F), Ch. 6(E)(1) above and Fritz Baur, "Entwicklungslinien des Zivilprozessrechts in den Jahren 1947 bis 1987", 40 *NJW* 2636, 2639 (1987).

105. ZPO §272(2).

106. See, e.g., Jauernig, §28(II); Rosenberg/Schwab/Gottwald, §106(II), p. 600; Prütting, in: *Münchener Kommentar zur Zivilprozessordnung*, §272, mn. 5 ff.

107. See Ch. 9(A)(1) below on default judgments.

108. The provisions of the Civil Procedure Code relating to service of process were simplified and updated in 2001 to reflect advances in information technology such as fax and e-mail. See Law for the Reform of Service of Process in Court Proceedings (*Gesetz zur Reform des Verfahrens bei Zustellungen im gerichtlichen Verfahren* or *ZustRG*) of June 25, 2001, BGBl. I 1206.

portunity to become aware of the contents of a legal document.[109] Service of a document can take place either at the instance of a party (*auf Betreiben einer Partei*) or at the request of the court (*von Amts wegen*).[110] Documents, "the service of which is prescribed by law or ordered by the court" are to be served at the request of the court.[111] Such documents include court papers, decisions, court notices, and the like as well as complaints and notices of appeal.[112] In exceptional cases parties may be required to arrange for service of certain court papers, such as attachment orders on third party debtors.

1. Service at the Request of the Court

Arrangements for service at the request of the court are made through the court clerk's office (*Geschäftsstelle*).[113] The party requesting service is required to provide the clerk of courts (*Urkundsbeamter*) with the requisite number of copies of the paper to be served.[114] The clerk of courts certifies the copies and arranges for them to be served on the designated recipients.[115]

The actual service can take place in a number of ways. Recent reforms have introduced various simplified means of service of process designed to save cost and time. If these are not successful, resort must be had to the traditional methods of in hand delivery and its substitutes.

a. Simplified Service of Process

The simplest means to effectuate official service of process is by delivery (*Aushändigung*) to the designated recipient at the clerk's office. In such case proof of service is noted in the case record by the official handing out the document.[116]

Service can be effected on certain persons such as lawyers, notaries, accountants, court executors, public officials, or other persons "who, by reason

---

109. See, e.g., Rosenberg/Schwab/Gottwald, §73(I), p. 403.

110. See ZPO §§166–190 for provisions governing service of process at the request of the court, and §§191–195 for additional provisions applying party-initiated service of process.

111. ZPO §166(2) ("...*deren Zustellung vorgeschrieben oder vom Gericht angeordnet ist*...").

112. See, e.g., ZPO §271 which requires a complaint to be served. ZPO §166(2) specifically provides that this service is at the request of the court.

113. ZPO §168(1)(1).

114. ZPO §133.

115. ZPO §§133, 169.

116. ZPO §173.

of their profession, can be assumed to be of heightened reliability" or on public bodies by any form of delivery against a simple acknowledgment of receipt (*Empfangsbekenntnis*) signed by the person served or a duly authorized representative.[117] Such service can be also effected by telefax so long as the document contains a legend to the effect that it is being served by telefax. The acknowledgment can be either in writing or by reply fax.[118] It is even possible to make official service by e-mail if the recipient is a person of heightened reliability or if the addressee has previously expressly consented to receive electronic transmittals. In such a case the document to be served should be provided with an "electronic signature" and be protected against unauthorized tampering by encryption or other means. The acknowledgment can be in any form, including e-mail.[119]

A common method of service at the request of the court is by registered mail with return receipt (*Einschreiben mit Rückschein*).[120] This method is generally employed when the person served is thought to be willing to accept the letter and sign the receipt. For instance, in the case of a complaint, the clerk's office usually sends a certified copy of the complaint along with other preparatory documents to the defendant at the address set forth by the plaintiff in the complaint.[121] In most cases the return of the registered mail receipt completes the service.

b. Other Means of Service of Process

If service cannot be effected by one of the simplified methods described above, one of the more traditional forms of personal service must be utilized. The clerk of courts is authorized to commission the postal service or, if necessary, a court official (*Justizbeamter*) to make the service by delivery of the process.[122]

The papers to be served are to be enclosed in a sealed envelope and are accompanied by a form for the return of service (*Zustellungsurkunde*).[123] The

---

117. ZPO §174(1) ("... *bei der aufgrund ihres Berufes von einer erhöhten Zuverlässigkeit ausgegangen werden kann*...").

118. ZPO §174(2).

119. ZPO §174(3). See Ch. 7(A) above on electronic pleadings.

120. ZPO §175. The return receipt signed by the addressee serves as the acknowledgment of service.

121. See Ch. 7(F)(5) below.

122. If the post office or a court official are unable to effectuate service, the court can commission a court executor (*Gerichtsvollzieher*) or other public authority (such as the police) to make service in the same manner. ZPO §168(2).

123. ZPO §176(1).

post office or other person making service is required to complete the service by either delivering the document to the defendant or by leaving it at the addressee's dwelling (*Wohnung*) or business premises (*Geschäftsräume*) with a family member, business associate, or other designated person.[124] If acceptance of the process is refused, it can be left with refusal noted and the service is valid.[125] If service is attempted at the addressee's dwelling or business premises but no-one is there to accept the papers, they may be deposited in any mailbox or similar mail receptacle identified with the specific dwelling or business premises, and such deposit qualifies as service.[126]

If all other means of personal service fail, the documents to be served may be lodged at a depository maintained by the post office or at the clerk's office of the local court for the district of the place where service was to be effected. Notice of such deposit is delivered to the person to whom mail addressed to the person to be served is given, or is tacked on the door of the addressee's dwelling or business premises. Service is effective with the delivery or tacking of the notice.[127]

c. *Service on Representatives*

Frequently service of court papers is made on authorized representatives of the persons to be served. A person who is not legally competent to litigate (*nicht prozessfähig*) can be served only by service on her or his designated legal representative (*gesetzlicher Vertreter*).[128] A person may also designate an agent for the service of process by written power of attorney, in which case service on the agent will be considered service on the principal.[129] In a pending case, if a party is represented by a lawyer, service may be made on the lawyer, who is required to return an acknowledgment of service to the court.[130]

---

124. ZPO §178. If the document is delivered to the addressee in person, service can be effected anywhere, ZPO §177.

125. ZPO §179.

126. ZPO §180. The person effecting service is also required to write the date of deposit on the outside of the envelope deposited.

127. ZPO §181.

128. ZPO §170(1).

129. ZPO §171.

130. See ZPO §§172, 174. If a party terminates a power of attorney or changes counsel, the party must notify the other parties and the court of the termination of representation and/or the new counsel. If the case is one in which representation by counsel is required, until such notification is received service on the previous counsel is valid. ZPO §87 (1). See Zöller/Stöber, §172, mn. 11, 12. Otherwise documents and notifications will be served on the party itself until a new attorney enters his appearance. Service of documents

An entity which is not a natural person can be served by serving the principal officer (*Leiter*) of the entity.[131] This can be done by simplified service or by all other means of service of process.

d. Service on Persons Abroad

Service of process within the European Union is largely governed by the EU Regulation of May 29, 2000 on the Service of Judicial and Non-Judicial Documents in Civil and Commercial Matters.[132] Outside the EU, most process is served pursuant to the Hague Convention on Service Abroad in Civil and Commercial Matters.[133] The German Civil Procedure Code authorizes service at the request of the court by registered mail with return receipt, provided that the state of the addressee is a signatory of a treaty or convention permitting this form of service abroad and that the state of the addressee has not excluded direct transmittal of registered mail by the postal service.[134] Absent an international treaty, service can be made by local authorities of the other state at the specific request of the presiding judge of the court in which the case is pending, or with the permission of the local authorities, by German consular officials.[135]

If a party is served abroad, the court may require the party to designate a domestic agent for the service of process in the ongoing proceeding.[136] If the party fails to do so, documents may be served by "deposit in the mail" (*Zustellung durch Aufgabe zur Post*) until the party designates such an agent.[137]

---

initiating an appeal can be made on the opposing party's lawyer for the instance from which the appeal is taken. ZPO §172(2).

131. ZPO §170(2).

132. European Regulation No 1348/2000 of 29 May 2000, OJ L 160, 30/06/2000, p. 37 (hereinafter the European Service Regulation). See ZPO §183(3).

133. For a discussion of the Hague Service Convention and other conventions regulating international jurisdiction of German courts and service of process in foreign countries see Ch. 12(B), (C) and (E) below.

134. ZPO §183(1)(1). For example, although the Hague Service Convention provides for service by direct transmittal of registered mail (Art. 10(a)), Switzerland has entered a reservation which bars direct transmittal of process from abroad. Hence such a procedure cannot be used by a German court to serve a Swiss domiciliary. Germany itself has also opted out of Art. 10(a) of the Hague Service Convention. See Ch. 12(E)(2)(a).

135. ZPO §183(1)(2). If the person to be served is a German official who has diplomatic immunity in the foreign country, service can be made by the German Foreign Office, ZPO §183(1)(3).

136. ZPO §184(1).

137. ZPO §184(1)(2) and (2). The court is required to notify the party of the consequences of failure to designate a local agent for service of process. Two weeks after deposit in the mail the document is deemed served. Notation in the record (*Akte*) of deposit of a

e. Service by Publication

In exceptional cases, if the location of a person is not known and the person has not appointed any kind of agent or representative, if the person lives abroad and it is impossible to effect service abroad, or if the person to be served lives in the dwelling of a person who is immune from judicial process, the court can authorize service of court documents by publication (*öffentliche Zustellung*).[138] The publication takes place by posting on the court bulletin board (*Gerichtstafel*) a notice containing the name of the person for whom service is effected, the name and last known address of the person to be served, the date, docket number and brief description of the subject matter of the document served, and designation of the place where the document may be retrieved. The notice must also warn of the consequences of failure to act in response to the notice.[139] In addition the court can, and usually does, order that the notice be published in the Federal Register (*Bundesanzeiger*) or in other publications.[140] The service by publication counts as effected one month after first posting of the notice unless the court sets a longer time period.[141]

The Federal Constitutional Court has decided several constitutional appeals based on misuse of service of process by publication. Because of the risk of infringement of the right to be heard (*rechtliches Gehör*) the statutory requirements for this form of service are strictly construed.[142]

f. Return of Service

In all cases where personal service must be made, the person making service (the postal clerk in the case of service by mail) is required to complete and return to the court a detailed return of service (*Zustellungsurkunde*) documenting the service or detailing the reasons service was not effected.[143] The

---

document in the mail establishes the time of deposit for the purposes of this provision, which can be considered a form of fictitious service.

138. ZPO §185. Authorization of service by publication must be by order of the court in which the case is pending. ZPO §186(1)(1).

139. ZPO §186(2).

140. ZPO §187.

141. ZPO §188 (fictitious service).

142. See, e.g., Federal Constitutional Court, 41 *NJW* 2361 (1988); generally 37 *NJW* 2567 (1984).

143. ZPO §182(1). A formal return of service is not required if one of the simplified methods of service is used.

return of service must include, among other things, the name of the addressee of the papers to be served, the name of the person to whom the papers were actually delivered, the proof of agency accepted in case of service on an agent, a description of the circumstances justifying one of the substituted methods of service such as leaving the documents in a mailbox or lodging them with the post office or court, confirmation that required notations of date and time of service had been made on the envelope served, the time and place of service, and the signature of the person making the service.[144]

2. Service at the Instance of a Party

Although most official court documents are served at the request of the court (*von Amts wegen*), some documents are served directly by the parties on each other or third parties.[145] Such service is arranged directly by the party or the party's lawyer, unless the papers to be served include some notification or order from the court to which a party is expected to react, in which case service is usually at the request of the court.[146]

In general the same provisions govern service whether performed at the request of the court or at the instance of a party *(auf Betreiben einer Partei)*.[147] The major differences are 1) that arrangements for service at the instance of a party are made by the party or its lawyer directly with the court executor (*Gerichtsvollzieher*) without the participation of the clerk's office, and 2) parties represented by counsel can serve each other by service "from lawyer to lawyer".[148] The court executor, like the clerk's office in the case of service at the request of the court, can commission the postal service to make service.[149] The court executor is responsible for making a return of service to the party

144. ZPO §182.

145. See ZPO §166(2) providing that service is to be at the request of the court where not otherwise provided.

146. Many of the documents which may be served at the instance of a party relate to attachment or execution, such as *ex parte* orders and decisions authorizing attachments, liens, and the like. See Rosenberg/Schwab/Gottwald, §73(III)(2), p. 405; Zöller/Stöber, §191, mn. 1; ZPO §829(2)(1) and Ch. 11(F)(1)(d) below (attachment order on third party debtors).

147. ZPO §191.

148. ZPO §§192, 195. In the local courts the parties can request the clerk's office to arrange for service of the papers by the court executor. ZPO §192(3). See Ch. 7(F)(3) below for service from lawyer to lawyer.

149. ZPO §194.

requesting that the document be served.[150] It is not clear whether the court executor can make use of the simplified methods of service such as delivery against acknowledgement or registered mail with return receipt.[151]

3. Service from Lawyer to Lawyer

When the parties are represented in the proceeding by lawyers, service of documents required to be served may be made "from lawyer to lawyer".[152] The lawyer effecting the service can simply mail a copy of the pleading or paper to the lawyer of the party to be served. The document should clearly indicate that it is being served "lawyer to lawyer."[153] Most lawyers also maintain mailboxes at the courthouses in which they customarily practice for the receipt of court-related papers. Lawyers maintaining such boxes are under an implicit professional duty to check them regularly, as deposit of papers in such boxes counts the same as mailing them to the lawyers at their offices.

Even certain pleadings and briefs ordinarily required to be served at the request of the court may be served from lawyer to lawyer if there is no court order to be communicated to the opponent at the same time.[154] The recent reforms to the service rules also authorize service of faxes and electronic documents from lawyer to lawyer.[155]

Service from lawyer to lawyer is effected when the addressee has received actual knowledge of the document and agrees to this form of service.[156] The lawyer receiving the service is therefore required to provide written acknowledgment of receipt of process on request of the lawyer effecting service.[157] In practice, service of litigation papers after the original complaint, is frequently "lawyer to lawyer".

---

150. ZPO §193.

151. Compare Zöller/Stöber, §191, mn. 3 (simplified methods may not be used) with Thomas/Putzo, *Zivilprozessordnung*, 25th ed. (2003), §174, mn. 1 (delivery against acknowledgment may be used).

152. ZPO §195 (*von Anwalt zu Anwalt*). This method of service applies only to those documents which are not accompanied by orders or other communications from the court, Thomas/Putzo, §195, mn. 2.

153. ZPO §195(1)(3).

154. ZPO §195(1)(2). Where the court has the ability to order the opponent to reply or take a position with respect to a submission within a specified time, ordinarily the paper to be responded to would be served along with the order at the request of the court.

155. ZPO §§195(1)(5); 174(2)(1), (3)(1).

156. German Constitutional Court, 54 *NJW* 1563, 1564 (2001).

157. ZPO §195(2).

4. Defects in Service of Process

A service of process which does not conform to obligatory legal requirements is invalid. However the German service regulations take a pragmatic attitude toward defects in service if the person to be served receives actual notice of the document to be served. In such cases, the document is deemed served at the point at which the document "actually reaches" (*tatsächlich zugegangen ist*) the person to be served.[158] Defects in service of process can also be cured retroactively by agreement of the party served.[159] In any event, objections to the sufficiency of service of process are usually waived if the party argues on the merits of the case (*zur Hauptsache verhandelt*).[160]

Defects in service made abroad under the Hague Service Convention may be cured retroactively to the extent that the Convention so provides, with reference to the law of the place of service. However according to prevailing opinion defects in service abroad which involve violations of foreign sovereignty may not be waived or cured.[161]

5. Service of the Complaint

Following the presiding judge's initial review of the complaint and her determination to employ either the early preliminary hearing or written proceedings to prepare the case for plenary proceedings, "the complaint is to be promptly served" on the named defendant or defendants.[162] This occurs regardless of the method of preparation chosen by the court. This service is a service at the request of the court and is arranged through the clerk's office.[163]

For purposes of the statute of limitations and other time limits the claim becomes pending upon receipt of the complaint at the court. The Civil Procedure Code requires that the complaint be served on the defendant "as soon as practicable" (*demnächst*) without setting a specific time limit. This has been

---

158. ZPO §189.

159. See Schellhammer, *Zivilprozess*, 10th ed. (2003), mn. 104.

160. ZPO §295.

161. German Federal Supreme Court, 46 *NJW* 598 (1993); see also European Court of Justice, Case 305/88, *Lancray v. Peters and Sickert*, ECR I-2725 (1990); Stürner, "Förmlichkeit und Billigkeit bei der Klagezustellung im Europäischen Zivilprozess", 47 *JZ* 35, 330 (1992).

162. ZPO §271(1) ("*Die Klageschrift ist unverzüglich zuzustellen.*"). See Zöller/Greger, §271, mn. 4. The complaint is to be accompanied by a notice urging the defendant to consult a lawyer if the defendant seriously intends to defend the case. ZPO §271(2).

163. ZPO §270(1).

interpreted, however, as permitting a window for the effectuation of service of approximately 6 weeks after filing. Additional time may be allowed if the delay is not the fault of the plaintiff.[164]

Accompanying the complaint for service is an order from the court addressing several preliminary matters. Typically these orders use pre-printed forms (*Vordrucke*) with applicable provisions or paragraphs indicated by check-marks and relevant dates or times filled in.

If the case is one for which an attorney is required (i.e. any case in the state district court or a family case in the local court), the order will remind the party served of the requirement of representation by counsel.

The remaining provisions of the initial procedural order of the presiding justice depend on whether she has determined that the case should be prepared by preliminary hearing or by written briefs.

If the court has decided that the case should be prepared via a preliminary hearing, the court order served with the complaint[165] will so specify and will set a date for the hearing.[166] The form order will also invite the parties and their counsel to attend, and may also set forth any special matters to be addressed.[167]

The order for a preliminary hearing will inform the defendant that if it contests the complaint, it must respond to the allegations of the complaint and set forth any defenses in a written answer (*Klageerwiderung*) to be filed with the court within a specified time.[168] The written answer may, but is not required to, state any counterclaim (*Widerklage*) the defendant may wish to assert against the plaintiff.[169] In the state district court (*Landgericht*) the defen-

---

164. See ZPO § 167; Zöller/Greger, §167, mn. 10–16.

165. In courts sitting in multi-judge panels, this preliminary action is taken by the presiding judge (*Vorsitzender*), ZPO §272(2).

166. The preliminary hearing is supposed to take place "as soon as possible" ("*so früh wie möglich*"), ZPO §272(3), but generally no sooner than two weeks after service of the complaint, ZPO §274(3).

167. ZPO §274.

168. ZPO §275(1). The time set for the written answer is usually at least two weeks after the time set for the appearance. ZPO §277(3). If no time for the written answer has been set and the answer or the reply has not been filed by the time of the preliminary hearing, the court will set time limits for the filing of these pleadings at the preliminary hearing. ZPO §275(3).

169. For rules of pleading counterclaims and claims against third parties, see Ch. 7(D) above and Ch. 7(J)(4) below. There is no "compulsory counterclaim rule" in Germany. When a party may choose to assert a claim is left to the party. Doctrines of *res adjudicata* or claim preclusion are based on the legal claims which are actually presented for decision, rather than any concept of claims that could have been litigated, but were not. See Ch. 9(F) below on the binding effect of judgments and res adjudicata.

dant will also be required to state any objections to having the case handled by a single judge (*Einzelrichter*) instead of a three-judge panel.[170] The court transmits a copy of the answer to the plaintiff or the plaintiff's lawyer as the case may be.

If the court has determined that the case should be prepared by written proceedings, the court will include with the copy of the complaint to be served on the defendant a summons (*Aufforderung*) requiring the defendant to advise the court by a specified time whether it will contest the complaint,[171] and if so, requiring the defendant to file an answer (*Klageerwiderung*) within an additional specified time period.[172] The summons from the court advises the defendant that failure to file the notification or the answer may result in a default judgment (*Versäumnisurteil*). Copies of the defendant's notification and the answer are served on the plaintiff or the plaintiff's attorney at the request of the court as the case may be.[173]

6. Informal Communication of Litigation Papers

A party or its lawyer is not required to serve all of its more informal communications with the court or other agencies on the opposing party or its counsel. Instead, the party is expected to "informally communicate" (*formlos mitzuteilen*) the document to the other party or its lawyer for information purposes. Most simple briefs and letters to the court are not required to be served formally on the opposing party, but must be simply informally communicated to the opponent.[174]

In most cases such informal communication takes place by simply sending a copy of the document to party or lawyer by ordinary mail or depositing a

170. ZPO §277(1). See Ch. 7(A)(4) and (E)(1).

171. ZPO §276(1). The minimum time is 2 weeks following service of the complaint. In courts in which representation by counsel is required the notification must include the appearance of a qualified attorney, ZPO §276(2). If the defendant is abroad and not represented by counsel admitted to practice in a German court the notification must include the appointment of an agent for the service of process as required by ZPO § 184; see Ch. 7(F)(1)(d).

172. Again, the minimum permissible time period is an additional two weeks after the notification, ZPO §276(1). The summons may also advise the plaintiff, to whom a copy is sent, of the time following receipt of the answer, within which any reply (*Replik*) or response (*Stellungnahme*) to a counterclaim must be filed, ZPO §276(3).

173. ZPO §276(1). In practice these papers are often served "from lawyer to lawyer" (*von Anwalt zu Anwalt*) if the plaintiff is represented by counsel.

174. ZPO §270(1).

copy in the opposing lawyer's courthouse mailbox. Informal communication is similar to service from lawyer to lawyer except that there is no requirement of indicating anything in the document nor is there any provision for acknowledgment of service by the recipient. When the communication is sent by mail it is presumed received on the second business day after being deposited in the mail.[175]

G. Pendency and Its Consequences

With the filing of the complaint in court and service of the complaint on the defendant, the case becomes *sub judice* or legally pending (*rechtshängig*) in court.[176] The claim remains pending until the complaint is withdrawn or dismissed, or until the court's final judgment has been issued. Pendency has certain important consequences. First, while a case is legally pending in one court, the subject matter of the case (*Streitgegenstand*) may not be raised by complaint or otherwise in any other court.[177] Second, the jurisdiction of the court, if originally properly invoked, will not be affected by subsequent changes in circumstances such as a change in residence of a party, decrease in the amount in controversy, and the like.[178] The defense that a claim is already pending in another court can be raised by a party or on the court's own motion, and leads to dismissal of the duplicative claim.[179]

When the second claim is completely duplicative of the first claim, dismissal is based on principles of *res adjudicata*. German law does not permit transfer of related actions among courts of differing subject matter jurisdictions or venues. However related claims pending in the same court may be consolidated for all or a part of ongoing proceedings.[180] In some cases a case related to, but not identical to, a case pending in another court may be stayed pending the outcome of the first case in the interest of judicial economy.[181]

---

175. ZPO §270(2).

176. ZPO §§261(1), 253(1). Additional claims raised during the course of a suit become pending when they are set forth in an oral proceeding in court or in a written pleading containing the elements of a complaint and served on the opposing side. ZPO §261(2).

177. ZPO §261(3)(1).

178. ZPO §261(3)(2). However the expansion of a claim for relief resulting in an increase in the amount in controversy beyond the jurisdictional limit of the local court may require referral of a local court case to the state district court . ZPO §506. See Ch. 5(B)(1) and (F) above.

179. See Jauernig §40(II), p. 162; Stein/Jonas/Schumann, §261, mn. 53 ff.

180. ZPO §147.

181. ZPO §148; Zöller/Greger, §148, mn. 1.

H. Preparation by Preliminary Hearing

The traditional manner by which German judges and lawyers shaped lawsuits for ultimate hearing and determination was by one or a series of preliminary hearings *(frühe erste Termine)* or conferences between parties, counsel and the court. The early preliminary hearing procedure is still followed in cases where the court's initial review of the complaint leads the court to believe that an early meeting of the parties and lawyers might likely lead to a rapid disposition of the case either by settlement or by an early ruling on some dispositive point.[182]

1. Preparation for the Preliminary Hearing

The May 2001 reforms to the Civil Procedure Code have laid more emphasis on the court's and counsel's complementary obligations to prepare in advance so that the preliminary hearing will be fruitful in preparing the case for further dispositive proceedings. Traditionally the court has been expected to identify in advance points or issues which the parties or their counsel would be asked to clarify or supplement at or prior to the hearing. The court has also been empowered to require the parties to be present in person at the preliminary hearing and to produce documents or allow inspection of premises or tangible things in connection with the preliminary proceedings or in anticipation of the plenary hearing.[183] The court could also summons witnesses identified by the parties in their pleadings or invite experts to the preliminary hearing if the court were of the view that their presence would foster efficient preparation of the case for further proceedings and disposition.[184]

The 2001 reforms have reinforced these traditional preparatory measures. Now following the receipt of the defendant's answer the court is also authorized to require third parties to produce relevant documents for the prelimi-

---

182. See Thomas/Putzo/Reichold, §272, mn. 6.

183. ZPO §§273(2)(1)–(3), 358a(2)(5). Such measures can be included either in the order setting the hearing which is served with the complaint on the defendant or in a later order timely issued before the hearing. They may be taken by the presiding judge or another judge designated by the court.

184. See ZPO §§273(2)(4), 358a(2)(4). The court can order the party with the burden of proof to advance the costs of such witnesses or experts. ZPO §§273(3), 379. The court is authorized to summon witnesses only after receipt of the defendant's answer in order to spare third parties potentially unnecessary burden from the litigation.

nary hearing and to order a view of relevant places or things within the control of third parties.[185]

It should be stressed, however, that these measures do not authorize a judge to take evidence of facts not asserted by the parties to litigation. There must be a contested *(streitig)* issue of fact. Although the court can order production of relevant documents and nominate an expert to resolve a contested factual issue, witnesses may not be summoned at any stage of the proceedings unless identified in the submissions of one of the parties.[186]

The extent to which these enlarged powers will be effectively used in preparation of cases by preliminary hearing is yet to be determined.

2. Conduct of the Preliminary Hearing

In earlier times the principle of orality (*Mündlichkeitsprinzip*)[187] required that everything of consequence in a civil law suit be stated orally to the court at a hearing and then summarized by the court and entered in the minutes. This tradition is reflected in the form of pleadings and written submissions which often start with phraseology like,

> "I enter my appearance as attorney for the Plaintiff and request that a hearing be scheduled at which I will request that Defendant be adjudged, . . . etc."[188]

Formerly it was customary for the attorneys to summarize or, even in special circumstances to read their written pleadings at the outset of a hearing. Nowadays the court will generally orally summarize the positions of the parties, incorporating the written submissions wholesale.[189]

Although in most cases the function of the preliminary hearing is to structure the proceeding for final disposition after one or more later hearings, in some cases the preliminary hearing may bring a final disposition. In every case

185. ZPO §§273(2)(5), 142, 144. See Ch. 7(L) below on production of documents and access to factual material.

186. See Musielak/Foerste, §273, Zöller/Greger, §273 mn. 3, 10. See also Ch. 8(C) below on the taking of evidence.

187. See Ch. 6(F)(1) above for a brief discussion of the principle of orality in German civil litigation.

188. *"Ich melde mich als Prozessbevollmächtigter des Klägers und bitte um Anberaumung eines Termins zur mündlichen Verhandlung, in dem ich beantragen werde: 1) Die Beklagte wird verurteilt...*"; see Zeiss, *Zivilprozessrecht*, 9th ed. (1997), p. 325 and ZPO §137(2) and (3).

189. ZPO §§139(1), 278(2)(2).

the preliminary hearing, any later hearings, and the plenary hearing (*Haupttermin*) collectively compose the unitary oral proceedings (*mündliche Verhandlung*) of the case. The record is cumulative, not discrete, and statements of the claims and defensive matters at issue, assertions of fact, stipulations, and resolutions reached at a preliminary hearing will govern proceedings at later hearings as well.[190]

A preliminary hearing may be held in a courtroom or in the chambers of the judge. Usually the parties as well as their counsel will be present. The judge might be assisted by a judicial intern (*Referendar*).[191] The judge orally outlines the issues of the case as disclosed by the pleadings filed to date, and may pose questions to the parties or their counsel in order to clarify unclear assertions of law or fact. The root of the inquiry is "How can this case be disposed of in the most expeditious and fair manner?"

Although settlement has always been a likely subject for discussion at a preliminary hearing, the latest revisions to the Code of Civil Procedure make a settlement conference mandatory before the convening of the preliminary hearing or the plenary oral argument (*Hauptverhandlung*).[192] These required settlement conferences are likely to take place in connection with preliminary hearings.

There may be a good deal of "back and forth" between judge, parties and counsel in an effort to shape the case for settlement or decision, if at all possible at a single plenary hearing. The effort is to eliminate unclarity and narrow the issues in dispute. If the court considers that a party's legal or factual position is unclear or incomplete in some material respect, the court may require the party to provide clarification orally at the hearing or in writing within some specified time period.[193]

Sometimes the result of a preliminary hearing is an agreement on the material facts leaving the only issue a question of law. If it appears that there is a

---

190. See, e.g., Jauernig, §28(IV), p. 110. Most rules governing the conduct of a plenary hearing apply to the preliminary hearing; see Ch. 8(B).

191. A judicial intern is a post graduate law student who has completed the first state examination and is completing a compulsory 2-year professional internship (*Referendariat*) composed of 4–9 month stints with judges, public prosecutors, practicing lawyers, governmental agencies, and (optionally) law firms abroad. See also GVG (*Gerichtsverfassungsgesetz*) §10 and Ch. 4(C)(3) above.

192. ZPO §278(2); see Ch. 7(M) and Ch. 8(B)(4) below on obligatory settlement conferences.

193. ZPO §273(2)(1). See Zöller/Greger, §273, mn. 6 and Ch. 6(C)(2) above for a discussion of the judge's duty to promote clarification and provide hints and feedback in civil cases.

legal issue which will likely dispose of the case, the court may require the parties to file briefs on that legal issue and be prepared to address it orally at a future hearing.

If the discussion at the preliminary hearing reveals that resolution of the case will require determination of disputed facts, the court will address how the facts are to be proved and provide in its minutes of the hearing or a subsequent order for the reception of evidence (*Beweisaufnahme*)[194] usually at a later hearing.[195] The court may also require one or both of the parties or designated third parties to produce documents or tangible things within their possession or control[196] and may initiate a request to public agencies for records or public documents.[197]

During and at the conclusion of the preliminary hearing the judge will create minutes (*Protokoll*)[198] of the proceedings including summaries of the parties' contentions, of any agreements reached, of any hints or feedback (*Hinweise*) from the court, of any interim orders or rulings (*Beschlüsse, Verfügungen*), and the like.[199] Typically the minutes are dictated into a dictating machine during pauses in the hearing and at the conclusion, and transcribed by court clerical personnel promptly thereafter. Parties and counsel listening are invited to suggest additions, corrections or rewordings.[200] The minutes become part of the official court record (*Akte*) and govern further proceedings.[201] Efficient and accurate condensation of the essence of a hearing is an important judicial skill.

The minutes of the preliminary hearing or a later interim ruling or decision issued by the court will constitute a sort of procedural road map to the ultimate determination of the case. In most cases, the goal will be no more

---

194. Stein/Jonas/Leipold, §273, mn. 15; Thomas/Putzo/Reichold, §273, mn. 2. See Ch. 8(C) below for procedures for the taking of proof of facts.

195. In rare cases, for instance if the proof is entirely documentary, it might be received at the preliminary hearing.

196. ZPO §§273(2)(5), 142, 144. See Ch. 7(L) below on preliminary disclosure of documents and proof and Ch. 8(C)(6) below on production of documents as proof in plenary proceedings.

197. ZPO §273(2)(2).

198. The function and importance of the minutes is discussed in greater detail at Ch. 6(D) above.

199. See ZPO §§139(4)(1), 159 and 160 for the requirement of minutes and specification of the contents.

200. Parties or counsel may also suggest revisions, additions or corrections to the minutes promptly following receipt of the transcript after the hearing. ZPO §§160a, 164.

201. E.g. formal mistakes in conducting the hearing can only be proved through the minutes. ZPO §165. See Ch. 6(D)(1) above.

than one further oral hearing for the reception of proof, presentation of oral argument, and reaching a decision.[202]

I. Preparation by Written Proceedings

In recent years the historical oral tradition of German civil procedure has been compromised and partially replaced by increasing use of and reliance on written pleadings and briefs (*Schriftsätze*). Parties may be required to file and exchange written pleadings and briefs to set forth contentions, clarify issues, respond to contentions of the opposing party or to hints from the court, and ultimately argue the law or the facts preparatory to final determination by the court. Since 1976 the ZPO has officially recognized a written preparation procedure as an alternate means to prepare cases for plenary hearing and determination.[203] By now the written preparatory proceeding has become the standard means for preparation of everyday cases in most courts.

If the case is prepared by written proceedings (*schriftliche Vorverfahren*), the parties must be particularly careful to include in their pleadings all of the potentially applicable legal contentions and claims as well as description of all potentially relevant facts and sources of proof. Under the written preparatory procedure, the parties rely on the exchange of their written pleadings and briefs to achieve the clarification and simplification of issues which otherwise occurs at the preliminary hearing.[204] The judge is expected to review the written submissions and to request by written order any necessary clarification from the parties.[205] The give-and-take in written proceedings is necessarily somewhat less spontaneous than that which occurs orally at the preliminary hearing. On the other hand, written exchanges can be more considered and

---

202. Reforms enacted in 1976 designed to expedite German civil litigation make resolution of the case in a single principal oral hearing a procedural priority. See ZPO §272(1); Stein/Jonas/Leipold, §273, mn. 1; Prütting, in: *Münchener Kommentar zur Zivilprozessordnung*, §272, mn. 1; Ch. 2(F), 6(E)(1) and Ch. 7(E)(2) above. There has been some debate as to the effectiveness and constitutionality of this reform, particularly with reference to revised ZPO §296 providing for preclusion of delayed assertions of fact. See, e.g., Jauernig, §28, esp. at (III)(2), p. 106; Federal Constitutional Court, 75 BVerfGE 302 (1987). On the other hand, see Baur/Grunsky, *Zivilprozessrecht*, 11th ed. (2003), mn. 51, 51a; Zuckerman, "Justice in Crisis: Comparative Dimensions of Civil Procedure", in: Zuckerman (ed.) *Civil Justice in Crisis* (1999), p. 31. See also Ch. 7(K) below.

203. ZPO §272(2); Stein/Jonas/Leipold, §273, mn. 1. See Ch. 2(F), Ch. 6(E)(1), Ch. 7(E)(2) above.

204. Thomas/Putzo/Reichold, §276, mn. 1.

205. See Zöller/Greger, §276, mn. 14.

clearly stated than oral assertions at a conference or preliminary hearing. In either case careful preparation under judicial oversight will minimize the risk that a party may appear later on at the plenary hearing and face preclusion of omitted factual or legal contentions.[206]

J. The Defendant's Answer

Regardless of whether the case is prepared by a preliminary hearing or the written procedure, the defendant is required to file a written answer (*Klageerwiderung*) to the factual and legal contentions of the complaint.

> "In the answer the defendant is required to bring forward his means of defense to the extent appropriate to a careful conduct of the proceedings keeping in mind the furtherance of the action at the then stage of proceedings."[207]

This does not mean that the defendant is required to bring forward every conceivable response and defense to the allegations of the complaint. Some discretion should be exercised.[208] If a particular defense or fact becomes relevant or important later in the proceedings, it may usually be raised at the time. On the other hand, the defendant may not withold important legal defenses or factual contentions until a late stage in the proceedings without risking preclusion if the court determines that they should have been raised earlier.[209]

1. Form of Answer

The defendant is expected to set forth fact and legal contentions as well as designations of expected sources of proof in the answer with the same specificity expected of the plaintiff in the complaint.[210] In responding to factual assertions in a complaint or other opposing pleading, parties and their lawyers

---

206. See Ch. 7(K) below for a discussion of the rules of preclusion of factual or legal assertions not timely raised.

207. ZPO §277(1) ("*In der Klageerwiderung hat der Beklagte seine Verteidigungsmittel vorzubringen, soweit es nach der Prozesslage einer sorgfältigen und auf Förderung des Verfahrens bedachten Prozessführung entspricht*").

208. See, e.g., Jauernig, §28(II) and (III)(2), pp. 103, 106; Zöller/Greger, §296, mn. 23; Grunsky, "Die Straffung des Verfahrens durch die Vereinfachungsnovelle", 32 *JZ* 201, 204 (1977).

209. See Ch. 7(K) and Ch. 8(A) below on preclusion of omitted claims and defenses.

210. See ZPO §130.

are admonished to be truthful and complete.[211] If the answer does not specifically deny an allegation in the complaint and indicate a factual basis for the denial, the allegation may be taken as admitted for the purposes of the suit.[212] A party may assert lack of knowledge of the truth or falsity of an opponent's factual allegation only if the facts alleged do not involve that party's own actions or and are not within the party's own scope of knowledge.[213] An answer in a case commenced in a state district court must also state whether the defendant objects to having the matter heard and determined by a single judge and the grounds for such objection.[214]

2. Challenges to the Complaint

The defendant can raise a variety of challenges to the allowability or sufficiency of the complaint.[215] First of all, the defendant's answer may attack the allowability (*Zulässigkeit*) of the complaint and argue that the complaint lacks one of the prerequisites to justiciability (*Prozessvoraussetzungen*) such as apparent jurisdiction, capacity to sue, required representation by counsel, etc. and should be dismissed.[216]

---

211. ZPO §138(1). A party is required to set forth its position with respect to the factual allegations of the opposing party. See ZPO §138(2). If the party charged with the burden of fact allegation does not have detailed knowledge of facts relevant to the case, the other party may be obliged to provide sufficient specification of those detailed facts which occurred in its sphere of knowledge. See Federal Supreme Court, 52 *NJW* 1404 (1999); 52 *NJW* 579 (1999); 50 *NJW* 128 (1997); 43 *NJW* 3151 (1990); Stürner, *Die Aufklärungspflicht der Parteien des Zivilprozesses* (1976), § 10(II), pp. 134 ff.

212. ZPO §138(3). "Facts which are not expressly controverted are to be regarded as admitted, unless the intention to controvert them appears from other statements by the parties" ("*Tatsachen, die nicht ausdrücklich bestritten werden, sind als zugestanden anzusehen, wenn nicht die Absicht, sie bestreiten zu wollen, aus den übrigen Erklärungen der Partei hervorgeht.*"). The court is required to advise the parties if it intends to draw such an inference. ZPO §139(1), see Stein/Jonas/Leipold, §138, mn. 31a.

213. ZPO §138(4). The party has an obligation to inform itself about facts which occurred within its own sphere of knowledge or within that of a subsidiary or other dependent entity. See Federal Supreme Court, 17 *NJW-RR* 612 (2002); 52 *NJW* 53 (1999); 43 *NJW* 453 (1990).

214. ZPO §277(1)(2).

215. See, e.g., Rosenberg/Schwab/Gottwald, §103 (I), p. 586; Jauernig, §43 (III), p. 170.

216. Such a dismissal would be a procedural dismissal (*Prozessabweisung*). See, e.g., Zöller/Greger, Vor §253, mn. 9. Defects which result from inadvertence may often be cured in a supplementary or amended pleading filed in response to the answer or as a result of a hint (*Hinweis*) from the court. ZPO §139(3). See Ch. 6 (C)(2)(e) above.

Or the defendant's answer may address the merits of the claim and assert that the claim is legally insufficient (*unschlüssig*) even assuming that the facts asserted are true. The answer can also assert that the facts as alleged in the complaint are untrue, or that there are additional facts which undermine the validity of the legal or factual basis of the claim. An answer may include both defenses of legal insufficiency and defenses based on disputes of fact as alternative grounds for dismissal.[217]

If the party asserts that the complaint lacks legal sufficiency, the facts alleged by the plaintiff are taken as true for the purpose of the defense. The answer argues why legally the facts asserted by the complaint fail to set forth a legally cognizable claim.

If the defendant contests the facts alleged, the answer must specifically deny the facts as controverted and gives the defendant's version of the relevant facts.[218] If the defendant asserts that there are additional facts which cast the allegations of the plaintiff in a different light and thus affect the legal sufficiency of the claim[219] those facts must be alleged with the same specificity as would be required in a complaint. Factual assertions in the answer, whether denying or supplementing those of the plaintiff, must be specific and accompanied by identification of the source of proof for those assertions.[220] In most cases the burden of alleging (and proving) the facts necessary to sustain a claim rests with the plaintiff.[221]

3. Affirmative Defenses and Setoffs

Some matters of legal sufficiency will be considered only if raised by the defendant. Prominent among these is the statute of limitations (*Verjährung*). If the defendant does not raise this defense in the answer, it will be considered waived, unless the court allows it to be raised at a later stage of the proceedings.[222] Other defects such as lack of capacity to sue may be raised or noticed by the court *sua sponte* at any stage of the proceedings.[223]

---

217. See Baur/Grunsky, §7(II)(2)(b)(cc), mn. 133; Rosenberg/Schwab/Gottwald, §103(I), p. 586.

218. There is no such thing as a "general denial" in German civil procedure. The degree of specificity required in a denial depends on the degree of specificity with which the facts are alleged in the complaint. See Zöller/Greger, §138, mn. 8a and Ch. 7(J)(1) above.

219. See Rosenberg/Schwab/Gottwald, §104(II)(2), p. 589.

220. ZPO §130(5).

221. See Ch. 8(C)(2) below on the burden of proof.

222. ZPO §§282(1)(3), 296(2)(3); Rosenberg/Schwab/Gottwald, §96(II), p. 537.

223. See Rosenberg/Schwab/Gottwald, §96(V)(2), p. 538.

A defendant's answer may raise matters of set-off (*Aufrechnung*) as well as counterclaims (*Widerklage*). A party may raise by way of setoff virtually any mature claim against the opposing party, regardless of whether the set-off claim is factually or legally related to the claim in chief.[224] Often set-offs are raised as alternative defenses. For example, the defendant may deny that a debt claimed by the plaintiff ever existed and simultaneously plead its own claim against the plaintiff as a set-off against any debt found to be due.

Setoffs present a variety of legal and procedural problems. While territorial jurisdictional limits and amount-in-controversy thresholds generally do not apply to claims in set-off, an opposing claim outside a court system's specialized jurisdiction (*Rechtswegfremd*) generally may not be pled as a set-off.[225] So, for instance, if a defendant in a case pending in the state district court (*Landgericht*) seeks to setoff a claim cognizable only by the administrative court (*Verwaltungsgericht*), the proper remedy is to seek a stay of the district court case pending a decision on the claim in the administrative court.[226]

In a case where the set-off is not factually or legally related to the plaintiff's claim, the court can order that the validity of the setoff be determined in a separate plenary hearing in the interest of avoiding undue delay or complication of the case in chief.[227] The court can then go ahead and enter a provisional judgment (*Vorbehaltsurteil*) on the plaintiff's claim, subject to later determination of the set-off.[228]

224. See BGB §387; Lüke, *Zivilprozessrecht*, §20(III), mn. 227.

225. See, e.g., Stein/Jonas/Leipold, §145, mn. 33; Zöller /Greger, §145, mn. 19a; German Federal Supreme Court, 16 BGHZ 124 (1955). See, however, Rosenberg/Schwab/Gottwald, §105(IV)(6), p. 598, criticizing this rule and suggesting that set-offs should be determined in the court hearing the principal claim, regardless of what court ordinarily would decide claims of that type. See also Baur/Grunsky, §11(I)(3), mn. 135; Jauernig/Stürner, *Bürgerliches Gesetzbuch*, 10th ed. (2002), §387, mn. 23; Schenke/Rutbig, "Die Aufrechnung mit rechtswegfremden Forderungen im Prozess", 45 *NJW* 2505 (1992); Ch. 5(A) and (C)(3) above.

226. See Zöller/Greger, §145, mn. 19a; Lüke, *Zivilprozessrecht*, §20(III), mn. 227; Rosenberg/Schwab/Gottwald, §105(IV)(6).

227. ZPO §145(III); Stein/Jonas/Leipold, §145, mn. 64; Rosenberg/Schwab/Gottwald, §105(IV)(5), p. 598.

228. ZPO §§145(III), 302. Judgments are discussed in greater detail in Ch. 9 below.

4. Counterclaims

A counterclaim (*Widerklage*) seeks relief against the plaintiff that may exceed or differ from the relief requested in the complaint.[229] The counterclaim must seek something other than the mere denial of the plaintiff's claim and therefor constitute its own legal subject matter (*Streitgegenstand*) outside the legal subject matter of the plaintiff's claim.[230] If the counterclaim is factually or legally related to the plaintiff's claim the venue for the complaint also applies for the counterclaim.[231]

It is still somewhat unclear whether there is any general requirement that a counterclaim bear a legal or factual relationship to the claims asserted in the complaint.[232] Currently the prevailing view of the commentators is that no such relationship is required unless the counterclaimant is relying on ZPO §33 to provide proper venue for a matter otherwise not subject to suit in the judicial district in which the complaint was filed.[233]

There is no particular time limit for the raising of a counterclaim, provided that the action is still pending and the plenary hearing has not been concluded.[234] However, if the claim becomes ready for decision before the coun-

---

229. The question of whether the counterclaim seeks relief in excess or different from the relief requested in the complaint is not always a clear one. See, e.g., Lüke, *Zivilprozessrecht*, §20(V), mn. 237.

230. A claim within the legal subject matter of the plaintiff's claim would be determined by the judgment on the plaintiff's claim. See, e.g., Musielak/Schmid, §33, mn. 8; Zöller/Vollkommer, §33, mn. 7.

231. See Ch. 5(C)(3) above and ZPO §33. For a detailed discussion whether a merely factual relation is sufficient see Stein/Jonas/Schumann, §33, mn. 17 f.; Lüke, *Zivilprozessrecht*, §20, mn. 236, 237; Jauernig, §46(II), p. 181. A state district court can consider an unrelated counterclaim which otherwise would fall below its jurisdictional minimum. However if the case is pending in the local court (*Amtsgericht*), and a counterclaim increases the amount in controversy above the jurisdictional limit of that court, the case must be transferred to the appropriate district court. See ZPO §506(I) and Ch. 5(B)(1) above.

232. Older case law appeared to require some sort of legal or factual relationship in all cases. See e.g. German Federal Supreme Court, 40 BGHZ 185, 187 (1964); 28 *NJW* 1228 (1975).

233. See Musielak/Schmid, §33, mn. 2; Zöller/Vollkommer, §33, mn. 1; Stein/Jonas/Schumann, §33, mn. 6 ff.; Jauernig, §46(II), p. 181; but see Rosenberg/Schwab/Gottwald, §98(II)(2)(d), p. 554. For venue by connection see further Ch. 5(C)(3) above.

234. See ZPO §296a; Zöller/Vollkommer, §33, mn. 9; Jauernig, §46(III), p. 182. ZPO §§282, 296 are not applicable to counterclaims. See, e.g., Zöller/Greger, §282, mn. 2a; Prütting, in: *Münchener Kommentar zur Zivilprozessordnung*, §296, mn. 40 ff.; Stein/Jonas/Leipold, §296, mn. 39; Rosenberg/Schwab/Gottwald, §98(II)(2), p. 553.

terclaim, a partial judgment may be rendered on the claim.[235] A counterclaim can join parties other than the original plaintiff as defendants on the counterclaim provided that such parties are within the territorial jurisdiction of the court.[236] Although not expressly sanctioned by the ZPO, various forms of contingent counterclaims can be asserted.[237]

K. Amendment of the Pleadings

German law is liberal in permitting parties to raise additional defenses and new legal and factual contentions until a late stage in the proceedings, but rather strict in regulating changes in the essential claims for relief (*Anträge)* as asserted in the complaint or counterclaim. This apparent inconsistency is related to the role of the claims as determining the legal subject matter of the proceeding (*Streitgegenstand*), which in turn defines the scope of legal pendency (*Rechtshängigkeit*) and *res adjudicata* (*materielle Rechtskraft*).[238]

1. Change in Assertions or Evidence Supporting or Opposing Claims for Relief

Written pleadings and assertions in support of the basic claims for relief or in defense against these claims can be amended and supplemented by later pleadings and briefs and by oral statements at hearings.[239] To the extent such supplementing and amending material is clarification of previous assertions in the complaint, or merely supports or implements the legal claims set forth in the complaint, it is generally received.[240]

---

235. ZPO §301(1). See Zöller/Greger, §33, mn. 9; Ch. 9(B)(1) below.

236. The ZPO has no provision expressly authorizing such joinder, but the German Federal Supreme Court has judicially sanctioned counterclaims joining third parties under condition that satisfy the requirements for an amendment of the claim, either agreement by the defendant or necessity in the interests of justice. 40 BGHZ 185 (1963); 131 BGHZ 76, 79 (1995). See Zöller/Vollkommer, §33, mn.18 ff.; Lüke, *Zivilprozessrecht*, §20, mn. 239; Zeiss, §54(II), mn. 406. See Ch. 7(B) above on joinder of parties and Ch. 7(K)(2) below on amendment of claims.

237. See, e.g., Federal Supreme Court, 21 BGHZ 13 (1956); 132 BGHZ 390, 397 ff. (1996); Zöller/Vollkommer, §33, mn. 26; Lüke, *Zivilprozessrecht*, §20, mn. 238.

238. See Ch. 9(F) below for a discussion of claims preclusion by prior judgment.

239. These are documented in the minutes of the hearing.

240. Indeed, such material can even be received when the case is on second instance appeal (*Berufung*). See Ch. 10(D)(2) below.

Parties are abjured to

> bring forward factual and legal material supporting claims and defenses, especially assertions, contraventions, objections, evidence and arguments on evidence as is appropriate to the state of the case and to a careful conduct of the litigation with a view to expedition of the proceeding.[241]

If the court believes that new assertions or material raised by either party should have been raised at an earlier point in the proceedings, and that consideration of the new material would delay the completion of the plenary hearing and disposition of the proceeding, the court can rule that the party is precluded from raising the new matter.[242] In ruling on the allowability of factual or legal assertions proffered at a late stage of the proceeding the court must strike a balance between competing policies. On the one hand requiring the parties to bring forward all of their potential contingent claims, defenses, and factual and legal materials at a single early point in the proceedings reduces the risk of unexpected delay or protraction of the proceedings from the introduction of new matter at a later stage in the proceedings.[243] On the other hand, economy in judicial proceedings is also fostered by a policy which permits the parties to withhold contingent and alternative claims, defenses and factual material in favor of concentrating on the primary claims and issues of the case without fear of being precluded from raising these other matters should it be come necessary to do so at a later time. The current balance between these policies is referred to as the principle of concentration *(Konzentrationsmaxime)* and is embodied in ZPO §296(1)–(3) in the following terms:

241. ZPO §282(1) ("*Jede Partei hat in der mündlichen Verhandlung ihre Angriffs- und Verteidigungsmittel, insbesondere Behauptungen, Bestreiten, Einwendungen, Beweismittel und Beweiseinreden so zeitig vorzubringen, wie es nach der Prozesslage einer sorgfältigen und auf Förderung des Verfahrens bedachten Prozessführung entspricht.*").

242. ZPO §296(2). See, e.g., Zöller/Greger, §296, mn. 26 and 8b ff.; Stein/Jonas/Leipold, §296, mn. 93 ff.

243. This policy is referred to as the principle of alternative pleading *(Eventualmaxime)*. Early reforms attempted to structure civil proceedings in stages, such as pleading claims, pleading defenses, proof, etc. In each stage each party was supposed to bring forward all potential claims, defenses, proof, etc. even if contingent. This system, which came from the old "common procedure" *(gemeiner Prozess)*, was abandoned because of its cumbersomeness. See Jauernig, §28(III)(1), p. 106; Schulte, *Die Entwicklung der Eventualmaxime* (1980); Ch. 2 (C) above.

(1) Means of prosecuting or defending a case which are first brought forward after the expiration of a deadline established therefore... may only be allowed, if according to the independent conviction of the court their allowance will not delay the determination of the case or if the parties have sufficient excuse for the lateness.

(2) Means of prosecuting or defending a case, which contrary to §282(1) are not timely brought forward or which contrary to §282(2) are not timely communicated to the opposing party may be disallowed if according to the independent conviction of the court their allowance would delay determination of the law suit and the lateness is the result of gross negligence.

(3) Delayed objections which address the allowability of the complaint, and which are waivable by the defendant, may only be allowed if the defendant has sufficient excuse for the delay.[244]

Traditionally German courts were very liberal in allowing late submission of factual or legal material to bolster a claim or defense. The standard set forth in ZPO § 296 above represents a legislative narrowing of this traditional liberality in an effort to reduce delay in German civil litigation.[245]

---

244. *(1) Angriffs- und Verteidigungsmittel, die erst nach Ablauf einer hierfür gesetzten Frist... vorgebracht werden, sind nur zuzulassen, wenn nach der freien Überzeugung des Gerichts ihre Zulassung die Erledigung des Rechtsstreits nicht verzögern würde oder wenn die Partei die Verspätung genügend entschuldigt.*

(2) Angriffs- und Verteidigungsmittel, die entgegen §282 Abs. 1 nicht rechtzeitig vorgebracht oder entgegen §282 Abs. 2 nicht rechtzeitig mitgeteilt werden, können zurückgewiesen werden, wenn ihre Zulassung nach der freien Überzeugung des Gerichts die Erledigung des Rechtsstreits verzögern würde und die Verspätung auf grober Nachlässigkeit beruht.

(3) Verspätete Rügen, die die Zulässigkeit der Klage betreffen und auf die der Beklagte verzichten kann, sind nur zuzulassen, wenn der Beklagte die Verspätung genügend entschuldigt.

245. Some courts and commentators believe that the standard set by ZPO § 296 and the preclusions resulting from application of that standard risk violating the constitutional right to judicial hearing (*rechtliches Gehör*). For a brief discussion of this issue see Jauernig, §28(III)(2), p. 106; Zöller/Greger, §296, mn. 2. The Federal Constitutional Court has suggested that §296 preclusions not be imposed in cases where the court itself has delayed the proceeding because of insufficient judicial clarification and case management. See 44 *NJW* 2373 (1990); 51 *NJW* 2044 (1998). There is some dispute as to what constitutes delay of the proceedings for the purpose of imposing preclusions. Some maintain that there is delay whenever it appears that admitting the new defense likely will mean that the proceeding will take longer than it would have had the defense been omitted (absolute standard). Others assert that there is relevant delay only if the admission of the defense at the time proposed would make the proceeding take longer than it would have had the defendant

2. Amendment of the Claims for Relief

Amendment of the essential claims for relief in the complaint or counterclaim (*Klageänderung*) is another matter. Once the complaint has been accepted by the court and is considered pending (*rechtshängig*), new claims for relief (*Anträge*) which change the subject matter of the proceeding (*Streitgegenstand*) may be added only under limited conditions. The defendant should have some assurance of what it is faced with before it tenders a defense. The claims for relief of the complaint define the extent of the bar that pendency of a case raises to the initiation of other proceedings. The subject matter of the lawsuit as defined by the claims of the complaint (or counterclaim) is important to application of the doctrine of *res adjudicata*. The essential claims for relief in the complaint cannot be a "moving target".[246]

The basic rule is that the legal claims raised by a pending complaint may be amended only if the defendant agrees to the amendment, or if the court determines that the amendment is necessary in the interests of justice.[247] As suggested above, the ZPO makes clear that changes or additions to factual or legal material in support of the claims are not to be considered amendments of the complaint.[248] It is also permissible to expand or restrict the amount of relief sought, so long as the basic cause of action is not affected.[249] And, if dur-

---

brought the defense forward at an earlier stage of the proceeding (relative standard). The Federal Supreme Court generally uses an absolute standard. The Federal Constitutional Court has affirmed the constitutionality of preclusions based on the absolute standard unless it is clearly evident that the determination of the case would have been delayed even if the party had brought forward the material at an earlier stage of the proceeding. See Federal Supreme Court, 86 BGHZ 31 (1983); 75 BGHZ 138 (1980); Federal Constitutional Court, 75 BVerfGE 302 (1987); 48 *NJW* 1417 (1995); Zöller/Greger, §296, mn. 19 ff.; Stein/Jonas/Leipold, §296, mn. 48 ff.

246. See, e.g., Lüke, *Zivilprozessrecht*, §15(II), mn. 161; Jauernig, §41, p. 163; Rosenberg/Schwab/Gottwald, §101, p. 572; Musielak/Foerste, §263, mn. 1.

247. ZPO §263 ("*Nach dem Eintritt der Rechtshängigkeit ist eine Änderung der Klage zulässig, wenn der Beklagte einwilligt oder das Gericht sie für sachdienlich erachtet*"). An amendment would generally be considered necessary in the interest of justice if it contributed to determining related matters in the same suit. See, e.g., Rosenberg/Schwab/Gottwald, §101(II)(2), p. 575 ; Zöller/Greger, §263, mn. 13; Stein/Jonas/Schumann, §263, mn. 12. For example, the court would likely allow amendment of a claim for unlawful exclusion of a member of a business association to include wrongful withdrawal of authority to act in behalf of the association. On the other hand, if the initial claim had been mere wrongful withdrawal of authority, an amendment to include wrongful exclusion might be less likely, since such a change would materially alter the subject matter of the litigation.

248. ZPO §264(1).

249. ZPO §264(2).

ing the pendency of the cause of action the circumstances of the claim itself change, the complaint may be amended to reflect these changed circumstances.[250] Frequently defendants consent to amendments of complaints which change the subject matter of cases in the interest of avoiding having to defend additional lawsuits.[251] Even if the defendant does not consent, if the prompt and efficient determination of all legally or factually related controversies between the parties would be served, an amendment to the complaint can be allowed by the court in the interest of justice.[252]

L. Production of Documents and Access to Proof in Preparatory Proceedings

German civil procedure does not know the kind of "pretrial discovery" practiced by parties and their counsel in American and English litigation. On the other hand, German civil procedure does provide for considerable production and exchange of factual information, especially documents, during the preparatory phases of the litigation prior to the taking of evidence in the plenary hearing. The practical effect of these activities is in many respects similar to that fulfilled by Anglo-American discovery, although the formal purposes of the activity may be somewhat different.

First of all, it should be kept in mind that parties are expected to make specific reference to sources of evidence in their pleadings, and to attach relevant documents whenever feasible.[253] Names and addresses of witnesses are to be included to the extent then known. Parties are also expected routinely to identify, produce and exchange all documents on which they intend to rely as proof of any matter of fact in the case. Parties may base their own claims on identified documents in the possession of their opponents and request their opponents to produce those documents to enable them to meet

---

250. ZPO §264(3). For instance if the plaintiff originally sued the defendant for the return of an automobile or other chattel, and the subject chattel was damaged or destroyed during the pendency of the suit, the plaintiff would be permitted to amend the complaint to assert a claim for money damages in lieu of the chattel. See, Zöller/Greger, §264, mn. 5; Rosenberg/Schwab/Gottwald, §101(I)(3)(c), p. 575; Lüke, *Zivilprozessrecht*, §15(II), mn. 171.

251. This might result in avoidance of having to pay another filing fee and another set of lawyer's fees.

252. ZPO §263. See, e.g., German Federal Supreme Court, 38 *NJW* 1841 (1985); Stein/Jonas/Schumann, §263, mn. 12; Rosenberg/Schwab/Gottwald, §101(II)(2)(b), p. 576.

253. See Ch. 7(A)(4) above.

their burdens of proof.[254] Parties can also ask their opponents to provide them with any known names and addresses of witnesses identified by either party as a source of likely evidence.[255] To the extent that a party's assertion of fact in a pleading is unclear, the opposing party may request that it be clarified.

In most cases these inter-party requests are made informally and complied with voluntarily. In the event of noncompliance, the party seeking the information may ask the court to order that it be provided. In most cases the court can also order production of this kind of information on its own motion.[256]

During the course of preparatory proceedings a party may also ask the court to appoint an expert witness on a particular issue of fact,[257] to request production of public documents by public agencies,[258] or to order third parties to produce identified documents in their possession.[259] Upon application of a party, the court may order third parties to give written answers to questions relevant to factual issues in the case.[260] Finally, on application of a party or on its own motion the court may make an inspection of premises or things[261] or order a medical examination of a party during the preparatory phase of the proceedings.[262]

The principal differences between American "discovery" and the development and clarification of factual assertions and sources of proof during preparatory proceedings in Germany appear to be:

a. There is greater participation by the judge in Germany, and less direct "party to party" interaction than is the case in the United States.

---

254. See ZPO §§421 ff. and ZPO §142.

255. See Federal Supreme Court, 13 *NJW* 821 (1960); 49 *NJW* 779, 780 f. (1996); 132 BGHZ 47, 50 f. (1996); Musielak/Foerste, §286, mn. 66; Stürner, *Die Aufklärungspflicht der Parteien des Zivilprozesses* (1976), p. 136.

256. See ZPO §§273(2), 141–144; Stürner, *Die richterliche Aufklärung im Zivilprozess* (1982), mn. 11, 71 ff.; for a description of the development of the judges' responsibility to take evidence *ex officio* see Peters, *Richterliche Hinweispflichten und Beweisinitiativen im Zivilprozess* (1983), pp. 12, 33, 47, 65, 92 ff.

257. ZPO §§144, 273(1).

258. ZPO §273(2)(2).

259. ZPO §§142, 273(2)(5).

260. ZPO 377(3); see Stadler, "Schriftliche Zeugenaussage und pre-trial discovery im deutschen Zivilprozess", 110 *ZZP* 137 (1997).

261. ZPO §§144, 273(2)(5).

262. See Supreme Court of the German Empire, 60 *RGZ* 147 (1904); Federal Supreme Court, 9 *VersR* 768 (1958); 25 *NJW* 1131 (1972); Stürner, *Die Aufklärungspflicht der Parteien des Zivilprozesses*, pp. 140 ff. For further details on the German evidentiary procedure see Ch. 7(L)(1) and (2) and Ch. 8(C) below.

b. In Germany there is ordinarily no oral examination of witnesses during the preparatory phases of the proceeding; if a witness is examined, it is always the judge who conducts the questioning.
c. The purpose of fact development during the preparatory phases of German litigation is somewhat different from the purpose of Anglo-American discovery. Discovery is aimed at informing parties and their counsel of relevant facts to prevent later surprise and help them prepare for a later trial at which the facts will be presented to the court. In Germany factual material provided to the court and parties during preparatory proceedings generally need not be adduced later on, and may, without more, be referred to by the parties and used by the court as the basis for argument and decision.

It also should be said that the scope of relevance of factual material produced both during the preparatory phase and during proceedings for the reception of evidence is somewhat narrower in Germany than in the United States.[263] In this sense the current state of affairs in Germany resembles recent developments in England, where pretrial production is governed by a more or less strict relevance standard, and material produced may be used as evidence without the need for later formal offer at trial.[264]

1. Production of Documents and Tangible Evidence

In Germany party and court access to third party private documents and tangible proof was traditionally quite limited. There was no right to compel production of such materials merely based on their relevance to some issue in a pending suit. A litigant seeking a document or thing in the possession of another party or a third party could obtain it only if the person with the document or thing was willing to produce it voluntarily or if she had an independent substantive right to possession or access.[265] In the case of a third party the litigant was required to proceed in an independent action against the third party to seek a turnover of the document or thing in question and the litiga-

263. See Materials of the German House of Representatives, *BT-Drucks.* 14/6036, p. 120.

264. See Stürner, "Transnational Civil Procedure: Discovery and Sanctions Against Non-Compliance", 2001 *Uniform Law Review* 871, 874 ff.

265. See ZPO §§422 f., 429(1). The latter was the entirety of this section before the May 2001 reforms.

tion in chief (*Hauptprozess*) would be stayed to allow the party reasonable opportunity to procure the proof.[266]

While stopping far short of the broad form of American "discovery", the 2001 reforms to the Civil Procedure Code have introduced new provisions requiring production of documents and other things by parties and third parties both at the preparatory and the plenary phases of civil cases. These new provisions may lead to some expansion of the access of parties and the court to factual material both at the preparatory and the evidentiary phases of civil proceedings.

The 2001 reforms have expanded the power of the court to order production of documents by parties and have given the courts for the first time the authority to order third parties to produce documents based solely on their potential relevance to the pending legal proceedings. The 2001 reforms amended Section 142 of the Civil Procedure Code to provide:

> The court can order that a party or a third party produce documents and other attachments in its possession to which a party has made reference. The court can set a time period for such production and can order that the documents produced shall remain at the court clerk's office for a period of time specified by the court.[267]

There is no express statutory threshold of relevance. The new statutory provision simply requires that a party have "made reference" to the document as evidence in a pleading or brief filed with the court. However the court must assess the relevance of any such document under the standards applicable to proof in general when issuing such orders.[268] If the court views the designated document as irrelevant, the court will not order production.

---

266. See ZPO § 431. This restrictive approach was based on the 19th Century liberalist concept that litigants should not be permitted to burden third parties with their dispute.

267. ZPO §142(1) ("*Das Gericht kann anordnen, dass eine Partei oder ein Dritter die in ihrem oder seinem Besitz befindlichen Urkunden und sonstigen Unterlagen, auf die sich eine Partei bezogen hat, vorlegt. Das Gericht kann hierfür eine Frist setzen sowie anordnen, dass die vorgelegten Unterlagen während einer von ihm zu bestimmenden Zeit auf der Geschäftstelle verbleiben*").

268. The statute says that the court "can" (*kann*) require a party or third party to produce documents. The statute contemplates that the documents produced will serve as evidence. There is no relaxed standard of relevance of such material as is the case with American discovery proceedings. See Hannich/Meyer-Seitz, *ZPO-Reform* (2002), § 142, mn. 8; Thomas/Putzo/Reichold, § 142, mn. 1; for a more generous approach Zöller/Greger, § 142, mn. 1 and 2; Musielak/Stadler, § 142, mn. 1.

The statute is silent as to the procedure to be employed in seeking an order requiring production of a document by party or a third party.[269] Presumably if the document were referred to in a party's complaint, answer, or other important pleading or brief and appeared to be of significance to the court upon reading the pleading, the court could on its own motion issue a procedural order to the party or third party that the document be produced.[270] If the court failed to order production of a document on its own motion, a party could move the court for an order of production. Such a motion (*Antrag*) would likely have to contain the same kinds of information statutorily required for an order of production of documentary proof by the opposing party.[271] One would anticipate, in particular, a requirement that the motion include a description of the importance of the document as proof of contested issues of relevant fact.

The statute protects the third party from having to produce documents to the extent that such production would be unreasonable (*nicht zumutbar*) or that the documents are protected by a statutory witness privilege. The procedures for claim of privilege and determination of such claims by the court are incorporated by reference.[272] If the document is in a foreign language, the court can order that it be translated.[273]

It should be noted that the documents are to be produced to the court, not directly to a party or its counsel. However if the documents are in the possession of the court they are accessible to the parties and their lawyers as well as those others given access to the record (*Akteneinsicht*).[274]

---

269. See Musielak/Stadler, §142, mn. 7 and 8; very critical Schellhammer, "Zivilprozessreform und erste Instanz", 55 *MDR* 1081, 1084 (2001). The new provision does specifically provide that the court can set a time period for the production to take place as well as a time period for the documents to remain at the clerk's office.

270. See Ch. 8 (C)(6) below on the power of the court to order on its own motion production of documents by parties as proof in plenary proceedings.

271. See Ch. 8 (C)(6) below on production of documents and other proof in connection with plenary proceedings. ZPO §§421–425 set forth the procedure for obtaining production of documents in the possession of the opposing party. ZPO §428 now authorizes a party to move for an order of production against third parties pursuant to ZPO §142.

272. ZPO §§142(2), 386–390; see Ch. 8(C)(10).

273. ZPO §142(3)(1). However the third party cannot be ordered to provide the translation. ZPO §142(3)(2).

274. See ZPO §299 which authorizes parties and their counsel to view and make copies of portions of the official case record (*Akte*). Non-parties are given access to the record only under limited circumstances. See Ch. 6(D)(3) above. As a matter of practice copies of documents produced by a party are sent automatically to the opposing party or its counsel.

2. Access to Objects and Premises for Examination

The 2001 reforms also expand the court's ability to order parties and third parties to produce or allow access to objects and premises for the purpose of obtaining proof by observation and examination (*Augenscheinbeweis*).[275] This includes both the production of things that can be produced and the allowance of examination of things such as premises that cannot be produced. The examination can be by the court directly or by an expert witness appointed by the court.

To the extent that the court can order the reception of proof by examination on its own motion, presumably the court could act on its own motion to enter an order against a party or third party. Otherwise a party can move that the court receive the proof and enter the appropriate order requiring the party or third party to cooperate. Third parties are not required to cooperate if the request is "unreasonable" (*nicht zumutbar*) or if they are protected by privileges.[276]

German civil procedure does not expressly authorize an order compelling any person to submit to a physical examination other than in paternity cases.[277] However a party who refuses to submit to a physical examination when such an examination would be highly relevant to a significant issue in the case risks an adverse inference by the court.[278] German courts cannot order physical examinations of third persons in ordinary civil litigation.[279]

---

275. ZPO §144 (as amended by May 2001 reform). See Ch. 8(C)(4) below for a discussion of proof by observation and examination of persons and things in plenary proceedings.

276. ZPO §144(2). The procedure for determining claims of privilege is incorporated by reference. See Ch. 8(C)(10) below. *Parties* are not protected from making production or giving access by any requirement of reasonableness or reference to privileges. If the court is convinced that a party is refusing access without reasonable grounds the court can draw an unfavorable inference on the likely results of such inspection based on the refusal. See ZPO §427; Musielak/Stadler, §§142, mn. 7, 144, mn. 8; Zöller/Greger, §§142, mn. 4, 144, mn. 4.

277. See ZPO §372a; Stein/Jonas/Chr.Berger, Vor §371, mn. 34.

278. See, e.g., Federal Supreme Court, 25 *NJW* 1131 (1972), where an adverse inference was drawn from a party's refusal to submit to an examination of its mental health status. However, this raises the constitutional question of whether such an inference is possible without a clear statutory basis. See Damrau, in: *Münchener Kommentar zur Zivilprozessordnung*, §371, mn. 7 ff. and especially Stürner, *Die Aufklärungspflicht der Parteien des Zivilprozesses* (1976), pp. 92 ff. and 140 ff.

279. This restraint appears to have been preserved in the 2001 reforms, which make no mention of examination of persons. See Materials of the German House of Representatives, *BT-Drucks.* 14/6036, p. 120 speaking of a "gently" increased duty of third persons.

By their terms these new provisions authorizing orders of production and access against parties and third parties appear to be aimed at expanding the court's access to evidence in plenary proceedings to decide issues of fact rather than providing access to factual material at an earlier stage of the proceedings. But as mentioned above, one must also consider the provisions expanding the court's authority to receive documentary evidence and proof by examination of premises and things at any stage of the proceedings.[280] Taken together these provisions not only expand the power of the court to obtain evidence and information from parties and third parties, they also provide for such activity at an early stage of the proceedings.[281] It can be inferred that the legislative intent may have been to give the court and parties access to fact information at an earlier stage of the proceedings to foster a more thorough preparation for plenary dispositive proceedings. In this sense the new provisions seem to be playing a role somewhat similar to that played by party discovery in Anglo-American procedure, although their scope is narrower because of the requirement of actual, rather than merely potential, relevance of the documents or things sought.[282]

M. Mandatory Settlement Conferences

Settlement has always been a high priority in German civil justice. The Civil Procedure Code has long required the civil court to "be mindful of a compromise settlement of the dispute or particular issues at all stages of the suit".[283] Traditionally German judges have raised the prospect of settlement whenever they have deemed such discussions likely to be productive, generally at the plenary hearing, in both first-instance and appeals cases.[284] The active role of

280. See ZPO §273(2)(5) and Ch. 7(H)(1) above.

281. See Ch. 8(C) below for a discussion of reception of evidence at plenary hearing and evidentiary proceedings in connection with plenary proceedings.

282. For a more detailed discussion of discovery problems see Stürner, *Die Aufklärungspflicht der Parteien des Zivilprozesses* (1976); Stadler, *Der Schutz des Unternehmensgeheimnisses im deutschen und U.S.-amerikanischen Zivilprozess und im Rechtshilfeverfahren* (1989); Junker, *Discovery im deutsch-amerikanischen Rechtsverkehr* (1987); Schlosser, "Die lange deutsche Reise in die prozessuale Moderne", 46 *JZ* 599 (1991); Katzenmeier, "Aufklärungs-/Mitwirkungspflichten der nicht beweisbelasteten Partei im Zivilprozess", 57 *JZ* 533 (2002).

283. ZPO §278(1) ("*... soll in jeder Lage des Verfahrens auf eine gütliche Beilegung des Rechtstreits oder einzelner Streitpunkte bedacht sein*"). See also Jauernig, §1(IV), p. 4; Musielak/Foerste, §278, mn. 1; Zöller/Greger, §278, mn. 1.

284. See Ch. 11(I)(1) below on case settlement in general and Ch. 8(B)(4) below on settlement discussions in plenary proceedings.

the German judge in promoting settlement has been seen as one of the reasons that to date there has been relatively little development of out of court ADR practice in Germany.[285]

On the other hand, in recent years the proportion of cases resolved in Germany before first instance judgment has tended to lag behind that of other jurisdictions such as the United Kingdom and the United States.[286] As a result of a perception of the somewhat lower percentage of cases resolved without a first-instance judgment as "unsatisfactory" (*unbefriedigend*), the 2001 reforms have reinforced and formalized the role of settlement facilitation in German civil procedure.[287]

The newly reformed Civil Procedure Code introduces the requirement of a formal "settlement conference" (*Güteverhandlung*) before the commencement of any oral preliminary or plenary proceedings in all civil cases unless such a settlement conference "appears clearly futile".[288] Such a settlement conference can take place in connection with any preliminary hearing in a case being prepared by preliminary hearing, at the same day the plenary hearing is scheduled but before the plenary hearing is opened, or at another date scheduled by the court before commencement of the plenary hearing.[289] The

285. Gottwald, "Civil Justice Reform: Access, Cost, and Expedition. The German Perspective", in: Zuckerman (ed.) *Civil Justice in Crisis* (1999), p. 230; Schütze, Alternative Streitschlichtung, 97 *ZvglRwiss* 117, 121 ff. (1998); Murray, "ADR und die amerikanische Justiz", in: Gottwald (ed.) *Aktuelle Entwicklung des europäischen und internationalen Zivilverfahrensrechts* (2002), pp. 25 ff.

286. It is estimated that over 90% of civil cases in Great Britain are settled prior to judgment. In the United States this figure is over 95%. In Germany the proportion of cases in the ordinary courts which are not resolved by contested judgment hovers around the 70% level. See Statistical Yearbook for the Federal Republic of Germany 2002, p. 342. The causes, as well as the benefits, of the very high ratios of cases resolved without a contested judgment in Anglo-American jurisdictions are the subject matter of considerable debate. See, e.g., Galanter/Cahill, "Most Cases Settle...", 46 *Stanford Law Review* 1339 (1992).

287. See Justification for the Government's Proposed Law for Reform of Civil Procedure (*Begründung des Regierungsentwurfs eines Gesetzes zur Reform des Zivilprozesses* or *BegrRegE*) of November 23, 2000, pp. 58 ff.

288. ZPO §278(2) (*...erscheint erkennbar aussichtslos*). Also excepted are cases which have already undergone settlement facilitation at a state sponsored settlement facility. See Section 11 (I) below for a brief description of such facilities.

289. The sole requirement seems to be that the "settlement conference takes place before the oral hearing" ("*Der mündlichen Verhandlung geht...eine Güteverhandlung voraus...*"). See Zöller/Greger, §278, mn. 12. The hope is to avoid an unnecessary court hearing and the activity of judges and lawyers associated with such proceedings. Another reason for requiring the settlement conference before the commencement of the plenary hearing might be to permit the parties to settle the case without incurring the additional statutory

key is to schedule and conduct the conference at a time when the parties and their counsel are likely to be in a position to address settlement in an informed and constructive manner.[290]

At the settlement conference the court is required to discuss the legal and factual issues in the case with the parties, and to the extent indicated, put questions to the parties and counsel designed to foster settlement. The personal participation of the parties in the settlement discussion is strongly encouraged. Parties who appear are to be heard by the court in person. The parties are to be summoned to the settlement conference. Failure to appear can be punished in the usual way by contempt fine, or by staying the proceedings if both parties to litigation are in default.[291]

The new provisions also permit the court to refer the parties to a delegated (*beauftragten*) member of the panel or commissioned (*ersuchten*) judge of another court for the settlement conference.[292] Such a measure might be employed if the parties live a great distance from the court where the case is pending, or if one or the other party is seriously reluctant to discuss the merits of the case or its position with the judge who would ultimately decide the case if the negotiations are unsuccessful. The court can even refer the parties to an out of court settlement facility (*Streitschlichtungstelle*) if the parties so agree and can stay the proceedings to permit the settlement process time to work.[293]

If the parties reach a settlement at the settlement conference, it can be made of record (*beurkundet*) at the same time and will have the effect of an "in-court settlement" (*gerichtlicher Vergleich*).[294]

The new reforms also facilitate settlement by authorizing the judge to send the parties a written settlement proposal. Such a proposal can be contained in an order incident to preparation of the case by written briefs, an order relating to a preliminary oral hearing, or in a written communication made for

---

attorneys fee associated with conduct of the plenary proceedings. See Ch. 9(E)(2) below on computation of statutory attorneys fees.

290. See Jauernig, §28(II), p. 103, for a critique that the new provisions may be requiring the parties to focus on settlement before they are sufficiently informed about the quality of their legal and factual positions to conduct meaningful negotiations.

291. ZPO §278(2)–(4). See also Foerste, "Die Güteverhandlung im künftigen Zivilprozess", 54 *NJW* 3103 (2001); Wieser, "Zivilprozessreform - Rechtliche Probleme der Güteverhandlung nach §278 ZPO n.F.", 56 *MDR* 10 (2002).

292. ZPO §278(5).

293. ZPO §278(5).

294. See Ch. 11(I)(3) below for a discussion of the special attributes of in-court settlement. The most important of these is that an in-court settlement can support direct execution.

that purpose. If both parties accept the proposal in writing, the judge can document the resulting settlement by simple court order with the effect of an in-court settlement.[295]

The new reforms have been met with some criticism by academics and others who have expressed the view that little is gained and some desirable flexibility is lost by requiring a formal settlement conference at an early stage of the process.[296] Time will tell whether this new feature has resulted in a net gain to German litigants and the lawyers and judges who serve them.

---

295. ZPO §278(6). See Ch. 11(I)(3) below.

296. E.g. Jauernig, §28(II), p. 103 and very critical Schellhammer, "Zivilprozessreform und erste Instanz", 55 *MDR* 1081, 1082 (2001).

CHAPTER 8

Plenary and Evidentiary Proceedings

A. Purpose and Scope of Plenary Proceedings

The heart of a German civil lawsuit is the oral plenary proceeding (*Hauptverhandlung*) at which the court and the parties discuss the issues of law, proof is had of disputed facts, and the issues are submitted for decision by the court. Conceptually this plenary proceeding is considered as a single integrated oral hearing, adjourned from time to time to suit the convenience of parties and court, and supplemented by written pleadings, memoranda and briefs. While recent reforms have attempted to concentrate the activity of the plenary phase into a single event,[1] adjournments and continuances of the plenary proceedings are commonplace in cases of more than trivial significance.

1. Purpose of Plenary Hearing

The plenary hearing is the key portion of the proceedings in which the court, counsel and parties address the dispositive legal and factual issues in the litigation by oral argument and reception of evidence. In a sense all that precedes the plenary hearing is considered "preparatory," even though cases are often disposed of by default judgment and otherwise before the plenary

1. ZPO §272(1), enacted in 1976, specifies that "The legal dispute should as a rule be resolved in a comprehensively prepared oral hearing (plenary hearing)." ("*Der Rechtsstreit ist in der Regel in einem umfassend vorbereiteten Termin zur mündlichen Verhandlung (Haupttermin) zu erledigen.*") In former times law suits were determined in a sequence of many relatively minor hearings and conferences similar to the French or Italian tradition. See Chs. 2(F), 6(E)(1), 7(E)(2) above.

phase is even reached. Although recent reforms have attempted to promote the concentration of plenary proceedings in a single plenary hearing,[2] as a matter of principle the plenary proceeding will extend from the time the first plenary hearing is opened by the court until the case is submitted for decision, even if this process requires several actual hearings or meetings.

In most cases the preparatory proceedings (described in Ch. 7 above) will have clarified the issues and focused attention on the legal and factual contentions in dispute before plenary proceedings are opened. In cases prepared by preliminary hearing, the minutes (*Protokolle*) of the preliminary hearing and any supplementary orders issued thereafter will pretty much set the stage for the plenary hearing. In cases prepared in writing, the combination of the parties' written submissions and the court's orders and preliminary dispositions will perform a similar role. The idea is to focus the plenary proceeding on one or more dispositive legal or factual issues which can be addressed and resolved in a single hearing.

If proof of facts is contemplated, the court's order will designate the documentary proof to be received and indicate which of the witnesses already named by one or other of the parties is to be summoned to give testimony.

An important function of plenary proceedings is to involve the parties directly in the oral argument and proof-taking functions. Ordinarily both parties as well as their respective counsel are expected to be present at the plenary hearing.[3]

2. Scope of Plenary Hearing

According to current practice, the plenary hearing will address all legal and factual issues necessary to reach a judgment disposing of the litigation. The issues for plenary discussion can include any relevant and unresolved issues raised by the parties' pleadings, issues raised by subsequent submissions and clarifications from the parties or their counsel during the preparatory phase, and even issues and contentions raised during the course of the plenary proceedings themselves.

---

2. The principle of concentration of proceedings (*Konzentrationsmaxime*) has been embodied in the 1976 "Stuttgart reforms", and further applied in the May 2001 reforms of the Civil Procedure Code. See Chs. 2(F), 6(E)(1), 7(E)(2) and 7(K) above.

3. See ZPO §§ 137(4), 141, 278(2)(3), 397(1) and (2). ZPO §141 requires the court to order the personal appearance of both parties at the plenary hearing "if this seems appropriate for clarification of the facts of the case" ("*wenn dies zur Aufklärung des Sachverhalts geboten erscheint*"). In this case the court sends the summons directly to the parties, even when they are represented by counsel. ZPO §141(2).

As suggested above, historically a German defendant and its counsel were comparatively free at various stages of the proceeding to make tactical selections from the then available legal and factual defenses and set-offs without fear of waiving the right to assert other defenses later on. There was no requirement that a party assert all conceivable defenses at the outset of the case. If one defense proved insufficient, the defending party was not precluded from asserting another later on. This regime enabled a defendant to present its defenses *seriatim* at a series of separate hearings in an effort to stave off a potentially unfavorable judgment and could result in protraction of proceedings to an unreasonable extent.

The reforms of the late 1970's attempted to introduce a bar to the unjustified late assertion of claims and defenses. This bar was somewhat reinforced by the 2001 civil procedure reforms. Today a German court can require the litigants to bring forward the most likely claims and defenses at a relatively early stage of the proceeding on pain of being precluded from doing so at a later time.[4]

The court now has the power to shape the scope of the plenary hearing in two ways. First of all, the court is authorized to set time periods and deadlines (*Fristen*) within the litigation framework for the parties to clarify their specific claims, defensive positions, assertions of fact or designations of evidence.[5] Such deadlines can be established in procedural orders (*Verfügungen*) and similar dispositions, provided that they are issued and signed by the presiding judge, another member of the panel or the single judge.[6]

If a party fails within the specified time to bring up additional clarifying matter, the party may be permitted to do so later on only if the court is convinced that the consideration of the omitted matter will not delay the disposition of the law suit or if there is satisfactory excuse for the delay.[7] So, if during the plenary hearing a party attempts to make new factual assertions or designations of evidence relative to an issue that was subject to such a dead-

4. See Ch. 7(K)(1) above for the obligation to raise claims and defensive material during preparatory proceedings. For further discussion of the dilemma faced by a German litigant under the current regime, see, e.g., Jauernig, *Zivilprozessrecht*, 28th ed. (2003), §28(III)(2); Lüke, *Zivilprozessrecht*, 8th ed. (2003), §17(IV), mn. 194.

5. ZPO §273(2)(1). See, e.g., Zöller/Greger, *Zivilprozessordnung*, 23rd ed. (2002), §271, mn. 1, 6.

6. See Chs. 2(D)(2)(b) and 7(E)(1) above. German law is relatively strict in establishing deadlines. Due regard for the right to be heard (*rechtliches Gehör*) requires a level of formality in setting any deadlines that might preclude a party's right to be heard on a relevant issue. See Federal Supreme Court, 76 BGHZ 236 (1980); Zöller/Greger, §296, mn. 9ff.

7. ZPO §296(1).

line, the party must be prepared to show that the new matter will not lead to a delay in the disposition of the case (such as by the need to summon witnesses not already present at the hearing), or that the party's delay in bringing the new matter forward was excusable. If there is a way in which the new material can be accommodated in the proceedings without causing material delay, the court is expected to take the necessary measures, including requiring the opposing party to address the new material on the spot, when such a measure would not cause that party unfair prejudice.[8] The most common kind of excuse is that the party was unaware of the new material and could not have learned of it by reasonable diligence within the time set by the court.[9]

The second restraint on late assertion of new matter during plenary proceedings is found in §282(1), which requires that:

> "In the plenary proceedings each party shall bring forward factual and legal material supporting claims and defenses, especially assertions, contraventions, objections, evidence and arguments on evidence, as is appropriate to the state of the case and to a careful conduct of the litigation with a view to expedition of the proceeding."[10]

This duty is accompanied by a statutory duty to make opposing counsel aware of means of attack or defense of a kind which the opponent would not be able to address without investigation (*Erkundigung*) in such time as to allow reasonable opportunity for investigation before the plenary hearing.[11]

If a party fails to abide by these requirements and proposes to raise new matter at the plenary hearing which would delay the conclusion of the pro-

---

8. See Zöller/Greger, §296, mn. 13–19. By the same token, the new material cannot be blamed for delaying the proceedings if it would be necessary to give a continuance for other reasons. There is some discussion in the case law about whether the "delay" (*Verzögerung*) contemplated by the statute means that the proceedings would last longer than they would without the new material at all, or whether preclusive delays are only those which would extend the proceedings longer than they would have lasted had the material been timely brought to the attention of the court and parties. Compare Federal Supreme Court, 86 BGHZ 31 (1983) with State Appeals Court of Hamburg, 32 *NJW* 1717 (1979) and German Constitutional Court, 75 BVerfGE 302 (1987) for different approaches to this issue. See Zöller/Greger, §296, mn. 20–23 and also Ch. 7(K)(1) above.

9. See Federal Supreme Court, 41 *NJW* 60, 62 (1988); Zöller/Greger, §296, mn. 24.

10. *"Jede Partei hat in der mündlichen Verhandlung ihre Angriffs- und Verteidigungsmittel, insbesondere Behauptungen, Bestreiten, Einwendungen, Einreden, Beweismittel und Beweiseinreden, so zeitig vorzubringen, wie es nach der Prozesslage einer sorgfältigen und auf Förderung des Verfahrens bedachten Prozessführung entspricht."* See Ch. 7(K)(1) above.

11. ZPO §282(2). The opposing counsel is to be notified by a "preparatory pleading or brief" (*vorbereitender Schriftsatz*). See Zöller/Greger, §282, mn. 4.

ceeding, the judge has the discretion to reject (*zurückweisen*) the new material if the judge is convinced that the delay was the result of gross negligence (*grobe Nachlässigkeit*) on the part of the party or its counsel.[12] Solicitude for the parties' right to be heard means that this power is very sparingly exercised, and only after the court has made a finding that the new material would cause delay and that the circumstances of failure to raise it earlier were egregious. The court's obligation to give hints and feedback requires it to advise a party of the possibility of rejection of late-submitted material and that the party have opportunity to argue that the new material would not cause undue delay or that the failure to raise it earlier was not the result of gross negligence.[13] The role of the preclusions is to provide some form and discipline to the proceedings, not act as a trap for the unwary.[14]

B. Conduct of the Plenary Hearing

While the proceedings at a plenary hearing may appear to be conducted and controlled by the judge, in actuality the parties and their lawyers play important roles. The respective claims and assertions, as well as the sources by which factual assertions are to be proven, remain the domain of the parties. The judge is forced to work with what the parties place before her.[15]

The plenary hearing in an ordinary civil action is conceptually structured into 7 more or less distinct phases or parts as follows:

1. Opening of the hearing (*Eröffnung der Verhandlung*),
2. Assertion of the legal claims and matters of defense at issue (*Stellung der Anträge*),
3. Hearing of the parties and argument of counsel (*Parteianhörung und anwaltlicher Vortrag*),
4. Attempts by the court to promote settlement (*richterliche Vergleichsbemühungen*),[16]

---

12. ZPO §296(2).

13. Zöller/Greger, §296, mn. 26f. and 32; see Chs. 7(K)(1) and 6 (C)(2) above on the court's obligation to give hints and feedback.

14. See Stein/Jonas/Leipold, *Kommentar zur Zivilprozessordnung*, 21st ed. (1997), §296, mn. 3.

15. See the discussion of the *Verhandlungsmaxime* in Ch. 6 (B) above.

16. Efforts by the court to promote settlement can take place at any stage of the proceeding. The recent 2001 reforms require that the court schedule and conduct a "settlement conference" (*Güteverhandlung*) before the commencement of plenary proceedings,

5. Taking of evidence (*Beweisaufnahme*),
6. Further argument by parties and counsel (*Erörterung des Sach- und Streitstandes durch die Parteien und Anwälte*),
7. Conclusion of the hearing (*Schluss der Verhandlung*).

In practice frequently these phases may appear to overlap and blend into each other. Sometimes also they may seem to repeat themselves, such as when the parties argue to the court before the taking of evidence, and then again after the evidence is taken.[17] While the form and order of these phases is not slavishly followed, they do serve to provide some structure to what may seem to an outsider a very loose and unstructured kind of court proceeding.

1. The Opening of the Hearing

According to the ZPO, the presiding judge "opens and conducts the oral proceedings."[18] At the plenary hearing, the judge's initial duty is to set forth the status of the suit and introduce the subject matter of the hearing. In cases where the parties feel sufficiently informed on the subject matter of the hearing and the issues to be addressed, they can waive the formal introduction by the presiding judge.[19]

The opening of the hearing is also the beginning of the minutes (*Protokolle*) which record and summarize the hearing and comprise a part of the record of the case (*Akte*).[20] Frequently the presiding judge will dictate the introductory matter into a dictaphone at the outset of the hearing, and then interrupt the hearing from time to time to summarize the proceedings into the dictaphone.

2. The Assertion of Claims and Matters of Defense

According to the ZPO the plenary proceedings are supposed to start with the assertion of the plaintiff's claims for relief and a counter-statement of the

---

See ZPO §278(1), (2); Ch. 7(M) above. For additional discussion of settlement activity in German civil litigation see Ch. 11(I) below.

17. See ZPO § 137(2) and § 279(3). Discussion of settlement can also be re-instituted after the taking of evidence. ZPO § 278(1) requires the court to consider settlement "at every stage of the proceedings" ("... *in jeder Lage der Verfahrens*...").

18. ZPO §136(1): "*Der Vorsitzende eröffnet und leitet die Verhandlung.*"

19. See ZPO §§ 136(2) and (3), 139(1)(1), 278(2)(2). In many cases, the introduction is a formality which all concerned are glad to dispense with in the interest of saving time. See Rosenberg/Schwab/Gottwald, *Zivilprozessrecht*, 15th ed. (1993), §106(III)(1), p. 602.

20. See Ch. 6(D) above for a discussion of the role of the case record and minutes of hearings and conferences.

defendant's defenses and application for dismissal.[21] The ZPO contemplates that the respective legal and factual assertions will be stated aloud by the parties or lawyers in comprehensive fashion.[22] Traditionally they were orally read aloud by the parties or lawyer from their respective pleadings.[23]

Although the statement of the claims and defensive matter at issue may seem like a mere formality, actually it serves two important procedural purposes. First, the statement of claims and defensive matter establishes the subject matter of the case (*Streitgegenstand*) for the purpose of applying doctrines of *res adjudicata*.[24] Second, according to the intentions of the legislature and drafters of the Civil Procedural Code, the assertion of the claims serves clearly to distinguish the oral proceedings from prior preparatory or preliminary proceedings and to signal that the most adversarial (*streitige*) phase of the proceedings has commenced. One of the effects of this is that the attorneys will be entitled to an additional unit of fees if the case is terminated after the opening of the oral hearing.[25]

In present-day practice the statement of claims and defenses by the parties or their attorneys can take place either immediately after the opening of the hearing by the presiding judge or can be postponed until after hearing from the parties and their attorneys.[26] Postponement of the assertion of claims and defenses may permit the judge to provide some hints and feedback based on interaction with the parties and their attorneys, which may, in turn, affect the form in which the claims are then stated.

Lengthy oral recitations of claims and defenses have been largely discontinued in favor of a brief oral summary of the various claims and contentions by counsel. In most simple cases where the claims have not been seriously al-

21. ZPO §137(1): "The oral proceedings will be commenced by the parties stating their claims for relief or dismissal." ("*Die mündliche Verhandlung wird dadurch eingeleitet, dass die Parteien ihre Anträge stellen.*") This is a reflection of the principle of orality (*Mündlichkeitsprinzip*), see Ch. 6(E)(1) above.

22. ZPO §137(2): "The parties are to state their claims and defenses freely to encompass all factual and legal aspects of the matter at issue." ("*Die Vorträge der Partein sind in freier Rede zu halten; sie haben das Streitverhältnis in tatsächlicher und rechtlicher Beziehung zu umfassen.*") If the lawyers state the claims and defenses, the parties are also to be given an opportunity to speak, ZPO §137(4).

23. ZPO §297(1)(1) prescribes that the "claims are to be read aloud from the pleadings". ("*Die Anträge sind aus den vorbereitenden Schriftsätzen zu verlesen.*")

24. See Ch. 9(F) below on the *res adjudicata* effect of judgments.

25. See BRAGO §31(1)(2) authorizing a full attorneys fee for the conduct of oral proceedings (*mündliche Verhandlung*). See also Ch. 4(H) above on lawyers' compensation and Ch. 9(E)(5) below on taxation of lawyers' fees in judgments.

26. See Ch. 8(B)(3) below.

tered or recast during the preparation process, counsel will briefly cite their respective pleadings, and the reference will be noted in the minutes.[27]

3. Hearing of the Parties and Argument of Counsel

German civil justice places some importance on the personal interaction between the parties and their judges. ZPO § 139(1) provides that the court is to discuss with the parties all relevant facts and issues in dispute. The court is empowered to require the parties to be present in person at the hearing and in most cases the court will issue an order to summon the parties. Normally the parties present will be heard in person by the court.[28] The direct party-judge dialogue furthers two important policies. First, the parties have direct communication with their judges, and can make sure that their claims and assertions are conveyed to the judges in their own words, unfiltered and undistorted by lawyers or other third parties. Second, the judges have direct access to the parties, and can immediately pin down and clarify factual assertions which their lawyers may have obfuscated or left ambiguous. The participation of the parties in the plenary hearing thus tends not only toward a fairer proceeding, but also a faster one.[29]

In a typical case the parties are asked by the presiding judge to clarify or restate factual assertions which may be unclear or disputed in the written pleadings. The judge speaks directly to the parties, both individually and collectively.[30] The purpose of the inquiry at this point is clarification of unclear factual assertions rather than proof of contested ones.[31] If a party's factual po-

---

27. Such incorporation by reference is specifically authorized by ZPO §§137(3) and 297(2). ZPO § 137(3) has been amended to provide that reading of pleadings aloud should ordinarily take place "only to the extent that their actual wording is of significance" (... *insoweit, als es auf ihren wörtlichen Inhalt ankommt*).

28. See ZPO §§ 137(4), 141, 278(2)(3). For a more detailed discussion of the courts responsibility to give hints and feedback (ZPO § 139(1)) see Ch. 6(C)(2) above.

29. See Rosenberg/Schwab/Gottwald, §106(III)(2), p.602; Musielak, *Kommentar zur Zivilprozessordnung*, 3rd ed. (2002), § 141, mn.1. This participation by the parties in direct oral dialogue with the judges is an aspect of the principle of orality (*Mündlichkeitsprinzip*) which forms an important tradition in German civil justice. See Ch. 6(E)(1) above.

30. See, e.g., Zöller/Greger, § 139, mn. 3. Such discourse takes place only in open court in the presence of the other party and its attorney. In principle there is to be no *ex parte* communication between party and judge. A judge may not accept communications about the case from a party in absence of the other party, except for communications concerning proceedings without notice and for routine procedural administration. Claims of judicial bias may be based on unjustified *ex parte* communication. See Ch. 6(C)(2)(f).

31. See Federal Supreme Court, 55 *NJW* 2247, 2249 (2002). If material facts are contested, evidence relevant to those facts would ordinarily be received in the phase of the ple-

sition on an issue as clarified leads to a particular disposition as a matter of law (usually against that party), the court can reach such a decision based on hearing of the parties without formally taking evidence.[32]

Although this discussion of the parties' factual contentions or assertions is not considered as evidence, "the parties are required to make their clarifications of factual circumstances completely and truthfully" to assist the court in determining what material facts are actually alleged and which of them are in dispute.[33] The attorneys may also contribute to the discussion, particularly if a party has mis-spoken or has obviously misunderstood the judge's question. The presiding judge can grant anyone present the right to address the court, and can also withdraw the right of address in cases of abuse or obstreperousness.[34]

The formal assertion of the claims and the hearing of the parties and their attorneys introduce the adversarial argument by parties and counsel. Each party argues for its position based on the record as developed to that stage of the proceeding. The proceedings are relatively informal. The presiding judge moderates the discussion, asks questions of parties and counsel, and may pro-

---

nary proceeding for reception of evidence. See Ch. 8(C) below. If other evidence does not suffice to support a determination of a contested factual issue the court can formally examine either or both parties in the evidentiary phase of the proceeding and may ultimately base its fact determination at least in part on party testimony. In evaluating that party testimony the court can consider assertions of the party made at the party-hearing phase of the proceeding. Federal Supreme Court, 45 NJW 1558 (1992); Thomas/Putzo/Reichold, Vor §445, mn. 2. See Ch. 8(B)(8) below on the taking of party testimony in evidentiary proceedings.

32. In-court fact clarifications which can lead to adverse legal consequences are considered "judicial admissions" (*gerichtliche Geständnisse*). See ZPO §§85(1)(2), 288. The extent to which a judge should warn a party of the legal effect of particular factual concessions or clarifications during oral proceedings depends on the circumstances of the individual case. See Stürner, *Richterliche Aufklärung*, mn. 66, p. 53. Such judicial admissions can be withdrawn only if they are factually erroneous and were made by mistake. ZPO §290. See generally Rosenberg/Schwab/Gottwald, §114(I)(1), p. 649ff.; Lüke, §20(II), mn. 223–225; Federal Supreme Court, 129 BGHZ 108, 111 (1995).

33. ZPO §138(1) ("*Die Parteien haben ihre Erklärungen über tatsächliche Umstände vollständig und der Wahrheit gemäss abzugeben*"). For the extent of this requirement see, e.g., Rosenberg/Schwab/Gottwald, §65(VIII), pp. 363ff.; Musielak/Stadler, §138, mn. 2ff. German procedural law recognizes a conceptual distinction between "facts" (*Tatsachen*) as alleged or ultimately found by the court, and "evidence" or "proof" (*Beweis*) offered to generate a belief in the existence of the facts. Most of the discussion in German civil procedure concerns facts rather than evidence. Only if there is ultimate disagreement about material facts is evidence adduced to prove them.

34. ZPO §136(2). See, e.g., Musielak/Stadler, §136, mn. 4.

vide hints and feedback on the points being discussed. In cases before three-judge tribunals the other judges may intervene to ask questions and make their own observations.[35]

During the course of the argument, counsel and parties may refer to facts asserted in the pleadings and deemed true because they were admitted, or at least not denied,[36] by the opponent, as well as facts supported by evidence received by the court during the course of preparatory proceedings.[37] If there is a possibility that the case can be decided on the basis of largely undisputed facts, the court will first attempt such a resolution before ordering the taking of evidence on disputed facts. If, however, it is clear from the start that the case can only be decided by hearing evidence, the court will generally proceed directly to the evidentiary portion of the plenary hearing, with further argument by the parties and counsel to follow. In some cases the parties' argument at the outset of the hearing makes it clear that evidence will have to be taken. In such a case the argument will be broken off, and the court will proceed to hear the evidence, if at all possible, in the same session of the plenary hearing.[38]

Adversarial argument is difficult to describe. The form of the argumentation is not statutorily regulated. The atmosphere in the courtroom varies from court to court and from case to case depending in part on the personalities of the judges and lawyers involved. It is not like the competitive presentations of common-law lawyers who argue their points of fact and law before largely pas-

---

35. The reporting judge (*Berichterstatter*) is often in a particularly good position to contribute to the discussion by reason of her more detailed knowledge of the legal and factual background of the case.

36. According to ZPO § 138(3), facts not expressly contested are to be treated as admitted unless the intention to contest them appears from the party's written or oral declarations. See, e.g., Rosenberg/Schwab/Gottwald, § 114(I)(2), p. 653f.; Zöller/Greger, § 138, mn. 9ff.; Ch. 6(B)(2) above.

37. This may include documents identified in the pleadings or at a preliminary hearing and produced by the parties or even third parties at or before the plenary hearing (see ZPO §142 and Ch. 7(L)(1) above) or reports or records of public agencies requested by the court pursuant to ZPO §273(2)(2) (see Ch. 7(H)(1) and (L) above).

38. One of the 1970s' reforms aimed at expediting and concentrating civil proceedings (see Ch. 2(F) above) was a provision requiring that "in the main hearing the taking of evidence should immediately follow the adversarial argument." ZPO §279(2). ("*Im Haupttermin soll der streitigen Verhandlung die Beweisaufnahme unmittelbar folgen*"). If the issue of fact arises unexpectedly and cannot be clarified, it may be necessary to order a continuance of the plenary proceedings or a special evidentiary hearing (*Beweisaufnahme*) at a later date to allow time for summoning any necessary witnesses and for preparation by the parties and their counsel. The evidentiary hearing is theoretically a continuation of the plenary proceedings. See ZPO §370 (1); Musielak/Stadler, § 370, mn. 1.

sive tribunals and juries. The German judge or judges are very much involved in the discussions. The proceedings perhaps resemble a somewhat formalized, sometimes animated, conference between judges, parties and lawyers. The parties and the lawyers seek to convince the judges of the validity of their respective positions, and to respond to the inquiries and hints and feedback from the court. Discussion is often very much "back and forth" among judges, parties and lawyers, with no discernable order of presentation. The presiding judge plays the leading role as moderator. She makes sure that the important issues are covered, keeps the argument on track, and brings the argument to a close when everything of importance seems to have been said, or when it is clear that an impasse of disputed facts has been reached so that the taking of evidence will be required.

In a sense the adversarial argument which takes place in the courtroom during the plenary hearing is but part of a continuum of adversarial argument which starts with the complaint, and continues both orally and in writing at all stages of the proceeding until the last appellate decision has been rendered. The importance of the judge's engagement in this discourse cannot be overstressed. The parties do not merely argue to the court, they argue with the judges, and expect and receive feedback on where the court stands and how they are doing.

If the taking of evidence is necessary during the course of the plenary hearing, the parties will be afforded an opportunity to argue once more following the taking of the evidence, in most cases with the benefit of feedback from the judge on the judge's impressions from the evidence.[39]

4. Efforts to Promote Settlement

The German court is statutorily mandated to encourage voluntary settlement of civil cases at all stages of the proceedings.[40] One of the 2001 procedural reforms now requires the court to schedule and hold a "settlement conference" (*Güteverhandlung*) before the adversarial oral argument.[41] In practice

---

39. ZPO §285(1) specifies that "the parties are to present argument based on the complete facts and circumstances resulting from the reception of evidence." (*"Über das Ergebnis der Beweisaufnahme haben die Parteien unter Darlegung des Streitverhältnisses zu verhandeln."*)

40. ZPO §278(1) (*Das Gericht soll in jeder Lage des Verfahrens auf eine gütliche Beilegung des Rechtsstreits oder einzelner Streitpunkte bedacht sein.*) For additional material on settlements in German litigation see Ch. 7(M) above and Ch. 11(I) below.

41. ZPO §278(2). See generally Zöller/Greger, §278, mn. 1 and 8ff.; Lüke, §17(V)(1), mn. 195a. For procedure in the labor courts see ArbGG §§54, 57(2). Labor courts are re-

such conferences are often combined with preliminary hearings in cases prepared by preliminary hearing. In cases prepared by exchange of written pleadings and briefs settlement conferences are early agenda items at the start of plenary proceedings. The court is also expected to raise settlement at other propitious points in the proceeding such as right after the adversarial argumentation (*streitige Verhandlung*) and again after any taking of evidence (*Beweisaufnahme*).[42] Special provisions of the ZPO regulate the allocation of costs and the availability of execution on judicially recorded settlements.[43]

"Settlement talk" between the court and the parties and counsel can take many forms. In some cases the court will merely mention the advantages of voluntary settlement, ask the parties or counsel if settlement has been attempted, and urge the parties to discuss settlement at an opportune time. The court is statutorily expected to order the parties' presence at the required settlement conference and any other occasions at which settlement efforts will be made.[44]

In many cases the court will take a more active role in the settlement discussions. The judge's underlying obligation to provide hints and feedback (*Hinweispflicht*) can often provide valuable guidance to the parties in settlement negotiations. German judges can, and often do, share with the parties their preliminary impressions of the case in the course of settlement negotiations. It is not at all uncommon for judges to propose specific settlement amounts and terms for discussion by the parties and counsel. The court can refer the case to a single member of the court or another available judge for the conduct of the initial settlement negotiations when such a referral would further the convenience of the court or the parties.[45] While the court is expected to initiate settlement discussions in the early stages of the proceeding before the first oral hearing, if the opportunity arises, settlement talk in court can occur at any stage of the proceeding, even on appeal.

---

quired to begin the proceedings with an effort at conciliation and to continue the effort throughout the proceedings.

42. See, e.g., Rosenberg/Schwab/Gottwald, §106(III)(3), p. 603; Lüke, §17(V)(2), mn. 195b; Stürner, "Grundfragen richterlicher Streitschlichtung", 54 *DRiZ* 202 (1976), and Stürner, "Richterliche Vergleichsverhandlung und richterlicher Vergleich aus juristischer Sicht", in: Meier (ed.) *Festschrift für Hans Ulrich Walder* (1994), p. 273.

43. See ZPO §98 (costs) and §794(1)(1) (execution); see also Ch. 9(E)(4) below on allocation of costs and attorneys fees in cases concluded by settlements.

44. ZPO §278(3). The new reforms provide that if the parties both fail to show up for the initial settlement conference, the case is to be stayed until the conference can be held, ZPO §278(4).

45. ZPO §278(5)(1). For instance, such a referral could be made if it were inconvenient for parties to attend a settlement conference because of distance or other factors.

If in litigated cases a settlement is reached as a result of either in-court or out-of-court negotiations,[46] the settlement must be judicially entered into the record of the case in order to entitle a party to obtain execution.[47] The substantive effect of a settlement is generally similar to that of a contractual novation.[48]

C. Proof of Facts and the Taking of Evidence

In cases which cannot be resolved without determining disputed facts, the taking of evidence accompanies, precedes, or follows the parties' argument. Often the need for evidence on disputed facts is foreseen from the beginning of the case, and the order scheduling the plenary hearing will have spelled out the issues on which evidence is to be taken and the means of proof to be examined. In such cases the taking of evidence would likely follow the formal assertion of claims for relief and applications for dismissal, and precede the principal argument.

In some cases the taking of evidence is deferred until the court and parties have addressed potentially dispositive legal issues which do not require the determination of disputed facts. Judicial economy and a standard of strict rele-

---

46. There is nothing to prevent the parties or their lawyers from negotiating settlement of a pending case out of court, with or without the assistance of ADR facilitation. The tradition of judicial promotion of and participation in settlement negotiations may be one reason why other forms of ADR have been slow to take hold in Germany. See, e.g., Gottwald, "Civil Justice Reform: Access, Cost, and Expedition. The German Perspective", in: Zuckerman et al. (ed.) *Civil Justice in Crisis* (1999), p. 207, 230; Schütze, "Alternative Streitschlichtung", 97 *ZVglRwiss* 117, 121ff. (1998). According to ZPO §278(5)(2) as enacted in 2001, the court may, with the consent of the parties, stay the proceeding for further out-of-court mediation. See Ch. 11(I)(1) below.

47. ZPO §160(3)(1); see, e.g., Zöller/Stöber, §160, mn. 5; Federal Supreme Court, 37 *NJW* 1465, 1466 (1984). ZPO §794(1) authorizes the issuance of execution based on settlements which are judicially made of record in litigated cases before German courts. (*Die Zwangsvollstreckung findet ferner statt: 1. aus Vergleichen, die zwischen den Parteien oder zwischen einer Partei und einem Dritten zur Beilegung des Rechtsstreits seinem ganzen Umfang nach oder in betreff eines Teiles des Streitgegenstandes vor einem deutschen Gericht.... abgeschlossen sind, sowie aus Vergleichen, die gemäss §118 Abs. 1 Satz 3 oder §492 Abs. 3 zu richterlichem Protokoll genommen sind...*). See Ch. 9(A)(4) below on other forms of judicially documented settlements and Ch. 11(F) below on executions.

48. See, e.g., Jauernig, §48 for a short and concise discussion of the procedural and substantive aspects of settlements of litigated cases; for details see Bork, *Der Vergleich* (1988); Röhl, *Der Vergleich im Zivilprozess* (1983); Wagner, *Prozessverträge* (1998).

vance of facts[49] will ordinarily impel the court to seek to decide the case on a legal or procedural ground which will dispose of the case with less investment of court and party effort than would be required for the clarification and determination of disputed facts.

If the court comes to the conclusion that the case is not susceptible of resolution without deciding some disputed facts, the parties and court may proceed with the evidence during the same session of the plenary hearing, or an evidentiary hearing might be scheduled for a future session. Nowadays the presumption is in favor of proceeding at the same session of the plenary hearing when at all possible without causing the parties unfair surprise or otherwise offending the parties' right to be heard.[50]

1. Scope of Factual Inquiry and Sources of Proof

a. *Framing the Facts in Dispute*

The parties initially define the scope of potentially relevant facts by their factual recitals in their pleadings (*Schriftsätze*) and by their representations to the court in preliminary proceedings. They are under an obligation to recite relevant facts with particularity and to be ready to argue the relevance of the facts asserted in terms of likely material inferences to be drawn from them. As noted above, relevant facts asserted with particularity by a party and not specifically denied or otherwise contested by the opponent are deemed admitted and do not require proof.[51] Such facts are treated as established by the court and ordinarily no proof of such facts will be received.

During the course of preliminary proceedings and plenary hearing the court will seek to clarify the parties' respective factual assertions and to refine any apparent disputes of fact. The idea is to focus the inquiry on disputes of fact

---

49. The principle of strict relevance in German civil procedure can be expressed by the maxim, "*Da mihi facta, dabo tibi ius*", literally, "You give me the facts and I will give you the law", or "It is the parties' duty to point to the facts in the case and the judge's to define the law applicable to those facts." See Rosenberg/Schwab/Gottwald, § 113(III), p. 648 and § 133(II)(2), p. 789; A. Blomeyer, *Zivilprozessrecht*, 2nd ed. (1985), § 18(II), pp. 112 ff.

50. ZPO §279(2). See, e.g., Zöller/Greger, § 279, mn. 3 f. on concentration of proceedings; see also Ch. 2(F), Ch. 6(E)(1), Ch. 7(E)(2), (H), (I), (K) and Ch. 8(A)(1) below.

51. See Ch. 6(B)(2) and ZPO § 138(3). This rule is subject to some exceptions in noncontentious proceedings (*freiwillige Gerichtsbarkeit*) where proof might be required of facts even in the absence of contest by an opposing party. The same is true for divorce cases. The court requires proof of the grounds for divorce regardless of whether the plaintiff's factual allegations are disputed by the other spouse. See, e.g., ZPO § 617 and Rosenberg/Schwab/Gottwald, § 165(V)(7), p. 1012.

which are relevant and important to decision of the case. In many cases serious differences in the facts set forth in the parties' initial submissions tend to disappear or become narrower in scope after discussion and dialogue between the court, counsel and the parties. During the course of argument counsel or the court may show that the disputed facts are in fact immaterial to the legal standard on which the case can be determined. Finally, in cases with more than one factual issue, the court may limit the scope of evidentiary inquiry to a single factual issue that might be determinative of the entire case in hopes of not having to engage in proof taking that would ultimately be unnecessary.[52]

Thus the scope of the evidentiary inquiry is ultimately the product of the initiative of the parties and their counsel as formed and shaped to a degree by the court. It is important to keep in mind, however, that the identification of potentially relevant facts, whether disputed or not, is a function of the parties. In rendering a decision, the court cannot take cognizance of a fact unless that fact has been advanced by one or the other party. In other words, the court cannot reach out beyond the scope of the relevant facts as conceived and advanced by one or the other of the parties and base its decision on some outside fact determined by the court to be relevant. If the court deems some fact not advanced by one or the other party to be potentially relevant, the court may call this potential fact to the attention of the parties and invite them to comment on it or incorporate it in their positions.[53]

b. Identification of the Means of Proof

To a large extent the identification of the means by which the facts are to be proved is also the exclusive province of the parties and their counsel. The

---

52. For instance, in a case on an assigned claim where the plaintiff's status as assignee is disputed, the court may well defer taking evidence on the underlying obligation and proceed first to take evidence on the plaintiff's status as creditor. This can be true even if the issue of the plaintiff's status as creditor is first raised by the defendant as an affirmative defense.

53. This is an instance of the court's exercise of its duty to provide hints and feedback (*Hinweispflicht*). See Ch. 6(C)(2) above. On the other hand, if the court pointed out a potentially dispositive fact that had not been adverted to by either party, there is some risk that the party disadvantaged would challenge the court's impartiality. See, e.g., Musielak/Stadler, § 139, mn. 5; Stürner, *Die richterliche Aufklärung im Zivilprozess* (1982), mn. 23 f. and Ch. 6(C)(2)(h) above. In any event, it would be a violation of the court's obligation to give hints and feedback if the court relied on such a fact to support its decision without calling it to the parties' attention and inviting their comments or argument. See ZPO § 139(2)(1); Musielak/Stadler, § 139, mn. 8; Zöller/Greger, § 139, mn. 5 ff. and Ch. 6(C)(2)(b) above.

parties nominate the witnesses when proof is to be had through witness testimony. In civil cases the court does not have authority to call witnesses who have not been nominated by one or the other of the parties.[54]

The parties also designate other forms of proof which they think will tend to establish facts potentially in dispute such as documents, records, tangible things, and views and indicate those facts which they think will have to be addressed by expert testimony. In the main the court confines its consideration of this kind of evidence to items proffered or identified by the parties. However the court is not quite as firmly bound to the parties' designations of these forms of proof as it is to their designation of live witnesses. If the court believes that a document or report not designated by a party may contain relevant evidence, the court can act on its own to request that document or report from either of the parties, from a public agency, or from a third party.[55] By the same token the court may order on its own motion production of real evidence, a view, or the appointment of an expert witness if the court considers such proof relevant to a fact placed in dispute by the parties. If the court decides to seek evidence from a source not identified by a party, the court is obliged to call this to the parties' attention in such a way that they have opportunity to address this new source of proof and to argue the appropriateness of any inferences to be drawn from it.[56]

c. *Orders for the Taking of Evidence*

If the court determines early on that proof of disputed facts will likely be necessary, the court may include a designation of factual issues for proof as well as names of witnesses to be summoned and a list of documents to be produced in a preliminary order preparatory to either a preliminary or the ple-

---

54. See ZPO §§273(2)(4), 373 and Ch. 7(L) above. On the other hand if the court thinks that a person not identified by either party might have relevant testimony, the court can inquire of the parties whether they have considered this person and why they have not called him as a witness. This kind of inquiry may well lead to the nomination of the witness by one or the other party. There may be instances when the court's duty to give hints and feedback could be said to require such an inquiry. See Stürner, *Richterliche Aufklärung*, mn. 72, 73, p. 57. However if the parties refuse to take the hint, the court is without power to override their decision and call the witness on its own.

55. See ZPO §§142–144 and Ch. 7(L)(1) and (2) above. The 2001 reforms to the Civil Procedure Code authorized the court for the first time to order third parties to produce documents and tangible things and to permit inspection of other places and things based solely on their relevance to civil litigation.

56. See ZPO §285(1); German Constitutional Court, 47 *NJW* 1210 (1994); Rosenberg/Schwab/Gottwald, §85(III)(1)(4), p. 457; Ch. 6(C)(2)(b) above.

nary hearing.[57] In many cases the factual issue or issues to be addressed and the evidence needed to resolve them first become clear at a preliminary hearing or even the plenary hearing and the evidence has to be taken at a later hearing. In such cases the factual issue and the sources of evidence to be examined are usually set forth in a separate "proof order" (*Beweisbeschluss*).[58] This order sets the time and date of the hearing, sets forth the issue on which proof is to be received, and identifies the witnesses and other evidence to be examined.[59] The order may be included in the minutes of an oral hearing or it may be separately issued by the court.[60]

Sometimes it is not known until the plenary hearing whether it will be necessary to resolve a factual dispute in order to reach a decision of the case. Argument of counsel and dialogue with the court can result in a kind of consensus that clarification of a fact dispute is necessary. This can lead directly to the taking of evidence in the same court session without formally incorporating this consensus in a preliminary proof order.[61] A proof order specifying the scope and content of an evidentiary proceeding can only be altered by agreement of the parties or by the court to the extent necessary to encompass evidence or additional witnesses relevant to the factual disputes identified.[62]

d. Disputed Facts Not Requiring Proof

Ultimately it is up to the court to determine whether a factual assertion is one "requiring proof."[63] Many facts need not be specifically proven. For instance, facts substantially admitted in a party's pleadings or oral representa-

57. See ZPO §273 and Ch. 7(H)(1) and (L) above. This kind of forethought implements the policy of expedition and concentration of oral proceedings underlying the 1976 procedural reforms.

58. ZPO §358 specifies that a proof order is required when the proof is to be obtained through a separate proceeding. See Thomas/Putzo/Reichold, §358, mn. 1.

59. For details see ZPO §359. The proof order must also set forth which party nominated each item of evidence to be received.

60. If the court anticipates the need for proof of some disputed fact before the preliminary hearing or the plenary proceeding, the court can issue a proof order beforehand and the proof can be taken at or even before the plenary hearing, ZPO §358a.

61. This kind of immediate taking of evidence can take place only if the witnesses or other evidence is already at hand. A reform proposed for 2004 provides for more liberalized procedures for taking of evidence with the consent of the parties. See Huber, "Modernisierung der Justiz?", 36 *ZRP* 268, 269 (2003).

62. ZPO §360.

63. (*beweisbedürftig*). See, generally, Rosenberg/Schwab/Gottwald, §114(I), pp. 649 ff.

tions, are considered "admissions"[64] for which no proof need be indicated or received. The admitting party is bound by the admission unless relieved by the court on a finding that the admission does not correspond to the truth and was the result of an error.[65] Factual assertions made in pleadings which are not expressly denied by the opposing party are, as a matter of principle to be treated as admitted.[66] No proof is required of "publicly known facts" ("*offenkundige Tatsachen*"), facts which are generally known in a community (*allgemeinkundige Tatsachen*) such as calendar events, geography, history, and the like, or facts known by the court *ex officio* (*gerichtskundige Tatsachen*) such as the result of the taking of real evidence in parallel proceedings.[67] Facts which are the subjects of presumptions (*Vermutungen*) need also not be proven, as long as the facts which invoke the presumption are the subject of proof.[68]

e. Hints and Feedback of the Court

Ultimately it is up to the court to be convinced of the facts. In a close case, the court would advise the parties of its doubts and suggest that a fact asserted by one of them might require proof,[69] or even take certain forms of proof on its own motion.[70]

---

64. ("*Geständnis*"). ZPO §§288–290. For a discussion of admissions and the circumstances under which they may be revoked, see Rosenberg/Schwab/Gottwald, §114(I)(1), pp. 649 ff.; Lüke, §20(II), mn. 223–225; Federal Supreme Court, 129 BGHZ 108, 111 (1995).

65. ZPO §290.

66. ZPO §138(3); see Ch. 6(B)(2) above. But according to the prevailing opinion ZPO §290, which has a severe binding effect, does not apply; see Federal Supreme Court, 44 *NJW* 1683 (1991); Musielak/Stadler, §138, mn. 15; Thomas/Putzo/Reichold, §138, mn. 18.

67. ZPO §291; see Rosenberg/Schwab/Gottwald, §114(I)(3), pp. 654 f. But the court should indicate to the parties that they may argue the appropriateness of any inferences to be drawn by the court. See ZPO §139(1) and Ch. 6(C)(2) above.

68. However the opposing party is not precluded from attempting to prove the nonexistence of the presumed fact. ZPO §292. See Rosenberg/Schwab/Gottwald, §114(I)(4), p. 655.

69. An example of the court's obligation to give hints and feedback (*Hinweispflicht*). See ZPO §§139(1) and (2), 279(3) and Ch. 6(C)(2)(e) above.

70. Especially likely in the exercise of the court's noncontentious jurisdiction (*freiwillige Gerichtsbarkeit*) or in uncontested divorce cases. See Rosenberg/Schwab/Gottwald, §114(II), p. 656.

2. Burdens of Proof

Under German civil procedure the allocation of the burden of proof of facts in dispute (*Beweislast*) is frequently of importance in structuring the proceedings and sometimes in the outcome. The broad concept of "burden of proof" encompasses the parties' fundamental obligation affirmatively to indicate in pleadings or oral representations to the court the means of proving all factual assertions that might be controverted.[71] This obligation is referred to as the "burden of production of proof" (*Beweisführungslast*). If a party fails or refuses to indicate any source of proof for an assertion of fact the court can disregard that assertion of fact.[72] Ordinarily a failure to indicate the source of proof of a fact needing proof is discerned and cured at a relatively early stage of the proceeding and is of little significance in the outcome of the case.

Of greater significance in case outcomes is the ultimate "burden of proof" (*Beweislast*) or risk of nonpersuasion of facts necessary to sustain a claim or defense. If there is a failure of evidence to support a particular fact, or if, after receiving all the evidence bearing on a particular fact, the court does not reach the required degree of conviction of a particular fact, the finding will be against the party with the burden of proof on that fact.[73]

The ordinary rule is that the party who asserts a fact favoring that party's claim or defense has the burden of proof of that fact.[74] So, for instance, if a plaintiff asserts that the defendant's negligent driving of her automobile caused the plaintiff's injuries, the plaintiff has the burden of proof of the defendant's negligence and of her own injuries. If the court is not convinced of both facts, the plaintiff fails in her burden of proof and will lose the case.

In specific cases and kinds of cases the burden of production of proof or the ultimate burden of proof may be specifically allocated or varied by pro-

---

71. See Rosenberg/Schwab/Gottwald, § 117(I)(3), p. 670; Stürner, *Die Aufklärungspflicht der Parteien des Zivilprozesses* (1976), § 2(II)(2), p. 8.

72. See Rosenberg/Schwab/Gottwald, § 117(I)(3)(a), p. 670; Lüke, §23(II), mn. 276. A party's initial failure to identify the means of proof of a fact assertion can be cured by a later oral or written specification. The court can also relieve a party of its failure to designate means of proof by taking certain kinds of proof (e.g. expert testimony) on its own motion.

73. For a discussion of the burden of proof in general see Rosenberg/Schwab/Gottwald, §117(I)(2) and (II), pp. 670 ff.; Lüke, §23(II); Jauernig, §50(III)

74. See Federal Supreme Court, 53 BGHZ 245, 250 (1970); 38 *NJW* 1774, 1775 (1985). For a discussion of the theoretical debate about the basic rule apportioning the burden of proof, see Rosenberg/Schwab/Gottwald, §117(II), pp. 670 ff.; Prütting, *Gegenwartsprobleme der Beweislast* (1983); Rosenberg, *Die Beweislast*, 5th ed. (1965); Musielak, *Die Grundlagen der Beweislast im Zivilprozess* (1975).

cedural or substantive law. For instance the provisions of the ZPO establishing special rules for "documentary and check process" (*Urkunden- und Wechselprozess*) provide that claims and defenses which cannot be substantiated with the kinds of documentary evidence admissible under those rules shall be dismissed.[75] Substantively BGB §280(1)(2) gives a defendant who claims that his failure of performance of an obligation was without fault the burden of proving that his failure was the result of circumstances outside his agency.[76]

Case law has recognized shifts in the burden of proof under specific circumstances. A physician proven to have committed serious malpractice is given the burden to prove that the patient's injuries were not caused by his misdeeds.[77] In products liability cases, if the plaintiff proves that the defendant's product was placed in commerce in a defective state, the defendant has the burden of showing that the defect arose without its fault.[78] These allocations of burden of proof often flow from considerations of relative accessibility and practicality of proof as well as other concerns of public policy.[79] Similar considerations can lead to relaxation or even shift in the burden of proof when a party has acted so as to frustrate the other party's ability to satisfy its burden of proof (*Beweisvereitelung*).[80] Provisions of procedural or substantive

75. ZPO §§597, 598. The court may dismiss the case without prejudice to the plaintiff to proceed in the ordinary way. When the court enters a provisional judgment against the defendant, the case remains pending to determine the sufficiency of the objection or defense on the basis of complete evidence. See ZPO §§597(2), 598–600 and Ch. 11(B), below.

76. BGB §280(1)(2): "...*wenn der Schuldner die Pflichtverletzung nicht zu vertreten hat.*" For other examples of allocations of the burden of proof by substantive law see BGB §§179, 345, 363.

77. See Federal Supreme Court, 41 *NJW* 2948 (1988); German Constitutional Court, 32 *NJW* 1925 (1979); Stürner, "Die Einwirkungen der Verfassung auf das Zivilrecht und den Zivilprozess", 32 *NJW* 2334 (1979); Rosenberg/Schwab/Gottwald, §117(II)(6)(b), p. 675.

78. Federal Supreme Court, 114 BGHZ 284 (1991); 67 BGHZ 359 (1976); see generally Rosenberg/Schwab/Gottwald, §117(II)(6)(c), p. 675. Similar provisions have been enacted by statutory law; see German Law on Product Liability of December 15, 1989 (BGBl. I, p. 2198) §1(2).

79. For a discussion of the theoretical bases for legislative or judicial alterations of the basic rule on burdens of proof, see Rosenberg/Schwab/Gottwald, §117(II), pp. 670 ff.; Prütting, *Gegenwartsprobleme der Beweislast* (1983).

80. See ZPO §§427(2), 444, 446. This is also largely a matter of case law. For instance, if a doctor sued for malpractice has lost or destroyed patient records or X-rays that would have been useful in proving malpractice or causation, the court may shift the burden of proof on the issue affected by the loss of the evidence to the defendant who caused or facilitated the loss. See generally Rosenberg/Schwab/Gottwald, §117(II)(6)(a), p. 674; Thomas/Putzo/Reichold, §286, mn. 17–19; Stürner, *Die Aufklärungspflicht der Parteien des*

law which create "presumptions" (*Vermutungen*) also have the practical effect of shifting the burden of proving the presumed fact once the basic fact has been established.[81]

Analysis of the respective burdens of proof and assessing the evidence on each proposition are part of the process of the evaluation of evidence and reaching a judgment in a logical and orderly manner.

3. Evidence

Outside of a number of relatively broad privileges[82] and the practical constraints of its procedure,[83] the German civil court is not bound by rules of admissibility in its reception of evidence relevant to disputed facts. Nor are there procedural rules governing the way in which specific kinds of evidence are to be weighed and evaluated by the court in resolving ordinary disputes of fact. The principle which governs the court's consideration of all evidence is the "free evaluation of proof" (*freie Beweiswürdigung*).[84]

This does not mean that there are no rules for the process of proof of facts. Proof (*Beweis*) is divided into 5 statutory classifications,

a. Proof by observation and examination of persons and things (*Augenscheinbeweis*),[85]
b. Proof by witness testimony (*Zeugenbeweis*),[86]
c. Expert testimony (*Beweis durch Sachverständige*),[87]
d. Documentary proof (*Beweis durch Urkunden*),[88]

Zivilprozesses (1976), pp. 138 ff., 153 ff., 234 ff.; German Federal Supreme Court, 99 BGHZ 391 (1987); 85 BGHZ 212 (1982); 55 *NJW* 825 (2002).

81. See, for instance, BGB §1117(3) providing that if a creditor is in possession of a mortgage deed, due delivery of the deed is presumed. For a detailed discussion of presumptions see Leipold, *Beweislastregeln und gesetzliche Vermutungen* (1966).

82. See Ch. 8(C)(10) below for a discussion of testimonial and evidentiary privileges.

83. For instance, the requirement that every witness be nominated by a party. ZPO §§273(2)(4), 373. This is a consequence of the principle of party control of the proceedings. See Ch. 6(B)(2) and Ch. 7(H)(1) and (L) above.

84. See Walter, *Freie Beweiswürdigung* (1979) and Ch. 8(D) below for a more comprehensive discussion of the process of the consideration of evidence and reaching of factual conclusions. A proposed 2004 reform will provide for liberalized procedures for taking of evidence with the consent of the parties. See Huber, 36 *ZRP* 268, 269 (2003).

85. See ZPO §§371–372a.

86. See ZPO §§373–401.

87. See ZPO §§402–414.

88. See ZPO §§415–444.

e. Proof by party testimony (*Beweis durch Parteivernehmung*).[89]

The ZPO prescribes sometimes different rules for the authentication, presentation and overall management of the different forms of proof.

4. Proof by Observation and Examination of Persons and Things

Proof by observation encompasses all forms of immediate appreciation of persons, places and things by the court. The court can observe a party's physical condition, the physical condition of premises, the smell emitted by a source of pollution, the damage done to a motor vehicle, the sound emitted by a siren, or the view from different perspectives at an intersection, and can use these observations as evidence in making a fact determination. Although the term "*Augenscheinbeweis*" would seem to connote visual observations, the concept includes any form of direct sensory appreciation by the finder of fact.[90] If the matter to be observed is of a specialized or technical nature the court can appoint an expert to assist the court in making the observations.[91] The observations are ordinarily to be made by the members of the court which will make the decision,[92] although when it is not feasible for all of the members of the court to observe the evidence, the observation can be delegated to a single member of the court, or even to another court.[93]

The court may observe persons, places and objects nominated by and within the control of either of the parties, as well as places and things which are publicly accessible or available. As of 2002 the court is also authorized to order third parties to make places or objects available to the court for proof by observation.[94]

---

89. See ZPO §§445–455.

90. Thus, a court can make observations by sight, hearing, smell and touch. See Rosenberg/Schwab/Gottwald, § 120(I), p. 693.

91. See ZPO §372(1).

92. Under extraordinary circumstances, where it is simply not feasible for the court to make the observations itself, the court can appoint another person to make the observations and report to the court. An observer (*Augenscheinsgehilfe*) might be appointed under circumstances where it would be physically difficult, dangerous or socially embarrassing (observations of parts of a person's body) for the court to make the observations itself. The court appointed observer reports in a manner similar to a witness. See, e.g., Rosenberg/Schwab/Gottwald, §120(IV), p. 696.

93. ZPO §372(2). The judge or court delegated to observe the evidence can also appoint an expert to assist in the view.

94. See Ch. 7(L)(2); ZPO §§144, 371(1)–(3). Such an order can include access to prem-

In cases to determine parentage the court is entitled to order blood tests or physical examinations of relatives of parties and other third parties.[95] In other kinds of cases German courts may not order parties or third parties to submit to compelled physical or mental examination. This is out of deference to constitutionally protected rights of personal privacy. However this does not prevent the court from finding against a party who has the burden of proof on some issue relating to his physical or mental condition but refuses voluntarily to permit an examination by a court appointed physician or psychiatrist. The court may also draw negative inferences if the opposing party refuses to submit to a medical examination highly relevant to the other party's case.

The court's sensory reception of verbal information from witnesses or documents is not considered proof by observation. Proof by observation is limited to direct sensory appreciation from persons, things and objects themselves, not receipt of abstract information through the verbal process. Verbalized information is classified either as proof by witness (*Zeugenbeweis*) or proof by documents (*Urkundenbeweis*) and is governed by different rules. However tape recordings of verbal statements and all forms of electronic data are considered proof by observation,[96] while ordinary print-outs of electronic data will qualify as documentary evidence.

The court is required to document proof by observation in the case record by drafting minutes (*Protokolle*) of the observation setting forth the important facts observed. As with other matters made of record, counsel may suggest amplification or correction of the court's record of the matters observed in the proof by observation.[97]

Unjustified refusal to permit or cooperate with the taking of evidence by observation can have serious consequences for the uncooperative party. If the recalcitrant party has the burden of proof, its unjustified refusal to permit the

---

ises other than the third party's dwelling. When a party to litigation refuses access to its dwelling, the court may draw negative inferences. See Musielak/Stadler, § 144, mn. 10.

95. See ZPO §372a. For a detailed discussion of the parties' burden to submit to a medical examination in other kinds of cases see Federal Supreme Court, 25 *NJW* 1131 (1972); Damrau, in: *Münchener Kommentar zur Zivilprozessordnung*, § 371, mn. 7 ff.; Stürner, *Die Aufklärungspflicht der Parteien des Zivilprozesses* (1976), pp. 92 ff., 140 ff. For the taking of evidence abroad in parentage cases see Federal Supreme Court, 42 *JZ* 42 (1987), and the comment of Stürner, 42 *JZ* 44 (1987).

96. See ZPO § 371(1)(2) as in force since 2002; see Musielak/Stadler, § 371, mn. 6; Ch. 8(C)(6) below.

97. See Ch. 6(D) above on the development of the case record. As a matter of practice the minutes of the observation are often dictated by the presiding or reporting judge during the observation or as soon as practicable after the observation is made.

observation may result in failure to sustain its burden of proof and an adverse decision. If the court finds that a party which does not bear the burden of proof has refused without justification to cooperate in proof by observation, the court can draw the inference that the proof by observation would not have favored the contentions of the refusing party.[98]

Traditionally the court did not have the power to punish third persons who refused to cooperate with the taking of evidence by observation. Any party who possessed an independent right of access to the place, person, or material in the control of the third party could bring a separate action against the third party to gain the access necessary to provide the proof by observation. In this event the principal lawsuit would be stayed to permit the institution and completion of the independent action.[99] This could be a time-consuming procedure.

The recent amendments to the Civil Procedure Code which authorized court orders to third parties for access to evidence for proof by examination also authorize the court to punish non-compliance with such orders in the same manner as non-compliance with a summons to a witness.[100]

5. Proof by Witness Testimony

Proof by witness testimony is one of the most important categories of evidence used for the resolution of fact disputes. The German law of proof differentiates between testimony provided by third-party witnesses and information and testimony provided by the parties. The ancient saying that "No person can be witness in his own cause!" still has some reflection, at least in form, in German evidence law. A party's contribution to clarification of facts in dispute is generally made in the course of the hearing of the parties (*Anhörung der Parteien*) in the plenary proceeding. Only where other kinds of evidence do not suffice to clear up factual disputes will the court take actual testimony from the parties. Party testimony and party interrogation are regulated by their own special rules.[101]

---

98. See ZPO §§ 144, 371(3), 427; Musielak/Stadler, § 144, mn. 8 and § 371, mn. 20.

99. See Rosenberg/Schwab/Gottwald, § 120(II)(2) and ZPO §§ 144(3), 371(2)(2), 428 ff., BGB § 809. According to the recent amendments a party may choose to utilize the traditional complicated procedure or to apply to the court for a subpoena order as described above.

100. See ZPO §§ 144(2)(2), 371(2)(1), 390 providing for monetary penalties and arrest in extreme cases. See Zöller/Greger §144, mn. 4.

101. See Ch. 8(C)(8) below for a discussion of party testimony.

Outside the parties almost any natural person is competent to give witness testimony.[102] Minority or lack of mental capacity are not per se disqualifications. Witnesses within the territorial jurisdiction of the German courts have a duty to appear when summoned.[103] A witness's duty to appear and give testimony includes the obligation to consult relevant documents to refresh his recollection of the events on which he will be examined. The witness is supposed to bring such documents with him to assist him in giving his testimony to the extent that he is permitted to do so.[104] However actual production of documents in court for use as proof or for examination by the parties is governed by the rules governing documentary evidence.[105]

Witness testimony is almost always given orally in open court. The court can order the witness to provide his testimony in a written statement when such a procedure seems likely to convey the witness's information completely and accurately.[106]

Witnesses are expected to testify based on their personal knowledge and in a matter of fact and non-conclusory form.[107] The testimony is supposed to be

102. Officers, directors and top management of a corporate party are generally considered as "parties" for the purpose of the conditional bar on party testimony. Other employees of corporate parties can be nominated and examined as witnesses. See ZPO §§455(1), 449; Thomas/Putzo/Reichold, §455, mn. 1 and Vor §373, mn. 6 and 7; for members of a commercial partnership see Federal Supreme Court, 42 BGHZ 230 (1964).

103. See ZPO §§380 ff. Although witnesses resident in foreign states may be invited to appear, the attendance of such witnesses is voluntary. See Ch. 12(E)(4) and especially (4)(d) below on procedures for obtaining testimony and evidence abroad.

104. ZPO §378. Traditionally if the owner of the documents did not permit the witness to bring them to court, the court did not have the authority to require him to do so (see Thomas/Putzo/Reichold, §378, mn. 3). If a party with an interest in having the documents available had an independent right of access to the documents, the party could bring an independent action to obtain such access and then make the documents available to the witness. Now the court has also been given the power to order third parties to make documents cited by the parties directly available to the court, which could presumably then make them available for a witness to use during testimony. See ZPO §§142(1) and(2), 390, 428 ff., 429(2); Ch. 8(C)(6) below.

105. See Ch. 8(C)(6) and (9)(b) below.

106. See ZPO §377(3). This alternate procedure, which was introduced in 1990, has been little used. The statute provides that the witness to whom the written questions are put is to be told that he can be summoned to testify in person. If the responses to the written questions are not clear, the court can order the witness to appear in person to clarify them. For further details see Stadler, "Schriftliche Zeugenaussagen und pre-trial discovery im deutschen Zivilprozess", 110 *ZZP* 137 (1997); for use in preparatory proceedings see Ch. 7(L) above.

107. See, e.g., Rosenberg/Schwab/Gottwald, §122(I), p. 704. See Ch. 8(C)(9)(a) below.

given in the presence of the actual judge or judges who will decide the case.[108] In cases where the decision is not likely to turn on the personal credibility of a witness, the court can delegate the taking of the witness testimony to a single member of the court (*beauftragten Richter*) or, if necessary, to a judge of another court commissioned to take the testimony (*ersuchten Richter*).[109] The statute specifically authorizes the court to delegate the taking of testimony to one of its members or another judge when the proposed witness is 1) outside the territorial jurisdiction of the German courts, 2) statutorily protected from having to attend court and give testimony,[110] 3) physically unable to attend the place of court, 4) likely to provide the most reliable and meaningful testimony if examined at a place other than that of holding court,[111] 5) of such relatively small importance and such a great distance away that it does not make sense to require the witness to appear in court in person.[112] The decision in such a case cannot be based on a determination of the credibility of a witness not actually heard by all the judges.[113]

Regardless of where and before whom the witness's testimony is given, the parties and their counsel have the right to be present,[114] and the plenary proceedings in civil cases are generally public.[115] A witness is entitled to the as-

---

108. ZPO §355(1). This is an expression of the principle of immediacy (*Unmittelbarkeitsprinzip*). See Ch. 6(E) above. The words of ZPO §355(1) only require that evidence be taken by the "court" which renders the judgment, not necessarily by the individual deciding judges in person. In case of a change of judge or judges of the same court between the taking of evidence and the decision, a repetition of the taking of evidence is only necessary, when the personal credibility of the witness is of decisive importance. See Federal Supreme Court, 50 *NJW* 1586 (1997); Ch. 8(C)(9) below.

109. ZPO §375(1). ZPO §375(1a) (added in 1990) authorizes such a delegation to a member of the court if the delegation leads to the simplification of the proceedings and the court can make its factual determination without the need for the presence of the witness. See Federal Supreme Court, 53 *NJW* 2024 (2000). A planned reform for 2004 provides for utilization of witness testimony taken in other court proceedings. See Huber, 36 *ZRP* 268, 270 (2003).

110. ZPO §375(1)(2). For instance, the President of the Federal Republic is to give testimony in his home. ZPO §375(2).

111. ZPO §375(1)(1).

112. ZPO §375(1)(3).

113. See Rosenberg/Schwab/Gottwald, §122(VII)(3), p. 712; Federal Supreme Court, 44 *NJW* 1302 (1991).

114. ZPO §357. This right of the parties to be present at all stages of the taking of proof by the court is referred to as the "principle of party-publicity" (*Parteiöffentlichkeitsprinzip*). It is an expression of the right to be heard. See Ch. 6(E)(2) and (3) above.

115. See Ch. 6(E)(2) above on the principle of publicity in German civil proceedings.

sistance of the witness's own counsel in preparation for and during the course of giving testimony.[116]

According to the ZPO witness testimony is generally supposed to be given under oath. The oath is to be administered after the conclusion of the witness's testimony.[117] The oath should be administered, when, in the sound discretion of the judge, the oath seems advisable because the witness's testimony is of such importance to the outcome of the case or because it is likely to lead to a truthful statement by the witness.[118] The oath is considered advisable when it may alleviate doubt about the credibility of a witness. When only a portion of a witness's testimony is deemed crucial to the court's decision, the oath can be restricted to that particular portion.[119]

In practice the oath is seldom administered. The court will assume that counsel's failure to request that the oath be administered is the equivalent of a waiver of the oath.[120] German courts are not eager to swear witnesses unless one or the other of the parties insist on it.[121]

6. Documentary Proof

a. Public and Private Documents

Documentary evidence (*Urkundenbeweis*) is any form of incorporation of information in verbal form in a written recording.[122] Photographs, drawings and other forms of literal depictions are not considered documents, but are objects subject to proof by observation. The same is true for tape recordings of verbal statements and all forms of electronic data.[123] But print-outs of elec-

116. See Rosenberg/Schwab/Gottwald, §122(VII)(4); for criminal matters see German Constitutional Court, 28 *NJW* 103 (1974).

117. ZPO §392. The witness is required to swear that "to the best of his knowledge he has spoken the entire truth and has not concealed anything" ("...*der Zeuge nach bestem Wissen die reine Wahrheit gesagt und nichts verschwiegen habe.*")

118. ZPO §391. Persons of less than 16 years of age or of impaired competence are not sworn, ZPO §393.

119. See Rosenberg/Schwab/Gottwald, §122(VI), p. 710.

120. Under ZPO §391 the oath is not to be administered if the parties both dispense with it.

121. If a party requests administration of the oath and the oath appears expedient to elicit truthful testimony, the oath must be administered. ZPO §391. For further details see Federal Supreme Court, 43 BGHZ 368 (1965).

122. See Zöller/Geimer, Vor §415, mn. 2; Federal Supreme Court, 65 BGHZ 300 (1975).

123. See ZPO §371(1)(2); Musielak/Stadler, §371, mn. 6; Thomas/Putzo/Reichold, Vor §371, mn. 6; Zöller/Geimer, Vor §415, mn. 2; Ch. 8(C)(4).

tronic data qualify as documentary evidence. There are no requirements as to form or signature of documents. All writings can be considered documentary evidence.

Within the broad category of documentary proof German procedure distinguishes between public or official documents (*öffentliche Urkunden*) and private documents (*Privaturkunden*). Public documents are defined as those documents created by a public official in the course of public duty.[124] The most important category of public documents is composed of documents created by public notaries (*Notare*). Such documents include wills, real estate deeds, certain kinds of private contracts, and incorporations.[125]

By statute a public document constitutes sufficient proof of the public proceedings reported in the document.[126] This means, for instance, that a document prepared by a public notary constitutes sufficient proof of the facts set forth in the document such as actions that occurred in the presence of the notary or public official which are then memorialized in the document.[127]

Private documents are all documents other than public documents. Private documents proved to have been signed by their issuers are proof that the statements contained are their issuers' statements. It is then up to the court to draw whatever conclusions are justified by the statements in the documents.[128] Normally the court will conclude that facts happened as declared in the document. For example, a receipt will be taken as confirmation of payment.

---

124. ZPO §415. Foreign public documents can also qualify as public documentary proof if adequately authenticated. ZPO §438(I).

125. The ancient institution of the public notary remains of considerable significance in the civil law world. While the precise qualifications and licensing of notaries is a matter for the German states (*Länder*), in general all real estate deeds, wills, incorporations, and certain contracts such as marriage settlements, must be drawn by licensed public notaries. For more particulars on the education, role and function of public notaries in modern Germany and Europe see Schilken, *Gerichtsverfassungsrecht*, 2nd ed. (1994), §32, pp. 415 ff.; Stürner, "Die notarielle Urkunde im europäischen Rechtsverkehr", 1995 *DNotZ* 343 (1995) and in French language "L'acte notarié dans le commerce juridique européen, 56 *Revue Internationale de Droit comparé* 515 (1996) et 100 *La Revue du Notariat (Montréal)* 251 (1998). For a discussion of the "Code Européen de Déontologie" of the notaries of the European Union see Schippel 1995 *DNotZ* 329, 334 (1995).

126. ZPO §415(1), 417, 418. This is an exception to the doctrine of free evaluation of evidence (*freie Beweiswürdigung*) which applies to most factual proof. See Ch. 8(I)(1) below. It does not foreclose proof that the document is not an accurate reflection of the action reported. ZPO §415(2).

127. See ZPO §§415, 418.

128. See ZPO §416; Federal Supreme Court, 55 *NJW* 2707 (2002). This is also true if the signature is authenticated by a notary.

Documentary proof is also categorized by function.[129] Documents are either dispositive documents (*wirkende Urkunde*) or reporting documents (*bezeugende Urkunde*). Dispositive documents are those which themselves constitute a legal act to be proved. They include deeds, judgments, wills, checks, and the like. Reporting documents contain information which is relevant to the determination of a fact in issue other than the legal effect of the document. They include all forms of records of public action, filings, reports, business records, diaries, letters and the like. A document's functional category does not affect its admissibility, but may play a role in its evaluation by the court.[130]

b. Production and Inspection of Documents

For a long time German civil procedure has empowered a party relying on a document in the possession or control of the opposing party to request the court to order production of the document for use as documentary proof in evidentiary proceedings if the requesting party had a legal right to possession or use of the document. Up until recently, however, there was no right to production if the request was based solely on the document's relevance to a decisive issue in the case. Since the 2001 reforms the court has the authority to order production of documents based solely on their relevance to disputed facts.[131]

The request for an order of production must identify the document requested with reasonable specificity, describe its relevance to some fact in issue, and set forth the basis for the belief that it is in the possession or control of the opponent. If the existence of the document or the opponent's obligation to produce it is contested, the court can decide the issue by simple order after hearing. Unjustified refusal to produce a document requested and ordered to be produced can be sanctioned by adverse inferences as to the document's contents.[132]

Traditionally the court also had no power to order third parties to produce documents solely on the basis of their relevance in litigation between others. If a party had a substantive right to possession of a document in the hands of a third party, that party could request that the proceeding be stayed to permit him to exercise his right to possession against the third party, if

129. See Rosenberg/Schwab/Gottwald, § 121(II)(2), p. 698.

130. See Ch. 8(D)(1) below.

131. See ZPO §§ 142(1) on the one hand and 421–427 on the other. See also Ch. 7(L)(1) above for required production of documents during preparatory proceedings.

132. See ZPO §§ 421 ff., 427 and for ZPO § 142(1) Musielak/Stadler, § 142, mn. 7.

necessary by independent litigation.[133] Otherwise documents not voluntarily made available by third parties could not be obtained by compulsory process.

The 2001 civil procedure reforms now give German courts the power to order third parties to produce unprivileged documents solely on the basis of their relevance to determine facts at issue in pending civil litigation. The court has authority to punish non-compliance by contempt sanctions. While the provisions authorizing such production are found in the parts of the Civil Procedure Code covering preparation for oral hearings, they have been incorporated by reference in the sections regulating documentary evidence, and can be used at any stage of the proceedings.[134]

c. *Authenticity of Documents*

Documentary evidence has probative value only when the document is deemed authentic (*echt*).

According to the statute production of the original signed counterpart of a public document should normally be required.[135] A certified copy or abstract (*beglaubigte Abschrift*) may also be used, subject to the power of the court to request production of the original.[136] The authenticity of an official document can be inferred from its appearance and apparent official origin.[137] In case of doubt the court can make inquiries with the originating public body either at the request of a party or on its own motion.[138] In practice plain photocopies of public documents are routinely used when there is little dispute as to their authenticity.

The original signed version of a private document is also preferred for evidentiary purposes, although the court may consider a certified or uncertified copy and give it such weight as the court finds appropriate.[139] When authenticity is not in question plain photocopies are the rule in practice.

---

133. ZPO §§428–431 (pre 2002 version).

134. See ZPO §§142, 390; 273(2)(5); 428, 429. For use in preparatory proceedings see Ch. 7(L)(1).

135. ZPO §435 (official documents).

136. ZPO §435. In cases when the court requests production of an original public document, the proponent of the document can explain the circumstances which prevent production of the original, in which case the court is required to give the certified copy such credence as the court finds appropriate.

137. ZPO §437(1).

138. ZPO §437(2).

139. Rosenberg/Schwab/Gottwald, §121(III)(1)(b), p. 699; Federal Supreme Court, 33 *NJW* 1047 (1980).

During the course of written or oral preparatory proceedings a party is expected to state its position with respect to the authenticity of all private documents referred to in the pleadings and briefs of the opponent.[140] Failure to do so will result in an inference that authenticity is not contested unless the context makes clear that the party intends to attack the authenticity of particular private documents.[141] If a party fails to specifically deny authorship of a private document attributed to him by the opposing party, authorship and authenticity are deemed admitted.[142] In the case of other private documents, if the opponent responds that the authenticity is unknown or contested, the party proposing the document has the burden of demonstrating its authenticity.[143]

The primary form of proof of authenticity of signed documents is proof of authenticity of the signature. Authenticity of a signature can be established by comparison of the signature with a specimen of known origin[144] either by the court or with the assistance of an expert witness.[145] If the signature on a private document is found to be genuine, the authenticity of the material in the document preceding the authentic signature may be inferred.[146] If the document is not signed, or if it is not feasible to authenticate the signature, its au-

---

140. ZPO §439(1). If a document is signed, the opposing party must state its position with respect to the authenticity of the signature. ZPO §439(2).

141. ZPO §439(3).

142. Rosenberg/Schwab/Gottwald, §121(III)(1)(b), p. 699.

143. See ZPO §§439(1), 138(3), (4), 440(1). The burden of proof of authenticity of private documents requested by the court on its own motion rests with the party whose position is favored by the documents.

144. ZPO §441. The party asserting the authenticity of the document has the responsibility to produce a specimen of established origin. ZPO §441(2). If authentic specimens can only be obtained from the opposing party the court has the authority to require the opponent to produce them on pain of a finding of authenticity by default. ZPO §441(3). If an authentic specimen can only be obtained from a third party the court may grant a continuance to permit the proponent to institute proceedings to obtain it. ZPO §441(4). According to the prevailing opinion, production cannot be ordered under ZPO §144 of a specimen of a third party's signature. See Zöller/Geimer, §441, mn. 2. A third party cannot be required to create a signature specimen if an existing specimen cannot be identified. Zöller/Geimer, §441, mn. 3.

145. See Deitigsmann, *Grundlagen und Praxis der gerichtlichen Handschriftenvergleichung* (1954).

146. ZPO §440(2). This is also true of private documents with notarially certified signatures and private documents with blank signatures. See Federal Supreme Court, 53 *NJW* 1179, 1181 (2000). There is no inference of authenticity for material *following* an authentic signature. See Federal Supreme Court, 113 BGHZ 48 (1990); Rosenberg/Schwab/Gottwald, §121(III)(1)(b), p. 699.

thenticity can be established by any form of proof calculated to convince the court that the paper before the court is in fact what it is purported to be by its proponent.

Documentary evidence is the one class of proof which is partially governed by specific rules of evaluation.[147] These rules modify and in some cases limit the principle of free evaluation of evidence (*freie Beweiswürdigung*) which governs consideration of almost all other forms of evidence.[148]

7. Expert Testimony

If the subject matter of factual inquiry is outside the knowledge or experience of the court, proof must be had through expert witnesses (*Sachverständige*) who are permitted to draw from the immediate facts conclusions which the court can adopt in its decision.[149] The high prevalence of technical and scientific evidence in modern day litigation make the use of expert testimony mandatory in a high proportion of litigated cases.

a. *Subject Matters for Expert Testimony*

Any matter of specialized expertise can be the subject matter of expert testimony. This includes matters of specialized life experience as well as those requiring technical or scientific education. An expert can be named to assist the court with specialized issues of foreign law. The parties can suggest the naming of an expert with respect to a factual contention, or the court can decide to name an expert witness on its own motion.[150] Generally the judge determines whether the issue to be addressed lies within her factual ability and experience or whether she will seek specialized assistance from an expert witness.[151] But failure to appoint an expert witness to provide support for a specialized finding or conclusion in a judgment can be a procedural error requiring correction on appeal.[152]

147. ZPO §§415–419.

148. See Ch. 8(D)(1) below.

149. For a comparative discussion of the advantages of the German approach to expert testimony, see Langbein, "The German Advantage in Civil Procedure", 52 *U. Chicago L. Rev.* 823, 841 (1985).

150. ZPO §§144, 273(2)(5), 403.

151. See Federal Supreme Court, 53 *NJW* 1946, 1947 (2000); Rosenberg/Schwab/Gottwald, §123(III)(2)(a). The court can take into account the expertise of individual members of the panel or of the first instance court (on an appeal) in determining whether additional expertise should be employed.

152. See, e.g., Federal Supreme Court, 53 *NJW* 1946, 1947 (2000) (medical findings). It is the court's responsibility to discuss the necessity of expert testimony with the parties

b. Court Appointed Experts

Although parties may propose and present reports and expert testimony in their briefs and pleadings and as a form of documentary evidence at hearings for the reception of evidence, the great bulk of expert testimony is presented through court appointed expert witnesses (*Sachverständige*) who are appointed by the court to address specific factual or legal issues.[153]

In most cases the parties will agree on the need for expert testimony and even the identity of the person to be the court appointed expert. Although the expert is in theory and in fact an aid to the court, in most cases of any consequence the parties exercise considerable influence on the naming of the experts.[154] There are no particular requirements for designation as an expert witness. The key is that the expert possess the particular knowledge and experience that will enable her to assist the court with respect to the issue designated for expertise.

It should be stressed that the expert witness is, in a sense, an official or arm of the court, rather than a witness for or against a particular party. German civil justice sets great store by the impartiality, diligence, and ability of court-appointed expert witnesses. Although the court appointed expert appears and delivers his expert testimony in the manner of a witness, in many respects he is regulated and performs more like a judicial officer, albeit appointed for a single case. A person named as an expert witness is expected to, and does, take his duties very seriously and render expertise of a high quality and diligence.[155]

---

and to give them the opportunity for comment. For a good survey see Thomas/Putzo/Reichold, Vor §402, mn. 3. See Generally Ch. 6(C)(2).

153. Expert evidence presented by parties is regarded with some suspicion and generally not accepted as the basis of proof of a contested fact. See Rosenberg/Schwab/Gottwald, §123(II)(4), p. 718. Written testimony of party expert witnesses may be used to challenge or point out weakness in the testimony of court appointed expert witnesses and may support requests for further questioning of court appointed experts or the appointment of additional experts. See Federal Supreme Court, 46 *NJW* 2382 (1993); 54 *NJW* 77 (2001); German Constitutional Court, 50 *NJW* 122 (1997); Thomas/Putzo/Reichold, Vor §402, mn. 5.

154. See ZPO §404. In fact, if the parties agree on a particular person as the expert, the court is required to honor their agreement and name that person as expert. The court is, however permitted, to restrict the parties' choice to persons on a particular list approved by the court. ZPO §404(4). A planned 2004 reform would allow utilization of expert evidence from other court proceedings. See Huber, 36 *ZRP* 268, 270 (2003).

155. See, e.g., Bayerlein (ed.), *Praxishandbuch Sachverständigenrecht*, 3rd ed. (2002); Jessnitzer/Ulrich, *Der gerichtliche Sachverständige*, 11th ed. (2000), on selection, naming, and subsequent treatment of court-appointed expert witnesses in German litigation.

In some cases expert witnesses are also fact witnesses. For instance, a doctor who has treated the injured plaintiff may be nominated by one of the parties as a fact witness to describe the injured party's injuries and treatment. The same individual may be appointed by the court as an expert witness to give an opinion about the patient's longer term prospects or any permanent disability.[156]

An expert witness may be appointed merely to provide specialized information as a matter of background to the factual or legal question at issue. This is often the case with experts on foreign law who describe the specialized law potentially applicable to the facts at issue, but leave it to the court to apply the law to the facts found.[157]

In many cases the expert is expected not only to impart the specialized knowledge in abstract form, but also apply that knowledge to the facts of the case and communicate her conclusions to the court. In such cases the expert is to state the specialized principles applied and describe her reasoning in applying those principles to the facts to the parties and the court.

Finally, the expert can be commissioned to make actual determinations of concrete facts if such determinations require a specific expertise. For instance many medical conditions can only be diagnosed by a qualified doctor. The expert's fact determinations can then be used as the basis for expert conclusions.

While a party may indicate in its pleadings or briefs that expert testimony will be required to establish a particular factual contention, the actual naming of the expert is a matter for the court.[158] If, however, the parties agree on a particular expert witness, the court is obliged to hear that expert.[159]

A party has the right to seek the disqualification of a proposed court appointed expert on the same grounds that a judge would be subject to dis-

---

156. See ZPO § 414 ("*sachverständiger Zeuge*"). It is said that fact witnesses are "irreplaceable" (*unersetzlich*) because of their unique knowledge of the facts of a given case. Expert witnesses, on the other hand, are defined by their expertise, not their acquaintanceship with the facts of a particular case, and have no particular connection with any particular case. See Rosenberg/Schwab/Gottwald, §123(II)(1), pp. 717/718. Expert witnesses who are acquainted with the facts of a particular case ("*sachverständige Zeugen*") fall in the borderline between testimony and expert testimony. See Rosenberg/Schwab/Gottwald, § 123(II)(2), p. 718.

157. See Rosenberg/Schwab/Gottwald, §123(I)(1), p. 717. This is also often the case with expert witnesses who describe customs or trade usages. Their testimony is limited to the existence of the custom or trade usage, and the court decides the applicability of such custom or usage in the case at bar.

158. See ZPO §§ 403, 404. When the proof is taken before a single member of the panel or another designated judge, that judge may select the expert. ZPO §§372(2), 405.

159. ZPO §404(4). The court may name on its own motion other experts on the same issue. See Thomas/Putzo/Reichold, § 404, mn. 2.

qualification.[160] These include well-founded doubts as to the expert's likely impartiality arising from the expert's relationship with a particular party or interest, or from the expert's conduct in the present or prior proceedings.[161] An application for disqualification is to be filed with the court or designated judge who has appointed the expert. The party seeking disqualification has the burden of convincing the court of the existence of grounds for disqualification.[162] The application should be filed as soon as the party is aware of the potential grounds for disqualification.[163] If a party waits to apply for disqualification until the expert has filed his testimony (*Gutachten*) the party must show why in the exercise of reasonable diligence the issue was not raised at an earlier time.[164] An order disqualifying an expert witness is non-appealable. Refusal to disqualify will support an immediate miscellaneous appeal.[165]

There is no particular procedure for finding and selecting a qualified person to serve as an expert witness in a particular case. In many cases the court can select experts from lists of qualified persons willing to serve provided by state licensing authorities for particular professions. The court may also request the parties to provide names of potential qualified experts.[166] In practice, the court usually discusses the naming of experts with the parties at a preliminary hearing or conference or during the plenary hearing and asks for their suggestions, or at least for their comments on experts whom the court may have in mind. This allows potential objections to an expert to be raised informally without the need for a formal application for disqualification.[167]

Expert witnesses are compensated under the auspices of the court. The expert's fee is usually determined at the time the expert is named. In many cases the amount of the fee is agreed on by the court, parties and expert. There is

---

160. ZPO §406. ZPO §41 sets forth the statutory grounds for disqualification of a judge. In addition a judge (and hence an expert witness) may be disqualified for well founded "apprehension of partiality" ("*Besorgnis der Befangenheit*"). ZPO §42. See also ZPO §408(3).

161. See, Rosenberg/Schwab/Gottwald, §123(III)(2)(d), pp. 720 f.

162. ZPO §406(3). An application for disqualification can also be made at a preliminary or plenary hearing or conference with the court.

163. ZPO §406(2)(1) specifies that the application shall be filed within two weeks of the naming of the expert if the cause for disqualification is known at that time.

164. ZPO §406(2)(2). If the cause for disqualification appears for the first time in the expert's testimony, the application must be filed at the earliest practicable time. See Rosenberg/Schwab/Gottwald, §123(III)(2)(d), p. 721.

165. ZPO §406(5).

166. ZPO §404(2) and (3).

167. If a party participates in the selection and naming of an expert, grounds for disqualification then known or ascertainable but not raised until later can be treated as waived. See Musielak/Huber, §406, mn. 16.

also a statute which prescribes ranges of fees for experts based in part on the difficulty of the expertise and the professional ranking of the expert witness, with the actual fee to be set by the court within the statutory range.[168] Payment of the expert's fee is the initial responsibility of the party who has the burden of proof on the issue to be addressed by the expert.[169] Ultimately the expert's fee like other fees and costs in the case will be assessed against the losing party.[170]

c. *Procedure on Expert Testimony*

The determination that expert testimony will be necessary and the naming of one or more court-appointed expert witnesses can take place at almost any stage of preliminary or plenary proceedings. When it is clear from the pleadings or discussions at a preliminary preparatory hearing that expertise will be required, the court will appoint the expert and specify the subject matter of the expert testimony requested before the plenary hearing. Sometimes it is only at the plenary hearing that it becomes clear that the case cannot be properly resolved without resort to expert testimony. In such a case the expert will be expected to deliver her testimony at a separate evidentiary hearing at a later time. The name of the expert, a description of the subject matter on which the expert is to testify, and any specific instructions to the expert or limitations on the expert's mandate will be set forth in a proof order (*Beweisbeschluss*) or in the minutes (*Protokolle*) of the preliminary or plenary hearing.[171]

The German civil procedure code imposes on persons who accept appointment as experts specific affirmative performance obligations. First of all,

---

168. See § ZPO 413 and Law on the Compensation of Witnesses and Expert Witnesses (*Gesetz über die Entschädigung von Zeugen und Sachverständigen* or *ZSEG*) § 3. If the statutorily prescribed fee is not sufficient to interest a qualified expert in the assignment the parties may, and as a practical matter often must, agree on a larger fee. See ZSEG § 7.

169. See ZPO §§ 379, 402; Zöller/Greger, § 411, mn. 2a; Federal Supreme Court, 62 *NJW* 2823 (1999). If the expert is named by the court on its own motion, the court will allocate initial responsibility for payment of the expert's fee at the time the expert is named—usually in accord with the court's impression of the party likely to be benefitted by the expert testimony. See Musielak/Huber, § 379, mn. 1 (unclear). If the party responsible for payment of an expert's fee is receiving legal aid (*Prozesskostenhilfe*) it is relieved of the obligation to advance expert witness fees. See ZPO § 122(1) and Ch. 4(I)(2)(a). If the party needs private expertise, the fee can be considered an attorneys's expense and paid by legal aid. See ZPO § 122; Zöller/Philippi, § 122, mn. 7 (expert witness fees advanced by legal aid attorney can be reimbursed by legal aid).

170. See Ch. 9(E) below.

171. See ZPO §§ 144, 273(2)(5), 358 ff., 358a; Ch. 7(L) and Ch. 8(C)(1)(c) above.

the expert has the obligation to consider the assignment and make sure that she or he is fully qualified by knowledge and experience and has the necessary time to render the expertise requested. A court appointed expert may not delegate her assignment to another, but may employ subordinate assistants to help with the work.[172] If the expert is in doubt about the scope of the project or the questions to be answered, she is expected to ask the court for clarification.[173] Above all, the expert undertakes the duty of timely and satisfactory delivery of the expert testimony sought.[174] Once the expert has been named and accepted the assignment, she can withdraw or resign only with the consent of the court and for good cause shown.[175]

In many cases the court will ask the expert for an opinion based on facts either agreed by the parties or found by the court and made known to the expert at the time of appointment.[176] In such a case the expert's function is to accept the facts as relayed to him and draw conclusions from those facts based on the expert's specialized knowledge and expertise.[177] If there are other facts which might be of consequence to the expert opinion, the expert is not at liberty to determine those facts for himself, but should either advise the court and ask for instructions or render the opinion in alternative form depending on what the other facts might be.[178]

In some cases the determination of the very facts in issue requires expertise.[179] In such a case the expert may well perform a fact-finding role. At the time the expert is named, the court is required to define the subject matter

---

172. ZPO §407a(1) and (2). The expert is required to identify any such assistants and describe their roles on the project.

173. ZPO §407a(3). The same is true if it appears that the expenses of the project will be out of proportion to the amount in controversy or will exceed the amount paid in advance.

174. See ZPO §407a(1)(1). Expert witnesses who are public officials or who maintain professional practices are assumed by virtue of their appointments to have undertaken to perform as experts when called on by courts. Other persons named as potential expert witnesses are expected affirmatively to indicate their readiness to undertake expert witness assignments and the duties which go with them. ZPO §407 and §407a(1)(2).

175. ZPO §408(1). An expert who without justification fails to deliver his expert testimony is responsible for the costs thereby incurred and may be fined. ZPO §409.

176. ZPO §404a(3).

177. This would be the case, for example, if the expert were appointed to give testimony on the applicability of foreign law to a particular fact situation.

178. See §404a(1) and (2); Federal Supreme Court, 37 BGHZ 389 (1962); Rosenberg/Schwab/Gottwald §123(III)(3)(a), p. 722.

179. For instance, when the factual issue is the medical condition of a party or the financial condition of a business enterprise.

and extent of fact finding authorized and the manner in which the parties will participate.[180]

The court can convey its instructions to the expert in writing, or at a hearing called for that purpose.[181] At such a hearing the court can discuss with the expert the factual scope of the investigation and the formulation of the questions to be submitted. The parties have the right to be present at such a hearing and to participate in communications between the court and the expert.[182] In practice more informal communications are often had by conference call. The court retains the responsibility to supervise the activities of the expert and to answer questions and clarify the expert's assignment as necessary.[183]

It is not clear how much of the contact between judge and expert must be on the record with the participation by the parties or their lawyers. A careful judge makes notes for the case record of any *ex parte* conversation or contact with an expert witness. The parties should always be consulted on important questions or issues, and should be notified if the expert communicates new or unexpected findings or discoveries to the court.

In most cases proceedings will be so structured that the expert testimony will be expected, at least in one alternative, to provide the basis on which the litigation can be disposed of and the case will be simply stayed pending receipt of the expert testimony. In other cases it is possible that other evidentiary proceedings or hearings for oral argument can take place during the interval given the expert to prepare the testimony.

---

180. ZPO §404a(4). The principle of party publicity (*Parteiöffentlichkeit*) requires that the parties be permitted to participate in any fact-finding to the extent feasible for them to do so. See German Constitution, Article 103(I); Ch. 6(E)(2) above. So, for instance, the parties and their lawyers would generally be given the opportunity to be present for any examination by the expert of concrete objects or corporate books and records, but not necessarily for laboratory experiments and never for medical examinations. To permit the parties to be present at a medical examination of a party or other person, even if the examination were required for expert testimony, would be a violation of the constitutional right of privacy. See Rosenberg/Schwab/Gottwald, §123(III)(3)(b), p. 722. The conflict between the principle of party publicity and the protection of trade secrets or other forms of confidentiality is resolved on a case-by-case basis. See German Constitutional Court, 47 *NJW* 2347 (1994); 48 *NJW* 40 (1995); 50 *NJW* 1909 (1997); Federal Supreme Labor Court, 46 *NJW* 612 (1993); Federal Supreme Court, 116 BGHZ 47 (1991). For a flexible approach see Stürner, *Die Aufklärungspflicht der Parteien des Zivilprozesses* (1976), § 14(III), pp. 208 ff., 218 ff.; Musielak/Stadler, §357, mn. 4 with further references.

181. ZPO §404a(2) and (5).

182. ZPO §404a(5). The parties are to receive copies of any written communications from the court to the expert.

183. ZPO §404a, esp. §404a(2).

In most cases the court will require the expert to provide his testimony in writing.[184] The form of the testimony can vary from simple completion of a preprinted report form to a detailed custom report. The written testimony should disclose the facts relied on or found, set forth any applicable abstract principles[185] and then set forth the expert's conclusions and the reasons for such conclusions.

When the testimony is rendered in writing the court will send copies to the parties or their counsel at the time the testimony is filed and solicit their comments, objections, further followup questions and any requests that the expert be heard orally.[186] Based on the responses received or on the court's own motion the court may pose additional followup questions to the expert to be answered in supplementary written testimony or may summon the expert to appear at a hearing to present and be questioned on his testimony orally.[187]

Upon receipt of the expert's written testimony the parties may suggest to the court additional questions to be posed to the expert in elaboration or clarification of the expert's testimony. The parties may also request that the expert be summoned to appear in person and be questioned at an oral hearing.[188] The parties may file written briefs arguing that the expert testimony should not be accepted or credited by the court.[189]

---

184. In such cases the expert is to file his written testimony with the court before a specified deadline, which can be enlarged for good cause. ZPO §411 regulates the process of written expert testimony.

185. For example, of law or science.

186. ZPO §411(3) and (4). The court can set time limits for the parties to file objections to the testimony, additional questions, or requests that the expert be summoned to appear at a hearing. The parties may request that the time limits be extended to permit them adequate time to address the expert's testimony, including, if necessary, to consult with their own experts. See Federal Supreme Court, 35 *NJW* 1335 (1982); 41 *NJW* 2302 (1988).

187. The court is required to summon the expert to appear for questioning if a party makes a timely and good faith request for a personal appearance. See German Constitutional Court, 51 *NJW* 2273 (1998); Federal Supreme Court, 50 *NJW* 802 (1997); 51 *NJW* 162 (1998).

188. If the appearance at an oral hearing will involve additional compensation to the expert beyond that already provided for, such appearance may be conditioned on prepayment of the additional fee by the party requesting the appearance. See ZPO §§379, 402; GKG §68.

189. These objections can include written testimony from party experts (*Privatgutachten*). See Ch. 8(C)(7)(b) below. If objections so raised cannot be reconciled with the written testimony the court may be constitutionally required to summon the court-appointed expert to an oral hearing to explain the testimony or address the objections. See German Constitutional Court, 50 *NJW* 122 (1997).

In some relatively simple cases the expert will not be required to file written testimony, but will merely appear at a hearing to give oral expert testimony. This is sometimes the case when the expert is also a fact witness, such as a treating physician in a personal injury case (*sachverständiger Zeuge*, ZPO §414).

If the expert has been appointed and the questions formulated during preliminary proceedings, the expert might well appear at an evidentiary hearing appended to the plenary proceeding. Otherwise the expert will appear at an evidentiary hearing specially scheduled to hear from the expert, with or without other evidence.

When an expert appears to be questioned at an oral hearing, he is treated like any other witness. Initial questioning is by the presiding judge. The judge may ask the expert to summarize his filed written testimony and then follow up with specific questions designed to clarify ambiguity, disclose underlying assumptions of fact, or challenge the expert's contentions or conclusions. The other judges, and then the parties and their counsel will then be allowed to pose questions as with other witnesses.[190] The court must make sure that the substance of the expert's oral testimony at the hearing is included in the minutes of the hearing.[191]

If the parties' written objections and questions or the proceedings at an oral hearing of an expert disclose serious deficiencies in an expert's testimony,[192] the court can appoint a second expert to address the same or a reformulated version of the questions originally committed to expertise.[193] In exceptional cases where the court has difficulty reconciling the differing expert testimonies of more than one expert witness, the court may appoint a "super expert" (*Obergutachter*) of exceptional specialized knowledge or ability to provide "review expert testimony" (*Obergutachten*) clarifying or reconciling any inconsistency or conflict among the other expert witnesses and assisting the court in analyzing their testimony.[194] The court can also summon disagreeing ex-

---

190. These questions by parties and counsel may be posed either through the court or directly. See ZPO §§396, 397; Ch. 8(C)(9)(a) below.

191. ZPO §160(3)(4). The expert's written testimony may be incorporated in the minutes of the hearing by reference. ZPO §160(5).

192. Such as incompleteness, an inadequate or unclear factual basis, apparent internal inconsistencies, outmoded scientific research procedures. See, e.g., Thomas/Putzo/Reichold, §412, mn. 1.

193. ZPO §412(1). This can also occur when an appointed expert is disqualified after filing his testimony, ZPO §412(2).

194. The ZPO contains no specific provision for appointment of an *Obergutachter*. The practice appears to have developed from case law. See Thomas/Putzo/Reichold, §412, mn. 3; Rosenberg/Schwab/Gottwald, §123(VI), p. 726.

pert witnesses to testify at the same hearing, with or without a "super expert". Sometimes such confrontations can generate free discussions among the experts from which surprising consensi can emerge.

Expert witnesses are rarely sworn. The court has the discretion to order that the expert be sworn if the issue on which the expert was heard is of great importance.[195] Alternatively the court may require the expert to acknowledge or refer to an oath which was given by the expert at the time the expert agreed to be listed by a licensing or trade organization as a person qualified and willing to give expert testimony. The oath is not to be used to help resolve the court's doubts concerning the truthfulness of an expert's testimony. In such a case the proper course of action is the appointment of another expert.[196]

d. Evaluation and Use of Expert Testimony

German judges typically set a high value on the testimony of qualified court-appointed experts. Although expert testimony, like all evidence, is subject to free evaluation (*freie Beweiswürdigung*) by the court, it is rare for a court judgment to depart from the opinion of a court appointed expert within the field of expertise.

The parties can and do argue against acceptance of expert conclusions contrary to their respective positions based on logical inconsistency, false or incomplete factual assumptions by the expert, or even lack of expert qualifications relevant to the opinions expressed.[197] Parties may provide reports of their own experts (*Privatgutachten*) contradicting or pointing our weaknesses in the position of the court appointed expert. Such submissions must be considered by the court[198] and may lead the court to avoid relying on a suspect conclu-

---

195. ZPO §410 with ZPO §391. Although ZPO §410 seems to contemplate routine swearing of an expert, either before or after rendering the testimony, in practice it occurs rarely. See Federal Supreme Court, 51 *NJW* 3355, 3356 (1998); Thomas/Putzo/Reichold, §410, mn.1. The form of the expert's oath is "that the expert will render or has rendered the testimony requested of him impartially and according to his best knowledge and belief" (*...dass der Sachverständige das von ihm erforderte Gutachten unparteiisch und nach bestem Wissen und Gewissen erstatten werde oder erstattet habe*).

196. See Rosenberg/Schwab/Gottwald, §123(IV)(C), p. 724; Thomas/Putzo/Reichold, §410, mn. 1.

197. As indicated above, if at any time an issue arises of possible bias of the expert toward or against one of the parties or interests represented, either party can seek disqualification of the expert. See ZPO §406; Ch. 8(C)(7)(b) above.

198. Refusal of the court to consider a submission by a party expert could be a violation of the right to a fair judicial hearing (*rechtliches Gehör*). See Ch. 6(E)(3) and Ch. 8(C)(7)(c) above.

sion of the court-appointed expert. The court might, and usually would, require the court appointed expert to address the divergent positions advanced by the party expert.[199] In rare cases and with the consent of the parties, the court might hear oral testimony from a party expert or even appoint the party expert as court appointed expert.[200] Fees and costs of a party expert whose opinion has had an effect on the judgment can be subject to reimbursement by the losing party.[201]

In some cases a dissenting private expert report may lead to the appointment of an additional expert or even a "super-expert". However the court would rarely reject a court appointed expert's opinion outright or come to a contrary conclusion within the realm of expertise without the support of another court appointed expert.

The high degree of acceptance of testimony by court appointed experts and the frequency with which German judges appoint experts to assist them with technical and other specialized questions in modern litigation have given rise to the concern that in some cases there may be an over-reliance on expert opinions in lieu of sound judicial fact finding and analysis.[202] It may sometimes be too easy for a busy judge to refer factually complex or difficult, but not necessarily expert, issues to a court appointed expert in order to avoid time-consuming analysis necessary to resolve them.[203] Once the expert has reported, it is tempting for the court simply to accept the expert's testimony as dispositive of the case.

The result can be increases in cost and delay to the parties. The parties may also find it more difficult to challenge of the conclusion of a court appointed expert witness than to attack or seek review of a conclusion arrived at directly by the court. Although the institution of the court appointed expert enjoys high acceptance in German civil justice, there is discussion of how over-use can be avoided.[204]

199. See Federal Supreme Court, 55 *NJW* 1651, 1654 (2002); Thomas/Putzo/Reichold, §411, mn. 5; see Ch. 8(C)(7)(c) above.

200. See Federal Supreme Court, 98 BGHZ 32, 40 (1986); 9 *NJW-RR* 255 (1994); Zöller/Greger, §402, mn. 2.

201. For an overview on the diverging case law see Thomas/Putzo, §91, mn. 48 ff.

202. See, e.g., Sendler, "Richter und Sachverständige", 39 *NJW* 2907 (1986).

203. It is, however, considered poor form, and in extreme cases error, for a judge simply to refer the case file to an expert with a general question which will dispose of the case.

204. See Sendler, 39 *NJW* 2907, 2909 (1986).

8. Proof by Party Testimony

Grounding judicial determinations on contested assertions of fact by interested parties is viewed with some reservation by German law and practice.[205] The interest of the immediate parties to the lawsuit disqualifies them from being called as ordinary witnesses (*Zeugen*). The parties make their primary contribution to clarification of the disputed facts during preparation of the case through written briefs or preliminary hearing and during the hearing of the parties (*Anhörung der Parteien*) in the plenary proceeding.[206] Disputes of fact remaining after this preliminary effort at fact clarification are preferably to be settled by forms of proof other than party testimony.[207]

Nonetheless, there are often facts crucial to the determination of a law suit which lie only within the knowledge of one or the other of the parties. Even in cases where there are third party witnesses, often the parties have the most extensive and immediate knowledge of the relevant facts. With due allowance for the effect of the parties' respective interests on the content and coloration of their testimony, the court can, and often must, ground its fact determinations on this form of proof.

---

205. See Coester-Waltjen, Oberhammer and Sutter-Somm, "Parteiaussage und Parteivernehmung am Ende des 20. Jahrhunderts", 113 *ZZP* 269, 296, 327 (2000). The use of party interrogation (*Parteivernehmung*) as a means of proof of facts was introduced in 1933 (see Ch. 2(F) above) as a replacement for the "party oath" (*Parteieid*). On motion of its opponent a party to litigation had to swear to the truth of factual assertions in his case (*zugeschobener Eid*). When the party swore the oath as demanded by her opponent, the court had to render judgment in favor of the swearing party without any deliberation on the evidence. If the party refused to do so, his case was lost. The party could also apply for the administration of the oath to the opponent, who would then have to swear to the reverse of the party's factual assertion (*zurückgeschobener Eid*). If the opponent did so, he would be the winner; if he refused to do so, he would lose. With the development of the principle of free deliberation and evaluation of proof (see Ch. 8(D)(1) below) this system of binding evidentiary rules was abandoned. For a survey see Coester-Waltjen, 113 *ZZP* 269 ff., 274 ff. (2000).

206. See especially Polyzougopoulos, *Parteianhörung und Parteivernehmung in ihrem gegenseitigen Verhältnis* (1976); Ch. 8(B)(3) above. Parties are also heard on the credibility of witnesses and the inferences to be drawn from evidence received by the court after the proof is received and before the court reaches its factual findings and conclusions. See ZPO §§279(3) and 285(1); Ch. 8(D)(2) below.

207. ZPO §445(1). A party "who has not satisfied its burdens of proof with other forms of proof, or who has not adduced other forms of proof" (*die den ihr obliegenden Beweis mit anderen Beweismitteln nicht vollständig geführt oder andere Beweismittel nicht vorgebracht hat*), can request that the opposing party be examined in proof of facts.

Party evidence can be taken either at the instance of the opposing party,[208] at the instance of the party whose evidence is proposed with the agreement of the opposing party,[209] or on the court's own motion "if the results of the oral argument and taking of other evidence do not suffice to support conviction as to the truth or lack of truth of a fact to be proved."[210] A party who wishes to offer his own testimony may apply for an order that the testimony be taken on the authority of the court if the agreement of the opposing party is not forthcoming.[211] Ordinarily the necessity for party evidence will be set forth beforehand in a proof order (*Beweisbeschluss*) which will also set forth the subject matter on which the party or parties are to give testimony.[212]

In some kinds of proceedings based entirely on documentary evidence such as checks or promissory notes party evidence can be used only under limited circumstances.[213] The legal representative of a legally incompetent or a corporate party (such as a guardian or a corporation director) would be considered the party for the purpose of party evidence. An incompetent party himself would be examined as a witness.[214]

---

208. ZPO §445. If the opposing party refuses to cooperate in providing the requested testimony, the court can consider the nature and circumstances of the non-cooperation and draw adverse inferences from it. ZPO §446.

209. ZPO §447.

210. ZPO §448 (*Wenn das Ergebnis der Verhandlungen und einer etwaigen Beweisaufnahme nicht ausreicht, um seine Überzeugung von der Wahrheit oder Unwahrheit einer zu erweisenden Tatsache zu begründen*...). See Federal Supreme Court, 50 *NJW* 3230 (1997); 51 *NJW* 814 (1998).

211. The European Court of Human Rights has recently indicated that the court's discretion on such an application is not unbounded. Ordinarily such an application should be granted when proof by testimony of the opponent has already been allowed ("procedural equality of the parties"). See European Court of Human Rights, *Dombo Beheer B.V. v. The Netherlands*, 18 EHRR 213 (1994); Federal Supreme Court, 52 *NJW* 363 (1999).

212. See ZPO §450. Such a proof order may be entered during the course of preliminary preparatory proceedings or in the earlier stages of the plenary hearing. If the party is not present in court at the time the proof order is entered, notice of the proof hearing and a summons to appear there are served on the party as if on a witness.

213. See ZPO §§592 ff., 595(2), 598 and Federal Supreme Court, 38 *NJW* 2953 (1985) for special rules governing document cases (*Urkundenprozess*). The special document case procedure is described in Ch. 11(B) below.

214. See ZPO §455(1). This is based on the principle that "whoever cannot be examined as a party will be examined as a witness." (*Wer nicht als Partei vernommen kann, wird als Zeuge vernommen*). See Thomas/Putzo/Reichold, Vor §373 mn. 7. Persons older than 16 years may be examined as a party (ZPO §455(2)), their legally competent representative as a witness. See also Ch. 8(C)(5) above.

Party evidence is taken by the court in the same manner as testimony is elicited from witnesses.[215] The parties ordinarily give evidence without the administration of any oath, although the court is required to advise the parties, like other witnesses, of the consequences of deliberately false testimony at the outset of the questioning.[216] However if the court finds a party's unsworn testimony insufficiently convincing, the court may order that the party be sworn with respect to some or all of the facts stated.[217] However if both parties have testified, the court can require an oath from only one of them.[218] In any event each party has the right to dispense with the administration of the oath to the opposing party, in which case the court cannot order it.[219]

9. Procedures for the Taking of Evidence

As noted above, evidence can be taken either during the plenary proceedings, generally immediately after the hearing of the parties and oral argument, or at a hearing specially scheduled for that purpose. The principle of immediacy (*Unmittelbarkeitsprinzip*) requires that oral witness or party evidence should be heard by the judges who are to decide the case.[220] The procedure for the reception of evidence tends somewhat to vary with the particular kind of evidence involved:

a. Witnesses

The names of the witnesses and the subject matters of their testimony must be specified in advance with sufficient particularity so that the parties and court can determine the relevance of the witness's testimony to one or more

---

215. See ZPO §451; for details see Zöller/Greger, §451, mn. 1 and 2.

216. ZPO §§395(1), 451.

217. ZPO §452(1)(1).

218. See ZPO §452(1)(2). Presumably this would be the party whose testimony the court found more convincing. Rosenberg/Schwab/Gottwald §124(III)(2), p. 732.

219. ZPO §452(3).

220. See Ch. 6(E) and Ch. 8(C)(5) above. When there is a change in the composition of the court to which the case is assigned the parties must be afforded at least one opportunity to argue before the members of the court who will decide the case. ZPO §309. A repetition of any preceding evidentiary proceedings is not required unless the court has doubts about the credibility of a witness who has testified and the new members wish to assess the witness's credibility for themselves. See Federal Supreme Court, 50 *NJW* 1586 (1997).

of the issues to be determined.[221] Evidentiary hearings are not to be used as fishing expeditions.[222]

As noted above, only witnesses nominated by one or the other party may be examined. If a party has identified a witness in the pleadings or briefs or in a preliminary oral proceeding, but not nominated the witness to testify, the court may ask why the witness was omitted and allow the party to make a late nomination. However the court is without the power to call on it's own motion a witness who has not been nominated by a party. If a party has nominated a witness, and later decides to dispense with the witness, the court similarly cannot call the witness unless the other party insists that the witness be examined.[223] Once the witness has been examined the witness's testimony is part of the case record and cannot be retracted.

Witnesses are examined individually by the court. As a rule witnesses are sequestered.[224] The presiding judge usually conducts the initial questioning. Ordinarily the presiding judge first asks the witness's identity and seeks to determine the witness's relationship to and interest in the proceedings in order to gain a sense of the witness's perspective and credibility.[225]

German procedure expresses a strong preference for witness testimony uninfluenced by either party preparation or suggestive questioning by the court. Normally German lawyers do not interview witnesses prior to their testimony in court. This is not because of any legal or ethical rule prohibiting attorneys from having prior contact with witnesses. A German lawyer would not be criticized for asking a potential witness what he intended to say in court.[226] How-

221. ZPO §373.

222. See Ch. 6(B)(2); Ch. 7(A)(4) and (L); Ch. 8(C)(1)(a) above; Federal Supreme Court, 36 *NJW* 2034 (1983) and 45 *NJW* 2489 (1992). When a party shows good cause for inability to provide sufficient specification of facts the court may give some weight to the possibility that necessary facts and evidence will develop later in the course of the taking of evidence. See Federal Supreme Court, 48 *NJW* 2111 (1995) and 17 *NJW-RR* 1433, 1435 (2002); Stürner, *Die Aufklärungspflicht der Parteien des Zivilprozesses* (1976), §9, pp. 106 ff.; Zöller/Greger, Vor §284, mn. 5 ff. According to ZPO §139(1) the court must give hints and feedback when specification of relevant facts and means of evidence does not suffice. See Ch. 6(C)(2).

223. ZPO §399. See Ch. 7(L) and Ch. 8(C)(1)(b) above.

224. ZPO §394(1).

225. ZPO §395.

226. Traditionally a German lawyer has not been allowed to utilize minutes of witness conferences as evidentiary documents. See Guidelines of Ethics §6 as in force until 1987:

> (1) An attorney may interview third parties likely to be a witness out of court, when this is necessary for clarifying the facts, giving good advice and properly representing the client.

ever if a witness admitted that he had reviewed his testimony with one or the other lawyer in advance of the hearing, the credibility of the witness with the judges could be seriously impaired.[227] It is primarily for this reason, rather than any legal or ethical prohibition, that lawyers in Germany do not generally prepare witnesses before they testify. Furthermore, German lawyers' fees and compensation are based on lump sums, not on hourly rates.[228] There is usually no additional compensation for time consuming witness interviews. The consequence is that this activity is not attractive for lawyers.

The statute specifically requires that the court's initial questions to the witness on the subject matter of his testimony be such as to allow the witness to give his own version of the testimony in terms of his own choosing.[229] Following the witness's initial narrative, the presiding judge as well as the other

---

> (2) He may inform and advise the third party of her rights and obligations.
> (3) It is permitted to create minutes of this preparatory examination and to ask the examined person for a written signed statement. The lawyer may utilize this minute or declaration in judicial proceedings as a basis for questions in case of divergences. However, he may produce the documents with the minutes themselves only in exceptional cases, for example when the witness cannot give testimony either by deposition before a delegated judge or by examination in a court hearing.

This rule of ethics was abandoned in 1987 (see Ch. 4(E)(1)) and the new Code of Ethics of 2001 does not any longer contain any provision on preparatory interviews of witnesses by lawyers. Preparatory interviews may be permitted if the lawyer does not unduly influence the witness and his testimony. For more details see Timmerbeil, *Witness Coaching und Adversary System*, Dissertation of the Faculty of Law of the University of Freiburg (2003), Ch. 3(VI)(2).

227. See Burckhard, "Die Fragwürdigkeit des Zeugenbeweises", 72 DRiZ 74 (1994); Court of Appeals of Hamburg, 52 *MDR* 496 (1998); 45 *MDR* 904 (1991); Court of Appeals of Dresden, 8 *OLG-NL* 97 (2001); Labor Court of Appeals of Frankfurt, 35 *ARST* 173 (1981). In some of these cases the "preparatory measures" included payments of compensation to the third party. Preparatory interviews of court appointed experts are not permitted; in case of unallowed consultations a court expert is subject to disqualification. See Court of Appeals of Hamm, 27 *MDR* 144 (1973); Federal Supreme Court, 28 *NJW* 1363 (1975); Ch. 8(C)(7)(b).

For a detailed discussion see Timmerbeil, *Witness Coaching*, Ch. 3(VI)(1)(b)(bb) and (d) above.

228. See Ch. 4(H) above.

229. ZPO §396(1) "The witness should be caused to set forth in narrative form his knowledge about the subject matter of the interrogation." (*"Der Zeuge ist zu veranlassen, dasjenige, was ihm von dem Gegenstand seiner Vernehmung bekannt ist, im Zusammenhang anzugeben."*) A witness may be permitted to give his initial narrative statement in writing, in which case the presiding judge is expected to go over the statement with the witness to make sure that it accurately reflects the witness's knowledge. Rosenberg/Schwab/Gottwald,

judges are free to pose follow up questions designed to clarify, supplement, or test the credibility of the witness's preceding narrative.[230]

Following an initial round of questioning by the judges, the parties and their counsel have the right to suggest additional questions to the court.[231] The party with the burden of proof on the issues on which the witness is examined generally goes first. If the questions seek relevant information and are not unduly repetitious or burdensome, the court is required to pose them to the witness.[232] Upon request the court may allow the parties, and must allow their respective counsel, to address their questions directly to the witness.[233] In most cases counsel ask their follow-up questions directly rather than posing them through the court.[234]

The purpose of the questioning by court and counsel alike is to clarify and test the credibility of the testimony. Both form and tone of the questions are adapted to this purpose. Witnesses may be asked for individual details from a comprehensive narrative. The court, a party or a lawyer, may confront a witness with an inconsistent prior statement whether made in court or outside and ask the witness to explain the inconsistency.[235] Questions designed to elicit a witness's bias or interest in the proceedings are fair game.

Strongly leading questions (*Suggestivfragen*) which put words in the witness's mouth and demand "yes" or "no" answers, are generally disapproved.[236] However the court or counsel are free to express skepticism about a witness's testimony and to question an evasive or recalcitrant witness in a manner calculated to extract the truth. Follow-up questioning of witnesses by German judges and lawyers has often been contrasted with Anglo-American cross examination. A casual observer might sense a considerable difference in tone

---

§122(VII)(5), p. 713; but see Zöller/Greger, §396, mn. 1 (disapproving of written submissions).

230. See ZPO§396(2) and (3).

231. ZPO §397(1).

232. See Federal Supreme Court, 50 *NJW* 802 (1997); Thomas/Putzo/Reichold, §397, mn. 1.

233. ZPO §397(2).

234. The right of counsel to ask questions to the witness may not be arbitrarily restricted by the judge without risk of infringement on the constitutional right to be heard. See Sachs/Degenhart, *Grundgesetz*, 3rd ed. (2003), Art. 103, mn. 29a; Dreier/Schulze-Fielitz, *Grundgesetz*, Vol. III (2000), Art. 103, mn. 66; German Constitutional Court, 49 *NJW* 2785, 2786 (1996) for criminal matters.

235. A lawyer may even attempt to hold or impeach a witness based on a prior inconsistent statement made by the witness to the lawyer outside of court, although lawyer interviews of witnesses prior to their appearances in court are relatively unusual in Germany.

236. See, e.g., Musielak/Huber, §397, mn. 2; Stein/Jonas/Berger, §396, mn. 7.

and rigor. In fact, though, follow-up and clarification questioning by German judges and attorneys tends to limit, clarify, undermine and impeach witness testimony in very much the same way cross examination accomplishes the same purposes in English or American trial practice, but in a more restrained and less dramatic fashion.[237]

The court has the power to rule on the admissibility (*Zulässigkeit*) of questions suggested or posed by the parties and counsel and can exclude questions which seek irrelevant evidence or go far beyond the subject matter of the hearing. The court can also exclude burdensome, repetitive, or harassing questions.[238] The court also enforces witness privileges.[239] Unjustified failure or refusal of a witness to answer a proper question posed by either the court or counsel can lead to assessment of costs against the witness, or in extreme cases, to fine or civil imprisonment.[240]

If the presiding judge refuses to permit a party or lawyer to pose a particular question to a witness, the issue is determined by interlocutory order (*Beschluss*) of the court before which the action is pending without right of interlocutory appeal.[241]

b. Documentary Proof

Documentary evidence can be introduced at any point during preparatory or plenary proceedings without the necessity of a separate evidentiary hearing. There is no requirement that documentary evidence be formally nominated by a party. Parties are automatically expected to produce all documents referred to in their pleadings and briefs.[242] During preparatory proceedings

---

237. StPO §239 specifically authorizes formal cross examination in criminal proceedings upon motion and agreement of the state prosecutor and the counsel of the accused. There is nothing in the Civil Procedure Code which prohibits the same procedure, but according to the prevailing opinion American-style declarative cross examination is not permitted in German civil procedure even with the consent of the parties to litigation. See Musielak/Huber, §397, mn. 1; Stein/Jonas/Berger, §397, mn. 1.

238. §ZPO §397(3). If a delegated or commissioned judge conducting the evidentiary hearing rules a party-propounded question out of order, and the panel decides that his ruling was in error, the court can order the re-examination of the witness in order to obtain the omitted testimony. ZPO §398(2).

239. See Ch. 8(C)(10) below.

240. ZPO §390.

241. ZPO §140. Such an error can be raised in the appeal from the final judgment and can be cured by allowing the question to be asked of the witness during second-instance proceedings in the appellate court. See Ch. 10(D)(2) and (3) below.

242. ZPO §131. See Ch. 6(B)(2) and (3); Ch. 7(A)(4) above.

the court can order the parties as well as third parties to produce any other relevant documents within their possession or under their control.[243] The court can also request public authorities to make available copies of public documents either at the request of a party[244] or on the court's own motion. The relevance and admissibility of the documents proposed by the parties or obtained by the court are subject to oral argument during the plenary proceedings.

There is no formal process of "offering" a document or other object in evidence at a hearing or trial. Documentary evidence is identified and referred to throughout the proceedings starting with the initial pleadings. Frequently documents relevant to a party's legal or factual position will be attached to the party's complaint, answer or to some other pleading or brief filed during the course of the case. If there is no objection to the document at the next reasonable opportunity, either in writing or at a hearing, the document becomes a part of the record and may be considered as evidence for any purpose in all subsequent proceedings. If there is objection to the consideration of documentary evidence identified by a party or the court, such objection is raised in a responsive pleading or brief or at a hearing and ruled on at a preliminary or plenary hearing or in a preliminary order. In this sense the treatment of documentary and other tangible evidence appears to be somewhat less formal than the treatment of witness testimony.

10. Evidentiary Privileges

German law recognizes a number of relatively wide ranging testimonial privileges (*Zeugnisverweigerungsrechte*) which may apply to deny access to testimony or other evidence in civil proceedings. These privileges can be classified in two groups, (1) privileges attaching to witnesses and (2) privileges based on the subject matter of questions. These legally based privileges entitle a person claiming them to refuse to appear as a witness,[245] to refuse to give testimony concerning a particular subject matter,[246] or to refuse to answer certain questions.[247] Privileges may also protect third parties from being required

243. ZPO §§142, 273(2)(5); see Ch. 6(C)(2); 7(H), (I) and (L)(1) above.

244. See ZPO §273(2)(2) and §432. A party may make application for such a court request only if the party does not have the legal ability to obtain the document from the public authority without the assistance of the court.

245. See ZPO §383(1)–(3).

246. See ZPO §383(4)–(6).

247. See ZPO §384.

to produce documents and tangible things or from compelled inspection of facilities and land.[248] They are contrasted to contractual obligations of confidentiality, which in and of themselves do not entitle a person called as a witness to refuse to answer questions or give testimony.[249]

a. Witness Privileges

First of all, certain government officials who are charged with preservation of confidential information may only be questioned concerning such confidential information with the permission of the relevant governmental organ.[250] On the other hand, once the requisite permission is obtained, the restriction disappears and the witness is obliged to answer.[251] The German Constitution also provides a testimonial privilege for members of the German Parliament (*Bundestag*).[252]

A party's spouse, present, past or future,[253] has a privilege to refuse to testify in a proceeding involving that party. The same is true of persons who are related to a party lineally or collaterally by blood or marriage until the third degree of kindred by blood and the second degree of kindred by marriage.[254] These privileges are considered to be so important that the court is required to advise potential family-member witnesses of the privilege at the time they appear and before they testify. If the court fails to so advise a family-member wit-

248. See ZPO § 142(2)(1) and § 144(2)(1); Ch. 7(H), (L)(1) and Ch. 8(C)(4) and (6)(b) above.

249. See Thomas/Putzo/Reichold, §383, mn. 1.

250. See ZPO §376. Protected officials include judges, officials (*Beamte*), other persons in public service (*andere Personen des öffentlichen Dienstes*) (§376(1)), members of the federal parliament, state legislatures, and federal and state governmental administrations as required by applicable regulations (§376(2)) and the President of the Federal Republic (§376(4)). The executive privilege of the President of the Federal Republic extends to testimony that in his judgment would disadvantage the welfare of the federation or of a German state.

251. See, e.g., DRiG §§46, 71 (judges), BMinG §6 (federal ministers), BBG §61 and BRRG § 39 (officials). Permission can only be denied for specified reasons and a party aggrieved by refusal of permission can bring an action in the Administrative Court (*Verwaltungsgericht*) to compel a senior official to give the requested permission. During the pendency of such review the underlying civil case will generally be stayed pursuant to ZPO § 148. See Federal Supreme Administrative Court, 24 *NJW* 160 (1971); Musielak/Huber, § 376, mn. 6. Termination of public service does not terminate the protection with respect to matters entrusted to public officials during public service.

252. German Constitution (*Grundgesetz*), Article 47.

253. ZPO §383(1)(1)–(2) applies to a party's fiancé(e) (*Verlobte*), as well as a party's spouse (*Ehegatte*), whether or not the marriage is still in force.

254. ZPO §383(1)(3).

ness, the court cannot base its findings on information obtained from the witness unless the privilege is later expressly waived.[255] There is no privilege for a living partner (*Lebensgefährte/-gefährtin*) to which a party is not married.[256]

The familial privileges do not apply to testimony concerning legal transactions as to which the privileged family member served as a formal witness,[257] to testimony concerning family relationships or family property matters,[258] and to situations in which the family member has been involved in the transactions in suit as predecessor in interest or agent of a party.[259]

It should be noted that this familial privilege belongs to the witness, not the party. If the witness chooses to waive the privilege and testify the related party is powerless to prevent it.

Clergypersons (*Geistliche*),[260] journalists,[261] and professional persons to whom confidential communications are entrusted[262] possess a privilege to refuse to testify concerning the subject matter of the confidential communications.

The clerical privilege covers matters communicated in the course of spiritual counseling.[263]

The journalists' privilege is intended to protect freedom of the press as guaranteed by the German Constitution.[264] It covers reporters and editorial per-

---

255. ZPO §383(2). See Federal Supreme Court, 38 *NJW* 1470 (1985); Zöller/Greger, §383, mn. 21.

256. See Zöller/Greger, §383, mn. 9. But living partners of the same sex who have applied for a formal registration of their relationship have the same procedural privileges as spouses. See ZPO §383(1)(2a).

257. ZPO §385(1)(1).

258. ZPO §385(1)(2),(3).

259. ZPO §385(1)(4).

260. ZPO §383(1)(4).

261. ZPO §383(1)(5).

262. ZPO §383(1)(6) "Persons, to whom information confidential by nature or legal requirement is entrusted by virtue of their office, their profession or their trade, with respect to the information covered by their obligation of confidentiality." ("*Personen, denen kraft ihres Amtes, Standes oder Gewerbes Tatsachen anvertraut sind, deren Geheimhaltung durch ihre Natur oder durch gesetzliche Vorschrift geboten ist, in betreff der Tatsachen, auf welche die Verpflichtung zur Verschwiegenheit sich bezieht.*") This privilege would cover, for instance, attorneys, who are required to maintain confidentiality by BRAO §43a(2); Code of Ethics of 2001 §2; European Code of Ethics Nō 2.3 (see Ch. 4(E)(1)); StGB (German Criminal Code) §203(1)(3), 204.

263. ZPO §383(1)(4) "Clergypersons, with respect to those things which are confided in them in the process of spiritual counselling." ("*Geistliche in Ansehung desjenigen, was ihnen bei der Ausübung der Seelsorge anvertraut ist.*")

264. See German Constitution, Article 5(1)(2).

sonnel of the printed press, radio and television and protects the names of their informants and sources of documents as well as disclosures from these sources.[265]

The professionals' privilege applies to a broad range of persons who receive confidential information and are required by the nature of the information or by law to maintain its confidentiality.[266] The privilege applies to officials such as legislators, judges, lay-judges (*Schöffen*), lenders, doctors, midwives, psychologists, accountants, tax accountants as well as attorneys and public notaries.[267] Agents and employees of covered professionals are similarly covered.[268] It extends only to those questions which seek information within the sphere of confidential disclosure. In framing questions to a cleric, journalist, or professional witness the court is required to avoid asking for information within the likely scope of the applicable privilege.[269] It is also asserted that a court cannot base its findings on any information obtained in violation of these privileges, although this contention is subject to debate and not fully accepted by the courts.[270]

Although the terms of these privileges give the witness the right to refuse to answer questions (*Zeugnisverweigerungsrecht*), in the case of the professional privileges, if the person who made the confidential disclosure waives the obligation of confidentiality, the privilege no longer applies and the professional person is obliged to answer the questions.[271] This means that in practical effect the person protected by the privilege and entitled to waive it is the professional's client.

---

265. ZPO §383(1)(5).

266. ZPO §383(1)(6).

267. Many of these persons are also bound by professional obligations of confidentiality which forbid disclosure of confidential information in out-of-court contexts. See StGB (German Criminal Code) §§203 f.; BRAO §43a(2); DRiG §§43, 45; BNotO §18; StBerG §83; WPO §64, etc.

268. See StGB (German Criminal Code) §203(3); Zöller/Greger, §383, mn. 17.

269. ZPO §383(3).

270. See Rosenberg/Schwab/Gottwald, §122(V)(3)(a), p. 708; Federal Supreme Court, 43 *NJW* 1734, 1735 (1990).

271. ZPO §385(2). This exception does not apply to the journalists' privilege which is based on different policy considerations. See Musielak/Huber, §385, mn. 6. Art. 9 of the *Reichskonkordat* of July 22, 1933, permits Catholic priests to claim the privilege for confidential communications made to them by their penitents regardless of a waiver by the person protected. There are various contracts between the individual German states and Protestant Churches providing certain Protestant clergymen with similar authority. See Musielak/Huber, §385, mn. 6; Rosenberg/Schwab/Gottwald, §122(V)(3)(a), p. 708.

b. Question-Based Privileges

In addition to those privileges which cover particular classes of persons and information imparted to or received by them, any witness may refuse to answer certain kinds of questions. First of all, a witness may refuse to answer a question if the answer would be likely to cause immediate financial harm (such as legal liability for damages) to the witness or any family member within the scope of the familial privilege.[272] This privilege is subject to the same exceptions as the family witness privilege, matters as to which the witness has served as an official witness, matters of family relationship and property, and matters in which the witness has served as predecessor in interest or agent of a party.[273]

Second, a witness has the right not to answer questions if the answer would dishonor[274] or tend to incriminate the witness or a near relative.[275]

Third, a witness does not have to answer questions which would require the disclosure of artistic or trade secrets.[276] This applies not only to the witness's own trade secrets, but also to trade secrets of others which have been imparted to the witness under a legal obligation of confidentiality.

---

272. ZPO §384(1) "Testimony can be refused with respect to questions if the answer to the questions would cause immediate proprietary harm to the witness or to any person to whom he stands in a relationship described in §383 (1)–(3)." (*"Das Zeugnis kann verweigert werden: (1) über Fragen, deren Beantwortung dem Zeugen oder einer Person, zu der er in einem der im §383 Nr. 1 bis 3 bezeichneten Verhältnisse steht, einen unmittelbaren vermögensrechtlichen Schaden verursachen würde."*)

273. ZPO §385(1).

274. This ground for refusing to answer a question is rarely encountered today. At one time it was applied to questions which would elicit admissions of adulterous sexual intercourse. For the current standard, see Court of Appeals of Karlsruhe, 47 *NJW* 528 (1994).

275. ZPO §384(2) "...if the answer would tend to dishonor or increase the danger of serious or minor criminal prosecution of the witness or a relative described by §383(1)–(3)." ("*...deren Beantwortung dem Zeugen oder einem seiner in §383 Nr. 1 bis 3 bezeichneten Angehörigen zur Unehre gereichen oder die Gefahr zuziehen würde, wegen einer Straftat oder einer Ordnungswidrigkeit verfolgt zu werden*"). For the foundation of this privilege see Stürner, *Die Aufklärungspflicht der Parteien des Zivilprozesses*, § 12(III)(3), pp. 184 ff. This German privilege against self-incrimination cannot be vitiated by offering the person claiming the privilege immunity from prosecution. For a more detailed discussion see German Constitutional Court, 34 NJW 1431 (1981); Stürner, "Strafrechtliche Selbstbelastung und verfahrensförmige Wahrheitsermittlung", 34 *NJW* 1757 (1981).

276. ZPO §384(3) "...if the witness could not answer without disclosing an artistic or trade secret." (*...die der Zeuge nicht würde beantworten können, ohne ein Kunst- oder Gewerbegeheimnis zu offenbaren.*) For further details see Stürner, "Die Geheimsphäre im Zivilprozess", 40 *JZ* 453 (1985); Stadler, *Der Schutz des Unternehmensgeheimnisses im deutschen und U.S.-amerikanischen Zivilprozess und im Rechtshilfeverfahren* (1989).

c. *The Scope and Significance of Witness and Party Privileges*

The expansive scope of witness privileges recognized in German civil litigation reflects the perception that the judge providing civil justice is an agent of the State and that the citizens require this kind of protection from excessive intrusion by such State agencies. It should be emphasized that in every case evidentiary privileges belong to and may be invoked only by witnesses or their clients. No party has the right to assert the privilege of another person. Moreover, the effect of these broad privileges is further limited in civil cases by the court's ability to draw an adverse inference if a party claims a privilege or refuses to give permission for a professional person to release information concerning a matter of likely relevance to the proceedings.

In Germany there is, for the most part, no express provision establishing and regulating claims of privilege by parties. Such claims are generally subject to judicial discretion. Assertion of a privilege by a party often ends up to the disadvantage of that party if the court draws a negative inference from the party's refusal to give information or to cooperate with the production of evidence.

Equal treatment of claims of privileges by parties and witnesses is under theoretical discussion but is not reality in German procedure. The privilege to refuse to provide testimony which will result in unfavorable consequences, in particular, is not a recognized privilege for parties and is not an accepted ground for refusing discovery and cooperation.

In American procedure parties may generally claim privileges to the same extent as non-parties. The option of contempt sanctions to require disclosure can be applied to witnesses and parties alike. Thus privileges in American procedure have to be defined more narrowly. Otherwise the substance of the case would be limited and discovery and preparation for trial could be burdensome and more difficult.[277]

Overall Anglo-American privileges are much narrower than those recognized by the German and continental tradition. For German parties, defendants in particular, this disparity in scope of privilege can be a serious problem. There is sometimes risk that a German defendant in an American court may infer that the suit was brought only to obtain disclosure of industrial or trade secrets that would have been protected in Germany.[278]

---

277. In some American jurisdictions the fact finder may draw an adverse inference from a party's claim of privilege. See Maine R. Ev. 513 (adverse inference may be drawn from party's claim of privilege in a civil case).

278. For consideration of party privileges when deciding whether to draw adverse inferences see ZPO §§371(3); 427(2), 446; Ch. 8(C)(10)(e) below. For further details see

d. Procedure on Claim of Witness Privilege

The requirement that the subject matter of a proposed witness's testimony be set forth with particularity in the proof order as well as the summons to the witness facilitates the timely raising and determinations of many issues of privilege. A person identified or summoned as a witness may assert a privilege either by appearing at the hearing and declining to testify, or by asserting a privilege in a written response to the summons.[279] In either case the witness must set forth the reasons the privilege applies.[280] A witness is always permitted to bring counsel to a hearing to advise the witness concerning privileges or to object in behalf of the witness to improper questions by the judge or a lawyer for one of the parties.[281] A witness can assert a privilege despite a waiver of the privilege on a prior occasion or in a prior stage of the proceedings.[282]

A question-based privilege can be asserted by refusing to answer the question and stating the grounds for the refusal on the spot.

If the party who nominated a witness[283] disputes the applicability of a privilege asserted by the witness, the court must decide the issue in an interlocutory proceeding (*Zwischenstreit*).[284] If the privilege has been asserted in

---

Stürner, *Die Aufklärungspflicht der Parteien des Zivilprozesses* (1976), § 12, pp. 174 ff. (self-incrimination), § 13, pp. 193 ff. (right of privacy), § 14, pp. 208 ff. (trade secrets and industrial secrets); Stürner, "Parteipflichten bei der Sachverhaltsaufklärung im Zivilprozess", 98 *ZZP* 237 (1985); Stürner, "Transnational Civil Procedure: Discovery and Sanctions against Non-Compliance", VI (NS) *Uniform Law Review* 871 (2001-4); Stürner, "US-amerikanisches und europäisches Verfahrensverständnis", in: Lutter et al. (eds.) *Festschrift für Ernst C. Stiefel* (1987), p. 763.

279. See ZPO §386. Another option for the witness is to appear in person at the office of the court before the date of the hearing and give an oral statement asserting the privilege and giving the reasons therefor. When the witness has properly asserted a privilege covering the entire subject matter designated for testimony, the witness is not required to appear at the hearing. ZPO §386(3).

280. The witness must make the reasons "credible" (*glaubhaft*). ZPO §§386(1) 294.

281. See Rosenberg/Schwab/Gottwald, § 122(VII)(4); for criminal matters German Constitutional Court, 28 *NJW* 103 (1974); Ch. 8(C)(5).

282. See Rosenberg/Schwab/Gottwald, §122(V)(3)(c), p. 709; Zöller/Greger, § 383, mn. 6. If a witness who testified at the first instance asserts a privilege on appeal, the appellate court may nonetheless accept and credit the testimony given at the first instance.

283. If that party decided to dispense with the witness's testimony rather than contest the privilege, the other party may be entitled to insist on the witness's testimony under ZPO §399 and take up the contest.

284. ZPO § 387. In practice separate interlocutory proceedings for determination of claims of privilege have become rare. Usually the determination is made at the hearing at which the witness is called to testify.

writing prior to the hearing, the reporting judge advises the court of the circumstances, the court hears argument from parties and witness, and the court decides whether the assertion of the privilege is justified.[285] The witness is summoned to the hearing for this purpose.[286] If the privilege is asserted at a previously scheduled hearing for the reception of evidence, the court will generally hear the parties and witness and decide the issue on the spot.[287]

The decision of the court is set forth in an interlocutory judgment which also assesses costs and attorneys fees related to the issue in accord with the outcome. A witness who fails to sustain the claim of privilege will thus be responsible for statutory attorneys' fees and costs of the party which successfully contests the claim.[288] Interlocutory judgments sustaining or overruling claims of privilege are subject to immediate miscellaneous appeal (*Beschwerde*) by the party nominating the witness or the witness, as the case may be.[289]

e. *Inferences on Claims of Privilege*

Ordinarily the consequences from the successful assertion of a privilege by a witness are merely that the party nominating that witness (*Beweisführer*) does not have the benefit of the witness's testimony.[290] Under some circumstances, however, a claim of privilege[291] by a witness with respect to a particular question or subject matter may give rise to a common-sense inference that the answer to the question would have favored a particular party or position.[292] Similarly, if a party refuses to answer questions put by the court or

285. See ZPO §387, 388. If the privilege is asserted in a hearing before a designated member of the tribunal or another judge, the judge reports the issue to the court before which the case is pending and oral argument is had before the full court. The full court decides the issue based on the factual material presented to the designated judge. ZPO §389.

286. The witness is entitled to bring counsel to any such hearing, but is not required to be represented by counsel. This is true even in those courts where party representation by counsel is mandatory. ZPO §387(2).

287. The court has the power to adjourn the proceedings to permit time for preparation.

288. See Rosenberg/Schwab/Gottwald, §122(V)(3)c), p. 709; Zöller/Greger, §387, mn. 5.

289. ZPO §387(3). An interlocutory judgment of the appellate court is generally final, ZPO §567(1). The decision of the appellate court on an interlocutory appeal is subject to miscellaneous appeal of law only when permitted by the appellate court. See ZPO §574(1)(2); Ch. 10(F)(4) below.

290. E.g., Jauernig, §53(II)(3)(c).

291. Including the privilege against self-incrimination.

292. For question-based privileges see Federal Supreme Court, 47 *NJW* 197, 198 (1994) and the example in Lüke, §26, mn. 300 of a paternity case in which the child's mother as-

counsel or refuses the production or inspection of documents or things, the court can draw a negative inference concerning matters to which the party's interrogation or cooperation would have related.[293] The same kind of inference can be drawn from the refusal of a party or witness associated with a party to give permission for a third person (such as a lawyer or accountant) to release pertinent confidential information.[294]

In any event such an inference is to be made with caution. A court inferring facts from a witness's privileged refusal to testify should be able to point to corroborating evidence as well as the particular facts and circumstances of the witness which make such an inference reasonable.[295]

If a party to litigation claims a privilege or refuses to give permission for a privileged witness or third person, the likelihood and force of an adverse inference will depend on the importance of the privilege and the perceived relevance of the information withheld. When the matter sought is of marginal relevance to the issues being determined and the grounds for assertion of the privilege appear weighty, the likelihood of a serious adverse inference will be small. An adverse inference is much more likely if it appears that a party is asserting a merely technical privilege to shield information important to the determination of facts at issue especially if the information withheld is decisive to the resolution of the dispute. Such an adverse interest will likely be a strong one if the party does not offer other appropriate evidence to clarify the relevant issue.[296]

---

serts her privilege against self-dishonor (ZPO §384(1), (2)) with respect to a question asking whether she had sexual relations with another man around the time of conception of the child. A claim of witness-based privilege (ZPO §383) normally does not support adverse inference by the court when deliberating the results of the taking of evidence. See Zöller/Greger, §383, mn. 7; Musielak/Huber, §383, mn. 10.

293. See ZPO §§371(3), 427(2), 446.

294. See Federal Supreme Court, 20 *NJW* 2021 (1967)—confidentiality of bank accounts; Court of Appeals of München, 2 *NJW-RR* 1021 (1987)—public notary; Court of Appeals of Frankfurt, 33 *NJW* 2758 (1980)—doctors and hospital staff; Zöller/Greger, §385, mn. 13; Musielak/Huber, §383, mn. 10. For details see Stürner, *Die Aufklärungspflicht der Parteien des Zivilprozesses* (1976), §13 IV, pp. 202 ff.; §14 IV, p. 229.

295. See Federal Supreme Court, 26 BGHZ 391, 400 (1958); Musielak/Huber, §384, mn. 2; Zöller/Greger, §384, mn. 3

296. For a discussion of details see Stürner, *Die Aufklärungspflicht der Parteien des Zivilprozesses* (1976), §15, pp. 234 ff.

D. Evaluation of Evidence and Fact Finding by the Court

1. Free Evaluation of Proof

If decision of the case requires resolution of a factual issue, the court is required to evaluate the evidence relating to that issue and make a factual determination based on that evidence. In performing this function the court is not constrained by rules or rankings of proof, but can evaluate most forms of evidence according to its sound judgment and common sense.[297]

ZPO §286 prescribes:

> "The court is to decide upon consideration of the entire content of the arguments and the results of reception of evidence according to its free conviction whether a factual assertion is to be regarded as true or untrue. The reasons which led to the court's convictions are to be stated in the judgment."[298]

The principle of "free evaluation of proof" (*freie Beweiswürdigung*) is only qualified with respect to certain forms of documentary evidence, which on some issues can be given either prima facie, or conclusive weight.[299]

At the same time, the court is not free to credit or discredit factual proof arbitrarily or whimsically. A German judge is expected to be able to articulate reasons for crediting or discrediting evidence and to explain the conclusions drawn from the evidence.[300] So, for instance, if the court believes the testimony of one fact witness in preference to that of another, the court must be

---

297. See, in general, Rosenberg/Schwab/Gottwald, §115, pp. 657 ff.; Lüke, §22(VIII), mn. 267–273; Walter, *Freie Beweiswürdigung* (1979), pp. 657 ff.

298. *"Das Gericht hat unter Berücksichtigung des gesamten Inhalts der Verhandlungen und des Ergebnisses einer etwaigen Beweisaufnahme nach freier Überzeugung zu entscheiden, ob eine tatsächliche Behauptung für wahr oder für nicht wahr zu erachten sei. In dem Urteil sind die Gründe anzugeben, die für die richterliche Überzeugung leitend gewesen sind."*

299. See ZPO §§415–419 (documents), Ch. 8(C)(6)(a) above; §165(2) (minutes of a judicial proceeding), Ch. 6(D)(1) above; §314 (factual content of pleadings).

300. ZPO §286(1)(2). See, e.g., Federal Supreme Court, 41 *NJW* 566 (1988); Federal Constitutional Court, 47 *NJW* 2279 (1994). The court is required to justify and articulate only those fact findings and conclusions which are material to determination of the case and need not analyze clearly irrelevant facts or evidence. Rosenberg/Schwab/Gottwald, §115(I)(1), p. 658; Federal Constitutional Court, 86 BVerfGE 133, 146 (1967); 52 *NJW* 1387, 1388 (1999).

in a position to give reasons for its choice in the judgment.[301] If the court draws a conclusion from proven facts, the court must be able to justify the conclusion by reference to either logic or experience.

2. Roles of Parties and Counsel

In analyzing the evidence, the court ordinarily will be bound by the parties' admissions and stipulations of fact (*Geständnisverträge*).[302] If the parties have agreed that the facts are to be determined based on a particular evidentiary record (e.g. solely from identified documents), their stipulation will be honored, except to the extent that the court can call for proof on its own motion (e.g. naming an expert witness).[303]

The court must also make sure that the parties have opportunity to comment on the evidence received and the conclusions to be drawn before the court reaches its own findings and conclusions of fact.[304] Following the reception of evidence "the court must discuss anew with the parties the factual and legal issues in the case and, to the extent then possible, the results of the reception of evidence."[305] The parties and their counsel are invited to address by oral argument the credibility of the evidence received as well as the conclusions to be drawn from it. If the proof is complex or circumstances otherwise suggest it, the parties are to be allowed reasonable opportunity to pre-

---

301. Failure to give sufficient rational or experiential foundation for factual findings is ground for setting a judgment aside on appeal for procedural error. See Federal Supreme Court, 44 *NJW* 1894 (1991).

302. On the other hand, once the parties have submitted evidence on disputed fact there is serious question about whether they can then determine how the court will evaluate that evidence. See Rosenberg/Schwab/Gottwald, §115(I)(3), p. 658. For admissions see Ch. 6(B)(2) and Ch. 8(C)(1)(a) and (d) above.

303. "Proof agreements" (*Beweisverträge*) addressing the drawing of factual conclusions by the court should be differentiated from "burden of proof agreements" (*Beweislastverträge)* by which the parties can stipulate which party bears the burden of production or the risk of non-persuasion on the case as a whole or on a particular issue. See Rosenberg/Schwab/Gottwald, §115(I)(3), p. 658 f.

304. See ZPO §§279(2), 285(1). ZPO §285(1) prescribes: "The parties are to argue concerning the results of the reception of evidence in the context of the issues of the case." ("*Über das Ergebnis der Beweisaufnahme haben die Parteien unter Darlegung des Streitverhältnisses zu verhandeln.*") This right may be waived if neither party feels the need for such argument. However the court is under an affirmative obligation to invite argument and comment from the parties. Such an invitation must be documented in the minutes of the hearing. Zöller/Greger, §279, mn. 7. See Ch. 6(C)(2)(e); Ch. 8(B)(3) above.

305. ZPO §279(3) (*...hat das Gericht erneut den Sach- und Streitstand und, soweit bereits möglich, das Ergebnis der Beweisaufnahme mit den Parteien zu erörtern.*)

pare their arguments and responses or to submit arguments in writing.[306] Sometimes the result of reception of evidence may lead a party to designate additional evidence that should be received in order that the court get a complete factual picture.[307] Proof which has not been exposed to party comment and argument may not be used as the basis for a judicial finding or determination.[308] This insistence on party input after evidence has been received is another expression of the constitutionally based right to be heard (*rechtliches Gehör*) in German civil justice.[309]

Usually this discussion with the parties and counsel occurs at the same hearing at which the evidence is presented. If the evidence was received by a single member of the panel or another judge, the parties are to be given the opportunity to argue the conclusions to be drawn from the evidence before the actual court which is to decide the case.[310]

The process of addressing the evaluation of evidence affords opportunity for the interplay between judge and parties which is an essential feature of German civil justice.[311] Good practice, if not specific rule language, mandates that the court share with the parties or their counsel its tentative conclusions and impressions from the reception of evidence, thus giving the parties opportunity to focus their arguments, to consider the offering of additional evidence, or to attempt to resolve the case.[312]

---

306. See Federal Supreme Court, 54 *NJW* 2796, 2797 (2001) and ZPO §139(5) providing for later written submissions when immediate response is not reasonably to be expected. See Ch. 6(C)(2)(d) above.

307. Such a late designation could be rejected under ZPO §296 if the court were convinced that the party should have been aware of the evidence and designated it at an earlier time. See Ch. 7(K)(1) above.

308. See Thomas/Putzo/Reichold, §285, mn. 1.

309. Zöller/Greger, §279, mn. 6; Federal Supreme Court, 43 *NJW* 120 (1990); Federal Constitutional Court, 47 *NJW* 1210 (1994). See Ch. 6(E)(3) above for a discussion of the right to be heard as a fundamental principle of German civil justice.

310. ZPO §285(2). Any facts (including observations of the demeanor of a witness) which might form the basis for a fact or credibility determination may only be used if they appear in the minutes of the evidentiary hearing and the parties have the opportunity to comment before the court decides the case. See Federal Supreme Court, 43 *NJW* 3088 (1990); 50 *NJW* 1586 (1997); 53 *NJW* 1420 (2000); Ch. 8(C)(5) and (9). Correspondingly an appellate court may not reach a conclusion about the credibility of a witness contrary to that of the court below without hearing the witness testify. See Federal Supreme Court, 52 *NJW* 2972 (1999); 53 *NJW* 217, 220 (2000); Musielak/Ball, §529, mn. 14, 15.

311. See Ch.6(C)(2) above for a discussion of the duty to give hints and feedback (*Hinweispflicht*) as a fundamental principle of German civil justice.

312. See ZPO §279(3) as in force since 2002 and Stürner, *Richterliche Aufklärung* mn. 71 ff.; Ch. 6(C)(2)(e).

The requirement that factual findings and conclusions be articulated and logically or experientially supported, as well as the opportunity for comprehensive review of such findings and conclusions on appeal, mean that considerable attention is paid to the logical and systematic evaluation of evidence by lawyers and judges. There is considerable literature on the process by which the judge evaluates evidence and draws factual conclusions.[313] Although German lawyers may appear to play a secondary role in connection with the reception of evidence by the court, their arguments on how the evidence should be analyzed and what conclusions should be drawn can have a crucial effect on what the court does with that evidence. The attorney must listen carefully to a witness's testimony, and then be in the position to argue effectively why the court should, or should not credit the testimony, and conclusions should or should not be drawn from it. These arguments are based on considerations of consistency of the testimony with undisputed facts, other testimony, the laws of nature or human experience, the existence of bias or interest which might color the testimony, likely innocent and nefarious causes for a witness's testimony to diverge from the attorney's version of the case, and similar common-sense matters.

3. Standard of Proof in Civil Cases

In order to determine a fact in dispute, the court must be "convinced" (*überzeugt*) that the fact exists, without setting an unrealistic standard of certainty.[314] Such a level of conviction may be difficult to describe. Termed sufficient have been "a degree of certainty useable for practical life,"[315] or "such a high degree of probability as would quiet, without eliminating, the doubts of a person of reasonable and clear perception of the circumstances of life."[316]

---

313. See, e.g., Bender/Nack, *Tatsachenfestellung vor Gericht*, 2nd ed. (1994); Brehm, *Die Bindung des Richters an den Parteivortrag und Grenzen freier Verhandlungswürdigung* (1982); Greger, *Beweis und Wahrscheinlichkeit* (1978); Schreiber, *Theorie des Beweiswerts für Beweismittel im Zivilprozess* (1968); Walter, *Freie Beweiswürdigung* (1979).

314. See ZPO §286(1); in general, Thomas/Putzo/Reichold, §286, mn. 2; Rosenberg/Schwab/Gottwald, §115(II)(1), p. 659.

315. (*"ein für das praktische Leben brauchbarer Grad von Gewissheit"*); see Federal Supreme Court, 46 *NJW* 935 (1993).

316. (*"ein für einen vernünftigen, die Lebensverhältnisse klar überschauenden Menschen so hoher Grad von Wahrscheinlichkeit, das er den Zweifeln Schweigen gebietet, ohne sie völlig auszuschliessen"*); see Federal Supreme Court, 53 BGHZ 245, 256 (1970); 53 *NJW* 953 (2000). This standard was originally formulated by the Reichsgericht for criminal cases; see Walter, *Freie Beweiswürdigung*, pp. 91 ff.

How high this probability must be is the subject of some dispute.[317] Some scholars suggest that "more likely than not" should suffice.[318] Others contend that a standard of probability akin to that of the common law would open the floodgates of liability.[319] In practice theoretical formulations of degrees of conviction may be of little importance. The court will in the final analysis base its determinations on such evidence as is reasonable to expect, considering the circumstances of the case, the nature of the issue and the kind and amount of evidence available.[320] One must remember that the German judge does not merely evaluate the presentation of others, but actively participates in the process of the reception and evaluation of the evidence, and in a sense, develops his own degree of conviction.

The requirement that the court have a subjective conviction of the truth of facts found and conclusions drawn does not prevent the court from relying on methods of proof which provide only a statistical likelihood of accuracy. For instance, blood tests or DNA-analyses, which associate persons to a high degree of statistical probability, can be used as the basis for a determination of parenthood.[321]

The court can also reach a fact conclusion based on *prima facie* evidence (*Anscheinsbeweis*) in the absence of a contrary explanation. In many kinds of cases direct evidence of a fact in issue may be difficult for the proponent of that fact to procure.[322] When in ordinary experience the facts proved are linked with a particular standard of care or causation, such standard of care or causation may be inferred in the absence of another explanation for the facts proved. So, for instance, if a motorist hits a pedestrian on the sidewalk, in the absence of other evidence the motorist's negligence can be inferred because in ordinary experience motor vehicles are not driven on the sidewalk unless the

---

317. A leading German commentator remarks, "According to the prevailing view, a (very) high probability corresponds to the required degree of security in the legal standard of proof set forth in §286." (*"Nach h. M. entspricht der erforderliche Grad an Sicherheit dem in §286 festgelegten gesetzlichen Regelbeweismass einer (sehr) hohen Wahrscheinlichkeit"*), Rosenberg/Schwab/Gottwald, §115(II)(2), p. 660. The encapsulation of the "very" in parenthesis epitomizes the difficulty of specifying a degree of conviction more precisely.

318. E.g., Bruns, *Beweiswert*, 91 *ZZP* 64 (1978).

319. E.g., Prütting, *Gegenwartsprobleme der Beweislast* (1983), p. 78.

320. See Rosenberg/Schwab/Gottwald, §115(II)(2), p. 660.

321. See Thomas/Putzo/Reichold, §372a, mn. 6 and 9; Federal Supreme Court, 44 *NJW* 2961 (1991).

322. E.g. in certain kinds of negligence cases or on issues of actual causation. See Rosenberg/Schwab/Gottwald, §115(III)(2)(a), p. 662; Federal Supreme Court, 114 BGHZ 284, 290 f. (1991).

driver is careless.[323] In the absence of an alternative explanation, prima facie evidence can give rise to a sufficiently convincing inference of the existence of the experientially-linked fact as to justify a fact finding.[324]

Proof of damages raises particular problems in a regime which requires reasoned justification for all findings and conclusions. It is often difficult to determine the amount of damages with enough logical particularity as to withstand rigorous rational analysis. For instance, how can the court determine with logical particularity the monetary amount of damages that should be awarded for pain and suffering sustained by an injured plaintiff? How can the court be "convinced" that any particular figure of damage is "true"? The same is often true of the causal link between the actions giving rise to legal liability and the damages assertedly flowing from those actions.

ZPO §287 attempts to mitigate the standard of conviction required for proof of damages or causation of damage. Issues of the degree or the causation of damage are to be determined by the court's "free conviction in consideration of all the circumstances."[325] This standard is generally believed to be somewhat less demanding than the standard of conviction required for other kinds of facts.[326] The court is authorized to determine in its discretion the extent of specific evidence or expert testimony to be required or allowed on issues of causation and extent of damage.[327] The court is required in its judgment to outline the "factual bases for the assessment" (*tatsächlichen Grundlagen der Schätzung*), but is not required to provide a logical justification of the details.[328]

The boundary between those facts subject to the "full conviction" standard of §286 and the relaxed standard of §287 is subject to dispute. The Federal Supreme Court has indicated that a claimant must fully convince the court that it was actually "affected" (*betroffen*) by the act or omission of the defendant.[329]

---

323. This example is from Lüke, §24(I), mn. 279.

324. For a more complete discussion of the use of prima facie evidence in German civil litigation, see Rosenberg/Schwab/Gottwald, §115(III), pp. 660 ff.; Walter, "Der Anwendungsbereich des Anscheinsbeweises", 90 *ZZP* 270 (1977).

325. ("... *unter Würdigung aller Umstände nach freier Überzeugung*"), ZPO §287(1).

326. See Thomas/Putzo/Reichold, §287, mn. 9–11; Lüke, §22(IX), mn. 269–272; Gottwald, *Schadenszurechnung und Schadensschätzung* (1979); Arens, "Dogmatik und Praxis der Schadensschätzung", 88 *ZZP* 1 (1975).

327. ZPO §287(1)(2). The court is also specifically authorized to examine the party with the burden of proof on the damages in order to obtain some basis for its award. ZPO §287(1)(3).

328. Thomas/Putzo/Reichold, §287, mn. 11.

329. See Federal Supreme Court, 58 BGHZ 48 (1972); 51 *NJW* 3417 (1998).

Once the affectedness (*Betroffensein*) has been shown to the complete conviction of the court, the milder standard of §287 applies to the determination of the extent of the affectedness and the numerical assessment of money damages.[330]

There are also judicial decisions which have allowed a relaxed standard of proof under circumstances when to require proof to a standard of "full conviction" (*volle Überzeugung*) would result in making a class of claim impossible of enforcement as a practical matter.[331] For instance, a party claiming casualty insurance proceeds based on theft of an auto which unexplainedly disappeared at night is not expected to prove to the full conviction of the court that it was stolen. Proof of circumstances consistent with theft will usually be accepted as sufficient.[332]

E. Conclusion of Plenary Proceedings

The plenary proceeding concludes with the submission of the case, or a potentially dispositive issue thereof, to the court for decision. The presiding judge has the responsibility for declaring the close of the plenary proceedings (*Schluss der Verhandlung*) when "in the view of the court the issue has been fully addressed" and when the matter is "ripe for decision" (*entscheidungsreif*).[333]

The formal close of plenary proceedings is important, for that is the time as of which the German law of *res adjudicata* applies. A judgment has res adjudicata effect based on the state of affairs as of the close of oral argument in the case in which it was rendered and does not adjudicate developments occurring thereafter.[334] By the same token, ordinarily no further factual submissions or arguments may be made following the close or plenary proceedings.[335]

Only under extraordinary circumstances may plenary proceedings, once closed, be reopened. A reopening of plenary proceedings (*Wiedereröffnung der Verhandlung*) may be ordered by the court only if the court determines that

---

330. See, e.g., Lüke, §22(IX), mn. 271–273; Thomas/Putzo/Reichold, §287, mn. 4 and 5; Federal Supreme Court, 51 *NJW* 3417 (1998); 53 *NJW* 1572 (2000).

331. See Zöller/Greger, Vor §284, mn. 28; Walter, *Freie Beweiswürdigung*, pp. 220 ff.

332. Federal Supreme Court, 44 *NJW* 2493 (1991).

333. ZPO §136(4) ("*wenn nach Ansicht des Gerichts die Sache vollständig erörtert ist.*"); see Zöller/Greger, §156, mn. 1; Lüke, §17, mn. 198.

334. E.g. Jauernig, §63(V); see Ch. 9 (F)(3) below on *res adjudicata* effect of judgments.

335. ZPO §296a. There is some debate about how late-submitted briefs (*nachgereichte Schriftsätze*) should be treated; i.e. whether they should be returned to the parties or left unread in the record (*Akte*). See Zöller/Greger, §132, mn. 4.

there was a material procedural error such as a violation of the judicial duty to give hints and feedback or a denial of right to be heard during the just-closed proceeding, if the court becomes aware of a circumstance that would sustain a post-judgment motion to reopen the proceedings, or if a judge dies or is otherwise unable to participate in the deliberation and decision of the case.[336] Reopening of the plenary proceedings is accomplished by issuance of a procedural order setting a time for continued oral plenary hearing, which is not confined to the grounds for reopening, but may encompass any open issue in the case.[337]

336. ZPO §156; Zöller/Greger, §156, mn. 2–5; Rosenberg/Schwab/Gottwald, §106(III)(9), p. 604. See Ch. 9(F)(4) below for a discussion of post-judgment reopening of proceedings.
337. Zöller/Greger, §156, mn. 1.

CHAPTER 9

Judgments and Other Case Dispositions

A judgment (*Urteil*) is the result of the joint efforts of parties and court to reach a binding determination of a lawsuit according to law. Approximately 30% of German civil lawsuits end in contested judgments (*streitige Endurteile*).[1] Most of these are reached following some sort of oral proceedings (*mündliche Verhandlungen*). A small number of contested judgments are entered after solely written proceedings (*Entscheidungen nach Lage der Akten, Entscheidungen ohne mündliche Verhandlungen*). A majority in number of all German civil case dispositions are by various kinds of uncontested judgments such as default judgments (*Versäumnisurteile*) and judgments by which one party voluntarily recognizes the validity of the other's position and agrees to the entry of an appropriate judgment (*Anerkenntnisurteile*). The parties may also end litigation by withdrawal of claims, by voluntary termination or by settlement. In any of these cases the court may enter a final cost order or document the settlement in the minutes of an oral hearing.

A judgment, which actually determines the parties' substantive rights and responsibilities, is to be contrasted with an interlocutory order (*Beschluss*) or procedural disposition (*Verfügung*) entered by the court or presiding judge during pendency of the case. These latter judicial acts address procedural matters rather than the merits of the issues in dispute. They are usually entered without oral argument by the parties, and may or may not be appealable.[2]

---

1. Rosenberg/Schwab/Gottwald, *Zivilprozessrecht,* 15th ed. (1993), §133(I), p. 784 (in 1989 contested judgments were entered in 30.1% of the Local Court cases and 31.2% of the District Court cases). For corresponding statistics showing similar though slightly decreasing numbers of contested judgments in 1996 see Gottwald, "Civil Justice Reform: Access, Cost, and Expedition. The German Perspective", in: Zuckerman et al. (eds.), *Civil Justice in Crisis* (1999), p. 207, 211.

2. See Ch. 10(F) below for a discussion of miscellaneous appeals of interlocutory orders (*Beschwerde*).

When a court sits in panels, the judgment is the combined product of the collegial court. The judgment is generally composed in writing, and orally announced in open court, if necessary at a special session called for that purpose.[3] The function of the judgment is not only to determine the issues in dispute and provide a "yes" or "no" answer or a monetary amount of damages. An essential component of almost every judgments is an exposition of the court's reasoning in reaching the result. The legal and logical consistency of such reasoning are as important as the ultimate correctness of the result in sustaining the judgment on appeal. The carefully reasoned and publicly announced judgment thus fulfils a function of educating the parties and the public about the law and its application to the facts of the case at bar.

German judges spend a considerable portion of their time and effort in the formulation and composition of judgments. A judge reasons and writes with care not only to avoid reversal on appeal. The quality of a judge's reasoning as described in her written judgments is important to her reputation among her peers and is a significant factor in promotion.

A. Uncontested Judgments and Case Terminations

A large number of cases in German courts are disposed of without actual judicial determinations of the merits of the parties' respective legal or factual contentions. Uncontested terminations of legal disputes are frequently based on agreements or acknowledgments by one or both parties. Such terminations sometimes represent parties' unilateral decisions not to contest their opponents' claims or to desist from prosecuting the terminating parties' own claims.

The legal effect of most forms of uncontested judgment is the same as that of a contested judgment. Uncontested judgments, like contested judgments, are generally enforceable by execution (*Zwangsvollstreckung*),[4] although there are differences among the various forms of uncontested judgments in treatment of costs and the ease in which they may be set aside on appeal or review. The main categories of uncontested civil judgments are default judgments

3. Most judgments also follow some kind of plenary hearing at which the parties appear and orally argue. This is a reflection of the principle of orality (*Mündlichkeitsprinzip*) underlying German civil justice. See Ch. 6(C)(1) above.

4. See Ch. 11(F) below.

(*Versäumnisurteile*), judgments by recognition (*Anerkenntnisurteile*) and judgments by relinquishment (*Verzichtsurteile*).

Uncontested termination of a litigated dispute by withdrawal of claim (*Klagerücknahme*) or voluntary termination (*Erledigung der Hauptsache*) generally do not result in uncontested judgments, although there is sometimes a final order for division of costs. Another form of uncontested termination of a civil proceeding is the formal settlement (*Prozessvergleich*), which can lead in appropriate cases to a stipulated disposition (*gerichtlicher Vergleich*) enforceable like a judgment.

1. Default Judgments

Many civil proceedings in Germany (as elsewhere) are determined by default judgments (*Versäumnisurteile*) when a party fails or declines to defend the claims asserted against him.[5] If, for instance, a party properly served with a complaint fails to file a written statement of intent to defend, the plaintiff can apply for the entry of a default judgment for the relief prayed for in the complaint.[6] A 1976 procedural reform allows the plaintiff to apply for the default judgment in writing without the necessity of attending an oral hearing.[7] Failure to file a written answer (*Klageerwiderung*) within the time set by a preparatory procedural order is not a default entitling the opponent to default judgment, but may result in preclusion from later assertion of defenses which should have been raised in the answer.[8]

Unjustified failure of a party to appear at a scheduled preliminary or plenary hearing can also be treated as a default entitling the opponent to seek a default judgment.[9] However failure to appear at a hearing for the reception of

5. Default judgments are rendered against defendants in about 25% of the cases in local courts and about 18% of the cases in state courts of general jurisdiction. Rosenberg/Schwab/Gottwald, §107(III)(4), p. 613.

6. ZPO §331. For implied application for default judgment from the demands of the complaint see Musielak/Stadler, *Kommentar zur Zivilprozessordnung*, 3rd ed. (2002), §331, mn. 5ff.; Federal Supreme Court, 37 BGHZ 79, 83 (1962).

7. ZPO §331(3). See, e.g., Jauernig, *Zivilprozessrecht*, 28th ed. (2003), §66 (III)(4); Rosenberg/Schwab/Gottwald, §107 (IV), p. 107; Bergerfurth, "Das Versäumnisurteil im schriftlichen Vorverfahren", 33 *JZ* 298 (1978).

8. ZPO §§276(1)(2), 296(1). See Ch. 7 (K) above.

9. ZPO §§330 331(1), (2). Failure of either party, or both parties, to appear at a plenary hearing can, at the election of the court, result in a determination of the case based on the state of the record (*Entscheidung nach Aktenlage*), if the facts have been sufficiently

evidence (*Beweisaufnahme*) or at a hearing for the announcement of a decision (*Verkündung einer Entscheidung*) is not the kind of default that can support a default judgment against the absent party.[10]

In the ordinary case, a default judgment can only be entered after a hearing.[11] The defaulting party must be properly summoned to the hearing.[12] At the outset of the hearing the court calls the case aloud (*Aufruf*) and requests the defaulting party to appear and participate in the hearing.[13] If the defaulting party does not appear, or if she appears, and does not defend, or does not address the opponent's argument or representations when requested by the court to do so, the opposing party may apply for the entry of a default judgment.[14] If the default is not cured before the conclusion of the hearing, the default judgment will be entered afterward. The judgment will generally be for the relief sought in the complaint and may be issued without the supporting reasoning generally required for contested judgments.[15] If the party appears before the end of the hearing and is prepared to participate, proceedings will continue as in any contested case.[16]

---

developed to permit such a determination. ZPO §§331a, 251a (added by the procedural reform of 1976).

10. Rosenberg/Schwab/Gottwald, §107(III)(1)(a)(1), p. 608. However, if oral argument has been scheduled to take place at the conclusion of an evidentiary hearing, failure to appear for the oral argument can support an application for default judgment.

11. ZPO §§331, 332; Lüke, *Zivilprozessrecht*, 8th ed. (2003), §32(II), mn. 372. An oral hearing may be dispensed with only when the defendant has failed to file a statement of intention to defend in response to a ZPO §276 order initiating written preparatory proceedings. ZPO §331(3).

12. ZPO §335(1)(2). See Thomas/Putzo/Reichold, *Zivilprozessordnung*, 24th ed. (2002), §335, mn. 3; Zöller/Herget, *Zivilprozessordnung*, 23rd ed. (2002), §335, mn. 3.

13. ZPO §220. For a description of an actual proceeding for the entry of default judgment, see Murray, "A Morning at the Amtsgericht: German Civil Justice in Practice", in: Nafziger/Symeonides (eds.), *Law and Justice in a Multistate World, Essays in Honor of Arthur T. von Mehren* (2002), p. 779.

14. The plaintiff can also be defaulted for failure to appear at a preliminary or plenary hearing, or the failure to argue to or address the opponent's position when requested to do so by the court. ZPO §§330, 333, 334. In courts where representation by attorneys is mandatory, the failure to appear by counsel can be a default. See Lüke, §32(II), mn. 372; Rosenberg/Schwab/Gottwald, §107(III)(1)(c), p. 609.

15. ZPO §§331(1) and (2), 313b(1);. See Rosenberg/Schwab/Gottwald, §107(III)(4), p. 612; Musielak/Stadler, §331, mn. 7 ff. This will ordinarily include court costs and attorneys' fees accrued to the stage of the proceeding at which the default occurred. See Ch. 4(H) above and Ch. 9(E) below for discussion of the allocation of court costs and attorneys' fees.

16. See ZPO §220(2); Federal Supreme Court, 46 *NJW* 861, 862 (1993).

Before a default judgment can be entered, the court must examine on its own motion the allowability (*Zulässigkeit*) of the complaint, at least on its face. Since a default judgment has the effect of a judgment on the merits (*Sachurteil*), the court must be satisfied of the existence of the prerequisites to suit (*Prozessvoraussetzungen*) before entering judgment. If the court finds some prerequisite to suit is lacking, the court must enter a procedural dismissal (*Prozessurteil*).[17] Other grounds for denying an application for default judgment include failure of the applicant to provide proof (*Nachweis*) of the prerequisites to suit,[18] or failure of the record to demonstrate timely notification of the defaulting opponent of a relevant time period or of the oral hearing.[19]

The court must also determine the legal sufficiency of the representations made by the party applying for the default judgment assuming that such representations are true (*Schlüssigkeitsprüfung*). If the facts alleged are not legally sufficient to support the claims for relief, the default judgment will not be granted and the complaint will be dismissed with prejudice.[20] A party aggrieved by such a dismissal has the right to lodge a second instance appeal (*Berufung*) as in any other case.[21]

A default judgment is strictly limited to the legal and factual assertions of record prior to the occurrence of the default. A party may not bring up new matter or enlarge a previously stated claim at a plenary hearing on an application for default judgment.[22] Under German law a party has the right to know what is at stake if he exercises the option to default. If there is doubt as to whether a defaulting party is aware of an assertion or claim for relief of the opponent, the hearing will be adjourned and rescheduled to

---

17. A dismissal of this kind is without prejudice to correcting the defect and filing a new action. Sometimes when a procedural judgment of dismissal is entered on a plaintiff's application for a default judgment, the judgment is called a "false default judgment" (*unechtes Versäumnisurteil*). See, e.g., Lüke, §32(II), mn. 372; Rosenberg/ Schwab/Gottwald, §107(II), p. 608.

18. ZPO §335(1)(1). However, this provision does not apply if the party represents that proof will be offered in due time. See, e.g., Federal Supreme Court, 14 *NJW* 2207 (1961); Thomas/Putzo/Reichold, §335, mn. 2 and Musielak/Stadler, §335, mn.2. Otherwise the claim will be dismissed by "false default judgment".

19. ZPO §335(1)(2) and (4). Zöller/Herget, §335, mn. 3, 5; Thomas/Putzo/Reichold, §335, mn. 3, 6.

20. ZPO §331(2); Rosenberg/Schwab/Gottwald, §107(III)(4)(b), p. 613; Jauernig §66 (III)(3)(b).

21. Jauernig §66 (III)(3)(b); Zöller/Herget, Vor §330, mn. 11.

22. ZPO §335 (1)(3). See also Zöller/Herget, §335, mn. 4; Musielak/Stadler, §335, mn. 4.

permit notification of the defaulting party and opportunity to appear and contest based on the new information.[23] A denial of an application for a default judgment can be reviewed by immediate miscellaneous appeal (*Beschwerde*).[24]

In cases where the defendant has failed to respond to an initial order invoking written preparatory proceedings and requiring notice of defense within a specified time,[25] a recently enacted provision of the ZPO authorizes application for issuance of a default judgment in writing.[26] Such a request can be contained in the complaint and must in any event be served on the defendant.[27] If the court is satisfied that the prerequisites to suit exist, the court may issue a default judgment based on the plaintiff's written representations of which the defendant has been made aware without the need of calling any oral hearing.[28] The judgment is announced by service.[29]

A party against whom default judgment has been entered has two weeks from the date of service of the judgment to file an objection (*Einspruch*) with the court that issued it.[30] The objection can address all, or only a portion of the default judgment.[31] The objecting party must set forth in the objection any legal and factual claims or means of defense to the case in chief, and refer to the sources of proof for factual contentions as it would in any

23. ZPO §§335(2) and 337. See Rosenberg/Schwab/Gottwald, §107(III)(2)(c), p. 610.

24. ZPO §336(1)(1). If the miscellaneous appeal is successful, a new hearing is scheduled on the application for default judgment. The defaulting party is not summoned to this hearing (ZPO §336(1)(2)). See, e.g., Rosenberg/Schwab/Gottwald, §107(III)(2)(c), p. 611. For a discussion of the procedure on a miscellaneous appeal see Ch. 10(F) below.

25. See Ch. 7(F)(5) above.

26. ZPO §331(3). This procedure was instituted as a part of the 1976 procedural reform. It can be considered an exception to the principle of orality (*Mündlichkeitsprinzip*), which usually would require an oral hearing prior to the issuance of a judgment on the merits. See Ch. 6(E)(1) above.

27. See ZPO §331(3)(2); Rosenberg/Schwab/Gottwald, §107(IV)(2), p. 615; State Court of Appeals of München, 34 *MDR* 235 (1980).

28. If, however, the defendant files its written statement of intention to defend before the judgment is issued, the application for default judgment must be denied and the action will proceed. ZPO §331(3)(1).

29. ZPO §310(3). See Musielak/Stadler, §331, mn. 23.

30. ZPO §339. If the judgment is announced by service (ZPO §§331(3), 310(3)), service on both parties is mandatory. See Federal Supreme Court, 47 *NJW* 3359, 3360 (1994).

31. ZPO §340(2)(2). See Prütting, in: *Münchener Kommentar zur Zivilprozessordnung*, 2nd ed. (1996), §340, mn. 10; Thomas/Putzo/Reichold, §340, mn. 4.

preparatory pleading or brief.[32] A copy of the objection is to be served on the opposing party.[33]

If the objection is in proper form and suggests an actual contest on the merits, the court will set a hearing on the objection, which may also become the plenary hearing in the underlying case if the objection is granted. An objection which is not in proper form or which on its face does not appear to be allowable (*statthaft*) can be overruled without a hearing.[34]

If the objector appears at the hearing on the objection and is prepared to proceed with oral argument, the default judgment is suspended and the case proceeds as if the default judgment had not been entered (ZPO §342). Although there is some dispute, the prevailing view is that if the defaulting party has been subject to factual preclusions for failure to address the opponent's factual assertions within a specified time period at an earlier stage of the proceedings,[35] the removal of the default judgment does not generally affect these preclusions.[36] A party may, however, be relieved from such preclusions by showing that the failure to respond was justified, or at least excusable, and that the relief requested will not unduly extend the proceedings.[37] To the extent that the decision reached by the court after hearing is identical with the decision set forth in the default judgment, the default judgment is upheld. To the extent the court's decision departs from the default judgment, the latter is set aside.[38]

It should be stressed that a party filing an objection to a default judgment within the prescribed time period is not required to show good cause or even excusable neglect for the default, but merely that he wishes to defend the case after all. An objection filed within the allowable time period must be granted

32. ZPO §340(3). Upon application of the objecting party the court can enlarge the time period for substantiation of the objection if it will not unduly prolong the proceedings or if there is good cause.

33. ZPO §340a. The copy is to be served irrespective of whether the objection is allowable and in proper form. See Zöller/Herget, §340a, mn. 2. Lack of service does not affect the validity of an objection, see Musielak/Stadler, §340a, mn. 1.

34. ZPO §341. See Prütting, in: *Münchener Kommentar zur ZPO*, §341, mn. 2. An order overruling an objection to a default judgment is subject to immediate miscellaneous appeal (*sofortige Beschwerde*). See Prütting, in: *Münchener Kommentar zur ZPO*, §341, mn. 17

35. See Ch. 7(K) above.

36. See, e.g., Lüke, §32(V), mn. 375; Rosenberg/Schwab/Gottwald, §107(V)(3)(c), p. 617; Zöller/Herget, §340, mn. 7; Prütting, in: *Münchener Kommentar zu ZPO*, §342, mn. 6; but see Thomas/Putzo/Reichold, §340, mn. 9.

37. Federal Supreme Court, 76 BGHZ 173 (1980). See also Prütting, in: *Münchener Kommentar zur ZPO*, §340, mn. 22 ff.

38. ZPO §343. State Court of Appeals of Köln, 29 *NJW* 113 (1976); Thomas/Putzo/Reichold, §343, mn. 4; Zöller/Herget, §343, mn. 2 ff.

regardless of the legal or factual sufficiency of the indicated defense. This generosity in setting aside defaults may reflect a conviction that it is easier to hear a defaulted case than to expend judicial resources in determining whether there was good cause for the default.[39]

If, on the other hand, the party raising the objection fails to appear at the hearing on the objection, the opponent may apply for a "second default judgment" (*zweites Versäumnisurteil*), which is not subject to being set aside on objection.[40] The only relief available to a party aggrieved by a second default judgment is by second instance appeal (*Berufung*) based on legal or factual insufficiency of the judgment.[41]

A party who successfully gets a default judgment set aside, in whole or in part, is responsible for the costs incurred by reason of the default, regardless of the allocation of the other costs and expenses of the law suit.[42] If the default judgment is ultimately reconfirmed in a contested judgment, the costs attendant upon the default proceedings are added to the other costs which that party must bear.[43]

2. Voluntary Termination of Claims

In some cases circumstances arising after the filing of suit may render a claim moot or otherwise legally hopeless. For instance, the defendant may voluntarily pay the amount due, a party to a divorce case may die, or a corporate plaintiff may lose the legal capacity to sue.[44] An action for declaratory

39. See Fasching, "Die Rechtsbehelfe gegen Versäumnisurteile im deutschen und österreichischen Zivilprozess", in: Grunsky/Stürner/Walter/Wolf (eds.), *Festschrift für Fritz Baur* (1981), p. 387; Bettermann, "Anfechtung und Kassation", 88 *ZZP* 365, 418 ff. (1975) for a discussion of the legal nature of the objection.

40. ZPO §345. However default in appearance at an oral hearing after the hearing on the objection is treated as a simple default and does not permit entry of a "second default judgment". If a party defaults a second time after securing removal of a first default judgment, the court may, on motion of the other party, exercise its discretion to enter a "decision based on the state of the record" (*Entscheidung nach Lage der Akten*), which is subject only to conventional appeal, ZPO §331(a). See Lüke, §32(V), mn. 376.

41. See ZPO §514(2). See Federal Supreme Court, 52 *NJW* 2120 (1999): Good cause for the second default is a sufficient basis of a second instance appeal. For procedures and grounds of various kinds of appeals see Ch. 10 below.

42. ZPO §344.

43. See Ch. 9(E) below on allocation of court costs and attorneys' fees.

44. For examples of circumstances in which lawsuits may become moot or invalid after their institution, see Rosenberg/Schwab/Gottwald, §132(I), p. 777; Lüke, §21(II), mn. 244.

judgment may be superseded by a later action seeking performance. So long as the claim was properly before the court at one time, German procedure offers the parties, or under some circumstances the claimant alone, the option of declaring the substantive dispute terminated (*die Hauptsache für erledigt erklären*), leaving the court only with the determination and allocation of costs.[45] Such voluntary terminations do generally dispose of the case on the merits, but they are not treated like outright dismissals or withdrawals for the purpose of assessment of costs and attorneys' fees.[46]

When a claimant becomes aware that its claim has become moot or legally invalid because of intervening circumstances, the claimant may propose that the parties declare a termination of the substantive dispute (*Erledigung der Hauptsache*), which will stop the lawsuit, leaving the court only with the task of fairly allocating the costs. Such declarations can be entered either orally or in writing. Usually they take the form of an oral or written statement of the claimant, which is agreed to or at least not disputed by the opponent. Once the parties have declared a suit terminated, the power of the court to determine the merits ceases, and the court's sole function is to assess costs.[47]

If the parties declare a case terminated, the court assesses costs and attorneys' fees not according to the usual "winner-loser" formula, but in its equitable discretion (*nach billigem Ermessen*) based on the parties' respective prospects up to the time of the declaration of termination.[48] In most circumstances such allocation of costs are likely to be more favorable to the claimant than on a withdrawal of the complaint or dismissal with prejudice.[49]

---

45. Approximately 1.5–2% of cases in the local courts and state courts of general jurisdiction are terminated in this manner.

46. Of course the claimant would also have the option of withdrawal of the claim (*Klagerücknahme*) or ceasing participation in the law suit and suffering default judgment of dismissal (*Versäumnisurteil*). However, in either of these instances the claimant would be treated as a 100% loser for the purpose of allocation of costs and attorneys' fees. See Ch. 9(E) below on assessment of costs and attorneys fees.

47. This is another example of the principle of party control of proceedings (*Dispositionsmaxime*). See, e.g., Rosenberg/Schwab/Gottwald, §132(II)(1), p. 778; Jauernig, §42 (VI)(1).

48. ZPO §91a, see Jauernig, §42(VI)(1). For an overview, see Bergerfurth, "Erledigung der Hauptsache im Zivilprozess", 45 *NJW* 1655 (1992).

49. If a claim is withdrawn, costs and attorneys' fees up to the time of withdrawal are assessed against the claimant. ZPO §269(3). If a claim is dismissed, costs and attorneys' fees, including a fee for the judgment dismissing the claim, are assessed against the claimant. See also Ch. 9(E) below.

In some cases a party will seek to declare a case terminated but the opponent will not join in the declaration. The opponent may object on the ground that the reason for failure of the claim existed at the time of the filing of the complaint or assertion of the claim, so that dismissal with prejudice and assessment of costs against the claimant is the proper disposition. If a party amends a complaint after an intervening circumstance has occurred, that party cannot thereafter seek termination of the amended claim based on that particular circumstance.[50] If there is objection to a proposed termination, the claimant may apply for a declaratory judgment on the contested termination and the court must decide whether the preconditions for termination exist, namely, whether there is a circumstance which renders a once valid claim moot or invalid and whether it arose after the claim was asserted.[51] If the court determines that the preconditions for a termination exist, it pronounces the claim terminated, and any costs and attorneys' fees attendant upon the process to determine the issue are awarded against the objector. If the court determines that the claim was invalid *ab initio*, or that the intervening circumstances have not rendered it moot, it will enter judgment of dismissal.[52]

A claimant may also make applications in the alternative. An application in chief to declare the original claim terminated can be accompanied by a subordinate application that the original claim be decided in the event that the court denies the application in chief. Such an application permits a claimant to avoid a loss on the merits if the preconditions for termination did not exist but the original claim was well founded.

3. Withdrawals of Claims

German law permits any claimant to effect withdrawal of a claim (*Klagerücknahme*) right up to the time of contested judgment. Counterclaims as well as initial claims are subject to voluntary withdrawal by the party originally asserting them. Withdrawal of a claim ends the proceedings based on the with-

50. The circumstance has become an existing circumstance with respect to the amended claim, so that the only proper remedy is dismissal or withdrawal. See Lüke, §21(II), mn. 247; Federal Supreme Court, 45 *NJW* 2235 (1992).

51. The theoretical bases and legal effect of contested terminations are much disputed in the literature. See, e.g., Rosenberg/Schwab/Gottwald, §132(III), p. 780; Lüke, §21(II), mn. 247; Lindacher, in: *Münchener Kommentar zur ZPO*, §91a, mn. 75 ff.

52. A judgment of dismissal results in an award of costs and attorneys' fees incurred up to the time of dismissal against the claimant. See Ch. 9(E) below.

drawn claim.[53] Although a claim withdrawal is not actually a judgment, a significant number of German civil proceedings end with voluntary withdrawals.[54]

A claimant has the right unilaterally to withdraw a claim up to the time of commencement of the opposing party's argument on the merits in the oral hearing (*mündliche Verhandlung*).[55] Thereafter a withdrawal of claim requires the consent of the opponent.[56] A claim can be withdrawn either orally or in writing.[57] There is no particular form required, as long as the intention is clear. A reduction in the amount or scope of a claim, without change in the legal basis, is treated as a partial claim withdrawal (*teilweise Rücknahme*).[58]

Withdrawal of a claim ends pendency (*Rechtshängigkeit*) of the case *ab initio*. Preliminary orders and provisional remedies, even partial or interlocutory judgments as well as judgments of a lower instance court (in the case of a withdrawal of a claim while on second instance appeal), are without effect without the necessity of a formal revocation.[59] The only matter left for the court to determine is the assessment of costs, which the court can make by order without oral argument.[60] Ordinarily costs and attorneys fees incurred up to the time of the withdrawal are assessed against the withdrawing party.[61]

---

53. However withdrawal of a claim does not terminate a counterclaim (*Widerklage*) asserted in the same proceeding. See Rosenberg/Schwab/Gottwald, §130(III)(1), p. 759 f.; Zöller/Greger, §269, mn. 17.

54. Approximately 17% of the cases filed in the local courts and 12% of the cases filed in the state courts of general jurisdiction are ended by withdrawals of claims. See Rosenberg/Schwab/Gottwald, §130(I), p. 755. See also Statistical Yearbook for the Federal Republic of Germany 2002, p. 342 for actual numbers of complaints filed and disposed of.

55. ZPO §269(1). So, for instance, if, during the oral hearing and before the defendant has been heard on the merits the plaintiff concludes that the claim has no chance, the plaintiff can withdraw the claim without seeking the defendant's consent. See Rosenberg/Schwab/Gottwald, §130(II)(2), p. 758.

56. ZPO §269(2). If the opponent does not consent to withdrawal the claim will proceed to either default or contested judgment on the merits.

57. ZPO §269(2). See Rosenberg/Schwab/Gottwald, §130(II)(1), p. 757; Zöller/Greger, §269, mn. 12a; Musielak/Foerste, §269, mn. 7.

58. Such a partial claim reduction is not subject to the requirements for an amendment of claim (*Klageänderung*). ZPO §264(2).

59. A party may, however, apply for a declaration to this effect by final court order. ZPO §269(3) and (4).

60. ZPO §§269(3) and (4), 128(4); Lüke, in: *Münchener Kommentar zur ZPO*, §269, mn. 53; Zöller/Greger, §269, mn. 19.

61. ZPO §269(3). However, if the court has already decided that certain costs are to be otherwise allocated, such a determination remains in force.

If, however, a complaint is withdrawn prior to service on the opposing party, the court may withhold or limit costs to the opposing party according to its equitable discretion based on the parties' respective prospects up to the time of the withdrawal.[62] Needless to say, if the withdrawal of the complaint is the result of an in or out of court settlement between the parties,[63] the allocation of costs and attorneys fees takes place in accord with the procedure for settlements, not unilateral withdrawals.[64]

A withdrawal is without prejudice to reassertion of the claim in a later proceeding.[65] However if the claimant has not paid the costs assessed against it with respect to the former proceeding, the defendant can object and obtain a stay of the new proceeding until the costs of the former case are paid.[66]

4. Stipulated Dispositions

In some cases the parties' negotiations (in or out of court) result in an agreed disposition of a case which they may wish to incorporate in a court document enforceable by process of execution. Such stipulated results are to be contrasted with simple out of court settlements not requiring any court activity[67] and with default judgments, terminations and withdrawals discussed above. The process by which civil cases are settled, and the role of the court in facilitating settlements is discussed in Ch. 11(I) below.

If the settling parties desire an immediately enforceable execution or a legally binding determination of status to implement their agreement, the settlement must generally be documented in an oral proceeding before a German court.[68]

---

62. See ZPO § 269(3)(3); Thomas/Putzo/Reichold, § 269, mn. 16.

63. See ZPO § 98; Federal Supreme Court, 12 *NJW-RR* 510 (1997). If the complaint is not withdrawn as stipulated in an out of court settlement, proof of the settlement will result in the complaint being dismissed as not allowable (*unzulässig*). See Lüke, §21(I), mn. 243; Zöller/Greger, §269, mn. 3.

64. Federal Supreme Court, 14 *NJW* 460 (1961); Rosenberg/Schwab/Gottwald, § 130 (III)(2)(b), p. 760; Zöller/Greger, §269, mn. 18a.

65. Supreme Court of the German Empire, 152 RGZ 46 (1937); Rosenberg/Schwab/Gottwald, §130(III)(4), p. 761; Zöller/Greger, §269, mn. 21; Musielak/Foerste, §269, mn. 18 ff.

66. ZPO §269(6). Federal Supreme Court, 45 *NJW* 2034 (1992); Thomas/Putzo/Reichold, §269, mn. 24.

67. Such settlements reached during pendency are often implemented by simple withdrawals or agreed on terminations of cases by the parties and without the participation of the court.

68. See ZPO §794(1)(1). If the court is one in which representation by counsel is mandatory, counsel must also be present. See, e.g., Musielak/Lackmann, §794, mn. 13;

The agreement must be orally read to the parties, assented to by them in the presence of the judge and then reduced to writing signed by the presiding judge and the attesting clerk (*Urkundsbeamten*) of the court in which the case is pending.[69] The function of the court is analogous to a notary, namely to ascertain the intention of the parties and reduce it to minutes (*Protokolle*) in the official case record. In most cases the court has no role to pass on the legality, fairness or appropriateness of the stipulated result. The court may comment to the parties or counsel on the reasonableness, apparent fairness or overall advisability of the proposed settlement under the circumstances and based on the legal positions of the parties. However, if the parties insist on settling the case on terms other than as recommended by the court, the court is generally required to honor their choice and document their settlement.[70]

The stipulated resolution ends the suit without a judicial judgment but can be enforced as a judicial execution.[71] Questions about the validity or effect of a stipulated disposition may generally be raised in the court in which the matter was pending at the time of the settlement and where the settlement was made of record.[72]

If the parties have not otherwise agreed, and the court has not already otherwise ordered, costs and attorneys' fees will be reciprocally suspended.[73] In most cases the parties agree on the allocation of costs and fees and their agreement is incorporated as a part of the settlement. Such agreements are usually

---

Rosenberg/Schwab/Gottwald, §131(III)(2)(g), p. 769; Jauernig, §48(III)(2). The court may also make a written settlement proposal. If both parties agree, the court may then document the settlement by court order. See ZPO §278(6) and Ch. 11(I)(3).

69. See Ch. 6(D). If the case has been referred to a single judge or designated judge of another German court for reception of proof or other ancillary proceedings, that judge is empowered to hear and document the settlement. See Lüke, §21(III), mn. 250; Rosenberg/Schwab/Gottwald, §131(I)(3), p. 763; Zöller/Stöber, §794, mn. 5.

70. Only in extreme cases, where the settlement would be considered to be void or contrary to public policy, could the judge properly refuse to make it of record. See Wolfsteiner, in: *Münchener Kommentar zur ZPO*, §794, mn. 43 ff.

71. ZPO §794(1)(1). See Zöller/Stöber, §794, mn. 14; Thomas/Putzo, §794, mn. 26 ff.

72. See Zöller/Stöber, §794, mn. 15a. For a detailed discussion of the different procedures to challenge or revoke settlements which have been made of record see Rosenberg/Schwab/Gottwald, §131(IV), pp. 771ff.; Baur/Stürner, *Zwangsvollstreckungs-, Konkurs- und Vergleichsrecht*, Vol. I, *Einzelvollstreckungsrecht*, 12th ed. (1995), mn. 16.11; Pecher, "Zur Geltendmachung der Unwirksamkeit eines Prozessvergleichs", 97 *ZZP* 139 (1984); Federal Supreme Court, 52 *NJW* 2903 (1999).

73. ZPO §98. See Ch. 9(E)(3) and (4) below; Federal Supreme Court, 18 *NJW* 103 (1965); Bergerfurth, "Vergleich ohne Kostenregelung", 25 *NJW* 1840 (1972).

based on the degree to which the settlement reflects their respective legal positions in the case.[74]

Parties represented by counsel can obtain the benefits of a judicially documented settlement, including immediate execution, without going to court, if their attorneys sign a document in which the debtor expressly submits itself to immediate execution. The document must be filed in the court competent to consider the dispute.[75] Out of court settlements which have not been made of record can be specifically enforced as simple contracts by independent actions.

5. Judgments by Acknowledgment or Relinquishment

German procedural law recognizes a judgment based on acknowledgment of a claim by the party against which a claim is asserted. Such a disposition, a "judgment by acknowledgment" (*Anerkenntnisurteil*), has the form and effect of a judgment on the merits, without requiring the court to make actual findings and conclusions.[76]

If a party against whom a claim for relief (*Antrag*) is asserted unconditionally acknowledges the claim at an oral hearing or in a written preparatory pleading or brief, the claimant may apply for judgment to be entered on the claim as acknowledged. In such a case the court is bound to enter judgment by acknowledgment without any investigation of the factual or legal basis for the judgment.[77]

Judgment by acknowledgment may be based only on an unconditional acknowledgment of a particular articulated claim. If the acknowledgment is conditional, or linked with defenses, there is as a matter of principle no basis for judgment by acknowledgment.[78] Nor may the judgment go beyond or differ

74. See Ch. 11(I)(2) below for a more complete discussion of allocation of costs in cases concluded by settlement.

75. See ZPO §§796a und 796b (added 1998). For an overview see Musielak/Voit, §796a, mn. 2 ff. At the option of the parties the document can also be filed in the office of a notary located in the district in which the court sits. See ZPO §796c and Ch. 11(I)(3).

76. It is said that the acknowledgment itself provides the grounds for the judgment. See Rosenberg/Schwab/Gottwald, §133(IV)(1), p. 791; Zöller/Vollkommer, §307, mn. 4; Musielak, §307, mn. 2.

77. ZPO §307. Federal Supreme Court, 46 *NJW* 1717, 1718 (1993). See Zöller/Vollkommer, §307, mn. 4; Rosenberg/Schwab/Gottwald, §133(IV)(1), p. 791; Lüke, §20(IV), mn. 233. This is an application of the principle of party control of litigation (*Dispositionsmaxime*).

78. Musielak, in: *Münchener Kommentar zur ZPO*, §307, mn. 4 ff., 8 ff.; Rosenberg/Schwab/Gottwald, §133(IV)(2), pp. 791 f. But if the defendant acknowledges liability but contests damages, the court may render an interlocutory judgment by acknowledgment on

from the exact claim as acknowledged. It is up to the court to determine whether the acknowledgment is sufficiently clear and unconditional so as to support judgment by acknowledgment.[79]

Acknowledgments usually occur during oral argument (*mündliche Verhandlung*) during the give and take between parties, attorneys and judges as the various claims and defenses are discussed. If a claimant believes that the opponent has acknowledged the validity of a claim, in whole or in part, the claimant may then and there orally apply to the court for judgment by acknowledgment on the claim as acknowledged. Sometimes an acknowledgment will be found in written submissions made during written preparatory proceedings (*schriftliches Vorverfahren*)[80] or in written proceedings by agreement (*schriftliches Verfahren*),[81] in which case the application for judgment by acknowledgment may be set forth in a subsequent written submission[82] or made at a later oral hearing. In any event, the acknowledgment, and the application for judgment thereon, if either occurs at an oral hearing, are to be noted in the minutes of the proceeding.[83] However a judgment by acknowledgment need not be orally rendered in the manner of other contested judgments.[84]

Closely related to the judgment by acknowledgment is the judgment by relinquishment (*Verzichtsurteil*). If a party who asserts a litigated claim voluntarily relinquishes the claim during litigation, the opponent may apply for judgment of dismissal to be entered on that claim by relinquishment.[85] Relinquishments, like acknowledgments, can occur during oral or written proceedings. Since judgment by relinquishment is also based on the principle of

---

her liability. See Rosenberg/Schwab/Gottwald, § 133(IV)(2), p. 792; Zöller/Vollkommer, §307, mn. 7.

79. The court may also determine whether the prerequisites to suit (*Prozessvoraussetzungen*) are present, but may not address the merits of the claim as acknowledged. See Zöller/Vollkommer, §307, mn. 4; Lüke, §20(IV), mn. 233.

80. See ZPO §276. See Zöller/Vollkommer, §307, mn. 3; Musielak, §307, mn. 9.

81. See ZPO §128. See Zöller/Vollkommer, §307, mn. 3; Thomas/Putzo, §307, mn. 4.

82. Indeed, the plaintiff's complaint (*Klage*) may contain an application for judgment by acknowledgment to the extent that the defendant may acknowledge the claim. When the acknowledgment and the application for judgment are both made in writing, judgment by acknowledgment may be entered and issued without any sort of oral proceedings. ZPO §307(2).

83. ZPO §160(3)(1) and (2).

84. ZPO §310(3). Such judgments may be rendered by service (*Zustellung*) on the parties.

85. ZPO §306. Since a judgment by relinquishment is a judgment on the merits, the court is obliged to assure itself of the prerequisites to suit (*Prozessvoraussetzungen*) before entering such a judgment. See Lüke, §20(IV), mn. 234.

party control of litigation, it is not as freely available in cases in which the court exercises a noncontentious jurisdiction (*freiwillige Gerichtsbarkeit*).[86]

An acknowledgment or relinquishment, once made, may be withdrawn prior to final judgment[87] only with the agreement of the opposing party, or upon a finding of particularly good cause, such as the subsequent discovery of documentary proof that would disprove the claim as acknowledged or a similar development that would constitute sufficient ground for reopening of a civil judgment.[88]

B. Contested Judgments

Law suits not resolved by agreement of the parties, by permitted unilateral withdrawal or by other voluntary terminations must be determined by judgment of the court. A final judgment (*Endurteil*) can dismiss a claim at issue, or grant some or all of the relief sought on the claim. The final judgment terminates the proceeding or at least a part of the proceeding in the instance in which it is rendered, subject to any rights of appeal.

1. Relationship of Judgment to Claims at Issue

A judgment on the merits is strictly limited by the claims placed at issue by the parties. No relief may be granted beyond or different than that prayed for by the plaintiff in its complaint or the defendant in its counterclaim.[89] A judg-

---

86. See Musielak, in: *Münchener Kommentar zur ZPO*, §306, mn.3 and §307, mn. 2. In marriage and family cases, judgment by relinquishment may only be entered with respect to those legal issues within the scope of party control. See Rosenberg/Schwab/Gottwald, §133(V)(2)(b), p. 798; Zöller/Vollkommer, Vor §306, mn. 8; Federal Supreme Court, 97 BGHZ 304, 309 (1986).

87. If judgment has been rendered by the court in which the acknowledgment was made, but the case is still subject to appeal or revision, an application to withdraw the acknowledgment may be made before the appellate court. See Rosenberg/Schwab/Gottwald, §133(IV)(6), p. 796.

88. See Zöller/Vollkommer, Vor §306, mn. 6, Musielak, §307, mn. 14; Rosenberg/Schwab/Gottwald, §133(IV)(6), p. 796; Federal Supreme Court, 80 BGHZ 394 (1981). For proceedings for reopening of civil judgments see Ch. 9(F)(4) below.

89. ZPO §308. See Zöller/Vollkommer, §308, mn. 2 ff.; Musielak," Die Bindung des Gerichts an die Anträge der Parteien im Zivilprozess", in: Gottwald et al. (eds.), *Festschrift für Schwab* (1990), p. 349. This limitation does not include costs and attorneys' fees, which are awarded even in the absence of a particular claim or particularization. ZPO §308(2). ZPO §308a authorizes the court in landlord-tenant cases involving residential real estate to declare in favor of the tenant an ongoing landlord-tenant relationship and its terms and

ment of dismissal relates only to the claims as asserted. There is no doctrine permitting the court to render judgment in a controversy other than as placed at issue by the parties' pleadings.[90] If the court renders relief different from or greater than that prayed for, the judgment is not invalid, but it may be attacked on appeal. On the other hand, within the scope of the claims placed at issue, the court is completely free to grant only a part of what is asked for.[91]

The strictness of this doctrine is somewhat mitigated by the power of the court to allow amendments of the claims during the course of litigation and the obligation of the court to provide parties and counsel with hints and feedback (*Hinweise*) as the case progresses.[92] If the original pleadings do not adequately address the real controversy, it is likely that the process of discussion of the claims with the court at the preliminary or plenary hearing will result in reformulation or restatement of the claims before the court comes to render judgment.[93]

In any event the court is not required to render judgment on all of the claims at issue at the same time. When, in the court's sound discretion it seems advisable, the court can render a partial judgment (*Teilurteil*) on only some or a part of the claims, leaving the other claims or remaining parts of the claim still pending.[94] In personal injury cases in which both liability and damages are disputed it is common for courts to give interlocutory judgments on liability (*Grundurteile*), leaving damages to later determination.[95] In many cases

---

duration even without particularized claim therefore in the pleadings or at an oral argument.

90. Under German law an award of relief different from that prayed for could implicate the constitutional right to be heard (*rechtliches Gehör*). See Rosenberg/Schwab/Gottwald, §133(I)(1)(b), p. 785; Musielak, §308, mn. 22.

91. Rosenberg/Schwab/Gottwald, §133(I)(1)(b), p. 785; Zöller/Vollkommer, §308, mn. 4; Musielak, in: *Festschrift für Schwab*, pp. 349, 352 ff.

92. See Ch. 7(K)(2) above on the procedure for amendment of claims for relief and Ch. 6(C) above on the court's obligation to give hints and feedback.

93. The constitutional right to be heard (*rechtliches Gehör*) requires that the opponent have the opportunity to be fully heard on any restated or amended claims prior to submission of the claims for judgment. See GG Article 103 and Ch. 6(E)(3) above. See Ch. 6(C)(2) above on the allowable scope of hints and feedback and Ch. 7(K)(2) above on the scope of allowable amendments of claims and defenses.

94. ZPO §301(1) provides that the court should decide individual claims or counterclaims when they are "ripe" (*reif*) for decision, but that the court has the discretion not to give partial judgment "when the court deems it would be inappropriate to do so under the circumstances of the case" ("*wenn es das Gericht nach Lage der Sache nicht für angemessen erachtet*"). ZPO §301(2). See Musielak, in: *Münchener Kommentar zur ZPO*, §301, mn. 4 ff., 18.

95. ZPO §304.

the judgment on liability will give the parties impetus to settle the pending damage claim making contested proceedings on damages unnecessary.[96] Ordinarily partial and interlocutory judgments on liability are appealable immediately. However, an appeal of a partial or interlocutory judgment does not automatically stay proceedings on the remaining issues in the case. That is up to the court's sound discretion.

2. Deliberations to Reach Judgment

Although today many civil cases in Germany are decided at least in the first instance by single judges,[97] the process envisioned by the Civil Procedure Code and the Court Organization Law (*Gerichtsverfassungsgesetz* or GVG) for reaching judgment is the collegial process of the multi-judge panel which was the norm in the state district courts (*Landgerichte*) and is still the norm on all appellate courts. Under that process the judges first engage in joint deliberations (*Beratung*) and then reach a decision by majority vote (*Abstimmung*).

Deliberations are expected to take place as soon as practicable following oral argument, often the same day. Only judges who have taken part in the last session of oral argument may participate in reaching the decision.[98] Deliberations and votes are conducted in secret.[99]

The presiding judge conducts the deliberations and collects the votes. However differences in opinion concerning the formulation and order of the issues or the effect of a vote are to be decided by the court as a whole.[100]

Judges are encouraged, at least when there is a difference of opinion, to consider and vote individually on elements of a cause of action and whether

96. See Zöller/Vollkommer, §304, mn. 1; Lüke, §27(IV), mn. 324.

97. E.g. in the local court (*Amtsgericht*) and in the state district court (*Landgericht*). See GVG §22(1) and ZPO §§348, 348a; Ch. 3(D)(1)(b) and (2)(b) and Ch. 7(E)(1) above.

98. ZPO §309. This is a result of the principle of immediacy (*Unmittelbarkeitsprinzip*), see Ch. 6(E) above. If during the interval between the last session of oral argument and the reaching of judgment a judge becomes unavailable, the presiding judge will schedule another session of oral argument before deliberating the case with a successor judge, ZPO §156(2)(3). See Zöller/Vollkommer, §309, mn. 4.

99. GVG §193. Court personnel and law interns (*Referendare*) assigned to the court may also be present. There are special provisions authorizing presiding judge to admit foreign judges and lawyers in research or educational programs to watch and listen to the deliberations on giving their promise to maintain confidentiality, GVG §193(2) and (3).

100. GVG §194(2). Written deliberations are permitted. See German Federal Supreme Administrative Court, 45 *NJW* 257 (1992). See also Breetzke, "Abstimmung, Spruch, Gründe", 40 *DRiZ* 5 (1962).

they have been factually substantiated.[101] When votes are taken, the reporting judge votes first, followed by the other judges in inverse order of seniority, with the presiding judge voting last.[102] Votes are oral, and each judge usually gives her reasons as she votes. All issues are decided by majority vote.[103] All judges are required to vote on all issues. A judge is not permitted to abstain from voting on an issue because she was in the minority on another issue.[104]

All judges who have participated in a decision, regardless of their votes, must sign the decision reached by majority vote.[105] There are no dissenting opinions in the ordinary German civil courts.[106]

3. Form of Judgment

In the interest of consistency, comparability and transparency of civil judgments among German courts the form of judgments is statutorily prescribed[107] and scrupulously followed. Requiring all courts to adhere to a single form of judgment is also thought to facilitate the appeals process.[108]

German judgments are captioned, "In the name of the people..."[109] signifying the source of judicial power being exercised. The caption (*Rubrum*) also contains the names of the parties and their attorneys, a designation of the court issuing the judgment, the names of the judges who took part in the decision, and an indication of the date on which oral argument was closed.[110]

---

101. See Rosenberg/Schwab/Gottwald, §22(VI)(1), p. 116.

102. GVG §197. See also Wacke, "Der Jüngste stimmt zuerst - Der Älteste teilt, der Jüngere wählt", 13 *JA* 176 (1981).

103. GVG §196. When there is no majority for a specific sum of damages, the votes are accumulated for the highest sum covered by a majority, GVG §196(2).

104. GVG §195. By the same token, a judge is not bound to vote on an issue consistent with her vote on prior issues. See Rosenberg/Schwab/Gottwald, §22(VI)(1), p. 116.

105. ZPO §315(1). However, the validity of a decision does not depend on the judges' signatures. See Federal Supreme Court, 13 *NJW-RR* 1065 (1998); Thomas/Putzo, §315, mn. 2.

106. Dissenting opinions are permitted in the Federal Constitutional Court (*Bundesverfassungsgericht*), BVerfGG §30(2). See Ch. 10(H) below for a description of constitutional appeals to the Federal Constitutional Court.

107. See ZPO §§311 ff.

108. See Zöller/Vollkommer, §313, mn. 2; Lüke, §28(II), mn. 336.

109. ("*im Namen des Volkes*"), ZPO §311(1). See Zöller/Vollkommer, §311, mn. 1.

110. ZPO §313(1)(1)–(3). The date on which oral argument was closed is of some importance because the judgment relates to the state of the record on that date. If, for example, a prerequisite of suit existing at the time of filing of the complaint had ceased to

Immediately following the caption is the mandate of the judgment (*Urteilstenor* or *Urteilsformel*) which sets forth the actual relief granted.[111] The mandate also addresses the award of costs and attorneys' fees and states whether the judgment shall be subject to immediate execution. This formulation enables the reader to learn the "bottom line" of a decision in the first few sentences of the judgment. It is the mandate of the judgment which counts in formulating the execution.[112]

The mandate is followed by the court's factual and legal substantiation (*Begründung*) for the judgment.[113] Usually the court's factual framework (*Tatbestand*) comes first, followed by an exposition of the court's actual reasoning and application of the law (*eigentliche Entscheidungsgründe*).[114]

The factual framework includes a brief recapitulation of the parties' contentions (*Ansprüche*) and the relevant supporting and opposing materials (*dazu vorgebrachten Angriffs- und Verteidigungsmittel*).[115] Usually the undisputed facts (*unstreitiger Sachverhalt*) come first, followed by the plaintiff's version of the disputed facts and the plaintiff's claims for relief (*Anträge*), and then followed in turn by the defendant's version of the disputed facts and formal pleading on the issues, usually a request for dismissal of the claim. The judgment then briefly summarizes the results of any reception of evidence (*Beweisaufnahme*).

The final part of the judgment is a brief exposition of the reasoning process by which the court reached its findings of disputed fact and application of the law. This part of the judgment includes a description of the court's evaluation of the evidence (*Beweiswürdigung*) and analysis of the law (*Rechtsausführungen*). The court is expected to articulate the factors which caused the judges,

---

exist by the time of completion of the oral argument, the court would be obliged to dismiss the complaint based on the state of affairs at that time. See Rosenberg/Schwab/Gottwald, §133(III)(2), p. 791.

111. ZPO §313(1)(4). See Thomas/Putzo/Reichold, §313, mn. 8 ff.; Zöller/Vollkommer, §313, mn. 8.

112. See Lüke, §28(II), mn. 337; Musielak, §313, mn. 6.

113. ZPO §313(1)(5)–(6). See Thomas/Putzo/Reichold, §313, mn. 12 ff., 27 ff.; Zöller/Vollkommer, §313, mn. 11 ff., 19 ff.

114. In cases where an appeal will "undoubtedly" (*unzweifelhaft*) not be lodged, the court can omit the findings of fact. The court can also omit the exposition of its reasoning in support of its decision if the parties agree to dispense with the same within 2 days of the conclusion of oral argument. ZPO §313a(1). Findings and conclusions cannot be dispensed with in certain cases such as divorce, cases involving future performance of obligations, and when it is expected that enforcement of the judgment will be sought abroad. ZPO 313a(4).

115. ZPO §313(2). The judgment may refer to pleadings and briefs, minutes of hearings and other documents for the details.

for example, to credit one witness rather than another, or to draw a particular inference or conclusion from facts proven.[116]

The court's legal reasoning usually includes a statement of the applicable law, and then a matching of the elements required by the applicable legal doctrine to the facts advanced by the parties[117] and either not disputed by the parties or found by the court to be proven by the evidence.[118]

The written judgment is signed by all members of the court rendering it.[119]

4. Rendition of Judgment

In accord with the principle of orality, almost all contested judgments are rendered orally, sometimes at the conclusion of the plenary proceedings or, more frequently, at a special court hearing called for that purpose (*Verkündungstermin*).[120] Indeed, a judgment is not valid until rendered.[121] Ordinarily judgment is to be rendered within three weeks of the completion of oral argument.[122] All judgments must be rendered at a public session of court.[123]

---

116. See ZPO §313(3); Rosenberg/Schwab/Gottwald, §60(II)(2)(e), p. 326.

117. Of course if a party has failed even to advance a factual element necessary to a cause of action, the party's claim will be dismissed regardless of the state of the proof. See Ch. 6(B)(2) and (3) above on the parties' responsibility to advance facts in support of their legal claims pursuant to the principle of party control of litigation (*Beibringungsgrundsatz*).

118. See Rosenberg/Schwab/Gottwald, §133(II), pp. 324 ff., for a description of the process by which German judges are expected to describe their reasoning in the finding of the law and application of the law to the facts of the case.

119. ZPO §315(1). See Thomas/Putzo, §315, mn. 1 ff. A signature can be made up at any time. See Federal Supreme Court, 52 *WM* 932, 933 (1998).

120. Exceptions are some default judgments (*Versäumnisurteile*) when a party has failed to indicate its intention to defend (see Ch. 9(A)(1) above) and judgments by acknowledgment (*Anerkenntnisurteile*) (see Ch. 9(A)(5) above). See ZPO §310(3). Ordinary default judgments and judgments without oral proceedings must be rendered orally. Rosenberg/Schwab/Gottwald, §60(I)(2), p. 323. The parties may not waive oral rendition of judgment. Supreme Court of the German Empire, 135 RGZ 118,119 (1932).

121. It is said that a written judgment is merely a proposed judgment, subject to change or reconsideration at any time until orally rendered by the court. See Federal Supreme Court, 14 BGHZ 39, 44 (1954); Zöller/Vollkommer, §310, mn. 1; Rosenberg/Schwab/Gottwald, §§60(I)(3), 62(III)(1)(b), pp. 324, 341.

122. ZPO §310(1). Rendition of judgment may be delayed beyond the three-week period only "when important causes, in particular the scope or difficulty of the case, so require" ("...*wenn wichtige Gründe, insbesondere der Umfang oder die Schwierigkeit der Sache, dies erfordern.*"). Some courts make generous use of this exception.

123. GVG §173(1). This is a reflection of the principle of publicity (*Öffentlichkeitsprinzip*). See Ch. 6(E)(2) above.

In some cases the judges retire and deliberate immediately after the close of oral argument and then return to the courtroom and render judgment at the same hearing. In such cases the rendition of judgment includes a reading aloud of the caption and the mandate of the judgment.[124] The mandate is usually written out before the judgment is rendered.[125] The judges may also either read aloud, or orally summarize portions of the factual findings or reasoning for their decision, but are not required to do so.[126] In any event the mandate of the judgment must be recorded in the minutes (*Protokolle*) of the hearing.[127] The actual presence of the parties at a hearing for rendition of judgment is not necessary so long as the hearing has been properly called.[128]

In most cases rendition of judgment takes place at a separate hearing. It is not necessary for all of the judges who decided the case to be present at such a hearing. The presiding judge may render the judgment alone.[129] It is also expected that the judgment will be completely composed and written out.[130] If the parties are not present at the hearing for the rendition of judgment, the mandate need not be read aloud in its entirety, but may be orally incorporated by reference.[131]

---

124. ZPO §311(2).

125. ZPO §311(2). See Zöller/Vollkommer, §311, mn. 2; Thomas/Putzo/Reichold, §311, mn. 2; German Federal Supreme Court, 38 *NJW* 1782 (1985); 52 *NJW* 794 (1999) (notes in shorthand are sufficient); Rosenberg/Schwab/Gottwald, §60(I)(2), p. 323. Exceptions are default judgments, judgments by acknowledgment or relinquishment and judgments following withdrawal of a claim, when the court has not had opportunity to write out the operative portions of the judgment in advance. In these cases judgment may be rendered by recital of the operative portions of the judgment without having it written in advance.

126. ZPO §311(3); Rosenberg/Schwab/Gottwald, §60(I)(2), p. 323; Zöller/Vollkommer, §311, mn. 5.

127. The judgment need not be read into the minutes, but, if already in written form, may be incorporated by reference. ZPO §160(3)(6)–(7), §160(5). A judgment not recorded in the minutes of the hearing is not invalid, but cannot be proven to have been rendered from the official record. See Rosenberg/Schwab/Gottwald, §60(I)(2), p. 323.

128. ZPO §312. Federal Supreme Court, 14 BGHZ (GS) 39 (1954).

129. ZPO §311(4).

130. ZPO §310(2). The validity of the rendition does not depend on the compliance with this provision, see Zöller/Vollkommer, §310, mn. 5; Federal Supreme Court, 41 *NJW* 2046 (1988). But written composition is mandatory during the next five months after rendition, see Federal Constitutional Court, 54 *NJW* 2161 (2001); Common Senate of the Federal Supreme Courts, 46 *NJW* 2603 (1993). Otherwise the judgment is subject to review appeal (ZPO §547(6)).

131. ZPO §311(2)(2). It is necessary, however, for the minutes (*Protokoll*) of the hearing to make reference to the rendition of judgment and the written judgment referred to in court.

C. Contested Judgments Without Oral Argument

Although the principle of orality has historically required that a court judgment, even a default judgment, be entered only after physical appearance and oral argument by the parties before the court, recent procedural reforms have made it possible in appropriate cases for the court to reach a decision and issue judgment based solely on the parties' written submissions.

Traditionally the only exception to the principle of orality was in cases of default. As indicated above, in default situations, the court may in its discretion reach a decision and enter judgment "based on the state of the record" (*nach der Lage der Akten*).[132] Where the court has ordered written preliminary proceedings and the defendant fails even to submit a statement of intention to defend, the court can also enter default judgment without oral hearing.[133]

The 1976 procedural reform attempted to reinforce procedures to reach a "decision without oral argument" (*Entscheidung ohne mündliche Verhandlungen*) where such a process would simplify and expedite the proceedings.[134] The parties' prior option to agree on a decision based on written submissions[135] was expanded to permit the court to specify a written procedure on its own motion in certain circumstances.[136] This expansion was reversed by the 2001 reform, so that now the court may on its own motion dispense with oral argument only in cost decisions and in small claims proceedings in local courts.[137]

When the parties so agree, any civil proceeding can proceed and be decided on the basis of written submissions without oral argument.[138] The willingness of each party can be expressed to the court either orally or in writ-

132. ZPO §331a. Ch. 9(A)(1) above.

133. ZPO §331(3). See Zöller/Herget, §331, mn. 12

134. For a brief discussion of the background of the 1976 reforms in this context, see Putzo, „Die Vereinfachungsnovelle", 30 *NJW* 1, 3 ff. (1977).

135. ZPO §128(2).

136. ZPO §§128(3) (pre-2001 version).

137. ZPO §§128(3) and 495a as amended by the *Gesetz zur Reform des Zivilprozesses* of July 20, 2001. See Zöller/Greger, §128, mn. 3; Musielak/Stadler, §128, mn. 22. ZPO §495a(2) provides that oral argument take place on motion of a party. See also Musielak/Huber, §495a, mn. 7; Thomas/Putzo/Reichold, §495a, mn. 2.

138. This includes special civil cases such as divorce cases, as well as appeals. See Rosenberg/Schwab/Gottwald, §109(I), p. 625; Musielak/Stadler, § 128, mn. 10.

ing.[139] Such an agreement relates only to the next upcoming decision in the suit. For instance, a party's agreement to a decision without oral argument in the first instance does not bind the party to such a process on appeal.[140] A party's agreement to proceed without oral argument can be revoked only with the permission of the court based on materially changed circumstances.[141] The court may, in its sound discretion, decline to accept the parties' agreement to proceed in writing, and require that the usual oral procedure be followed.[142]

The purpose of the written procedure by agreement is to permit a rapid resolution of the case. For this reason, a decision without oral argument is not allowable more than three months after the parties agreement thereto.[143]

D. Amendment of Judgments

It is a basic principle of German law that once a German court has rendered judgment, that court is bound by the judgment as rendered.[144] The judgment may become the basis for further proceedings, but the court may not entertain additional party submissions on the claims for relief (*Anträge*) which have already been decided.[145]

A German court may revoke or amend its own judgment only under very limited circumstances. For instance, a default judgment (*Versäumnisurteil*) may be removed on objection (*Einspruch*) of the defaulting party.[146] A provisional judgment (*Vorbehaltsurteil*) in set-off cases or documentary proceedings may be revoked or modified by the final judgment on the overall merits of the case.[147]

---

139. See Rosenberg/Schwab/Gottwald, §109(I)(1)(b), p. 626. Submission by telephone does not suffice. See German Federal Supreme Administrative Court, 34 *NJW* 1852 (1981). If one party agrees after the other one has revoked her submission, a valid agreement is not achieved. See Federal Supreme Court, 54 *NJW* 2479 (2001). See also Thomas/Putzo, §128, mn. 24.

140. See Rosenberg/Schwab/Gottwald, §109(I)(1)(d), p. 626; Lüke, §33(1), mn. 378.

141. ZPO §128(2). But a party may revoke her agreement as long as the other party did not agree. See Federal Supreme Court, 54 *NJW* 2479 (2001).

142. Lüke, §33(1), mn. 378; Thomas/Putzo/Reichold, §128, mn. 30; Zöller/Greger, §128, mn. 7.

143. ZPO §128(2)(3).

144. ZPO §318. This principle applies both to judgments orally rendered and those rendered by service on the parties.

145. See, e.g., Rosenberg/Schwab/Gottwald, §61(I)(1), p. 331. See Ch. 9(F) below on binding effect of judgments and res adjudicata.

146. See Ch. 9(A)(1) above.

147. See Ch. 7(J)(3) and Ch. 11(B).

The court also has a limited power to issue a judgment correcting or completing a judgment which it has already rendered. The same court panel (*Kammer*)[148] which issued a judgment can correct "typographical errors, errors in arithmetic, and similar apparent mistakes" at any time.[149] When a court is asked to correct language in a judgment, the issue can be whether the claimed error is simply an error of expression (*Ausdrucksfehler*), which is correctible, or an error of judgment, which is not.[150] Even relatively gross mistakes, such as a judgment which purports to adjudge the defendant's complaint dismissed can be corrected in this manner.[151] Such mistakes can be corrected at any time, even during appeal or after the judgment becomes final without appeal.[152]

The court panel which issued a judgment can also correct mistakes, omissions and ambiguities in the factual framework (*Tatbestand*) or legal reasoning (*Entscheidungsgründe*) portions of the judgment (other than mistakes of the kind correctable under ZPO §319) upon written application filed within two weeks of service of the judgment.[153] If the factual framework omits reference to evidence relevant to the issues decided, or if it is based on a misapprehension of the content of a document, a party can move for correction of the asserted mistake.[154] Such an application initiates a special proceeding before the judges who participated in the decision.[155] Oral hearing is scheduled on the motion and the judges are required to determine the issue based on the record of the case as supplemented by their memories, but without taking of additional evidence. Their decision is incorporated into an order (*Beschluss*) which is appended to the judgment.[156] This mechanism for correcting errors

148. See Ch. 3(D)(2)(b) and (c) above on court structure.

149. ZPO §319 (*"Schreibfehler, Rechnungsfehler und ähnliche offenbare Unrichtigkeiten"*).

150. The material content (*sachlicher Gehalt*) of a judgment can be neither corrected nor enlarged. See Rosenberg/Schwab/Gottwald, §61(I)(3), p. 332; Zöller/Vollkommer, §319, mn. 4; Thomas/Putzo/Reichold, §319, mn. 2 ff.

151. See Rosenberg/Schwab/Gottwald, §61(I)(3)(a)(2), p. 333.

152. ZPO §319(1); Rosenberg/Schwab/Gottwald, §61(I)(3)(a)(2), p. 333. This kind of error in a judgment can be corrected without the need of oral proceedings. However the fact and nature of the correction must be noted on the judgment, ZPO §319(2). The court's refusal to grant an application for correction is not appealable as such. An order (*Beschluss*) correcting a judgment is subject to immediate miscellaneous appeal (*sofortige Beschwerde*). ZPO §319(3).

153. ZPO §320(1). The application must at the very latest be made within 3 months of the date of rendition (*Verkündung*) of the judgment. ZPO §320(2)(3).

154. See, e.g., Rosenberg/Schwab/Gottwald, §61(I)(3)(b), p. 334.

155. ZPO §320(3), (4); Thomas/Putzo/Reichold, §320, mn. 4; Zöller/Vollkommer, §320, mn. 11 ff.

156. See ZPO §320(4)(5); Rosenberg/Schwab/Gottwald, §61(I)(3)(b), p. 334. The cor-

in factual framework is important in second instance appeals, since there is no opportunity for re-examination of facts in review appeal (*Revision*) to the Federal Supreme Court.[157] Correction of these portions of a judgment does not affect the mandate (*Tenor*), which can be substantively changed only on second instance appeal (*Berufung*) or on review appeal (*Revision*) to the Federal Supreme Court.[158]

If a judgment has apparently unintentionally omitted to resolve an integral issue in the case, a party can apply to the court for "supplementation of the judgment" (*Ergänzung des Urteils*).[159] So, for instance, if the judgment omits the allocation of litigation costs, a party can apply for supplementation of the judgment to include the judgment as to costs. If one of several claims for relief is not addressed in the judgment, and the omission appears to be one of oversight, a similar application to supplement the judgment to decide the claim would be in order.[160] A written application for supplementation must be filed within two weeks of service of the judgment.[161] Proceedings on the application for supplementation of judgment are similar to those for correction of the substantive parts of the judgment. On motion of a party there is an oral hearing limited to the issues not decided in the prior judgment, after which the court may issue a supplementary judgment (*Ergänzungsurteil*).[162]

---

rective order is not subject to further application for correction, nor may it be the subject of a separate appeal, ZPO §320(4)(4). Refusal to correct the substance of a judgment is also not subject to separate appeal at the time. See Thomas/Putzo/Reichold, §320, mn. 6.

157. See, e.g., Jauernig, §58(III)(2); Musielak, §320, mn. 1.

158. See Ch. 10(D) and (E) below on second instance and review appeals.

159. ZPO §321. However an intentional failure to decide a particular issue or claim in a case can be attacked only on second instance or review appeal. See Rosenberg/Schwab/Gottwald, §61(1)(4), p. 335; Zöller/Vollkommer, §321, mn. 2.

160. See Rosenberg/Schwab/Gottwald, §61(I)(4), pp. 335 for a discussion of the grounds and procedures for supplementation of judgments.

161. ZPO §321(2), see Thomas/Putzo, §321, mn. 4.

162. ZPO §321(3), (4). See Zöller/Vollkommer, §321, mn. 10. The supplementary judgment is, in principle, appealable in its own right. See Federal Supreme Court, 53 *NJW* 3008 (2000). If a supplementary judgment is entered within the time limit for filing an appeal from the judgment supplemented, that time limit begins anew with the service of the supplementary judgment. Appeals from both the supplementary and supplemented judgment will be consolidated. ZPO §518. See Ch. 10(D) and (E) below for discussion of procedures on second instance and review appeals respectively.

E. Judgments for Litigation Costs

As a rule the final judgment in any German litigated matter must also apportion the parties' respective liabilities for "litigation costs" (*Prozesskosten*) incurred in the litigation. These are generally composed of court costs (*Gerichtkosten*) and attorneys' fees and expenses (*Anwaltskosten*).[163]

It can be said that Germany observes the "loser pays" rule on court costs and attorneys' fees more faithfully than any other modern jurisdiction.[164] The basic principle is that a party whose claim is sustained in court should not have to pay the cost for achieving vindication. A party who fails to sustain his position in court must not only pay his own costs of litigation, but must defray the litigation costs of his victorious opponent as well.[165]

The law governing the allocation of litigation costs as part of the process of judgment and the assessment of costs following judgment is highly developed and intricate. As a rule both court costs and attorneys fees are computed according to the amount in controversy and the stage the proceeding has reached. This permits German lawyers to estimate their ongoing risk of having to pay the opponent's costs and attorneys fees with some exactitude. They can and do take into account potential liability for court costs and attorneys fees of the ongoing proceeding in deciding whether to settle or withdraw claims or prosecute them further at every stage of a lawsuit.

Legal aid recipients are not required to pay court costs in order to initiate or defend litigation in which they are involved. Nor will the court enter any judgment against a legal aid recipient ordering him to pay court costs of the opponent, regardless of the outcome of the case. If a successful opponent of a legal aid recipient has paid court costs in advance, the court will return the costs advanced and there will be no claim for reimbursement against the legal aid recipient.[166]

---

163. See Ch. 4(H) above and for a brief overview see, e.g., Jauernig, §93; Thomas/Putzo, Vor §90, mn. 1 ff.

164. Although many jurisdictions in Europe, Asia and Latin American provide some fee-shifting in civil litigation, in most jurisdictions only a portion of the attorneys fees are shifted from the winner to the loser. In Germany the loser is expected to pay the winner's entire statutory attorneys fee, which is the winner's entire fee in many cases. See Ch. 4(H) above.

165. ZPO §91; Rosenberg/Schwab/Gottwald, §87(I), p. 464; Thomas/Putzo, §91, mn. 1 ff.

166. See Musielak/Fischer, §123, mn. 2 ff., Federal Constitutional Court, 52 *NJW* 3186 (1999) and Ch. 9(E)(1)(c) below.

Attorneys fees are treated somewhat differently in legal aid cases. Legal aid only defrays the recipient's own attorney's fees and expenses. It does not protect the legal aid recipient against a judgment for attorney's fees of a successful opponent.[167] Attorneys fees are assessed in favor of or against legal aid recipients at the full statutory rates according to the standard criteria.[168] However, collectibility of attorneys fees from a legal aid recipient may be another matter.[169]

1. Court Costs

The cost of access to the German courts is not insignificant. Court costs paid by civil parties defray a considerable portion of public expenditure for civil justice.[170] For example, a plaintiff suing to enforce an obligation which he values at 5,000 Euro is required to be prepared to pay 363 Euro, or 7.2% of the amount in controversy as a basic court fee, exclusive of costs of service, any witness or expert witness fees, and any costs for execution.[171] For smaller amounts in controversy, the courts costs represent a greater proportional burden, for larger amounts in controversy a lesser one.

In Germany it can fairly be said that the state is obliged to provide high quality civil justice but the parties, at least those able to do so, are expected to contribute toward the cost of the justice they receive. Moreover the relatively healthy court costs implement a policy to discourage unnecessary litigation.[172]

Court costs include both statutorily established court fees and certain court-administered expenses, such as expert witness fees, other witness fees and expenses, costs to effect service, and the like. Court costs and how they are determined and taxed are regulated by the Court Costs Law (*Gerichtskostengesetz* or *GKG*) which supplements provisions of the ZPO in the spe-

---

167. See ZPO §123; Musielak/Fischer, §123, mn. 1. In contrast, legal costs insurance (*Rechtsschutzversicherung*) typically pays the fees and expenses of the insured's own lawyer as well as indemnifies against awards of attorneys fees for the opponent's representation. See Ch. 4(J) above for a brief description of German legal costs insurance.

168. See Ch. 4(I)(2)(c) above for a more complete discussion of taxation of legal aid costs.

169. The criteria for legal aid are nearly the same as for exemption from execution. Compare ZPO §115 with ZPO §§850, 850a–850k. See Ch. 11(F)(1)(a) and (d) below.

170. See Ch. 3(J)(3) above on financial support of the German civil justice system; Franzen/Apel, "Prozessaufwand bei Gericht und Anwalt - betriebswirtschaftlich und anschaulich - mit Folgerungen", 41 *NJW* 1059 (1988).

171. *Gerichtskostengesetz* (GKG) §11, Attachment 1, No. 1210.

172. See Lüke, §49, mn. 493; Stürner, *Die Aufklärungspflicht der Parteien des Zivilprozesses* (1976), §17(1), pp. 261 ff.

cific area of court costs. The provisions for levying court costs and ultimately assessing them against the respective parties are intricate. The magnitude of these costs, however, means that potential responsibility for various levels of court costs is often a material element in making strategic and tactical choices in litigation.

a. *Determination of Court Costs*

Court costs (as well as statutory attorneys fees) are based on the amount placed in controversy (*Streitwert*) by the claims for relief of the parties' respective pleadings, and the stage of the proceeding reached at the time they are assessed. Basic court costs are not directly related to the amount of time or effort expended by the court in resolving the matter.[173]

The amount in controversy is set forth in the plaintiff's complaint. If the defendant believes that the amount in controversy alleged by the plaintiff is inaccurate, either too large or too small, the defendant can contravene the plaintiff's assertion and make his own representation of the amount in controversy. Disputes over the amount in controversy are frequently resolved informally at preliminary hearings, but are sometimes left to be determined as a part of the final judgment.[174]

The amount in controversy used for determination of statutory costs is also used for determination of statutory attorneys fees. The effect of the amount in controversy on the compensation of the parties' lawyers is large enough to make determination of the right amount in controversy of considerable interest to parties and lawyers alike.[175] The implications of the amount in controversy on court costs are generally subsidiary to this issue's impact on attorneys' fees.[176]

---

173. There is some dispute within the EU about whether this kind of scheme leads to an unfair burden on litigants with large amounts in controversy, who may end up paying court costs which exceed the fair value of the work done by the courts in resolving their cases. For instance, a case with an amount in controversy of 20 Million Euro will generate court costs of some 184,000 Euro, regardless of the work done. See GKG §11, Attachment 1, No. 1210. A cost-of-living increase in court costs is proposed for 2004.

174. GKG §25(2), (3). In cases where the court must fix the amount in controversy in order to decide which court has subject matter jurisdiction or whether an appeal is allowable, the court's determination for that purpose also generally governs the assessment of costs. GKG §24.

175. See Ch. 4(H) above on attorneys' compensation and Ch. 9(E)(2) below on taxing attorneys fees in final judgments.

176. For a discussion of the concept of "amount in controversy" and how it is determined see Ch. 5(B)(1) above.

Court costs also depend on the stage the proceeding has reached before termination. Attachment 1 to the Court Costs Law sets forth the number of "fee units" (*Gebühren*) associated with various stages and activities of litigation in the various courts. Costs for a given case are determined by multiplying the level of court costs for the amount in controversy according to the Court Costs Law § 11 by the number of fee units for the activities that have taken place according to Attachment 1.

For instance, the court costs for processing a first instance case to judgment in either a local court or a state district court are based on 3 fee units.[177] If the amount in controversy were 300 Euro, the court costs would be 75 Euro.[178] If, on the other hand, the amount in controversy were 10,000 Euro, the court costs would amount to 588 Euro.[179]

There are special and additional court costs imposed for such activities as execution, applications for prejudgment attachment or other preliminary measures, and for all levels of appeal. At the appellate level there is a basic fee for the appeal itself and additional fees for judgment (with or without reasons) on the appeal.[180] On the other hand, if a case is resolved by acknowledgment or withdrawal of claim the usual court costs are reduced. The same is true for cases which are settled prior to judgment.[181]

Court costs in family law cases generally carry a smaller number of fee units. For instance, the basic suit cost of a first instance marital proceeding (*Ehesache*) is 1 fee unit rather than 3 as charged for ordinary civil litigation. This fee is waived if the complaint is withdrawn before plenary oral argument.[182]

b. Initial Payment of Court Costs

The party who seeks the aid of the court bears the initial responsibility for the court costs for the matter at issue.[183] This responsibility can then be shifted by the court in its judgment. However the original "cost debtor" (*Kostenschuldner*) remains secondarily liable for court costs if the person adjudged liable for the costs cannot pay them.[184] Multiple parties are generally jointly and

177. GKG, Attachment 1, No. 1210.

178. Three fees each of 25 Euro, GKG §11, Attachment 1, No. 1210 and Attachment 2.

179. Three fees each of 196 Euro. GKG §11, Attachment 1, No. 1210 and Attachment 2.

180. See GKG, Attachment 1, Nos. 1220–1249.

181. If a settlement is reached before a first-instance judgment, the basic suit cost of three fee units is reduced by one fee unit, GKG, Attachment 1, No. 1211(c).

182. GKG, Attachment 1, No. 1510.

183. GKG §§49, 65.

184. GKG §58(2). See Hartmann, *Kostengesetze*, 32nd ed. (2003), §58 GKG, mn. 11 ff.

severally responsible for the entire costs assessed against their side unless the court has apportioned liability for costs among them.[185]

In most civil cases the plaintiff must pay the basic court costs for processing of a civil case in the court of first instance upon filing of the complaint.[186] If the plaintiff's complaint is amended to enlarge the claim, the additional costs associated with the larger amount in controversy must be paid before the oral hearing. There is no requirement for advance payment of court costs in most family cases or for counterclaims.[187] Court costs on appeals are generally not required to be paid in advance.[188] If some judicial activity will involve actual cash outlay, such as appointment of an expert witness, the parties are generally ordered to advance such costs, with the ultimate liability to be determined in the judgment.[189]

Advance payment of court costs is waived if the plaintiff is a recipient of legal aid and can also be delayed or dispensed with if the court finds that requiring immediate advance payment will constitute an unreasonable hardship or that delay in commencing the case (in order to raise the fees) will cause irreparable injury.[190]

To the extent that court costs are not required to be paid in advance, they must be paid by the party responsible when due following final judgment or other termination of the case. If a party has been required to pay costs in advance, and the other party is adjudged liable for costs, the party liable is required to reimburse the party who paid in the same manner as with attorneys fees.[191]

---

185. GKG §59. However, if a party is affected by only a part of the matter in controversy (*Streitgegenstand*), that party's responsibility for initial payment of costs is measured by the level of costs associated with the amount in controversy with which she is associated.

186. GKG §65. If the case starts out as a warning proceeding (*Mahnverfahren*) the plaintiff pays a greatly reduced fee on filing of the application for a warning notice, but must pay costs associated with a regular civil case if the defendant objects and the plaintiff wishes to go forward. See Ch. 11(C) below for a discussion of civil warning proceedings. GKG §65 does not apply in labor court proceedings. ArbGG §12(4).

187. GKG §65(1),(2).

188. See Hartmann, §65 GKG, mn. 4.

189. GKG §68. Hartmann, §68 GKG, mn. 6 ff. See Ch. 8(C)(7)(b) above for court appointed experts.

190. GKG §65(7)(1). In the latter two instances the court must find that the complaint does not appear to be without chance of success or frivolous (*aussichtslos oder mutwillig*), GKG §65(7)(2).

191. See ZPO §91(1); Rosenberg/Schwab/Gottwald, §87(III), pp. 465 ff.; Thomas/Putzo, Vor §91, mn. 7 ff.

c. *Waiver of Court Costs*

Parties who are indigent can receive partial or complete waivers of liability for court costs upon application to the court for legal aid (*Prozesskostenhilfe*).[192] Anticipated court costs are included in litigation costs when computing an applicant's eligibility for legal aid. If the applicant is adjudged to be entitled to full legal aid, all court costs otherwise payable are advanced by the state.[193] If the legal aid recipient prevails, the state is entitled to collect the costs for the case, including any that would have been paid in advance by the indigent party, from the losing opponent. The losing indigent party is to reimburse the opponent's attorney fees, but not court costs advanced by the opponent. In such a case the court will return the opponent's court costs.[194]

2. Statutory Attorneys' Fees

As indicated above, in most cases German lawyers are paid for their services in litigated matters according to a statutory schedule of fees.[195] Attorneys fees, as well as court costs are considered "litigation costs" (*Prozesskosten*) which are subject to allocation among the parties by the court in a final judgment.

Attorneys fees, like court costs, depend on the amount in controversy and the stage to which the litigation has reached. The Federal Attorneys Fees Law (*Bundesgebührenordnung für Rechtsanwälte* or *BRAGO*) sets forth the number of fee units which apply to various litigation stages and activities as well as the amount to be associated with each fee unit at every amount in controversy.[196]

---

192. See Ch. 4(I)(2) above for a discussion of the process for obtaining legal aid.

193. If partial legal aid is granted, the applicant may be responsible to reimburse the state for a part of the costs and attorneys fees disbursed. See Ch. 4(I)(2)(a) above.

194. For further discussion see Musielak/Fischer, §123, mn. 2 ff. and Federal Constitutional Court, 52 *NJW* 3186 (1999). See Ch. 9(E) before (1) above.

195. See Ch. 4(H) above.

196. See BRAGO §§31–71 for provisions setting numbers of fee units for various litigation activities and BRAGO §11 and Attachment for the table of fee unit values based on the amount in controversy. The most recent draft of a proposed New Law Regulating the Compensation of Lawyers is designed to simplify taxation of costs, to improve the income of lawyers and to encourage out of court settlements. Although the fundamental principles of compensation will not change, the draft of August 2003 provides for two significant alterations. The "evidence fee" (*Beweisgebühr*) will be discontinued and replaced by an increased "suit fee" (*Prozessgebühr*) and "oral argument fee" (*Verhandlungsgebühr*). Statutorily specified attorneys' fees for out-of-court activities will also be dropped beginning in 2006. See *Frankfurter Allgemeine Zeitung*, September 3, 2003.

In general, a lawyer is entitled to charge a "suit fee" (*Prozessgebühr*) for preparation and institution of a civil action, an additional "oral argument fee" (*Verhandlungsgebühr*) if the case goes to oral argument, and a third "evidence fee" (*Beweisgebühr*) if there is reception of evidence by the court. If there is no oral argument, but there are one or more conferences at which the case is presented or settlement is discussed the lawyer may charge a "discussion fee" (*Erörterungsgebühr*).[197] If the lawyer settles a case at any stage, the lawyer is entitled to an additional "settlement fee" (*Vergleichsgebühr*).[198]

The Attorneys Fee Law identifies a number of activities incident to litigation as "special undertakings" (*besondere Angelegenheiten*) for which the lawyer can charge an additional fee or fraction of a fee. For instance, an application for preliminary attachment is considered a special undertaking for which an additional fee is to be charged.[199] Warning proceedings (*Mahnverfahren*) are to be handled at fractions of the fee units applicable to conventional litigation.[200]

Ordinary office overhead is considered covered by the statutory fee structure. However, actual out of pocket disbursements for telephone, postage, travel expenses, photocopies are subject to reimbursement by the client. They are also added to the statutory attorneys fees for purpose of taxation of costs pursuant to final judgment.[201]

Attorneys are permitted, within bounds, to arrange with their clients for payment of fees in excess of those allowable by statute.[202] However, only the statutory fees may be taxed to the opposing party based on the outcome of the litigation.[203]

Attorneys whose clients qualify for legal aid are paid by the state at special "legal aid" rates. If a legal aid client prevails and litigation costs are assessed against the opposing party, the latter is liable for attorneys fees at the full statutory rate, regardless of the legal aid. The claim for reimbursement of litigation costs belongs to the state. If the state actually collects an amount over its

---

197. BRAGO §31. See Hartmann, §31 BRAGO, mn.1 ff. for an overview and mn. 11 ff. for details of the particular fees.

198. BRAGO §23. If the settlement takes place before suit is started, the settlement fee is 1.5 fee units.

199. BRAGO §40. See Hartmann, §40 BRAGO, mn. 2 ff.

200. BRAGO §43. See Hansens, "Anfall und Erstattungsfähigkeit der Rechtsanwaltsvergütung im Mahnverfahren", 97 *Rpfleger* 487 (1989).

201. See BRAGO §§25–29. Travel by the lawyer's own auto is subject to reimbursement at kilometer rates prescribed by statute. See BRAGO §28(2)(1).

202. See Ch. 4(H) above.

203. ZPO §91(2)(1). See also Baumbach/Lauterbach/Albers/Hartmann, *Zivilprozessordnung*, 59th ed. (2001), §91, mn. 41.

outlays for legal aid in the case, the lawyer may be paid from the excess toward the difference between the legal aid fee and the full statutory fee [204]

Although lawyers fees become legally due and owing when the project for which the lawyer was retained is completed, a lawyer is entitled to require payment of a "reasonable advance" (*angemessenen Vorschuss*) against foreseeable fees and disbursements before filing suit or at any time during the engagement.[205] If the case is successful the client may recover some or all of the fees advanced from the opposing party. If the opposing party is unable to pay the fees, it is the client, not the lawyer, who bears the loss.

Ordinarily the court's determination of the amount in controversy at the outset of the case for the purpose of assessing court costs will also apply to the determination of the statutory attorneys' fees for both parties. Each lawyer has the right on his own behalf to contest the court's determination of the amount in controversy and to appeal such determination.[206]

If the amount in controversy (*Streitwert*) originally fixed for purposes of court costs does not correspond to the "value of the subject matter of the representation" (*den Wert des Gegenstands der anwaltlichen Tätigkeit*) for purposes of attorneys fees, or if the court has failed to set the amount in controversy, on application of either party or lawyer the court is required to determine the value of the subject matter of the representation for attorneys fees purposes at the time the compensation is due.[207]

If there is a dispute as to the appropriate amount of statutory attorneys fees to be charged for a particular litigated matter, the client or the lawyer may apply to the court of first instance for a judicial assessment (*gerichtliche Festsetzung*) of the correct attorneys' fee.[208] Such an application may be made when the fee is due, usually at the conclusion of the matter. The court may be asked to fix a fee regardless of whether the fee will be paid by the original client or reimbursed by the opposing party. The procedure is similar to

204. See Ch. 4(I)(2)(b) and (c) above for a more complete description of payment and reimbursement for attorneys fees in legal aid cases.

205. BRAGO §§16, 17. A "reasonable advance" may generally cover the complete fee and can be paid in cash or by providing appropriate security. See Hartmann, §17 BRAGO, mn. 13 ff.

206. BRAGO §9(2).

207. BRAGO §10. There are no court costs or allowable attorneys fees associated with this proceeding. Any affected party can take a miscellaneous appeal (*Beschwerde*) from the decision if the amount involved is more than 50 Euro.

208. BRAGO §19(1). This provision does not apply to arbitral procedures; see State Court of Appeals of Berlin ("*Kammergericht*"), 106 *Rpfleger* 171, 172 (1998).

the procedure for assessment of taxable litigation costs.[209] In most cases the decision will be made by a magistrate (*Rechtspfleger*), subject to review by the court.[210]

3. Adjudicating Liability for Court Costs and Attorneys' Fees

Liability for court costs and attorneys fees is adjudicated or allocated by the court in the final judgment.[211] If the final judgment does not contain an allocation of costs and attorneys fees, either party may apply to have the judgment completed.[212]

If a case is terminated without a final judgment, such as by withdrawal of claims or by voluntary termination of claims, the court on its own motion (voluntary termination) or on motion of either party (withdrawal) renders an order with respect to costs and attorneys fees.[213] The court may decide the issue without oral argument in a simple order.[214]

As noted above, the general rule is that ultimate responsibility for litigation costs is imposed on the loser, who must reimburse the winner if the latter has been required to advance costs or pay attorneys fees.[215] In a case where neither party has achieved 100% judicial vindication of its claims or defenses, the court can order that costs will be reciprocally suspended (*gegeneinander aufgehoben*) or that costs will be allocated among the parties in proportion to their relative success (*verhältnismässig geteilt*).[216] In considering the parties' relative success, the court will generally look at the ultimate result achieved as com-

---

209. BRAGO §19(2). If there is objection to a lawyer's fee by a party required to pay the fee by virtue of cost shifting in the judgment, the formal determination of the correct amount of the fee may be made in the proceedings for taxation of costs.

210. See Ch. 3(H)(2) on the activities of the magistrates.

211. The court is required to rule on liability for costs on its own motion even if neither party has requested it. See ZPO §308(2) and Rosenberg/Schwab/Gottwald, §87(II)(1), p. 464.

212. See Ch. 9(D) above.

213. See Ch. 9(A)(2) and (3) above on voluntary termination of claims and withdrawal of claims.

214. See ZPO §§91a(1), 269(4), 128(3); Rosenberg/Schwab/Gottwald, §87(III)(7), p. 469.

215. ZPO §91(1)(1). See Baumbach/Lauterbach/Albers/Hartmann, Vor §91, mn. 3; Thomas/Putzo, §91, mn. 1 ff.

216. ZPO §92. If costs are suspended each party will be responsible for one half of the court costs and its own attorney's fees and expenses.

pared with a party's original or amended claims (*Anträge*).[217] If a plaintiff seeks 100,000 Euro, and the defendant concedes owing 10,000, a judgment for the plaintiff of 20,000 Euro would generally result in an award of costs mainly in favor of the defendant.

If a party has received some, but not all that she originally sought, the court may nonetheless award full costs against the opponent if the "excess claim" (*Zuvielforderung*) was relatively trivial and did not cause the opponent to incur special costs, or if the determination of the correct amount of the claim was a matter for expert testimony or sound judicial discretion (*richterliches Ermessen*). This rule can be applied in personal injury cases, enabling plaintiffs who have received awards smaller than those originally claimed to receive full reimbursement of costs even if their lawyers somewhat overestimated the values of their claims when drafting their complaints. As a practical matter this provision plays no role if courts permit complaints without any definite enumerated money demand or with a demand expressed merely in order of magnitude.[218]

In family cases there are special rules for allocation of costs. For instance, in a case for divorce or annulment of marriage costs are not allowed to either party unless the judge makes a specific discretionary allowance based on unreasonable hardship to either party or if a non-allowance of costs in a property settlement dispute appears to be unfair (*unbillig*) to a party.[219] In paternity cases, no costs are allowed if paternity is successfully challenged, but the usual rules otherwise apply.[220] In cases for support of minor children costs may be assessed in the court's discretion based on the degree to which the party charged has failed to make prompt and accurate disclosure of his income and financial circumstances.[221]

There are also special rules for evictions of residential premises (*Wohnraum*). If a tenant has asserted the right to continue a tenancy and the landlord has failed to apprise the tenant of a supervening landlord interest suffi-

---

217. For an overview see Zöller/Herget, §92, mn. 2 ff.

218. ZPO §92(2)(1) and (2). See Thomas/Putzo, §92, mn. 7 ff.; Lüke, in: *Münchener Kommentar zur ZPO*, §253, mn. 116 ff.; v. Gerlach, "Die prozessuale Behandlung von Schmerzensgeldansprüchen", 51 *VersR* 525 (2000) and Ch. 7(A)(2) above.

219. ZPO §93a. For instance, if a party to a proceeding for distribution of property incident to divorce had maintained an extreme position and the court decided essentially in accord with the position of the opposing party, the court could also tax the "losing" (*unterliegende*) party with part or all of the costs and attorneys fees of the winner. See Thomas/Putzo, §93a, mn. 6.

220. ZPO §93c (no judicial discretion), Baumbach/Lauterbach/Albers/Hartmann, §93c, mn. 12.

221. ZPO §93d. See also Furtner, *Das Urteil im Zivilprozess*, 5th ed. (1985), p. 38.

cient to support eviction, the landlord may be required to bear part or all of the costs of the eviction. The same may be true if the tenant agreed to vacate promptly on receipt of the landlord's notice of termination of tenancy and then requested a period of time to do so not greater than the time ultimately allowed by the court in the eviction judgment.[222]

A party who has suffered a default judgment (*Versäumnisurteil*), but has set the judgment aside and defended on the merits is liable for the court costs associated with the default judgment even if he ultimately prevails on the merits.[223] Parties whose conduct results in unnecessary judicial activity may also be assessed court costs associated with the activity regardless of the outcome of the case.[224]

A party who unsuccessfully appeals will be responsible for costs on the appeal regardless of which party won below.[225] However, if the appeal is successful, the judgment on appeal can change the allocation of costs below to accord with the ultimate result in the case.

As a general rule if a judgment on appeal reverses or modifies the judgment below, the appellate court will include in its decision an allocation of litigation costs in the current instance and all prior instances of the case. On the other hand, if the appellate judgment affirms the prior court's determination, the appellate judgment will only address the litigation costs on the appeal, and the lower court's decision on costs for that instance will stand. These general rules are subject to exceptions, such as when specific costs are allocated based on a party's action or inaction at some stage of the proceeding.[226]

4. Court Costs and Attorneys' Fees in Settled Cases

As indicated above, if a case is settled during the first instance or terminated by certain other consensual dispositions at any instance there is a reduction of the number of fee units of court costs otherwise payable. By the same token, the lawyers who settle the case are entitled to charge an extra fee

222. ZPO §93b.

223. ZPO §344. See Ch. 9(A)(1) above on default judgments.

224. E.g. ZPO §§93, 95, 96. For §93 see, e.g., Stürner, *Die Aufklärungspflicht der Parteien des Zivilprozesses*, §18, pp. 269 ff. For the party's right to be heard see Zöller/Herget, §95, mn. 6; State Court of Appeals of Hamm, 10 *NJW-RR* 1406 (1995).

225. ZPO §97(1). However, if the appeal was successful by reason of material that could have been brought before the court below, the winning party may be charged with a part or all of the costs of the appeal. ZPO §97(2).

226. See Rosenberg/Schwab/Gottwald, §87(IV), p. 471; Zöller/Herget, §97, mn. 11 ff.

unit for their efforts in concluding the settlement. These modifications of the fee structure for contested cases are intended to foster and encourage settlements and consensual case dispositions.[227]

In the usual case the allocation of responsibility for costs incurred prior to settlement is agreed on as a part of the settlement. Court costs are often substantial components of litigation exposure and few parties are likely to reach settlements without covering costs in the agreement. Parties' agreement as to division and allocation of court costs are treated by the court like other party stipulations and agreements for purposes of documenting and enforcing settlements.

In many cases the parties' agreement on court costs will mirror the kind of allocation that the court would be expected to make based on their relative success in the settlement outcome. Thus, if a plaintiff received by way of settlement 80% of what he originally claimed, it would be common for the parties to agree on a parallel division of court costs, with the plaintiff bearing 20% of the costs and the defendant 80%. Sometimes if the parties are having difficulty reaching agreement on the division of costs as a part of the settlement, a hint or suggestion from the court can facilitate an agreement without requiring the court to enter a formal decision.[228]

The law also provides a default rule for costs in settled cases if the parties do not otherwise agree. ZPO §98 specifies that liability for litigation costs incurred prior to settlement and not otherwise allocated by agreement or judicial action is "reciprocally suspended" (*gegeneinander aufgehoben*). This means that court costs are divided equally between the parties, but that each party is responsible for the fees of her own attorney.[229]

Some uncontested terminations, such as withdrawals or recognition of claims, do not always involve express negotiation and agreement among the parties. In such cases the Civil Procedure Code provides default rules on liability for costs designed to encourage such dispositions in appropriate cases. For example, if a defendant immediately acknowledges the amount claimed by the plaintiff and has not previously given cause for the initiation of suit, the costs of a case terminated by judgment by acknowledgment (*Anerkenntnisurteil*) are to be borne by the plaintiff.[230] If the parties have either orally or in writing declared the claim terminated (*die Hauptsache erledigt*), the court

227. BRAGO §23. See Hartmann, §23 BRAGO, mn. 2. For allocation of costs in cases concluded by settlement see Ch. 9(A)(4) above and Ch. 11(I)(2) below.

228. For an example of this process, see Murray, in: *Essays in Honor of Arthur T. von Mehren*, p. 779.

229. See Zöller/Herget, §92, mn. 1 and Ch. 9(E)(3) above.

230. ZPO §93. See Chs. 9(A)(5) , 9(E)(3) above on judgments by acknowledgment.

can determine the allocation of costs in a simple order based on its sound discretion (*nach billigem Ermessen*) according to the status of the proceedings at the time of termination.[231]

5. Taxing Court Costs and Attorneys' Fees

If the parties or their lawyers are able to agree on the actual amounts of litigation costs as allocated by the court and if the judgment will be paid without the need for execution, then there is no need for any proceeding to fix the actual amount of the costs to be taxed. This happens in a large number of cases. However, if the parties are not able to agree on the actual amounts of taxable costs, or if there will be a need for execution, the court of first instance will on request tax the monetary amount of litigation costs to be paid by the respective parties in accord with the allocation of costs in the final judgment.

The determination of the monetary amount of costs (*Kostenfestsetzung*) that each party will be required to bear is the responsibility of the magistrate (*Rechtspfleger*).[232] A party seeking formal taxation of costs must file in the court of first instance a written application for taxation of costs (*Kostenfestsetzungsantrag*) supported by appropriate bills and accountings as well as a copy of the judgment on which the application is based.[233] A copy of the materials must be served on the opponent, who is given opportunity for comment before the magistrate issues the taxation order.[234] If the costs are to be divided, the magistrate requests the other party to file information on costs incurred by his side along with comments on the initial submission.[235]

If judgment has not been rendered, the person seeking taxation of costs can file the accountings and supporting materials and costs will be taxed automatically in the judgment when rendered and issued. Or if judgment has been orally rendered, but the written judgment has not been issued and served, a

231. ZPO §91a. See Ch. 9(A)(2) above on voluntary terminations of claims.

232. ZPO §104. Such proceedings belong to the category of matters which the Civil Procedure Code (ZPO) gives the judges of the respective courts, but which the Magistrates Law (RPflG) delegates to the courts' magistrates. See RPflG §21(1).

233. See ZPO § 103(2)(2); Rosenberg/Schwab/Gottwald, §88(I)(1), p. 476. The application may be filed by a party *pro se* even in the state district court where ordinarily representation by counsel is required, RPflG §13.

234. ZPO §103(2)(2); Rosenberg/Schwab/Gottwald, §88(III)(1), p. 480; Zöller/Herget, §104, mn. 7.

235. ZPO §106. The magistrate must follow the requirements of law in the taxation of costs and does not exercise judicial discretion. See Zöller/Herget, §106, mn. 1; State District Court of Berlin, 13 *NJW-RR* 215, 216 (1998).

party may file an application for taxation of costs with supporting documentation and request that the taxation of costs be included in the judgment when issued. These simplified measures are intended to streamline the cost-fixing process and save time, but are rarely used in practice.[236]

The standard of proof of the existence and amount of costs and attorneys fees and expenses is that of "reasonable plausibility" (*glaubhaft machen*). For instance, a statement by an attorney that telephone or photocopying costs have been incurred in a specific amount is accepted as sufficient proof of these items without further substantiation.[237] The magistrate's decision is generally based on the parties' written submissions, but oral argument may be scheduled if the magistrate deems it necessary.

The magistrate is bound by the court's order in allocating the court costs and attorneys' fees, but the opposing party may challenge the amount of any court cost or attorneys fee, whether the item was necessary, or whether it was incurred in the proceeding at hand.[238] The order taxing costs must be served on the opposing party unless it is included with the final judgment.[239]

The Magistrate's order taxing court costs and attorneys fees or refusing to do so may be appealed to the next higher court by immediate miscellaneous appeal (*sofortige Beschwerde*).[240] Payment of costs by the party adjudged liable is due when the judgment establishing liability for the costs is final or when the proceeding is terminated by settlement, withdrawal of claim or other consensual disposition.[241] Unpaid litigation costs bear interest at from the time of initiation of the proceedings for taxation of costs.[242]

6. Security for Court Costs and Attorneys' Fees

As a rule no party is required to post security for court costs and attorneys fees as a condition to maintaining or defending a suit. However, a plaintiff who does not maintain a usual residence (*gewöhnlichen Aufenthalt*) in the Eu-

---

236. ZPO §105. See Musielak/Wolst, §105, mn. 1; Belz, in: *Münchener Kommentar zur ZPO*, §105, mn. 1.

237. ZPO §§294, 104(2). See also Marx, "Zur Glaubhaftmachung von Kostenansätzen", 107 *Rpfleger* 157 (1999); Thomas/Putzo, §104, mn. 3; Zöller/Herget, §104, mn. 8.

238. See Rosenberg/Schwab/Gottwald, §88(III)(2), p. 480; Zöller/Herget, §104, mn. 8.

239. ZPO §§104(1)(3), 105(1)(2). However, if the application is denied the denial must be served on the applicant. ZPO §104(1)(4).

240. ZPO §104(3). See Zöller/Herget, §104, mn. 9 ff. See also Ch. 10(F) below on the procedure on miscellaneous appeals.

241. GKG §63.

242. ZPO §104(1)(2). Currently the rate is 5% over the base rate (*Basiszinssatz*).

ropean Union or the European Free Trade Area may, upon request of the opposing party, be required to post security for the foreseeable costs and attorneys fees that may be sustained by the opposing party in the event the complaint is not successful. If international law or a treaty prohibits awards of costs or requiring security for costs or if the defendant has real estate in Germany, no security for costs may be required. Nor may security for costs be required on counterclaims.[243] If the conditions justifying security disappear, the security must be released on request of the party furnishing it.[244]

F. *Res Adjudicata* Effect of Judgments

A German judgment which is not subject to further appeal (*formelle Rechtskraft*) stands as the conclusive adjudication of the claims submitted for adjudication and can be raised as a defense to any later effort by either party to submit the same claims for adjudication in another proceeding. That judgment must also be followed in any later proceeding in which the same claims constitute a material element of the matter in dispute. The German doctrine of *res adjudicata* (*materielle Rechtskraft*) serves to guarantee certainty in litigation and to preclude repeated relitigation of matters already litigated and decided.[245]

---

243. ZPO §110. The former version of this provision permitted German courts to require security for costs for all foreign parties, including residents of the European Union. This provision was challenged by the European Court of Justice, Case C-122/96, *Stephen Austin Saldanka v. Hiross Holding AG*, 1997 ECR I 5325 (1997). If security is requested by the defendant, the court must allow the plaintiff a reasonable time to post it. Upon failure timely to post security the complaint is deemed withdrawn. ZPO §113.

244. ZPO §109. This provision applies to all kinds of security. See Thomas/Putzo, §109, mn. 1a.

245. This doctrine is analogous to the doctrine of *res adjudicata* in Anglo-American jurisprudence, although the scope and effect of the doctrine are somewhat different. For a discussion of the various theories supporting the binding effect of judgments in German procedural law, see Schwab, *Der Streitgegenstand im Zivilprozess* (1954); Habscheid, *Der Streitgegenstand im Zivilprozess und im Streitverfahren der freiwilligen Gerichtsbarkeit* (1957); Jauernig, *Verhandlungsmaxime, Inquisitionsmaxime und Streitgegenstand* (1957); Zeuner, *Die objektiven Grenzen der Rechtskraft im Rahmen rechtlicher Sinnzusammenhänge* (1959); Rimmelspacher, *Materiellrechtlicher Anspruch und Streitgegenstandsprobleme im Zivilprozess* (1970); Gaul, "Rechtskraftlehre seit Savigny", in: Jakobs et al. (eds.), *Festschrift für Flume* (1978), pp. 443 ff.; Koussoulis, *Beiträge zur modernen Rechtskraftlehre* (1986); Stürner, "Rechtskraft in Europa", in: Geimer (ed.), *Wege zur Globalisierung des Rechts. Festschrift für Schütze* (1999), pp. 913 ff.; Nelles, *Anspruch, Titel und Vollstreckung im internationalen Rechtsverkehr* (2000).

1. Kinds of Judgments Entitled to Binding Effect

In general, only judgments (*Urteile*) not subject to further appeal are entitled to *res adjudicata* effect so far as future legal proceedings are concerned. Court orders (*Beschlüsse*) other than formal judgments may also be given *res adjudicata* effect when they are not subject to alteration in further proceedings or on appeal.[246]

Judgments entitled to *res adjudicata* effect include not only contested final judgments (*streitige Endurteile*) but also default judgments (*Versäumnisurteile*) to which objection has not been raised, judgments resolving procedural issues (*Prozessurteile*), and partial final judgments (*Teilurteile*). Judgments which dissolve other judgments in order to continue legal proceedings, or (on appeal) which vacate judgments entered below and remand cases for further proceedings are not entitled to *res adjudicata* effect.[247] The same is true of procedural orders and other dispositions before final judgment. Termination of a case by withdrawal of the complaint (*Klagerücknahme*) does not qualify as a judgment entitled to binding effect.[248] On the other hand, a judgment by relinquishment (*Verzichtsurteil*) is considered a judgment on the merits and is given *res adjudicata* effect.[249]

Settlements, whether made of record or not, are not entitled to *res adjudicata* effects as prior judgments.[250] There is no concept of "consent judgment" in German civil practice.[251] A prior settlement may be raised as an accord and satisfaction in later litigation. However, it is not considered a judgment and the rules of *res adjudicata* do not apply.

---

246. See Lüke, §31(II), mn. 357; Thomas/Putzo/Reichold, §322, mn. 3; Zöller, Vor §322, mn. 9.

247. See Lüke, §31(II), mn. 355.

248. Such withdrawals are analogous to voluntary dismissals without prejudice in American procedural law.

249. See., e.g., Zöller/Vollkommer, Vor §322, mn. 8. Such a judgment is analogous to a dismissal with prejudice. See Ch. 9(A)(3) above on withdrawals and abandonments of claims.

250. See Ch. 9(A)(4) above and Ch. 11(I) below on settlements and the procedure for documenting them in court.

251. See, however, ZPO §1053, which authorizes an arbitral tribunal to make awards by consent, which may be given the legal effect of a court judgment by ZPO §1055. See Münch, in: *Münchener Kommentar zur ZPO*, §1053, mn. 18. For a comparative survey see Stürner, "Formen der konsensualen Prozessbeendigung in den europäischen Zivilprozessrechten", in: Breidenbach et al. (eds.), *Konsensuale Streitbeilegung. Akademisches Symposium zu Ehren von Peter F. Schlosser* (2001), p. 5.

2. Scope of *Res Adjudicata* Effect

The scope of *res adjudicata* effect of a civil judgment is defined by the parties to the litigation and the formal claims (*Ansprüche*) which were submitted to the court for decision. The basic rule is that a judgment binds the parties and their successors in interest with respect to the subject matter of the claims actually asserted and decided. As a rule non-parties are not bound. Nor are the parties themselves bound with respect to actual or potential claims not actually submitted for adjudication.

a. As Defined by Claims for Relief

The binding effect of a judgment is limited to the "subject matter of the controversy" (*Streitgegenstand*) upon which it was issued. The subject matter of the controversy is in turn defined by the actual claims (*Ansprüche*) asserted by the respective parties and explicitly or implicitly decided by the court.[252]

Thus if a plaintiff sought damages for injuries sustained from a defective consumer product, the final judgment issued in the litigation would be *res adjudicata* only to the extent of the claims (*Ansprüche*) at issue. It would not necessarily cover all claims related to the product, or to injuries received from it. If the plaintiff's claim were limited to a claim for personal injury, an adverse judgment on that claim would not preclude the same party from suing the same defendant for property damage sustained in the same event. Binding effect extends only to claims which were actually at issue, not those which could have been raised or which may have arisen out of the same transaction or occurrence. German civil procedure does not recognize the concept of claim preclusion in the broad sense as is the case in common law countries.

So, for example, if a creditor claimed to be owed 30,000 Euro by a debtor, the creditor could file a partial suit (*Teilklage*) for any portion of the total claim. The judgment rendered would be neither preclusive or conclusive on a subsequent suit for a further part or the unpaid balance of the total claim.[253]

---

252. ZPO §322(1): "Judgments are capable of binding effect only to the extent that a claim raised by the complaint or a counterclaim has been decided." (*"Urteile sind der Rechtskraft nur insoweit fähig, als über den durch die Klage oder durch die Widerklage erhobenen Anspruch entschieden ist."*); see Thomas/Putzo/Reichold, §322, mn. 17 ff.

253. Lüke, §31(IV), mn. 360. The decision would, however, be binding as to the portion of the claim adjudicated. There is some diversity of opinion on how to apply a final judgment in a partial claim when a later partial claim is asserted. A complaint which discloses that the particular sum sued for is part of a larger legal claim is referred to as an "open partial complaint" (*offene Teilklage*). In this case a later partial claim is clearly per-

By the same token, the legal theory on which the claim was decided is immaterial. The legal grounds (*Entscheidungsgründe*) for a decision are not entitled to any binding or limiting effect.[254] If the plaintiff sued for personal injuries arising from medical malpractice based on a tort theory, the judgment in that case would bar a claim for breach of contract asserting the same claims for relief, but on a different legal theory. And a court judgment deciding a claim on a different legal theory than that originally suggested by the plaintiff would prevent relitigation of the actual claims adjudicated based on any legal theory.

When the issue of *res adjudicata* is raised, the court is required to examine and compare not only the formal claims for relief, but also the factual content of the current claim with that of the decided case in order to determine whether they are in fact the same claim.[255] A difference in the operative facts can be sufficient to save the second case from dismissal. An example would be a case in which a purchaser of goods paid for them with a check and then stopped payment on the check. An adverse judgment on the seller's claim based on the check would not necessarily bar a second claim, identical in amount, to recover the purchase price of the goods under the sales contract, since the factual bases of the two claims are not the same. The check claim would be based on issuance and delivery of the check while the contract claim would be founded on conclusion and performance of the contract.[256]

As a rule German law does not recognize issue preclusion short of entire claims. Dismissal of a claim for restoration of converted property on the

---

missible. When the claimant does not specify the partial nature of the claim, the complaint is a "hidden partial complaint" (*verdeckte Teilklage*). Although there has been dispute about the extent of the *res adjudicata* effect of a judgment rendered on a "hidden partial complaint" (see Federal Supreme Court, 34 BGHZ 337 (1961)), it is now the prevailing opinion that additional later claims are not precluded by an adverse judgment on the preceding hidden partial claim. See Federal Supreme Court, 135 BGHZ 178, 181 (1998). For further details see Leipold, "Teilklagen und Rechtskraft", in: Bettermann et al. (eds.), *Festschrift für Zeuner* (1994), p. 431; Marburger, "Rechtskraft und Präklusion bei der Teilklage im Zivilprozess", in: Schön (ed.), *Gedächtnisschrift für Knobbe-Keuk* (1997), p. 187; Gottwald, in: *Münchener Kommentar zur ZPO*, §322, mn. 118 ff.; Ch. 7(A)(5) above.

254. See, e.g., Rosenberg/Schwab/Gottwald, §153(III) pp. 922 ff.; Thomas/Putzo/Reichold, §322, mn. 28 ff.; Zöller/Vollkommer, Vor §322, mn. 31 ff.; Federal Supreme Court, 53 *NJW* 3492 (2000); 56 *NJW* 1044 (2003).

255. This process is referred as "dual analysis of the scope of the controversy" (*zweigliedriger Streitgegenstand*).

256. See Federal Supreme Court, 54 *NJW* 157, 158 f. (2001); 56 *NJW* 585 (2003); Thomas/Putzo/Reichold, Einl. II, mn. 24.

ground that the plaintiff had failed to prove ownership would not prejudice the plaintiff in a later suit for damages based on the same event. By the same token, a judgment for the plaintiff in an action for restoration of converted property, would not preclude the defendant from challenging the plaintiff's title again in a later action for damages to the converted property.[257] Only a final declaratory judgment directly deciding on the ownership will be given *res judicata* effect to preclude a party from litigating this issue in a later action.[258]

When the defendant's response raises matters of set-off and the court enters a judgment determining the set-off, the judgment will be given *res judicata* effect with respect to the claim pleaded as a set-off against the defendant's obligation.[259] This special form of *res judicata* effect may be considered as an exception from the concept of non-recognition of issue preclusion in German civil procedure.

b. Parties Bound

A judgment is *res adjudicata* only between the parties to the litigation and those persons claiming by, through or under those parties.[260] Third parties who claim by, through or under parties to the litigation are bound by the judgment and cannot relitigate the matter in controversy. A transferee of an object or a successor to a legal claim is generally bound by prior judgments affecting the object or claim unless she qualifies as a good faith transferee without notice.[261] Heirs of a litigant are bound by judgments rendered for or against their testator.[262]

Parties whose legal rights are made legally dependent on the rights of another may be bound by judgments affecting those rights. Thus a member of a registered partnership may be bound by a judgment against the partnership having to do with the business of the partnership because of the provisions of

257. See Federal Supreme Court, 17 *NJW-RR* 516 (2002); 123 BGHZ 137, 140 (1993); Thomas/Putzo/Reichold, §322, mn. 28 f. A form of issue preclusion may be a factor in some cases of third party practice like intervention or notice of pending suit to third parties. See Ch. 7(C) and (D) above.

258. See ZPO §256(2) and Ch. 9(F)(3) below.

259. See ZPO §322(2); Thomas/Putzo/Reichold, §322, mn. 44 ff. For set-offs see Ch. 7(J)(3) and Ch. 9(D) above.

260. Rosenberg/Schwab/Gottwald, §156(I), p. 935.

261. ZPO §325(1) and (2). See Rosenberg/Schwab/Gottwald, §156(II)(2)(a), p. 936; Zöller/Vollkommer, §325, mn. 2 f.

262. See Rosenberg/Schwab/Gottwald, §156(II)(2)(a), p. 936.

law making members of a partnership legally responsible for the liabilities of partnerships to which they belong.[263]

There are a few other exceptions to the doctrine limiting the effect of civil judgments on non-parties to the litigation. Certain kinds of judgments which affect legal status also bind third parties (*Gestaltungswirkung*). For instance, a judgment of divorce concludes the marriage not only between the parties to the litigation but also as to many others who may be affected.[264] The Patent Court can enter a judgment in a case between two private parties that invalidates a patent for the world.[265]

Because a judgment is only *res judicata* between the parties to litigation and has no issue-preclusive effect, it does not operate as collateral estoppel to prevent a party to the case from relitigating the same issue of law or fact against other parties in other cases.[266] Thus, if a passenger recovers against her driver for negligence in an automobile accident case, that judgment and its underlying finding of the driver's negligence will not bind the driver in a case brought by the driver of the other car, or even by another passenger in his own car.

3. Effect of the Prior Judgment

A prior judgment may prevent a party from raising the same claim in a future proceeding, or may prejudge the decision in a later action. In the first sense the prior judgment is treated as a barrier to the future claim. In the second the prior judgment serves as a prejudgment of a material element of the second action.

If the subject matter of a newly filed complaint is the same as that of a prior case concluded by final judgment, the final judgment in the former case is a "negative pre-requisite to suit" (*negative Prozessvoraussetzung*) in the new case.[267] The prior judgment may be raised by the opposing party. The court

---

263. See HGB §129(1); Schmidt, *Gesellschaftsrecht*, 4th ed. (2002), §49(VI)(1), p. 1439; Rosenberg/Schwab/Gottwald, §156(II)(4), p. 939. By the same token, the heirs to an estate may be bound by a judgment in an action between the executor and a third party. ZPO §327.

264. See Rosenberg/Schwab/Gottwald, §94(III)(1), p. 529.

265. However, a judgment sustaining the patent will not be conclusive against other parties who may wish to challenge the patent. See van Venrooy, „Rechtskraftwirkung des klageabweisenden Urteils im Patentnichtigkeitsverfahren", 93 *GRUR* 92 (1991).

266. See, e.g., Zöller/Vollkommer, Vor §322, mn. 32 f. and §325, mn. 3 ff.; Stein/Jonas/Leipold, §322, mn. 84 ff. and §325, mn. 1 ff. For the binding effect of a decision in favor of an interest group against the defendant in later individual law suits see Ch. 5(B)(5). A planned reform for 2004 provides a special form of issue preclusion based on the results of evidentiary proceedings in related criminal cases. See Huber, 36 *ZRP* 268, 271 (2003).

267. See Rosenberg/Schwab/Gottwald, §151(III)(1)(a), p. 917.

is also required to consider on its own motion any prior judgments of which it has knowledge. Once noticed the prior judgment makes the subsequent claim unallowable (*unzulässig*) and requires dismissal.[268]

In some cases the prior judgment establishes beyond contest an element of a second claim. For instance, a declaratory judgment of ownership of real estate or personal property may be pled as the legal basis for a complaint between the same parties seeking possession of the real estate or thing or for reimbursement for damage to the premises or thing in question. This does not mean that there is issue preclusion in Germany. Only a final judgment which directly establishes a material element of the second claim will be given this *res adjudicata* effect.[269] Within the narrow scope of *res adjudicata* in Germany, a prior civil judgment binds not only subsequent court proceedings, but also administrative proceedings and even criminal proceedings involving the same parties.[270]

A judgment is binding not only on the party which commenced the case, but also on the defendant. So, for instance, a defendant who was adjudged liable to the plaintiff in a case for damages may not bring his own action against the plaintiff seeking a declaratory judgment of non-liability or any limitation of liability directly inconsistent with the prior judgment.[271]

A final judgment speaks always to the state of affairs as of the conclusion of oral argument on the facts (*Tatsachenverhandlungen*) in the proceeding in which it was rendered. If the case were appealed, this would include the oral argument at the second instance appeal, but not the oral argument on review appeal.[272] Facts of consequence which arise after the last oral argument may form the bases for legal claims and defenses not subsumed by the former judgment. For instance, in a family support case a prior judgment may be modified when it appears that changed circumstances may affect the obligation to support spouse and children as adjudicated by the judgment.[273] Payment of a claim occurring after oral argument can be raised as a claim or defense in a

268. See, e.g., Thomas/Putzo/Reichold, §322, mn. 11; Zöller/Vollkommer, Vor §322, mn. 19.

269. See Jauernig, §63(III)(2); Rosenberg/Schwab/Gottwald, §151(III)(2), p.917 f.; Stein/Jonas/Leipold, §322, mn. 204 ff.; Ch. 9(F)(2)(a) above.

270. Rosenberg/Schwab/Gottwald, §151(III)(5), p. 918 f. and §10(II), p. 52.

271. See Rosenberg/Schwab/Gottwald, §154(II)(1), p. 927; Zöller/Vollkommer, Vor §322, mn. 21; Federal Supreme Court, 123 BGHZ 139 (1993).

272. This is because new facts may not be received at the review appeal level. See Ch. 10(E)(2) below.

273. See ZPO §323; Brudermüller, in: Johannsen/Henrichs (eds.), *Eherecht*, 3rd ed. (1998); Rosenberg/Schwab/Gottwald, §158, pp. 952 ff.

subsequent proceeding or sometimes in an action to arrest execution.[274] In general, material facts existing before the conclusion of oral argument in the prior proceeding but not brought forward or considered in the prior judgment cannot be raised as the basis for new proceedings inconsistent with the prior judgment.[275] If the additional facts are newly discovered and could not have been brought forward in the proceeding by the exercise of reasonable diligence, they may form the basis of a motion for reopening the former proceeding on the ground of newly discovered evidence.[276]

Under the German law of transnational civil procedure the circumstances under which a judgment becomes final and binding is a matter for the law of the jurisdiction in which the judgment was rendered. On the other hand, the effect of a prior judgment on a later proceeding may be affected or even determined by the principles of law of the forum in which the subsequent case is brought.[277]

4. Proceedings for Reopening of Civil Judgments

Even after all appellate measures have been exhausted, in rare cases a civil judgment may be reopened by the court which rendered it if manifest injustice would otherwise result. The grounds for reopening can be described in general terms as a "particularly serious lack of correct procedure" or an "obvious disintegration of the correctness of the judgment".[278]

There are two procedural routes by which a reopening of a final judgment can be sought. A complaint for nullity of judgment (*Nichtigkeitsklage*) addresses certain very serious procedural defects such as incorrect composition of the court, failure of required representation of a party, or lack of impartiality of a judge.[279] A claim for nullity based on incorrect composition of the court or improper participation by a judge who had been disqualified may be

274. ZPO §767. See Ch. 11(F)(3)(b) below on actions to arrest execution.

275. See ZPO §767(2); Rosenberg/Schwab/Gottwald, §155(II), p. 931 ff.

276. See Ch. 9(F)(4) below.

277. See Schack, *Internationales Zivilverfahrensrecht*, 3rd ed. (2001), mn. 774 ff., 791 ff.; Rosenberg/Schwab/Gottwald, §151(III)(3), p. 918 and §157(I)(4), pp. 946 f. See Ch. 12(C) below on recognition of foreign judgments.

278. For details see Braun, *Rechtskraft und Restitution*, Vol. I (1979) and Vol. II (1985); Rosenberg/Schwab/Gottwald, §159, pp. 961 ff.; for a survey see Lüke, §38(I), mn. 427 ("*besonders schwere Verfahrensmängel... offensichtliche Erschütterung der Richtigkeit des Urteils*").

279. ZPO §579. A complaint for nullity based on lack of impartiality of a judge must allege either that the judge was statutorily disqualified from deciding the case or that the judge continued to sit after being disqualified for lack of impartiality (*Befangenheit*) in that case. For statutory disqualification and disqualification based on lack of impartiality, see ZPO §§41 ff. If a party failed to seek disqualification for lack of impartiality during the

filed only if the party is unable to raise these issues by appeal. Participation in the case by a statutorily disqualified judge can form the basis for a nullity complaint regardless of whether it could also be raised in a pending appeal. The same is true of failure of required representation by a party. In these cases the plaintiff does not have to show that the defect alleged actually affected the judgment.[280]

A complaint for restitution of judgment (*Restitutionsklage*) addresses a wider range of serious defects in the prior proceedings or judgment. Grounds for reopening a judgment via complaint for restitution include false material statement under oath by the opposing party, forgery of documents received in evidence, false testimony by a witness or expert, or criminal conduct by a party or judge in connection with the judgment. In the case of criminal conduct, a sentence by a criminal court must, in principle, precede the civil complaint for restitution of the prior judgment. A party may also bring an action for restitution of judgment if she finds a prior judgment covering the same subject matter (*Streitgegenstand*) or if she is placed in the position to use a newly discovered document (*Urkunde*) that would have led to a more favorable judgment.[281]

A complaint in restitution may not, however, be based on any defect that was, or in the exercise of reasonable diligence by parties or counsel, could have been addressed during the first instance proceeding or during any second-instance appeal.[282] Moreover, in contrast to a complaint for nullity of judgment, only defects that were causal of the judgment below may be the basis for reopening the proceedings.[283]

The allowable ground for reopening based on newly discovered documentary evidence does not apply to other forms of evidence such as witness testimony or evidence by examination (*Augenscheinsbeweis*).[284] The newly discov-

---

pendency of the case, the party may not raise it later on. See ZPO §43 and Federal Supreme Court, 34 *NJW* 1273, 1274 (1981).

280. ZPO §579(2); Lüke, §38(II), mn. 430; Zöller/Greger, §579, mn. 1 ff.

281. ZPO §§580 f. See also ZPO §641i, which authorizes reopening a judgment of paternity if contrary expert evidence such as blood or DNA tests later becomes available. For a discussion of the individual grounds for a restitution of judgment complaint see Rosenberg/Schwab/Gottwald, §160(II)(3), pp. 967 ff.; Musielak, §580, mn. 6 ff.

282. ZPO §582; see Rosenberg/Schwab/Gottwald, §160(II)(1), p. 966; Musielak, §582, mn. 2 ff.

283. See Musielak, §580, mn. 3 ff. However a defect which affected a preliminary finding or decision upon which the judgment was ultimately based can be raised in a proceeding to set aside the judgment, ZPO §583.

284. Proof based on the content of files kept on a computer (as opposed to computer printouts) is currently considered as proof by examination. See Ch. 8(C)(3)(a) above on

ered document must be of moment to the outcome of the case without the need for explanatory or supplementing expert or lay testimony. Documentary evidence which merely casts doubt on the credibility of witness testimony is usually not sufficient. The party seeking reopening must be able to show that the document existed at the time of the prior proceeding, but that she was unaware of its existence or was unable to have access to it before the judgment in question became final.[285]

A complaint to set aside a judgment must be filed within a month of the time the plaintiff becomes aware of the ground for the complaint and in any event within 5 years of the date the judgment becomes final.[286] Such complaints are examined with care by the court in order to determine whether all of the legal prerequisites are set forth with particularity as required by the statute.[287]

If a party alleges with specificity a ground for setting aside a judgment by complaint for either nullity or restitution, the court will process the complaint as any civil proceeding. The court may hear and consider the allegations and supporting facts relating to reopening as a preliminary matter, or may consolidate the issue of reopening with further oral argument on the merits of the matter as reopened.[288] If the court decides to reopen the case, the argument is treated as a continuation of plenary proceedings in the reopened case and the parties are as free to make additional assertions or bring forward additional proof as they would have been in the original plenary hearing, had it continued.[289] The court may allow the reopening in an interlocutory judgment

---

proof by examination. There is some discussion about whether such proof should be considered as documentary evidence for the purpose of restitution complaints. See Zöller/Greger, §580, mn. 16, arguing that the exclusion of computer files may be no longer justified in the light of the most recent reforms concerning the use of electronic signatures. But see Federal Supreme Court, 65 BGHZ 300 (1976) which limits strictly the scope of ZPO §580(7)(b) to conventional documents in a case concerning a photograph.

285. See Rosenberg/Schwab/Gottwald, §160(II)(3)(d), p. 969 for a discussion of actions in restitution of judgment based on newly discovered documents.

286. ZPO §586. These facts include facts relating to the timeliness of the complaint, which are to be shown to a plausibility (*glaubhaft*). ZPO §589(2).

287. See ZPO §589(1); Zöller/Greger, §589, mn. 1 ff.

288. ZPO §590. In the latter case the argument on the reopening will precede any argument on the merits. If the complaint seeks reopening of a proceeding at the stage of revision appeal, the Federal Supreme Court is authorized to hear and consider factual evidence on the grounds for reopening, even though it would otherwise be required to accept facts as found below. See Zöller/Greger, §590, mn. 2.

289. ZPO §590(1), (2). The scope of the reopened proceedings would be subject to procedural preclusions already existing in the case and not affected by the ground for reopening. See Rosenberg/Schwab/Gottwald, §161(IV)(3), p. 977; Musielak, §590, mn. 4 f.

(*Zwischenurteil*), or may incorporate the reopening in the final judgment (*Endurteil*) in the case as reopened.[290]

A judgment reopening a prior judgment on one of the allowable grounds for a nullity complaint or a complaint for restitution has the effect of retroactively vacating the reopened judgment. The *status quo ante* is restored to the extent practicable.[291] The court thereupon reaches and issues a new judgment based on the proceedings as reopened. The new judgment may be different or even contrary to the original judgment. However, once the court has determined to reopen the proceedings, a new judgment must be issued to conclude the case even if the court comes to exactly the same conclusion as the prior judgment.[292] If a case is reopened, both the reopening judgment and the new judgment on the merits are subject to the usual appellate remedies.[293]

5. *Res Adjudicata* and European Law

Civil procedure law seldom offers a good opportunity for the development of common European Law affecting a core procedural issue. Such development has, however occurred, in case subject matter and *res adjudicata* doctrine.

Articles 27(2) and 34(3) of the European Regulation on Jurisdiction and Enforcement (Brussels Regulation, BRJE) raise the question of whether the subject matter of a pending case for purposes of *lis pendens* or the subject matter of a prior judgment for purposes of *res adjudicata* effect should be determined under national procedure law or whether common European standards should develop. The European Court of Justice has decided in favor of a development of common European standards. In analyzing issues of claimed "identity of the subject matter" of two actions the court has developed a criterion of identity of the essential core issues ("core issue theory").[294]

290. See Rosenberg/Schwab/Gottwald, §161(IV)(2), p. 976; Zöller/Greger, §590, mn. 4.

291. See Rosenberg/Schwab/Gottwald, §161(IV)(2), p. 976. Reopening a judgment does not affect the intervening rights of a good faith purchaser protected by BGB §§892, 932.

292. See Rosenberg/Schwab/Gottwald, §161(IV)(3), p. 978; Lüke, §38(V), mn. 437; Musielak, §590, mn. 9. This is in contrast with the simple affirmance that is entered if a motion to set aside a default judgment is unsuccessful. See ZPO §343, Ch. 9(A)(1). It is, however, suggested that simple affirmance should also be allowed in motions for reopening proceedings. See, e.g., Zöller/Greger, §590, mn. 16; Thomas/Putzo, §590, mn. 5.

293. ZPO §591. A refusal to reopen a judgment may also be appealed.

294. See European Court of Justice, Case 145/86, Hoffman v. Krieg, 1988 ECR 645 (1988); Case 144/86, Gubish v. Palumbo, 1987 ECR 4861 (1987); Case 406/92, The Tatry v. Maciej Rataj, 1994 ECR I-5439 (1994); see Ch. 12(C)(2)(b) and (E)(1).

Thus, the ECJ has established within the framework of the Brussels Regulation a *res judicata* doctrine that tends to follow the common law model of issue preclusion and expands the res adjudicata effect to material elements of a judgment.

As of the time this text is written the traditional German doctrine of *res judicata* stands undisturbed when domestic or non-EU cases are involved.[295] It can be argued that all in all the more simple and restrained *res adjudicata* doctrine of German civil procedural law would appear preferable to the broader approach of the common law when ascertaining the preclusive effect of a foreign judgment. It takes into consideration that a correct detailed analysis of a judgment rendered under foreign law in a foreign language is difficult and will often require knowledge of foreign law that the judge of the recognizing state may not have.[296] The ALI/UNIDROIT Principles of Transnational Civil Procedure recommend that the scope of claim and issue preclusion by foreign judgments be limited in accord with the German model.[297]

---

295. For a detailed discussion see Rüssmann and Walker, "Die Streitgegenstandslehre und die Rechtsprechung des EuGH - nationales Recht unter gemeineuropäischem Einfluss?", 111 *ZZP* 399 and 429 (1998).

296. See Stürner, "Rechtskraft in Europa", in: Geimer (ed.), *Festschrift für Schütze* (1999), pp. 913 ff., 933 f.

297. See The American Law Institute (ed.), *ALI/UNIDROIT Principles and Rules of Transnational Civil Procedure*, Discussion Draft No. 4 (April 2003), Principle 28.

CHAPTER 10

Appellate Justice

A. Purpose and Function of Appellate Justice

German civil justice has traditionally offered numerous appellate remedies (*Rechtsmittel* or *Rechtsbehelfe*) to parties aggrieved by judicial findings, determinations or final orders at almost any stage of the proceedings. In almost every case an appellant has at least two potential levels of resort beyond the first instance local court or state district court proceeding. In fact, the large number of lower court orders subject to appeal, the generous scope of review and the ease by which appellate remedies can be invoked all have tended to result in delay in some cases, especially those in which a recalcitrant party insists on exhausting all of its appellate options.

For a long time the German bench, bar and legislature have debated the wisdom of reforms calculated to streamline the German appellate structure and limit the scope of review in many matters. In July 2001 this debate culminated in legislation implementing some, but not all of the proposed reforms.[1] The following discussion reflects the current appellate system and practice as it has been modified by the new legislation.

The function and purpose of the appellate process in German Civil Justice is threefold. The first of these is to offer in most cases some opportunity to reexamine the facts relevant to the controversy, in some cases including facts not brought before the court of first instance. The second major purpose of appellate process is to correct errors of interpretation and application of the law. The third aim is to maintain and enforce correct procedure.

---

1. See Law for the Reform of Civil Procedure (*Zivilprozessreformgesetz*) of July 27, 2001, BGBl. 2001(I), p. 1887.

The task of determining the validity of post-constitutional legislation under the German Constitution is not the province of the ordinary appellate courts, although such courts do take the Constitution into account when determining the correct interpretation of statutory provisions and regulations.[2] Claims that a statute is unconstitutional may be raised in the Federal Constitutional Court (*Bundesverfassungsgericht*), either by reference from one of the other courts or by constitutional appeal (*Verfassungsbeschwerde*) by a private party. The Federal Constitutional Court also exercises a relatively strict control over the constitutionality of statutory interpretation and case law of the other courts through a quasi-appellate jurisdiction over the decisions of all of the other courts in constitutional matters.[3]

The somewhat pervasive abundance of appellate remedies may seem extreme to a foreign observer. In some cases the frequent resort to layers of appellate remedies can result in delay. However one must be cautious in regarding this system as a redundancy that can be easily abbreviated or cut back. First instance judges act with relative speed and efficiency in processing a case from complaint to judgment. This efficiency gives the litigants the benefit of an early decision of their case. The availability of comprehensive appellate remedies provides litigants with a second look in those cases where the relatively speedy first instance disposition might not have given due attention to a fact of importance or a nuance in the law. Said another way, the quality guarantee of strong appellate remedies makes possible a relatively quick and inexpensive route to an initial decision. Many litigants will find the first instance decision acceptable, in which case both time and money will have been saved. The appellate remedies provide extra time and judicial attention for the minority of cases in which at least one party believes that it has not been well served by the expeditious initial determination.[4]

---

2. The ordinary courts may, however, determine the constitutionality of legislation enacted prior to adoption of the German Constitution in 1949. See German Constitutional Court, 4 BVerfGE 331, 339 ff. (1956); 66 BVerfGE 248, 254 (1984); Jarass/Pieroth, *Grundgesetz für die Bundesrepublik Deutschland,* 5th ed. (2000), Art. 100, mn. 8. If pre-constitutional statute law is incorporated into a post-constitutional revision or re-codification, even those provisions which survive unaltered are considered post-constitutional.

3. For a brief description of the jurisdiction, composition and procedure of the Federal Constitutional Court see Ch. 3(E) above and Ch. 10(H) below.

4. See Ayad, „Optimierung des Rechtsschutzes und effektiverer Richtereinsatz?", 33 *ZRP* 229, 233 (2000); Dauster, „Eckpunkte einer Justizreform", 33 *ZRP* 338, 342 (2000); Schellhammer, „Zivilprozessreform und erste Instanz", 55 *MDR* 1081 (2001); Flotho, „Schneller - besser - billiger?", 31 *BRAK-Mitt.* 107, 108 (2000); Stürner, „Eckpunkte einer Justizreform", 53 *NJW Beilage Heft* 25, 31 (2000).

For this reason, reform proposals designed to reduce appellate process and its consequent costs and delays must give some consideration to the first instance procedure. It may well be that more effort and deliberation would have to be expended in all cases at the initial instance in order to compensate for a potential reduction in appellate options.[5] This interrelationship may be the reason that the reforms in appellate procedure ultimately enacted in July 2001 were relatively modest and did not seriously abbreviate or curtail appellate options in most civil cases.

B. Kinds of Appellate Remedies

In ordinary civil litigation appellate remedies (*Rechtsmittel*) are classified in three categories, the second instance appeal of facts and law (*Berufung*), the review appeal on law and procedure only (*Revision*) and the miscellaneous appeal (*Beschwerde*) from an interlocutory order or relatively minor decision.[6] In addition there are a number of other legal remedies (*Rechtsbehelfe*) which involve reconsideration or review of different kinds of court decisions and actions, but which probably should not be considered appeals. These latter include the application to set aside a default judgment (*Einspruch*), the objection to warning proceedings (*Widerspruch*), and certain objections (*Erinnerungen*) seeking judicial review or reconsideration of actions of magistrates (*Rechtspfleger*) and court executors (*Gerichtsvollzieher*) in the performance of their judicial functions.[7]

In general a second instance appeal (*Berufung*) is taken from a judgment (*Urteil*) of a court of first instance to a court exercising appellate jurisdiction. Most civil judgments of the ordinary courts of first instance are subject to second instance appeal.

A review appeal (*Revision*) is usually a second level of appeal after the second instance appeal of facts and law. Review appeals are limited to issues of

---

5. See Gottwald, "Civil Justice Reform: The German Perspective", in: Zuckerman (ed.), *Civil Justice in Crisis* (1999), pp. 224–230; Greger, "Justizreform - und nun?", 57 *JZ* 1020 (2002).

6. For the purposes of this work these three kinds of appeals will be denominated "second instance appeal", "review appeal" and "miscellaneous appeal" respectively.

7. These various kinds of review or reconsideration proceedings will not be treated in detail here, but are mentioned at various points in connection with the activities to which they relate. See, e.g., Ch. 9(A)(1) above (objection to default judgment); Ch. 11(F)(3) below (review of actions of court executors), and Ch. 3(H)(2) above (review of actions of magistrates).

law and procedure only. In civil cases review appeals go only to the Federal Supreme Court (*Bundesgerichtshof*).[8] Cases started in the state district courts (and family cases from the local courts) have second instance appeals to the state court of appeals and then may seek a review appeal to the Federal Supreme Court. Local court cases other than family cases have a second instance appeal to the state district courts,[9] with the possibility of a review appeal to the Federal Supreme Court.[10]

Miscellaneous appeals (*Beschwerde*) may be taken from a variety of court decisions other than formal judgments as authorized by statute. In most cases the miscellaneous appeal goes to the next higher court in the appellate hierarchy. The diversity in form and content of such appeals makes their classification almost impossible.

C. Prerequisites and Principles Applicable to All Appellate Remedies

The circumstances and grounds under which the various appellate remedies may be invoked are statutorily prescribed for each appealable act or decision. Compliance with the statutory prerequisites is necessary in order to invoke the appellate jurisdiction.

There are also certain principles which apply to appellate remedies in general. An appellant must show some aggrievement (*Beschwer*) in the decision subject to appeal.[11] Aggrievement is determined with reference to the party's formal claims for relief (*Anträge*) as presented to the court below in the complaint (*Klage*) or other pleading[12] as amended by subsequent briefs (*Schriftsätze*) or oral submissions at hearings or oral argument.[13] In general, if the

8. Subject to the jurisdictional limitations of that court. See Ch. 3(D)(4) above.

9. Each of the German States has the option to channel these appeals to the state appeals courts rather than the district courts. GVG § 119(3). This provision is effective only up to December 31, 2007. See Thomas/Putzo, *Zivilprozessordnung*, 24th ed. (2002), GVG § 119, mn. 21.

10. Such appeals are very rarely granted. See Ch. 10(E) below.

11. See German Federal Supreme Court, 3 *NJW-RR*, 959 (1988); Rosenberg/Schwab/Gottwald, *Zivilprozessrecht*, 15th ed. (1993), § 136(II)(3), pp. 809 ff.; Lüke, *Zivilprozessrecht*, 8th ed. (2003), § 34(III)(2), mn. 386.

12. Such as the answer (*Klageerwiderung*) or counterclaim (*Widerklage*) for a defendant. See Ch. 7(J) above.

13. See Rosenberg/Schwab/Gottwald, § 136(II)(3)(a), pp. 810 f.

party received in the decision all that it requested from the court below, there is no legal aggrievement to support an appeal from that decision.[14] If the judgment awards a plaintiff all that was sought in the plaintiff's formal claims for relief, the plaintiff has no legal aggrievement to support its appeal. In some situations, however, a defendant may be substantively aggrieved even though its formal claims for dismissal were granted. For example, if a defendant has sought dismissal of a claim as legally or factually unsubstantiated, and it is in fact dismissed, but without prejudice for some procedural ground, the defendant does have sufficient aggrievement to sustain an appeal from the decision apparently in its favor.[15]

In general, a party cannot be made worse off by its own appeal. The principle prohibiting a change for the worse[16] permits a party to lodge an appeal without the fear that the appeal may leave it worse off than before. This principle is partially reflected in ZPO §528, which prohibits granting relief on an appeal in excess of that which is requested by a party.[17]

While the operative portion of an appellate judgment cannot give an appealing party less than he obtained below, this does not mean that the appellate court cannot change the grounds on which the judgment is supported. Moreover, if a party appeals a judgment of dismissal on procedural grounds, and if the appellate court finds the grounds for dismissal insufficient, the court can go ahead and affirm the dismissal based on the claim's lack of substantive merit.[18]

An opposing party cannot receive new benefit at the appellate level without lodging its own appeal. If a plaintiff has received an award, albeit a smaller one than it sought, and the defendant appeals, unless the plaintiff lodges its own appeal the plaintiff will not be permitted to ask the appellate court to award it any more than was awarded in the court below. In order to reduce pressure on a party to appeal solely in order to protect its options in case of appeal by the opponent, the Civil Procedure Code permits a non-appealing party to lodge a

---

14. In these circumstances if the claim were not barred by *res adjudicata*, the party's remedy would be to commence a new action for the additional relief. See Ch. 9(F)(2)(a) above.

15. See Federal Supreme Court, 28 BGHZ 349 (1959). This is because a dismissal as unsubstantiated (*unbegründet*) would be a judgment on the merits and bar future prosecution of the claim, while a procedural dismissal (*Prozessurteil*) without prejudice would not. See Ch. 6(C)(2)(c) and (d); Ch. 7(E).

16. *Verbot der reformatio in peius* or *Verschlechterungsverbot*.

17. However, a party against whom an appeal has been lodged may file a cross appeal from those parts of the decision which do not favor it. See Ch. 10(C) below.

18. See ZPO §538(1) and §528; Federal Supreme Court, 46 BGHZ 281, 283. (1967); Rosenberg/Schwab/Gottwald, §140(II)(2), pp. 848 f.

cross appeal (*Anschlussberufung*) at any time up to one month after service on it of the opponents brief in support of appeal (*Berufungsbegründungsschrift*).[19] If the cross appeal was filed after the time limit for filing appeals from the judgment in question (*Berufungsfrist*), it automatically disappears if the opposing party's appeal is withdrawn.[20] If the cross appeal is filed within the time limit, it is considered an independent appeal (*selbstständige Anschlussberufung*) and stands on its own feet regardless of the fate of the opponent's appeal.[21]

When a court has decided an issue but has issued its decision in an incorrect form, a party aggrieved by the substance of the decision may elect either the form of appeal prescribed for the form of decision issued, or the form of appeal prescribed for the correct form of the decision rendered.[22]

A party lodging an appeal retains the right to waive appeal or withdraw the appeal without the consent of the court or opposing party right up to the time of rendition of the appellate judgment.[23] This is a corollary of the principle of party control of proceedings (*Dispositionsmaxime*).[24]

---

19. ZPO §524. The provisions regulating cross appeals were amended and simplified in the July 27, 2001 reform. For instance, under prior procedure a cross appeal could be filed at any time up to close of oral argument on the opponent's appeal. See Klamaris, *Das Rechtsmittel der Anschlussberufung* (1975); Rosenberg/Schwab/Gottwald, §138, pp. 830 ff. for a detailed discussion of the cross appeal and its procedures, most of which remains applicable under the amended statute. Cross appeals may be lodged both in second instance appeals (*Berufung*) and in review appeals (*Revision*). In review appeals the cross appeal must be lodged within one month of service of the notice of appeal (*Revisionsschrift*). See ZPO §554 and Ch. 10(E)(3).

20. See ZPO §524(4). Such a cross appeal is termed a "dependent cross appeal" (*unselbstständige Anschlussberufung*).

21. This was clearly the law prior to the recent July 27, 2001 reform. That law repealed the specific provision (ZPO §522(2) a.F.) defining the "independent cross-appeal". The proposition that a cross appeal filed within the time for a regular appeal stands on its own two feet regardless of the fate of the opponent's appeal should still apply despite the repealer of the express language. See Zöller/Gummer, *Zivilprozessordnung*, 23rd ed. (2002), §524, mn. 1; Musielak/Ball, *Zivilprozessordnung*, 3rd ed. (2002), §524, mn. 4.

22. For instance, if a court issued a judgment (*Urteil*), when the matter legally should have been decided by simple order (*Beschluss*), an aggrieved party would have the option of filing second instance appeal (*Berufung*) from the judgment or filing miscellaneous appeal (*Beschwerde*) from the simple order that should have been utilized for the decision. See Federal Supreme Court, 98 BGHZ 362 (1986); Rosenberg/Schwab/Gottwald, §135(II), pp. 806 ff.; Lüke, §34(III)(5), mn. 392.

23. ZPO §§515, 516. Withdrawal of claim (see Ch. 9(A)(3)) above, voluntary termination of appeal and withdrawal of appeal should be distinguished. See Federal Supreme Court, 51 *NJW* 2453 (1998).

24. See Ch. 6(B)(1) above for a discussion of this fundamental principle of German civil justice.

D. Second Instance Appeals

A second instance appeal[25] has traditionally been considered a complete second instance reexamination of facts and law. It has been close to "a second bite at the apple" in that practically everything that was before the first-instance court was subject to reconsideration by the appellate court. In traditional terms the goal of the appeal of facts and law was,

> "...not only the correction of errors of the lower court in matters of fact or law, but rather a completely new decision of the controversy through continuation of the argumentation and with ius novorum, that is, basic admissibility of new evidence in support of claim and defense..."[26]

It has been also easily possible to raise in the appellate court certain factual material which becomes known or relevant after the first instance proceedings are completed. Traditionally the appellate court was free to find the facts and draw factual inferences different from those found by the first instance court.

That having been said, the scope of the second instance appeal and the ability of the appellate court to consider new theories and new factual submissions have been subject to gradual constriction over a long time, culminating in the most recent reforms of July 2001.[27] Under the current standard of review, the appellate court is required to accept factual findings of the first-instance court "insofar as there is no clear indication of doubt of the correctness or completeness of the fact determinations material to the decision and therefore indication for a new fact determination."[28]

---

25. Also termed the "second instance" (*zweite Instanz*).

26. Rosenberg/Schwab/Gottwald, § 134(I)(2)(a), p. 802 ("*...nicht nur die Korrektur von Fehlern des Untergerichts in tatsächlicher oder in rechtlicher Beziehung, sondern eine völlig neue Entscheidung des Rechtsstreits durch Fortsetzung und Erneuerung der Verhandlung und mit dem ius novorum, d.h. der grundsätzlichen Zulässigkeit neuer Angriffs- und Verteidigungsmittel...*").

27. See Reforms of February 13, 1924 and October 27, 1933 and the Simplification Reforms of 1976. For preparatory research before the most recent reforms see Rimmelspacher, "Funktion und Ausgestaltung des Berufungsverfahrens im Zivilprozess", Bundesministerium der Justiz (ed.), 52 *Bundesanzeiger* No. 216a (2000); Brehm, "Verfahrenskontrolle und Entscheidung des Berufungsgerichts", 107 *ZZP* 463 (1994); Rimmelspacher, "Tatsachen und Beweismittel in der Berufungsinstanz", 107 *ZZP* 421 (1994); E. Schmidt, "Der Zugang zur Berufungsinstanz", 107 *ZZP* 499 (1994).

28. ZPO § 513(1) and § 529(1)(1) ("*...die vom Gericht des ersten Rechtszuges festgestellten Tatsachen, soweit nicht konkrete Anhaltspunkte Zweifel an der Richtigkeit oder Vollständigkeit der entscheidungserheblichen Feststellungen begründen und deshalb eine erneute*

The appellate court is not to re-examine matters not seriously in dispute, or where there is no likelihood of a different outcome. On the other hand, if an appellant can raise some real doubt about the fact findings below, the appellate court can re-examine the facts de novo, and if necessary, receive anew evidence submitted below or even entertain new evidence not considered by the first instance court. While the appellate court can take new evidence, or re-take evidence submitted to the first instance court, it does so in a minority of cases.

Second instance appeals generally lie only from final judgments (*Endurteile*), including partial judgments (*Teilurteile*), and some interlocutory and provisional judgments (*Zwischenurteile* and *Vorbehaltsurteile*),[29] but not default judgments (*Versäumnisurteile*).[30] Some court orders (*Beschlüsse*) are made expressly non-appealable.[31] Others are subject to immediate miscellaneous appeal (*sofortige Beschwerde*). Interlocutory decisions (*Vorentscheidungen*) not statutorily declared unappealable or expressly made reviewable by miscellaneous appeal are subject to review in the second instance appeal from the final judgment.[32]

A second instance appeal is subject to a jurisdictional minimum amount in controversy (*Beschwerdegegenstand*) of 600 Euro unless the court which issued the judgment gives permission for appeal.[33] Permission is granted based on a finding that the case raises an issue of "fundamental significance" (*grundsätzliche Bedeutung*) or that "the development of the law or the preservation

---

Feststellung gebieten"). This definition of the scope of factual review was introduced in the July 27, 2001 reform law. The extent to which it restricted the scope of fact review or merely clarified prior practice is subject to debate. See for a detailed discussion Ebel, "Die Berufung im Zivilprozessrechtsreformgesetz", 34 *ZRP* 309, 312 (2001); Schellhammer, *Zivilprozess*, 9th ed. (2001), mn. 1040; Heiderhoff, "Die Tatsachenbindung des Berufungsgerichts nach der ZPO-Reform", 58 *JZ* 490 (2003); Grunsky, "Zum Tatsachenstoff im Berufungsverfahren nach der Reform der ZPO", 55 *NJW* 800 (2002); Greger, "Zweifelsfragen und erste Entscheidungen zur neuen ZPO", 55 *NJW* 3049 (2002); restrictive Court of Appeals of Saarbrücken, 18 *NJW-RR* 139 (2003).

29. For a description of some of the more common forms of judgment, see Ch. 9 above.

30. See Rosenberg/Schwab/Gottwald, § 135, pp 804 ff. However a "false default judgment" (*unechtes Versäumnisurteil*) which has the effect of a judgment on the merits is appealable as any other final judgment. See Ch. 9 (A)(1) above.

31. See Rosenberg/Schwab/Gottwald, § 135(I)(3), pp. 805 f.

32. ZPO § 512. See Thomas/Putzo/Reichold, § 512, mn. 3.

33. ZPO § 511. The appellant has the burden of making a showing of satisfaction of the jurisdictional minimum. See Thomas/Putzo/Reichold, § 511, mn. 11. For the right to remonstration in case of violation of the right to be heard, see Ch. 10(H)(1) below.

of a unified doctrine" (*die Fortbildung des Rechts oder die Sicherung einer einheitlichen Rechtsprechung*) require an appellate decision.[34]

1. Procedure on Second Instance Appeals

The reforms of July 2001 have attempted to streamline the statutory procedure for appeals of law and fact. The procedure applies both to appeals from judgments of the local courts to the state district courts and appeals from first instance judgments of the state district courts to the state appeals courts.[35] The new reforms provide for expedited screening and dismissal of frivolous or totally unfounded appeals, the greater use of single-judge courts in certain appellate matters, and a stricter standard for allowability of newly adduced material in support of claims or defenses.

A second instance appeal is taken by filing a notice of appeal (*Berufungsschrift*) in the appellate court with jurisdiction for appeals from the judgment in question.[36] The notice of appeal must designate the judgment (*Urteil*) being appealed and state that an appeal is being taken from this judgment.[37] Ordinarily a certified copy of the judgment is to be attached to the notice of appeal.[38] Since both the state district courts and the state appeals courts require representation by counsel, the notice of appeal must be signed by an attorney authorized to practice in a German court.[39]

The notice of appeal must be filed within a month from the date of service of the complete judgment and in no event later than 5 months after rendition (*Verkündung*) of the judgment.[40] If a judgment is retroactively

34. ZPO §511(4). The appellate court is bound to accept the appeal if the permission is given. Often the necessary finding is included in the judgment itself. Lack of venue or subject matter jurisdiction is not a basis for a second instance appeal. See ZPO §513(2). International jurisdiction may be made the subject of second instance appeal. See Federal Supreme Court, 57 *NJW* 426 (2003); Ch. 5(F) above and Ch. 10(E)(2), Ch. 12(B)(5) below.

35. Appeals of law and facts from judgments of the local courts in family law matters generally also go to the state appeals courts. See Ch. 3(D), Ch. 5(B)(2) above and Ch. 11(A) below.

36. ZPO §519(1).

37. ZPO §519(2). The judgment is properly designated by naming the court which rendered the judgment, the parties to the case, the date of rendition, and the case file number, see Federal Supreme Court, 54 *NJW* 1070 (2001). See also Thomas/Putzo/Reichold, §519, mn. 13 ff. for further details concerning the contents of a notice of appeal.

38. ZPO §519(3).

39. See Ch. 4(D)(2) above on current requirements for admission to practice before German courts.

40. ZPO §517. See Thomas/Putzo/Reichold, §517, mn. 2 regarding incomplete judgments.

amended or completed (*ergänzt*), the time for appeal begins anew with the service of the amended judgment.[41] The time for filing the notice of appeal is jurisdictional and cannot be extended. However if a party fails, without fault (*ohne ihr Verschulden*), to file a notice of appeal within the required time period, it may apply to the court for an order restoring the prior status (*Wieder - einsetzung in den vorigen Stand*) so that the necessary notice can be filed.[42]

The appellant is also required to file a brief in support of appeal (*Berufungsbegründung*) no later than 2 months after service of the complete judgment.[43] In many cases the brief is filed with the notice of appeal. Fax and electronic transmission of briefs are being introduced in many state courts of appeal.[44]

The required content of a brief in support of appeal is now prescribed by ZPO §520. A brief in support of appeal must set forth with particularity the extent to which the judgment is attacked, and the precise changes in the judgment sought by the appeal (*Berufungsanträge*). The brief also must describe the circumstances which constitute any error of substantive or procedural law and the significance of the error to the decision under appeal.

With respect to facts and fact findings, the 2001 reform requires briefs to contain

> "3. designation of concrete indications which justify doubt of the correctness or completeness of the fact findings in the judgment appealed from and which therefore indicate the need for renewed fact findings".[45]

---

41. ZPO §518. See Ch. 9(D) above.

42. ZPO §233; see Lüke, §35(II), mn. 395. Fault of the lawyer in failing to make a timely filing is chargeable to the client. However this is not the case if the filing was delayed through fault of a non-lawyer employee. See Thomas/Putzo, §233, mn. 12.

43. ZPO §520. The time can be enlarged by order of the presiding judge either with the consent of the opposing party, or without the opposing party's consent for not more than one month if the judge is of the view that the determination of the controversy will not be unduly extended (*verzögert*) or if the appellant shows substantial justification (*erhebliche Gründe*) for such enlargement. The appellant may also file a brief in support of appeal before service of the complete judgment, see Federal Supreme Court, 52 *NJW* 3269, 3270 ff. (1999).

44. See ZPO §130a; Zöller/Gummer, §519, mn. 18c and §520, mn. 7. This has been facilitated by enactment of a new Law for the Adaption of Form Requirements of Private Law and Other Form Requirements to Modern Electronic Commerce (*Gesetz zur Anpassung der Formvorschriften des Privatrechts und anderer Vorschriften an den modernen Rechtsgeschäftsverkehr*) of July 13, 2001, BGBl. 2001 (I), p. 1542. See Ch. 7(A)(1).

45. ZPO §520(3)(3) ("*die Bezeichnung konkreter Anhaltspunkte, die Zweifel an der Richtigkeit oder Vollständigkeit der Tatsachenfeststellungen im angefochtenen Urteil begründen und deshalb eine erneute Feststellung gebieten*").

This requirement goes somewhat beyond the pre-2001 standard, which required mere identification of the grounds for the appeal and designation of the new facts, sources of proof and any objections to such proof.[46]

If the appellant proposes that the appellate court entertain new evidence not adduced in the court below, the brief must describe the new evidence and set forth the circumstances justifying the consideration of such new evidence. The 2001 reforms have clarified and somewhat constricted the circumstances under which an appellate court can receive new evidence.[47] Evidence which has been correctly disallowed by the court below cannot be re-offered as new evidence in a second instance appeal.[48] Ordinarily new evidence can only be considered if it (1) relates to a point which the court below apparently overlooked or considered insignificant (*übersehen oder für unerheblich gehalten worden*), (2) was not considered because of a procedural error in the proceeding below, or (3) was not considered in the first proceeding without neglect on the part of the party offering it in the appeal (*ohne dass dies auf einer Nachlässigkeit der Partei beruht*).[49]

The brief in support of appeal must also set forth the value of the subject matter of the appeal (*Beschwerdegegenstand*) in cases other than simple money judgments to the extent necessary to determine the allowability of the appeal.[50] Finally, the appellant must indicate in its brief on appeal any reason why the appeal cannot be considered and decided by a single judge.[51]

---

46. See ZPO § 519(3)(2) pre-2001 version: ("... *die bestimmte Bezeichnung der im einzelnen anzuführenden Gründe der Anfechtung (Berufungsgründe) sowie der neuen Tatsachen, Beweismittel und Beweiseinreden, die die Partei zur Rechtfertigung ihrer Berufung anzuführen hat*"); see Hartmann, „Zivilprozess 2001/2002: Hunderte wichtiger Änderungen", 54 *NJW* 2577, 2590 (2001); Zöller/Gummer, § 520, mn. 33 ff.

47. Prior to the July 2001 reforms new evidence could be entertained on an appeal of facts and law if the appellate court deemed that consideration of the new evidence would not unduly protract the proceeding and that its non-production below was without the fault of the offering party or was due to the excusable neglect. See ZPO § 528 pre-2001 version.

48. ZPO § 531(1). Of course if the appellate court were to find that the lower court's refusal to consider the evidence was a procedural error, the appellate court could, on motion of a party, either remand the matter to the lower court with instructions to receive and consider the excluded evidence, or take the evidence itself and consider it in its decision. See Ch. 10(D)(4) below.

49. ZPO § 531(2). See Zöller/Gummer, § 531, mn. 22 ff. regarding new evidence.

50. ZPO § 520(4)(1). An appeal is only allowable if the subject matter of the appeal is at least 600 Euro unless the court below gives express permission to appeal. See ZPO § 511(2), Ch. 10(D) above.

51. See ZPO §§ 520(4)(2), 526. The use of single judges on civil appeals is a new procedure introduced by the July 2001 reforms. Prior thereto, although single judges often prepared appeals for oral argument, the actual decision was by a panel of three judges. The

Both the notice of appeal and the brief in support of the appeal must be served on the opposing party. Ordinarily this would be done at the request of the court, but service by the lawyer for the appealing party by simply sending a copy of each pleading to the opposing lawyer in the mail or by leaving it in the opposing lawyer's mailbox at the courthouse will not affect the validity of the appeal.[52] At any time following the filing of the notice of appeal the presiding judge of the appellate court can set a time within which the opponent may file a brief in opposition to the appeal (*Berufungserwiderung*) and a time thereafter within which the appellant may file a reply brief (*Stellungnahme auf die Berufungserwiderung*).[53]

The appellate court is required to review the notice of appeal and brief in support of appeal to determine whether or not the appeal is filed within the time limit and is otherwise in proper form and sets forth a justification for the appeal as a matter of law. If one of these prerequisites is lacking the court can dismiss the appeal by simple order (*Beschluss*).[54] Traditionally many appellate courts have used this required preliminary review as an opportunity to look briefly at the merits of the appeal. If the appeal looks completely hopeless, in some cases the presiding judge might informally advise the appellant of the court's preliminary appraisal, and give the appellant the opportunity to withdraw the appeal before incurring the obligation for court costs and attorneys fees.[55]

The July 2001 reforms have introduced an additional opportunity for the court to dispose of patently non-meritorious appeals in a summary manner. If as a result of the preliminary review the appeals court is of the unanimous conviction that 1) the appeal has no chance of success (*keine Aussicht auf Erfolg*), 2) the legal issue has no fundamental significance (*keine*

---

recent change appears to implement and extend the trend to single-judge decisions brought into the state district courts by the 1976 reforms and also extended by the 2001 reforms. See Ch. 3(D)(2)(b) and Ch. 7(E)(1) above.

52. ZPO §§521(1), 166(2); Federal Supreme Court, 65 BGHZ 114 (1975). See Ch. 7(F) above for procedures on service of process and court papers.

53. ZPO §521(2). See Thomas/Putzo/Reichold, §521, mn. 2 ff.

54. ZPO §522. A party aggrieved by such a dismissal can file a miscellaneous appeal of law (*Rechtsbeschwerde*) in the Federal Supreme Court. See ZPO §522(1)(3); Zöller/Gummer, §522, mn. 18.

55. This practice, which occasionally takes place by telephone, is not entirely free from possible criticism on the ground of infringement of the right to be heard (*rechtliches Gehör*) of the opposing party. See Court of Appeals of Oldenburg, 16 *NJW* 451 (1963); Stürner, *Die richterliche Aufklärung im Zivilprozess* (1982), mn. 32; Zöller/Greger, §139, mn. 4; Ch. 6(C)(2)(f).

grundsätzliche Bedeutung), and 3) the development of the law or the preservation of a unified case law does not require a decision of the appellate court, the court can dismiss the appeal as unmeritorious. The dismissal is by simple order (*Beschluss*) rather than complete judgment (*Urteil*). Before entering any such dismissal, the court or the presiding judge must advise the appellant of its intention to do so and the reasons for the contemplated dismissal, and give the appellant time to file written comments (*Stellungnahme*). The court's reasons for the dismissal must be included in the order of dismissal if not already disclosed in the required prior notification to the appellant.[56] An appeal dismissed as unmeritorious is not subject to further appeal.[57]

During this preliminary phase the court also decides whether the appeal should be referred to a single judge for all further proceedings including decision. Prior to the July 2001 reforms all second instance appeals in the state district courts (from non-family court judgments and decisions of the local courts) and in the state appeals courts (from judgments and decisions of the state district courts and of the local courts in family cases) were heard and decided by panels of three judges unless the parties both consented to a decision by a single judge. The role of a single judge was limited to preparatory proceedings and certain other procedural matters.[58]

The new reforms have attempted to enlarge the role of the single judge also at the appellate level. Now an appellate court can refer a second instance appeal (*Berufung*) to a single one of its members for all further proceedings, including argument and decision if, 1) the decision subject to appeal was rendered by a single judge, 2) the case does not present special difficulties of a factual or legal nature (*keine besonderen Schwierigkeiten tatsächlicher oder rechtlicher Art*), 3) the legal controversy has no fundamental significance, and

---

56. ZPO §522(2). For a detailed discussion of this new opportunity to dispose of appeals see Piekenbrock, "Nichtannahme der Berufung? - Kritische Gedanken zu §522 ZPO", 57 *JZ* 540 (2002).

57. ZPO §522(3). This does not prevent an appellant from raising constitutional issues in a constitutional appeal to the Federal Constitutional Court or from applying for a new hearing under ZPO §321a if the right to be heard is affected (see Court of Appeals of Celle, 56 *NJW* 906 (2003); Thomas/Putzo/Reichold, §522, mn. 22). See Ch. 10(F) below for constitutional appeals. If the procedure of the first instance court infringes a party's constitutional rights a summary order will be unconstitutional (Federal Constitutional Court, 56 *NJW* 1924 (2003)), even when the requirements of ZPO §522(2) are met.

58. See ZPO §524 pre-2001 version.

4) oral argument on the merits has not yet been held.[59] A decision referring an appeal to a single judge is not appealable.[60]

If during the course of an appeal referred to a single judge the referee judge decides that by reason of changed circumstances the appeal does present special factual or legal difficulties or the issue is of fundamental significance, the judge may request the appellate court to recommit the case to the 3-judge panel from which it was referred. If after hearing the parties the appellate court agrees, the matter will be returned to the panel. The parties may also unanimously request such a re-committal, but the appellate court is not bound to grant their request. Orders granting or denying requests for re-committal are not subject to appeal. Once recommitted to a panel, the case may not be re-referred to a single judge.[61] This particular provision of the 2001 reform was somewhat controversial among judges and lawyers,[62] and it remains to be seen how much use will be made of it by the appellate courts.

Even if the matter is not referred to a single judge for decision, in second instance appeals many of the preparatory proceedings can be conducted by a "preparing single judge" (*vorbereitender Einzelrichter*).[63] In ordinary civil matters any member of the panel can be designated as the preparing judge. In matters before commercial panels, the presiding judge is automatically designated the preparing judge.[64]

It is the task of the preparing judge to conduct the proceedings to such a point so that they can be disposed of in a single oral argument before the panel. The single judge can even receive oral testimony and other evidence to be reported to the panel "to the extent desirable for simplification of the proceed-

---

59. ZPO § 526(1). If the appellate court is a commercial panel (*Handelskammer*) of the state district court, a referral to a single judge can only be to the presiding judge. ZPO § 526(4). For the use of single judges in state district courts and state courts of appeals see Ch. 3(D)(2)(b) and (3)(b) and Ch. 7(E)(1) above.

60. ZPO § 526(3). See Court of Appeals of Düsseldorf, 34 *NJW* 352 (1981).

61. ZPO § 526(2), (4).

62. See Kraushaar, „Reform der Zivilprozessordnung - Mutig oder mutwillig", 33 *ZRP* 463 (2000); Dauster, „Eckpunkte einer Justizreform - Quo vadis?", 33 *ZRP* 387, 392 ff. (1999); Stürner, "Eckpunkte einer Justizreform", 53 *NJW* Beilage Heft 25, 31 (2000).

63. ZPO § 527(1). The frequency of use of this procedure varies from court to court and panel to panel.

64. ZPO § 527(1)(2). This is to spare the honorary judges (*ehrenamtliche Richter*) who make up the rest of the panel, and as lay persons, would not be in the position to make the legal determinations incident to preparation of the case for oral argument. See Ch. 3(D)(2)(c) above for information on the composition and function of the commercial panels in the state district courts.

ings before the appellate court, if it is anticipated that the appellate court will be able to evaluate the proof without personal impression of the taking of evidence."[65]

If either party defaults or the appeal is withdrawn a single judge of the appeals court, almost always the preparing judge, has the authority to enter any necessary dispository orders and to decide certain subsidiary issues such as liability for costs (to the extent that this was not adjudicated in the court's decision on the merits), the determination of the amount in controversy, and the amounts of costs, fees and expenses.[66]

2. Scope of Review

Although the July 2001 reforms have somewhat restricted the scope of review of facts on appeal, the appeals court continues to exercise a wide ranging oversight over the quality and fairness of the decision below in the interest of reaching a fair and correct ultimate decision of the underlying controversy.

The old Civil Procedure Code provision simply stating that "the controversy as defined by the claims will be argued anew"[67] has been replaced by a more specific provision defining the scope of appellate review. New ZPO § 529 specifically provides that the appeals court is to proceed on the basis of fact findings of the previous instance "so far as no concrete points of reference cast doubt on the correctness or completeness of findings material to a decision and therefore indicate a renewed fact finding"[68] and may entertain new facts "to the extent that their consideration is permissible."[69] Defects in procedure which are not so fundamental as to be subject to review on the court's own motion, may only be noticed if raised in the notice of appeal or an appeal brief

65. ZPO § 527(2)(2) ("*...soweit dies zur Vereinfachung der Verhandlungen vor dem Berufungsgericht wünschenswert und von vornherein anzunehmen ist, dass das Berufungsgericht das Beweisergebnis auch ohne unmittelbaren Eindruck von dem Verlauf der Beweisaufnahme sachgemäss zu würdigen vermag.*"). This provision is slightly altered from the pre-July 27, 2001 version, which had the connotation that reception of proof by a single judge would be the exception, rather than the rule. See ZPO § 524(2) pre-2001 version: "...this may only occur..." ("*...dies darf nur insoweit geschehen...*").

66. ZPO § 527(3).

67. ZPO § 525 pre-2001 version ("*...wird der Rechtsstreit in den durch die Anträge bestimmten Grenzen von neuem verhandelt*").

68. "*...soweit nicht konkrete Anhaltspunkte Zweifel an der Richtigkeit oder Vollständigkeit der entscheidungserheblichen Feststellungen begründen und deshalb eine erneute Feststellung gebieten*".

69. "*...soweit deren Berücksichtigung zulässig ist*".

(*Berufungsschriftsatz*). Otherwise the appeals court is not bound by the asserted legal grounds for review, and may reach a just result within the scope of the claims submitted for review (*Berufungsanträge*), which continue to govern the overall scope of the controversy.[70]

The new law is somewhat more specific than prior law about the court's power to decline to entertain new designations of facts and means of proof in support of a claim (*Angriffsmittel*) or defense (*Verteidigungsmittel*). Assertions of fact and means of proof made and properly dismissed in the first instance are not subject to revival on appeal.[71] Revised ZPO §531 provides that new designations of fact and means of proof may be considered on appeal only 1) if they address a point which was patently overlooked or erroneously considered insignificant by the court of the first instance,[72] 2) were not brought up in the first instance because of a defect in procedure,[73] or 3) were omitted in the first instance proceeding without neglect by the party asserting them on appeal.[74] The appellate court may require that the party making the new designations of fact and means of proof make a plausible showing that they are allowable under these terms.

The extent to which these specific provisions will actually narrow the scope of second instance appeals is currently unclear. While the language is somewhat less permissive than the prior formulation,[75] the express authority to consider new designations of fact and means of proof which were omitted below without neglect should permit the appeals court to entertain new facts and proof under most circumstances when such consideration would be in the interest of justice. Commentary to date on the new provision generally is of the

70. ZPO §528.

71. ZPO §531(1). If the dismissal was unlawful, the appellate court may not uphold it on other grounds, see Federal Supreme Court, 83 BGHZ 371, 378 (1982). However, this provision does not apply if the respective statement becomes non-controversial, see Federal Supreme Court, 76 BGHZ 133, 141 (1980).

72. ZPO §531(2)(1). ("*...einen Gesichtspunkt betreffen, der vom Gericht des ersten Rechtszuges erkennbar übersehen oder für unerheblich gehalten worden ist...*").

73. ZPO §531(2)(2). ("*...infolge eines Verfahrensmangels im ersten Rechtszug nicht geltend gemacht wurden...*").

74. ZPO §531(2)(3). ("*...im ersten Rechtszug nicht geltend gemacht worden sind, ohne dass dies auf einer Nachlässigkeit der Partei beruht*").

75. Prior law allowed new causes of action and defenses when "according to the free conviction of the court the allowance would not delay conclusion of the litigation or if the party gave sufficient excuse for the delay". ZPO §528 pre-2001 version ("*...wenn nach der freien Überzeugung des Gerichts ihre Zulassung die Erledigung des Rechtsstreits nicht verzögern würde oder wenn die Partei die Verspätung genügend entschuldigt*").

view that the traditional scope of second instance appeal will not be fundamentally affected by the new reforms.[76]

The new law has continued prior requirements for timely designations of fact and means of proof within the appellate process. Failure to refer facts or means of proof in the notice of appeal or appeal brief can result in a preclusion from relying on them in the appeal.[77] Waivable objections to the allowability (*Zulässigkeit*) of a complaint which were not included in the notice of appeal or appeal brief may be later asserted only if the movant shows sufficient excuse for the delay.[78] Amendments of the complaint and the assertion of setoffs and counterclaims can take place on appeal with the consent of the opposing party or with leave granted by the appeals court, provided that the amendment, setoff or counterclaim "is supported by facts which the appeals court may in any event consider on the appeal according to ZPO § 529."[79]

Formal stipulations of the parties (*gerichtliche Geständnisse*)[80] and waivers of procedural objections[81] which took place in the first instance proceeding continue to be effective in the second instance appeal.[82]

3. Plenary Proceedings in Second Instance Appeals

Plenary proceedings in a second instance appeal take place before the entire panel of three judges unless the parties have agreed on decision by a single judge (ZPO § 527(4)), or the court has referred the case to a single judge under new ZPO § 526. Proceedings in the appellate courts "are subject to the provisions governing first instance proceedings before the state district courts to the extent that they would not result in deviation from the provisions of

76. See Schellhammer, „Zivilprozessreform und Berufung", 55 *MDR* 1141, 1144 (2001); Schneider, "Die missglückte ZPO-Reform", 54 *NJW* 3756 (2001); Heiderhoff, "Die Tatsachenbindung des Berufungsgerichts nach der ZPO-Reform", 58 *JZ* 490 (2003); Musielak/Ball, § 529, mn. 1; Zöller/Gummer, Vor § 511, mn. 1, who states that one has to wait and see.

77. ZPO §§ 530, 296.

78. ZPO § 532. The fact that the party submitted facts with respect to a favorable decision on the merits is no sufficient excuse for the delay. See Federal Supreme Court, 38 *NJW* 743, 744 (1985).

79. ZPO § 533 ("...*diese auf Tatsachen gestützt werden können, die das Berufungsgericht seiner Verhandlung und Entscheidung über die Berufung ohnehin nach § 529 zugrunde zu legen hat*"). This last provision is a new addition from the July 2001 reform.

80. See Ch. 8(C)(1)(d) above.

81. Under ZPO § 295 if a party fails promptly to object to a procedural defect or to assert the objection at the next scheduled oral argument the defect is generally waived.

82. ZPO §§ 534, 535.

this subpart [regulating appeals]"[83] Oral argument follows a form similar to that in the first instance. The presiding judge opens the proceedings, the parties state their respective claims and requests for relief, and the court enters into a dialogue with the lawyers and occasionally directly with the parties if they are present.[84] If there is additional proof to be heard by the entire tribunal, it is usually taken at this time.[85]

There is no requirement for an early settlement conference as is newly the case with the first instance.[86] However that does not mean that the court does not encourage or participate in settlement discussions at the appellate stage. If either the preparing judge or the panel of deciding judges see an opportunity for a settlement, they can and do raise the topic and pursue the settlement discussions with the parties at the plenary hearing.[87]

Failure of the appellant to participate in oral argument can result in a default judgment dismissing the appeal.[88] If the appellee does not appear, and the appellant moves for a default judgment, the court will decide issues raised by the appeal taking the factual assertions of the appellant to be true.[89]

4. Judgments in Second Instance Appeals

If the grounds asserted for a second instance appeal do not satisfy the appeals court of the error or incompleteness of the decision below, the appellate court can simply affirm the decision of the first instance court . If, on the other hand, the second instance appeal proceedings convince the court that the first instance court erred, the appeals court may either vacate the first instance de-

---

83. ZPO § 525 ("*...sind die im ersten Rechtszuge für das Verfahren vor den Landgerichten geltenden Vorschriften entsprechend anzuwenden, soweit sich nicht Abweichungen aus den Vorschriften dieses Abschnitts ergeben*").

84. As is the case with the first instance, the court can summon the parties to be present at the oral hearing. See ZPO §§ 525, 141, 273(2)(3); Ch. 7(H)(1) above.

85. In cases when the court is of the view "that an immediate impression of the taking of proof" ("*unmittelbarer Eindruck von dem Verlauf der Beweisaufnahme*") is necessary for the evaluation of the proof, the reception of the evidence is not delegated to the preparing judge, ZPO § 527(2).

86. ZPO § 525(2).

87. ZPO § 278(1) applies in the second instance appeal with as much force as in the initial proceeding. See Thomas/Putzo/Reichold, § 525, mn. 2.

88. ZPO §539(1). The provisions relating to default judgments in the state district court apply to default judgments entered on appeals.

89. ZPO § 539(2). The appellant may also request that the court decide the appeal on the basis of the record (*Entscheidung nach Lage der Akten*). See Rosenberg/Schwab/Gottwald, § 139(V)(4), p. 847.

cision and remand the case with instructions to the court below correcting the error or the appeals court may enter its own judgment determining the merits of the case.

According to the new reforms to the Civil Procedure Code the appeals court is generally expected to enter its own decision of the case rather than remand the case to the first instance court for correction of the error.[90] This is true even if the appeals court reaches a result different from the first instance judgment based on new evidence heard for the first time in the appeals court. There is no requirement that the first instance court have the "first crack" at fact finding if the appeals court finds that the evidence justifies a different result.[91] The competence and duty of the appeals court to reach a decision on the merits reflects the policy in favor of streamlining proceedings rather than protracting them by remands.

On the other hand, the appeals court is authorized and expected to remand a case to the first instance court for further proceedings on motion of a party in a number of circumstances. Remand is justified, for example, if the appellate court finds that the procedure in the first instance "suffered from a material defect" (*an einem wesentlichen Mangel leidet*) and because of this defect, a "comprehensive or detailed reception of evidence is necessary."[92] Cases may also be remanded if the decision reversed was an early dismissal on the ground of legal unallowability (*Unzulässigkeit*), when an application to set aside a default judgment was originally disallowed, and in a number of other circumstances where the first instance court did not have opportunity to consider the factual merits of the claim.[93] The idea is that if the first instance court has not had a chance to consider any facts relative to the case, it may be more efficient to remand the case in hopes that the first instance court will render a decision acceptable to the parties. However if the case has proceeded through a more or less complete process of consideration by the first instance court, the appeals court should enter its own decision on the merits in the interest of sparing the litigants further procedural delay.[94]

Judgment in a second instance appeal can be rendered either at the end of the plenary hearing or at a special hearing convened for that purpose. The

90. ZPO §538(1).

91. This does not mean that litigants can ignore the first instance. As indicated in Ch. 10(E)(2) and (3) above, the appeals court can consider causes of action and evidence not offered in the first instance only under limited circumstances.

92. ZPO §538(2)(1) (*eine umfangreiche oder aufwändige Beweisaufnahme notwendig ist*).

93. See ZPO §538(2) for a listing of the circumstances under which remand is authorized.

94. See, e.g., Rosenberg/Schwab/Gottwald, §140(IV)(5), p. 854; Lüke, §35(IV), mn. 403; Federal Supreme Court, 46 *NJW* 2318 (1993); 55 *NJW* 2795 (2002).

form of judgment generally follows that of all German civil judgments.[95] The new reforms require judgments of appellate courts to refer to facts found by the first instance court which were relied on by the appellate court, to describe any alterations or departures from the first instance fact findings, and briefly to explain the reasons for alteration, vacation or affirmance of the judgment under appeal.[96] If the judgment is rendered at the end of the plenary oral argument, the references to the fact findings and any departures or revisions can be made orally and incorporated in the minutes (*Protokolle*) of the hearing.[97] The time for further appeal begins to run with the service or rendition of the appellate judgment.[98]

Following rendition of the judgment the appellate court is required to return the cumulative record of the case including a certified copy of the judgment on appeal to the court of the first instance.[99]

E. Review Appeals

The second instance appeal (*Berufung*) is intended to provide comprehensive review of the legal and factual regularity of a civil judgment and the proceedings in which it was rendered. Further judicial review beyond the second instance appeal is limited to what is in effect a discretionary review appeal (*Revision*) on issues of law and procedure only to Germany's Federal Supreme Court.[100] The purpose of such review appeal is not primarily to obtain correct justice in the individual case. More important to the court's willingness to decide any given review appeal is the significance of the issue presented to the system of justice as a whole. The decisions of the Federal Supreme Court of Justice serve to unify and rationalize Germany's entire system of civil justice.

---

95. See Ch. 9(B)(3) above on form of civil judgments.

96. ZPO §540. The appellate court may also render the judgment pursuant to ZPO §313, see Thomas/Putzo, §540, mn. 1.

97. Judgments in which no further appeal is conceivable, default judgments, and the like may be abbreviated. See ZPO §§540(2), 313a and 313b.

98. See Ch. 10(E)(1) below.

99. ZPO §541(2).

100. For a description of the composition and jurisdiction of the Federal Supreme Court see Ch. 3(D)(4) above. Appeals from state appeals courts in Bavaria which predominantly raise issues of Bavarian state law can be filed in the Bavarian State Supreme Court (*Bayerisches Oberstes Landesgericht*), which can then proceed also to decide contested issues of federal law. See Keidel, „Die Revision in Zivilsachen gegen Urteile bayerischer Oberlandesgerichte (Landgerichte)", 14 *NJW* 2333 (1961); Zöller/Gummer, EGGVG §8, mn. 3 ff.

The July 2001 German civil procedure reforms have replaced the former jurisdiction of the Federal Supreme Court of Justice, which was based partly on jurisdictional amount, with a pure discretionary jurisdiction limited to cases in which permission to appeal have been granted by state appeals courts or the Federal Supreme Court itself.[101] This reform has rationalized and streamlined a jurisdiction which had previously generated an overburden of review appeals as of right[102] which of necessity were disposed of by summary decisions.[103] The reforms should enable the Federal Supreme Court to concentrate its energies on its fundamental responsibility to render authoritative construction, interpretation and unification of the law of Germany.[104]

1. Initiation of Review appeals

A party seeking discretionary review appeal from a judgment rendered in a second instance appeal must first apply to the court which rendered the decision in question. The second instance appellate court[105] has the authority to make a determination binding on the Federal Supreme Court that a case before it is of "fundamental significance" (*grundsätzliche Bedeutung*) or that "the development of the law or the securing of a unified case law requires a decision of the Federal Supreme Court" (*die Fortbildung des Rechts oder die Sicherung einer einheitlichen Rechtsprechung eine Entscheidung des Revisionsgerichts erfordert*) and thereby authorize a review appeal from its judgment to the Federal Supreme Court.[106] Ordinarily this determination is to be contained in the judgment itself. If the judgment is silent on the point, presumably a party may be

101. See ZPO §§542, 543(1).

102. Under the previous regime a party could file a review appeal as of right to the Federal Supreme Court if the amount in controversy exceeded 60,000 DM. This jurisdiction resulted in a large number of appeals raising questions of relatively little legal significance. For instance, in 1998 some 6096 cases were appealed to the Federal Supreme Court, the great bulk of them based on the jurisdictional amount. For details and references see Ch. 3(D)(4) and (K) above.

103. For instance, in 1998 the Federal Supreme Court disposed of some 2141 of the cases appealed to it by summary decision as insubstantial. See Ch. 3(D)(4) and (K) above.

104. This purpose of the reform is severely criticized by the German Lawyers Association; see "Thesen des Deutschen Anwaltsvereins", 2000 *AnwBl.* 178 (2000); Büttner, "Revisionsverfahren - Änderungen durch das Zivilprozessreformgesetz", 55 *MDR* 1201 (2001).

105. The state district court in second instance appeals from decisions of the local courts and the state appeals court in second instance appeals from decisions of the state district courts. See Ch. 3(D) above.

106. ZPO §543(1). See Thomas/Putzo/Reichold, §543, mn. 12.

entitled to apply for a completion or alteration of the judgment.[107] If the judgment contains the necessary determination, the party aggrieved must file its notice of appeal within one month of service of the second instance appellate judgment and in no event later than 5 months after rendition of the judgment.[108]

The notice of appeal (*Revisionsschrift*) need only contain a designation of the judgment from which review appeal is being taken and a statement that the appellant is appealing on grounds of law or procedure from this judgment.[109] The notice of appeal must be accompanied by a certified copy of the judgment under appeal. The court must serve a copy of the notice of appeal on the opposing party.[110]

The notice of appeal and any other papers filed with the Federal Supreme Court in civil cases must be signed by a member of the bar of that court. As indicated above[111] the bar of the Federal Supreme Court consists of a small, select group of appellate specialists who limit their practices to Federal Supreme Court appeals. Although the lawyer who handled the case below may participate in the preparation of briefs and other papers to be filed, a Federal Supreme Court practitioner must have the final word on all written filings and presentations and will conduct the entire oral argument.[112]

If the second instance appellate court refuses to give permission for a further appeal of law and procedure, the party aggrieved can lodge a miscellaneous appeal from denial of permission (*Nichtzulassungsbeschwerde*) with the Federal Supreme Court of Justice within one month of service of the appeals court judgment.[113] There is an expedited procedure for consideration of these appeals. Written substantiation (*Begründung*) of the miscellaneous appeal must be filed within two months of service of the appeals court judgment. The substantiation must describe the issue sought to be appealed with particularity and address the criteria for allowance set forth in ZPO §543(2). The opposing party is then given an opportunity for comment (*Stellungnahme*)

---

107. For a description of these procedures see Ch. 9(D) above. See Thomas/Putzo/Reichold, §543, mn. 7; Zöller, §319, mn. 16; Federal Supreme Court, 16 *NJW-RR* 61 (2001).

108. ZPO §548.

109. ZPO §549.

110. ZPO §550. See Ch. 10(D)(1) above for parallel provisions in case of second instance appeals.

111. See Ch. 4(D)(5) above.

112. The lawyer who conducted the second instance appeal may be present at the oral argument along with her Federal Supreme Court colleague, and might be permitted to answer a question from one of the judges or make supplementary comments or remarks.

113. ZPO §544(1). The lodging of the procedural appeal suspends the legal effectiveness (*Rechtskraft*) of the judgment appealed from, ZPO §544(5).

and the Federal Supreme Court of Justice decides the issue by summary order (*Beschluss*). An adverse decision should be briefly supported with written reasons (*begründet*) unless the court does not deem reasons necessary to give guidance to the bar about the conditions under which permission is generally granted or denied.[114] If the Federal Supreme Court denies the miscellaneous appeal, the judgment appealed from becomes final and not subject to further appeal.[115]

If the miscellaneous appeal is sustained (*stattgegeben*) the case proceeds as a review appeal in the Federal Supreme Court. The timely initiation of the miscellaneous appeal counts as filing a notice of appeal with permission.[116] The time for filing the brief in support of the review appeal starts to run with the service of the decision granting the miscellaneous appeal.

This new process of screening virtually all review appeals based on the significance of the legal issue may present constitutional questions. The pre-reform framework provided for discretionary acceptance of review appeals with amounts in controversy less than the 60,000 DM jurisdictional minimum based on a similar standard.[117] The Federal Constitutional Court ruled, however, that to apply a standard that required a minimum level of legal significance to some, but not all appeals, could violate the right of a fair legal hearing. The Constitution would permit the Federal Supreme Court to reject a legally insignificant appeal only if it would also have no chance on the merits.[118] The new statutory regime subjects all appeals, regardless of amount in controversy, to the same standard for acceptance. This circumstance should suffice to differentiate the current statutory arrangement from the scheme which aroused the concern of the Federal Constitutional Court.

---

114. ZPO §544(3) and (4).

115. ZPO §544(5). This does not prevent a party from attacking the constitutionality of the judgment by constitutional appeal (*Verfassungsbeschwerde*) to the Federal Constitutional Court. A judgment may be unconstitutional if a statute on which it is based, the interpretation of a statutory provision, or case law created by the decision does not conform to the requirements of the German constitution. For a most recent example see Federal Constitutional Court, 56 *NJW* 1924 (2003). See Ch. 3(E) above on the jurisdiction of the Federal Constitutional Court and Ch. 10 (H) below for a brief description of the process of constitutional appeals.

116. ZPO §§544(6), 549, 551(2).

117. See ZPO §546 pre-2001 version.

118. Federal Constitutional Court, 49 BVerfGE 148 (1979). The plenum of the Federal Constitutional Court later decided that former ZPO §554b should be construed as a basis for rejection for non-meritorious appeals rather than a process for discretionary acceptance of some, but not all appeals. See 54 BVerfGE 277 (1981).

The debate surrounding the adoption of the new standard of acceptability for review appeals to the Federal Supreme Court continues even after the legislation has come into effect. The main issue is the construction and interpretation of the requirement that acceptance of the appeal further the interest of "securing a unified case law."[119]

The Federal Supreme Court has adopted a very restrictive understanding of this requirement for permission to lodge a review appeal. A showing that the decision of the court below may be the result of a serious error of substantive law or procedure is not enough. According to the narrow construction of the Federal Supreme Court the requirement of "securing a unified case law" is met only by a case which actually diverges from existing case law or which poses real danger that the same or other courts will repeat or imitate the same error.[120]

An infringement of constitutional rights that could support a constitutional appeal to the Federal Constitutional Court may also fulfill the requirements of "fundamental significance" or "securing of a unified case law".[121] Acceptance of such cases gives the ordinary courts opportunity to correct constitutional errors themselves without burdening the Federal Constitutional Court.[122]

The future development is not foreseeable. It is possible that the Federal Supreme Court may yield to the influence of very critical comments of scholars and practitioners or perhaps a future decision of the Federal Constitutional Court and adopt a broader construction of the requirements for permission to lodge a review appeal. The present understanding is very narrow and may create injustice and dissatisfaction.[123]

2. Scope of Review

The basic premise for review by the Federal Supreme Court is that the decision under appeal "rests on a violation of federal law or of some other legal provision that has a realm of application greater than a state appeals court dis-

---

119. ZPO § 543(2)(2) (*die Sicherung einer einheitlichen Rechtsprechung*).

120. See Federal Supreme Court, 55 *NJW* 2957 (2002); 56 *NJW* 754 (2003); 56 *NJW* 831 (2003); 56 *NJW* 2012 (2003).

121. Federal Supreme Court, 56 NJW 65 (2003); 56 NJW 2011 (2003).

122. See Federal Constitutional Court, 56 *NJW* 1924 (2003) (en banc decision with further references).

123. For detailed discussion see Piekenbrock/Schulze, "Die Zulassung der Revision nach dem ZPO-Reformgesetz", 57 *JZ* 911 (2002); Nasall, "Irrwege. Wege. - Die Rechtsmittelzulassung durch den BGH", 56 *NJW* 1345 (2003).

trict."[124] If the issue in dispute is one of state law, and the state is composed of a single appeals court district, the Federal Supreme Court will not intervene. A review appeal cannot be based solely on the claim that the court of the first instance erred in the assumption or declination of subject matter jurisdiction or venue.[125]

A reviewable violation of federal law can consist either of a failure to observe correct procedure in the lower court's conduct of the case (*Prozessverstoss*) or the court's failure to observe and properly apply a provision of substantive law in its decision (*Verletzung des materiellen Rechts*). A violation of substantive law can occur when the court applies a legal rule in the absence of the required fact findings or fails to apply a legal rule despite findings of facts indicating that the rule should be applied.[126]

ZPO § 547 sets forth a number of circumstances under which it is conclusively presumed that the judgment below rests on a failure to observe correct procedure (*absolute Revisionsgründe*). These range from improper composition of the court below, to violations of the requirement of publicity for plenary hearings, to failure of the decision under review to contain a written explanation of the court's reasons (*Gründe*) when such reasons are required by statute.

The court may review errors not only in the final judgment (*Endurteil*) but also in decisions preceding the final judgment which have affected the final judgment and are not independently subject to review. The court is obliged to consider only matters within the scope of the claims for relief asserted by the parties. However the court is not bound to the reasoning of the parties concerning substantive law. Procedural errors not required to be noticed on the court's own motion will be considered only if substantiated in a party's brief.[127]

---

124. ZPO § 545 ("...*auf der Verletzung des Bundesrechts oder einer Vorschrift beruht, deren Geltungsbereich sich über den Bezirk eines Oberlandesgerichts hinaus erstreckt.*"). Law is "violated" (*verletzt*) when a legal norm is not applied, or not correctly applied in the decision under review. ZPO § 546. An appeal to the Bavarian State Supreme Court requires an issue of Bavarian state law. See EGGVG § 8(2).

125. ZPO § 545(2). But improper assertion of international jurisdiction can be the basis for review appeal. See Federal Supreme Court, 94 BGHZ 156 (1985); 57 *NJW* 426 (2003). See Ch. 5(F) and Ch. 10(D) above, Ch. 12(B)(5) below.

126. Rosenberg/Schwab/Gottwald, § 143(IV), p. 875. The failure can be the result of oversight, improper interpretation of the law, or improper application of the law to the relevant facts.

127. ZPO § 557. See Ch. 7(E) above for procedural matters which the court must consider on its own motion.

Review of facts and fact findings on review appeal is very limited. There is no provision for taking of additional evidence at this stage of the proceedings. The Federal Supreme Court is obliged to rely on fact findings of the decision below as supplemented by minutes of the state appeals court hearings (*Sitzungsprotokolle*) for all facts relevant to the substantive issues under consideration. If the state appeals court has determined a party's assertion of fact to be true or untrue, the Federal Supreme Court must, in principal, accept the appeals court's determination. This does not, however, mean that the court must accept findings which were reached in violation of correct procedure or which conflict with the processes of rational reasoning, the laws of nature or established scientific knowledge.[128]

Additional facts not referred to in the findings and minutes below may be considered on review appeal only if they appear in the record of the case (*Akte*) and were not previously considered as a result of procedural error by the lower court.[129] In this limited sense it is sometimes possible for the review appeals court to base its decision on facts not considered by the second instance court.[130]

In transnational cases the correct application of foreign law may be in dispute. The rules of choice of law or conflicts of laws are federal law and their improper application is a reviewable violation of federal law.[131] The rules of the foreign law themselves are in some respects treated like facts which must be proved.[132] It is the responsibility of the court to clarify the content of foreign statutory and case law and to take evidence when the content of foreign law is in dispute. This is true even when the parties to litigation agree on the content of foreign law if there are remaining contradictions or inconsistencies that recommend further clarification.[133]

A review appeal may be based on improper application of evidentiary rules when clarifying the contents of foreign law. Usually the court has to order expert evidence for reliable clarification of questions of foreign law. A lack of

---

128. See ZPO §559; Thomas/Putzo/Reichold, §559, mn. 15 ff.

129. ZPO §559(1)(2) and §551(3)(2)(b). See Thomas/Putzo/Reichold, §559, mn. 10.

130. See Rosenberg/Schwab/Gottwald, §146(II)(2)(b), pp. 890 f.

131. See Federal Supreme Court, 136 BGHZ 380, 386 (1997); Thomas/Putzo/Reichold, §545, mn. 10.

132. See ZPO §293. The wording of this section is ultimately somewhat unclear as to who bears the responsibility of educating the court in foreign law and how this is to be accomplished.

133. See Federal Supreme Court, 49 *NJW* 54, 55 (1996); 45 *NJW* 2026, 2029 (1992); 17 *NJW-RR* 1359 (2002); 136 BGHZ 380, 386 (1997); Thomas/Putzo/Reichold, §293, mn. 4.

expert evidence supporting a significant provision of governing foreign law is generally considered as a violation of evidentiary rules.[134]

3. Procedure on Review Appeal

An appellant has up to two months following service of the judgment within which to file a review appeal brief (*Revisionsbegründung*) explaining its grounds for the review appeal.[135] The review appeal brief must set forth the appellants "claims on appeal" (*Revisionsanträge*), consisting of an explanation of the extent to which the judgment is being appealed, i.e. the scope of the appeal, plus a specification of what changes are being sought in the judgment below.[136] The brief must also particularize the circumstances constituting the claimed violation of law by the court or courts below, and set forth a specific description of any facts forming the basis of a claimed violation of procedural requirements.[137] Finally, the brief in support of the appeal also sets forth the appellant's written arguments supporting its claim of error in the decision below, together with citations to statutory authority, case law, and scholarly commentary.

Upon the filing of the brief in support of the appeal, the court is required to determine on its own motion whether the appeal appears to be allowable (*an sich statthaft*) and has timely been filed and supported with an appeal brief in proper form. If no brief is filed or if any of these requirements is not met, the appeal will be dismissed by simple order (*Beschluss*).[138]

If the appeal is deemed allowable, the court will set a date for oral argument and so advise the parties.[139] In the meantime, the opposing party will

---

134. See Federal Supreme Court, 45 *NJW* 2026, 2029 (1992); 55 *NJW* 3335 (2002); Thomas/Putzo/Reichold, §293, mn. 10. For further details see Spickhoff, "Fremdes Recht vor inländischen Gerichten: Rechts- oder Tatfrage?", 112 *ZZP* 265 (1999). For expert testimony see Ch. 8(C)(7) above.

135. This time is automatically enlarged when the appeal is permitted by allowance of a procedural appeal from a denial of permission. The time may be further enlarged by the presiding judge upon agreement of the parties or for up to two months without agreement if the presiding judge believes that enlargement would not materially delay decision of the case or if the appellant raises substantial grounds for the enlargement. ZPO §551(2). Such enlargements of time are relatively common in practice.

136. ZPO §551(3)(1).

137. ZPO §551(3). If permission to appeal was given by decision of a procedural appeal from a state appeals court denial of permission, the appeals brief can only advance grounds for appeal which were contained in substantiation of the procedural appeal. ZPO §551(3)(2).

138. ZPO §552.

139. ZPO §553.

be given opportunity to file its own brief in opposition to the appeal, and to lodge its own cross review appeal (*Anschlussrevision*).

A cross review appeal can raise any error of law or procedure in the judgment or proceedings below that could have been raised by the cross-appellant on its own appeal. The notice of cross appeal (*Anschlussschrift*) must be filed within a month of the filing of the appeal brief (*Begründung*) of the original appellant, and must include the elements required in a substantiating brief such as the claims for relief on the cross appeal (*Anschlussrevisionsanträge*), description of the errors alleged, legal arguments, etc.[140] A party can file a cross review appeal even if the time for filing an original appeal has run or if it has already waived its right to appeal. Permission for a cross appeal is not required. However if the appeal in chief is dismissed as not allowable (*unzulässig*) or is withdrawn, the cross appeal lapses.[141]

Subsequent procedure on review appeal follows a pattern similar to the procedure on second instance appeals before the state appeals courts.[142] Because the issues are limited to issues of law and correct procedure, preparatory hearings or proceedings before a preparing judge (*vorbereitender Richter*) are not common. There is no provision for referral of review appeals to a single judge for decision. Nor is there any kind of settlement conference required.[143]

4. Oral Argument in the Federal Supreme Court

The principal of orality (*Mündlichkeitsprinzip*) applies to proceedings in the Federal Supreme Court with as much force as in the other courts. No judgment will be rendered on a contested review appeal without hearing the parties at oral argument.[144] Unless an appeal is dismissed early on as legally unallowable (*unzulässig*), the parties and their counsel can expect to be heard by a panel of the Federal Supreme Court in plenary proceedings.

---

140. ZPO §554(3).

141. ZPO §554(4). This means that a party who wishes to be sure of obtaining review of the judgment below regardless of the fate of an opponent's appeal cannot rely on a cross appeal but must obtain permission and lodge its own appeal. For second instance cross appeal see Ch. 10(C) above.

142. See ZPO §§525, 555.

143. See ZPO §555. However the admonition of ZPO §278(1) that the court should encourage the parties to settle the case at all stages of the proceeding applies even at the review appeal stage, and cases are sometimes settled in the course of review appeal proceedings.

144. If the appellee fails to appear at oral argument and if the appeal is justified the court can issue a default judgment (*Versäumnisurteil*). ZPO §§331, 555. See Thomas/Putzo/Reichold, §555, mn. 5; Zöller/Gummer, §555, mn. 4.

In general the oral argument takes place before a panel of at least 5 judges from one of the 12 civil senates. Cases are assigned to senates based on the subject matter of the case.[145] The presiding justice of each senate assigns cases to panels of the senate based on a case assignment plan of general applicability.[146]

Each case is generally assigned to one of the members of the panel who acts as "reporting judge" (*Berichterstatter*) and carefully reviews the case record and briefs prior to the oral argument. The reporting judge will generally prepare a memorandum of opinion (*Gutachten*) or recommended decision (*Votum*) and circulate it among the colleagues on the panel to prepare them for the oral hearing.

The oral proceedings in one of the hearing rooms of the Federal Supreme Court in Karlsruhe can be impressive. The judges are clad in maroon robes and traditional headware. Counsel are attired in robes of their own. The judges occupy a long, sometimes curved bench along one wall of the room, counsel are situated at small tables with podia on either side, and there is generally space for the clients or onlookers on benches at the back of the chamber.

Counsel for each party are invited to address the court on the issues raised by the review appeal.[147] Although the tone and order of argument is more formal than in the lower courts, questions from the presiding judge, the reporting judge, or other members of the panel are common, and it is not unusual for the court to go back and forth between the two lawyers on a particular point or issue.

Since the advocates come from a small exclusive group well known to the judges of the court,[148] the tone of the argument is that of a respectful conversation among colleagues rather than that of a speech or oration. Argumentation is usually concise and logically rigorous. Raised voices and appeals to emotion are out of the question.

Even at the review appeal level, the judges use the oral argument to give the parties judicial hints and feedback (*richterliche Hinweise*) on their tentative eval-

145. See GVG §21e. The various senates have different subject matter focuses. See Ch. 3(D)(4) above for a discussion of the composition and expertises of the various senates.

146. The idea is that the case assignments should not depend on the individual cases or the personnel involved. See GVG §21g; GG Article 101(1)(2); Federal Constitutional Court, 50 *NJW* 1497 (1997). The case assignment plan is decided on by a majority of the members of the senate at the beginning of each year.

147. Although the parties may be, and often are, present for the oral argument, the court does not generally address them directly. Their respective contentions are stated through their counsel.

148. For a description of the composition of the bar of the Federal Supreme Court see Ch. 4(D)(5) above.

uations of the issues.[149] Sometimes a lawyer can straighten out a wrong assumption or misconception in these exchanges. In any case, the lawyers are apprised of the court's likely direction and can marshal their best arguments.

As is the case with other judgments, the judgments of the Federal Supreme Court are rendered orally. Sometimes the oral rendition of judgment will take place the same day as the oral argument.[150] Otherwise the court will convene a session for the rendition of judgments (*Verkündungstermin*) at a later date.[151]

5. Judgments on Appeals of Law and Procedure

The senates of the Federal Supreme Court reach their decisions based on a process of collegial deliberation (*Beratung*) and vote (*Abstimmung*). Only those members of the senate who participated in the oral hearing may deliberate and vote on the decision.[152]

Deliberation is secret. Usually the members of the panel assemble to consider several appeals. The memorandum or proposed judgment often forms the basis for the discussion. The presiding judge presides over sessions for deliberation, although the reporting judge will often take a leading role in the discussion of a particular case.

Once the matter has been discussed to the satisfaction of the presiding judge and other members of the panel it is in order for vote. Decisions are based on a majority vote of the panel. Once a panel has voted on a particular disposition, that becomes the judgment of the senate, and the reporting judge or other member assigned to draft the judgment is required accurately to incorporate the result and reasoning of the majority whatever may be her personal opinion.[153] The majority judgment is then signed by each member of the court, again regardless of personal opinion, and becomes the judgment of the court. Dissenting opinions are not permitted.

Judgments of the Federal Supreme Court follow the form of other civil judgments and contain the same elements.[154]

---

149. See Ch. 6(C)(2) above on the duty to give judicial hints and feedback.

150. It is not uncommon for the court to hear oral argument during the morning and then reassemble after lunch to render judgments in those cases ripe for rendition at that time.

151. See Ch. 9(B)(4) above for the procedure on rendition of judgments.

152. ZPO §§ 555, 309. For the process of deliberation of judgments see Ch. 9(B)(2) above.

153. In cases where the reporting judge is in the minority another judge may be assigned to draft the key portions of the judgment.

154. See Ch. 9(B)(3) above for the form and contents of civil judgments.

If the court finds legal error (*Rechtsverstoss*) in the judgment or proceedings below and the error had a causal effect (*ursächlich war*)[155] on the lower court's judgment, the appeal is justified (*begründet*). On the other hand, a finding of no error, or that any error did not affect the judgment below results in a dismissal of the appeal as unfounded (*unbegründet*).[156]

Once the Federal Supreme Court has determined that a review appeal is justified, the court has several choices for disposition. Its decision can vacate the decision below to the extent that the latter rests on errors of law or resulted from errors in procedure.[157] In many cases correction of the error of the court below will require that the case be remanded to the lower court, which can then reconsider the case based on correct procedures and any additional facts rendered relevant by the applicable law as determined by the Federal Supreme Court.[158] The Federal Supreme Court must set forth in its decision the legal analysis (*rechtliche Beurteilung*) which led to the vacation of the lower court's decision.[159] If the lower court's error was one of law, but no additional fact findings would be necessary or appropriate to reach a decision based on the correct legal rule, the Federal Supreme Court may apply the correct legal rule to the facts found by the courts below and decide the case itself.[160] In all cases, however, when additional fact determinations would be potentially relevant to a proper application of the law, the Federal Supreme Court must remand to the second-instance court for the necessary fact finding.[161]

---

155. Errors in substantive law would generally be considered causal if the decision cannot be supported on another legal basis. However procedural errors may or may not affect the substantive correctness of the judgment rendered in the proceeding in which they occur. Ordinarily the appellant has the burden of convincing the court that a procedural error led to a defect in the judgment rendered. ZPO § 545. Certain serious errors of procedure or a cumulation of several procedural errors are presumed to have affected the correctness of the judgment and can support a review appeal without the need to prove special causality. See ZPO § 547 and Ch. 10(E)(2) above.

156. ZPO § 561.

157. ZPO § 562.

158. ZPO § 563(1). In extreme cases of gross substantive error or procedural misconduct the Federal Supreme Court may remand the case to a panel of the state appeals court or state district court other than the panel which rendered the decision below.

159. ZPO § 563(2). The Federal Supreme Court may remand the case to the first-instance court if it determines that the appellate court itself should have remanded the case. See Federal Supreme Court, 53 *NJW* 575 (2000); Thomas/Putzo/Reichold, § 563, mn. 15. For appellate judgments of remand see Ch. 10(D)(4) above.

160. See ZPO § 563(3); Federal Supreme Court, 122 BGHZ 308, 316 (1993).

161. See, e.g., Rosenberg/Schwab/Gottwald, § 146(II)(2), pp. 889 f.

When a matter is remanded to the lower court based on a finding of substantive or procedural error by the Federal Supreme Court, the lower court is bound by the law or procedural rule as announced by the Federal Supreme Court in all further proceedings in that case.[162] Other lower courts are not so bound although they pay serious attention to published Federal Supreme Court decisions as indicators of likely dispositions in review appeals of their own judgments. According to the prevailing opinion, in future review appeals in the same case, the Federal Supreme Court is itself bound to the law as declared by it in prior appeals in that case.[163] In any event, the Federal Supreme Court is never bound to follow its prior legal rulings in other cases, although it gives prior rulings considerable deference in the interest of maintaining the consistency and predictability of the law.[164]

6. Direct Review Appeal

In certain cases where the facts found by the first-instance court are not in dispute, and where the issue on appeal is solely a question of law, the aggrieved party may elect to bypass the second-instance appeal and seek permission for a direct review appeal (*Sprungrevision*) in the Federal Supreme Court.[165] The idea is to avoid the cost and delay of a superfluous second-instance appeal and obtain an authoritative determination of the disputed legal issue directly from the highest court.

The preconditions for seeking a direct review appeal are agreement by the parties[166] and an important substantive legal issue[167] which does not require additional fact finding beyond that which occurred in the first-instance proceeding. The standard of significance of the legal issue is the same as for review appeals by permission of the state appeals court, namely that the issue is

---

162. ZPO §563(2); see Rosenberg/Schwab/Gottwald, §146(III)(3), pp. 891 ff.; Lüke, §36(III), mn. 417; Federal Supreme Court, 132 BGHZ 6, 10 (1995).

163. See Federal Supreme Court, 25 BGHZ 200, 203 (1958); Thomas/Putzo/Reichold, §563, mn. 10. However, the Federal Supreme Court is not bound if it has published a differing decision in another case. See 60 BGHZ 392, 397 ff. (1973).

164. Although German courts do not formally recognize the doctrine of *stare decisis*, as a practical matter case law of the Federal Supreme Court plays an important role in filling out the general and abstract provisions of codified law in German civil justice.

165. ZPO §566.

166. ZPO §566(1)(1) and (2)(4). A statement of agreement signed by the opponent's lawyer must be included with the application or filed with the Federal Supreme Court within the time for filing an appeal. See Rosenberg/Schwab/Gottwald, §142(I)(3), p. 864.

167. An asserted procedural error cannot be used as the basis for a direct review appeal. ZPO §566(4)(2).

of "fundamental significance" (*grundsätzliche Bedeutung*) or that the "development of the law or the securing of a unified case law requires a decision of the Federal Supreme Court."[168]

Application for permission for direct review appeal is filed in the Federal Supreme Court. The application must set forth the same kind of information that would be contained in a notice of review appeal.[169] The opponent has the right to file written comments, which must confirm the opponent's agreement to the request, but may also argue that the legal issue does not meet the criteria for acceptance by the review appeals court. There is no oral argument on the application for permission for direct appeal. Decision of the court is by simple order. If the permission is granted, the filing of the application counts as the initiation of the appeal and subsequent time periods start to run with the service of the order granting permission.[170]

Denial of permission for direct review appeal is not subject to further appeal or reconsideration and makes the judgment below final.[171] Having elected to seek a direct review appeal, the disappointed applicant does not have the option to proceed with a regular second instance appeal. This feature, as well as the relatively low percentage of acceptances of direct review appeals, have meant that the direct review appeal procedure is seldom used.

F. Miscellaneous Appeals

In many cases a party or other affected person[172] aggrieved by a court order or disposition (*Beschluss, Verfügung*) other than a judgment (*Urteil*)[173] may obtain review of the order or disposition by miscellaneous appeal (*Beschwerde*). Miscellaneous appeal is available in all cases in which it is authorized by statute as well as in all cases "in which a request by a party which would affect the on-

168. ZPO §566(4)(1) and (2) ("...*die Fortbildung des Rechts oder die Sicherung einer einheitlichen Rechtsprechung eine Entscheidung des Revisionsgerichts erfordert*").

169. See ZPO §§566(2)(1), 548–550 and Ch. 10(E)(1) above.

170. ZPO §566(7). If the direct review appeal results in a remand, that remand is to the first instance court from which the direct review appeal was made. ZPO §566(8).

171. ZPO §566(6).

172. Such as a defaulting witness ordered to pay costs under ZPO §380. See Rosenberg/Schwab/Gottwald, §147(III)(5)(b), p. 898.

173. As a matter of principle the criterion distinguishing between judgments (*Urteile*) subject to second instance appeal and orders and dispositions (*Beschlüsse* and *Verfügungen*) subject to miscellaneous appeal is whether the law required oral hearing prior to entry of the decision, not whether oral proceedings in fact took place. Rosenberg/Schwab/Gottwald, §147(III)(4)(a), p. 897.

going proceedings is denied by a decision not requiring oral hearing and argument."[174] Case law also permits miscellaneous appeals of otherwise unappealable orders in certain extreme cases in which the order lacks any legal basis and is in content alien to law.[175] Examples of the kinds of orders and dispositions which are subject to miscellaneous appeal include orders on applications for recusal of a judge,[176] orders of the clerk of courts setting court costs,[177] decisions on applications for legal aid,[178] denials of applications for default judgments,[179] decisions on evidentiary privileges of witnesses[180] and contempt rulings (*Ordnungsmittel*) against parties and others.[181]

Traditionally there was no particular time period for lodging many miscellaneous appeals, and the procedure under which they were handled tended to extend and slow the case. The July 2001 reform has introduced a general time period for lodging a miscellaneous appeal and has otherwise sought to tighten and streamline the miscellaneous appeal procedure without otherwise restricting availability of the remedy. It remains to be seen whether these measures will affect the time required to bring a case to a final judgment.

1. Initiation of Miscellaneous Appeals

A miscellaneous appeal is filed either in the court which issued the order or disposition challenged, or in the next higher court (*Beschwerdegericht*),

174. ZPO § 567(1)(2) ("...*es sich um solche eine mündliche Verhandlung nicht erfordernde Entscheidungen handelt, durch die ein das Verfahren betreffendes Gesuch zurückgewiesen worden ist*").

175. Federal Supreme Court, 28 BGHZ 349 (1958). See Rosenberg/Schwab/Gottwald, §147(III)(3), pp. 896 f. However, after the new legislation of July 27, 2001, the allowability of an extraordinary miscellaneous appeal is again in dispute. According to recent decisions of the Federal Supreme Court, if a decision violates constitutional rights, the party aggrieved may lodge a remonstrance in the court making the decision in question. See ZPO § 321a. If that court does not remedy the remonstrance, its decision may only be appealed to the Federal Constitutional Court. See Federal Supreme Court, 55 *NJW* 1577 (2002); Federal Supreme Tax Court, 56 *NJW* 919 (2003). The most recent decision of the Federal Constitutional Court (56 *NJW* 1924 (2003)) demands a legislative solution that would broaden the scope of ZPO § 321a. See Ch. 10(H) below.

176. ZPO § 46(2).

177. ZPO § 104(3).

178. ZPO § 127(2), (3).

179. ZPO § 336(1).

180. ZPO § 390(3).

181. GVG § 181(1).

which is usually the court in which second instance appeals would be filed.[182] Ordinarily the notice of appeal (*Beschwerdeschrift*) is in writing, although in local court cases in which representation by counsel is not mandatory, the appeal may be lodged orally at the clerk's office.[183] There is no prescribed form for the notice of appeal. It must merely identify the order or disposition that is challenged and state that an appeal is being taken from that order or disposition.[184]

The newly reformed Code of Civil Procedure requires that all miscellaneous appeals be lodged within two weeks of service of the order or disposition on which they are based.[185] The opposing party then has the right to file a cross appeal.[186] If the appeal is lodged in the court issuing the order in question, that court must examine the notice of appeal and, in effect, reconsider the action in question in light of the assertions of the appeal. If the court becomes of the view that the appeal has merit, the court is under a duty to grant relief (*abhelfen*) and rescind or amend the order or disposition appealed.[187] Otherwise the court is required to transmit the appeal directly (*unverzüglich*) to the appellate court.

The lodging of a miscellaneous appeal automatically stays only orders imposing civil fines or orders of contempt (*Ordnungs- oder Zwangsmittel*).[188] If

---

182. ZPO §569(1). Motions for reconsideration (*Erinnerungen*) of actions of delegated or commissioned judges (*beauftragter oder ersuchter Richter*) or of a clerk of courts (*Urkundsbeamter*) must be submitted to the court in which the action is pending within two weeks of the action in question. If the court refuses to reconsider, the aggrieved party may lodge a miscellaneous appeal to the next higher court. ZPO §573.

183. ZPO §569(3). Oral miscellaneous appeal is also permitted for parties seeking legal aid, witnesses, experts, or third parties affected by court orders. Oral notices of appeal are minuted and the minutes are transmitted to the court.

184. ZPO §569(2). The term „*Beschwerde*" does not have to be used. See Federal Supreme Court, 45 *NJW* 243 (1992).

185. ZPO §569(1). Previously the two-week time period applied only to the "immediate miscellaneous appeal" (*sofortige Beschwerde*), which was specifically authorized by statute in a limited number of circumstances. Other miscellaneous appeals were not subject to time limits, although lapse of time or intervening circumstance could make the appeal moot. Now all miscellaneous appeals must follow the timetable and procedure that previously applied only to immediate miscellaneous appeals.

186. ZPO §567(3).

187. ZPO §572(1)(1). This obligation to reconsider orders and dispositions previously entered is an exception to the principle that ordinarily a court is bound by its previous decisions in the same case. ZPO §318. See Lüke, §37, mn. 423. A court judgment subject to miscellaneous appeal need not be reconsidered by the court which rendered the judgment. See ZPO §§572(1)(2), 318.

188. ZPO §570(1).

the appeal is lodged with the court issuing the order, that court may grant a temporary stay of the order, even if it decides not to grant any other relief on the appeal.[189] The appellate court may also grant provisional measures including a stay of the order appealed pending decision of the appeal.[190]

2. Procedure on Miscellaneous Appeals

The appellate court must examine the notice of appeal and any supporting documentation to determine whether the appeal is allowable (*statthaft*) and was lodged in proper form within the statutory time period. If the court determines that any of these prerequisites is lacking, the appeal may be dismissed by simple order.[191] Actions taken by a single judge in the court below may be reviewed by a single judge of the appellate court, unless the judge refers the matter to the usually constituted panel because it appears to be of unusual difficulty or of fundamental legal significance.[192]

Parties to a miscellaneous appeal are not confined to the record before the court below, but may adduce additional legal and factual support (*neues Vorbringen*) for their respective contentions on appeal. The court however, may set a time for the production of factual assertions and designations of proof (*Angriffs- und Verteidigungsmittel*), after which such material will only be received in cases of excusable delay.[193]

If the reviewing judge or panel is of the view that the appeal is allowable (*zulässig*), the court will either request written comments (*Erklärungen*) from the parties' counsel[194] or set the appeal for oral argument. Since the decisions of miscellaneous appeals appear as simple orders, not judgments, there is no statutory requirement of oral hearing. However the principles of fair judicial

---

189. ZPO §570(2).

190. ZPO §570(3).

191. ZPO §572(2).

192. ZPO §568. This measure came from the July 2001 reforms and is designed to speed proceedings by increasing the authority of single judges. However it can be argued from the terms of the Law Implementing the Brussels Regulation (*Gesetz zur Ausführung zwischenstaatlicher Verträge und zur Durchführung von Verordnungen der Europäischen Gemeinschaft auf dem Gebiet der Anerkennung und Vollstreckung in Zivil-und Handelssachen* - AVAG) that miscellaneous appeals relating to international execution matters must still be heard by three-judge panels. See Thomas/Putzo/Reichold, §568, mn. 2.

193. ZPO §571(2) and (3).

194. See ZPO §571(4)(1) and (2). If the appeal is one which may be orally lodged, the comments of the parties may be given orally in the same manner. ZPO §571(4)(2).

hearing (*rechtliches Gehör*) still apply.[195] Oral hearing may be scheduled if the fair and proper disposition of the issue requires hearing orally from the parties or their counsel.[196] The court may also order the reception of testimony or other proof in connection with a miscellaneous appeal if the circumstances warrant.[197]

3. Disposition of Miscellaneous Appeals

The decision of a miscellaneous appeal is in the form of a simple order (*Beschluss*) regardless of whether oral argument has taken place. If the appeal is ultimately unjustified (*unbegründet*) it will be simply dismissed. If the appellate court finds the appeal to be meritorious, it can vacate the decision below and either remand the matter to the court below to consider the issue again based on the reasoning of the appellate court or it can decide the matter and enter a new order in its place.[198]

4. Miscellaneous Appeals of Law to the Federal Supreme Court

A party or affected person may request a miscellaneous appeal of law (*Rechtsbeschwerde*) to the Federal Supreme Court from a decision of an appellate court on a miscellaneous appeal, from an order other than a judgment entered during the course of a second instance appeal, and from an order of the state appeals court in the exercise of first-instance jurisdiction under limited circumstances.[199] A miscellaneous appeal of law may be taken if specifically authorized by statute and if the question raised by the appeal is of fundamental significance or the development of the law or securing of a unified interpretation of law requires a decision of the Federal Supreme Court on the

---

195. See German Constitutional Court, 7 BVerfGE 95 (1958); 36 BverfGE 85 (1974); Rosenberg/Schwab/Gottwald, § 148(IV)(4), p. 905.

196. See ZPO §§ 572(4), 128(4). Ordinarily the appellate court will give the opposing party opportunity for oral argument before reaching a decision if a hearing could be helpful and if the decision could be to the party's substantive or serious procedural disadvantage.

197. Rosenberg/Schwab/Gottwald, § 148(IV)(5), p. 905; Lüke, § 37, mn. 424.

198. See ZPO § 572(3). Rosenberg/Schwab/Gottwald, § 148(V), pp. 905 f. In some cases the court is required to enter its own decision rather than remand the case to a lower court.

199. ZPO § 574(1)(2). For instance in the execution of arbitral awards. See ZPO §§ 1062, 1065 and Ch. 11(F)(3) below.

issue raised.[200] In a situation where a miscellaneous appeal of law is not specifically authorized by statute such an appeal may be taken only if the court issuing the order in question gives permission for the appeal.[201] This procedure for limited discretionary miscellaneous appeals of law was introduced in the July 2001 reforms and replaces a prior provision allowing a further miscellaneous appeal (*weitere Beschwerde*) from an appellate court decision by a party newly burdened by the appellate court decision on the first appeal.[202]

The procedure is similar to that on review appeal (*Revision*) from a decision of a second instance appeal. If the miscellaneous appeal of law is not authorized by statute, appellant must request permission from the appellate court.[203] Permission may be granted in the appellate court decision and is binding on the Federal Supreme Court. Unlike review appeals, however, if the appellate court refuses to grant permission for a miscellaneous appeal of law,[204] there is no resort to the Federal Supreme Court by way of appeal from the denial of permission. Appeals may be premised only on errors of federal law or of law applicable to a region larger than a state appeals court district. The scope of review is analogous to that on review appeals of final judgments.[205]

The miscellaneous appeal of law is initiated by filing a notice of appeal (*Rechtsbeschwerdeschrift*) in the Federal Supreme Court within a month of service of the decision or order appealed from.[206] The opposing party has the right to file a cross appeal of law within a month of filing of the appellant's brief in justification of the appeal.[207]

The notice of appeal must designate the decision appealed from and indicate that appeal of law is being lodged against the decision. Ordinarily a copy of the decision is to be attached to the notice of appeal. In many cases the notice of appeal will also set forth the legal justification of the appeal. Oth-

---

200. ZPO §§574(1)(1) and (2)(1), (2).

201. ZPO §574(1)(2). Permission is based on the same criteria for appeals authorized by statute, namely, significance of the question or need for unified interpretation of law. ZPO §574(3).

202. See ZPO §568 pre-2001 version.

203. This can be the appellate court in the miscellaneous appeal, the second instance appellate court, or the state appeals court in some relatively rare first-instance matters. ZPO §574(1)(2).

204. See Ch. 10(E)(1).

205. See ZPO §576.

206. ZPO §575(1)(1).

207. ZPO §574(4). However if the notice of cross appeal is not filed within a month of service of the decision and the appeal is later dismissed or withdrawn the cross appeal lapses.

erwise a brief in support of the appeal (*Rechtsbeschwerdebegründung*) must be filed, also within a month of the service of the decision appealed from.[208]

The notice of appeal or brief in support of appeal must set forth with particularity the extent to which the decision below is challenged and the specific relief requested (*Rechtsbeschwerdeanträge*). For miscellaneous appeals of law not requiring permission of the court below, the justification must also address the statutory criteria of unusual significance or need for unified interpretation. Finally, the justification must include specific designation of the legal grounds on which the claimed error (*Rechtsverletzung*) is premised and the relevant facts.[209]

The Federal Supreme Court is required on its own motion to examine miscellaneous appeals of law for the statutory prerequisites and will dismiss any appeals not meeting them. If the court is of the view that a statutorily authorized appeal does not pose an issue of fundamental legal significance or one which requires a unified legal interpretation, the appeal will also be dismissed.[210]

Miscellaneous appeals of law may be decided with or without oral hearing. If the court is inclined to grant relief on such an appeal, the court will give the opposing party prior opportunity to file a brief in opposition or hear the parties in oral argument. Although the Federal Supreme Court is bound by the parties' specific designations of error and requests for relief (*Beschwerdeanträge*), the court is not bound by their reasoning.[211] If the decision is correct, but for a different reason than that adopted by the court below, the appeal will be dismissed.[212]

As is the case with review appeals, the decision of the Federal Supreme Court may either dismiss the miscellaneous appeal of law, may remand the matter to the lower court for further proceedings, or, when there is no need for additional fact finding, substitute a new decision of its own.[213]

G. Costs and Attorneys' Fees on Appeals

Every appellate measure involves court costs (*Gerichtskosten*) and almost all also involve attorneys' fees and expenses (*Anwaltskosten*). A party filing a notice of second instance appeal (*Berufungsschrift*) from a judgment of the local court or state district court will be required to pay court costs based on the

208. ZPO §575(2).
209. ZPO §575(3).
210. ZPO §577.
211. ZPO §577(2).
212. ZPO §577(3).
213. ZPO §577(5).

amount in controversy (*Wert des Streitgegenstandes* or *Streitwert*) in the appeal.[214] Additional court costs are also levied on the initiation of review appeals to the Federal Supreme Court and on the initiation of miscellaneous appeals from decisions other than judgments. In each case the court costs are payable to the court offering the appellate remedy sought.[215]

Court costs on appeal are based on the amount placed in controversy by the appeal, not to exceed the amount in controversy in the instance below. So, for instance, if a defendant who was originally sued for 50,000 Euro files a second instance appeal from an adverse judgment of 20,000 Euro, the court costs on the appeal would be computed based on an amount in controversy of 20,000 Euro. However if the plaintiff filed a cross appeal based on the contention that the judgment should have been 50,000 Euro, the amount in controversy would be increased to 50,000 Euro.[216]

Court costs for appellate remedies are somewhat higher than the corresponding first-instance court costs for the same amount in controversy. The costs for a second instance appeal proceeding in general are computed at 1.5 units of costs and there is an additional court fee of up to three units of costs if the second-instance court is required to issue a judgment or other order disposing of the proceeding.[217] There is a corresponding upcharge for proceedings before the Federal Supreme Court.[218] By way of contrast, miscellaneous appeals are frequently cost free, or bear only minimal court costs.[219]

Although a party becomes liable for costs by lodging an appeal or cross appeal, court costs on appeal are generally not actually paid until the appeal is resolved.[220] However any actual court expenditures necessitated by an appeal or required to be incurred in connection therewith must be paid in advance.[221]

---

214. GKG §§49, 61.

215. GKG §4. Usually the payment facilities for all state courts are located at the offices of the local courts in the localities where the other courts also sit.

216. GKG §19. In this case the original appellant would bear initial responsibility for costs based on 20,000 Euro and the cross appellant would be responsible for costs based on 30,000 Euro. Ultimately costs would be assessed against the losing party based on the combined sum.

217. GKG, Attachment 1, Nos. 1220–1229.

218. There the fee for the proceedings in general is 2 units, but the fee for a fully reasoned judgment is an additional 4 units. See GKG, Attachment 1, Nos. 1230–1249.

219. See GKG, Attachment 1, Nos.1911–1957.

220. See Rosenberg/Schwab/Gottwald, §86(II)(4), p. 462; GKG §§61, 63, 65(1). This is to be contrasted with first instance proceedings, where the fee for the proceeding in general (*Gebühr für das Verfahren im allgemeinen*) must be paid before the court takes any action or schedules any proceedings. See GKG §§61(1)(1), 65(1)(1).

221. GKG §68. E.g. fees for witnesses or experts.

Taxation of costs on appeal parallels taxation of costs in first-instance proceedings.[222] The judgment in a second instance appeal or review appeal will ordinarily contain a provision assessing the costs against the losing party,[223] or in some cases dividing the costs among the parties. The actual computation of the amounts is usually done by the clerk of courts (*Urkundsbeamter*).

When an appellate court reverses a lower court decision the appellate court decision addresses costs in both instances. However when an appeal is dismissed, the appellant must bear the costs of the second instance and the costs decision below remains unaffected. Cases which involve multiple parties and changing amounts in controversy can generate very complicated costs decisions.[224]

In certain cases a part of the costs can be assessed against a party who ultimately prevails. For instance, if a party prevails on appeal based on a legal or factual contention that was brought forward for the first time on appeal, but which the party could have presented below, the appellate court can assess all or a part of the court costs for the appellate proceedings against that party.[225] Victorious parties can also be taxed with costs for unnecessary continuances or hearings, and for default judgments or for costs in connection with transfer of cases brought in the wrong court for subject matter jurisdiction or venue purposes.[226]

Attorneys fees on appeal follow a pattern similar to court costs. The Attorneys Fee Law (BRAGO) permits attorneys to charge separately for the lodging of second instance, review and miscellaneous appeals. Each instance (*Rechtszug*) (including a review appeal) justifies a separate full attorneys fee for the basic pleadings (*Prozessgebühr*), for representation in oral argument (*Verhandlungsgebühr*), and for taking of proof (*Beweisgebühr*) if proof is received.[227] In addition, the amount in controversy is automatically increased by 30% if a case goes before an appellate court and by 100% if the case is appealed to the Federal Supreme Court.[228] If the case is remanded, the proceedings before the court below on remand are considered a separate instance for the purpose of computing fees.[229] Miscellaneous appeals (*Beschwerde*) and mo-

---

222. See Ch. 9(E) above on judgments for costs and attorneys fees.

223. See ZPO §97(1).

224. See Pantle, *Die Praxis des Zivilprozesses*, 2nd ed. (1992), mn. 532 ff.; Schumann, *Die Berufung in Zivilsachen*, 5th ed. (1997), mn. 612 ff.

225. ZPO §97(2).

226. See Ch. 9(E)(3) above; Rosenberg/Schwab/Gottwald, §87(IV)(2), pp. 471 f. for some of the circumstances when costs or partial costs may be assessed against a victorious party.

227. BRAGO §31.

228. See BRAGO §11(1)(3) and (4).

229. BRAGO §15. However, the attorney gets the fee for the basic pleadings only if the case is remanded to a court that has not handled the case before.

tions for reconsideration (*Erinnerungen*) are not considered "instances" for the assessment of attorneys fees. In general such appeals justify only reduced fees.[230]

The same rules that apply to court costs also govern awards of attorneys fees when decisions are reversed or modified on appeal or when appeals are dismissed.[231]

H. Constitutional Appeals to the Federal Constitutional Court

A final judgment in a civil case may be "appealed" to the German Federal Constitutional Court (*Bundesverfassungsgericht*) based on the assertion that a judgment rests on a statute, a judicial interpretation of statutory law, or a doctrine of case law that violates fundamental rights guaranteed by the German Constitution.[232] Such appeals by aggrieved parties are separate from and in addition to the process by which courts refer constitutional questions arising during the course of civil proceedings to the Federal Constitutional Court for an authoritative decision.[233]

A litigant's right to lodge a constitutional appeal (*Verfassungsbeschwerde*) is guaranteed by the German Constitution.[234] At the same time the Federal Constitutional Court has taken pains to make it clear that the constitutional ap-

230. BRAGO §61. For most miscellaneous appeals the attorneys fees are reckoned at 50% of the "instance" fees. However certain cases, such as miscellaneous appeals from orders implementing divorce judgments, are considered full instances for purposes of attorneys fees. BRAGO §61a.

231. See Ch. 9(E) above on apportionment of attorneys fees in case of partial success or based on special circumstances.

232. For a brief description of the composition and jurisdiction of the Federal Constitutional Court see Ch. 3(E) above.

233. See Ch. 3(E) for a description of the referral process. The Federal Constitutional Court has many functions in addition to deciding constitutional issues arising during the course of private litigation. See GG Article 93 for a list of the kinds of controversies within the Federal Constitutional Court's constitutional responsibility. Some of the more important include the determination of constitutional issues raised by queries from the legislature or executive government and banning of political parties.

234. Article 93(4a) of the German Constitution provides that the Federal Constitutional Court will decide "constitutional appeals which can be lodged by any person based on the assertion that a fundamental right or a right guaranteed by Articles 20(4), 33, 38, 101, 103 and 104 has been infringed by state action". ("*Verfassungsbeschwerden, die von jedermann mit der Behauptung erhoben werden können, durch die öffentliche Gewalt in einem seiner*

peal is not to be considered as another level of appellate review in the ordinary case, but is rather an "extraordinary remedy provided to a citizen with which to avert state power from infringing his fundamental rights".[235]

A constitutional appeal may be lodged only after all other judicial remedies are exhausted (*Erschöpfung des Rechtsweges*).[236] Premature constitutional appeals are subject to summary dismissal on the court's own motion. In exceptional cases the Federal Constitutional Court can entertain a constitutional appeal before exhaustion of all conventional judicial remedies if the court is convinced that the case is of widespread significance (*von allgemeiner Bedeutung*) or if the appellant would suffer a serious and unavoidable detriment (*schwerer und unabwendbarer Nachteil*) if required to fully exhaust all potential judicial remedies.[237]

Constitutional appeals are also subject to an acceptance proceeding (*Annahmeverfahren*) which serves to weed out cases of little significance or hope of success.[238] Thus, although there are a great number of constitutional appeals filed in the Federal Constitutional Court each year, the majority of them are dealt with in a more or less summary fashion leaving a much smaller caseload for plenary consideration on the merits.

1. Grounds for Constitutional Appeal

A constitutional appeal may be lodged by any person, natural or juristic, which is vested with rights protected by the German Constitution.[239] The appellant must be able to point to a violation of one of its fundamental constitutionally protected rights by "state power" (*öffentliche Gewalt*). Actions by private persons, by foreign states, or by organizations not encompassed within

---

Grundrechte oder in einem seiner in Artikel 20 Abs. 4, 33, 38, 101, 103 und 104 enthaltenen Rechte verletzt zu sein."). See also BVerfGG § 90(1).

235. German Constitutional Court, 18 BVerfGE 315, 325 (1965) („*ein dem Staatsbürger eingeräumter ausserordentlicher Rechtsbehelf, mit dem er Eingriffe der öffentlichen Gewalt in seine Grundrechte abwehren kann*"); see also Schlaich, *Das Bundesverfassungsgericht*, 3rd ed. (1994), § 4(5)(A), mn. 187.

236. See BVerfGG § 90(2)(1). Federal Constitutional Court, 63 BVerfGE 77, 78 (1983); Schlaich, § 4(5)(A), mn. 192.

237. BVerfGG § 90(2)(2).

238. BVerfGG §§ 93a ff.

239. The Federal Constitutional Court has ruled that certain juristic persons created by public law such as localities (*Gemeinden*) may sometimes raise constitutional appeals when special constitutional rights are affected by state action. See BVerfGG § 91 and Schlaich, § 4(5)(B)(I), mn. 200.

the German state (such as the EU) do not as a matter of principle qualify as German state power.[240]

In an ordinary civil case a constitutional appeal is usually based on the allegation that the judgment appealed from rests on a statute, statutory interpretation or case law doctrine that offends a fundamental right guaranteed by the German Constitution. The constitutional right infringed can either be a substantive right such as the right of personal autonomy and the freedom to conclude contracts,[241] or it can be a procedural right, such as the right to be heard (*rechtliches Gehör*) guaranteed by Article 103 of the German Constitution.

The appellant must allege and be prepared to show that he was "personally, presently and immediately harmed with respect to her constitutionally protected position."[242] In the case of a civil judgment, this means that the appellant must demonstrate that the unconstitutional statute, interpretation or case law directly resulted in an adverse judgment. A constitutional appeal will not lie if the judgment can be supported on a legal basis consistent with the Constitution.

In some cases it might be difficult to show that a procedural omission that arguably deprived a litigant of a fair judicial hearing affected the judgment. In such cases it is usually enough if it reasonably appears that the procedural error had some impact on the judgment. A procedural defect that did not likely affect the judgment is not cognizable on an ordinary appeal and will not support a deprivation of constitutional right.[243]

Within these parameters the Federal Constitutional Court has been receptive to the assertion of constitutionally protected interests in a wide variety of

---

240. This generally includes regulations or actions of the European Union, even when they have the effect of law within Germany and are carried out by German authorities. So long as the European Court of Justice provides a guarantee of protection of constitutional rights against acts of the European Union (see Ch. 3(F) above), the Federal Constitutional Court will not grant additional or concurring protection. See Federal Constitutional Court, 89 BVerfGE 155, 175 (1993); 102 BVerfGE 147 (2000); 54 *NJW* 2705 (2001); Lecheler, "Zum Bananenmarktbeschluss des Bundesverfassungsgerichts", 41 *JuS* 120 (2001); for execution of European foreign judgments based on the Brussels Regulation (see Ch. 12(A)) especially Stürner, "Anerkennungsrechtlicher und europäischer Ordre Public als Schranke der Vollstreckbarerklärung", in: K. Schmidt et al. (eds.), *50 Jahre Bundesgerichtshof - Festgabe aus der Wissenschaft*, Vol. III (2000), pp. 677 ff.

241. As guaranteed by Article 2(1) of the German Constitution; see Federal Constitutional Court, 47 *NJW* 36 (1994).

242. Federal Constitutional Court, 53 BVerfGE 30, 48 (1980) ("...*selbst, gegenwärtig und unmittelbar in seiner grundrechtlich geschützten Position verletzt*..."); Schlaich, §4(B)(IV)(2), mn. 223; Sachs/Sturm, *Grundgesetz*, 3rd ed. (2003), Art. 93, mn. 80 ff.

243. See Federal Constitutional Court, 13 BVerfGE 132, 144 f. (1961). Ch. 10 (D) above (ordinary appeals); Schlaich, §4(B)(IV)(1), mn. 217 (constitutional appeals).

legal relationships. For instance, the landlord-tenant relationship as regulated by statute law interpreted by ordinary courts can be viewed in light of the landlord's constitutionally protected property interests and the tenant's interest in fair procedure, personal autonomy and its own property interests. Any decision of a court in a landlord tenant dispute is likely to implicate these interests.[244] Does this mean that a litigant dissatisfied with the treatment afforded these interests by statute law and the ordinary courts can file a constitutional appeal based on the assertion that the adverse lower court judgment infringed the constitutionally protected interest? In a number of cases deemed to be more or less extreme the Federal Constitutional Court has accepted constitutional appeals from ordinary court cases which raised constitutional issues in this indirect manner.[245]

Serious errors by an ordinary civil court in interpretation and application of substantive law can rise to constitutional dimensions. A judicial decision, which is based on an "objectively untenable and therefore arbitrary interpretation of the written substantive law," can be seen as a violation of a person's basic constitutional right to be free from arbitrary state action.[246] The Constitutional Court has had some difficulty in defining which judicial errors in application of law are of such magnitude as to constitute constitutional deprivations.[247]

The constitutionally guaranteed rights to a fair judicial hearing and to be heard (*rechtliches Gehör*)[248] are frequently invoked to support constitutional appeals. In a number of cases the Federal Constitutional Court has held that procedural errors in civil litigation can be so egregious as to constitute deprivations of these rights.[249] The theory is that a failure to observe the procedures

---

244. See Federal Constitutional Court, 46 *NJW* 2035 (1993); 45 *NJW* 2752 (1992); Baur/Stürner, *Sachenrecht*, 17th ed. (1999), §29(E), mn. 64 ff., pp. 346 ff. For a general survey Diederichsen, "Das Bundesverfassungsgericht als oberstes Zivilgericht", 198 *AcP* 171 (1998).

245. See Schlaich, §4(B)(IV)(1), mn. 210–217. The Constitutional Court has held that the right to live and conduct business freely as guaranteed by GG Article 2(1) is potentially infringed by practically any form of governmental regulation, thus subjecting all regulatory statutes to Constitutional Court review for reasonableness and proportionality. Federal Constitutional Court, 80 BVerfGE 137 (1990).

246. See Federal Constitutional Court, 18 BVerfGE 85, 92 f. (1964); 64 BVerfGE 389, 394 (1984) (*objektiv unhaltbare und deshalb willkürliche Auslegung des geschriebenen materiellen Rechts*); 56 *NJW* 1924, 1928 (2003).

247. See Schlaich, §4(B)(IV)(1), mn. 214–215.

248. See GG Article 103(1).

249. In fact, nearly 50% of all constitutional appeals are based on alleged violations of those constitutional norms which define and constrain the institutions of justice (*Justizgrundrechte*) as set forth in Articles 19(4), 101(1)(2), 103(1), and 104 of the German Constitution. Schlaich, §4(E)(II)(3), mn. 311–314.

provided by law results in a denial of the fair judicial hearing guaranteed by the Constitution.[250] This approach has tended to subject almost all claims of serious procedural error to Constitutional Court review. More recently the Constitutional Court has attempted to narrow its scope of review of procedural errors to those which infringe the "measure of fair judicial hearing specifically guaranteed by the Constitution," which may be different from and less than that provided by the Code of Civil Procedure and to make clear that primary responsibility for maintaining correct application of procedural law should lie with the ordinary courts.[251]

The most recent reforms of 2001 enacted a new ZPO § 321a providing a right to remonstrance when decisions of lower courts are not subject to ordinary second instance appeal and a party to litigation asserts a violation of the right to be heard (*Anhörungsrüge*).[252] The Federal Supreme Court prefers a very broad application and construction of this provision to avoid an increase of review appeals based on a violation of the right to be heard.[253] The Federal Constitutional Court has issued a demand for a legislative solution by broadening the scope of ZPO § 321a to avoid an increase of constitutional appeals.[254] The federal legislature has now to decide whether a general right to remonstrance should be introduced to protect the right to be heard without creating a permanent overload of the Federal Supreme Court and the Federal Constitutional Court. It is evident that a general right to remonstrate to correct a violation of the right to be heard may conflict with the principles of finality and res judicata.

German lawyers have been ingenious in arguing that a wide range of claimed errors in interpretation and application of substantive law as well as claimed lapses in correct procedure can implicate the rights guaranteed by the German Constitution.[255] The Constitutional Court's somewhat expansive conception of its own jurisdiction in ordinary civil cases has not only caused its caseload of constitutional appeals to burgeon, but has also generated criticism

---

250. Federal Constitutional Court, 62 BVerfGE 320 (1983); Schlaich, § 4(E)(II)(3), mn. 313.

251. ("...*spezifisch verfassungsrechtlich gewährleistete Ausmass an rechtlichen Gehör.*"); Federal Constitutional Court, 60 BVerfGE 305, 310 (1982); Schlaich, § 4(E)(II)(3), mn. 314.

252. See ZPO §§ 321a, 511(2).

253. See Federal Supreme Court, 55 *NJW* 1577 (2002); Ch. 10(F) before ( ).

254. See Federal Constitutional Court, 56 *NJW* 1924 (2003).

255. For a discussion of the various kinds of cases in which the Federal Constitutional Court has found violations of constitutional norms in judgments of the civil courts see Schlaich, § 4(E)(I–II), mn. 271–316; Schumann, „Bundesverfassungsgericht, Grundgesetz und Zivilprozess", 96 *ZZP* 137 (1983); Stürner, „Die Kontrolle zivilprozessualer Verfahrensfehler durch das Bundesverfassungsgericht", 41 *JZ* 526 (1986).

from some academics, who have come to refer to the Federal Constitutional Court as "Germany's supreme civil court".[256]

2. Procedure on Constitutional Appeal

A notice of constitutional appeal (*Verfassungsbeschwerdeschrift*) must be filed with the Federal Constitutional Court within one month of service of the judgment or decision raising the constitutional issue.[257] The appellant's notice of constitutional appeal must set forth the constitutional right that was infringed and must describe with particularity the particular aspect of the judgment or decision that infringed the designated constitutional right.[258] In almost every case the notice of constitutional appeal will also elaborate the arguments of the appellant in support of the appeal, since the court will have to decide whether to entertain the appeal based largely on the notice itself. Although a party can initiate a constitutional appeal pro se, representation by counsel is required at any oral argument.[259]

The notice of constitutional appeal is initially referred to one of the three-judge panels of the senate to which it relates.[260] The panel is required to review the legal prerequisites for the appeal on its own motion. If the appellant has not exhausted all judicial remedies or if some other prerequisite is lacking, the appeal will be dismissed by simple order.[261] After having any other in-

---

256. See especially Diederichsen, 198 *AcP* 171 (1998); Stürner/Schumacher, "The Role of the Supreme Courts at the national and international level", in: Yessiou-Faltsi (ed.), *The Role of the Supreme Courts* (1998), pp. 207 ff., 212.

257. BVerfGG § 93(1). If the judgment is not formally served, the time begins to run at the time the appellant receives notification of the complete contents of the decision. If the appellant is prevented without fault of his own from filing the notice of constitutional appeal in a timely manner, upon application the court may enlarge the time to allow filing of the appeal. Such an application must be filed within two weeks of the end of the period of hindrance and in any event within a year of the expiration of the original time period. A litigant is bound by the lapses of its counsel with respect to this filing. BVerfGG § 93(2).

258. BVerfGG §§ 23, 92.

259. BVerfGG § 22. There is no special bar for the Federal Constitutional Court. Any lawyer authorized to appear before a German court may appear in the Federal Constitutional Court.

260. The Federal Constitutional Court is divided into two 8-judge senates to which matters are assigned based on their subject matters. See Ch. 3(E) above. Most constitutional appeals in ordinary civil litigation are referred to the First Senate. See BVerfGG § 14.

261. BVerfGG § 24. For a detailed discussion of the legal prerequisites that must be set forth in a notice of constitutional appeal see Schlaich, § 4(B), mn. 198–249.

terested parties served with notice of the appeal and allowing opportunity for comment (*Stellungnahme*)[262] the panel also considers the merits of the issue raised in order to determine whether the appeal should be considered by the full senate or whether it can be disposed of in summary fashion.[263]

The notion of a screening or acceptance proceeding for constitutional appeals was first introduced in the 1950s and such proceedings have taken several forms since. The current version limits acceptance of constitutional appeals to cases "to which is attributed fundamental constitutional significance...in the effectuation of rights enumerated in §90(1), which can also be the case if the appellant would sustain a severe disadvantage from a denial of a decision on the merits."[264] With the aid of the notice of appeal and any comments filed by the opposing party the panel must consider whether the issues raised meet these criteria. If the panel unanimously decides that the appeal does not meet the statutory threshold the appeal is dismissed by simple order, which need not set forth any reasoning for the dismissal.[265] If, on the other hand, the panel unanimously determines that the appeal satisfies the statutory criteria and that the "questions necessary for decisions of the constitutional appeal have already been decided by the Federal Constitutional Court,"[266] the panel can summarily sustain an appeal which appears to be justified. So far as the parties are concerned, the decision of the panel is of the same legal effect as a decision of the senate. If, however, the issue is one of the constitutionality of a statute, any decision having the effect of rendering the statute unconstitutional must be rendered by the entire senate.[267] So long as the proceeding is pending before the panel, the panel has the power to issue procedural rulings and adopt provisional measures, providing that a provisional measure that suspends operation of a statute can

---

262. BVerfGG §23(2).

263. Technically speaking, the preliminary examination of legal prerequisites (*Zulässigkeitsprüfung*) precedes the acceptance proceeding (*Annahmeverfahren*) in which the panel addresses the apparent merits of the questions presented. However as a practical matter the two issues are often handled together. See Schlaich, §4(C), mn. 250.

264. BVerfGG §93a(2) ("*soweit ihr grundsätzliche verfassungsrechtliche Bedeutung zukommt,...wenn es zur Durchsetzung der in §90 Abs. 1 genannten Rechte angezeigt ist; dies kann auch der Fall sein, wenn dem Beschwerdeführer durch die Versagung der Entscheidung zur Sache ein besonders schwerer Nachteil entsteht*").

265. BVerfGG §93d(1).

266. BVerfGG §93c(1) ("*...und ist die für die Beurteilung der Verfassungsbeschwerde massgebliche verfassungsrechtliche Frage durch das Bundesverfassungsgericht bereits entschieden*").

267. BVerfGG §93c(1)(2).

only be adopted by the senate.[268] An order by a panel unanimously rejecting or sustaining a constitutional appeal is final and not subject to further appeal.[269]

If the panel does not unanimously reject or grant the appeal, the entire senate will determine whether the appeal will be accepted. The votes of three members of the senate are sufficient for acceptance.[270]

If the appeal is accepted by the senate, the matter may be set for oral argument before the senate in Karlsruhe.[271] If the appeal implicates a federal or state statute or attacks the action of a federal or state agency or minister, the organs of government involved will be given opportunity to file written comments and to appear at any oral argument.[272] In all cases the opposing party which was favored by the ruling under attack will be given opportunity to comment and appear at any oral argument that is scheduled.[273] If the parties unanimously agree, or if the court determines in the exercise of its judicial discretion that an oral hearing may not advance the matter, the court can dispense with oral argument and decide the case by simple order based on the papers.[274]

Oral proceedings before the Federal Constitutional Court are similar to those before the ordinary appellate courts such as the state appeals courts or the Federal Supreme Court.[275] In cases appealed from the ordinary courts the Constitutional Court will generally base its fact findings on the facts as found by the other courts.[276] Although the Constitutional Court is empowered to "seek the evidence necessary to ascertain the truth,"[277] it rarely receives evidence itself. When it does decide to receive proof of facts relevant to a constitutional issue, the Court can designate a judge of the Constitutional Court or another court to receive the evidence and report to the full senate.[278]

---

268. BVerfGG §93d(2).

269. BVerfGG §93d(1).

270. BVerfGG §§93b, 93d(3).

271. See BVerfGG §25.

272. BVerfGG §94(1), (2) and (4).

273. BVerfGG §94(3).

274. BVerfGG §§25(1), 94(5)(2). If public organs are entitled to be heard the public organs must waive oral argument. BVerfGG §94(5)(2).

275. The law requires that minutes of the proceedings be kept and that the proceedings be preserved on a tape recording. BVerfGG §25a.

276. See Schlaich, §4(E)(II)(1), mn. 278.

277. BVerfGG §26(1) ("*Das Bundesverfassungsgericht erhebt den zur Erforschung der Wahrheit erforderlichen Beweis*"). This formulation suggests that in constitutional matters the principle of party control of proof (*Beibringungsgrundsatz*) may be subject to a duty of the court to make an effort to determine objective truth.

278. BVerfGG §26. In constitutional appeals from civil judgments the provisions of the

In appropriate cases the Constitutional Court can call for specialized opinions from third parties and appoint experts to report on specific legal issues and factual matters.[279] Law professors or judges of other courts are sometimes called on to render opinions on complex or portentous legal matters. When such comments and opinions are received the parties to the appeal are given opportunity to comment on the third party views.

3. Decisions and Judgments of the Constitutional Court

Following oral argument or submission of the issue on written briefs the senate deliberates and decides each appeal in confidential session by majority vote. One of the members of the senate is designated to write the judgment, which is signed by all of the judges who participated in the decision. Unlike the case in all of the other German courts, a Constitutional Court judge who does not agree with the reasoning of the majority may dissent and may file a dissenting opinion setting forth the grounds for the dissent.[280] According to the statute a decision is supposed to be rendered within three months of the completion of oral proceedings, although this time period may be, and frequently is, enlarged by simple order of court.[281]

If the case was heard in oral argument, the decision of the Constitutional Court takes the form of a judgment (*Urteil*) which is orally rendered at a session called for that purpose.[282] Otherwise the decision is rendered as a simple order (*Beschluss*) which is filed and served on the parties.

A decision of the Federal Constitutional Court can either dismiss the appeal as unjustified or can grant the appeal in whole or in part. Like other courts, the Constitutional Court is not bound by the legal theories advanced by the parties in their submissions and oral presentations.[283] If the appeal is granted, the decision should set forth exactly which constitutional requirement is infringed and by what decision or action. The decision can also include a declaration that repeated action of the same kind would infringe con-

---

Civil Procedure Code apply to the taking of evidence in Constitutional Court proceedings. BVerfGG §28.

279. BVerfGG §27a. For an example see Stürner, *Der straffreie Schwangerschaftsabbruch in der Gesamtrechtsordnung* (1994).

280. BVerfGG §30(2).

281. BVerfGG §30(1).

282. BVerfGG §§25(2), 30(1). See Ch. 9(B)(4) above on the rendition of judgments.

283. See Federal Constitutional Court, 86 BVerfGE 133, 144 (1993); Lechner/Zuck, *Bundesverfassungsgerichtsgesetz*, 4th ed. (1996), §30, mn. 4.

stitutional requirements. In most cases the judgment below will be vacated and the case will be remanded to the court from which it came for further proceedings consistent with the judgment of the Constitutional Court.[284]

Decisions of the Federal Constitutional Court, whether denominated as judgments or court orders, are given special status by the German Constitution and statutory law. First of all, Constitutional Court decisions "are binding on all constitutional organs of the Federal Government and the states as well as all courts and public agencies."[285] Second, even in constitutional appeals from decisions in civil litigation, a decision of the Constitutional Court that a law is constitutional, unconstitutional or void acquires the force of law (*Gesetzeskraft*).[286] The Court has declared that this applies even to the Court's material legal reasoning in support of its decision.[287] All such decisions must be published in the Federal Legal Register (*Bundesgesetzblatt*).[288] In this sense decisions of the Federal Constitutional Court are of stronger precedential authority than decisions of the Federal Supreme Court. Constitutional Court decisions are thus frequently cited as case law even with respect to ordinary legal issues.[289]

284. BVerfGG §95.

285. BVerfGG §31(1) (*...binden die Verfassungsorgane des Bundes und der Länder sowie alle Gerichte und Behörden*).

286. BVerfGG §31(2)(2).

287. See Federal Constitutional Court, 1 BVerfGE 14, 37 (1952); 40 BVerfGE 88, 93 ff. (1976).

288. BVerfGG §31(2).

289. This circumstance may contribute to the concern that the Constitutional Court has become Germany's highest court with respect to the interpretation and application of ordinary civil law. See Diederichsen, 198 *AcP* 171 (1998).

CHAPTER 11

Special Proceedings

Most civil matters in the courts of ordinary jurisdiction follow the pattern described in the foregoing chapters. As noted above proceedings in the specialized courts are modified to a greater or lesser extent to reflect the particular interests at stake and the policies of the systems in which they function.[1]

Even in the ordinary courts, there are modified forms of procedure in certain specialized groups of cases. These modified forms of procedure are designed to address particular needs of certain kinds of cases, or to protect special interests. The following brief description addresses only the most significant of these special proceedings. This chapter also includes an overview of the German law of execution and insolvency.

A. Family Court Proceedings

Although procedure in family cases in the local courts follows in general the pattern of ordinary civil actions, there are several special features of family court procedure designed to implement governmental policies favoring the maintenance of the family unit and to address the special needs of family cases.[2] Some of these special provisions apply to all family cases (*Familiensachen*), while others affect only a subset of family cases such as marriage cases in general (*Ehesachen*) or divorce cases (*Scheidungssachen*) in particular. Many, but not all of the special provisions regulating family court procedure are collected in §§606–661 of the Civil Procedure Code.[3]

---

1. See Ch.3(B) and (C) above.

2. The special procedures for various kinds of family cases were newly arranged and codified in 1976 and 1998 legislative reforms. See Diederichsen, "Das Verfahren vor den Familiengerichten", 30 *NJW* 649 (1977); Gressmann, *Neues Kindschaftsrecht* (1998).

3. Other provisions affecting family court procedure are found in the Court Organization Law (GVG), in individual sections of the Civil Procedure Code and in the Law on Noncontentious Jurisdiction (*Gesetz über die Angelegenheiten der freiwilligen Gerichtsbarkeit* or FGG).

The borderline between cases subject to the special jurisdiction and rules of the family courts and other civil cases subject to the ordinary rules is not always clear.[4] Family cases include not only all cases in which the validity or termination of a marriage is at stake, but also cases concerning the custody and support of illegitimate or legitimate children and for support or other protection within an ongoing marriage.

Even if the statute does not formally consign a proceeding to the family court, it will be considered a family court proceeding if it is factually related to a family court case (*Familiensachen kraft Sachzusammenhangs*).[5] There is some dispute as to whether execution proceedings on a money or property family court judgment are also family court proceedings.[6] Taxation of costs and attorneys fees relating to a family case qualifies as a family case, while a claim by a lawyer against a client for a fee earned in family court representation does not.[7]

In the great bulk of marital and family matters the parties must be represented by counsel admitted to a court in Germany.[8] Judgments of the local courts when sitting in family court matters are appealed not to the state district courts, but directly to the state appeals courts.[9] Most proceedings in family court cases are not open to the public.[10]

There is some special terminology in family court. For instance many (but not all) family cases are not initiated by a complaint (*Klage*), but by a written application (*Antragsschrift*).[11] The initiating party is called the "applicant" (*Antragsteller*) and the opposing party is the respondent (*Antragsgegner*).

1. Special Procedures in Marital Cases

Cases involving the existence, validity or termination of a marriage are subject to special rules which recognize the state's interest in the marital institu-

---

4. See, e.g., Lüke, *Zivilprozessrecht*, 8th ed. (2003), §46(II)(1), mn. 469 ff.; Thomas/Putzo, *Zivilprozessordnung*, 24th ed. (2002), §621, mn. 6 ff.; Zöller, *Zivilprozessordnung*, 23th ed. (2002), §621, mn. 2 ff.

5. German Federal Supreme Court, 31 *NJW* 1571 (1978); see Lüke, §46(I), mn. 470.

6. See Rosenberg/Schwab/Gottwald, *Zivilprozessrecht*, 15th ed. (1993), §166(I)(3), p. 1022. The prevailing opinion is that they are not. German Federal Supreme Court, 32 *NJW* 1048 (1979); Thomas/Putzo, §621, mn. 20.

7. Rosenberg/Schwab/Gottwald, §166(I)(4), p. 1022.

8. ZPO §78(2) and (3). For requirements and procedures for admission to practice before German courts see Ch. 4 (D) above.

9. GVG §119(1). See Ch. 3(D)(1) and (3)(a), Ch. 5(B)(2) above.

10. GVG §170. See Ch. 6(E)(2) above.

11. See, e.g., ZPO §622(1).

tion. Many of these rules are designed to discourage hasty action terminating a marriage or to protect the weaker party in marital disputes.

First of all, all marital cases must be commenced by written application (*Antragsschrift*) signed by an attorney. Permissible counter-applications are limited to claims addressing the marital relationship.[12] The optional written preparatory procedure does not apply to marital cases, which must be prepared by preliminary hearing.[13] The court is given authority to enter a variety of temporary orders (*einstweilige Anordnungen*) regulating custody, visitation, child support, possession of marital premises, and marital support.[14]

In general the marital case rules are more liberal than the rules for ordinary cases in permitting late withdrawal or amendment of pleadings.[15] On the other hand, late assertion of new facts in support of a claim or defense can be overruled "if the court is convinced that their introduction would delay determination of the proceeding and the lateness is the result of gross negligence."[16]

The principles of party control of proceedings (*Dispositionsmaxime*) and party responsibility for facts and proof (*Verhandlungsgrundsatz*) are modified in marital proceedings to recognize the interest of the state in marital matters.[17] There can be no default judgment against a defendant in a marital case.[18] The court is also not bound by the parties' admissions and stipulations of fact.[19]

The court is required to summons both parties to appear in person at a court hearing, where they are subject to interrogation without any special

---

12. ZPO §§609, 610.

13. ZPO §611(2).

14. ZPO §620. An application for a temporary order can be filed at any time after the case becomes pending. If the issue relates to custody or support of children, the Office of Childrens' Services (*Jugendamt*) is notified and requested to comment. ZPO §620a. Even during the continuance of an ongoing marriage one of the marriage partners can apply for court regulation of custody, support and similar matters pursuant to other statutory authority. See, e.g. BGB §1666, ZPO §§642 ff.

15. For details see Rosenberg/Schwab/Gottwald, §165(V)(3) and (4), p. 1010 and ZPO §611.

16. ZPO §615 (*...wenn ihre Zulassung nach der freien Überzeugung des Gerichts die Erledigung des Rechtsstreits verzögern würde und die Verspätung auf grober Nachlässigkeit beruht*).

17. See Lüke, §46(II)(2), mn. 472–473; Thomas/Putzo, Einl I, mn. 6 ff.; Zöller/Greger, Vor §128, mn. 9 ff., 12. For the principles of party control over the scope of the proceedings and over facts see Ch. 6(B)(1) and (2).

18. ZPO §612(4). This means that even if the defendant does not appear, the plaintiff is required to prove all relevant facts in order to obtain the relief requested. See Rosenberg/Schwab/Gottwald, §165(V)(10), pp. 1014 f.

19. ZPO §617.

proof order.[20] The court has the authority to order all forms of proof on its own motion and, after hearing both parties, can consider matters of fact which neither party has asserted.[21]

As in other cases, the court is required to explore all possibilities of settlement.[22] If the court believes that the purposes of potential settlement will be served, the court may suspend the proceedings, and the court is obliged to do so in divorce cases if there is a reasonably concrete prospect of continuance of the marriage (*konkrete Aussicht auf Fortsetzung der Ehe*) or if the plaintiff requests such a suspension.[23]

In marital matters the court is required to issue a comprehensive judgment determining all issues raised as to the existence and termination of the marriage. A partial judgment (*Teilurteil*) determining some, but not all, of these matters is not permissible.[24]

In a divorce case ancillary applications (*Folgesachen*) for marital support, division of marital property, and care, custody and support of minor children, may be joined with the original application for divorce and may be adjudicated along with the divorce, if granted.[25] In practice, many ancillary applications are handled as separate matters. The court often will first decide the application for divorce and then take up the ancillary applications.[26] If the parties present an agreed plan for the care and custody of minor children, the court must normally confirm this plan and use it as a basis of other necessary ancillary decisions (support, division of marital property, etc). If the court refuses to confirm the agreed plan as in the children's interest, the court is required to address this issue first and reach a decision on care and custody of children before adjudging the divorce and related matters.[27]

---

20. ZPO §613.

21. ZPO §616. In divorce or annulment cases if either party objects, the court may consider facts outside the parties' assertions only inasmuch as they tend to support the existence or continuance of the marriage. ZPO §616(2).

22. ZPO §§608, 278, 614.

23. ZPO §614(2) and (3). See Rosenberg/Schwab/Gottwald, §165(V)(9), pp. 1013 f.

24. Rosenberg/Schwab/Gottwald, §165(V)(6), pp. 1011 f.

25. ZPO §623. Legal aid granted for the divorce itself will support representation in the proceedings on an ancillary application for distribution of pensions between the divorced spouses unless the order granting the legal aid otherwise indicates. ZPO §624(2).

26. ZPO §628.

27. ZPO §627.

2. Procedures in Other Family Cases

Family cases involving the determination of parenthood, or the care, custody or support of minor children, whether joined with a divorce case or maintained independently during or after marriage, almost always involve the interest of the state as protector of the minor children. Proceedings in such cases are regulated partly by the Civil Procedure Code (ZPO) and partly by the Law on Noncontentious Jurisdiction (*Gesetz über die Angelegenheiten der freiwilligen Gerichtsbarkeit* or FGG).[28] Although representation by counsel is compulsory in all divorce cases and ancillary proceedings involving a marriage or its property, in some non-marital family cases such representation is not required.[29] On the other hand, in any case in which the welfare of a child is involved, the family court is required to notify and hear from the Office of Childrens' Services (*Jugendamt*) before making a decision.[30] Moreover, if the court deems it advisable for the protection of the interests of a minor child, the court can name a guardian ad litem (*Pfleger für ein seine Person betreffendes Verfahren*) to appear for the child in a family court proceeding.[31]

In any case involving the custody or care of a child, each parent has the right to be heard in person by the court, regardless of whether that parent has custody of the child at the time.[32] The court must also hear from the child in person if the child is 14 years old, or court is of the view that hearing from the child in person would be of value in determining an issue in the case.[33]

The Law on Non-Contentious Jurisdiction imposes on the family court the responsibility to strive toward a resolution of child care and custody matters by agreement, and requires the court to consult with the parties early and often on potential settlements and to advise the parties of public resources for counseling and conciliation. The court is authorized to suspend

---

28. See, e.g., ZPO §§621, 621a; ZPO §640(1) and BGB §1600e(2) with FGG §§55b, 55c.

29. ZPO §§78(3), 621. For example, in a proceeding between unmarried parents for a custody of a minor child the parents would not be required to have lawyers.

30. FGG §49a. The Office of Childrens' Services may be represented in the proceedings by a non-lawyer. ZPO §78(4).

31. FGG §50. The law suggests that such a guardian ordinarily should be named if the interests of the child and its ordinary legal representative stand in conflict or if there is a possibility of withdrawal of the child from the care of its parents or other caregiver, and that a guardian ordinarily should not be named if the child is represented by its own attorney.

32. FGG §50a

33. FGG §50b. See German Federal Constitutional Court, 34 *NJW* 217, 218 (1981).

the proceedings if the parties are ready to enter into counseling or conciliation or if the court believes that such a suspension would lead to settlement of the dispute.[34]

Cases for the determination of the existence of a parent child relationship (*Klage auf Feststellung des Bestehens eines Eltern-Kind-Verhältnisses*) can be brought either by (on behalf of) the child, by the child's mother, or by the putative parent (usually seeking a declarative judgment of non-parenthood).[35] Generally they must be brought in the judicial district in which the child resides.[36] The final judgment establishes the status of parenthood effective against the parties and, in principle, against the world.[37] Pending final judgment the court may enter orders for temporary custody and support of the child and its mother as in a divorce case.[38] Procedure, including the right of the court to order evidence on its own motion, and the rights of key parties (such as the parent, putative parent, childrens' services officer and the child) to participate and be heard in person, parallel other family court proceedings.[39]

When there is no question about the parentage of a minor child, there is a simplified procedure for assessment of support against a parent not having physical custody.[40] Upon application by the custodial parent the court notifies the putatively responsible parent of the application and the amount that would be due under the support guidelines.[41] If there is no contest by the respondent the court goes on to determine the liability of the respondent for periodic payments and assess the amount due as of the time of the application.[42] In the ordinary case there is no oral hearing. If there is a serious dispute about the amount or liability for support, the proceeding will be governed by the ordinary rules governing family court actions.[43]

---

34. FGG §§52, 52a.

35. ZPO §640.

36. ZPO §640a(1)(1). A claim brought by the mother can also be lodged in the court where the mother resides (ZPO §640a(1)(2)). For further exceptions and details see ZPO §640a(1)(3) and (1)(4).

37. ZPO §640h.

38. ZPO §641d. If parenthood is not proven, a putative parent ordered to pay temporary support can recover amounts paid from the party which obtained the temporary order. ZPO §641(g).

39. ZPO §640(1).

40. ZPO §§645–660.

41. See BGB §§1629(2)(2) and (3)(1), 1626a(2) and 1666, 1671, 1672; ZPO §647.

42. ZPO §§648–649.

43. ZPO §651.

The simplified procedure is only valid for support claims up to 1.5 times the amount that would be payable under the statutory support guidelines.[44] Applications are based on pre-printed forms which can be submitted and filed without the assistance of a lawyer.[45]

B. Documentary and Check Proceedings

The German civil justice system has long recognized a special accelerated procedure for claims based solely on checks, other negotiable instruments, and similar documents.[46] If a claim is for a sum certain and the cause of action can be proved solely through documentary evidence the plaintiff has the option to follow the special written document and check procedure (*Urkunden- und Wechselprozess*).[47] The idea is to provide a relatively fast and inexpensive means to collect sums due where all of the material relevant to the cause of action is in writing.[48]

If the documentary and check process is elected, the plaintiff must so indicate in the complaint and attach all checks, notes or other documents on which the claim is based.[49] Counterclaims are not permitted.[50] The only admissible proof is documentary proof (*Urkundenbeweis*) which the court can consider without the need for witness testimony to establish relevance or authenticity. Witness testimony, views, expert testimony and party interrogation

---

44. See ZPO §645, BGB §§1612a ff.

45. ZPO §§657–659. In order to facilitate efficient handling of these cases, the statute permits delegation of these proceedings to a single local court serving several local court districts. See ZPO §660.

46. In 1989 approximately 5% of the civil cases in the local courts and 2.2% of the cases in the state district courts were governed by the documentary and check procedure.

47. ZPO §592. Included are claims for foreclosure of a mortgage on default of payment. If only a part of the claim is based on documentary evidence, the documentary process may be used for this part of the claim. German Federal Supreme Court, 21 *WM* 367 (1967).

48. Check cases and many other documentary cases within the subject matter jurisdiction of the state district court are referred to the commercial panels (*Handelskammern*). See GVG §95(1)(2) and (3) and Ch. 3(D)(2)(c) above. In both the local and the district courts they are often batched for efficient handling using mechanized procedures for notice and printed forms of judgments and orders.

49. ZPO §593(2). The documents may also be attached to a later written memorandum or brief, or filed at an oral hearing. An exemplified copy is allowed. See State Appeals Court of Frankfurt, 49 *WM* 2079, 2081 (1995); Thomas/Putzo/Reichold, §593, mn. 3.

50. ZPO §595(1).

at the instance of the court are not permitted.[51] If it turns out that the plaintiff's cause of action cannot be sustained solely by documentary proof, the plaintiff has the option of withdrawing the case from the documentary procedure,[52] or the court will dismiss the case without prejudice to the plaintiff to proceed in the ordinary way.[53]

The defendant may raise objections (*Einrede*) to the cause of action asserted by the plaintiff, and may substantiate the objections with documentary proof of its own.[54] If the court finds the complaint legally sufficient and supported by the documentary evidence, and finds any objections of the defendant legally insufficient, or insufficiently supported, the court will enter judgment for the plaintiff in the amount substantiated by the documentary evidence. If the documentary evidence supports the position of the defendant, the complaint will be dismissed. If the defendant raises a legally sufficient objection or defense (*Einrede*) which will require proof beyond the documentation submitted by the parties, the court enters a provisional judgment (*Vorbehaltsurteil*) against the defendant "reserving his rights",[55] and the case remains pending for ancillary proceedings (*Nachverfahren*) to determine the sufficiency of the objection or defense.[56] The plaintiff may obtain execution on the provisional judgment,[57] but if the ancillary proceedings result in vacation of the judgment, the plaintiff will be liable for damages sustained by the defendant by reason of execution of the vacated judgment.[58]

---

51. ZPO §595. On application of the plaintiff party interrogation (*Parteivernehmung*) may be used to authenticate documents signed by or obtained from the opposing party or to give evidence for contested facts asserted in the claimant's reply. See Thomas/Putzo/Reichold, §595, mn. 3.

52. ZPO §596. However if the case is on second instance appeal before an appellate court, the plaintiff may withdraw from documentary procedure only in accordance with ZPO §263 (cf. German Federal Supreme Court, 29 BGHZ 337, 339 (1959)), and he cannot withdraw at all if the case is on review appeal to the Federal Supreme Court. See Thomas/Putzo/Reichold, §596, mn. 3.

53. ZPO §597(2). See Supreme Court of the German Empire, 148 RGZ 199, 201 (1935); Thomas/Putzo/Reichold, §597, mn. 3.

54. ZPO §598. Applications for interrogation of parties are also permitted; see ZPO §§598, 595(2).

55. (...*Ausübung seiner Rechte vorzubehalten*...). See ZPO §599(1).

56. See ZPO §600.

57. ZPO §§599(3), 708(4). The provisional judgment is also subject to appeal if the defendant believes that it was improperly granted.

58. See ZPO §§600(2), 302(4)(3) and (4); Lüke, §46, mn. 461.

The ancillary proceedings go forward like an ordinary case without restriction as to mode of procedure or proof.[59] If the court finds in favor of the plaintiff on the defendant's objections and defenses, the provisional judgment is made final. If it turns out that the plaintiff's claim is not justified, the provisional judgment is vacated and the claim dismissed.[60]

If the claim is based on a check (*Wechsel or Scheck*), the procedure is even more simplified and expedited.[61] Venue in a check case may, at the option of the creditor, be laid at the place of payment of the check (often the place of the creditor's place of business) rather than the residence of the debtor.[62] The time within which the defendant must answer or appear can be significantly shortened, from a minimum of two weeks in the ordinary civil case, to as little as 24 hours in a check case if the summons is served in the same locality where the court sits.[63] Proof of delivery of the check can consist simply of a request for party interrogation of the defendant.[64]

So, for example, if a plaintiff produces the defendant's check, but the defendant claims that the goods purchased with the check were defective, the plaintiff will be able to obtain a provisional judgment. However this may be revoked if the defendant is ultimately able to convince the court in the ancillary proceedings of the defects in the goods.

C. Civil Warning Proceedings

If a creditor believes that its claim is not likely to be contested by the debtor, and wishes to avoid the cost and expense of commencing an ordinary lawsuit, it may elect to use the "civil warning procedure" (*Mahnverfahren*) to collect the claim. In a large number of cases the receipt of the official warning notice from the court will produce voluntary payment. If the claim is actually not

---

59. See ZPO §600(1). The ancillary proceedings are considered a part of the initial documentary case. During the ancillary proceedings it is possible for both parties to go beyond the bounds of the strict documentary procedure in both pleading and proof. Rosenberg/Schwab/Gottwald, §163(III)(6), p. 990.

60. ZPO §§600(2), 302(4)(2).

61. See ZPO §§602–605.

62. ZPO §603. If several obligors are sued in the same case, venue may be laid in the judicial district in which any of the obligors reside.

63. ZPO §604.

64. ZPO §605. If the defendant defaults, delivery is admitted. See Rosenberg/Schwab/Gottwald, §163(IV)(2)(d), p 992; Thomas/Putzo/Reichold, §605, mn. 1.

disputed, the warning procedure can result in an enforceable court order and execution. If the defendant gives notice that the claim is disputed (*Widerspruch*), it will proceed as an ordinary lawsuit.

The warning procedure is popular among German creditors.[65] As noted above,[66] court costs for filing ordinary civil cases are relatively hefty. The court costs for issuance of a warning notice are relatively minimal.[67] Most warning proceedings are commenced by the creditor itself without the use of an attorney. And if an attorney is used, the fees for making out the application for a warning notice are modest.[68] Use of the warning procedure is an inexpensive way to jog a dilatory debtor to pay, and to get an execution if the debtor fails to do so.[69] Recent amendments to the Civil Procedure Code have authorized widespread use of mechanized facilities for processing of claims including the filing of claims in electronic form, and the automated issuance of warning notices (*Mahnbescheide*).[70]

1. Claims Eligible for the Warning Procedure

The warning procedure is available for a liquidated claim payable inside Germany in European currency.[71] If the debtor lives outside Germany in a state which is a Member State of the European Union, a signatory to the Lugano Convention, a signatory to the Hague Convention on the Recognition of Decisions for Family Support, or a state which is a party to a special bi-lateral treaty, the debtor will be subject to the German warning procedure according to the provisions of the European Regulation or the individual international

65. In 1989 there were some 5.3 million warning proceedings filed in local courts in Germany. Objections were raised by the debtors in only about 11% of these.

66. See Ch.9(E)(1)(b) above.

67. Court costs of proceedings for the issuance of a warning notice are computed at ½ of one unit of cost. See GKG, Attachment 1 No. 1100. An ordinary civil case is computed at 3 units of cost, reduced to one if the case is settled by agreement or by withdrawal of the claim before judgment. See GKG, Attachment 1 No. 1210, 1211; for more details see Ch. 9(E)(1)(a). For instance, the cost of obtaining a warning notice for a claim of 600 EuR would be 17.50 EuR, while the cost of asserting the claim as an ordinary civil action would be 105 EuR.

68. See BRAGO §43.

69. If, however, the debtor objects to the warning notice, the case becomes an ordinary civil case and the ordinary fees are payable.

70. ZPO §689(1), (3).

71. ZPO §688(1) and (3). Claims in a foreign currency may be converted into Euro. See Federal Supreme Court, 104 BGHZ 268 (1988).

treaty. In such case any execution notice (*Vollstreckungsbescheid*) issued in such a procedure will be enforceable in the foreign state of the debtor's residence.[72]

The claim may be any kind of claim for the payment of money, whether based on a contract, tort, or other cause of action, so long as performance by the creditor of any corresponding obligation is completed and there is no requirement of future performance.[73] If the claim is subject to the consumer credit law (*Verbraucherkreditgesetz*) and bears interest, the warning procedure is available only if the rate of interest provided in the contract did not exceed the base interest rate of the European Central Bank by 12% as of the time the contract was formed.[74] The warning procedure cannot be used if service of the warning notice (*Mahnbescheid*) would have to be by public notice (*öffentliche Bekanntmachung*).[75]

2. Procedure in Warning Proceedings

The warning procedure is conducted by the magistrates (*Rechtspfleger*) in the local courts, which have jurisdiction of warning proceedings regardless of amount in controversy.[76] Exclusive venue is laid at the location of the creditor's residence or corporate "seat".[77]

The proceeding is commenced by application filed by the creditor, usually on pre-printed forms supplied by the court, or electronically, seeking the issuance of a warning notice ordering the defendant to pay the claim. The application must set forth all pertinent details of the parties and the claim, including interest, and the fact that no performance is due on the part of the creditor, and also designate the court which would have subject matter jurisdiction and venue were the case to be handled as a contested proceeding (*strei* -

72. ZPO §688(3); Law Implementing European Regulations and International Conventions on Recognition and Execution of 2001/2002 (*Anerkennungs- und Vollstreckungsausführungsgesetz*), §32. See also Einhaus, „Die internationale Reichweite des deutschen Mahnverfahrens im Anwendungsbereich des EuGVÜ", 50 *AnwBl* 557 (2000). For details on relevant European Regulations and international conventions see Ch. 12(A) and (D) below.

73. See ZPO §688(2)(2).

74. ZPO §688(2)(1). This is a form of consumer protection.

75. ZPO §688(2)(3).

76. ZPO §689(2)(1); RPflG §20(1).

77. See ZPO §§689(2), 13, 17, 18 and Ch. 5(C)(1). If the *defendant* has no place of usual residence or no "seat" in Germany, the exclusive venue is in the local court which would be a proper venue for an ordinary suit based on the claim. See ZPO §703d and Ch. 12(B)(1) below.

tiges Verfahren).[78] An application submitted in writing must be signed by the creditor or authorized representative.[79]

The magistrate reviews each application for prerequisites to justiciability (*Prozessvoraussetzungen*) and for the particular warning procedure requirements.[80] If the magistrate finds a defect in an application, she notifies the applicant and gives the applicant an opportunity to respond to her concern. If the defect is not corrected or the magistrate's concern is not resolved to the magistrate's satisfaction, the application is returned to the applicant.[81] Such a return (*Zurückweisung*) is not a formal dismissal of the claim, but operates merely as a declination by the court to entertain it as a warning proceeding. The creditor is free to recast the application and try again, or to commence a regular proceeding.[82]

If the application survives the magistrate's initial review, the magistrate will send the debtor a warning notice (*Mahnbescheid*), advising the debtor of the creditor's application and ordering the latter to pay the creditor's claim, with interest and related costs or to notify the court of its objections to any part of the claim within two weeks of receipt of the notice.[83] The warning notice must specifically state that the court has not examined the sufficiency of the creditor's claim.[84] It must also state that if the debtor does not raise a timely ob-

---

78. ZPO §690. If the identity of the parties is clear, a lack of their exact names will not affect the validity of the warning notice. See German Federal Supreme Court, 50 *NJW* 1584, 1586 (1997).

79. ZPO §690(2). Signature can be dispensed with on applications submitted electronically if there is a system to insure that applications can only be filed with the authorization of the creditor. ZPO §690(3).

80. Rosenberg/Schwab/Gottwald, §164(III)(3), pp. 995 f. The magistrate does not generally examine the complaint for the legal sufficiency (*Schlüssigkeit*) of the claim. In consumer credit matters the magistrate must determine whether the claim satisfies the maximum interest requirements of the consumer credit law. ZPO §§690(1)(3), 688(2)(1).

81. ZPO §691. If the defect is of a kind that could be cured by the applicant, the magistrate might also issue an interim order calling the defect to the applicant's attention and setting a brief time period to cure it. See German Federal Supreme Court, 52 *NJW* 3717, 3718 (1999).

82. If the application has been used to toll the statute of limitations, the tolling will be continued if a civil complaint is filed within a month of the time the application is returned and if the complaint is promptly served. ZPO §691(2). Delay of service of the complaint will not affect the tolling if the delay is not the fault of the plaintiff. See German Federal Supreme Court, 53 *NJW* 2282 (2000) and ZPO §167; for details Ch. 7(F)(5) above.

83. ZPO §692(1). If objections are to be filed on a specific form, the warning notice must attach a copy of the form and advise that additional forms can be obtained from the local court. ZPO §692(1)(5).

84. ZPO §692(1)(2).

jection, an execution notice (*Vollstreckungsbescheid*) will issue, which may ultimately lead to involuntary execution (*Zwangsvollstreckung*). The warning notice must also identify the court in which contested proceedings would take place if objections to the warning notice are filed.[85]

The warning notice is served on the debtor in the manner prescribed for civil complaints, usually by mail to the address of the debtor as listed in the application.[86] Objection may be filed with the court in writing, or given orally to the clerk of courts at the clerk's office at any time after receipt of the warning notice.[87] Although there are forms which debtors may use in filing objections, such forms are not obligatory and any format which communicates the fact and nature of the debtor's objection will suffice.

If the debtor fails to file objection to the warning notice within two weeks of effective service of the notice on him, the creditor may apply for an execution notice (*Vollstreckungsbescheid*).[88] The application must recite that two weeks have elapsed since service of the warning notice and must itemize any payment received by the creditor since filing of the application for the warning notice. This application is also reviewed by the magistrate. If she notices defects in the warning procedure or the lack of any prerequisite to suit, the application will be denied and the warning notice will be extinguished.[89]

If the application for an execution notice is in order, the magistrate will issue the notice and it will be served on the debtor. In the ordinary course service is on the court's own order, and usually is by mail. If a creditor wishes to arrange service itself and so requests in the application, the execution notice will be delivered to the creditor for service.[90] Like warning notices, execution notices can be issued on an automated basis.

The execution notice has the legal effect of an immediately executable default judgment (*Versäumnisurteil*). The creditor can begin execution proceedings immediately,[91] subject, however to possible liability for damages if a

---

85. ZPO §692(1)(4) and (1)(6). The notice must advise that determination of subject matter jurisdiction and venue is reserved to the designated court.

86. See Ch. 7(F)(5) above on procedures for service of process. The warning procedure is not available for claims which must be served by public notice. See ZPO §688(2)(3) and Ch. 11(C)(1) above.

87. ZPO §§694, 702.

88. ZPO §699. The application must be filed within 6 months of the issuance of the warning notice or the warning notice will become null and void. ZPO §701.

89. Rosenberg/Schwab/Gottwald, §164(IV)(3), p. 1001.

90. ZPO §699(4).

91. See ZPO §§700(1), 708(2).

timely objection is filed and the court ultimately adjudges his claim to be worth less than his execution.[92]

If the debtor files an objection (*Einspruch*) with the court within 2 weeks of issuance of the execution notice, further proceedings will be had as if objection had been timely lodged to a default judgment in an ordinary case.[93] If no objection is lodged, the execution notice becomes final and has the effect of a final judgment by default.

3. Procedure if Objection Is Raised

If the recipient of a warning notice files an objection with the court issuing the notice within the 14 day period (or afterward but before the magistrate has taken up the issuance of the execution notice), the warning proceeding, as such, is terminated. On application of either party the case will be transferred to the court which appears to have proper subject matter jurisdiction and venue so that it can proceed there as an ordinary civil action.[94] The court that issued the warning notice will transmit the record of the case to the court in which the case will proceed. If the record is promptly (*alsbald*) forwarded, the pendency (*Rechtshängigkeit*) established by the service of the warning notice is not interrupted.[95]

The court receiving the transfer is not bound by the action of the magistrate transferring the record so far as its jurisdiction and venue are concerned. That court must of its own motion examine the record received to make sure of the prerequisites of justiciability (*Prozessvoraussetzungen*) as it would examine the complaint in an ordinary case.[96] The court then requests the applicant to transform its claim as set forth in the application for a warning notice into the form of a conventional complaint (*Klageschrift*) within a specified

---

92. See ZPO §717(2); for proceedings on execution see Ch. 11(F) below.

93. See ZPO §700(3) and Ch. 9(A)(1) for proceedings following objection to a default judgment.

94. ZPO §696(1). Ordinarily the case will be transferred to the court identified by the plaintiff in the application as the court in which an ordinary suit on the claim could be brought. However the parties may agree to transfer of the case to another court.

95. ZPO §696(3). Delay in forwarding the records will not affect pendency so long as the delay is not attributable to the applicant. German Federal Supreme Court, 103 BGHZ 20 (1988).

96. ZPO §696(5). If the court is of the view that jurisdiction or proper venue is lacking, the case will be transferred to the proper court or dismissed without prejudice. See Ch. 5(F) above. Deferring the examination of jurisdiction and venue to the court receiving the transfer is designed to permit automated handling of the transfers by the originating court.

time, generally two weeks.[97] The resulting pleading, called a "justification of claim" (*Anspruchsbegründung*) serves the function of the complaint (*Klage*) in the ongoing civil action. The restrictions on the nature of the claim or relief requested which applied at the beginning of the warning proceedings no longer apply. The plaintiff is also required to advance the difference between the court fee for an application for a warning notice and the court fee on filing of a complaint.[98]

Procedure after the filing of the justification of claim follows the course of ordinary civil actions. The defendant may be required to file an answer after service of the justification of claim. The court may order the optional written preparatory procedure or prepare the case by a preliminary hearing (*früher erster Termin*). Court costs and attorneys fees are the same as for a civil case commenced in the conventional way.

D. Pre-Judgment Attachment and Provisional Measures

A party who has a legitimate basis for concern that time or intervening events may hinder or prevent successful execution of a future civil judgment can initiate a special proceeding for prejudgment attachment (*Arrest*) or other preliminary measures (*einstweilige Verfügungen*) to provide security for the potential future judgment or temporarily to regulate the parties' legal relationship pending final judgment.[99] This special expedited proceeding is usually carried out in the court in which the underlying claim is pending or will be filed. Attachment or other preliminary relief may also be sought in the local court for the district in which the property to be attached is found or in which the subject matter of the litigation is located.[100] Resort to a court other than

---

97. ZPO §697(1). If the justification of claim is not timely filed, the opponent can move to have the court set a definite time for filing the justification upon pain of dismissal of the claim. ZPO §697(3) and Thomas/Putzo/Reichold, §697, mn. 8.

98. See GKG §65(1)(2).

99. See ZPO §§916–945; for more details see Baur/Stürner, *Zwangsvollstreckungs-, Konkurs- und Vergleichsrecht*, Vol. I: Einzelvollstreckungsrecht, 12th ed. (1995), mn. 51.1 ff., 53.1 ff. For a survey on the law of the European countries see Stürner, "Einstweiliger Rechtsschutz", in: Storme (ed.), *Procedural Laws in Europe* (2003), pp. 143 ff.; for provisional measures in aid of foreign courts compare Ch. 12(D)(3) below.

100. See ZPO §§919, 937(1), 942(1). The prejudgment attachment is not necessarily limited to the particular object that is the subject matter of the litigation. See Thomas/Putzo/Reichold, §919, mn. 7.

the court of the action in chief is only permissible in pressing circumstances (*in dringenden Fällen*), such as risk of imminent dissipation of the property.[101]

The "attachment court" (*Arrestgericht*) or the "court of preliminary measures" (*Gericht der einstweiligen Verfügung*) can order attachment of property sufficient to satisfy a judgment based on a money-claim, or a variety of other preliminary measures designed to safeguard the realization of the claims in suit. Such measures can include an order of sequestration of specific property in contention, a preliminary injunction forbidding disposition of property or restraining specific actions in question, a series of preliminary orders designed to maintain the status quo pending decision of the underlying litigation, or temporary measures to regulate the parties' conduct or provide interim support or payments pending final judgment.

A plaintiff can seek an attachment or other preliminary measures in connection with an initial claim just as can a defendant in connection with a counterclaim. A party may seek preliminary relief before the commencement of an action, at any stage during the prosecution of the case or even on appeal. An important safeguard for the person whose property is attached or who is otherwise constrained by a preliminary measure is a claim for damages if the plaintiff's claim is adjudged to be without merit or if the attachment turns out to be too large or otherwise unjustified.[102]

1. Prejudgment Attachment

A party who has a claim for the payment of money only[103] and who justifiably fears that execution of a judgment may be frustrated by lapse of time or other event outside his control[104] can initiate a summary proceeding seeking a judicial attachment (*Arrest*) of sufficient described property of the defendant to satisfy the claim and costs of suit. The petition for attachment (*Arrestgesuch*)[105] must set forth the underlying claim (*Arrestanspruch*) with particularity and make a plausible (*glaubhaft*) showing of success on the merits. The pe-

---

101. ZPO §§937, 942.

102. ZPO §945; for details Baur/Stürner, *Einzelvollstreckungsrecht*, mn. 52.23 ff., 54.21 ff.

103. ZPO §916(1). Included are non-money claims which can be converted into money claims, e.g. a claim for delivery of individual goods may turn into a claim for damages in case of non-performance. See Thomas/Putzo/Reichold, §916, mn. 4; BGB §§433(1)(1), 280 ff.

104. ZPO §917.

105. See ZPO §920(1) and(2). It is also possible to make an oral petition for attachment at the clerk's office (*Geschäftsstelle*). The clerk's minutes of the oral request form the basis for the court's action. ZPO §920(3).

tition must also make a plausible showing of the circumstances which justify the prejudgment intervention of the court (*Arrestgrund*). Attachment of a debtor's property currently located in Germany can be ordered if it would otherwise be necessary to execute the judgment in a foreign country that is not a Member State of the European Union or a party to the Lugano Convention.[106] Other grounds include apparent wasteful dissipation of the debtor's assets through unfavorable conduct of business, specific likelihood of sale or encumbrance of the debtor's property, frequent change of the debtor's abode, and similar developments which would endanger the currently available prospects for satisfaction of the creditor's claim.[107] Fears of competitive claims of other creditors are not grounds for a preferential attachment. The primary purpose of prejudgment attachment is not to improve the creditor's position with respect to the debtor's assets but merely to prevent deterioration of that position.[108]

Depending on the nature of the circumstances, the court may order notice to the debtor and set a time for a written response, schedule an oral hearing, or, in exceptional cases, enter a decision *ex parte*.[109] Although the statute leaves

---

106. ZPO §917(2)(1). However if there is no danger that the debtor's German assets will be removed before the time when final judgment would be expected, or if the creditor possesses sufficient security for its claim in other forms, mere foreign residence of the debtor will not support a prejudgment attachment. Thomas/Putzo/Reichold, §917, mn. 3, 4. See ZPO §917(2)(2). The exception to the general rule justifying attachment of a foreign defendant's German property is the consequence of a decision of the European Court of Justice, 47 *NJW* 1271 (1994). The ECJ held that allowing attachment of the German property of other EU-citizens only because their main assets were located in another Member State of the EU is a forbidden discrimination against citizens of EU Member States. See Baur/Stürner, *Einzelvollstreckungsrecht*, mn. 51.3.

107. See Thomas/ Putzo/Reichold, §917, mn. 1, 2; Baur/Stürner, *Einzelvollstreckungsrecht*, mn. 51.3.

108. German Federal Supreme Court, 131 BGHZ 95, 105 (1997). Attachments made within one month of filing of a bankruptcy proceeding are automatically voided by the court order initiating the insolvency proceeding ("opening order"); see InsO §88. Older attachments may be subject to avoidance by virtue of one of the avoidance powers given the bankruptcy trustee. See Ch. 11(G)(2) below on bankruptcy procedure and the powers of the bankruptcy trustee. Attachments not subject to avoidance in bankruptcy support priority claims to the proceeds from the attached assets when those assets are liquidated by the trustee. See InsO §§50, 166 ff. When ordinary execution is taken against a debtor existing attachments are given priority in the order of time based on when the attachment orders were served. See Ch. 11(F)(1)(a) below.

109. ZPO §922(1). An order may be made without giving prior notice to the other party only upon proof of urgent necessity and a preponderance of considerations of fairness. See German Constitution Art. 103(1) and Federal Constitutional Court, 9 BVerfGE

the question of whether to order oral hearing to the discretion of the court, the principle of fair judicial hearing requires that hearing be dispensed with only in cases of good cause.[110]

Although it is possible for the court to receive oral testimony in connection with a request for attachment, ordinarily the court's decision is based on the parties' written submissions and representations at any oral hearing. The court may condition any attachment on the posting of security by the creditor if the court believes that the petitioner has failed to make a fully plausible showing of either the strength of the legal claim or the circumstances justifying pre-judgment relief, or if the circumstances otherwise justify such an order (such as would be the case with an *ex parte* proceeding).[111] In any event, an order granting an attachment must set forth the amount for which attachment is authorized and the amount of security that the debtor may furnish to prevent the attachment or to secure release of the property attached.[112] The court's decision on the petition is embodied in a judgment (*Urteil*) if rendered after oral hearing, and in a simple order (*Beschluss*) if rendered without oral hearing. An order of attachment must be promptly served on the opposing party at the instance of the applicant.[113] Judgments and orders of attachment are both subject to appeal.[114] If the claim on which the attachment is based is not already pending (*anhängig*), the attachment court must, on request of the debtor, specify a time period within which action on the claim must be commenced. If the party securing the attachment fails to commence a lawsuit within the time specified, the attachment is subject to dissolution.[115]

89, 98 (1959). If the court proceeds *ex parte* and decides not to grant the creditor's request, the request and the denial are not to be disclosed to the debtor. ZPO §922(3).

110. The decision to proceed without oral hearing must be made by the entire court, and is not subject to appeal.

111. ZPO §921(2), Thomas/Putzo/Reichold, §921, mn 3.

112. ZPO §923.

113. ZPO §922(2). This is one of the relatively few situations in which process is served at the instance of a party rather than at the instance of the court. See Ch. 7(F) above.

114. A judgment granting or denying an attachment after hearing is subject to second instance appeal (*Berufung*). An ex parte denial of attachment is subject to miscellaneous appeal (*Beschwerde*). See Ch. 10(D) and (F) for procedures on these appeals. A grant of an order of attachment without oral hearing is subject to review by objection (*Widerspruch*). The objection is heard by the court issuing the order. The attachment order is not stayed by lodging of the objection, but may be rescinded, modified, or confirmed subject to security in a judgment after hearing. ZPO §§924, 925. The court's decision on the objection is usually given after hearing as a judgment (*Urteil*) and is subject to second instance appeal. See Baur/Stürner, *Einzelvollstreckungsrecht*, mn. 51.15 ff., 51.21 ff.

115. ZPO §926. The debtor can also request dissolution or modification of the at-

Simple attachments of tangible personal property are executed by the court executor (*Gerichtsvollzieher*). Attachment of real estate or intangible personal property is by court order recorded in the real estate registry or served on the third party debtor as the case may be. Prejudgment attachments proceed in the same manner as attachments in process of execution,[116] except that the property is merely attached, not liquidated.[117] If the attaching creditor subsequently obtains a judgment in the case in chief, the judgment creditor may proceed directly to liquidate the attached property in order to satisfy the judgment.[118] On the other hand, if it turns out that the creditor is unable to sustain his underlying claim or if the attachment was otherwise defective or legally unjustified, the party whose property was attached may seek damages sustained by virtue of the attachment, including the costs of posting any security to remove the groundless or improper attachment.[119]

2. Other Preliminary Measures

Claimants seeking protection of interests other than simple claims for money judgments may petition the court in which the case in chief is pending or, if there is no case pending, the court in which a case could be filed for preliminary measures (*einstweilige Verfügungen*) designed to safeguard their rights to effective relief.[120] Section 935 of the Civil Procedure Code provides:

---

tachment based on change in circumstances affecting either the merits of the underlying claim (e.g. payment), or the need for security (e.g. provision of security for the judgment by the debtor or others). See ZPO §927 and Thomas/Putzo/Reichold, §927, mn. 12–15.

116. See Ch. 11 (F)(1) below on procedure on personal property execution.

117. ZPO §§928–932. The attachment must be completed within a month of oral rendition or service of the attachment judgment or order on the attaching creditor. ZPO §929(2).

118. See Thomas/Putzo/Reichold, §930, mn. 3; Baur/Stürner, *Einzelvollstreckungsrecht*, mn. 52.10 ff., 52.20; see also Ch. 11(F)(1) below on procedures on liquidation of attached property on execution.

119. ZPO §945. The scope of damages is defined by BGB §249. See Thomas/Putzo/Reichold, §945, mn. 1 ff., 7 ff. and Baur/Stürner, *Einzelvollstreckungsrecht*, mn. 52.23 ff. for a discussion of the circumstances under which damages would be recoverable.

120. For details see Baur, *Studien zum einstweiligen Rechtsschutz* (1967); Jauernig, "Der zulässige Inhalt einweiliger Verfügungen", 79 *ZZP* 321 (1966); Leipold, *Grundlagen des einstweiligen Rechtsschutzes* (1971); Schilken, *Die Befriedigungsverfügung* (1976); Heinze, *Einstweiliger Rechtsschutz im Arbeits- und Wirtschaftsrecht* (1981); Walker, *Der einstweilige Rechtsschutz im Zivilprozess und im arbeitsgerichtlichen Verfahren* (1993); Heinze, "Die Leistungsverfügung", in: K. Schmidt et al. (eds.), *Festgabe für den Bundesgerichtshof*, Vol. III (2000); pp. 569 ff.

> Preliminary measures with respect to the subject matter of the controversy are permissible when there is justified concern that the realization of the rights of a party could be frustrated or seriously impeded by a change in the current circumstances.[121]

This broad provision can be invoked to authorize a preliminary order sequestering identified property in dispute, enjoining the debtor from disposing of or encumbering described property, or prohibiting the debtor from engaging in described deleterious or assertedly illegal conduct in business or personal affairs.[122] The court is authorized to order that a notice of any provisional measure affecting the ownership of real estate, ships or other registered property be recorded in the appropriate registry to prevent the owner from disposing of this property to a third party.[123] The precise form and content of the preliminary measure is left to the sound discretion (*freie Ermessen*) of the court.[124] Like the prejudgement attachment, the idea is to secure the eventual effectuation of a final judgment.

Preliminary measures are also authorized to regulate legal relationships between litigating parties and establish a kind of "legal peace" (*Rechtsfrieden*) during the litigation.[125] When a long-standing legal relationship breaks down, and the interests of one party or the other are threatened, the court can intervene to re-establish the relationship or establish a new one in order to avoid potential injury or disadvantage to one of the parties pending the litigation. For instance, if a supplier refuses to deliver goods to a long term distributor based on a dispute as to the meaning of the distributorship agreement, the court can order that deliveries continue pending the outcome of the litigation in order to save the distributor from potentially serious harm from the supplier's unilateral ac-

---

121. ZPO §935. (*Einstweilige Verfügungen in Bezug auf den Streitgegenstand sind zulässig, wenn zu besorgen ist, dass durch eine Veränderung des bestehenden Zustandes die Verwirklichung des Rechtes einer Partei vereitelt oder wesentlich erschwert werden könnte*).

122. ZPO §938. For details see Baur/Stürner, *Einzelvollstreckungsrecht*, mn. 53.10 ff.

123. ZPO §§938, 941. Such a measure can consist of a warning notation against a putatively wrong registration (*Widerspruch*), an outright prohibition of transfer (*Veräusserungsverbot)* or a mere pre-registration of transfer of an interest in land (*Vormerkung*) in the appropriate registry. Warning notations and pre-registrations do not prevent the debtor from making an assignment or transfer of the property, but do prevent the purchaser from claiming status as a good faith purchaser. The result would be that the purchaser's title may be subject to the plaintiff's claim. See Baur/Stürner, *Sachenrecht*, 17th ed. (1999), §20(VII), mn. 67 ff.; Kohler, *Das Verfügungsverbot gemäss §938 Abs. 2 ZPO im Liegenschaftsrecht* (1984).

124. ZPO §938(1).

125. ZPO §940.

tion.[126] If a party claims that another party is violating a trademark or patent right, or engaging in unfair competition, the court can restrain such behavior pending final judgment in the case. A party seeking such relief must make a plausible showing of the necessity for preliminary relief. Delay in resort to the court can be seen as evidence that the need for relief is not pressing.[127]

While the primary purpose of preliminary measures is to safeguard rights from frustration due to alteration of the thing or legal relationship in controversy, the statute has been construed to permit preliminary measures to protect from frustration of legal right due to the circumstances of the plaintiff as well. In certain cases security for the eventual satisfaction of a plaintiff's claim will not suffice to give the plaintiff complete justice. A spouse or child with a claim to periodic payments of support may not be able to wait for relief until final judgment.[128] A person injured in an accident may lack funds to pay ongoing medical bills. The case law supports use of the court's power to grant preliminary relief in a number of such cases when final judgment may come too late.[129]

Preliminary measures may be used to grant needy parties a portion of the ultimate relief sought only under exceptional circumstances, when "the applicant requires immediate satisfaction so pressingly that he can not wait out an ordinary proceeding without sustaining disproportionately great, practically irreparable, damage."[130] The circumstances that have been held to justify this exceptional kind of preliminary relief are many and various. In all cases, however, the person seeking the relief must make at least a plausible showing of success on the merits and a strong showing of the exigency justifying relief before legal entitlement has been established in the ordinary manner.[131]

---

126. See State Appeals Court of Stuttgart, 5 *NJW-RR* 940 (1990); State Appeals Court of Koblenz, 36 *WRP* 412, 413 (1991); Stürner, "Einstweilige Verfügung auf Durchführung von Austauschverträgen", in: Bettermann et al. (eds.), *Festschrift für Zeuner* (1994), pp. 513 ff.

127. Thomas/Putzo/Reichold, §940, mn.5 ("*Selbstwiderlegung*").

128. The family court has specific authority to adopt preliminary measures (*einstweilige Anordnungen*) concerning temporary support, occupation of real estate, custody of children, and use of property pending final judgment of the underlying case. See Ch. 11(A) above.

129. See State Appeals Court of Cologne, 13 *MDR* 398 (1959) (funds to pay ongoing medical bills); State Appeals Court of Karlsruhe, 42 *FamRZ* 1424 ff. (1995) (payments of support).

130. Thomas/Putzo/Reichold, §940, mn. 6. See State Appeals Court of Cologne, 10 *NJW-RR* 546 ff. (1995); State Appeals Court of Düsseldorf, 11 *NJW-RR* 123, 124 (1996).

131. Lüke, §89(III), mn. 724. See Baur/Stürner, *Einzelvollstreckungsrecht*, mn. 53.23 ff.; Thomas/Putzo/Reichold, §940, mn. 6–17 for a discussion of the various situations in which preliminary partial relief has been ordered on this theory.

Although all such dispositions are preliminary and are subject to the court's final decision on the merits, in many cases the circumstances of the parties make the court's preliminary order final in practical effect. Payments to an impecunious claimant for periodic support or medical bills may be impossible to recover even if the court finally rules that there was no legal entitlement to them. The court may require security for repayment of sums advanced pursuant to preliminary order, and in most cases preliminary payments will be ordered only for a limited time.[132]

The court's authority in non-family cases[133] to order a party to vacate residential premises is limited to situations of recent trespass in order to avoid resort to self-help (*Eigenmacht*).[134] In most cases a tenant cannot be forced to vacate his residence prior to final judgment.

Application for preliminary measures other than simple attachment must be made to the court in which the case in chief (*Hauptsache*) is, or will be, pending.[135] Only in exceptionally pressing cases may the plaintiff resort to the local court where the thing in controversy is located.[138] In such cases the local court may grant temporary relief for a specified limited time only, subject to renewal of the request in the court of the case in chief.[139]

Procedure on requests for preliminary measures parallels the procedure on motions for simple attachment.[140] However, as a rule preliminary measures

---

132. A number of decisions have specified 6 months as the maximum permissible duration of such payments on the theory that most litigants should be able to obtain a first-instance judgment in such a time period. See State Appeals Court of Hamm, 1 *NJW-RR* 943 (1986); State Appeals Court of Koblenz, 35 *FamRZ* 527 (1988) and other cases collected at Thomas/Putzo/Reichold, §940, mn. 9.

133. In family cases, the court may order that a party vacate the marital premises and otherwise regulate use and access to the family residence. ZPO §620(7) and (9).

134. ZPO §940a. However, if there is a concrete danger of bodily harm the court may also order a party to vacate residential premises.

135. ZPO §937(1). If the case is on appeal, this will be the court in which the appeal is lodged. ZPO §943(1).

138. ZPO §942. If the preliminary relief requested is merely a warning notation against a putatively wrong registration (*Widerspruch*) or a pre-registration of transfer of an interest in land (*Vormerkung*) in a real estate registry maintained by that local court, there is no requirement of exceptional necessity and no requirement of resubmission to the court of the case in chief unless the opposing party so requests. ZPO §942(2).

139. ZPO §942(1). In these exceptionally pressing cases the local court may act *ex parte*, but any renewal of the preliminary order would take place only after notice and hearing of the parties. If the request for preliminary relief is not renewed within the specified time, the local court is required to vacate the preliminary order on request of the opposing party. ZPO §942(3).

140. ZPO §936.

other than simple attachment are only ordered after oral hearing. The court may, however, deny a request for preliminary relief without hearing, and may grant such relief without hearing in pressing cases (*dringende Fälle*).[141] Usually requests for preliminary measures in cases being heard by panels in the state district court or in the state appeals courts are decided by the entire panels, although in exceptional circumstances which require prompt relief without notice or oral hearing, the presiding justice can act in behalf of the court.[142]

The existence of alternative forms of security for the applicant's claim is to be taken into account in determining whether preliminary measures should be ordered. If the court orders a preliminary measure, the opposing party may obtain the dissolution of the preliminary restraint by posting alternative security if the alternative security would fully protect the interests safeguarded by the preliminary measures.[143]

As is the case with simple attachment, the court is authorized to enter other preliminary measures conditioned on the applicant's furnishing security for any damages caused by the preliminary restraint in the event that the preliminary measures prove unjustified, either because of lack of merit of the underlying claim or other cause.[144]

3. Claim for Unjustified or Improper Attachment

A party whose property has been attached or against whom other preliminary relief has been ordered has a right to damages from the attaching creditor or the party who obtained the preliminary relief in the event that the attachment or preliminary order is vacated or ultimately determined to be

---

141. ZPO §937(2). Pressing cases include situations where the effectiveness of a preliminary measure would be jeopardized by the delay necessary to call a hearing. But the right to be heard (*rechtliches Gehör*) would permit the court to act without at least requesting a written response from the opposing party only in the most extreme cases, usually when prior notice to the debtor would endanger the effectiveness of the provisional measure. See Baur/Stürner, *Einzelvollstreckungsrecht*, mn. 54.4.

142. ZPO §944. In a case which is assigned to a single judge, the single judge will act on requests for preliminary measures. See Ch. 3(D)(2)(b) and Ch. 7(E)(1) above.

143. ZPO §939. For instance an artisan might apply for a preliminary order of sequestration to protect his lien to secure payment for work done on an item of moveable personal property. The property owner would likely be able to secure vacation of the preliminary order by posting money security for the artisan's claim. See Thomas/Putzo/Reichold, §939, mn. 2.

144. ZPO §§921, 936.

unjustified by the outcome of the underlying suit.[145] The claim must be based on a defect which existed at the time the attachment or preliminary measure was ordered. Later developments affecting the basis for the pre-judgment attachment or provisional measure (such as payment) cannot support a claim for damages. The decision of the attachment court approving an attachment or other preliminary measure is, in principle, not res adjudicata on the substance of the later damages claim.[146] However a specific determination in the case in chief that no valid claim existed as of the date of the attachment would be given effect in the subsequent damages claim.[147]

The right to damages pursuant to ZPO § 945 extends only to damages sustained by the opponent, and does not cover collateral harm to third parties. The claimant must show that the damage claimed was the direct result of the attachment or other preliminary restraint, and not some other cause.[148] Elements of damage can include the cost of posting security, any costs attendant on efforts to dissolve the attachment or restraint, and consequential damages suffered by reason of the existence of the attachment or restraint.[149] A creditor who obtains an attachment or other preliminary restraint based on a questionable claim or shaky procedural basis does so at his peril.

E. Non-Contentious Civil Proceedings

A good portion of the activity of the local courts involves the exercise of non-contentious jurisdiction (*freiwillige Gerichtsbarkeit*) in more or less non-adversarial matters such as guardianship, probate, registration of real estate,

145. ZPO § 945. This right also exists if an attachment is granted prior to suit, and suit is not brought within the prescribed time.

146. See Baur/Stürner, *Einzelvollstreckungsrecht*, mn. 52.23 ff.; 54.21 ff.; Thomas/Putzo/Reichold, § 945, mn. 9, 10. Some courts, however, have held that a decision of the attachment court dissolving an attachment based on a defect existing at the time it was made is binding in a subsequent action for damages. German Federal Supreme Court, 75 BGHZ 1 (1980). It is also prevailing opinion that the finding of the attachment court on the reason for attachment (*Arrestgrund*) or need for other provisional measure may not be challenged in a subsequent suit for damages.

147. See Federal Supreme Court, 41 *NJW* 3268 (1988); 122 BGHZ 172, 175 (1993); Baur/Stürner, *Einzelvollstreckungsrecht*, mn. 52–25; Thomas/Putzo/Reichold, § 945, mn. 9.

148. See BGB §§ 249 ff. In rather exceptional cases third parties may be entitled to damages under the provisions of substantive law, e.g. on the basis of breach of contract or negligence, etc.

149. See Thomas/Putzo/Reichold, § 945, mn. 15; Baur/Stürner, *Einzelvollstreckungsrecht*, mn. 52.25.

maintenance of business registers, and the like.[150] Many of these matters involve the interests of parties not well positioned to protect themselves, or some aspect of the public interest. Much of non-contentious jurisdiction partakes of an ongoing administrative or supervisory character. For these reasons, the principle of party control of proceedings (*Verhandlungsprinzip*) does not apply to many non-contentious proceedings and the court is often given a direct responsibility to examine the sufficiency or regularity of a transaction or state of affairs.

1. Non-Contentious Jurisdiction

The boundary between contentious and non-contentious jurisdiction is not always very clear. Some family law proceedings confided to the non-contentious jurisdiction can be very contentious in fact, and include oral argument, taking of proof and rendition of decision in a manner very similar to conventional civil actions.[151] On the other hand, many so called "contentious" cases are resolved by agreement. It is hard to find a governing principle according to which one can authoritatively assign cases to contentious or non-contentious jurisdiction.[152] In general, cases which involve matters of legal status (e.g. guardianship, business register), or which involve several involved parties (inheritance, condominium matters) are likely to be confided in whole or in part to the non-contentious jurisdiction.

Many more or less administrative or ministerial court functions in the exercise of non-contentious jurisdiction are performed by the magistrates (*Rechtspfleger*).[153] Matters of greater legal difficulty or importance are generally assigned for decision by local court judges (*Amtsrichter*).[154] Decisions of a magistrate are generally subject to miscellaneous appeal (*Beschwerde*) to the appellate court. In most case this would be the state district court.[155]

---

150. See Baur/Wolf, *Grundbegriffe des Rechts der freiwilligen Gerichtsbarkeit*, 2nd ed. (1980), pp. 18 ff.; Rosenberg/Schwab/Gottwald, § 11(I), pp. 53 f. for a listing of some of the more common functions within the non-contentious jurisdiction of the local courts.

151. See Rosenberg/Schwab/Gottwald, § 11(II)(1), p. 54. See Ch. 11(A)(2) above for family cases.

152. See Baur, *Grundbegriffe der freiwilligen Gerichtsbarkeit* (1973), pp. 13 ff.

153. See RpflG § 3 and Ch. 3(H)(2) above.

154. See RpflG §§ 5, 14 ff.

155. See RpflG § 11 as enacted in 2001.

2. Procedure in Non-Contentious Proceedings

Proceedings in non-contentious jurisdiction are governed in large part by the Law on Non-Contentious Jurisdiction (*Gesetz über die Angelegenheiten der freiwilligen Gerichtsbarkeit* or FGG), supplemented by the Civil Procedure Code (ZPO). Many sections of the FGG simply incorporate sections of the ZPO by reference. Proceedings in non-contentious jurisdiction matters are often commenced by filling out specialized forms such as the forms for entry of a business entity in the business register, or for probating an estate. There are special subsections of the FGG dealing with procedural aspects of some of the more common (and adversarial) matters within the non-contentious jurisdiction such as guardianship or ongoing care and custody of minor children (*Vormundschaftssachen* and *Familiensachen*) and civil commitment proceedings (*Unterbringungssachen*).[156]

Sometimes there is a question about the binding effect of a decision rendered in the exercise of non-contentious jurisdiction on a court hearing a later contentious proceeding. In general the proceedings are independent and a party to a later contentious proceeding is not bound by a prior decision in a non-contentious proceeding.[157] In some cases, where the parties to the contentious proceeding also took significant part in the non-contentious proceeding, they may be bound by the decision of the non-contentious proceeding.[158]

The multiplicity of different kinds of non-contentious proceedings, and the variety of interests and functions served, makes it difficult to make meaningful generalizations.[159] However it should be noted that the legal structures of all of these proceedings are carefully designed to preserve rights of appearance and hearing as well as opportunities for appeal and review to all parties conceivably affected by the proceeding. Although "non-contentious" this jurisdiction is in no way "non-judicial".

---

156. See FGG §§35 ff., 65 ff., 70 ff. For family cases see also Ch. 11(A) above.

157. Rosenberg/Schwab/Gottwald, § 11(III)(2), p. 57. For example, issuance of a certificate of inheritance by the probate court does not bind a court in a later contentious proceeding between rival claimants to inheritances in the subject estate.

158. E.g. when a non-contentious proceeding determines disputes about money claims between a condominium as a whole and owners of individual units. See WEG §§ 43 ff. (German Law on Condominiums). On the other hand, in many cases a judge in the non-contentious jurisdiction will not be bound by a decision between two parties in a contentious case because of the additional and different interests which the non-contentious judge must consider. See Rosenberg/Schwab/Gottwald, § 11(III)(3)(b), pp. 57 f.

159. For an effort to rationalize and explain the law on non-contentious jurisdiction and procedure in non-contentious proceedings, see Baur, *Grundbegriffe*, p. 13 ff.

F. Execution of Civil Judgments

If a court judgment is not paid or complied with, the holder of the judgment must have a means of enforcing it. The German civil justice system provides an intricate mechanism for the execution of civil judgments. Statutory mechanisms for involuntary execution (*Zwangsvollstreckung*) of civil judgments attempt to strike a balance between speed and effectiveness of remedy on the one hand and scrupulous protection of the rights of the parties, particularly the judgment debtor, on the other.[160]

Most executions are carried out under the supervision of the local courts in their role as "execution courts" (*Vollstreckungsgerichte*).[161] This does not mean that the court issuing the judgment never has a role in the execution. Some functions related to the execution must be performed by the "deciding court" (*Prozessgericht*).[162] However the ongoing supervision of the execution process and the determination of issues arising in connection with that process are generally the responsibility of the local courts.

The first prerequisite for execution is a "title of execution" (*Vollstreckungstitel*), an official court document identifying the judgment debtor and the judgment creditor and confirming that the creditor has a right to execution against the debtor in a certain amount or for a certain kind of described performance based on a court judgment or the legal equivalent. Most execution titles are final court judgments (*Endurteil*), partial judgments, default judgments or execution notices in warning proceedings.[163]

---

160. Execution of civil judgments against property of judgment debtors involves elements of property law and the rights of third party owners and lienors in addition to the procedures of civil justice between the parties. Execution is also a quintessential example of intervention of state power in private dealings. For this reason, German law of execution is very intricate and detailed. The following description and analysis is not intended to do this body of law justice, but merely to sketch the outlines of some of the more common forms of execution. For a more complete and authoritative treatment see Baur/Stürner, Zwangsvollstreckungs-, Konkurs- und Vergleichsrecht, Vol. I: *Einzelvollstreckungsrecht,* 12th ed. (1995); Rosenberg/Gaul/Schilken, *Zwangsvollstreckungsrecht,* 11th ed. (1997).

161. ZPO §764.

162. See ZPO §§887 ff. (execution of judgments for specific performance, see Ch. 11(F)(2)(b) below), ZPO §767 (action to arrest execution, see Ch. 11(F)(3)(b) below).

163. See Ch. 11(C)(2) above for the procedure to obtain an execution notice (*Vollstreckungsbescheid*) in warning proceedings.

Judgements not subject to further appeal are enforceable without any security.[164] Judgements subject to appeal are also immediately enforceable, but in many cases security may be required from the creditor as a condition of immediate enforcement or from the debtor as a condition for granting a stay from execution.[165] If a judgment subject to further appeal is vacated, the creditor will be liable for damages sustained by the debtor by reason of execution of the vacated judgment.[166]

Some execution titles result from settlements documented of record.[167] In the case of a court judgment, the mandate of the judgment (*Urteilstenor*) itself is the title of execution. In the case of a settlement, the execution title is prepared by the court clerk from the minutes of the hearing at which the settlement was made of record.[168]

The second prerequisite for execution is, in principle, the court's certification of enforceability of the execution title (*Vollstreckungsklausel*).[169] This certificate of execution is prepared by the court clerk and appended to the judgment or other execution title to be executed.[170] The exact text of the certification is:

> "The above copy is issued to [name of the creditor] for the purpose of execution".[171]

In case of a conditional execution title the certification will generally be issued only when any special preconditions for the commencement of execu-

---

164. See ZPO §§704, 705.

165. For an overview see Lüke, §58(II), mn. 527–534; for details see ZPO §§708 ff. and Baur/Stürner, *Einzelvollstreckungsrecht*, mn. 14.1 ff., 15.1 ff.

166. See ZPO §717(2) and (3); Baur/Stürner, *Einzelvollstreckungsrecht*, mn. 15.32 ff.

167. ZPO §794(1)(1). German law also permits a party to subject itself to immediate execution on a promissory note or similar obligatory document executed before a notary. Such "executable documents" (*vollstreckbare Urkunde*) are frequently used in connection with real estate mortgages and financing transactions secured by personal property. See ZPO §794(1)(5); Baur/Stürner, *Einzelvollstreckungsrecht*, mn. 16.14 ff.; Wolfsteiner, *Die vollstreckbare Urkunde* (1978); Münch, *Vollstreckbare Urkunde und prozessualer Anspruch* (1989); Ch. 12(C)(1) below.

168. See Ch. 11(I) below for the procedure for making settlements of record.

169. See ZPO §724.

170. See Ch. 3(H)(1) above for description of the functions of the court clerks..Certifications of enforceability of executable documents are prepared and issued by public notaries. ZPO §797(2). Some execution titles need no execution certificate, e.g. determinations of the monetary amount of costs (see ZPO §795a and Ch. 9(E)(5) above), other execution titles only under special circumstances, e.g. execution notices (see ZPO §796).

171. *(Vorstehende Ausfertigung wird dem [Bezeichnung der Partei] zum Zwecke der Zwangsvollstreckung erteilt).*

tion (e.g. finality of the judgment of divorce in case of a settlement in an ancillary family dispute) have been made of record by public or authenticated documents.[172] The certification of enforceability may permit execution for or against successors of the original parties to the litigation.[173]

The third and last prerequisite for execution is service of the execution title on the debtor.[174] The service of the title may grant the debtor a last opportunity for voluntary execution. The execution title can be served by the creditor directly and need not go through the court.

1. Execution on Money Judgments

The holder of a money judgment has the option of several means of obtaining execution of the judgment against different kinds of assets of the judgment debtor. The court official who performs executions against tangible personal property is the court executor (*Gerichtsvollzieher*), who acts upon application by the creditor directly or in exceptional cases through the clerk's office (*Geschäftsstelle*) of the court to which she is attached.[175] It is the court executor's job to collect the sum provided in the execution title, to receipt for same, and when the judgment is satisfied in full, to deliver the execution title to the judgment debtor.[176]

a. Execution Against Tangible Personal Property

In the ordinary case the court executor is expected to go to the premises of the debtor and search there for property with which the judgment can be satisfied. If the debtor refuses access to the premises, the court executor can obtain an order granting access from the local court in the district where the premises are located.[177] If the court executor finds property of the debtor which is subject to execution, she levies an attachment (*Pfändung*) on sufficient property to satisfy the judgment. Some items of household, trade and farm use, however, are not subject to execution. Exempted are items of the debtor's "personal or household use" (*dem persönlichen Gebrauch oder dem Haushalt dienende Sachen*), sufficient food and fuel for the debtor and family for a four week period (or the money to buy

---

172. ZPO §726.

173. ZPO §§727 ff.

174. ZPO §750.

175. ZPO §753. For more details on the office and function of the court executor see Ch. 3(H)(3) above.

176. ZPO §§754, 757.

177. ZPO §758a.

the same), pets and household farm animals, sufficient farm implements and tools for support of the debtor and his family, tradesmen's tools and equipment, books, clothing and uniforms, some personal jewelry and the like.[178]

If the court executor finds money, valuables or personal property not exempt from execution, she makes levy on the assets by taking them into her possession or otherwise giving notice that the assets have been levied on. Money, securities and small items of valuable personal property are usually physically taken by the court executor for safekeeping.[179] Bulky items such as furniture, or equipment, are constructively seized by affixing an official seal to the item in a prominent location.[180] In all events the debtor is to be notified of which items have been seized. Once an item of property is subject to levy, the debtor may not avoid the attachment by selling, transferring or concealing the property. If the debtor transfers the attached property to a third party, the purchaser's title is subject to the creditor's levy.[181] If there is property of the debtor in the possession of a third party, levy can be made directly against the third party, provided that the latter is prepared to surrender the property.[182]

When the court executor performs an execution and does not find sufficient property of the debtor to cover the judgment, she is authorized to question the debtor about the existence of other tangible or intangible property that might potentially be available for execution.[183] She is also authorized to ask other parties in the debtor's household the name and address of the debtor's employer, although these parties are not required to respond. Any information received is to be relayed on to the creditor.[184]

In keeping with the policy favoring composition and compromise settlement, the statute specifically charges the court executor with promoting vol-

---

178. See ZPO §811.

179. ZPO §808(1).

180. ZPO §808(2).

181. But the purchaser may claim the status as a good faith purchaser. See Baur/Stürner, *Sachenrecht*, §55(D)(III)(1).

182. ZPO §809. If the third party refuses to surrender the property, or asserts an interest of his own, the judgment creditor may attach the judgment debtor's right to possession of the property and assert this right to possession against the third party. See Baur/Stürner, *Einzelvollstreckungsrecht*, mn. 28.10 ff. The creditor may also proceed under the Law on Fraudulent Transfers (*Anfechtungsgesetz* or AnfG) to set aside the transfer to allow levy on the property. For details see Baur/Stürner, *Einzelvollstreckungsrecht*, §26.

183. See ZPO §806a(1). Another remedy of the judgment creditor would be to request that the debtor be ordered to file a disclosure under oath (*eidesstattliche Versicherung*). See Ch. 11(F)(1)(c) below.

184. ZPO §806a(2).

untary settlement of the judgment debt under execution. If she does not find assets which can be readily seized, but the debtor undertakes to pay the judgment in installments within a reasonable time, she is authorized to collect the installments with the consent of the creditor.[185]

Items of personal property in the immediate or mediate custody of the court executor are subject to subsequent attachment (*Anschlusspfändung*) to secure other judgments of the original judgment creditor or the claims of other judgment creditors. The court officer merely notes the subsequent attachment in his minutes (*Protokolle*). Attachments in execution of money judgments have priority in the proceeds of the attached property in order of time of attachment.[186]

When the property attached is money (*Geld*), realization on the attachment is simple. The court executor simply turns the money over to the judgment creditor. Payment is deemed to take place as of the time of seizure of the money.[187]

In the more common case, when the personal property attached is a moveable other than money, the court executor must sell the attached property at auction (*Versteigerung*). Unless the property is of a kind that immediate disposition is economically necessary, the auction sale cannot take place earlier than a week after the attachment. Unless the parties otherwise agree, the sale takes place in the district in which the attachment was made, and must be publicly advertised with reasonable designation of the items to be sold.[188]

At the auction the attached property must be sold to the highest bidder, who must pay cash. The property may not, however, be sold at a price less than half of its regular market value (*gewöhnlicher Verkaufswert*).[189] This minimum bid (*Mindestgebot*) must be made known to the participants at the beginning of the auction.[190] The creditor may bid at the auction and need not produce cash up to the amount of the judgment.[191]

---

185. ZPO § 806b.

186. See ZPO § 826 (*Anschlusspfändung*) and ZPO §§ 804(3), 827(2), 872 ff. (priority rule); Baur/Stürner, *Einzelvollstreckungsrecht*, mn. 28.27, 29.15; Lüke, § 75(I)(5), mn. 624.

187. ZPO § 815(1) and (3). For the protection of the interests of third parties see ZPO § 815(2) and Ch. 11(F)(3)(c) below.

188. ZPO § 816.

189. ZPO § 817a(1) and (2). Items of gold and silver must be sold for a price at least equal to their bullion value. ZPO § 817a(3).

190. ZPO § 817a(1) and (2).

191. For details of the auction procedure see ZPO § 817. If the creditor buys the property in against the judgment claim, the claim is satisfied to the extent of the winning bid. ZPO § 817(4).

The announcement of the award to the highest bidder does not pass title to the attached goods. It creates a special kind of public contract for the conveyance of the goods.[192] Title passes when the winning bidder pays the purchase price and the goods are delivered to the purchaser by the court executor.

In most cases the purchaser at an execution sale acquires good title to the attached property free and clear of liens and claims of third parties.[193] This is true if the attached property was not actually owned by the judgment debtor, if the property sold was legally exempt from attachment and even if the claim on which attachment was made did not exist at the time of attachment.[194] On the other hand, if the attachment is void (*unwirksam*) because of non-compliance with fundamental requirements of the authorizing statute, the purchaser may acquire no valid title.[195]

Receipt of the proceeds of sale by the court executor counts as payment by the debtor to the extent of the net proceeds received.[196] The court executor is obligated to deliver the net proceeds of the sale after payment of costs of sale to the judgment creditor to the extent of the judgment, unless other parties have established prior claims to the proceeds.[197] If there are multiple attachments, the court executor satisfies them in the chronological order the attachments were made. If there is dispute among the attaching judgment creditors, the money is placed in escrow, and the dispute is resolved by the execution court.[198]

---

192. Baur/Stürner, *Einzelvollstreckungsrecht*, mn. 29.6 ff. If the court executor fails to deliver the goods to the highest bidder, the correct remedy is an exception (*Erinnerung*) under ZPO §766.

193. See Federal Supreme Court, 119 BGHZ 75, 76 f. (1992); Baur/Stürner, *Einzelvollstreckungsrecht*, mn. 29.7. The policy behind this rule is to encourage bidders to participate and pay higher prices in execution sales.

194. These defects must be raised by other proceedings such as actions in arrest of execution (*Vollstreckungsgegenklage*), objection (*Erinnerung*), or third party claims (*Drittwiderspruchsklage*). After distribution of the proceeds the debtor or third party may sue the creditor based on a theory of unjust enrichment (BGB §812(1)(1)); see Baur/Stürner, *Einzelvollstreckungsrecht*, mn. 27.12 f., 29.18 ff. and Ch. 11(F)(3) below for an explanation of these remedies.

195. See Lüke, §75(II), mn. 628; Baur/Stürner, *Einzelvollstreckungsrecht*, mn. 29.7. This occurs rarely.

196. ZPO §819.

197. See ZPO §815(1). See Ch. 11(F)(3)(c) below on claims for prior satisfaction from proceeds.

198. ZPO §§827, 872 ff. The court executor provides a report to the execution court of the amount and timing of the competing attachments and other relevant details.

b. Execution against Real Estate

A judgment creditor may proceed to satisfy its claim from the debtor's real estate either through an involuntary lien procedure (*Zwangshypothek*), which gives the judgment creditor a priority interest in the property, but does not immediately liquidate it, or by an execution sale procedure (*Zwangsversteigerung*), which leads to prompt sale of the property and application of the proceeds to valid consensual and non-consensual liens in order of priority. Property which produces income or which can only be liquidated over time may be subject to involuntary administration proceedings (*Zwangsverwaltung*). Procedures for involuntary sale and administration of real estate are largely governed by the Law on Involuntary Sale and Administration (*Gesetz über die Zwangsversteigerung und die Zwangsverwaltung* or *ZVG*). A creditor can elect any one or a combination of these remedies.[199]

The local court for the district in which the real estate is located becomes the execution court for all real-estate related execution measures. If the real estate is located in more than one local court district, the district, or even state appeals court whose territorial jurisdiction includes all of the real estate will specify the local court to serve as execution court. That local court will then notify all other local courts in whose districts the debtor's real estate is located.[200]

An involuntary lien (*Zwangshypothek*) may be obtained by filing an application with office for the registration of real estate (*Grundbuchamt*), generally located at the local court for the district in which the debtor's real estate is located.[201] The application must include the judgment creditor's execution title. The registration office enters a security lien (*Sicherungshypothek*) in the amount of the judgment in the real estate registry (*Grundbuch*). The creditor's security lien is deemed to arise as of the time of entry of the lien in the real estate registry.[202]

---

199. ZPO §866. For details on the execution against real estate see Baur/Stürner, *Einzelvollstreckungsrecht*, §§34–38, mn. 34.1 ff.; Böttcher, *ZVG*, 3rd ed. (2000); Stöber, *ZVG*, 17th ed. (2002); for a short survey see Lüke, §§80–83, mn. 664 ff.

200. See ZVG §§1, 2; ZPO §§36, 37. The state appeals court designates the execution court if the debtor's real estate is located in more than one district court judicial district. In extreme cases, if the debtor's real estate is located in more than one appeals court district, the designation must be made by the Federal Supreme Court of Justice.

201. GBO §1.

202. ZPO §867(1). The minimum amount for which a lien will be noted is more than 750 Euro (ZPO §866(3)). If there are more than one parcel of real estate involved, the creditor must apportion the lien by monetary amount among the various parcels registered to the debtor. ZPO §867(2).

The establishment of a security lien protects the creditor's interest in the real estate against future consensual or non-consensual liens to the same extent as would a consensual mortgage, but does not lead directly to satisfaction of the judgment. Entry of the security lien similarly does not discharge the debtor's obligation. In order for the judgment to be paid and the debtor's obligation extinguished, the creditor must take further steps to cause the property to be sold to a third party or administered so as to generate cash proceeds.[203]

Independent from the lien procedure a judgment creditor can apply to the execution court to initiate proceedings for an involuntary sale of the debtor's property.[204] There is no requirement that the judgment creditor have already obtained a judgment lien (*Zwangshypothek*). However, by obtaining a judgment lien the judgment creditor can protect himself from transactions and certain other liens which might arise before an opportune time for a sale. The execution sale can only address property registered in the name of the judgment debtor.[205]

If the application is in order and the court is satisfied that the debtor is the registered owner of property in the district, the court issues an order that the sale take place and that structures the conditions of the sale (*Anordnungsbeschluss*). This order has the effect of a seizure of the debtor's property and gives the creditor the right to satisfaction of his claim from the property.[206] A copy of the order must be promptly served on the debtor and the court's action is duly noted in the real estate registry.[207]

The terms and conditions of the actual execution sale of the debtor's real estate are very precisely regulated by statute.[208] All proceedings are taken under the auspices of the execution court. Following the issuance of the structuring order seizing the property, the court must issue an order for the actual auction-sale proceeding (*Versteigerungstermin*). The order sets the place and date for the auction proceeding,[209] lists the registered owners and registered value

203. See ZPO §867(3).

204. ZVG §§15, 16. The application must include the judgment creditor's execution title.

205. ZVG §17. The execution sale can also cover the judgment debtor's interest as heir of the registered owner of the property.

206. ZVG §§10(1)(5), 20.

207. ZVG §§19, 22.

208. See ZVG §§15–144.

209. Usually the sale is to take place within 6 months of the order, and either at the courthouse or some other place within the judicial district (such as on the premises being sold). ZVG §36.

of the real estate, requests all persons claiming any interest in the real estate to quantify and register their interests before bids are solicited at the auction, and similarly invites all persons with a right to prevent the auction to take action before the sale takes place.[210] The notice must be served on the debtor and all persons with registered interests in the real estate, published in the local organ for publication of court notices and posted on the courthouse bulletin board.[211] The auction must be scheduled for a date at least 6 weeks after the issuance of the notice.[212]

At the beginning of the auction proceedings the court must first identify any third parties' interests in or claims secured by the real estate which have priority over the claim of the judgment creditor seeking the sale. These can be freeholds, easements, claims of mortgagees and other lienors as well as claims of other judgment creditors holding prior judgment liens or seizures. The court then determines the minimum bid (*geringstes Gebot*) for which the property can be sold and sets the conditions of the sale.

Under German law property subject to prior liens or interests in land is sold at execution sale subject to the prior liens or interests. The purchaser thus acquires only the equity of the debtor. The interests of third parties subordinate to the interest of the judgment creditor seeking the sale are extinguished. The minimum bid must be one which will be sufficient to cover all prior liens and interests plus the costs of the sale.[213] When payment is made, the amount of prior liens and interests is deducted and payment is made in the net amount (*Bargebot*).[214] Sale at any amount in excess of the minimum bid will yield at least something to the judgment creditor who sought the sale.

Bids are generally orally tendered at the execution sale, with the court retaining authority to determine the acceptability of any bid.[215] When the bidding stops, the court announces the highest bid and invites the parties to comment on the proposed award (*Zuschlag*) of the property to the highest bidder.[216] At or following the conclusion of the auction proceeding the court

210. ZVG §§37, 38.

211. ZVG §§39–41.

212. ZVG §43. The issuance of the notice must comply with the requirements prescribed by ZVG §37. See State Appeals Court of Karlsruhe, 101 *Rpfleger* 256, 257 (1993); State Appeals Court of Hamm, 108 *Rpfleger* 172, 173 (2000).

213. ZVG §§44, 52, 91.

214. See ZVG §49. In exceptional circumstances the purchaser may be required to discharge the prior liens. See ZVG §50.

215. ZVG §§71f.

216. ZVG §§73, 74.

issues its award order (*Zuschlagsbeschluss*),[217] which becomes effective on rendition (*Verkündung*).[218] The award order includes terms evicting the debtor from the property and requiring the debtor to relinquish possession of the property in favor of the purchaser; it permits involuntary execution against the debtor.[219] Interests of claimants junior to that of the creditor effecting the sale are extinguished. If there are any sales proceeds left after satisfying the judgment and paying the sales expenses, the excess will be applied to the junior creditors' claims in order of priority in time.[220] The award order is subject to miscellaneous appeal (*Beschwerde*).[221] If the appeal is sustained, the title of the purchaser can be vacated.[222]

In cases where the creditor seeks satisfaction from the income of the debtor's property, the creditor can seek to have the property subject to involuntary administration (*Zwangsverwaltung*) by a court appointed administrator (*Zwangsverwalter*) until sufficient funds have been generated and paid over to satisfy the judgment. Application is made to the execution court, which by order seizes the income, rents or fruits of the real estate, removes the debtor from possession of the property and installs a court appointed administrator.[223] The administrator is required to manage the property in a prudent manner considering all relevant interests (including the interest of the debtor) and generate income or proceeds from such administration to satisfy the claim of the judgment creditor.[224] The administrator is subject to the oversight of the execution court and renders periodic accountings to the court with copies to the interested parties.[225] The administration is terminated when the creditor's claim is paid or when the real estate is seized for execution sale.[226]

---

217. ZVG §§81, 82.

218. ZVG §§87–89. When the court does not render the award order orally it becomes effective on its service. See State Appeals Court of Cologne, 90 *Rpfleger* 113 (1982).

219. ZVG §93.

220. ZVG §§91, 92. If there are several claimants to the cash proceeds from the sale, the court can convene a distribution proceeding (*Teilungsverfahren*) for the determination of their relative priorities and for adoption of a plan (*Teilungsplan*) for division of the proceeds among them. See ZVG §§105–115.

221. ZVG §96.

222. ZVG §90.

223. See ZVG §§146, 148, 150.

224. See ZVG §152. The funds are disbursed according to a distribution plan (*Teilungsplan*) approved by the court. ZVG §§155 ff.

225. ZVG §153, 154. For details see Baur/Stürner, *Einzelvollstreckungsrecht*, mn. 37.3 ff.

226. ZVG §161.

c. Disclosure under Oath

A judgment creditor can request the court executor to conduct the disclosure of the debtor under oath (*eidesstattliche Versicherung*) in order to discover assets or income for the satisfaction of the judgment. Disclosure is in order if the creditor makes a showing (*glaubhaft macht*) that efforts to levy on the assets of the judgment debtor have not resulted in full satisfaction of the judgment or are not likely to do so, that the debtor has refused to permit the court officer to search through his premises, or that the court executor has not found the debtor in his premises in repeated visits after sufficient notice and without excuse.[227]

Upon receipt of a proper request for disclosure, the court executor must notify the debtor and set a time for the disclosure hearing at least 2 weeks but not more than four weeks following receipt of the request.[228] Upon notification by the court executor the judgment debtor is required to provide a written disclosure under oath (*eidesstattliche Versicherung*) of all of his tangible and intangible property as well as all claims against third parties.[229] The disclosure must include all transfers of property to a relative or close associate (*nahestehende Person*) made within two years before the disclosure hearing, and all gifts and transfers of property without full consideration to anyone made within four years of the disclosure hearing.[230]

If the debtor makes a showing that he will pay and discharge the judgment within a time period of not more than six months, the court executor must delay the disclosure hearing to give him a chance to do so.[231] At the disclosure hearing, the court executor may question the debtor about the disclosure in order to clarify ambiguity and insure completeness. The debtor then swears

---

227. ZPO §807.

228. ZPO §900(2). If the parties do not object, the court executor can arrange for an immediate disclosure.

229. ZPO §807.

230. ZPO §807(2). Excepted are customary occasional gifts of relatively little value. Such a disclosure can be used to prepare for a proceeding under the Law on Fraudulent Transfers (*Anfechtungsgesetz*), which permits a creditor to seek a court order setting aside a fraudulent transfer and allowing levy on transferred property. See Ch. 11(F)(1)(a) above and Baur/Stürner, *Einzelvollstreckungsrecht*, §26.

231. ZPO §900(3). With the consent of the parties, the court executor may receive the debtor's installment payments and remit them to the creditor. If the debtor has paid three-fourths of the judgment within the extension period, the court may, but is not required to, delay the hearing for another two months to permit him to complete the payments. This leeway is given to protect the debtor against a possible unnecessary registration of the disclosure and its consequences. See Ch. 11(F)(1)(c) below.

an affidavit to the accuracy and completeness of his written disclosure as supplemented at the hearing. A debtor can be subject to a repeated disclosure within three years only if the creditor makes a plausible showing that the debtor has acquired new property or income in the interval since the last disclosure.[232]

If a judgment debtor does not respond to the summons to the disclosure hearing from the court executor, the execution court may issue an arrest order (*Haftbefehl*) ordering that the defaulting debtor be taken into custody until he has provided the disclosure.[233] A debtor in custody has the right to be brought before the court executor of the district in which he is in custody and to give his disclosure at any time, upon which he will be released.[234] If the failure to provide the disclosure is inaccessibility of the necessary information, the arrest order will be suspended for a reasonable time to permit the debtor to get the information and present it at a new disclosure hearing.[235]

If a debtor has been required to make disclosure or has been subject to an arrest order, the execution court enters the debtor's name on a special "black list" (*schwarze Liste*) which is accessible to the public.[236] A debtor's name is removed from the black list upon satisfaction of the judgment on which disclosure was made, or on the expiration of three years, whichever occurs first.[237] The copying and publishing of the black list and information taken from the list is subject to detailed statutory regulation designed to limit the use of the information to legitimate credit and business purposes and prevent harassment of the debtor or undue invasions of his privacy.[238]

d. Execution against Intangible Property

In many cases the judgment debtor's most valuable property will be intangible property, such as bank accounts, uncertificated securities or claims against third parties. While evidence of this kind of property may be discovered by the court officer in searching through the debtor's premises, or may

---

232. ZPO § 903.

233. ZPO § 901. This provision is not unconstitutional. See Federal Constitutional Court, 36 *NJW* 559 (1983).

234. ZPO § 902.

235. ZPO § 902(3).

236. ZPO § 915. The information from the black list is to be used only for effecting executions or for determining the debtor's creditworthiness. ZPO § 915(3).

237. ZPO § 915a.

238. ZPO §§ 915b–915h.

be disclosed by the debtor in a disclosure under oath, actual realization upon such property usually involves a third party, such as a bank, an issuer of securities, or a third-party debtor.

A judgment creditor desiring to levy against a claim of its judgment debtor against a third party makes written application to the execution court designating the judgment debtor and the third party debtor (*Drittschuldner*).[239] The creditor is not required to convince the execution court of the validity of the debtor's claim against the third-party debtor, a mere assertion of such a claim suffices.[240] Neither the debtor nor the third-party debtor are notified of the filing of the notice. The court decides ex parte based on the application and other papers of record in the proceeding[241] and issues an order of attachment (*Pfändung*). The order forbids the debtor from transferring or collecting the attached claim and forbids the third party debtor from paying it to the debtor.[242] The creditor is responsible for serving a copy of the attachment order on the third-party debtor. The court executor is required to serve a copy of the attachment order and a copy of the return of service (*Zustellungsurkunde*) on the judgment debtor.[243] The attachment becomes valid on service of the order of attachment on the third-party debtor.[244]

If the claim which is attached is secured by a mortgage of real estate, the mortgage certificate must be secured by the court executor.[245] If the mortgage is not certificated, the attachment must be noted in the real estate record book (*Grundbuch*).[246]

If the claim is based on a negotiable instrument such as a promissory note or check which can be transferred by indorsement, the court officer must take

---

239. See ZPO §§828 ff.

240. Lüke, §76(III), mn. 635; Thomas/Putzo, §829, mn. 9.

241. ZPO §834. The particular circumstances of this procedure and the ability of the debtor to lodge a prompt objection following issuance of the order justify this procedure in light of the right to be heard (*rechtliches Gehör*). See Federal Constitutional Court, 9 BVerfGE 98 (1959).

242. ZPO §829(1).

243. ZPO §829(2). This service is coordinated so that the debtor does not learn about the order before the third-party debtor receives notification. For further details on service see Ch. 7(F) above and for return of service see Ch. 7(F)(1)(f) above.

244. See ZPO §829(3).

245. All mortgages are registered in the real estate record book. German law also recognizes certificated mortgages, which can be transferred by written assignment of the claim secured accompanied by delivery of the mortgage certificate, without the need to register the transfer in the real estate record book. See BGB §§1113 ff., 1154 and Baur/Stürner, *Sachenrecht*, 17th ed. (1999), §§36 ff.

246. ZPO §830.

possession of the instrument itself in order to make a valid attachment of the claim.[247] Negotiable instruments payable to bearer or otherwise transferrable without the need of indorsement are treated like tangible personal property.[248] Attachment of a claim for ongoing payments, such as the monthly earned income of an employee, reaches not only those payments due at the time of the attachment, but future payments as they become due.[249] Attachment of the portion of a debtor's income that is necessary for the debtor's maintenance and that of his family would result in additional burden on the public social welfare system. A monthly amount of a debtor's income equal to the monthly amount of social welfare support is therefore, in principle, not subject to execution.[250]

Attachment of the claim merely holds the claim in suspense for the potential satisfaction of the judgment creditor. In order to realize on the attached claim, the judgment creditor must obtain an order of assignment (*Überweisungsbeschluss*) of the claim. In practice, the order of attachment and order of assignment are almost always contained in the same order.[251]

There are two methods by which the creditor can realize on the attached claim. The creditor may cause the claim to be assigned to him at face value for payment in place of the debtor (*Überweisung an Zahlungs Statt zum Nennwert*), in which case the claim becomes his property to deal with as he wishes. Upon election of this form of assignment, the creditor takes the claim subject to any defenses the third party debtor may have against the judgment debtor and subject to the ability of the third party debtor to pay. In any event the debtor is discharged to the extent of the face amount of the claim.

Alternatively, the judgment creditor may merely take assignment of the right to receive payment of the claim (*Überweisung zur Einziehung*), in which case the judgment debtor is credited only with the actual amount of money received on the claim by the judgment creditor. If the third-party debtor does not pay the assigned claim, the judgment creditor cannot execute directly against the defaulting third party. The creditor must initiate an independent

247. ZPO §831.

248. See ZPO §831 and Thomas/Putzo, §831, mn. 1–3.

249. ZPO §832. See German Federal Supreme Court for Labor and Employment Cases, 46 *NJW* 2699 ff. (1993).

250. See ZPO §§850 ff.; for details see Baur/Stürner, Einzelvollstreckungsrecht, mn. 24.1 ff. Similar exemptions from execution in tangible personal property are discussed in Ch. 11(F)(1)(a) above.

251. See ZPO §§835 ff.; Lüke, §76(VII), mn. 646. If the order of assignment is separate, it must be served on the debtor and the third-party debtor in the same manner as the attachment order. ZPO §835(3).

action on the claim against the third party and obtain its own execution title.[252]

Execution against intangible personal property other than money claims or accounts such as patents, copyrights, various kinds of annuity charges secured by real estate (*Rentenschulden*), and future interests (*Anwartschaftsrechte*) requires the execution court to enter a special order directed to the judgment debtor and any third parties involved prohibiting the judgment debtor from realizing financial benefit from these assets and making appropriate provision, including special administration (*Verwaltung*), to divert the economic value of these assets to satisfy the judgment creditor's claim.[253]

2. Enforcement of Non-Monetary Judgments

German civil procedure provides a variety of remedies for the enforcement of judgments not for money, but for delivery of a specific thing, for the performance or abstention from performance of specified conduct, or for the establishment of specific stati or obligations.[254] In general these remedies are structured so as to require the minimum amount of actual coercion of the judgment debtor.

a. *Judgments for Delivery of Possession of Tangible Personal Property or Real Estate*

Judgments requiring the judgment debtor to deliver to the judgment creditor possession of tangible personal property are enforced by the court executor, who simply takes possession of the designated item and turns it over to the judgment creditor.[255] The same is true if the creditor is entitled to a designated quantity of fungible property.[256] If the court executor cannot find the

252. A separate action is required to insure that the third party is in no way disadvantaged by the proceedings to collect a judgment between the judgment creditor and its judgment debtor. See Lüke, §76(VII), mn. 649. The judgment debtor must cooperate with the judgment creditor in providing information necessary to collect the claim. In default of voluntary cooperation, the debtor may be required to disclose such information under oath. ZPO §836(3).

253. See ZPO §857; Lüke, §78, mn. 657 ff.; For details see Baur/Stürner, *Einzelvollstreckungsrecht*, mn. 32.1 ff.

254. Enforcement of orders requiring delivery of children (BGB §1632) in family court matters is governed by the Law on Non Contentious Jurisdiction. E.g. FGG §33.

255. ZPO §883.

256. ZPO §884.

property, the debtor can be required to give a disclosure under oath as to its existence and whereabouts.[257] If the property is in the possession of a third party and the latter will not voluntarily turn it over to the court executor, the creditor must levy on the debtor's right to possession of the property (*Anspruch des Schuldners auf Herausgabe*) and then bring an appropriate action against the third party to secure possession.[258]

Judgments requiring the debtor to surrender possession of real estate are also executed by the court executor, whose assignment is to remove the judgment debtor from possession and place the judgment creditor in possession.[259] If the debtor has personal property in the seized premises, the court officer is required to deliver the personal property to the debtor, the debtor's designee, or a member of the debtor's family.[260] If no authorized recipient can be found, the court officer makes arrangements to store the personal property at the expense of the debtor. If the property is not claimed and the storage costs paid within two months, the court officer can have the property sold and the money deposited for safekeeping and ultimate delivery to the debtor or entitled party.[261]

Judgments of eviction from residential real estate (*Wohnungsräumungen*) are subject to various tenant-protective rules. For instance, the court hearing the eviction proceeding can order in the judgment of eviction a stay of execution.[262] Following issuance of the eviction judgment, the debtor can apply to the court of first instance[263] for a stay of execution, or an enlargement of a stay of execution, as the case may be.[264] Execution cannot be stayed for more than a total of one year from the effective date of the eviction judgment.[265] Even if the eviction is the result of a compromise agreement between the parties (*Räumungsvergleich*), the local court retains the right to order a delay of

257. ZPO §883(2).

258. ZPO §886.

259. ZPO §885(1).

260. ZPO §885(2).

261. ZPO §885(3) & (4).

262. ZPO §721(1). The stay may be granted on application of either party or on the court's own motion.

263. ZPO §721(4). Generally the local court in the district in which the real estate is located. See ZPO §29a and GVG §23(2)(a) and Ch. 5(B)(2) and (C)(2) above.

264. The debtor's application for a stay must be filed no less than two weeks before the date of execution or expiration of a previous stay. A stay may be granted without oral hearing, provided that the opposing party is given prior opportunity to comment. The stay of execution may be conditioned on paying current rent, giving security, or other performance or forbearance by the debtor. See ZPO §§721(1), (3), (4); 732(2).

265. ZPO §721(5). If the case is on appeal the appellate court can order the eviction stayed pending the outcome of the appeal. See ZPO §§719(1), 707.

eviction under terms similar to those pertaining to forcible evictions.[266] Finally, substantive law contains additional tenant-protective provisions that affect the process of eviction.[267]

b. Judgments for Specific Performance

German substantive and procedural law offers specific performance as a remedy of first resort to vouchsafe for the claimant exactly that to which she is legally entitled without exposing her to the risk that she would not be able to obtain full reimbursement via damages.[268] The manner of execution of judgments for specific performance differs with the various kinds of specific performance that can be compelled by civil judgment. In one class are various kinds of actions (*Handlungen*) and restraints or forbearances (*Unterlassungen oder Duldungen*). Performances requiring declarations of the actor's will (*Willenserklärungen*) such as property conveyances or apologies, are treated as a separate class.

If the actions required by the judgment are of a kind that can be performed by someone other than the judgment debtor (*vertretbare Handlungen*), on motion by the creditor the court will authorize the creditor to have the action performed by a person of the creditor's reasonable choice at the cost of the debtor.[269]

If the action required by the judgment is one that only the debtor can perform, and performance lies within the debtor's power, the court has the power to force the debtor to render actual performance.[270] However the court does not have the power to compel a judgment debtor to perform or

266. ZPO §794a. This provision does not apply to settlements which are not made of record in the court. See State District Court of Wuppertal, 20 *NJW* 832 ff. (1967) and Zöller/Stöber, §794a, mn. 1. But see State District Court of Essen, 21 *NJW* 162, 163 (1968) and State District Court of Ulm, 34 *MDR* 944 (1980) for a contrary view.

267. Probably the most significant of these is contained in BGB §574(1), which gives a tenant the right to resist eviction and require continuation of the landlord-tenant relationship if "termination of the tenancy would mean for the tenant, his family or another member of his household a hardship which is not justifiable in consideration of the legitimate interests of the landlord." (*...Beendigung des Mietverhältnisses für den Mieter, seine Familie oder einen anderen Angehörigen seines Haushaltes eine Härte bedeuten würde, die auch unter Würdigung der berechtigten Interessen des Vermieters nicht zu rechtfertigen ist*). Much landlord-tenant litigation revolves around this provision.

268. See, e.g. ZPO §893.

269. ZPO §887(1). The court order can require the debtor to pay the costs of the third-party performance in advance. Recovery of the cost from the debtor is by the conventional means of execution for money judgments. ZPO §887(2).

270. ZPO §888(1). For instance, a business person can be forced to prepare financial accounts, a party to a divorce case can be compelled to provide financial information, or a debtor can be required to give a disclosure under oath.

create a work of art, or to perform actions when the actions require cooperation of others not under the debtor's control.[271] If the debtor refuses to perform the action as required by the judgment, the court rendering the judgment may append fines and imprisonment as inducements to perform (*Beugemittel*).[272]

Injunctive judgments and orders requiring the judgment debtor to refrain from certain described action (*Unterlassung*) or to allow another to perform described actions (*Duldung*) are common in intellectual property and unfair competition cases as well as in family cases and even disputes among neighbors. Such judgments must be precise in describing the action that is proscribed or to be tolerated and the circumstances under which it is forbidden or to be allowed. The judgment itself, or a supplementary order, must also give the debtor notice of the consequences of failure to abide by the terms of the order.[273] Actions which are the substantial equivalent of the action proscribed are generally also covered.[274] For example, in patent infringement or unfair competition cases it is often difficult to describe potential infringements or violations with particularity in advance. On an application to enforce the judgment the court must determine whether the conduct proved is sufficiently similar to that described in the judgment to warrant sanctions.

If the judgment debtor violates the terms of such a judgment, the creditor may apply to the court rendering the judgment for an order of civil contempt of court requiring a monetary penalty (*Ordnungsgeld*).[275] This fine is a penalty for proven disobedience of the court order rather than an inducement to render performance as is the case with fines imposed to encourage a debtor to perform a required act.[276] If the fine is not paid or is ineffective in curbing the

---

271. See, e.g., Baur/Stürner, *Einzelvollstreckungsrecht*, mn. 40.13, 40.14; Lüke, § 85(II), mn. 701 f. In such cases the creditor's sole remedy is damages.

272. See ZPO § 888. Fines cannot exceed 25,000 Euro and are payable to the state treasury, not the creditor. Sometimes as a result of a settlement of an antitrust or business tort case a party may contractually agree to a penalty in an amount greater than the statutory maximum for failure to comply with the terms of the settlement. Such private penalties are enforceable when they are a part of an enforceable settlement (see Ch. 7(M), Ch. 9(A)(4) above and Ch. 11(I) below). See BGB §§ 339 ff. Imprisonment cannot exceed 6 months, and must be terminated if the debtor indicates willingness to perform or gives a sufficient ground for inability to perform. See ZPO §§ 909–913 for provisions regulating civil arrest and imprisonment. Use of the arrest remedy is extremely rare.

273. ZPO § 890(2).

274. See for details Baur/Stürner, *Einzelvollstreckungsrecht*, mn. 40.21 ("*Kerntheorie*").

275. ZPO § 890(1). The fine cannot exceed 250,000 Euro per imposition.

276. Although traditionally there was dispute over whether contempt proceedings were in the nature of civil inducements or criminal punishments, since a 1975 amendment of

judgment debtor's misconduct, the court may order imprisonment (*Ordnungshaft*).[277] The debtor must be heard before the imposition of any order of fine or imprisonment.[278] Upon proof of violation of an injunctive judgment or court order the judgment debtor can also be required to post security against costs and damages arising from any future violation.[279] If the judgment debtor seeks to interfere with another party's action which he has been ordered to permit, the court executor may take action to physically prevent such interference.[280]

If the action required is one of declaration of will (*Willenserklärung*), such as by a conveyance of real or personal property, there is no need to compel the debtor to go through the motions render the legal act required. The judgment itself will serve as the legal declaration required and replaces the legal act in the form customarily required.[281] However it is up to the creditor to see to it that the judgment is recorded in the appropriate book or register or served on the appropriate parties or officials. If the required legal act involves both a declaration of will and some concrete action, such as with transfer of tangible personal property,[282] the creditor cannot rest on a judgment declaring the judgment debtor's will to transfer, but he must also obtain possession. This he can do with the assistance of the court executor, who will take the personal property from the judgment debtor.[283]

Settlements (*Prozessvergleiche*) cannot pass title under ZPO § 894 because they are not final judgments of a court. Suit can be brought on the settlement

---

ZPO § 890 the prevailing view has been that they are punishments for past misdeeds (disobedience of the order), and hence in some respect subject to criminal rules of proof, including proof of criminal liability (*Verschulden*). See Lüke, §85(III), mn. 704; Baur/Stürner, Einzelvollstreckungsrecht, mn. 40.27 f.; Federal Constitutional Court, 34 *NJW* 2457 (1981); A *prima facie* case is sufficient. See Federal Constitutional Court, 34 *NJW* 3139 (1991).

277. ZPO § 890(1). Imprisonment may be ordered for up to 6 months for each occurrence but cannot exceed 2 years in total.

278. ZPO § 891.

279. ZPO § 890(3).

280. ZPO § 892.

281. ZPO § 894. So, for instance, a judgment can replace a notarial document (*notarielle Beurkundung*) such as a deed. The legal act is effective when the judgment becomes final and is not subject to further appeal (*rechtskräftig*). This is important because German substantive law requires an express declaration of will to complete a transfer of personal property or realty. Such a declaration must be independent from any sales contract, which merely creates the obligation to make such a declaration, but does not make it. See Baur/Stürner, *Sachenrecht*, 17th ed. (1999), § 5(IV), pp. 47 ff.

282. See BGB § 929.

283. ZPO § 897(1).

in order to gain a real court judgment to render the fictive legal act on behalf of the judgment debtor or the creditor can apply for a court order of specific performance implementing the executable settlement.[284]

3. Remedies of Judgment Debtors

German civil procedure provides judgment debtors and third parties with abundant means to protect themselves from judicial error or overreaching by judgment creditors in the process of execution. These include procedures to review actions taken in the execution process as well as means to forestall, delay or terminate execution proceedings.

a. Appellate Review of Execution Proceedings

Defects in the steps of the execution process may be raised by debtors, creditors, or even affected third parties simply by filing an objection (*Erinnerung*) with the execution court.[285] Most actions of the court executor (*Gerichtsvollzieher*) are subject to review by objection.[286] This is also true of some *ex parte* or ministerial actions of the execution court such as issuance of an execution lien order (*Pfändungsbeschluss*).[287]

Decisions (*Entscheidungen*) of the execution court rendered in the course of execution proceedings are subject in almost every case to miscellaneous appeal (*Beschwerde*) to the state district court.[288]

Sometimes the boundary between steps in the execution process reviewable by objection and decisions reviewable by miscellaneous appeal is difficult to discern. It does not necessarily depend on whether the action at issue was taken by the magistrate (*Rechtspfleger*) or by the local court judge. Generally speaking, if the execution court denies an application to undertake a means of execution (*Vollstreckungsmassnahme*), or if the execution court authorizes a means of execution after notice to the debtor and opportunity for hearing

---

284. See Federal Supreme Court, 98 BGHZ 127, 129 (1986); Baur/Stürner, *Einzelvollstreckungsrecht*, mn. 41.6; Lüke, §86, mn. 709. Such a supplementary proceeding is not needed if the necessary declaration of will is contained in the settlement agreement itself. Sometimes failure to include such a declaration in a settlement agreement can be an expensive mistake for which the lawyer can be held responsible.

285. ZPO §766(1). The execution court can also decide on the appropriateness and formal legality of measures of execution which the court executor has failed or refused to perform on request of the creditor (ZPO §766(2)).

286. For exceptions see Zöller/Stöber, §766, mn. 5.

287. ZPO §§829, 834.

288. See Ch. 10(F) above.

(*Anhörung des Schuldners*), the correct remedy for the aggrieved party is miscellaneous appeal.[289] There is dispute about the correct way to appeal measures taken when there is no opportunity for hearing to the debtor.[290] To the extent that the court issuing the underlying judgment (*Prozessgericht*) becomes involved in the execution (as with enforcement of injunctions) the remedy is exclusively by miscellaneous appeal.[291]

Miscellaneous appeals are decided by the state district court by court order (*Beschluss*), and are subject to miscellaneous appeal of law (*Rechtsbeschwerde*) to the Federal Supreme Court with permission of the state district court.[292]

b. Actions to Arrest Execution

A judgment debtor can bring a complaint in arrest of execution (*Vollstreckungsgegenklage* or *Vollstreckungsabwehrklage*) if defenses to the claim represented by the judgment have arisen since the judgment became final (*rechtskräftig*).[293] The most common of these are payment, accord and satisfaction or counterclaims arising from post judgment payments, performances or other circumstances.

The discovery of new evidence bearing on the validity of the claim represented by the judgment does not justify a complaint in arrest of execution. Newly discovered evidence may, however, support a reopening of the proceedings (*Wiederaufnahme des Verfahrens*).[294]

A complaint in arrest of execution may be filed in the court of first instance which issued the execution title at any time after the execution title is issued and effective.[295] It is directed against the judgment creditor and must contain all objections which the debtor has at the time of filing the complaint.[296] The

289. E.g. Baur/Stürner, *Einzelvollstreckungsrecht*, §43(I)(2), mn. 43.4.

290. See Lüke, §70(I), mn. 582.

291. ZPO §§887 ff., 793.

292. ZPO §§793, 574. See Ch. 10(F)(4) above.

293. See Ch. 9(F)(3) above.

294. See Ch. 9(F)(4) above.

295. ZPO §767. If the title itself is defective, the debtor may lodge an appeal in the appellate court or object to the certification of enforceability according to ZPO §732 (for certification of enforceability see Ch. 11(F) above). There is some dispute about whether the debtor has the free choice between these remedies and the action to arrest execution if an execution title is defective *and* defenses to the claim have arisen since the execution title was issued. See Baur/Stürner, *Einzelvollstreckungsrecht*, mn. 45.4; Federal Supreme Court, 118 BGHZ 229, 231 (1993).

296. ZPO §767(3). This is an exception to the usual rule in civil cases, which permits parties to raise defenses and objects seriatim, subject to preclusion only when unreason-

filing of the complaint itself does not result in stay of execution. However once the proceeding is commenced, the debtor may apply to the court in which it is pending for provisional measures (*einstweilige Anordnungen*) staying the execution or permitting it to proceed only upon furnishing of security by the creditor.[297] The debtor has to make a plausible showing of merit to one or more of the grounds for arrest of the execution and at least assert the likelihood of harm if the execution goes forward.[298] The court can confirm, modify, or terminate the provisional measures. In pressing cases (*dringende Fälle*) the execution court may also grant a stay and may set a time limit within which the petitioner must obtain a decision from the court of first instance which rendered the judgment, in default of which the execution will go forward.[299]

The grounds for objection (*Einwendungen*) to execution must be circumstances which affect the claim on which the judgment is based in whole or in part. They can include payment, accord and satisfaction, waiver, substituted performance, and setoff.[300] For instance, if the judgment debtor has paid a part of the claim after the judgment was rendered but the creditor seeks execution in the full amount, the debtor can bring an action to restrain execution of the paid portion of the claim.

The action in arrest of execution can be based only on grounds for objection arising after the last oral argument on the facts (*Tatsachenverhandlung*) in the case in chief. All grounds which arose before then are precluded by *res judicata*.[301] Sometimes it is hard to determine when a ground for objection arose. For instance, there is dispute about whether a right of setoff should be deemed to arise when the facts supporting the setoff came into existence, or when the debtor declared a setoff based on those facts.[302] The current practice in court as well as the policy in favor of expedition of the proceedings

---

able delay would result. In proceedings to arrest execution, the policy against permitting a debtor to delay the inevitable with multiple complaints to arrest execution results in the tighter requirement. See Lüke, §71(II), mn. 589.

297. ZPO §769(1)(1).

298. ZPO §769(1)(2).

299. ZPO §769(2). The petitioner is usually the judgment debtor.

300. Parties can also contractually restrict the mode and timing of execution. If a judgment creditor violates such an agreement, it is disputed whether the proper remedy is objection or complaint in arrest of judgment. See Baur/Stürner, *Einzelvollstreckungsrecht*, mn. 10.7; Lüke, §68, mn. 579.

301. See Ch. 9(F)(3) above.

302. Under German substantive law a setoff must be declared by the party entitled to it. See BGB §§387 ff., 388 ("declaration of setoff").

(*Prozessbeschleunigung*) favor the time the right of setoff arose (*entstand*) as the relevant time. However according to strong opinion in the literature the time of exercise (*Ausübung*) of the right of setoff is controlling, subject to preclusion only in cases of inexcusable delay.[303]

There are a number of circumstances under which the court executor or execution court is required to suspend or restrict execution. One is a court decision on an action in arrest of execution or otherwise ordering that the execution be suspended, modified, or delayed, either temporarily or permanently, or allowing the execution to go forward only on furnishing of security.[304] Execution must also be suspended if the judgment provides for a stay of execution upon furnishing security for the judgment or depositing sufficient funds to satisfy the judgment in an appropriate escrow account and if the debtor produces official documentary confirmation that these requirements have been satisfied.[305] The court officer may not proceed if the debtor produces an official or private post-judgment document from the judgment creditor acknowledging payment or agreeing to suspension or delay of execution or a receipt from a bank indicating that sufficient funds to pay the judgment have been deposited to the credit of the judgment creditor or are available to be drawn on by him.[306] If the creditor has already enough security for his claim through a consensual security interest, the debtor can raise objection (*Erinnerung*) to execution of the judgment against other property of the debtor.[307]

c. *Protection of the Interests of Third Parties*

The Civil Procedure Code permits a third party claiming an interest in property subject to execution to bring a third party complaint (*Drittwiderspruchsklage*) to establish its interest in the property and protect itself from seizure and sale of the property on execution.[308] The action may be maintained

---

303. See Federal Supreme Court, 123 BGHZ 49, 52 (1993); for details see Baur/Stürner, *Zwangsvollstreckungsrecht*, §45(III)(1)(b)(bb), mn. 45.14; for a brief survey see Lüke, §71(III), mn. 591.

304. ZPO §775(1), (2).

305. ZPO §775(3). For security as a condition to grant a stay of execution see Ch. 11(F) above.

306. ZPO §775(4), (5).

307. ZPO §777.

308. ZPO §771. See Picker, *Die Drittwiderspruchsklage in ihrer geschichtlichen Entwicklung als Beispiel für das Zusammenwirken von materiellem Recht und Prozessrecht* (1981); Prütting/Weth, "Die Drittwiderspruchsklage gemäss §771 ZPO", 17 *JuS* 505 (1988); Baur/Stürner, *Einzelvollstreckungsrecht*, §46(A), mn. 46.1 ff.

by any claimant with a "right in the property that hinders sale."[309] This includes not only beneficial owners of the property (such as lessors of personal property), but also may include those creditors who hold "ownership" of the property as security for payment of a debt.

The interests of rival claimants to real estate in general are made known through notation in the real estate registry (*Grundbuch*), and therefore such interests are generally recognized and protected during the execution process.[310] German law also recognizes unregistered ownership or security interests of third parties in tangible personal property in the possession of a judgment debtor. Seizure of property in the possession of the debtor may jeopardize these interests.

The court officer is not required to make a determination of the existence, validity or amount of third party ownership or security interests in tangible personal property in the debtor's physical possession (*Gewahrsam*). It is his duty to seize the property, even if the debtor insists that it belongs to a third party or that a third party has a security interest in it.[311] Seizure of the property and its subsequent sale are effective against not only the debtor, but also the third-party owner or lienor.

A seller of goods may enter into a contract of "retained ownership" (*Eigentumsvorbehalt*) with the purchaser, under which the seller remains owner of goods delivered into the possession of the purchaser until payment of the purchase price in full. It is generally recognized that such an owner may bring a third party action to establish his interest and prevent the sale of the goods on execution.[312] It is also possible for a lender to take a contractual "security transfer" (*Sicherungsübereignung*) of personal property owned by its debtor as collateral for a loan. It is disputed whether the interest created by such an arrangement qualifies as the kind of interest which will sustain a third party action, or whether such a creditor's sole remedy would be for priority treatment from the proceeds of the execution sale.[313]

---

309. ZPO §771(1) (*ein die Veräusserung hinderndes Recht*).

310. See ZVG §§17, 37(4) and (5), 44 f., 52; Ch. 11(F)(1)(b) above. A third party real property interest which is not registered is an exception. If such an interest exists, a third party complaint may be necessary for the protection of the third party's interests. See Baur/Stürner, *Einzelvollstreckungsrecht*, mn. 34.4.

311. See ZPO §808; Ch. 11(F)(1)(a) above.

312. 54 BGHZ 218 (1971). See Lüke, §72(II), mn. 597; Baur/Stürner, *Sachenrecht*, 17th ed. (1999), §59.

313. See Baur/Stürner, *Einzelvollstreckungsrecht*, §46(II)(1)(b)(bb), mn. 46.8; Lüke, §72(II), mn. 598. See Ch. 11(F)(3)(c) below on determination of claims to proceeds of personal property sold on execution.

Similar problems may arise if a judgment debtor has made an assignment of a claim or other intangible property.[314] In such a case the assignee may maintain a third party complaint to protect its interest.

The third party proceeding is commenced by the third party claimant against the judgment creditor in the court in the district in which the execution is taking place.[315] A third party complaint cannot be filed until an actual execution has commenced or the items to be seized have been identified. On the other hand, if the court executor has already held the sale and distributed the proceeds it is too late.[316] The plaintiff must show that its sale hindering rights (*veräusserungshindernde Rechte*) are inconsistent with sale of the property on execution, and hence, that the execution is not allowable (*zulässig*). A decision in favor of the plaintiff will forbid the sale on execution, but does not amount to a binding declaratory judgment of ownership for other purposes.[317]

Third parties who have non-possessory liens (not considered "ownership") on tangible personal property are not entitled to proceed in arrest of execution.[318] However they may seek prior satisfaction of their claims out of the proceeds. A complaint for "prior satisfaction from the proceeds" (*vorzugsweise Befriedigung aus dem Erlös*) may be filed in the execution court or in the state district court in the district in which the execution court is located, depending on amount in controversy, and may name the attaching judgment creditor, the debtor, or both as opposing parties, depending on who is contesting the priority of the third party interest.[319] If the third party satisfies the court of the existence and priority of its interest, an amount of the proceeds of sale of the collateral sufficient to satisfy the claim will be set aside for the third party.[320]

---

314. See Baur/Stürner, *Einzelvollstreckungsrecht*, §46(II)(1)(b)(bb), mn. 46.8; Thomas/Putzo, §771, mn. 19.

315. ZPO §771(1). The subject matter jurisdiction is determined by amount in controversy.

316. This does not mean that the third party is wholly without recourse. One option would be to sue the judgment creditor for the proceeds on a theory of unjust enrichment. BGB §812(1)(1). See Lüke, §72(III), mn. 604 and Baur/Stürner, *Einzelvollstreckungsrecht*, mn. 42.26 for a discussion of other routes such a third party might follow. Compare Ch. 11(F)(1)(a) above for other kinds of claims based on unjust enrichment.

317. Lüke, §72(III), mn. 605. For the scope of *res adjudicata* see Ch. 9(F)(2)(a) above.

318. E.g., the non-possessory lien of the landlord on goods of the tenant to secure unpaid rent (BGB §§562 ff.).

319. ZPO §805(1)–(3).

320. ZPO §805(4). For the remedy of the holder of a contractual security interest see Ch. 11(F)(3)(c) above.

G. Bankruptcy and Insolvency

In Germany the ordinary courts (*ordentliche Gerichte*) exercise jurisdiction in bankruptcy. Bankruptcy proceedings are governed by the Federal Bankruptcy Law (*Insolvenzordnung* or *InsO*).[321] Space does not permit any detailed description or analysis of German bankruptcy law or procedure. A brief sketch, however, may give an idea of how this specialized procedure relates to the overall structure, goals and function of the German civil justice system.[322]

1. Purpose and Structure of Insolvency Proceedings

The primary purpose of insolvency proceedings under German law is the common and equal satisfaction of the claims of creditors either from the orderly sale of the debtor's assets and division of the proceeds or through adoption of a plan of reorganization that maintains the business entity. Bankruptcy proceedings also give a debtor who is a natural person the opportunity eventually to obtain a discharge from remaining unsatisfied indebtedness.[323]

In each state district court judicial district one of the local courts is designated the insolvency court (*Insolvenzgericht*) for that judicial district.[324] The insolvency court has exclusive subject matter jurisdiction over all proceedings brought pursuant to the Insolvency Law. Exclusive venue for insolvency proceedings is laid in the insolvency court for the judicial district in which the

321. For more details see Bork, *Einführung in das neue Insolvenzrecht*, 2nd ed. (1998); Häsemeyer, *Insolvenzrecht*, 2nd ed. (1998); Uhlenbruck (ed.), *Insolvenzordnung Kommentar*, 12th ed. (2002); Kirchhof/Lwowski/Stürner (eds.), *Münchener Kommentar zur Insolvenzordnung*, Vol. 1-3 (2001/2002). The current Insolvency Law was enacted in 1994 as a complete recodification and modernization of German bankruptcy law. Bankruptcy law was first codified for the German nation in 1877. For a short history see Baur/Stürner, *Zwangsvollstreckungs-, Konkurs- und Vergleichsrecht*, Vol. II: *Insolvenzrecht*, 12th ed (1990), mn. 3.1 ff.; or Stürner, in: *Münchener Kommentar zur InsO*, Einleitung, mn. 5 ff.

322. For a short overview in German language see Stürner, in: *Münchener Kommentar zur InsO*, Einleitung, mn. 1–24.

323. See InsO § 1. Availability of a discharge for a debtor who is a natural person is a feature first introduced into German bankruptcy law with the 1994 recodification.

324. InsO § 2. By default this is the local court in whose district the seat of the district court is located. The state governments are authorized to change this designation and designate additional local courts as insolvency courts.

debtor is jurisdictionally resident.[325] Procedure in insolvency proceedings is governed by the Insolvency Law as supplemented by the Civil Procedure Code.[326] Many, but not all of the orders and dispositions of the bankruptcy court are subject to immediate miscellaneous appeal (*Beschwerde*) to the state district court.[327] A miscellaneous appeal of law (*Rechtsbeschwerde*) to the Federal Supreme Court may be taken from a state district court decision on the immediate miscellaneous appeal.[328]

The new Bankruptcy Code combines three previously existing modes of insolvency into a single unitary form of proceeding, which can be transformed from a liquidation proceeding to a reorganization and vice versa as the circumstances of the case may dictate. Regardless of expected outcome, all proceedings are commenced in the same manner with an "opening proceeding" (*Eröffnungsverfahren*). Either the debtor or a creditor can file an application to open a bankruptcy proceeding based on the existence of a ground for insolvency (*Insolvenzgrund*). Statutory grounds of insolvency include excess of debts over assets (*Überschuldung*), inability to pay debts as they become due (*Zahlungsunfähigkeit*), or (on an application by a debtor), anticipated inability to pay debts as they become due (*drohende Zahlungsunfähigkeit*).[329]

2. Bankruptcy Procedure

Upon filing of an application for bankruptcy, the insolvency court is required to examine the application to determine whether a sufficient ground for insolvency exists and whether the debtor's apparent assets will be sufficient to cover the costs of the bankruptcy proceeding.[330] If the application is insuf-

---

325. InsO §3. If the debtor has an independent business with a center of gravity in another district, venue is laid in the district in which the business is located. If more than one court has jurisdiction, commencement of a proceeding in the first court with jurisdiction excludes later proceedings. For venue based on residence see Ch. 5(C)(1) above.

326. InsO §4.

327. InsO §6. For instance, decisions opening and declining to open a proceeding (InsO §34); terminating a proceeding (InsO §216); confirming or declining to confirm a plan of reorganization (InsO §253), granting or declining to grant a discharge (InsO §289) are all subject to immediate procedural appeal.

328. InsO §7, ZPO §574. See Ch. 10(F)(4) above for procedure on miscellaneous appeals of law.

329. See InsO §§11 ff.

330. Court costs for bankruptcy proceedings are governed by the Court Costs Law (*Gerichtskostengesetz*). See Ch. 9(E)(1) above. In general, the costs for filing the proceeding are based on the gross amount of the assets in the bankrupt estate. See GKG §37.

ficient in either respect, it will be dismissed on the court's own motion.[331] Pending decision on the application the court is authorized to order provisional measures to secure the estate such as the appointment of a temporary trustee (*vorläufiger Insolvenzverwalter*), injunction against transfer of the debtor's assets or levy of execution against them and the like.[332]

If the court determines that the application is in order the court will enter an "opening order" (*Eröffnungsbeschluss*) commencing the formal proceedings. The opening of a bankruptcy proceeding operates as an automatic stay of any pending civil proceedings against the debtor.[333] In the opening order the court ordinarily names an insolvency trustee[334] and requires all creditors of the debtor to file their claims with the insolvency trustee within a specified period of time. The order notifies persons owing the debtor that they should render performance only to the trustee.[335] The opening order also sets the dates for meetings of creditors (*Gläubigerversammlungen*) for the purpose of proving claims and determining the course of future proceedings.[336]

The insolvency trustee has the responsibility to assemble and evaluate the debtor's bankruptcy estate (*Insolvenzmasse*)[337] and to report to the court and

---

Debtors who are natural persons and who plan to seek a discharge of a part of the indebtedness may request that payment of costs be deferred until issuance of the discharge. The court also has the power to appoint counsel for the debtor at public expense in whole or in part. See InsO §§4a–4d.

331. InsO §§26, 34(1).

332. InsO §21. See Haarmeyer, in: *Münchener Kommentar zur InsO*, §21, mn. 46 ff., 88 ff.

333. ZPO §240. The trustee in bankruptcy (*Insolvenzverwalter*) has the option to take up any stayed action for the benefit of the estate. See InsO §§85 ff.; Rosenberg/Schwab/Gottwald, §126(II), pp. 744 ff.; Baur/Stürner, *Insolvenzrecht*, mn. 9.79 ff.

334. InsO §§27, 28. The insolvency trustee must be a person of suitable business acumen who is independent from either debtor or creditors. InsO §56. The creditors may nominate a trustee of their own choice at the first meeting of creditors following the appointment of the trustee, and the court is obligated to honor their choice if the nominee is otherwise qualified. InsO §57.

335. InsO §§27, 28. The opening order is to be served on the debtor and known creditors, entered in the real estate and any applicable business registries, and published in an appropriate publication. InsO §§30–32. The purpose of this publicity is to prevent persons acquiring interests in property of the bankruptcy estate from claiming the status of good faith purchaser.

336. See InsO §39.

337. The insolvency estate includes the non-exempt assets of the debtor at the time of commencement of the bankruptcy and all assets acquired during the course of administration. InsO §§35, 36.

the creditors on the economic situation of the debtor and its causes.[338] The trustee has the right to request complete information from the debtor on all aspects of the bankruptcy.[339] The trustee's avoidance power embraces his right to set aside fraudulent conveyance and other transfer unfavorable for the estate made during statutorily fixed periods before rendition of the opening order or inability to pay debts.[340]

Based on the information received, the creditors reach a collective decision on whether any enterprise of the debtor should be continued or immediately liquidated. Although the trustee has broad powers in the conduct of the debtor's business for the benefit of the bankruptcy estate, important decisions such as the borrowing of money or initiation of significant litigation require approval of the creditors or of a creditors' committee appointed by the court.[341]

Insolvency creditors are those persons with claims against the debtor as of the time of commencement of the insolvency proceedings and who do not have a right to separation of specific property (*Aussonderungsrecht*).[342] Written registrations of claim (*Anmeldungen von Forderungen*), which may include supporting documents, must be filed within a time set by the court (*Anmeldungsfrist*). If no objection is raised by the trustee or another creditor within a further specified time, the claim is treated as established.[343] If the claim is contested, the creditor has the burden of establishing the claim in a conventional civil proceeding in the form of a declaratory judgment (*Feststellungsklage*) in the court which has subject matter jurisdiction for the claim and which is located in the district of the bankruptcy court.[344] Creditors who claim

---

338. InsO §§148–156. The trustee operates under the general oversight of the court. The court can request clarification and information from the trustee on issues arising during the course of administration. InsO §58. The trustee is required to render periodic accountings of his administration to court and creditors and a final accounting at the conclusion of the bankruptcy. InsO §66.

339. See InsO §§97 ff.

340. See InsO §§129 ff.; for execution measures before commencement of insolvency proceedings see Ch. 11(D)(1) above.

341. InsO §§157 ff., 160ff. Lack of approval, however, does not generally affect the validity of measures taken by the trustee. See InsO §164.

342. See Inso §§38, 47.

343. InsO §§174 ff., 178. If only the debtor objects, the administration continues, but the registration of the claim is not given *res adjudicata* effect against the debtor. See InsO §201(2).

344. InsO §§179, 180. Cases pending at the time of bankruptcy can be continued in the courts in which they were started. See ZPO §240 and InsO §180(2).

retention of title (*Eigentumsvorbehalt*) in assets in the possession of the debtor can bring claims for separation (*Aussonderung*) of the property subject to their ownership interests.[345]

The insolvency trustee takes possession of the debtor's assets. If the proceeding is to be handled as a liquidation, the trustee proceeds to administer and liquidate them for the benefit of the bankruptcy estate and the creditors.[346] Assets subject to security interests other than retention of title are generally administered or liquidated by the trustee and the secured creditors are given priority claims to the proceeds.[347] The creditors may be called upon to decide by vote at a creditors meeting on whether particular assets should be sold piecemeal, or whether efforts should be made to preserve value of a going business.[348] The trustee then commences distribution (*Verteilung*) of the proceeds of the assets among the creditors in accord with their respective priorities.[349]

If the most likely route to satisfaction of the creditors' claims is liquidation by arrangement or some sort of reorganization, either the debtor or the trustee in bankruptcy presents a plan of liquidation or reorganization for consideration and adoption by the creditors.[350] The plan must describe the current state of affairs and the proposed liquidation or reorganization, taking care to treat various classes of creditors fairly and equitably, and in no event less favorably than would be the case in the event of a liquidation.[351] If adopted by majorities in both number and amount of claims in each creditor class, the plan may be confirmed by the bankruptcy court and carried out according to its terms, with or without supervision by the trustee.[352] If a class refuses to consent to a plan, the court can dispense with consent based on a finding that the creditors have no good basis for refusing consent and that the plan is no less favorable to them than would be a liquidation.[353] Under certain circumstances it is possible for a debtor to administer the bankruptcy estate (*Eigenverwal-*

345. InsO § 47. For details see Ganter, in: *Münchener Kommentar zur InsO*, § 47, mn. 54 ff.; Baur/Stürner, *Insolvenzrecht*, mn. 14.7ff. and Baur/Stürner, *Sachenrecht*, § 59, mn. 26 ff.

346. See InsO §§ 148 ff., 156 ff., 159.

347. InsO §§ 49–52, 166 ff.

348. InsO §§ 156, 157.

349. See InsO §§ 187 ff. With the consent of any creditors' committee the trustee is authorized to commence partial distributions (*Abschlagsverteilungen*) as soon as practicable following the expiration for the time for proofs of claim. InsO § 187(2).

350. See InsO §§ 217 ff.

351. InsO §§ 219 ff., 222 ff., 251.

352. InsO §§ 235 ff., 260 ff.

353. InsO § 245.

tung) under the oversight of an examiner (*Sachwalter*).[354] The reformed German reorganization provisions were modeled on the provisions of Chapter 11 of the American Bankruptcy Code.[355]

If at any time it appears that the assets available will not cover the costs of the proceeding, the proceeding may be terminated by the court on its own motion unless a party advances the probable costs or the court orders that they be deferred.[356] Proceedings may also be terminated on motion of the debtor with the consent of all creditors, or if the grounds for insolvency no longer exist.[357] Upon termination of bankruptcy the debtor's ability to deal with his property is restored and any restraint on creditors is removed.[358]

3. Relationship to Basic Principles of Civil Procedure

The principle of party control of proceedings (*Verfahrensmaxime or Dispositionsgrundsatz*) applies in large part to procedures in bankruptcy. Bankruptcy proceedings are commenced by party action and many important decisions during the process require party consent, in some cases by vote. On the other hand, the ability of particular parties to steer bankruptcy proceedings or secure favorable outcomes is severely limited by the principles of equality of treatment of creditors (*gleichmässige Gläubigerbefriedigung*) and universality (*Universalitätsgrundsatz*).[359]

The principle of party control of facts and proof (*Beibringungsgrundsatz*) applies to determination of the validity of specific claims in proceedings brought in the courts of general jurisdiction for that purpose. However the bankruptcy court and the trustee have an independent responsibility to in-

---

354. See InsO §§270 ff. This provision is modeled after the American concept of "debtor in possession" in corporate reorganization proceedings. See Stürner, in: *Münchener Kommentar zur ZPO*, Einleitung, mn. 21.

355. See Baur/Stürner, *Insolvenzrecht*, mn. 4.47, 39.91ff. and Stürner, "Kurt Hans Nadelmann und Stefan Riesenfeld und ihr Einfluss auf das deutsche und europäische Insolvenzrecht", in: Lutter/Stiefel/Höflich (eds.), *Der Einfluss deutscher Emigranten auf die Rechtsentwicklung in den USA und Deutschland* (1993), pp. 493 ff.

356. InsO §§4a–d, 207.

357. InsO §§212, 213.

358. InsO §215. However all creditor claims registered in the bankruptcy without objection by the debtor, another creditor, or the trustee are deemed to be established with the effect of judgments and are entitled to execution to the extent not satisfied during the course of the bankruptcy. InsO §§201, 202, 215(2). For potential discharge of claims see Ch. 11(G)(4) below.

359. See Stürner, in: *Münchener Kommentar zur Insolvenzordnung*, Einl., mn. 47 ff., 62 and 64; Kübler/Prütting, *Kommentar zur Insolvenzordnung* (1999 ff.), Einl., mn. 63 ff.

vestigate the status of the debtor and its assets at the outset of every bankruptcy proceeding.[360] The principle of orality (*Mündlichkeitsprinzip*) applies to many, but not all bankruptcy court proceedings. Some submissions are required to be made in writing without oral presentation.[361]

By their very nature bankruptcy proceedings tend to be extended over some time and to involve a number of conferences and hearings. They give relatively little opportunity for implementation of the principle of concentration (*Konzentrationsmaxime*). The court is given power to expedite the proceedings and concentrate them to the extent feasible. The principle of the right to be heard (*rechtliches Gehör*) is observed in all proceedings for determination of legal rights or property interests, but does not require that affected parties be notified and heard in more administrative or executory court functions.[362]

4. Discharge in Bankruptcy

A new concept embodied for the first time in the 1994 Insolvency Law is that of potential discharge of the debtor following the conclusion of bankruptcy proceedings. In general bankruptcy only divides the debtor's assets as of the time of the bankruptcy and satisfies claims only to the extent of payment received, thus leaving creditors free to obtain and realize on executions for the unsatisfied balances of their claims from assets or income received after bankruptcy. Bankrupts who are natural persons, however, have the option of seeking a discharge of unsatisfied pre-bankruptcy claims, which discharge may be granted after a six-year post-bankruptcy period of assignment (*Abtretungserklärung*) during which the debtor assigns all non-exempt assets and net non-exempt income to a trustee (*Treuhänder*) for the satisfaction of pre-bankruptcy creditors on an equal basis.[363] The bankruptcy court appoints the trustee at the time of closure of the liquidation proceedings, and grants the discharge at the end of the period of assignment provided that the debtor has fulfilled all the conditions of the assignment.[364]

Bankrupts who are not natural persons do not have any right to discharge, although in some cases rights of particular creditors may be affected and even

---

360. InsO §§5, 97 ff.

361. See Stürner, in: *Münchener Kommentar zur InsO*, mn. 53 f.

362. See Kübler/Prütting, §5, mn. 21 ff.; Stürner, in: *Münchener Kommentar zur InsO*, Einl., mn. 60.

363. See InsO §§286 ff. The assignment includes a portion of assets received by gift or inheritance during the assignment period. InsO §295(1).

364. InsO §300.

abbreviated by plans of liquidation or reorganization approved by creditors collectively.[365]

5. Consumer Bankruptcy

The new Insolvency Law provides for a special simplified "consumer insolvency proceeding" (*Verbraucherinsolvenzverfahren*) for debtors who are natural persons and who do not conduct any kind of independent business with more than 20 creditors or any claims of employees.[366] Such debtors can apply for the optional "debt cleansing" (*Schuldenbereinigung*) procedure.[367] The application must establish the eligibility of the debtor for the special procedure, recite an unsuccessful effort at a composition of creditors within six months before the filing of the application, describe in detail the debtor's assets, list all creditors and their claims, and set forth a plan for the full or partial satisfaction of all claims, with due regard for existing mortgages, liens and other security arrangements. The debtor must also indicate whether a discharge of unpaid indebtedness is being sought.[368]

If there is no objection by any creditor to the proposal, it is deemed accepted and is duly confirmed by the court.[369] The court may also confirm a plan if a majority of the creditors in number and amount consent and the court determines that the non-consenting creditors would not fare worse under the plan than under a straight liquidation of the debtor's assets with subsequent discharge.[370] If the plan is accepted, completion of the terms of the plan results in the cleansing of the claims covered.

If the plan is not confirmed, the debt-cleansing procedure is transformed into a simplified insolvency proceeding. Based on the submissions of the debtor and after hearing the creditors the court may specify a sum in money to be raised by the debtor as equivalent to the amount that the creditors could expect to realize from the debtor's bankruptcy estate. If the debtor pays this

365. See Stürner, in: *Münchener Kommentar zur InsO*, mn. 71.

366. See InsO §§304–314.

367. A qualified debtor against whom a straight insolvency proceeding has been commenced can apply for the debt cleansing plan and thereby obtain a stay of the creditor proceedings until determination of the application for debt cleansing. InsO §306.

368. InsO §305. The Federal Ministry of Justice is authorized to develop simplified paper and electronic forms for use in describing assets and claims. Debtors may be represented in debt cleansing and simplified insolvency proceedings by suitable individuals and employees of credit counseling agencies who are not lawyers. InsO §305(4) and (5).

369. InsO §308.

370. InsO §309.

sum to a trustee[371] within a specified time the court may grant a discharge from further liability, subject to the 6-year period of assignment of all non-exempt assets and income. Otherwise the proceeding will follow the form of a conventional liquidation.

H. Arbitration

Arbitration has been recognized and available in Germany for a long time. In the past certain provisions of the Civil Procedure Code disfavored arbitral proceedings and hindered parties from obtaining the flexibility and economy generally associated with the remedy. For this reason and other reasons, traditionally Germany was not the locus of a great deal of international arbitration, although arbitration has been used in German domestic matters to a degree comparable with other European jurisdictions.

By law adopted December 22, 1997, the German Bundestag sought to effect a major modernization of the provisions of the Civil Procedure Code governing arbitration to make arbitration in Germany, both in domestic and international matters, more attractive to parties, particularly commercial firms.[372] It is too soon to say whether these changes will make Germany into a leading forum for international commercial arbitration. In any event, German parties in certain specialized circumstances, such as building projects, partnership and corporate ownership disputes, and franchise and other commercial disputes, are increasingly resorting to various forms of arbitration in the hopes of obtaining resolution of their disputes in a specialized forum and procedure.

1. Availability of Arbitration

Arbitration is available for any civil claim, whether of a property or non-property character, over which the parties are legally empowered to reach an

371. Of the kind used to collect income and distribute it during the post-bankruptcy assignment period in liquidation proceedings when discharge is sought. InsO §§313, 292.

372. See Law on the Reorganisation of Arbitration Proceedings *(Gesetz zur Neuregelung des Schiedsverfahrensrechts - SchiedsVfG)* of 22.12.1997, BGBl. I, 3224. This law was based to a large extent on the UNCITRAL Model Law on Arbitration adopted by the UN General Assembly in 1995. For details see Berger, *Das neue Recht der Schiedsgerichtsbarkeit* (1998); Münch, in: *Münchener Kommentar zur ZPO*, Vol. 3 (2002), §§1025 ff.; Schwab/Walter, *Schiedsgerichtsbarkeit*, 6th ed. (2000); P. Schlosser, *Das Recht der internationalen privaten Schiedsgerichtsbarkeit*, 2nd ed. (1989).

agreed settlement.[373] Thus claims in which the state has an interest, such as most family law claims, may not be submitted to arbitration. Specifically excepted from arbitrability are most claims for eviction from residential premises.[374]

An arbitration agreement is considered to be a procedural contract (*Prozessvertrag*), which must relate to a specific legal relationship (*Rechtsverhältnis*) or dispute.[375] The arbitration agreement can be a free standing agreement (*Schiedsabrede*), or it can be a clause in another agreement between the parties (*Schiedsklausel*). In either event, the agreement to arbitration must be in writing, either a document signed by the parties,[376] or an exchange of letters, electronic messages, or other form of communication designed to memorialize the agreement.[377] An arbitration clause can be incorporated by reference.[378]

The defendant in a civil case in court may raise an arbitration agreement as a defense at any time up to the beginning of oral argument in plenary proceedings (*mündliche Verhandlungen zur Hauptsache*). If the court finds that the agreement exists and is valid, the action is to be dismissed without prejudice.[379] If there is dispute about arbitrability, the court may adjudicate this issue so long as the arbitral tribunal has not been formed. Under appropriate circumstances the court may adopt provisional measures to protect the subject matter of the controversy or preserve the status quo pending the outcome of the arbitration.[380]

2. The Arbitral Tribunal

The parties may agree on the number of arbitrators. In default of agreement, the panel is to consist of three arbitrators.[381]

---

373. ZPO § 1030.

374. ZPO § 1030(2).

375. ZPO § 1029(1). See German Federal Supreme Court, 40 *NJW* 651, 652 (1987).

376. ZPO § 1031(1). An arbitration agreement involving a consumer (*Verbraucher*) must be set forth in a separate individual document and it must be signed by both parties in their own hands. An electronic version must comply with the Electronic Signature Act (BGB § 126a). ZPO § 1031(5).

377. ZPO § 1031(1). A document proposing an arbitration clause and making it clear that failure to object will be considered acceptance can also suffice. ZPO §1031(2).

378. ZPO § 1031(3). The arbitration clause may be on the back of a written contract. See Bavarian State Supreme Court, 14 *NJW-RR* 644, 645 (1999).

379. ZPO § 1032. However that provision does not apply to check proceedings. German Federal Supreme Court, 47 *NJW* 136 (1994). See Ch. 11(B) above.

380. ZPO § 1033.

381. ZPO § 1034(1).

If the arbitration agreement contains no provision for choosing a panel or if the parties cannot agree on the composition of the entire panel, they each nominate an arbitrator, and the two nominees attempt to agree on a third. If they fail to agree on the third arbitrator, or if the parties fail to agree on the single arbitrator in a one-arbitrator proceeding, the arbitrator will be named by the state appeals court in the district in which the arbitration is taking place.[382] The statute requires the court to follow any requirements of the agreement and to consider the nature and purpose of the arbitration in exercising its power to name arbitrators.[383]

A party is required to disclose all circumstances bearing on the independence and objectivity of any arbitrators nominated by it. Persons nominated as arbitrators are in turn charged at all times with making any such circumstances known to both parties. An arbitrator can be disqualified if there are "justified doubts as to his impartiality or independence".[384] If the parties have not agreed on a procedure for requests to disqualify, the party seeking disqualification must lay its concerns in writing before the tribunal. If the tribunal fails to act, the party may seek disqualification from the court, provided that a request to disqualify does not as such operate as a stay of proceedings or restraint on the participation of the arbitrator in question.[385] Failure of an arbitrator to perform his office can similarly lead to an application to the court to terminate his appointment.[386]

It might be noted that service as an arbitrator is one of the few extra-curricular activities permitted a sitting judge in Germany, provided that the judge-arbitrator has the consent of both parties and the approval of the ministry of justice of the state in which she is appointed.[387]

Under the new law the arbitration panel is given the power to determine questions relating to its own jurisdiction, including the existence of a valid arbitration agreement.[388] The arbitration panel is also authorized to adopt provisional measures to secure the subject matter of the controversy or preserve

---

382. ZPO § 1035(1) and (3). The state appeals courts have jurisdiction to exercise judicial power to the extent authorized by law in the arbitration process and enforcement or revocation of arbitral awards. See ZPO § 1062.

383. ZPO § 1035(5).

384. See ZPO § 1036 *(berechtigte Zweifel an seiner Unparteilichkeit oder Unabhängigkeit)*.

385. ZPO § 1037. A party may generally seek disqualification only before rendition of the final award. See Thomas/Putzo/Reichold, § 1037, mn. 9.

386. ZPO § 1038.

387. DRiG § 40. The requirement that both parties consent has the effect that judges usually serve as sole arbitrators or as presiding members of three-arbitrator tribunals.

388. ZPO § 1040. Any objection to the jurisdiction of the arbitration tribunal must be raised at the latest in the defendant's answer (*Klagebeantwortung*). ZPO § 1040(2).

the status quo. If enforcement of a provisional measure is required, a party may apply to the state appeals court for an appropriate order.[389]

3. Procedure on Arbitration

The form of proceedings before the arbitral tribunal may be agreed on by the parties, provided that certain principles are observed. These are:

a. The parties are to be treated equally,[390]
b. Each party is to be afforded the right to be heard,[391]
c. Representation of parties by lawyers may not be excluded.[392]

To the extent that the parties do not agree on particular procedures, the arbitral tribunal is authorized to proceed in its discretion, subject, however to the foregoing principles. Unless the parties otherwise agree the proceeding begins with an application for arbitration (*Antrag, die Streitigkeit einem Schiedsgericht vorzulegen*).[393] The parties file complaint (*Klage*) and answer (*Klagebeantwortung*) respectively within times set by the tribunal.[394] There is supposed to be at least one oral hearing unless the parties have agreed otherwise.[395] The form and language of written and oral communications and presentations is up to the arbitral tribunal, so long as all meetings of the tribunal, all submissions to the tribunal and all communications and dispositions from the tribunal are promptly communicated to both parties.[396]

Default by the plaintiff in filing its complaint at the start of an arbitration results in a simple termination of the proceeding. On the other hand, if the defendant fails to file an answer or either party fails to file later pleadings or attend scheduled hearings of the tribunal, the proceeding goes forward in the defaulting party's absence and may result in an award.[397]

---

389. ZPO §§1041, 1062.

390. ZPO §1042(1)(1) (*Die Parteien sind gleich zu behandeln.*).

391. ZPO §1042(1)(2) (*Jeder Partei ist rechtliches Gehör zu gewähren.*).

392. ZPO §1042(2) (*Rechtsanwälte dürfen als Bevollmächtigte nicht ausgeschlossen werden.*).

393. ZPO §1044.

394. ZPO §1046.

395. ZPO §1047(1). Even if the parties have agreed otherwise, the arbitral tribunal is authorized to order an oral hearing in order to ensure the right to be heard. See Thomas/Putzo/Reichold, §1047, mn. 1.

396. ZPO §§1045, 1047.

397. ZPO §1048. The consequences of the failure of a party to participate are not necessarily legal default, but may depend on the circumstances or be agreed on by the parties.

An arbitral tribunal does not have the power to summon and compel the attendance of witnesses or the production of documentary evidence. However if a party to an arbitration proceeding wishes to compel attendance of a reluctant witness or wishes access to other proof, the party may apply to the court for assistance in the taking of proof (*Beweisaufnahme*) or the rendering of other judicial measures (*Vornahme sonstiger richterlicher Handlungen*) in assistance to the arbitration. The court is authorized to grant the assistance requested and conduct a hearing for the reception of proof at which the parties to the arbitration and the arbitrators may also participate and ask questions in the same manner as in a civil case.[398] The arbitration tribunal may, however, appoint an expert witness to prepare an expert report and appear before the tribunal for questioning as in a civil action.[399]

If the parties reach a settlement during the pendency of the arbitration, the proceedings are concluded. On application of either party, the tribunal will embody the settlement in an arbitral award by agreement (*Schiedsspruch mit vereinbartem Wortlaut*). Such an arbitral award is to follow the form of and has the same legal effect and enforceability as any other award.[400] A settlement reached during an arbitration may thus acquire a kind of res adjudicata effect, even though a settlement reached during ordinary civil proceedings would not be entitled to such effect.[401]

ZPO § 1048(4). For the different consequences of default in normal German civil procedure see Ch. 9(A)(1) above. The rules on default in German arbitration proceedings adopt the prevailing solution in international arbitration. For a comparative survey see Stürner, "Parteidisposition über Tatsachen und Beweismittel im Zivilprozess ausgewählter europäischer Staaten", in: Bork (ed.), *Festschrift für Helmuth Kollhosser* (2004).

398. ZPO § 1050. For the taking of evidence by witness testimony, by observation or examination of persons and things or by production of documents in court proceedings see Ch. 8(C)(4), (5), (6), (9) and (10) above.

399. ZPO § 1049. For expert testimony in civil actions see Ch. 8(C)(7) above.

400. ZPO § 1053. An award by agreement may be enforced through the process of court execution like normal arbitration awards (see Ch. 11(H)(6) below). But with the consent of the parties the certification of enforceability for an award by agreement may also be rendered by a notary in the district of the court having jurisdiction to review the arbitral proceeding. ZPO § 1053(4).

401. See Münch, in: *Münchener Kommentar zur ZPO*, § 1053, mn. 18; Stürner, "Formen der konsensualen Prozessbeendigung in den europäischen Zivilprozessrechten", in: Breidenbach et al. (eds.), *Konsensuale Streitbeilegung* (2001), pp. 5 ff.; see also Ch. 9(F)(1) above on res adjudicata and claim preclusion.

4. The Arbitral Award

If the proceedings are not otherwise settled or terminated, the arbitrators must render their award (*Schiedsspruch*). Unless the parties have otherwise agreed, the arbitrators may decide by majority vote. The award must be in writing and signed by all the arbitrators. If an arbitrator refuses to vote or to sign the award, the majority can vote and sign the award without him. If an arbitrator refuses to participate in a vote, this fact is to be made known to the parties.[402]

Unless the parties have otherwise agreed, the award must be legally justified (*begründet*) based on the facts and applicable substantive law.[403] The arbitration tribunal must apply the substantive law on which the parties have agreed. When such agreement is lacking, the law with the most significant connection to the substance of the dispute may govern the case. The tribunal may decide the dispute on the basis of fairness and justness or the rules of *lex mercatoria* only with the express consent of the parties.[404] The award must contain the date and place at which it was issued. Signed counterparts must be given to all parties.[405] If the award is incomplete or unclear, any party may apply to the tribunal for supplementation or clarification of the award.[406]

Ordinarily the arbitral award marks the conclusion of the arbitral proceedings, although the tribunal may end the proceedings without award if the plaintiff fails to file its complaint, the parties agree to terminate the proceedings without award, or both parties fail, despite reminders from the tribunal, to participate in the arbitral proceedings.[407]

5. Costs and Attorneys Fees in Arbitration

In contrast to ordinary civil litigation, where the court's discretion to vary the statutory allocation of costs and attorneys fees is rather limited,[408] in arbitration, the tribunal is given wide discretion in the award of costs and attorneys fees among the parties, "in consideration of the circumstances of the

402. ZPO §§ 1052, 1054(1).
403. ZPO § 1054(2); Rosenberg/Schwab/Gottwald, § 174(III), p. 1102.
404. See ZPO § 1051.
405. ZPO § 1054(3) and (4).
406. ZPO § 1058. Unless the parties have otherwise agreed, such application must be made within one month of issuance of the award. The tribunal may also supplement or clarify the award on its own motion.
407. ZPO § 1056.
408. See Ch. 9(E) above.

individual case, especially the outcome of the proceedings."[409] Ordinarily the allocation of costs is included in the arbitral award, if not, the tribunal may tax costs in a subsequent supplementary award.[410]

While the allocation of costs and attorneys fees among the parties is within the tribunal's discretion, the fees which attorneys may charge for representation in arbitration and which may be taxed against their opponents are regulated by the Attorneys Fee Law, which applies to arbitrations with some slight modifications.[411]

6. Review and Enforcement of Arbitral Awards

The Civil Procedure Code specifically provides that an arbitral award "has among the parties the effect of a legally effective court judgment."[412] Absent agreement of the parties, arbitral awards are not appealable, and are subject to very limited judicial review.

A party may apply to the state appeals court specified in the agreement for arbitration or in the absence of such a specification, the appeals court for the district in which the arbitration took place[413] for judicial revocation (*gerichtliche Aufhebung*) of an arbitral award based on a limited list of grounds, namely:

a. lack of legal capacity of a party to conclude an arbitration agreement, or substantive invalidity of the agreement under governing law,
b. lack of sufficient notice of the arbitration so as to permit meaningful participation in the proceedings and access to means of proof or defense
c. scope of the award in excess of the issues properly subjected to arbitration
d. defects in the constitution of the arbitral panel as required by the Civil Procedure Code or the parties' agreement which affected the arbitral award,
e. lack of arbitrability of the subject matter of the dispute according to German Law, and

---

409. ZPO § 1057 (...*unter Berücksichtigung der Umstände des Einzelfalles, insbesondere des Ausgangs des Verfahrens*).

410. ZPO § 1057(2).

411. BRAGO §67.

412. ZPO § 1055 (*Der Schiedsspruch hat unter den Parteien die Wirkungen eines rechtskräftigen gerichtlichen Urteils.*). For the effects of a judgment see Ch. 9(F) above.

413. See ZPO §§ 1059, 1062.

f. violation of public policy (ordre public) from enforcement or recognition of the award.[414]

Unless the parties have otherwise agreed, an application for revocation of an arbitral award must be filed within three months of receipt of the award by the applicant.[415] Under appropriate circumstances the court may remand the proceedings to the arbitration tribunal, or may simply revoke the award.[416]

An arbitral award may be enforced through the process of court execution, provided that the state appeals court in the district in which the arbitration took place has made an appropriate declaration to that effect. A party seeking execution of an arbitral award must first apply to the court for a declaration of the executability (*Vollstreckbarerklärung*) of the award. A copy of the application must be served on the opposing party, who may raise any ground for revocation of the award as would justify an independent application to that effect.[417] If substantial objection is raised, the court must conduct a hearing, otherwise it may proceed without hearing and decide the application by simple decision and order (*Beschluss*).[418] Once the court has declared an arbitral award subject to execution, the party benefitted has the full range of execution measures available to attempt to collect or enforce the award.[419] If the award requires the performance of or forbearance from action or conduct, the court processes are similarly available to secure enforcement.

---

414. ZPO §§ 1059, 1062. As a matter of principle a party may not waive her right to apply for judicial revocation in advance. See Federal Supreme Court, 39 *WM* 1487 (1985). But judicial revocation cannot be based on defective constitution of the arbitral panel affecting the award if the parties have agreed on an award without reasoned explanation according to ZPO § 1054(2).

415. ZPO § 1059(3). However an application for revocation cannot be filed if a German court has previously declared the award to be subject to execution (*vollstreckbar*).

416. ZPO § 1059(4).

417. See ZPO §§ 1060, 1062. Most grounds for revocation must be raised within the time allowed for filing an independent application for revocation (*Aufhebungsantrag*), namely 3 months absent party agreement otherwise. ZPO § 1060(2). This time limit does not apply when revocation is based on lack of arbitrability or violation of public policy. If an application for revocation is already pending, the application for declaration of executability must be deferred until decision on the other application. If an application for revocation has been dismissed with prejudice, the party is precluded from raising the same grounds for revocation in a later proceeding for declaration of executability.

418. ZPO § 1063. The court may permit use of certain execution measures (*Vollstreckungsmassnahmen*) provisionally pending decision of a contested application to the extent necessary to secure eventual payment of the award. ZPO § 1063(3).

419. ZPO § 1060(1).

Recognition and enforcement of foreign arbitration awards is to be sought under nearly the same rules governing the declaration of enforceability of domestic arbitration awards.[420] German law provides for recognition and enforcement of all foreign arbitration awards according to the UN-Convention on the Recognition and Enforcement of Foreign Arbitration Awards 1958 independently from ratification of this convention by the state where the arbitration award was rendered.[421] The grounds for non-recognition according to the UN-Convention and the grounds for revocation and refusal of enforcement under national German law are more or less the same.[422]

I. Case Settlement and Alternative Dispute Resolution

The policy favoring voluntary settlement of legal disputes finds expression at many points in the German civil justice system and in German procedural law. Lawyers are encouraged and compensated to negotiate settlements for their clients even before filing suit.[423] In certain of the specialized court systems, participation in a conciliation procedure is a precondition to filing suit,[424] in others such proceedings take place immediately after filing of claim and before any other judicial activities.[425]

---

420. See ZPO §§1061, 1062–1065.

421. See Ch. 12(C)(1) below.

422. Compare ZPO §1069(2) and Article V UN-Convention on Recognition and Enforcement of Foreign Arbitration Awards 1958.

423. See Ch. 4(H) above and Ch. 11(I)(2) below.

424. In administrative and social welfare courts, parties filing claims must demonstrate that they have participated in administrative adjustment proceedings as a precondition to suit. See, for instance, VwGO §§80 ff. and SGG §78. The requirement that a party lodge objection with the administrative agency involved before starting a case in the administrative court is partly calculated to increase chances of informal resolution of the problem at the agency level. See Ch. 3(C)(2) and (3) above; for details Meyer-Ladewig, *Sozialgerichtsgesetz*, 7th. ed (2002), vor §77, mn. 1.

425. Most labor court proceedings commence with a required informal conciliation proceeding conducted by the presiding judge of the panel. See ArbGG §54 and for details Kramer, *Die Güteverhandlung: prozessuale Schlichtung in Arbeitssachen* (1999). These conciliation proceedings have generated an enviable record of success resolving nearly 79 per cent of cases filed in the labor court, see Lewerenz/Moritz, "Durchsetzung des Arbeitsrechts im Prozess oder interessengerechte Konfliktlösung? Vergleich und Urteil im Kündigungsschutzprozess", in: Walther et al. (eds.), *Der Prozessvergleich* (1983), p. 73.

In most kinds of disputes brought before the ordinary courts there is no specific requirement that parties undergo any form of conciliation or alternative dispute resolution as a condition to filing or maintaining a law suit. A recent reform has authorized the various states to require that parties undergo mandatory conciliation before filing certain kinds of small claims and other actions.[426]

Once litigation has started, however there are many features of the process designed to encourage voluntary settlement, and German judges are expected to take active roles to help settle cases when appropriate.[427] The most recent reforms in the Civil Procedure code have promoted settlement during litigation by requiring, at least in principle, an initial settlement conference before the plenary hearing in all civil cases.[428]

1. Role of the Judge in Case Settlements During Litigation

In all civil proceedings, the judge plays an important role in fostering resolutions by agreement.[429] In this role the judge functions under the following statutory admonition:

> The court shall be mindful at all stages of the proceedings of the potential for an agreed disposition of the legal dispute or individual issues thereof.[430]

The civil procedure reform of July 27, 2001 requires a settlement conference (*Güteverhandlung* or *Gütetermin*) before the oral preliminary or plenary hearing unless there was a prior formal attempt to reach a settlement at an out-of-

426. EGZPO § 15a (money claims up to 750 Euro, disputes between neighbors, certain libel and slander claims). For details and exceptions see Zöller/Gummer, § 15a EGZPO, mn. 3 ff.

427. See Ch. 4(H); Ch. 7(M); Ch. 8(B)(4); Ch. 9(A)(4) and (E)(4) above.

428. ZPO §278(2) (as amended by Law of July 27, 2001). See Thomas/Putzo/Reichold, §278, mn. 6 ff.; Zöller/Greger, §278, mn. 8 ff.

429. For details see Stürner, "Grundfragen richterlicher Streitschlichtung", 54 *DRiZ* 202 (1976); id., in: W. Gottwald et al. (eds.), *Der Prozessvergleich* (1983), p. 151; id., "Richterliche Vergleichsverhandlungen und richterlicher Vergleich aus juristischer Sicht", in: Meier (ed.), *Festschrift für Hans Ulrich Walder* (1994), p. 273; M. Wolf, "Normative Aspekte richterlicher Vergleichstätigkeit", 89 *ZZP* 260 (1976); Röhl, *Der Vergleich im Zivilprozess* (1983); Breidenbach, "Aussergerichtliche Streiterledigung - Sinn und Zusammenspiel mit dem Gerichtsverfahren", in: P. Gottwald (ed.), *Aktuelle Entwicklungen des europäischen und internationalen Zivilverfahrensrechts* (2002), p. 117.

430. ZPO §278(1).

court conciliation facility (*Gütestelle*)[431] or unless such a conference appears to be without prospect of success (*aussichtslos*).[432]

The court is expected to order the personal appearance of the parties at the settlement conference with the court. The court may also refer the parties to a judge designated from the panel (*beauftragter Richter*) or to a judge in another judicial district (*ersuchter Richter*) for the initial settlement conference.[433] A new feature of the 2001 reform is the court's authority in appropriate cases to propose to the parties an out of court mediation or other settlement process.[434]

As an experienced observer of the German litigation process observes, for judges in the facilitation of settlement negotiations during litigations, "The untrammeled discretion of the judge ('can') has transformed itself into an official duty ('should')".[435] Most modern German judges take their role as facilitators of settlements very seriously and place a premium on getting as many civil disputes as possible resolved by voluntary party settlement. The result of this positive policy slant has been a perceived increase over the last decades in the number of cases resolved by in-court settlement.[436]

At the same time, the German justice system strives to guarantee that a litigant who is seeking justice as dispensed by the court will not be placed under undue economic, procedural or judicial pressure to accept a settlement.

> But settlement may not squeeze final judgment from the litigation process, because the community of law needs judgments. The law is preserved in judgments, and only judgments can develop and prop-

431. As mentioned above, German states are authorized to establish conciliation facilities to assist parties in resolving disputes out of court and to require resort to such facilities in limited categories of cases. See EGZPO § 15a.

432. ZPO § 278(2).

433. ZPO § 278(3), (5). Attendance of the parties at such conferences can be compelled in the same way as can attendance at any hearing for oral argument when party presence is required. If neither party appears at the settlement conference, the case is stayed and continued indefinitely. ZPO § 278(4).

434. ZPO § 278(5)(2). For the development of out of court mediation in Germany see Ch. 11(I)(4) below.

435. Schellhammer, *Die Arbeitsmethode des Zivilrichters,* 12th ed. (1997), § 9(1)(1), mn. 492 (*Das freie Ermessen des Richters ('kann') verwandelte sich in eine Amtspflicht ('soll').*).

436. See Rosenberg/Schwab/Gottwald, § 131, p. 762; Hendel, "Der Prozessvergleich als Instrument der Ressourcenökonomie. - Zielverschiebungen in der Vergleichspraxis und daran anknüpfende rechtspolitische Empfehlungen", in: Walther et al. (eds.), *Der Prozessvergleich* (1983), p. 125, 128. In 1989 about 25 per cent of all cases were resolved by in-court settlement (local courts: 9.4 per cent; district courts: 12.6 per cent; state appeals courts: 16.8 per cent).

> agate the law. The constitution speaks only about justice, not mediation (GG Art. 92). The judge, who is bound to the law and justice (GG Art. 20 III), may not misuse his authority in settlement negotiations to deny a party a judgment. There will always be persons, rational as well as irrational, who ultimately want a judgment and no settlement, even if it costs them the suit. The judge may not undermine such persons' right to receive such a judgment through brainwashing.[437]

The positive role of the judge as a sort of mediator or facilitator of settlements is a measure designed to be productive of high quality settlements in cases where settlements are appropriate. Settlement technique and style vary with the backgrounds, depths of experience and personalities of the judges themselves. However there are several techniques and tools which German procedural law places in the hands of judges for their use in facilitate inter-party settlement discussions.

First of all, the authority of the judge to require the parties to sit face to face and state their respective positions and demands can ease or eliminate many differences caused by poor communication. Parties are forced to confront and relate to their opponents on a person-to-person basis. For many people dealing with a real person whom they can see and speak to directly is far different than dealing with a stylized opponent through lawyer, pleadings and structured litigation process. Sometimes just getting the parties together in the same room and requiring them to address the issue is enough to result in a settlement.

Perhaps the most powerful tool of the judge in encouraging good settlements is the judge's power and duty to clarify and give preliminary evaluative feedback (*Hinweise*) on the parties positions as they are stated and understood by the judge. The judge's duty to hints and feedback on the legal and factual

437. Schellhammer, §9(1)(1), mn. 942 (*Aber der Vergleich darf das Urteil nicht aus dem Prozess hinausdrängen, denn die Rechtsgemeinschaft braucht es. Im Urteil bewährt sich das Recht, nur das Urteil kann es entwickeln und fortbilden. Das Grundgesetz spricht nur von Rechtsprechung, nicht von Schlichtung (Art. 92 GG). Der Richter, gebunden an Gesetz und Recht (Art. 20 III GG), darf seine Autorität bei Vergleichsverhandlungen nicht missbrauchen, der Partei das Urteil zu verweigern. Es wird immer Menschen geben, vernünftige wie unvernünftige, die partout ein Urteil wollen und keinen Vergleich, auch wenn es sie den Prozess kostet. Ihnen darf der Richter den Anspruch auf das Urteil nicht durch eine Gehirnwäsche vereiteln*). See also Stürner, 54 *DRiZ* 202 (1976) and Federal Supreme Court, 19 *NJW* 2399 (1966) for an example of undue judicial pressure which resulted in voidability of the judge-mediated settlement.

sufficiency of the parties' positions is at the core of the judicial function in civil litigation. The recent reforms stress the judge's obligation to make use of this tool at the required initial oral settlement conference.

> In the settlement conference the judge is to give free consideration to all circumstances in discussing the factual and legal issues of the case with the parties and to the extent appropriate, should ask questions. The appearing parties should be personally heard on the issues.[438]

This kind of judicial participation is especially helpful to parties as they consider settlements. Clarifications offered by a judge can often assist a party in overcoming limitations of its own perspective and can reduce the risk that a party will settle (or continue to litigate) out of ignorance or selective blindness.[439]

Performance of this duty to give hints and feedback requires a particular kind of intellectual discipline on the part of the judge. The judge must be able to give meaningful evaluation of the parties' respective positions based on the judge's knowledge of the case to date, without undermining their belief in her impartiality if it is necessary for her to decide the case later on.[440] The judge must resist the temptation slightly to slant the "clarifications" in order to induce a recalcitrant party to settle. The theory is that the more the parties know about their cases and their respective strengths and weaknesses on both sides, the more likely they will be able to come to a sensible compromise resolution.

> "Only the enlightened party can decide freely for or against a settlement. The clarification should convince, not persuade. The judge plays the role of an honest broker. Inasmuch as he enlightens the parties neutrally on the legal or factual situation presented, he is serving the principle of freedom of contract."[441]

---

438. ZPO §278(2) (*Das Gericht hat in der Güteverhandlung den Sach- und Streitstand mit den Parteien unter freier Würdigung aller Umstände zu erörtern und, soweit erforderlich, Fragen zu stellen. Die erschienenen Parteien sollen hierzu persönlich gehört werden*).

439. See Schellhammer, §9(2)(4), mn. 499.

440. See Ch. 6(C)(2) above on the judge's conflicting considerations when giving "hints and feedback".

441. Schellhammer, §9(2)(4), mn. 499 (*Nur die aufgeklärte Partei kann sich frei für oder gegen den Vergleich entscheiden. Die Aufklärung soll überzeugen, nicht überreden. Der Richter spielt die Rolle des ehrlichen Maklers. Indem er die Parteien neutral über die Sach- und Rechtslage aufklärt, dient er der Vertragsfreiheit*).

The judge is empowered to use the tool of time to encourage the parties to settle. Sometimes a "cooling off period" will lead parties to reconsider and seek compromise. In domestic relations cases, there is specific statutory authorization for the judge to postpone or even suspend the proceedings for time periods running into the months if so doing is likely to lead to settlement or abandonment of the proceedings. The Law on Unfair Competition authorizes a stay of litigation on motion of a party in order to permit opportunity for settlement negotiations.[442] In ordinary civil litigation the judge may continue a conference at which a settlement proposal has been discussed to a future date to allow the parties time to digest the proposal and maturely react to it.[443]

Although the new reforms lay emphasis on the new required preliminary settlement conference, settlement discussions are not confined to a particular preliminary stage of the proceedings. Parties can settle at any point, right up to the time of issuance of final judgment and even thereafter if the case is appealed. Moreover, the judge may raise the subject of settlement at virtually every stage of the proceeding. If the tenor of the proceedings indicates that the time may be ripe, or if a particular point is approaching when the judge thinks that the parties might be more amenable to negotiate, the judge can raise the issue on her own motion. An unsuccessful attempt to broker a settlement at one stage of the litigation does not preclude the judge from attempting to do so later.

Needless to say, the latitude allowed the judge in the use of time to foster potential settlements is not unbounded. The power of the judge to postpone or suspend proceedings in domestic relations cases has statutory limits. In the ordinary civil case abuse of the power to schedule hearings in order to place a party under undue settlement pressure could generate an appeal to the Constitutional Court (*Verfassungsbeschwerde*)[444] or an action to void any resulting settlement on grounds of undue judicial influence.[445]

---

442. UWG §27a(10).

443. See ZPO §227(1)(2) and Zöller/Greger, §278, mn. 19; Schellhammer, §9(2)(5), mn. 500.

444. See Zöller/Geimer, Einleitung, mn. 120; Maunz/Schmidt-Bleibtreu/Klein/Ulsamer, *Bundesverfassungsgerichtsgesetz*, §90, mn. 155 and Federal Constitutional Court, 47 *NJW* 719 (1994) for unjustified delay to render a judgment. However, case settlements themselves are not subject to constitutional appeal. See Bavarian Constitutional Court, 47 *NJW* 2281 (1994).

445. See Federal Supreme Court, 19 *NJW* 2399 (1966); for state liability in case of wrongful documentation by the judge see Stürner, 54 *DRiZ* 202, 204 (1976); for the liability of lawyers see State Appeals Court of Frankfurt, 41 *NJW* 3269 (1988); State Appeals Court of Hamm, 43 *VersR* 1404 (1992).

The judge has the power to divide and structure the proceedings in order to encourage partial and provisional settlements. Claims subject to potential settlement can be severed in order to facilitate the settlement.[446]

Often reaching a viable settlement of a case requires a certain kind of judicial creativity to transcend the stylized assertions of legal claim and defense and espy the real interest of the parties and craft an arrangement to meet those interests.[447] Such an ability can be hard to teach, but may be the result of experience combined with a curious and engaging attitude on the part of the judge.

Traditionally the active role of the judge in promoting settlement has meant that for a long time out of court mechanisms of alternative dispute resolution have not been perceived to be necessary and have not developed to a really remarkable degree. As mentioned above, the recent reforms have introduced the option of a formal referral of the parties to out of court settlement facilities and of a stay in the proceedings (with the consent of the parties) in order to accommodate such referral.[448] It remains to be seen whether this legislative authorization will foster the development of a new market for the professional activities of lawyers or other dispute resolution professionals.[449]

2. Costs and Attorneys Fees in Cases Settled During Litigation

If the parties settle a case during litigation both the overall amount of court costs and attorneys fees payable and the way the costs and attorneys fees are allocated among the parties will be affected. The idea is to provide incentives to the parties to settle rather than burden the courts with unnecessary judgments.

---

446. See ZPO § 145(1) and Ch. 7(A)(5).

447. It is undisputed that a judge's "rights-based" suggestions for settlement may never justify an application for disqualification even when the judge's suggestion seems to be partial in the eyes of a party. See Federal Constitutional Court, 42 BVerfGE 78 (1976); State Appeals Court of Stuttgart, 54 *NJW* 1145 (2001); Kammergericht (State Appeals Court of Berlin), 99 *KGR* 187 (1999); Zöller/Greger, § 278, mn. 2. However, if a judge makes "interests-based" suggestions for settlements that include elements of the parties' conflict which are not within the frame of reference of the parties' claims for relief and factual assertions, the judge may be risking disqualification based on introducing issues beyond the subject matter in dispute (*Streitgegenstand*) without the consent of both parties. See Zöller/Greger, § 278, mn. 3; very generous Kammergericht (State Appeals Court of Berlin), 24 *NJW-RR* 1164, 1166 (2000). See Ch. 11(I)(4) below on "interests-based" mediation.

448. ZPO § 278(5). See also UWG § 27a(10).

449. See for more details Ch. 11(I)(4) below.

If a case is settled at any stage of a civil proceeding prior to judgment of the first instance court, the total court costs otherwise payable as of that stage of the proceeding are reduced by two units. So, for instance, if an ordinary civil case were settled at some point prior to the rendition of judgment, the three units of court costs ordinarily payable would be reduced to one unit.[450] If the settlement is reached on second instance or review appeal, costs are reduced by one and a half units or three units respectively from the costs that would have been imposed if a reasoned judgment were rendered.[451]

By the same token, in computing attorneys fees, reaching a settlement is counted as a unit of performance for both counsel in computing their fees. Thus, if an ordinary civil case is settled after the initiation of plenary proceedings, but before judgment, the lawyers for both parties would be entitled to compensation from their clients based on three units of performance, the basic suit fee, the plenary proceedings fee, and the settlement fee.[452] This provides lawyers with a positive incentive to settle cases rather than leave them to be decided by the court. Sometimes when a case is settled early in the proceedings, the lawyers will delay the formalization of the settlement until the opening of the plenary hearing to increase their fee bases from two to three units (including the settlement fee).[453]

The Civil Procedure Code authorizes the parties to agree on the allocation of court costs and attorneys fees in case settlements.[454] In most cases this is what happens, and the agreement concerning fees and costs is incorporated as a part of the settlement when the latter is documented of record.[455] Allocations of fees by agreement often tend to be based on the extent to which the settlement favors the position of one party or the other.[456] Thus, a plaintiff

---

450. See GKG Attachment 1, No. 1211.

451. GKG Attachment 1, Nos. 1220 and 1224, 1231 and 1236.

452. BRAGO §31.

453. This is particularly likely if one or both of the parties have legal costs insurance. See Ch. 4(J) above; Murray, "A Morning at the Amtsgericht: German Civil Justice in Practice", in: Nafziger et Symeonides (eds.), *Law and Justice in a Multistate World, Essays in Honor of Arthur T. von Mehren* (2002), p. 779. The court may, on the other hand, suggest that the parties document the settlement before the commencement of plenary proceedings if the court has the impression that three units of costs would be excessive compensation under the circumstances.

454. ZPO §98. However the court is not bound by a cost agreement of the parties in marriage cases. See ZPO §93a(1)(3).

455. See Ch. 11(I)(3) below.

456. This is by analogy to the result that would have been obtained had the court reached a decision sustaining each party's position in part. See Ch. 9(E)(3) above; ZPO §92.

who obtained in settlement three-quarters of what he had sought in the suit would expect the opponent to agree to bear the burden of three-quarters of the costs and attorneys fees for both parties. The parties can also agree to submit the allocation of costs for decision by the court.[457] If, however the parties do not reach any agreement on cost allocation in an otherwise settled case, the Civil Procedure Code provides for suspension (*Aufhebung*) of liability for costs as a default solution.[458]

3. Formalities of In-Court Case Settlements

An important feature of German civil justice gives parties settling most kinds of civil cases the ability to embody their settlements in forms equivalent to execution titles (*Vollstreckungstitel*).[459] German law permits parties who negotiate resolutions during litigation to make the settlements of record (*beurkunden*) in the litigation.[460] As a rule, settlements made of record can be enforced with all the tools available to holders of final judgments.[461] This advantage means that many settlements of cases reached during litigation are made of record with the court.

The requirements for an in-court settlement of a litigated case are set forth in §794 of the Civil Procedure Code, which authorizes involuntary execution:

> (1) based on settlements, which have been concluded between the parties...for the resolution of a legal dispute...before a German court, or before a settlement facility established or recognized by the state

457. See Rosenberg/Schwab/Gottwald, §87(II)(4), p. 465. German Federal Supreme Court, 18 *NJW* 103 (1965). The court would likely decide the issue based on the same criteria applicable to cost allocation in the event of voluntary termination (see CH. 9(A)(2) above), namely "according to its sound discretion having due regard for the circumstances of the case." ZPO §91a (*...unter Berücksichtigung des bisherigen Sach- und Streitstandes nach billigem Ermessen...*). This occurs relatively infrequently, since the parties generally will not reach a settlement that leaves an important issue open.

458. ZPO §98. This means that the parties would split the costs of court and each would be responsible for its own attorneys fees and expenses.

459. For enforcement of settlements made outside of court see Ch. 11(I)(3) below.

460. Settlements made of record in the court are called "in-court settlements" (*Prozessvergleiche*) in order to differentiate them from settlements not made of record.

461. For the various measures for execution on and enforcement of final judgments, see Ch. 11(F) above. If the settlement requires the performance of an executory act such as a conveyance or assignment, the act itself must be accurately set forth and incorporated in the settlement as made of record with the court, since otherwise it would be difficult to effect execution. See Ch. 11(F)(2)(b) above.

ministry of justice, as well as settlements which have been made of judicial record according to § 118(1)(3) or § 492(3).[462]

The in-court settlement process applies to negotiated resolutions other than a simple withdrawal of the complaint (*Klagerücknahme*), suffering of default judgment (*Versäumnisurteil*), judgment by acknowledgment or waiver (*Anerkenntnisurteil*), or similar stipulated disposition.[463] The procedure is designed to make sure that the parties are aware of the settlement and its consequences, and to insure that the parties' settlement agreement is clear and unambiguous enough to enable execution or enforcement if necessary.

Under the traditional approach the settlement is supposed to be reached or at least announced at a hearing, usually before the court in which the case is pending. Under some circumstances, if settlement discussions are being conducted by a designated or referred judge, that judge can document any resulting settlement.[464] The parties agreement must be embodied in the minutes of a judicial hearing before a judge or in a document incorporated in the minutes by reference. The settlement agreement must also be read aloud to the parties, or they must at least orally acknowledge having read it.

The new reforms have introduced a procedure whereby the judge can make a written settlement proposal to the parties. The acceptance of the proposal in written form has the effect of documenting the settlement by court order.[465] As already mentioned above, parties represented by counsel may obtain the benefits of an in-court settlement, including immediate execution, outside of court if their lawyers sign a document in which the debtor expressly submits to immediate execution.[466] The document is to be filed in a local court where one of the parties has its residence or "seat".[467] The creditor may apply for a declaration of executability in the court competent to consider the settled dispute whenever involuntary execution becomes necessary.[468] At the parties' option the document may be filed in the office of a notary located in the district

462. ZPO § 794 (*aus Vergleichen, die zwischen den Parteien... zur Beilegung des Rechtsstreits... vor einem deutschen Gericht oder vor einer durch die Landesjustizverwaltung eingerichteten oder anerkannten Gütestelle abgeschlossen sind, sowie aus Vergleichen, die gemäss § 118 Abs. 1 Satz 3 oder § 492 Abs. 3 zu richterlichem Protokoll genommen sind.*).

463. See Ch. 9(A) above for a discussion of various forms of stipulated disposition.

464. Rosenberg/Schwab/Gottwald, § 131(I)(3), pp. 763 f.

465. See ZPO § 278(6).

466. See Ch. 9(A)(4) above.

467. ZPO § 796a(1) and §§ 12–18; see Ch. 5(C)(1) above.

468. See ZPO §§ 796a, 796b (added 1998). For discussion of the similar declaration of executability of arbitration awards see Ch. 11(H)(6) above.

where the local court competent for filing the documented settlement sits; the notary may also issue a declaration of executability when necessary.[469]

4. Alternative Dispute Resolution

The active role of German judges in promoting settlements may be the most significant reason why mechanisms of out of court dispute resolution have not developed to the extent as is the case in the United States.[470] It should be stressed, however, that a broader scope and application of ADR are being given ever more consideration.[471] As mentioned above, the German legislature encourages out of court settlements by mandatory conciliation before filing certain kinds of small claims[472] and by optional referral of the parties to out of court settlement facilities.[473] Stay of proceedings to give an opportunity for out of court mediation is also the preferred model of the modern French and English civil procedure.[474] The American ideas of a "multidoor-courthouse" and of mandatory court-annexed mediation[475] have not yet been implemented in Germany by legislative measure. Experiments with similar ADR models are being encouraged and subsidized in a number of German courts on a voluntary basis by the ministries of justice of some German States.[476] Mediators in divorce and family disputes, at present the most important fields

469. See ZPO §796c.

470. See Murray, "ADR und die amerikanische Ziviljustiz", in: Gottwald (ed.), *Aktuelle Entwicklungen des europäischen und internationalen Zivilverfahrensrechts* (2002), p. 25.

471. For more details see Breidenbach, *Mediation. Struktur, Chancen und Risiken von Vermittlung im Konflikt* (1995); Breidenbach/Henssler (eds.), *Mediation für Juristen* (1997); Haft/Schlieffen (eds.), *Handbuch der Mediation* (2002); Günter Hager, *Konflikt und Konsens* (2001); for a good overview on the German present status see Breidenbach, "Aussergerichtliche Streiterledigung - Sinn und Zusammenspiel mit den Gerichtsverfahren, in: Gottwald (ed.), *Aktuelle Entwicklungen* (2002), p. 117.

472. See EGZPO §15a and Ch. 11(I) above.

473. See ZPO §278(5) and UWG §27a(10); Ch. 11(I)(1) above.

474. See Articles 131-1 ff. of the French Civil Procedure Code and Part 26(4) CPR England; Stürner, in: Breidenbach et al. (eds.), *Konsensuale Streitbeilegung* (2001), p. 13.

475. See Frank Sander, "Varieties of Dispute Processing", 70 *F.R.D.* 111 (1976); Goldberg/Sander/Rogers, *Dispute Resolution* (1992); for a survey on the recent development see Murray, "Civil Justice Reform in America: The Civil Justice Reform Act of 1990 and its Consequences", 3 *ZZPInt* 319 (1999); id., "ADR und die amerikanische Ziviljustiz", in: Gottwald (ed.), *Aktuelle Entwicklungen* (2002), pp. 26 ff., 32 f.

476. For a survey see Breidenbach, in: Gottwald (ed.), *Aktuelle Entwicklungen* (2002), pp. 117 ff.

for mediation, have their own well established professional organization.[477] The Association of German Lawyers has decided to set up a special commission for mediation development.[478] In a growing number of contracts mandatory mediation has begun to replace dispute resolution by arbitration especially in cases of outstanding economic significance.[479]

Future developments may bring an increase of various forms of mediation. Lawyers and other professions are discovering the advantages of this new market and are undertaking mediation as a profitable and remunerative business. The nearly complete lack of professional ethics for this new profession and its services may encourage abuses and doubtful techniques which produce outcomes which are successful in the sense of "getting to yes".

The development of the rule of law and of abstract rules of procedural and substantive law has been important to the progress of human culture. The step from a "rights-based" dispute resolution procedure through public courts to an "interests based" process through private mediation could result in loss of fairness especially for the weaker party of a conflict. This might be especially likely if a mediator does not respect traditional principles of fair procedure and justice. The development of professional ethics, mediator liability and mediation law must accompany the growth of mediation in Germany as elsewhere.[480]

---

477. Bundesarbeitsgemeinschaft für Familien-Mediation e.V.; see Breidenbach, in: Gottwald (ed.), *Aktuelle Entwicklungen* (2002), p. 125.

478. Ausschuss für Mediation der Bundesrechtsanwaltskammer; see 30 *BRAK-Mitt.* 25 f. (1999).

479. See Eidenmüller, "Hybride ADR-Verfahren bei internationalen Wirtschaftsverfahren", 48 *RIW* 1 ff. (2002).

480. See for the U.S. Murray, in: Gottwald (ed.), *Aktuelle Entwicklungen* (2002), pp. 26 ff., 30 ff.

CHAPTER 12

German Civil Justice in International Matters

Since the physical and economic world is not governed by a single regime but by many different political, economic and legal systems, it has become necessary for the various civil justice systems to develop and enforce rules allocating the decision of disputes among the various systems as well as rules determining which jurisdiction's law will apply. The process of creation of rules governing the jurisdiction of the national courts of the various nations of the world has been informed by international customary law, which has tended to give shape both to international jurisdiction-allocating conventions and to national law governing jurisdiction in international matters. Germany's law governing jurisdiction in international civil matters, recognition of foreign judgments, and proceedings in aid of foreign jurisdiction thus contains elements of customary international law, international and European conventions and regulations, and national statutory law.

Although it is not the aim of this work to provide an exhaustive analysis of the German law of international civil procedure (*internationales Zivilprozessrecht*), a brief sketch of some of the salient doctrines governing the interaction of Germany's civil justice system with Europe and the rest of the world is important to gaining some understanding of the workings of the system as a whole.[1]

A. Sources of International Civil Procedure Law

German law of international jurisdiction, recognition of foreign judgments, and proceedings in aid of foreign jurisdiction is based on a combination of

---

1. For a more complete treatment of German international civil procedure law see Geimer, *Internationales Zivilprozessrecht*, 4th ed. (2001); Schack, *Internationales Zivilverfahrensrecht*, 3rd ed. (2002).

international customary law, international conventions to which Germany is a party, regulations of the European Union binding on Germany as a Member State, and national statute law. Together these sources of law have contributed to the regimen which establishes, defines and limits the role of German civil justice in international matters.

International customary law forms an important foundation for the international jurisdiction of all states. The basic principle that a state must respect the territorial sovereignty of other states restricts a state from exercising acts of sovereignty over foreign territory. No state can conduct judicial proceedings on the territory of another state without that state's express permission. The same principle tends to restrain a state from exercising jurisdiction over matters so connected with the persons, things, and interests of another state that the jurisdiction cannot be properly exercised without, in effect, judicially invading the other state.[2] On the other hand, customary international law does not prevent courts from giving notice to parties or other litigation participants such as experts, who are located in other countries.

Whether a dispute must have some minimal recognized connection (*anerkanntes Anknüpfungsmerkmal*) with a particular state in order to support that state's civil jurisdiction to resolve is subject to debate.[3] As a practical matter, customary international law has not developed any clear code of international civil jurisdiction. There is room for differing views of how far any particular state may go in adjudicating disputes involving disputants, property, and issues not located within its geographic borders. One restraint on a state's unilateral assertion of jurisdiction considered exorbitant by the international community is the likely refusal by other states to enforce or recognize judgments based on the exorbitant jurisdiction.[4]

An important source of law governing the international jurisdiction of German courts and the recognition of foreign judgments are international con-

---

2. See Geimer, Part 1 Chapter 5(I)(1), mn. 121–122; Stürner, „Der Justizkonflikt zwischen den U.S.A. und Europa", in: Habscheid (ed.), *Der Justizkonflikt mit den Vereinigten Staaten von Amerika* (1986), p. 3; Bertele, *Souveränität und Verfahrensrecht* (1998), pp. 63–195.

3. See Geimer, Part 1 Chapter 5(I)(3), mn. 126–128b; Schack, §1(III)(1), mn. 21; §8(I)(1) mn. 186. The Federal Constitutional Court requires a minimal measure of reasonableness (*Mindestmass an Einsichtigkeit*) as a precondition for exercise of jurisdiction to prescribe and adjudicate. 63 BVerfGE 343, 369 (1983).

4. See Ch. 12(C)(1) below for examples of refusal by German courts to recognize judgments of American courts based on exercise of extra-territorial jurisdiction considered exorbitant in Germany.

ventions to which Germany is a party and, more recently, regulations of the European Union. In 1968 Germany and the ten other then members of the European Community entered into the so-called "Brussels Convention" providing for regulation of the signatories' respective assertion of international jurisdiction and recognition of foreign judgments involving the Member States.[5] The Lugano Convention of September 16, 1988 extended the schema of the Brussels Convention to a number of additional European states not members of the European Community.[6] These two multiparty international treaties specify the extent to which the parties may exercise extraterritorial jurisdiction in certain civil and commercial litigation vis à vis each other, and the extent to which civil judgments in such cases rendered by the courts of a party state will be recognized and enforced by the other party states. They are both "double" conventions, in that they specify both the extent to which the exercise of jurisdiction is permissible and the extent to which it is forbidden. They are also both self-executing conventions, in that they may be directly applied by the courts of the Member States, without the need of comprehensive enabling legislation.

On December 22, 2000 the European Union enacted the terms of a reformed Brussels Convention as a Regulation of the European Union.[7] The effect of this change is that as new members join the EU there is no need for them formally to adopt the Brussels Convention as was the case in the past. Other EU regulations affecting the international jurisdiction of courts of the Members States include regulations on jurisdiction and recognition and enforcement of judgments in family law matters,[8] the service of process and

---

5. Brussels Convention of September 27, 1968 on Jurisdiction and Enforcement of Judgments in Civil and Commercial Matters. The Brussels Convention was amended and extended to Great Britain, Ireland and Denmark by the first Accession Treaty of October 9, 1978, to Greece by the second Accession Treaty of October 25, 1982, to Spain and Portugal and Greece through the Third Accession Treaty of May 26, 1989 and to Austria, Finland and Sweden by the Fourth Accession Treaty of November 29, 1996.

6. In 1988 the Lugano Convention included the then 12 members of the European Community and the then six Member States of the European Free Trade Association (EFTA), Finland, Austria, Iceland, Switzerland and Norway. The first three of these subsequently joined the European Union and the Brussels Convention. Poland was invited to join the Lugano Convention as of January 2, 2000. Liechtenstein joined in 1991.

7. European Union Regulation No. 44/2001 of December 22, 2000 on Jurisdiction and Recognition and Enforcement of Decisions in Civil and Commercial Matters, OJ L 012, 16/12/2001, p. 1 (hereinafter referred to as the "Brussels Regulation" or "BRJE"). The Regulation binds and benefits all members of the European Union except for Denmark. BRJE Article 1(3).

8. European Union Regulation No. 1347/2000, OJ L 160, 30/06/2000, p. 19.

other documents in civil and commercial matters,[9] insolvency proceedings,[10] and judicial cooperation in taking of evidence in civil and commercial matters.[11] The European Court of Justice has jurisdiction to decide questions referred to it by the courts of the Member States on the construction and application of the Brussels Regulation.[12] The incorporation of the Brussels Convention into an EU Regulation does not affect the provisions of the Lugano Convention which continues to regulate international jurisdiction among the EU Member States and the other parties to that convention.[13]

In addition to the more or less comprehensive provisions of the Brussels Regulation and the Lugano Convention for civil and commercial matters, there are a number of other multilateral treaties regulating jurisdiction and recognition of foreign judgments in specific classes of matters.[14]

There are also many international treaties and less formal international arrangements with parties outside the European Union which play a role in civil litigation. The most important of these are the Hague Conventions on Service of Process Abroad[15] and the Taking of Evidence Abroad.[16] There are

---

9. European Union Regulation No. 1348/2000, OJ L 160, 30/06/2000, p. 32.

10. European Union Regulation No. 1346/2000, OJ L 160, 30/06/2000, p. 1.

11. European Union Regulation No. 1206/2001, OJ L 174, 27/06/2001, p. 1.

12. Treaty of the European Community, Article 234. This was also the case with the Brussels Convention by virtue of the Protocol of Interpretation of 1971. See Geimer, Part 1 Chapter 5(III)(3), mn. 246j. See Kropholler, *Europäisches Zivilprozessrecht*, 7th ed. (2002), Introduction(II)(1)(a)–(c), mn. 30–39 and Schack, §3(IV)(2), mn. 85–89 for a discussion of the role of the European Court of Justice in interpreting the Brussels Convention and Regulation. According to Art. 68(1) of the Treaty of the European Community judicial cooperation matters are now subject to certification only by the Member States' highest appellate courts. See Ch. 3(F) above.

13. There is no institution with the authority to maintain the unitary construction and application of the Lugano Convention. This remains the province of the national courts of the parties to the treaty. Decisions of the European Court of Justice construing the Brussels Convention or Regulation are of persuasive authority, and there is a system for the exchange of information on construction and application of the Lugano Convention among the party states. See Kropholler, Introduction (III)(5), mn. 71–78; Geimer, Part 1 Chapter 5(IV), mn. 247c–247f.

14. See Schack, §3(I)(1)–(3), mn. 54, 55 for a catalog of some of the many multilateral and bilateral conventions and treaties affecting international jurisdiction and recognition of foreign judgments in specific matters and classes of matters.

15. Hague Convention of November 15, 1965 on the Service of Process and Documents Abroad.

16. Hague Convention of March 18, 1970 on the Taking of Evidence Abroad in Civil and Commercial Matters.

also Hague Conventions on recognition of foreign adoption,[17] on recognition of judicial separation and divorce,[18] and on enforcement of child support and protection orders.[19]

The role of international conventions in defining the permissible limits of international civil jurisdiction and providing for the recognition of foreign judgments may be greatly expanded if the currently pending Hague Convention on Jurisdiction and Recognition of Judgments is finalized and adopted by a large number of states, notably the United Sates, which is not a party to the major European conventions and regulations.[20]

The German Constitution also plays a role in defining the minima and limits of the international jurisdiction of German courts. The principle of the rule of law (*Rechtstaatsprinzip*) embodied in the German Constitution requires the state to provide free recourse to justice. This principle prevents arbitrary or discretionary restrictions on court jurisdiction, even in international matters.[21] On the other hand, the right to a fair judicial hearing, also embodied in the Constitution, restrains the German state from burdening potential international defendants with having to appear and defend under unreasonable circumstances. These constitutional guarantees are also reflected in the rules regulating the recognition and enforcement of foreign judgments, prohibiting recognition of judgments not based on a minimally fair process.[22]

It must be kept in mind that international civil procedure law (*internationales Zivilprozessrecht*) relating to civil jurisdiction in international matters

---

17. Hague Convention of November 15, 1965 on the Jurisdiction of Officials, the Applicable Law and the Recognition of Decisions in the Area of Adoptions.

18. Hague Convention of July 1, 1970 on Recognition of Divorces and Judicial Separations.

19. Hague Convention of October 2, 1973 on the Recognition and Enforcement of Support Orders. The United States is not a party to this convention. See Geimer, Part 1 Chapter 5(II)(4), mn. 244a for a catalog of these and other Hague Conventions affecting international civil procedure law of Germany.

20. Current negotiations on a comprehensive convention do not seem to be very promising. There may be potential for progress on questions of jurisdiction by party agreement. See for an up-to-date documentation of the negotiations http://www.hcch.net/e/workprog/index.html and for the history of the Hague negotiations Nygh, "Arthur's baby: The Hague Negotiations for a World-Wide Judgments Convention", in: Nafziger/Symeonides (eds.), *Law and Justice in a Multistate World, Essays in Honor of Arthur T. von Mehren* (2002), p. 151. See further Baumgartner, *The Proposed Hague Convention on Jurisdiction and Foreign Judgments* (2003).

21. See Ch. 12(B) below.

22. See Geimer, Part 1 Chapter 6, mn. 249–256a for a discussion of the constitutional aspects of international jurisdiction and recognition of foreign judgments.

and recognition and enforcement of foreign judgments is not the same as international choice of laws (*internationales Privatrecht*). Although some of the same policies are implemented by both bodies of law, the determination of what state has civil jurisdiction over a dispute and what state's law will provide the rule of decision proceed from different legal bases and frequently involve different considerations of law and policy.[23] Often a German court will have civil jurisdiction to decide a matter that is governed by the law of another state. Sometimes choice of laws doctrine of a foreign state will require courts of that state to apply German law to a dispute before pending in that state. German choice of laws doctrine is a fertile field of inquiry, but is outside the scope of this work.[24]

B. Jurisdiction of German Courts in International Matters

The jurisdiction of German courts in international matters is prescribed by national statutory law. However in many cases the Brussels Regulation, the Lugano Convention or specific treaty obligations are of greater practical significance.

In general, the provisions of the German Civil Procedure Code specifying venue (*örtliche Zuständigkeit*) for civil actions within Germany also describe the extent to which German courts claim jurisdiction to adjudicate in international matters.[25] However the application of these provisions to international matters may sometimes require more restrictive constructions of these provisions than is the case when they are applied within Germany. And in many cases they are overruled by provisions of the Brussels Regulation, other treaties or other elements of international law. The following brief treatment

---

23. See Geimer, Part 1 Chapter 2, mn. 19–58 for an analysis of the relationship of international civil procedure law with international choice of laws.

24. See Reimann, *Conflict of Laws in Western Europe; A Guide Through the Jungle* (1995), for a recent analysis of European conflicts of laws doctrine. Leading German texts on choice of law include Kegel/Schurig, *Internationales Privatrecht*, 8th *ed.* (2000); Kropholler, *Internationales Privatrecht*, 4th ed. (2001); von Hoffmann, *Internationales Privatrecht* 7th ed. (2002); v. Bar/Mankowski, *Internationales Privatrecht*, Vol. I, *Allgemeine Lehren*, 2nd ed. (2003); v. Bar, *Internationales Privatrecht*, Vol. II, *Besonderer Teil* (1991).

25. For a discussion of the "double function" of the German rules on venue (*örtliche Zuständigkeit*) as also defining international jurisdiction, see Geimer, Part 4 Chapter 3(II), mn. 943–973; Schack, §8(II)(1)(b), mn. 236–237.

of the jurisdiction of German civil courts in international matters will attempt to make note of the most common circumstances under which the Brussels Regulation or the Lugano Convention provide for a result different from that provided by purely German law on international jurisdiction, which applies with respect to parties or cases from other parts of the world.

German law on international jurisdiction does not as a matter of principle recognize the concept of *forum non conveniens* as a basis for discretionary non-exercise of civil jurisdiction in favor of the courts of another state where suit would arguably be more convenient for parties and witnesses.[26] Both under German statute law and under the Brussels Regulation, if jurisdiction exists, as a matter of principle the court is required to entertain the action unless restricted from doing so by some other statute or regulation of international law, or in some cases, by valid agreement of the parties.

1. Jurisdiction Based on the Defendant's Domicile

The foundation of German and European doctrine concerning civil jurisdiction is the principle that the defendant is generally susceptible to suit in the state of his domicile (*Wohnsitz*).[27] Both the German Civil Procedure Code and the Brussels Regulation specify that for all matters other than those for which an exclusive jurisdiction is prescribed, a person has a general susceptibility to be sued (*allgemeine Gerichtstand*) in the state of his domicile.[28] For purposes of ZPO §13, the particular elements of domicile (*Wohnsitz*) are spelled out in German Civil Code §§7–11. "Domicile" is not specifically defined in the Brussels Regulation. According to Article 59 of the Brussels Regulation the law of the forum governs the determination of domicile, provided that if the party is not a domiciliary of the forum state, but may be a domiciliary of another

26. Geimer, Part 4 Chapter 6, mn. 1073–1094; Schack, §10(II), mn. 493–502. Some, however, assert that the German doctrine that a party must have a need for legal protection in order to invoke the aid of the courts can be applied analogously to *forum non conveniens* to require the court to determine that the German court is, in comparison with other potential fora, "suited to provide an economical, just and accurate decision of the case in question" („*geeignet... im konkreten Fall Prozessökonomie, Verfahrensgerechtigkeit und richtige Beurteilung des Sachverhalts zu gewährleisten.*"): Wahl, *Die verfehlte internationale Zuständigkeit* (1974), p. 126. Where only the location of property is a ground for personal jurisdiction, principles similar to those supporting the *doctrine of forum non conveniens* may apply; see Ch. 12(B)(2)(c) below.

27. Geimer, Part 4 Chapter 8(III), mn. 1138–1144.

28. ZPO §§12, 13 and BRJE Article 2(1), codifying the principle of „*actor sequitur forum rei*", see Zöller/Vollkommer, *Zivilprozessordnung*, 23rd ed. (2002), §12, mn. 2.

EU state, the court shall apply the law of that other EU state to determine whether the party is domiciled there.

Under German law a legal person such as a corporation has its domicile at its "seat" (*Sitz*).[29] Frequently the seat of a corporation is specified by the corporate charter. In default of such specification, the seat of a legal person is the location where the administration (*Verwaltung*) of the entity is conducted.[30] The Brussels Regulation is slightly more generous to plaintiffs. According to Article 60 the domicile of a legal person is alternatively its "statutory seat," the place where it has its "central administration" or its "principal place of business".[31]

General susceptibility to suit means susceptibility to all kinds of suits that may be asserted against the defendant, regardless on what law they may be based or what kind of relief is requested, with the exception of those kinds of claims for which an exclusive international jurisdiction (*ausschliess icher internationaler Gerichtstand*) is prescribed,[32] such as claims affecting title to land[33] or actions against consumers.[34]

General susceptibility to suit cannot be based on an agreement. Agreements conferring jurisdiction are only authorized for "disputes which have arisen or may arise in connection with a particular legal relationship."[35]

A person who does not have a known domicile, either in Germany or elsewhere, is generally subject to suit in Germany based on sojourn (*Aufenthalt*) there.[36] In order to determine whether such a person may be subject to suit in Germany, the German court must determine whether the person is a domiciliary of some other state. There is some question whether German law or the law of the asserted state of domicile applies to this determination.[37] This jurisdiction is not affected by the Brussels Regulation, which applies only to persons who have a domicile in one of the EU Member States.[38]

29. ZPO §17(1)(1).

30. ZPO §17(1)(2). ZPO §17(3) provides the opportunity to create an *additional* seat by the corporate charter. See Zöller/Vollkommer, §17, mn. 13.

31. BRJE Article 60(1). The domicile of a trust is to be determined according to the conflicts of laws rules of the forum Member State. BRJE Article 60(3).

32. ZPO §12; see Geimer, Part 4 Chapter 9(II)(10), mn. 1282–1284.

33. See Ch. 12(B)(3)(a) below.

34. See Ch. 12(B)(3)(c) below.

35. BRJE Article 23 and similarly ZPO §§38, 40(I). See Ch. 12(B)(4) below.

36. ZPO §16. If the place of sojourn of such a person is not known, he or she may be sued in Germany if that person had a domicile in Germany at some time in the past. See also Geimer, Part 4 Chapter 9(II)(2), mn. 1266.

37. See Schack, §8(II)(2)(a), mn. 247.

38. BRJE Article 4. However if it is asserted that a person has a domicile in another EU Member State, the German court must apply the law of the state of asserted domicile. BRJE

2. Jurisdiction Based on Specific Connections

The only circumstances supporting more or less unlimited susceptibility to suit are domicile in Germany, and in the case of those relatively few persons who have no domicile anywhere, sojourn in Germany. All other bases for international jurisdiction are associated with specific persons, or kinds of persons, and are grounded, at least in part, on the nature of the claim asserted or are limited to certain kinds of claims. Some of the principal "person-associated" (*personbezogene*) or other circumstantial bases for jurisdiction follow.

a. Activities of a Branch Business

A natural or legal person with a domicile abroad, but with a German branch office or place of business (*Niederlassung*) "from which direct business transactions are concluded" may be sued in Germany for matters based on the conduct of business (*Geschäftsbetrieb*) for which the branch was established.[39] This branch-jurisdiction is recognized in the Brussels Regulation in similar, but not identical, terms.[40]

Although jurisdiction based on a branch office represents an expansion of jurisdiction over multi-national enterprises with their seats outside Germany, it does not confer jurisdiction over a foreign entity merely because it may do some isolated business in Germany. Jurisdiction under this provision is limited to more or less permanent branch establishments which are authorized to conclude business transactions out of the branch. Moreover, jurisdiction only extends to matters arising out of the activities of the branch. There is no jurisdiction over unrelated activities of the main office or parent organization based on this provision. Sometimes, however, a German parent company, which has functioned like a branch of a wholly-owned foreign subsidiary, can subject the foreign subsidiary to international jurisdiction in Germany.[41]

Article 59(2). See also BRJE Articles 22 and 23, which apply even if some or all of the parties lack an EU domicile.

39. ZPO §21(1) ("*von der aus unmittelbar Geschäfte geschlossen werden*"). The same statute authorizes parallel jurisdiction over a foreigner who administers real estate in Germany for matters arising out of the administration of the real estate. ZPO §21(2).

40. Article 5(5) of the Brussels Regulation provides for jurisdiction, "as regards a dispute arising out of the operations of a branch, an agency or other establishment , in the courts for the place in which the branch, agency or other establishment is located."

41. European Court of Justice, Case 218/86, *SAR Schotte v. Parfums Rothschild*, 1987 ECR 4905 (1987) construing Article 5(5) of the Brussels Convention. See Kropholler, Art. 5, mn. 97; Geimer, Part 4 Chapter 9(VIII)(1), mn. 1445.

b. Extended Sojourn

German international jurisdiction extends to economically based claims (*vermögensrechtliche Ansprüche*) against persons without a domicile in Germany, who are there on temporary sojourns for extended periods of time (*Aufenthalt von längerer Dauer*), such as students, employees, household workers, apprentices, and the like.[42] There is no requirement that the claim be related to the purpose of the defendant's sojourn or his activities in Germany.

This extended form of jurisdiction based on sojourn is not formally recognized in the Brussels Regulation. Although it is not formally excluded[43] because the Brussels Regulation is a mandatory and exclusive regulation of international jurisdiction within the EU, one would expect that the European Court of Justice would not recognize this form of international jurisdiction as applied against a defendant with a regular domicile in another EU state.[44]

c. Location of Property

A somewhat controversial provision of German statute law extends jurisdiction of the German courts in civil actions asserting economically based claims (*vermögensrechtliche Ansprüche*) over any person, natural or juristic, who does not have a domicile in Germany, but who has property (*Vermögen*) there.[45] Neither the statutory language nor the gloss of interpretation added by German case law requires that the claim be related to the property located in Germany. Nor is the German court's jurisdiction limited by the amount or value of the property in Germany.

Originally ZPO §23 was designed to give creditors in Germany—regardless of their own citizenship—the ability to bring actions against debtors residing abroad or moving around within Germany without a fixed domicile.[46]

---

42. ZPO §20. This jurisdiction even extends to vacationers and inmates of prisons and hospitals. See Zöller/Vollkommer, §20, mn. 5.

43. See BRJE Article 3(2) and Annex 1, establishing a list of exorbitant international jurisdictions asserted by national law but specifically disavowed by the Brussels Regulation within the EU.

44. See BRJE Articles 3 and 4. Zöller/Vollkommer, §20, mn. 4.

45. ZPO §23(1). The same section also extends jurisdiction if a "thing claimed by the complaint" ("*mit der Klage in Anspruch genommene Gegenstand*") is located in Germany. The property in Germany can consist of real estate, tangible personal property, or intangible property such as a bank account with a German bank or a debt owed by a German debtor. Zöller/Vollkommer, §23, mn. 8.

46. See Federal Supreme Court, 115 BGHZ 90 (1992).

Some commentators have advanced the notion that possession of property in Germany evidences an "affinity to Germany" (*Affinität zu Deutschland*) which supports the jurisdiction of Germany's courts, at least to the extent of economically based claims.[47] In 1991 the Federal Supreme Court suggested that this jurisdiction is present only when there is a "sufficient domestic association with the litigation."[48] What is a "sufficient domestic association" has not yet been spelled out. The 1991 decision seems to be applying principles similar to those supporting the doctrine of *forum non conveniens* in American jurisprudence.[49]

Under the most extreme construction of ZPO §23 a person who possesses even a small amount of tangible or intangible property (*Vermögen*) in Germany is susceptible to suit in Germany by any German or foreign plaintiff based on any economically based claim, regardless of amount or relationship to the defendant's property in Germany. While this broad extension of jurisdiction has been stoutly defended[50] theorists and reformers have questioned whether it is justifiable for all claims regardless of whether Germany has any other interest in either the parties or the claim, and for amounts in excess of the value of the property in Germany.[51]

The Brussels Regulation specifically denies effect to any jurisdiction under ZPO §23 if the defendant is a domiciliary of one of the Member States.[52] This means that an EU domiciliary cannot be sued in Germany solely because she has property there.[53] However the Brussels Regulation does not prevent Germany from asserting this jurisdiction over most persons who do not have domiciles within the European Union.[54] Other EU domiciliaries are also free

47. See, e.g., Geimer, Part 4 Chapter 9(IV)(1/5), mn. 1347, 1356.

48. Federal Supreme Court, 115 BGHZ 90 (1992) (*hinreichender Inlandsbezug des Rechtsstreits*) noted by Schlosser, 12 *IPrax* 140 (1992); Lüke, 105 *ZZP* 314 (1992).

49. See Schack, §8(II)(7), mn. 325 for a critical view of the position of the Federal Supreme Court. For the *doctrine of forum non conveniens* see Ch. 12 (B) before (1).

50. See Geimer, Part 4 Chapter 9(IV)(5), mn. 1356–1357; Schack, §8(II)(7), mn. 330.

51. See Pfeiffer, *Internationale Zuständigkeit und prozessuale Gerechtigkeit* (1995), pp. 532ff.

52. BRJE Article 3.

53. The Brussels Regulation does permit provisional measures (attachment, preliminary injunctions) against EU domiciliaries based on an otherwise exorbitant international jurisdiction such as that provided by ZPO §23 so long as another EU court has jurisdiction over the case in chief. BRJE Article 31, see Schack, §8(VII)(3), mn. 424; Kropholler, Art. 31, mn. 17; Ch. 12(C)(I) below.

54. The Lugano Convention prohibits the exercise of this jurisdiction with respect to domiciliaries of Norway, Iceland, Switzerland and Liechtenstein. See Lugano Convention, Article 3.

to avail themselves of this jurisdiction against non-EU domiciliaries.[55] This circumstance can lead to the somewhat anomalous result that an American domiciliary with property in Germany may be subject to suit there by any person, EU domiciliary or not, and the ensuing judgment will be enforceable throughout the European Union.[56]

d. Location of Tortious Conduct

Both the German Civil Code and the Brussels Regulation confer international jurisdiction on German courts in cases in tort (*unerlaubte Handlung*) if the tortious conduct took place in Germany. Section 32 of the Civil Procedure Code requires that the tort be committed in Germany but is also interpreted to include actions to enjoin imminent future torts (*vorbeugende Unterlassungsklagen*).[57] The language of the Brussels Regulation is somewhat more liberal, authorizing jurisdiction "in the courts for the place where the harmful event occurred or may occur."[58]

Some cases, such as automobile accidents in Germany involving foreign drivers, are clear. In such cases the tortious behavior and at least some of its immediate consequences occurred in Germany, and German courts have jurisdiction to entertain claims against the responsible parties regardless of their domicile. However where the tortious conduct occurs outside Germany, but the event causing immediately the harm, or the mere suffering of the harm, occurs within Germany, jurisdiction may be less clear. For instance if a defective machine is manufactured outside Germany and then used and causes injury in Germany, the culpable act is the negligent manufacture of the machine, which took place abroad. A literal reading of the German statute, which seems to focus on the actor's conduct as the key element, would raise at least a question about German international jurisdiction in such a case. Nonetheless, case law under the German statute as well as the language of the Brussels Regulation[59] and the decisions of the European Court of Justice sustain international jurisdiction in such a case based on the theory that the tort is "committed" both at the place where the tortfeasor acted (*Handlungsort*)

---

55. BRJE Article 4(3).

56. See Geimer, Part 4 Chapter 9(IV)(22), mn.1382–1384.

57. ZPO §32 specifies the court "in whose district the conduct was committed" ("*in dessen Bezirk die Handlung begangen ist*") as the proper venue for tort claims, thus indirectly asserting German courts' international jurisdiction for such claims.

58. BRJE Article 5(3). See Kropholler, Art. 5, mn. 68; Schack, §8(II)(4), mn. 292.

59. The Brussels Regulation, which identifies the "harmful event" as the touchstone for jurisdiction, appears to be more liberal.

and where the results of such action have occurred (*Erfolgsort*), i.e. where someone is injured or a legally protected interest (e.g. ownership) is infringed.[60] However, solely economic consequences of an injury or infringement which occurred elsewhere are not enough to support jurisdiction under these provisions.[61]

A libel case can be brought in any jurisdiction in which the defamatory writing was circulated. Even though the original tortious publication may have taken place abroad, if the publication was circulated in Germany, the tort is committed in Germany and the courts of Germany have jurisdiction.[62] Within the EU, a claim for all damages sustained anywhere resulting from a libel can be brought in the forum where the defendant publisher has its seat. However if jurisdiction is based on circulation of the libelous material, the damages are limited to those sustained in the forum jurisdiction where the material was circulated.[63]

e. *Location of Performance of a Contract*

In cases brought to enforce performance of a contract or for damages from breach of contract, German law establishes international jurisdiction in the courts "of the place of performance of the obligation in dispute."[64] The place of performance is determined by reference to German Civil Code §269, which specifies that if the place of performance cannot be inferred from the circumstances, it can be considered as the place of the domicile of the obligor (*Schuldner*) at time of the creation of the obligation.[65] The jurisdiction extends

60. See Federal Supreme Court, 40 BGHZ 395 (1964); 52 BGHZ 111 (1970); 124 BGHZ 245 (1994); Zöller/Vollkommer, §32, mn.16, 17 and European Court of Justice, Case 21/76, *Bier v. Mines de Potasse d'Alsace*, 1976 ECR I 1735 (1976).

61. See European Court of Justice, Case 364/93, *Antonio Marinari v. Lloyds Bank*, 1995 ECR I 2719 (1995); Zöller/Vollkommer, §32, mn. 16; Geimer, Part 4 Chapter 9(XI)(4), mn. 1501.

62. See Federal Supreme Court, 30 *NJW* 1590 (1977); Geimer, Part 4 Chapter 9(XI)(6), mn. 1513–1515.

63. European Court of Justice, Case 68/93, *Shevill v. Presse Alliance*, 1995 ECR I 415 (1995), noted by Wagner, 62 *RabelsZ* 243 (1998) and critically by Rauscher, 1 *ZZP Int.* 145 (1996).

64. ZPO §29(1)(„...*des Ortes..., an dem die streitige Verpflichtung zu erfüllen ist.*").

65. This is true even if the obligor later changes his domicile and does not live in Germany at the time of institution of suit. See Zöller/Vollkommer, §29, mn. 24. This is true also for obligations of payment (BGB §§270(1) and (4), 269(3)). Under German law, payment must be sent to the location of the creditor's domicile, but payment is considered to be performed by the obligor once she has caused the payment to be sent to the creditor or its bank, ("*Schickschuld*"). Thus the domicile of the debtor would be the place of performance of the obligation of payment. However in cases governed by the Vienna Con-

not only to suits to enforce a contractual obligation, but also to suits seeking negative declaratory judgments restricting the meaning or application of a contract.[66]

Under Article 5(1)(b) of the Brussels Regulation jurisdiction over cases arising out of contracts for the sale of goods is placed where the goods are or should be delivered. This is true for all claims related to such contracts, including simple claims for payment.[67] There is a parallel rule for contracts for the performance of services. Jurisdiction over all claims is in the courts of the place where the services were or should be performed. In all other cases, the "location of performance" is determined according to the law governing the contract, which may establish different locations of performance for the different claims arising out of the same contract.[68]

Frequently parties to a contract will specify the place of performance in the contract. Under German law a contractual specification of Germany as the place of performance will sustain international jurisdiction only if the parties to the agreement are merchants (*Kaufleute*), which includes all corporations, or public entities (*juristische Personen des öffentlichen Rechts*).[69] This limitation parallels the statutory limitations on the parties' ability to agree directly on jurisdiction and venue before the actual controversy arises.[70] On the other hand, the Brussels Regulation is somewhat more liberal. The European Court of Justice has held that an agreement on the place of contract performance that does not comply with the Article 23 requirements for an agreement on

---

vention on the Sale of Goods the domicile of the creditor is frequently deemed to be the place of performance for obligations to pay, thus permitting a German creditor to sue in his own domicile for the contract price, but not for other relief relating to the contract, Article 57(1)(a). See Schlechtriem/Hager, *Commentary on the UN Convention on the international sale of goods*, 2nd ed. (1998), Article 57, mn. 4 ff.; Geimer, Part 4 Chapter 9(X)(7), mn. 1489. This doctrine does not apply to claims against consumers where the Brussels Regulation or Lugano Convention provide an exclusive international jurisdiction for suits against consumers. See BRJE Article 16 (2), Ch. 12(B)(2)(g) and (3)(c) below.

66. Geimer, Part 4 Chapter 9(X)(5), mn. 1487.

67. Kropholler, Art. 5, mn 21.

68. BRJE Article 5(1)(a). This is the interpretation of the European Court of Justice of Article 5(1)(a) of the Brussels Convention, which is identical with BRJE Article 5(1)(a), but has been supplemented in the Regulation with Article 5(1)(b). See European Court of Justice, Case 12/76, *Tessili v. Dunlop*, 1976 ECR 1473 (1976). See also Kropholler, Art. 5, mn. 15–20; Schack, §8(II)(3), mn. 269–273.

69. ZPO §29(2). See German Federal Supreme Court, 49 *NJW* 1411 (1996); Thomas/Putzo, *Zivilprozessordnung*, 24th ed. (2002), §29, mn. 2, 10.

70. See ZPO §38; Ch. 12(B)(4) below (international jurisdiction) and Ch. 5(D) above (venue).

international jurisdiction may be used indirectly to support international jurisdiction via Article 5(1) so long as it complies with the requirements of a valid agreement under governing law.[71] This decision has drawn criticism, and more recently the ECJ has held that "place of performance" terms in contracts that are in reality substitutes for agreements on international jurisdiction (*abstrakte Erfüllungsortvereinbarungen*) must satisfy the requirements of BRJE Article 23 for such agreements.[72]

f. Claims for Support

A German domiciliary may bring a claim for support (*Klage in Unterhaltssachen*) against a defendant not generally susceptible to suit in Germany (*Person, die im Inland keinen Gerichtsstand hat*) in a German court based on the plaintiff's own German domicile.[73] This rule is based on a policy in favor of permitting support claimants easy access to court in order to secure funds for support.[74] An even more extended form of international jurisdiction based on sojourn of a support claimant is recognized by the Brussels Regulation and the Lugano Convention.[75]

g. Claims by or against European Consumers, Insureds and Employees

European Law provides for special "claimant friendly" international jurisdiction to support claims by consumers against firms doing business with consumers, claims by insureds, policy holders or beneficiaries against insurance companies, and claims by employees against their employers. By the same token, within the EU consumers, insureds and employees are protected from suit in any jurisdiction other than that of their domicile.

The Brussels Regulation applies the special consumer rules to "a contract concluded by a person, the consumer, for a purpose which can be regarded as being outside his trade or profession" if it is an installment sales contract or loan to finance the purchase of goods, or if

---

71. European Court of Justice, Case 56/79, *Zeljer v. Selinitri*, 1980 ECR 89 (1980).

72. European Court of Justice, Case 106/95, *MSG v. Les Gravières Rhenanes*, 1997 ECR I 11 (1997). See Kropholler, Art. 5, mn. 28, 29; Schack, §8(II)(3), mn. 277.

73. ZPO §23a. This jurisdiction extends to both legal and contractual claims for support. It is somewhat expanded and altered by the special Civil Procedure Code provisions establishing jurisdiction and venue in family cases. See ZPO §§35a, 642 and Ch. 5(C)(2) above.

74. See Schack, §8(IV)(3), mn. 379.

75. See BRJE Article 5(2).

> "the contract has been concluded with a person who pursues commercial or professional activities in the Member State of the consumer's domicile or by any means directs such activities to that Member State, or to several states including that Member State, and the contract falls within the scope of such activities."[76]

A European consumer is given the option of bringing suit on a consumer contract either in the courts of the Member State of the commercial party's domicile, or, significantly, in the courts of the domicile of the consumer.[77] Thus among the members of the European Union, a commercial organization which conducts programs of advertising or solicitation within Germany will be subject to suit in Germany by consumers with reference to the business so advertised.[78] This substantially extends the traditional "branch" jurisdiction provided for in German law and elsewhere in the Brussels Regulation[79] in consumer matters and provides consumers with a ready forum for their legal grievances.

More significantly, the Brussels Regulation provides that the state of the consumer's domicile is the exclusive international jurisdiction for suits against consumers, thus precluding international jurisdiction based, for instance, on place of fulfillment of contract.[80] This exclusive jurisdiction can be waived by agree-

---

76. BRJE Article 15(1)(c).

77. BRJE Article 16(1).

78. The term "directs activities" to a Member State was designed to address various kinds of international E-commerce. With the evolution of the Internet, the question has arisen whether a business which maintains a Web Site accessible to domiciliaries of a Member State thereby "directs activities" to a Member State so as to be subject to suit there under this provision. Some commentators suggest a distinction between a passive web site, which merely advertises products or services, and an active web site, through which consumers can place orders. Permitting consumers from a particular Member State to place orders through an active web site may be sufficient to ground jurisdiction of that Member State under this provision. See Committee on Legal Affairs and the International Market, Report on the Proposal for a Council Regulation on Jurisdiction and the Recognition and Enforcement of Judgments in Civil and Commercial Matters, A5-0253/2000, September 18, 2000; Kropholler, Art. 15, mn. 23–25; Bampiniotis, "Jurisdiction over e-Commerce Disputes in the European Union under Regulation 44/2000: Terra Incognita", LLM Thesis, *Harvard Law School Library* (2001) and the Joint Council and Commission Statements of December 14, 2000 on Article 15 et al., Council document 14139/00.

79. See Ch. 12(B)(2)(a) above.

80. BRJE Article 16(2). This does not prevent a party contracting with a consumer from bringing a counterclaim in a suit brought by the consumer against it in a forum other than the consumer's domicile. BRJE Article 16(3).

ment only under limited circumstances.[81] Thus, an EU consumer need not fear that she will be subject to suit in an EU creditor's jurisdiction based on either contractual agreement or on doctrines of international jurisdictional law.

A similar scheme governs suits on individual contracts of employment. An employee may sue her employer not only in the Member State of the employer's domicile or in which the relevant branch is located,[82] but in addition in any Member State in which the employee "habitually carries out his work" or last did so.[83] On the other hand, the employer may bring suit against an employee only in the courts of the Member State in which the employee is domiciled, regardless of where the work was carried out.[84] These employee-protective provisions may be waived or bargained away by contract only under limited circumstances.[85]

An insurer is subject to suit by a policyholder, an insured, or a beneficiary not only in the Member State of its domicile,[86] but also in the Member State of the plaintiff's domicile.[87] Liability insurers and real estate casualty insurers are also subject to suit in the courts of the Member State where the "harmful event" occurred.[88] Where local law permits direct actions by an injured party against the tort-feasor's insurance company, the injured party is given the same status as an insured or beneficiary for the purpose of international jurisdiction.[89] Waiver of these protections by agreement is also limited.[90]

---

81. See Ch. 12(B)(2)(i) below on jurisdiction by waiver and Ch. 12(B)(4) below on international jurisdiction by agreement.

82. BRJE Article 18(2) provides that in employment matters an employer's maintenance of a branch, agency or establishment in a Member State is the equivalent of domicile there for employment matters arising out of operations of the branch, agency or establishment.

83. BRJE Article 19(1) and (2)(a). If there is no single Member State in which the employee's work was habitually carried out, suit may be brought in the "courts for the place where the business which engaged the employee is or was situated." BRJE 19(2)(b).

84. BRJE Article 20. As is the case with consumers, counterclaims against an employee may be brought in the courts in which the employee's suit was brought.

85. See Ch. 12(B)(2)(i) below on jurisdiction by waiver and Ch. 12(B)(4) below on jurisdiction by agreement.

86. See BRJE Article 9(1)(a). Insurers who maintain branches, agencies or other establishments in Member States are considered domiciliaries of such Member States for matters arising out of the activities of the branches, agencies or establishments. BRJE Article 9(2).

87. BRJE Article 9(1)(b). Co-insurers may be sued in the courts of the state in which proceedings are brought against the lead insurer. BRJE Article 9(1)(c).

88. BRJE Article 10. Liability insurers may also be joined in proceedings brought by the injured party against the insured where local law permits. BRJE Article 11.

89. BRJE Article 11(2) and (3).

90. BRJE Article 13. See Ch. 12(B)(4) below on jurisdiction by agreement.

It should be stressed that these Brussels Regulation consumer-, employee-, and insured-friendly provisions apply only within the European Union. Consumers who are not domiciled in a Member State may not avail themselves of the jurisdictional provisions of the Brussels Regulation. Nor do the Brussels Regulation provisions apply to enterprises contracting with consumers, employers, or insurers who are not domiciliaries of the Union and do not maintain a branch, agency or other establishment there.[91] International jurisdiction in transactions involving such parties must be determined by German statute law, which does not recognize protected categories parallel to those of the Brussels Regulation.[92] Thus, for example, an American consumer could be sued in Germany based on a contract with a German company either if the place of fulfillment of the contract was Germany,[93] or if the American consumer merely was sojourning there as a student at the time suit was brought.[94] Legislation regulating particular kinds of businesses sometimes provides a basis for international jurisdiction of claims by or against those businesses which is different than the general provisions of the German Civil Procedure Code.[95]

h. Jurisdiction by Joinder of Parties or Claims

The Brussels Regulation also provides for international jurisdiction when suit is brought against multiple defendants based on claims "which are so closely connected that it is expedient to hear and determine them together to avoid the risk of irreconcilable judgments from separate proceedings."[96] If at least one of the defendants is domiciled within a Member State, courts of that state have international jurisdiction over the claims against them all.[97] The

---

91. BRJE Article 4. Note, however, that maintenance of a branch, agency or establishment in a Member State is considered domicile in that Member State for the purpose of the consumer, employee and insured international jurisdiction provisions. See Thomas/Putzo/Hüsstege, Art. 1 EuGVVO, mn. 1.

92. See Geimer, Part 4 Chapter 8(IX)–(XI), mn. 1187–1190.

93. ZPO §29(1); see Ch. 12(B)(2)(e) above.

94. ZPO §20; see Ch. 12(B)(2)(b) above.

95. For instance a consumer domiciled in Germany may bring an action based on a door-to-door sales transaction (*Haustürgeschäft*) subject to BGB §312 in the German courts by virtue of ZPO §29(c)(1). Section 26(1) of the Law Regulating Consumer Protection in Distance Learning Transactions (*Fernunterrichtsschutzgesetz*) contains a similar provision for consumer claims based on distance learning contracts. See BGB §312b(3)(1).

96. BRJE Article 6(1).

97. Note that jurisdiction by joinder must be based on a general susceptibility to suit of one of the defendants by reason of domicile. Jurisdiction by joinder cannot be built on

qualification that the claims have to be so closely related as to raise the danger of irreconcilable judgments if determined separately is designed to limit the use of this jurisdictional ground for the purpose of forum shopping.

German statute law is unique in Europe in its failure to allow international jurisdiction over parties by virtue of joinder in an action properly brought before a German court. In fact, German law does not recognize any form of international jurisdiction by joinder.[98] If a claim is asserted against multiple defendants, there must be a basis for jurisdiction against each of them regardless of how closely the claims are related.[99] ZPO §36(1) authorizing the next higher court to specify venue in a case brought against multiple defendants proceeds from the basis that international jurisdiction exists for each defendant and does not create international jurisdiction by joinder.[100]

The Brussels Regulation also recognizes international jurisdiction over third-party claims in the court which has jurisdiction over the original case.[101] However the German Civil Procedure Code does not permit the joinder of claims against a third party for indemnity or guaranty in the case in chief. If a defendant has a possible claim for indemnity or guaranty of the claim asserted against her, she may notify the potential indemnitor or guarantor and give them the opportunity to intervene in the pending case.[102] Such interventions do not require any new basis for international jurisdiction. Article 65 of the Brussels Regulation exempts Germany (and Austria, which has a similar procedural wrinkle) from applicability of Article 6(2) of the Brussels Regulation, but provides that German defendants may make use of the suit notification procedure even if the affected parties are from other Member States.[103]

---

one of the other person-associated bases for international joinder such as place of performance of a contract or place of commission of a tort. See Kropholler, Art. 6, mn. 12.

98. See Ch. 5(C)(3) and (E) on venue by connection and venue by judicial specification. An impressive comparative analysis is given by Otte, *Umfassende Streitentscheidung durch Beachtung von Sachzusammenhängen* (1998), pp. 490–815.

99. Schack, §8(III)(6), mn. 357. For some very limited exceptions see Kropholler, Art. 6, mn. 4; Otte, Chapter 2 §1(B)(1), pp. 654–665.

100. Schack, §8(III)(6), mn. 358.

101. BRJE Article 6(2). Such jurisdiction does not apply if the original proceedings were instituted "solely with the object of removing [the third party defendant] from the jurisdiction of the court which would be competent in his case."

102. See Ch. 7(C)(1) and (D) above for a description of the suit notification and intervention procedure.

103. Schack, §8(III)(7)(b), mn. 367. The effects of the German suit notification procedure on third parties are required to be recognized even in other Member States. See Kropholler, Art. 6, mn. 23.

On the other hand, Article 65 does not protect defendants domiciled in Germany (or Austria) from being sued under Article 6(2) in other Member States.[104]

Under both German law and the Brussels Regulation a defendant need not have independent ground for international jurisdiction for the assertion of a counterclaim. ZPO §33 applies to extend both international jurisdiction and venue over a related counterclaim between the original parties to the action. The Brussels Regulation requires that the counterclaim arise "from the same contract or facts on which the original claim was based,..."[105] The German Civil Procedure Code specifies that the counterclaim must "be related to the claim set forth in the complaint or to the means of defense brought forward by the defendant."[106] Both terms seem to be intended to reach the same result.[107]

Setoffs (*Aufrechnungen*) which are related to the case in chief should be treated like counterclaims.[108] Unrelated setoffs are not specifically addressed in the Brussels Regulation. The European Court of Justice seems to be of the view that the allowability of setoffs is a matter of national procedural law rather than an issue of international jurisdiction.[109] Under German national law a court may exercise jurisdiction over an unrelated claim asserted solely by way of setoff only if that claim 1) falls itself within the court's international jurisdiction, 2) is uncontested, or 3) is represented by a judgment.[110]

i. *Jurisdiction by Waiver*

Both the German law and the Brussels Regulation provide for international jurisdiction if the defendant acknowledges jurisdiction or waives objection

104. Kropholler, Art. 6, mn. 20–21. Judgments rendered in other Member States of the EU based on such third-party jurisdiction are enforceable in Germany and Austria under the BRJE. This is not true for judgments against third parties from other foreign jurisdictions where the "mirror image principle" (*Spiegelbildprinzip*) is a prerequisite for recognition and enforcement. See Ch. 12(C)(1) below. For a more generous point of view see Geimer, Part 4 Chapter 1(I)(2), mn. 858.

105. BRJE Article 6(3).

106. ZPO §33 ("... *mit dem in der Klage geltend gemachten Anspruch oder mit den gegen ihn vorgebrachten Verteidigungsmitteln in Zusammenhang steht*"). See Ch. 7(J)(4) above.

107. Schack, §8(III)(5)(b), mn. 352.

108. Schack, §8(III)(5)(b), mn. 353; Kropholler, Art. 6, mn. 42.

109. European Court of Justice, Case 341/93, *Danvaery Production v. Schuhfabriken Otterbeck,* 1995 ECR I 2053 (1995); Kropholler, Art. 6, mn. 43–45. Schack, §8(III)5)(c), mn. 355.

110. This is somewhat disputed. For details see Zöller/Greger, §145, mn. 19; Thomas/Putzo/Hüsstege, Art. 6 EuGVVO, mn. 7; Federal Supreme Court, 46 *NJW* 2753 (1993); 55 *NJW* 2182 (2002).

thereto by addressing the merits of the case. ZPO §39 provides that objections to improper venue (and thus indirectly to international jurisdiction) will be waived if the defendant, without raising any objection to jurisdiction, argues the merits of the case (*zur Hauptsache mündlich verhandelt*).[111] The Brussels Regulation is a little different, allowing jurisdiction if the defendant "enters an appearance" (other than solely to contest international jurisdiction).[112] There is no jurisdiction by consent under the Brussels Regulation or German statute law if the courts of another state have exclusive international jurisdiction over the matter.[113]

3. Exclusive International Jurisdiction

Both German statute law and the Brussels Regulation provide that the courts of Germany have exclusive international jurisdiction in a number of specified situations. Some rules of exclusive jurisdiction are based on the notion that certain matters are so connected with a particular locality and the legal system governing that locality that the courts of that jurisdiction should adjudicate those matters exclusively regardless of circumstances that may otherwise ground jurisdiction elsewhere. Other rules are based on a desire to protect the interests of particular parties, such as consumers, tenants, etc.[114]

In general, exclusive international jurisdiction is mandatory and may not be dispensed with by waiver or agreement. The following are some of the areas in which German courts have exclusive international jurisdiction.

a. *Matters Related to Real Estate*

German courts possess exclusive international jurisdiction to adjudicate cases in which the title, boundaries, or possession of German real estate is at

111. However if the case is brought in a local court (*Amtsgericht*) where representation by counsel is not required, the waiver will be effective only if the court has called this issue to the defendant's attention pursuant to ZPO §504. This is true regardless of whether the defendant in fact has counsel in the proceeding. Zöller/Vollkommer, §39, mn. 10.

112. BRJE Article 24; but see for Articles 13, 17, 21 Ch. 12(B)(3)(c) below. Under the Brussels Convention objections to international jurisdiction were required to be raised before other objections or defenses. Failure to raise an objection to international jurisdiction at the outset was considered a waiver. The language of the Brussels Regulation appears to be consistent with this result. See for details Kropholler, Art. 24 EuGVO, mn. 7.

113. BRJE Article 24; Schack, §8(II)(5)(b), mn. 311; *contra:* Geimer, Part 4 Chapter 2(VI)(2), mn. 929.

114. For a discussion and critique of the theoretical basis for exclusive international jurisdiction in Germany see Geimer, Part 4 Chapter 2, esp. mn. 878 ff.

issue.[115] This exclusive jurisdiction also includes cases seeking to establish or determine the validity of liens or encumbrances (*Belastungen*) on German real estate. The exclusivity of the jurisdiction bespeaks the generally recognized strong local interest and competence in deciding issues involving local real estate. The Brussels Regulation recognizes the exclusive jurisdiction of the courts of the Member State in which the property is located "in proceedings which have their object rights in rem in immovable property or tenancies of immovable property."[116]

b. Public Registrations

German courts have exclusive international jurisdiction in matters relating to the validity of entries in public registers such as business registers (*Handelsregister*) or land registers (*Grundbücher*) maintained in Germany.[117] This exclusive jurisdiction is necessary for the integrity and usefulness of these public records. The administration of some public registers is a non-contentious activity carried on under the auspices of the Local Courts.[118]

The German courts also have exclusive international jurisdiction over cases involving the validity or registration of German patents, trademarks or other registered business rights. This is true not only for national patents, but also for European patents granted for Germany.[119] This exclusive jurisdiction does not extend to actions for the infringement of such rights, which are subject to the usual rules on international jurisdiction.

---

115. ZPO §24. Zöller/Vollkommer, §24, mn. 6a. See also ZPO §29a which establishes exclusive jurisdiction for landlord-tenant cases in the court of the district in which the subject premises are located. A court possessing exclusive jurisdiction to adjudicate a real estate case may on motion of a party also decide related personal claims. See ZPO §§25, 26 and Ch. 5(C)(2) above.

116. Article 22(1). This is subject to a small exception for disputes relating to temporary tenancies for private use of not more than 6 months if the landlord and the tenant are domiciliaries of the same Member State. Such disputes may be adjudicated by the courts of the parties' domicile even if the property is not located there.

117. BRJE Article 22(3). German statutory jurisdiction to determine the validity of entries in these registers is sometimes derived from ZPO §24 (land register) or from the provisions delegating the maintenance of the registers to the Local Courts in the exercise of their non-contentious jurisdiction. See, e.g., Land Register Regulation (*Grundbuchordnung*) §1.

118. See Ch. 11(E) below for a brief description of the local courts' non-contentious jurisdiction.

119. BRJE Article 22(4).

c. *Actions against Consumers, Insureds and Employees*

European law provides for a special exclusive jurisdiction for an action brought by a business against a consumer, for an action by an insurer against an insured, policy holder or beneficiary and for an action by an employer against an employee.[120] These special exclusive international jurisdictions are intended to provide special protection for the weaker party in cross-border litigation arising from one of the identified relationships. The protections provided by these provisions may only be waived in advance of litigation under limited circumstances.[121]

This exclusive jurisdiction applies only to domiciliaries of the European Union. Consumers, insureds, beneficiaries, policyholders, or employees domiciled elsewhere are subject to the statutory rules of German international jurisdiction.[122]

4. International Jurisdiction by Agreement

Both German and European law recognize, within limits, the ability of parties to agree on the international jurisdiction of courts of a particular state to adjudicate claims between or among them. Article 23 of the Brussels Regulation provides that a domiciliary of a Member State may agree with another party that "the courts of a Member State are to have jurisdiction to settle any disputes which have arisen or which may arise in connection with a particular legal relationship."[123] German statute law is more or less simi-

---

120. Article 16(2) of the Brussels Regulation provides that "Proceedings may be brought against a consumer by the other party to the contract only in the courts of the Member State in which the consumer is domiciled." Article 20 provides that "an employer may bring proceedings only in the courts of the Member State in which the employee is domiciled." Article 12 authorizes an insurer to bring proceedings "only in the courts of the Member State in which the defendant is domiciled, irrespective of whether he is the policyholder, the insured or a beneficiary." See Ch. 12(B)(2)(g) above.

121. See BRJE Article 13 (insured); Article 17 (consumer) and Article 21 (employee). Once litigation has commenced, this exclusive jurisdiction can be waived under Article 24 of the Brussels Regulation by entering an appearance that is not limited to the purpose of contesting international jurisdiction. See Ch. 12(B)(2)(i) above.

122. However parties contracting with consumers, insurers and employers elsewhere, are bound by this term in connection with any claims they may bring in any court against a consumer, insured, beneficiary, policyholder or employee who is an EU domiciliary. See Kropholler, Art. 12, mn. 1. Judgments obtained in violation of these protections would have difficulty gaining recognition or enforcement within the EU.

123. BRJE Article 23(1). The agreement may be with another EU domiciliary or an outside party. This provision and the corresponding provision in the German Civil Procedure Code reflect the strong public policy in favor of allowing competent parties to achieve

lar.[124] A valid choice of jurisdiction by agreement makes the chosen jurisdiction exclusive as long as it is clear that the parties did not intend to agree merely on additional jurisdiction to that which was otherwise available.[125] Note however, that the choice must be made with respect to a "particular legal relationship".[126] Agreements purporting to choose jurisdiction in advance for disputes arising out of a broad range of relationships or circumstances may be invalid.[127]

The Brussels Regulation requires a relatively low degree of formality. The agreement must be in writing or evidenced by a writing, or in some other form customary in the parties' trade or commerce, or in a form which the parties have established or adopted between themselves. Electronic communications which provide some form of durable record will suffice.[128]

An agreement conferring international jurisdiction will not be recognized if it is contrary to the exclusive jurisdictions for cases against consumers, insureds or employees, or to other provisions making certain jurisdictions exclusive.[129]

Because the Brussels Regulation applies to cases in which any party to an agreement conferring jurisdiction on courts of a Member State is a domiciliary of a Member State, German national law on jurisdiction by agreement will apply only in a limited number of cases where neither party is a domiciliary of the EU[130] or where the parties agree on international jurisdiction of a non-member state's court.[131] For example, if suit is brought by a non-EU domicil-

---

greater legal security (*Rechtssicherheit*) and predictability by choosing jurisdictions to resolve their disputes in most cases. See Geimer, Part 4 Chapter 10(I), mn. 1596–1599a.

124. ZPO §38.

125. See BRJE Article 23(1)(2); for German law Thomas/Putzo, Vor §38, mn. 8.

126. See BRJE Article 23(1)(1) and ZPO §40(1).

127. See European Court of Justice, Case 214/89, *Duffryn plc v. Petereit*, 1992 ECR I 1756, 1769 (1992); Geimer, Part 4 Chapter 10(XVI)(3), mn. 1682, 1683.

128. BRJE Article 23(1) and (2).

129. BRJE Article 23(5); ZPO §40(2)(2). See Ch. 12(B)(3) above.

130. BRJE Article 23(1). See Geimer, Part 4 Chapter 10(III)(1), mn. 1605; Kropholler, Art. 23, mn. 12. There is some dispute over whether the Brussels Regulation should apply if only one party is a Member State domiciliary and the contractual transaction bears no particular relationship to any Member State. This would be the case, for example, if a German and an American contracted with reference to activity in America. Some authors argue that the Convention and Regulation are aimed solely at regulating legal affairs between Member States, so that such transactions should not be covered. See, however, European Court of Justice, Case 412/98, Group Josi Reinsurance Company v. Universal General Insurance Company, 2000 ECR I 5925 (2000); Case 387/98, Coreck Maritime v. Handelsveem, 2000 ECR I 9337 (2000) and 54 *NJW* 501 (2001); Kropholler, Art. 23, mn. 4–10 for arguments to the contrary.

131. See Kropholler, Art. 23 EuGVO, mn. 14; European Court of Justice, Case 387/98, Coreck Maritime v. Handelsveem, 2000 ECR I 9337 (2000) and 54 *NJW* 501 (2001).

iary against another non-EU domiciliary based on the latter's sojourn in Germany and the defendant asserts that the parties have agreed on the jurisdiction of the courts of another state, the validity and effect of the agreement would be determined by ZPO §38.[132] The same would be true if domiciliaries of Member States were to agree on personal jurisdiction of a U.S. court.

The provisions of ZPO § 38 are somewhat more restrictive than the Brussels Regulation. Merchants and corporate entities are relatively free to choose jurisdiction by means of any "express or implicit agreement" (*ausdrückliche oder stillschweigende Vereinbarung*).[133] If at least one of the non-merchant parties is not a German domiciliary, an agreement in writing or confirmed in writing (such as by exchange of letters) will suffice to choose jurisdiction either before or after a particular dispute has arisen.[134] Otherwise, the agreement on jurisdiction must be express and in writing and must be entered into after the dispute has arisen or must be directed to relocation of a party's domicile or place of sojourn after conclusion of the contract.[135] As is the case with agreements under the Brussels Regulation, statutorily exclusive jurisdictions cannot be altered by agreement.[136]

---

132. If the parties agree on jurisdiction of another Member State's court, the German court may deny its jurisdiction on the basis of German procedural law or stay its proceedings until the other Member State's court decides finally the jurisdictional issue. See BRJE Article 23(3); Kropholler, Art. 23 EuGVO, mn. 12. If the other Member State's court dismisses the case because of a lack of jurisdiction, the German court may proceed on the merits if German jurisdiction exists according to German law.

133. ZPO §38(1). Both parties to the agreement must be merchants, corporations or public entities. Otherwise the agreement is subject to the requirements for agreements among non-merchant natural persons. Geimer, Part 4 Chapter 10(III)(5), mn. 1625. See Ch. 5(D) above on agreements specifying subject matter jurisdiction or venue within Germany.

134. ZPO §38(2). However if one party is a German domiciliary, the agreement on German jurisdiction may only choose the courts in which that party is susceptible to suit or in which a special jurisdiction is statutorily provided.

135. ZPO §38(3). This is especially true if both parties are residents of Germany. See Geimer, Part 4 Chapter 10(III)(4), mn. 1622. A written agreement will also be given effect if the domicile or sojourn of the defendant is unknown at the time suit is brought.

136. ZPO §40(2). Agreements conferring or restricting jurisdiction are prohibited with respect to "non-economic claims" (*nichtvermögensrechtliche Ansprüche*) if they fall within the jurisdiction of the local courts regardless of the amount in controversy. ZPO §40(2)(1). Thus, agreements conferring jurisdiction are not permitted in marital cases (*Ehesachen*). See Zöller/Vollkommer, §40, mn. 5.

5. Jurisdiction to Determine International Jurisdiction

Germany stands firmly by the principle that a court has jurisdiction to determine its own international jurisdiction. German courts at each level of proceedings are required to examine international jurisdiction on their own motion.[137] Unlike subject matter jurisdiction and venue, which are not subject to reexamination on second instance or revision appeal, lack of international jurisdiction can be raised or noticed at any stage of the proceeding.[138]

This does not mean that a litigant sued in Germany can ignore the German proceedings and later assert that the German court lacked international jurisdiction. Under German national law a final determination by a court that it has international jurisdiction over a particular litigant is not subject to collateral attack. The result is that a litigant sued in Germany must raise any objection to the German court's international jurisdiction in the pending proceeding.

If the defendant does not appear the court considers the factual allegations of the plaintiff as true (*Geständnisfiktion*).[139] The only exceptions to this principle are allegations of an agreement conferring jurisdiction or an agreement establishing place of performance of a contract. According to the literal words of the statute other allegations of fact relating to jurisdiction (*zuständigkeitsbegründende Tatsachen*) cannot be challenged by the defaulting defendant later on.[140] Some writers argue that this construction is too harsh and that the conclusive effect of ZPO §331 should not be applied to any fact allegations which are necessary to establish international jurisdiction.[141]

For litigants who are EU domiciliaries, the Brussels Regulation permits a court asked to enforce a judgment from another Member State to review the international jurisdiction of the court rendering the judgment only for applicability of the rules restricting international jurisdiction in cases against consumers and insureds and the rules establishing exclusive jurisdictions. The reviewing court may not recognize or enforce the prior judgment if the

137. This requirement that the court examines jurisdiction on its own motion is carried forward in Article 25 of the Brussels Regulation.

138. Federal Supreme Court, 44 BGHZ 46 (1966); 57 *NJW* 426 (2003). See Schack, §8(V)(1), mn. 385. See ZPO §§513(2) and 545(2) prohibiting reconsideration of subject matter jurisdiction and venue on appeal; Chs. 5(F), 10(D), 10(E)(2) above.

139. ZPO §331. See Ch. 7(J)(1) above on the effect of uncontroverted allegations in pleadings.

140. See Schack, §8(V)(1), mn. 386.

141. See Geimer, Part 4 Chapter 11(III)(2), mn. 1822.

judgment was rendered in violation of these rules.[142] Otherwise a finding by a court of a Member State that it has international jurisdiction is not subject to collateral attack in the courts of another Member State.[143]

The doctrine giving conclusive effect to a foreign court's finding of jurisdiction does not apply outside the EU. German courts do not regard non-EU foreign courts' findings of jurisdiction to be conclusive.[144] Germany recognizes judgments of other states only if the foreign courts' assertions of jurisdiction is consistent with international jurisdiction according to German law.[145]

C. Recognition of Foreign Judgments

As is the case with international jurisdiction, the extent to which German courts will recognize and enforce civil judgments entered by foreign courts is regulated differently within and without the European Union. The basic German rule for recognition of foreign judgments is set forth in §328 of the Civil Procedure Code. Rules regulating the procedure for obtaining enforcement of foreign judgments in Germany can be found in ZPO §§722 ff. Recognition of judgments issued by judicial organs of other Member States of the European Union is governed by Articles 32–37 of the Brussels Regulation and enforcement of such judgments is covered by Articles 38–56.[146]

In addition to the general provisions of German statutory law and the Brussels Regulation, a number of multilateral treaties and conventions also address the recognition and enforcement of foreign judgments, generally in specific categories of matters.[147] To this body of law can be added a number

---

142. BRJE Article 35(1). The reviewing court is, however, bound by any findings of fact on which the prior Member State court based its finding of jurisdiction. Article 35(2).

143. BRJE Article 35(3). Nor may the court refuse to recognize the judgment on the grounds that the originating court's finding of international jurisdiction is contrary to the public policy of the recognizing state.

144. See Ch. 12(C)(1) below. The Lugano Convention also requires the courts of the signatories to respect each other's determinations of international jurisdiction. Absent a specific treaty requirement, German courts are not bound by jurisdictional findings of foreign courts when it comes to recognition of foreign judgments.

145. See Ch. 12(C)(1) below.

146. Parallel provisions of the Lugano Convention regulate recognition and enforcement of civil judgments by party states. For recognition of judgments in family law matters see European Union Regulation No. 1347/2000, OJ L 160, 30/06/2000, p. 19.

147. Some of the more significant of these include:

Hague Convention of October 2, 1973 on the Recognition and Enforcement of Orders of Support;

of bilateral treaties with states not members of the EU or parties to the Lugano Convention such as Israel or Tunisia.[148] While the provisions of these specialized multilateral and bilateral treaties generally parallel those of the Brussels Regulation, any detailed discussion of their provisions is outside the scope of this work.

1. The Basic Rules for Recognition of Foreign Judgments

ZPO § 328 now applies only to recognition of judgments issued by states outside the European Union. The statute speaks by negative implication, specifying circumstances under which a foreign judgment will not be recognized. The key circumstances under which German courts will not recognize judgments of foreign courts are:

a. If the courts of the state which rendered the judgment would not have jurisdiction according to German law;[149]
b. If the defendant has neither entered an appearance nor been served with a written document commencing the proceeding by a legally sufficient means of service of process;[150]
c. If the judgment conflicts with another German or previously rendered foreign judgment adjudicating the same subject matter in controversy but entered in another suit;[151]
d. If recognition of the judgment "leads to a result that is irreconcilable with material principles of German law, especially if recognition is irreconcilable with constitutional rights;"[152]

European Convention of May 20, 1980 on the Recognition of Judgments in Custody Matters;

Hague Convention concerning the Jurisdiction of Authorities and the Law applicable in Respect to the Protection of Minors of October 5, 1961;

Convention on Contracts for the International Carriage of Goods by Road (CMR) of May 19, 1956.

See Geimer, Part 12 Chapter 1(II)(2), mn. 2758–2761 for a list of others.

148. Israel, Treaty of July 20, 1977; Tunisia, Treaty of July 19, 1966.

149. ZPO §328(1)(1).

150. ZPO §328(1)(2).

151. ZPO §328(1)(3). The same applies if recognition of the judgment would conflict with a case already pending in Germany.

152. ZPO § 328(1)(4) ("... *zu einem Ergebnis führt, das mit wesentlichen Grundsätzen des deutschen Rechts offensichtlich unvereinbar ist, insbesondere wenn die Anerkennung mit den Grundrechten unvereinbar ist*").

e. If reciprocity is not guaranteed.[153]

Most foreign judgments which do not run afoul of the foregoing limitations are entitled to recognition and enforcement within Germany.

A key prerequisite to recognition in Germany is that the foreign judgment partake of the characteristics of a judicial act which finally decides an actual controversy between parties. In contrast to the Brussels Regulation, German statute law is that foreign notes or security documents which purport to grant the right of immediate execution (*vollstreckbare Urkunde*) do not qualify.[154] Recognition and enforcement of orders entered in the exercise of non-contentious jurisdiction are governed by the German Non Contentious Jurisdiction Law.[155]

The judgment in question must be issued by a state judicial organ. Recognition and enforcement of foreign awards of arbitrations or private tribunals must be sought under the UN-Convention on the Recognition and Enforcement of Foreign Arbitration Awards of June 6, 1958, to which Germany is a

---

153. ZPO §328(1)(5).

154. Schack, §17(III)(1), mn. 811. German law permits a party to subject itself to immediate execution on a promissory note or similar document executed before a notary (ZPO §794(1)(5)). "Executable documents" (*vollstreckbare Urkunde*) are frequently used in connection with real estate mortgages and other financing transactions to secure immediate execution in real estate or tangible and intangible personal property. See Ch. 11(F) above. If the document does not support execution because of intervening performance or other event (e.g. in case of payment of a loan), the debtor may file an action to arrest execution. See Ch. 11(F)(3)(b) above. The burden of proof for both parties is the same as in normal actions. The creditor has to give evidence of the factual basis of his claim for execution, the debtor must similarly support his affirmative defense (e.g. payment, etc.). There is no shifting of the burden of proof to the obligor. See Baur/Stürner, *Zwangsvollstreckungs-, Konkurs- und Vergleichsrecht*, Vol. I, *Einzelvollstreckungsrecht*, 12th ed. (1995), §12(IV), mn. 16.14 ff., 16.23; Federal Supreme Court, 54 *NJW* 2096 (2001). Most continental European countries permit immediate execution of all documents executed by notaries. For details see Leutner, *Die vollstreckbare Urkunde im europäischen Rechtsverkehr* (1997); BRJE Article 57 provides for recognition and execution of all executable documents within the European Union, although the domestic law of Great Britain and some other countries does not provide for this form of stipulated executable act.

155. See FGG §16a. The Brussels Regulation does not generally exempt non-contentious matters from its scope of applicability. However Article 1(2) does expressly exempt the most important traditional non contentious matters of family law and the law of succession. See Kropholler, Art. 1, mn. 12 and 21–30. The new regulation on jurisdiction, recognition and enforcement of judgments in family matters (see Ch. 12(A)) covers divorce judgments and decisions connected with divorce cases. A regulation on other family and succession cases is being drafted. For ongoing European legislation see http://europa.eu.int/comm/justice_home/fsj/civil/fsj_civil_intro_en.htm.

signatory.[156] On the other hand, German courts will recognize judgments of foreign courts staffed by lay judges and decisions of some administrative agencies which function as courts in civil and commercial matters.[157]

Settlements even when documented in court also do not qualify as judgments entitled to recognition under German law, although the Brussels Regulation[158] and several multilateral and bilateral treaties provide for their recognition. American "consent judgments" may obtain recognition in Germany only if the court's approval of the judgment clearly goes beyond a mere documenting of the agreement reached by the parties.[159]

German statute law as well as the Brussels Regulation accords recognition to judgments issued in civil and commercial matters (*Zivil- und Handelssachen*). Decisions partaking of a criminal nature or which adjudicate tax liability or administrative law matters are entitled to recognition only to the extent that specific laws or regulations so provide.[160] Contempt sanctions issued to punish or compel parties or others to obey court orders other than as a part of the execution process fall within this category, although frequently the judgments resulting from such enforcement measures will be recognizable and enforceable in Germany.[161] On the other hand, the mere fact that a

---

156. See Ch. 11(H)(6) above and ZPO §§1061, 1025 ff.

157. Courts staffed by lay judges include, e.g., the *tribunaux de commerce* on the French model (Court of Appeals of Saarbrücken, 41 *NJW* 3100 (1988)) or American juries. Administrative agencies in some countries such as Denmark establish responsibility for child support. See Schack, §17(1)(III), mn. 813.

158. See BRJE Article 58; Ch. 12(C)(2)(e) below.

159. See Hess, "Die Anerkennung eines Class Action Settlement in Deutschland", 55 *JZ* 373, 377 (2000); Schack, §17(III)(1)(c), mn. 816; Geimer, Part 12 Chapter 1(IX)(1), mn. 2860. However a settlement of an arbitration proceeding can be incorporated into an agreed award and thereby gain enforceability in Germany. ZPO §§1053(2), 1055, 1061 (following the UNCITRAL Model Law; see Münch, in: *Münchener Kommentar zur ZPO*, § 1061, mn. 5). This development may herald greater future generosity in the recognition of judicial dispositions by agreement on the Anglo-American model. For a survey on consent judgments in Europe see Stürner, "Formen konsensualer Prozessbeendigung in europäischen Zivilprozessrechten", in: Breidenbach et al. (eds.), *Konsensuale Streitbeilegung* (2001), p. 6.

160. Punitive damages awards of American courts are considered to be decisions in civil matters in so far as the amount awarded has to be paid to the party to litigation and not to the state. See Stiefel/Stürner/Stadler, "The Enforceability of Excessive U.S. Punitive Damage Awards in Germany", XXXIX *The American Journal of Comparative Law* 779, 785 (1991); Federal Supreme Court, 118 BGHZ 312 ff., 336 ff. (1992); but see Ch. 12(C)(2)(c) below.

161. See Schack, §17(III)(1)(e), mn. 817–818. According to BRJE Article 49 fines and similar measures (such as *astreinte* in France) levied against parties during execution pro-

judgment is issued by a specialized court, such as a labor court, will not preclude recognition if it is basically civil or commercial in character.

Under German law only judgments which have the effect of *res adjudicata (rechtskräftig)* in the states of issuance are entitled to recognition. Provisional judgments (*Vorbehaltsurteile*) or interlocutory decisions which may be subject to immediate execution in the state rendering them are not entitled to recognition unless specifically made recognizable by some multilateral or bilateral treaty. The same is generally true of provisional measures (*einstweilige Verfügungen or Massnahmen*).[162] Judgments which are subject to execution but do not have res adjudicata effect and many provisional measures are, however, enforceable within the EU by virtue of the Brussels Regulation.[163]

The European Court of Justice has restricted recognition and enforcement of provisional measures rendered by European courts. When provisional measures are granted without giving notice to the opponent (*ex parte* procedure) the decision is not generally enforceable in other countries of the European Union.[164] If a court's jurisdiction for provisional measures is not based on the Brussels Regulation but on provisions of national law,[165] enforcement of the provisional measures in other Member States of the European Union will not be required.[166] Thus, a provisional measure of a French court ordering payment or performance of a contractual obligation, based on traditional French

---

ceedings are to be recognized and enforced within the EU. Judgments granting damages for economic loss or damages for pain and suffering entered in proceedings annexed to a criminal procedure (*Adhäsionsverfahren*) are civil matters and must therefore be generally recognized and enforced within the EU. See European Court of Justice, Case 172/91, *Sonntag v. Waidmann*, 1993 ECR I-1963 (1993); Case 7/98, *Krombach v. Bamberski*, 2000 ECR I-1935 (2000), but see Ch. 12(C)(2(c) below.

162. See Schack, § 17(III)(1)(e), mn. 821 f. Exceptions may be made for provisional measures in lieu of a decision of the main proceeding with the express or implied consent of the parties to litigation. See also Ch. 12(E)(3) below for provisional measures of German courts to secure claims pending abroad.

163. See BRJE Article 32; Schack, §17(III)(1)(f), mn. 823–826; Kropholler, Art. 32, mn. 20–23. Treaties and conventions on enforcement of judgments and orders in family law matters frequently provide for recognition and enforcement of various kinds of preliminary or temporary orders issued in such cases.

164. European Court of Justice, Case 125/79, Denilauler v. Couchet Frères, 1980 ECR 1553 (1980).

165. BRJE Article 31 permits provisional measures based on otherwise exorbitant national jurisdiction. See Ch. 12(B)(2)(C) above.

166. See European Court of Justice, Case 99/96, Mietz v. Internship Yachting Sneek, 1999 ECR I 2277 (1999).

jurisdiction over cases where French nationals are claimants, will not be recognized and enforced in Germany, if French courts do not have jurisdiction for the main procedure according to the provisions of the Brussels Regulation.[167] Enforcement will be limited to assets of the German defendant located in France. The European Court of Justice utilizes this restriction to prevent national courts from shifting jurisdiction over transnational cases to domestic courts by means of provisional measures which replace a main procedure not subject to domestic jurisdiction according to the Brussels Regulation.

German courts will recognize a foreign judgment only if the foreign court had international jurisdiction over the subject matter and parties of the controversy. If Germany and the other jurisdiction are parties to a multilateral or bilateral agreement or convention regulating international jurisdiction, generally that agreement will specify the kind of international jurisdiction that will require enforcement of resulting judgments. In other cases, a German court will apply the "mirror image principle" (*Spiegelbildprinzip*). This principle is embodied in ZPO §328(1)(1) which prohibits recognition of a foreign judgment "if the courts of the state to which the foreign court belonged do not have jurisdiction according to German laws."[168] Under the mirror image principle a German court will generally recognize a foreign court's determination of its own international jurisdiction if a German court in its place would have decided that it had international jurisdiction according to the German rules.[169] Thus a decision of a foreign court based on international jurisdiction considered exorbitant by German standards would not be entitled to recognition. Similarly, a German court will not recognize a foreign judgment adjudicating a matter which under German law would be subject to exclusive international jurisdiction of a state other than that rendering the judgment.[170] This reexamination of international jurisdiction under the mirror image prin-

---

167. See BRJE Article 31; Art. 14 of the French Civil Code.

168. ("*...wenn die Gerichte des Staates, dem das ausländische Gericht angehört, nach den deutschen Gesetzen nicht zuständig sind.*")

169. Another way of thinking of the mirror image principle is as a "hypothetical application of the German rules of jurisdiction" (*hypothetische Anwendung der deutschen Zuständigkeitsregeln*). For a discussion and explanation of the ramifications of the mirror image principle see Schack, §17(III)(2)(a), mn. 831–840; Geimer, Part 12 Chapter 1(XII)(3)(b), mn. 2896–2898; Stürner, "Die neue schweizerische internationale Zuständigkeit im internationalen Vergleich", in: Gottwald (ed.), *Festschrift für Karl-Heinz Schwab* (1990), p. 465.

170. For instance, if a foreign court judgment purported to adjudicate matters relating to the title of real estate located in Germany or a state other than the state rendering the judgment. See Schack, §17(III(2)(b), mn. 835. For exclusive jurisdiction in matters related to real estate, see Ch. 12(B)(3)(a) above.

ciple does not extend to either the venue or subject matter jurisdiction of the foreign court, which are exclusively matters for the foreign courts rendering the decisions.[171]

Although the mirror image principle may restrict recognition of some foreign judgments based on international jurisdictions not recognized in Germany, in some instances it may work to the disadvantage of defendants sued abroad. For instance, Germany recognizes international jurisdiction by waiver.[172] Thus a defendant sued in a foreign court who fails to object to the international jurisdiction of the foreign court may be subjecting himself to a judgment that can be enforced in Germany. Moreover, the mirror image principle does not require that the ground for exercise of international jurisdiction used by the foreign court and that which a German court would have used under like circumstances be the same. For instance, a foreign judgment expressly based on some ground for international jurisdiction not recognized in Germany is entitled to recognition in Germany if some other basis for international jurisdiction that would suffice in Germany also exists in the foreign state.[173]

Certain kinds of international jurisdiction asserted by United States courts do not pass muster in Germany under the mirror image principle. For instance the assertion of "general jurisdiction" over a foreign firm or enterprise that does business in the United States unrelated to the claim on which suit is brought would not result in a judgment that would be recognized or enforced in Germany.[174]

When considering whether to recognize or enforce a judgment of an American state court, a German court will apply the mirror image principle to the international jurisdiction of the individual state, not to the United States as a whole. For instance, a harm occurring in Arizona[175] would not support international jurisdiction of a state court in California. However according a decision of the German Federal Supreme Court the mirror image principle should be applied to judgments of American federal courts based on the international jurisdiction of the United States as a whole, regardless of whether

171. Schack, §17(III)(2)(b), mn. 836.

172. See Ch. 12(B)(2)(i) above.

173. For instance, if the defendant possessed property in a non-EU foreign state and the foreign judgment was rendered in a case involving money or property. See ZPO §23; Schack, §17(III)(2)(b), mn. 837; Zöller/Geimer, §328, mn. 96b; Federal Supreme Court, 141 BGHZ 186, 289 ff. (1999).

174. See Ch. 12(B)(2)(a) and (e) above.

175. For international jurisdiction see ZPO §32; Ch. 12(B)(2)(d) above.

the American federal court jurisdiction was based on diversity of citizenship or a federal question. In the context of the above example, this means that a judgment of a California federal court sitting in diversity would be entitled to recognition in Germany even when the same judgment rendered by a California state court would not.[176]

According to German statute law, a German court is not bound by the jurisdictional determination of the foreign court of its own international jurisdiction, but is entitled and expected to examine the grounds for international jurisdiction of the foreign court in light of the mirror image principle before recognizing the foreign judgment.

Within the EU the principles of recognition of judgments are straightforward. The basic rule is that a final judgment of a court of a Member State in a civil or commercial matter is entitled to recognition by the courts of the other Member States subject to a small number of exceptions and limitations.[177] The same is now true in divorce matters and connected child custody and protection matters.[178] Moreover, the international jurisdictional determination of the court issuing a judgment is final and not subject to reexamination by other EU courts in proceedings for recognition or enforcement of the judgment.[179]

EU proposed regulations providing a similar solution in other family law and in probate matters are drafted and under discussion.[180] There is a similar proposal for a speedier and more straightforward procedure for recognition

---

176. German Federal Supreme Court, 141 BGHZ 286, 292 (1999), annotation by von Hoffmann/Hau, 44 *RIW* 344 (1998); Geimer, Part 12 Chapter 1(XII)(3), mn. 2900. *Contra:* Stürner/Bormann, "Internationale Anerkennungszuständigkeit US-amerikanischer Bundesgerichte und Zustellungsfragen im deutsch-amerikanischen Verhältnis", 55 *JZ* 81, 85 (2000); Roth, "Zur Anerkennung der internationalen Zuständigkeit US-amerikanischer Bundesgerichte", 112 *ZZP* 484 (1999); Schack, §17(V), mn. 906.

177. BRJE Article 32 ff. The exceptions are set forth in Articles 34 and 35 and are discussed below.

178. See European Union Regulation on Jurisdiction and Recognition of Judgments in Matrimonial Matters, Articles 14 and 15. This regulation is sometimes referred to as "Brussels II."

179. See BRJE Article 35(3); Ch. 12(B)(5) above; Schack, §17(III)(2)(d), mn. 840; Kropholler, Art. 33, mn. 3. The only exceptions are for cases where international jurisdiction is exclusive and cases involving consumers, insureds, beneficiaries, and policyholders. See BRJE 35(1); Ch. 12(B)(3) above.

180. See the Commission's proposal for a Council regulation concerning jurisdiction and the recognition and enforcement of judgments in matrimonial matters and in matters of parental responsibility of May 3, 2002, COM 222 (2002). This proposal is supposed to supplement the above mentioned regulation.

and enforcement of existing executions and "undisputed actions" such as default judgments, documents granting the right of immediate execution and the like.[181]

2. Grounds for Non-Recognition

German courts may not recognize otherwise eligible foreign judgments which run afoul of the prohibitions of ZPO §328 or, within the EU, the prohibitions of Articles 34 and 35 of the Brussels Regulation. A German court asked to recognize a foreign judgment must make its own determination of the applicability of these limitations.

a. Default Judgments without Opportunity for Defense

Under both German statute law and the Brussels Regulation, a foreign default judgment issued in proceedings in which the defendant was not served in a time and manner calculated to permit him to prepare a defense will not be recognized or enforced in Germany.[182] This limitation implements the German constitutional right[183] to be heard (*rechtliches Gehör*) which encompasses the concept of a fair judicial hearing. Application of the limitation can require the court asked to recognize the foreign judgment to make its own determination of the timing and sufficiency of service or notice in the court proceeding in which the judgment was rendered.[184]

---

181. See the Commission's proposal of April 18, 2002, COM 159 (2002); Schollmeyer, "Europäisches Mahnverfahren", 22 *IPRax* 478 (2002). It is at least doubtful whether such a Regulation would be conform with the subsidiarity principle of EC Treaty, Article 5(2). See Bross, "Überlegungen zum gegenwärtigen Stand des Europäischen Einigungsprozesses - Probleme, Risiken und Chancen", 29 *EuGRZ* 574, 577 (2002); Stürner, "Stellungnahme vom 25. Juni 2002 für den Deutschen Juristentag" (not published).

182. BRJE Article 34(2); ZPO §328(1)(2).

183. German Constitution Article 103. This right is also embodied in the European Convention on Human Rights Article 6. See Ch. 6(E)(3) above.

184. See European Court of Justice, Case 166/80, Klomps v. Michel, 1981 ECR 1593 (1981); Case 228/81, Pendy Plastic v. Pluspunkt, 1982 ECR 2723 (1982); Case 49/84, Debaecker v. Bouwman, 1985 ECR 1779 (1985); Case 305/88, Lancray v. Peters, 1990 ECR I 2725 (1990); Federal Supreme Court, 44 *NJW* 641 (1991); 141 BGHZ 286, 295 ff. (1999); Schack, §17(III)(3), mn. 850; Stein/Jonas/Roth, §328, mn. 115; Stürner, "Förmlichkeit und Billigkeit bei der Klagzustellung im Europäischen Zivilprozess", 47 *JZ* 325 (1992); Stürner/Bormann, "Internationale Anerkennungszuständigkeit US-amerikanischer Bundesgerichte und Zustellungsfragen im deutsch-amerikanischen Verhältnis", 55 *JZ* 81 (2000); for more details see Ch. 12(E)(2) below.

American class action judgments (other than punitive damages awards) may be recognized and enforced in Germany in favor of the members of the class even if the class members were not individually served with legal process as long as the defendant was appropriately served and the other prerequisites to recognition exist. However a settlement or adverse decision in such a class action will not be recognized to bar a member of the class from bringing an action in a German court based on the same subject matter as the American class action unless the plaintiff was duly served with process according to German standards in connection with the class action.[185]

b. *Irreconcilability with Local Judgment*

Another ground for refusal to recognize a foreign judgment is that the foreign judgment is not reconcilable with a judgment rendered between the same parties by a German court either before or after the rendering of the foreign judgment.[186] This rule, which gives precedence to the German judgment regardless of when rendered, differs from the rules regulating conflicts between judgments entered within Germany and the rules regulating such conflicts among foreign judgments. Conflicts between judgments rendered by different German courts are usually resolved according to the priority principle (Prioritätsprinzip)—"first in time, first in right".[187] The same is true of conflicts between otherwise recognizable judgments of courts of other Member States of the European Union or of foreign states.[188] There are also treaties which specify a "last in time" preference for reconciling conflicts in foreign judgments in certain kinds of matters, such as court orders relating to the care and custody of children.[189]

Sometimes it is not clear whether two judgments are in fact "irreconcilable" (*unvereinbar*). The European Court of Justice has ruled that judgments are ir-

185. This issue has not yet been expressly determined by the Federal Supreme Court but non-recognition would be probable in light of prior judgments. See 120 BGHZ 305, 309–313 (1992) and 141 BGHZ 286, 302–304 (1999); similarly Hess, 55 *JZ* 373, 378 (2000). This result is similar to the result that obtains with respect to interest group complaints (*Verbandsklage*) within Germany. See Ch. 7(B)(5) above.

186. See ZPO §328(1)(3); BRJE Article 34 (3).

187. See ZPO §580(7) authorizing an action to set aside a judgment (*Restitutionsklage*) based on the existence of an earlier binding judgment between the same parties. See Ch. 9(F)(4) above.

188. BRJE Article 34(4); Schack, §17(III)(4), mn. 855.

189. European Union Regulation on Jurisdiction and Recognition of Judgments in Matrimonial Matters Article 15(II)(e), (f).

reconcilable if their respective legal consequences "mutually exclude each other" or the essential core issues of the cases are the same.[190] The German law of *res judicata* based on the "subject matter of the controversy" (*Streitgegenstand*) is relatively narrow. However it does not prevent a German court from declining to recognize a foreign judgment based on a functional conflict with a domestic judgment or another foreign judgment under these rules.[191] The same is true, with some modifications, of the law of *res adjudicata* in most of continental European states.

c. *"Ordre Public"*

An important ground for refusal to recognize a foreign judgment is incompatibility with the "public order" (*ordre public* or *öffentliche Ordnung*) of Germany.[192] The concept of "public order" is somewhat narrower than "public policy". Public order relates to the fundamental values of a state's system of justice. The Brussels Regulation denies recognition to foreign judgments if recognition would be "manifestly contrary to public policy of the Member State in which recognition is sought."[193]

---

190. (*"Sich gegenseitig aussschliessen"*), European Court of Justice, Case 145/86, *Hoffman v. Krieg*, 1988 ECR 645 (1988); for details see Ch. 9(F)(5). See Schack, §17(III)(4), mn. 858 and Kropholler, Art 34, mn. 49, who argue in favor of a narrow interpretation of "irreconcilable" in order to encourage recognition of foreign judgments. The same problem arises in application of the doctrine of *lis alibi pendens*. See Ch. 9(F)(5) above and Ch. 12(E)(1) below.

191. See Schack, §17(III)(4), mn 859. See also Ch. 9(F) above for a more detailed discussion of German law of *res judicata*.

192. See generally Stürner, "Anerkennungsrechtlicher und europäischer Ordre Public als Schranke der Vollstreckbarerklärung - der Bundesgerichtshof und die Staatlichkeit in der Europäischen Union", in: K. Schmidt et al. (eds.), *50 Jahre Bundesgerichtshof - Festgabe aus der Wissenschaft*, vol. III (2000), p. 677.

193. BRJE Art. 34(1). Each Member State retains the right to determine the meaning of "*ordre public*" in the context of its own legal, political and cultural values. This determination may not, however, conflict with common European values and the policy favoring a free market within the EU. The European Court of Justice exercises an overall control on the application of individual states' public policy values in this context. See Case 7/98, *Krombach v. Bamberski*, 2000 ECR I 1956 (2000), noted by Pieckenbrock, 20 *IPRax* 364 (2000); Geimer, 21 *ZIP* 859 (2001) and Case 38/98, *Renault v. Maxicar*, 2000 ECR I 2973 (2000), noted by Hess, 21 *IPRax* 301 (2001). See also Leipold, „Neuere Erkenntnisse des EuGH und des BGH zum anerkennungsrechtlichen ordre public", in: Hohloch et al. (eds.), *Festschrift für Hans Stoll* (2001), p. 625. For the proposition that further elaboration of a common European *ordre public* might play a major role in the future development of recognition and enforcement of judgments within the EU see Föhlisch, *Der gemeineu-*

The parallel provision of German statute law is more restrictively worded. Recognition will be denied if recognition of the judgment "leads to a result that is irreconcilable with material principles of German law, especially if recognition is irreconcilable with constitutional rights."[194]

Conflict with *ordre public* can be based on the procedures under which the foreign judgment was obtained or on the substantive law on which it is based. A judgment resulting from procedures which plainly violate the right to a fair judicial hearing (*rechtliche Gehör*) guaranteed by the German Constitution[195] or the right to a fair judicial procedure guaranteed by Article 6 of the European Convention on Human Rights will not be recognized.[196]

Extensive discovery orders proceedings in American courts which involve foreign parties or third parties can raise a question of *ordre public* if recognition or enforcement of the resulting judgments is sought in Germany. Extensive discovery proceedings are foreign to German civil justice.[197] However they may not be so alien as to be "irreconcilable with fundamental principles of German law". Recognition may depend on a case-by-case examination of the circumstances under which the proceedings took place and the extent of burden placed on the responding parties.[198] Generally ordinary American discovery is not a bar to recognition in Germany.

Most issues of *ordre public* arise in connection with substantive law supporting foreign judgments. This does not mean that the recognizing court re-examines the legal correctness of the foreign judgment. The issue is whether the judgment appears to be based on a legal principle which is so inimical to the local public order that the recognition of the judgment would be seen as

---

ropäische ordre public (1996); Stürner, in: *50 Jahre Bundesgerichtshof – Festgabe aus der Wissenschaft*, vol. III, p. 677.

194. ZPO §328(1)(4) ("...*zu einem Ergebnis führt, das mit wesentlichen Grundsätzen des deutschen Rechts offensichtlich unvereinbar ist, insbesondere wenn die Anerkennung mit den Grundrechten unvereinbar ist*").

195. GG Article 103(1).

196. For instance, a French "judgment of adhesion" will not be recognized within the European Union if the procedure does not permit an absent defendant to be represented by defense counsel. European Court of Justice, Case 7/98, *Krombach v. Bamberski*, 2000 ECR I 1935 (2000). For other examples see Schack, §17(III)(5)(b), mn. 864–865; Stein/Jonas/Roth, §328, mn. 139–143.

197. See Ch. 7(A)(4), (J)(1) and (L); Ch. 8(C)(1)(a) and (b) above.

198. See Federal Supreme Court, 118 BGHZ 312 (1993) (on punitive damages); Stiefel/Stürner, "Die Vollstreckbarkeit US-amerikanischer Schadensersatzurteile exzessiver Höhe", 38 *VersR* 830 (1987); Stiefel/Stürner/Stadler, "The Enforceablitiy of Excessive U.S. Punitive Damage Awards in Germany", XXXIX *The American Journal of Comparative Law* 779 (1991); Schack, §17, mn 865.

a betrayal of that local public order.[199] Judgments that have little actual effect on local persons or institutions are less likely to offend ordre public than judgments which directly impact German residents or institutions. A court called upon to recognize a foreign judgment is not bound by the form of the judgment or by its statement of grounds, but may reexamine the facts to determine whether a conflict with *ordre public* exists.[200]

American judgments for punitive or treble damages have been denied enforcement in Germany based on ZPO §328(1)(4) because German law regards damages in civil cases as strictly compensatory in character.[201] In a recent mass-media case the German Federal Supreme Court indicated a willingness to consider a kind of punitive damage award in order to insure that a wrongdoer should not profit from his wrongdoing. This may suggest that in some circumstances the German Federal Supreme Court might someday consider recognition of at least some kinds of punitive damages awards, although at present it seems unlikely that this will really happen.[202]

d. Reciprocity

Finally, a German court is required to deny recognition to a judgment of a court of a state unless that state guarantees recognition of German judg-

---

199. Compare Federal Supreme Court, 123 BGHZ 268 (1993) (personal liability of a school teacher for negligence during an excursion under Italian law is incompatible with German public policy) with Federal Supreme Court, 140 BGHZ 395 (1999) (surety of the indigent brother for business debts of the sister and her husband under French law is compatible with German public policy (for the constitutional right of personal autonomy and the freedom to conclude contracts see Ch. 10(H)(1) above)).

200. Schack, §17(III)(5), mn. 868.

201. Federal Supreme Court, 118 BGHZ 312 (1993), noted by Koch, 45 *NJW* 3073 (1992); Schack, 106 *ZZP* 104 (1993); Bungert, 14 *ZIP* 815 (1993). See Schack, §17(III)(5), mn 869; Geimer, Part 12 Chapter 1(XII)(4), mn. 2974; Brockmeier, *Punitive damages, multiple damages und deutscher ordre public* (1999), pp. 88–140; Stiefel/Stürner, 38 *VersR* 830 (1987); Stiefel/Stürner/Stadler, XXXIX *TheAmerican Journal of Comparative Law* 779 (1991)

202. Federal Supreme Court, 128 BGHZ 1 (1996) "*Caroline v. Monaco I*"; 49 *NJW* 984 (1996) "*Caroline v. Monaco II*" and 49 *NJW* 985 (1996) "*Caroline v. Monaco III*". It is not yet clear whether this is a general development of German law of damages or whether it will remain a limited phenomenon in restrictively selected cases such as massive infringements of the right to privacy (*allgemeines Persönlichkeitsrecht*) by mass-media. See Stürner, "Persönlichkeitsschutz und Geldersatz", 29 *AfP* 1 (1998) (with respect to parallel developments in media law throughout Europe). The Federal Constitutional Court may be receptive to a more generous practice. See 48 *NJW* 649, 650 (1995) (*obiter dictum*). See, however, Zekoll/Ralph,"U.S.-amerikanische Antitrust-Treble-Damages Urteile und deutscher ordre public", 54 *JZ* 384 (1999).

ments.[203] While this seems like a reasonable requirement, it can raise problems if the state rendering the judgment also requires reciprocity. "Who goes first?"[204]

Another concern about this rule is that a restrictive practice of a foreign state may disadvantage litigants who are compelled to use that state's courts, regardless of the litigants' nationality. This problem has led to a relaxation of the rule in certain matters, such as, for instance, family matters.[205]

For these reasons German case law tends to interpret the reciprocity requirement fairly flexibly, requiring that the conditions for recognition of German judgments by the originating state generally approximate those required by Germany. Even if requirements as to presence or international jurisdiction differ in some respects, to the extent that they overlap, recognition can be afforded.[206]

When the judgments of American courts are involved, the requirement of reciprocity applies to the individual American states. This is also true of judgments of American federal courts grounded on diversity of citizenship.[207] Presumably federal court judgments based on federal question jurisdiction would be considered on a national standard of reciprocity.

e. Recognition of Consent Judgments and Settlements

Within the EU, each Member State, including Germany, is required to recognize and enforce "a settlement which has been approved by a court in the course of proceedings and is enforceable in the Member State in which it was

---

203. ZPO §328(5). This problem does not, of course, arise within the EU, since the Brussels Regulation provided for reciprocal recognition of judgments by all Member States.

204. Sometimes the circularity can only be circumvented by attempting to predict whether courts of the originating state would recognize judgments of the recognizing state based on a review of legislation, court dicta or scholarly writings. Frequently a statement by a state's ministry of justice will help. See Schack, §17(III)(6)(a), mn. 872, 876. Commentaries such as Stein/Jonas/Roth, §328 mn 162–183 offer lists of countries with respect to which reciprocity is rendered.

205. See ZPO §328(2) authorizing recognition of judgments regardless of reciprocity primarily in certain kinds of family matters. Compare FGG §16a which does not contain a requirement of reciprocity.

206. Federal Supreme Court, 42 BGHZ 194 (1965); 52 BGHZ 251 (1970) (recognition of South African judgments against South African domiciliaries even though South Africa does not recognize judgments based on all German grounds for international jurisdiction).

207. Federal Supreme Court, 141 BGHZ 286, 299 (2000). See Stürner/Bormann, 55 *JZ* 81, 85 (2000); Roth, 112 *ZZP* 483, 486 (1999). Compare this rule with the application of the mirror image principle, which treats diversity cases and federal question cases alike and applies a national standard to both. See Ch. 12(C)(1) above.

concluded."[208] The court approving the settlement is required to provide a special certificate in a form prescribed by the Regulation for use in obtaining enforcement of the settlement in other Member States.

A settlement reached in a state not in the European Union is not entitled to recognition as a judgment in Germany unless it is approved by a court by a process which goes beyond the mere acknowledging or recording of the settlement. This is because German statute law provides only for recognition of actual court judgments (*Urteile*), not settlements.[209] For example, American class action settlements stand a good chance of receiving recognition in Germany, at least to the extent of the benefit conferred on the members of the class, because they are subject to required judicial examination and approval.[210]

3. Procedure for Recognition of Foreign Judgments

Under German law foreign judgments are entitled to automatic recognition subject to the limitations discussed above. This means that there is no requirement of a formal court proceeding to obtain a declaration of recognition before the foreign judgment will be recognized by a court in a civil proceeding in Germany.[211] It is up to the German court to determine whether the judgment is entitled to recognition according to law. The court has the responsibility on its own motion to examine the judgment for the existence of the prerequisites of recognition, and the absence of barriers to recognition.[212] A decision to recognize a foreign judgment, or not to recognize a foreign judgment in a pending civil matter is not appealable as such, but would be reviewed in an appeal from a judgment or order based on the recognition or non-recognition of the foreign judgment.

Organs other than civil courts may also be presented with foreign judgments and asked to recognize them. For instance, foreign judgments awarding damages for personal injury or disability may be important to applications for social benefits. The organ presented with the foreign judgment has the responsibility to determine its recognizability.

---

208. BRJE Article 58.

209. ZPO §328(1); Stein/Jonas/Roth, §328, mn. 5. See Ch. 12(C)(1) above.

210. But not to the extent of any punitive damages awards. See Ch. 12(C)(2)(c) above.

211. Schack, §17(IV)(1)(a), mn. 879. This is true throughout the EU by virtue of Article 33(1) of the Brussels Regulation.

212. Schack, §17(IV)(1)(c), mn. 882. The ZPO §328(2) ground for non-recognition of a foreign default judgment based on absence of an opportunity for the defendant to defend should, as a practical matter, be raised by the defendant, unless the inadequacy of service was patent on the court record as transmitted to the German court.

While the absence of a required preliminary determination facilitates the use of foreign judgments, there is a risk that different courts or governmental organs may reach differing decisions on the recognition of a single judgment or series of judgments.[213] Reconciling such differing initial determinations by the appellate process can be a laborious and costly exercise. A litigant concerned about whether a foreign judgment will be recognized in Germany can initiate an action for declaratory judgment (*Feststellungsklage*) pursuant to ZPO §256 to establish the recognizability of the foreign judgment.[214]

Because of the importance of consistency in the recognition of judgments of family status and obligations there is a special procedure for recognition of judgments in specified family matters.[215] Before German officials and agencies can take official action based on a foreign judgment changing marital status or establishing or changing family obligations of custody and support the judgment must be submitted for examination by the appropriate Ministry of Justice to the Ministry of Justice in the German state of the affected parties' residence or sojourn, which conducts a special proceeding to determine whether it is entitled to recognition.[216] Excepted from this requirement is a judgment rendered by a foreign court of the state of domicile of both spouses at the time the judgment was rendered.[217] Such judgments are treated like other judgments and do not require formal proceedings for recognition.[218] Under the new EU Matrimonial Regulations the special procedure is also no longer required for divorce judgments of an EU Member State.[219]

4. Effects of Recognition of Foreign Judgments

The law of the jurisdiction in which the judgment or order was rendered determines the finality and binding character of a decision.[220] The effects of a

---

213. See Schack, §17(IV)(1)(a), mn. 879.

214. Zöller/Greger, §256, mn. 4. The Brussels Regulation also envisions a procedure whereby an "interested party who raises the recognition of a judgment as the principal issue in a dispute may,... apply for a decision that the judgment be recognized." Article 33(2).

215. See Law on the Alteration of Family Law Rules (*Familienrechtsänderungsgesetz or FamRÄndG*) Art. 7, §1(1)(1).

216. For a description of the procedure before the Ministries of Justice see Schack, §17(IV)(3)(a), mn 898; Geimer, Part 12 Chapter 1(XV)(1), mn. 3015.

217. FamRÄndG Art. 7, §1(1)(3).

218. See Schack, §17(IV)(3)(a), mn. 893–894.

219. Article 14, European Union Regulation Nr. 1347/2000, OJ L 160, 30/06/2000, pp. 19, 23–24.

220. See Schack, § 17(I)(1)(a), mn. 776.

prior judgment on a later proceeding may be governed alternatively by the principles of the law of the state rendering the decision or the law of the recognizing state. Neither the wording of the Brussels Regulation nor the wording of German national law gives any help for a solution of this problem.[221] According to the effects doctrine ("*Theorie der Wirkungserstreckung*") it is the law of the state rendering the judgment which determines the effects of judgments to be recognized. Under this doctrine American judgments would be given American claim and issue preclusion effect in Germany, though German law does not know issue preclusion and limits claim preclusion to a very small scope.[222] The European Court of Justice shows some sympathy with this understanding of effects of foreign judgments, though a clear decision does not exist.[223] The Federal Supreme Court argues that the effect of German and foreign judgments should be equal developing the doctrine of equal treatment ("*Gleichstellungstheorie*").[224] The prevailing German opinion takes the effects doctrine as a basis but limits effects of a foreign judgment by German standards.[225] In the end Germany does not recognize American issue preclusion and the claim preclusion effect of a decision will be reduced to German dimensions.

D. Enforcement of Foreign Judgments

While the recognition of foreign judgments in German judicial proceedings and by official agencies generally requires no special judicial proceeding, enforcement of foreign judgments by German judicial authorities is another matter. Before a holder of a foreign judgment can obtain enforcement of such a judgment in Germany the holder must obtain a German judgment of enforceability (*Vollstreckungsurteil*) of the judgment or a declaration of enforceability (*Vollstreckbarerklärung*) in a special proceeding commenced for that purpose.[226]

Only judgments requiring performance (*Leistungsurteile*) may be given enforcement. Judgments establishing or altering legal relationships (*Gestaltungsurteile*) or judgments declaring legal rights (*Festellungsurteile*) may be recog-

221. See ZPO §328 and BRJE Article 26(1).

222. See Ch. 9(F)(2) and (3) above.

223. European Court of Justice, Case 145/86, Hoffman v. Krieg, 1988 ECR 645 (1988).

224. Federal Supreme Court, 36 *NJW* 5143 (1983); 36 *NJW* 1976, 1977 (1983).

225. See Schack, §17(I)(3), mn. 791 ff.

226. See ZPO §722(1) - judgment of enforceability; BRJE Article 38(1) - declaration of enforceability. Also known as *exequatur* (from French practice).

nized in German judicial proceedings relating to their subject matters, but are not susceptible of direct enforcement.[227]

Judgments of foreign courts which merely recognize or declare enforceable judgments of other foreign courts are also not entitled to enforcement in Germany. Only an "original" court judgment which adjudicates rights between the parties is enforceable in Germany.[228] According to a decision of the Federal Supreme Court this doctrine does not, however, bar German courts from recognizing foreign court judgments which give enforcement to arbitral awards issued in the state of the foreign enforcing court.[229]

Both German statute law and the Brussels Regulation establish procedures whereby holders of foreign judgments can seek judgments or declarations of enforceability.[230] Holders of judgments from outside the European Union must go through the standard statutory procedure set forth in ZPO §§722 ff. Holders of judgments issued by other Member States of the European Union may follow a simplified 2-stage procedure spelled out in the Brussels Regulation. This procedure is designed to speed and reduce the cost of obtaining enforcement of EU judgments.[231]

1. Judgment of Enforceability - German Statutory Procedure

A holder of a foreign judgment not entitled to use the simplified Brussels Regulation procedure must file a complaint for execution (*Vollstreckungsklage*)

---

227. See Zöller/Geimer, §722, mn. 5.

228. This prohibition of the double declaration of enforceability (*Verbot des Doppelexequatur*) is based on the doctrine that every state should have the right to decide for itself which judgments of foreign courts it will recognize and enforce and that no state should be able to prescribe recognition of judgments by other states. See Schack, §18(I)(2), mn. 936.

229. Federal Supreme Court, 30 *RIW* 557 (1984). Some commentators do not agree. See Zöller/Geimer, §722, mn. 8; Schack, §18(I)(2), mn. 937. According to the new German law regulating arbitration (ZPO §§ 1025 ff.) foreign arbitral awards are subject to direct and simplified recognition and enforcement in Germany pursuant to the New York Convention, see ZPO §1061 and Ch. 12(C)(1) above. This may mean that the ongoing validity of the Federal Supreme Court decision may be questionable.

230. See ZPO §§722, 723; BRJE Articles 38–56.

231. Similar simplified procedures are available to holders of judgments issued in states signatory to the Lugano Convention as well as certain other international treaties providing for recognition and enforcement of judgments in specific kinds of matters. See Lugano Convention Articles 31ff.; and, e.g., Hague Convention on the Recognition and Enforcement of Decisions relating to Maintenance Obligations of October 2, 1973 Article 17.

in either the local court or the state district court of the district in which the defendant is domiciled or in which the defendant has property (*Vermögen*). Choice of court depends on the court's subject matter jurisdiction.[232] Complaints for enforcement of foreign family-law decisions must be brought in the family court divisions of the local courts.[233]

A defendant in an action for execution based on a foreign judgment may raise all grounds for non-recognition or non-enforcement of the foreign judgment (such as denial of right to fair judicial hearing in the foreign proceeding or *ordre public*)[234] as well as grounds in defense of execution such as later payment or satisfaction of the judgment of which enforcement is sought.[235] The plaintiff has the burden of establishing the grounds for enforceability. The court is also under an obligation *ex officio* to examine the foreign judgment for its compliance with the requirements of ZPO §328.[236] No judgment of enforceability can be issued until the court is satisfied that the underlying judgment has *res judicata* effect (*Rechtskraft*) according to the law of the court which issued it.[237]

A successful action for enforceability of a foreign judgment will result in a judgment of enforceability (*Vollstreckungsurteil*). An abstract of the judgment of enforceability prepared by the court clerk can be used in dealing with court executors and in implementing other execution measures.[238] Even if the judgment of enforceability is granted, the debtor retains the same right to initiate later actions to forestall execution (*Vollstreckungsabwehrklage*) based on circumstances arising since the judgment of enforceability as would be available with respect to a German judgment.[239]

---

232. ZPO §722(2). See Ch. 5(B) above for a discussion of subject matter jurisdiction of the local courts and the state district courts.

233. Zöller/Geimer, §722, mn. 31. But see Ch. 12(C)(3) above for initial examination of certain decisions in divorce and family matters by the Ministry of Justice.

234. See ZPO §328; Ch. 12(C)(2)(a)–(d) above on the various grounds for denial of recognition of a foreign judgment.

235. In the course of the action for execution the defendant must assert all grounds in defense of execution based on circumstances which occurred since the foreign judgment to be enforced was rendered. Such defenses may be precluded in later proceedings. See Baur/Stürner, *Zwangsvollstreckungs-, Konkurs- und Vergleichsrecht*, Vol. I Einzelvollstreckungsrecht, 12th ed. (1995), mn. 57.3.

236. ZPO §723(2)(2).

237. ZPO §723(2)(1).

238. See ZPO §724; Ch. 11(F) above on the available measures of execution.

239. ZPO §767. See Ch. 11(F)(3) above on actions to prevent execution.

2. Declaration of Enforceability - EU Procedure

Holders of judgments rendered by EU courts may utilize a simple two-step procedure designed to avoid consideration of issues of recognizability if such issues are not raised by the debtor. The procedure is partly spelled out in the Brussels Regulation and partly left to local law.[240] The foreign judgment creditor must file an application for enforcement in the state district court for the district in which the judgment debtor is domiciled or where the execution is to take place.[241] The application must include an authenticated copy of the foreign judgment together with a certificate of the issuing court setting forth particulars such as the date of service of process on the defendant, names of parties receiving legal aid, text of the mandate of the judgment, and a statement that the judgment is enforceable in the state in which it was issued.[242]

The application is referred to the presiding judge of the panel assigned to enforcement of foreign judgments. The presiding judge initially examines only the apparent regularity of the judgment on its face. There is no inquiry at this stage into any of the grounds for non-recognition provided for in Articles 34 and 35.[243] If the application and supporting documents appear to be in order, the presiding judge enters a simple order (*Beschluss*), from which the clerk of the court prepares an execution clause (*Vollstreckungklausel*) to attach to the foreign judgment.

This document is served by the court on the debtor, who has a month within which to file a miscellaneous appeal (*Beschwerde*) to the state appeals court.[244] The debtor may raise on such appeal any of the grounds for non-

---

240. BRJE Articles 39 ff. Local law includes the German Law Implementing International Conventions on Recognition and Enforcement of Judgments (*Gesetz zur Ausführung zwischenstaatlicher Anerkennungs- und Vollstreckungsverträge in Zivil- und Handelssachen* or *AVAG*). See Baur/Stürner, *Einzelvollstreckungsrecht*, mn. 55.9 ff.

241. BRJE Article 39, Annex II.

242. See BRJE Articles 40(3), 53, 54, Annex V.

243. BRJE Article 41(1). See Ch. 12(C)(2)(b)–(d) above on the various grounds for non-recognition set forth in Articles 34 and 35. The Lugano Convention still requires (as did the former Brussels Convention) that the presiding judge examine the judgment for its apparent enforceability under the law of the issuing state and its recognizability under the terms of the Convention. See Schack, §18(III)(1), mn. 950; Kropholler, Art. 41, mn. 5.

244. BRJE Articles 42(2) (service), 43 (conditions and time of appeal). During this one-month period the judgment creditor may proceed with measures of execution only to the extent of "protective measures against the property of the party against whom enforcement is sought", BRJE Article 47(3), AVAG §§ 18 ff. The scope of activity allowed the execution creditor under this provision is left to the law of the Member State. See Schack, §18(III)(2), mn. 953, 954. For a detailed discussion of permissible protective measures in Germany see Kropholler, Art. 47, mn. 12–13; Baur/Stürner, *Einzelvollstreckungsrecht*, mn. 55.16 ff.

recognition specified in Articles 34 and 35 of the Brussels Regulation as well as any ground for objection to execution of a German judgment such as later payment, satisfaction, etc.[245] An action to forestall execution (*Vollstrekkungsabwehrklage*) based on developments occurring after issuance of the declaration remains available even after the decision of the state appeals court.[246] Further appeal is limited to miscellaneous appeal of law (*Rechtsbeschwerde*) to the Federal Supreme Court.[247]

3. Proceedings Following a Judgment or Declaration of Enforceability

Once a decision of the appropriate German court on the complaint for execution or the simplified application under the Brussels Regulation has become final (*rechtskräftig*), proceedings on execution or other enforcement of the foreign judgment are the same as for a German judgment.[248]

Difficulties can be encountered with foreign judgments expressed in foreign currencies. If the judgment specifically requires payment in a specified foreign currency, some authors maintain that only payment in the specified currency can avert execution activity.[249] The more pragmatic view is that a debtor should be able to invoke statutory remedies to avert execution by payment in a sufficient sum of local currency to equal the amount of the foreign judgment according to the prevailing rate of exchange, generally at the time of execution, but in some cases, such as with damages awards, at another more suitable time to avoid unjust enrichment.[250]

---

245. Kropholler, Art. 43, mn. 24–30; AVAG §12. See Ch. 11(F)(3)(b) above on objections to execution.

246. AVAG §14, ZPO §767.

247. BRJE Article 44, Annex IV, AVAG §§15ff. See Ch. 10(F)(4) above on miscellaneous appeals of law to the Federal Supreme Court.

248. See Ch. 11(F) above.

249. See Schack, §19(I)(d), mn. 963. In such case the court officer might attach enough local funds to satisfy the judgment when converted into the designated foreign currency.

250. See Stein/Jonas/Münzberg, §704, mn. 161; Hanisch, "Umrechnung von Fremdwährungsforderungen in Vollstreckung und Insolvenz", 9 *ZIP* 341, 346 (1988); Baur/Stürner, *Zwangsvollstreckungs-, Konkurs- und Vergleichsrecht*, vol. I, *Einzelvollstreckungsrecht*, 12th ed. (1995), §55, mn. 28 and generally Bachmann, *Fremdwährungsschulden in der Zwangsvollstreckung* (1994).

4. Alteration of Foreign Judgments

Although the traditional view was that a German court does not have authority to alter a foreign judgment, that view has been modified in recent years. Now it is well established that German courts can modify certain kinds of recognized foreign judgments to take into account changes in conditions since the time the judgments were rendered. Foreign as well as domestic judgments requiring periodic payments for spousal or child support are particularly likely to be susceptible of alteration based on changed circumstances.[251] In both cases the same considerations favor compromising *res judicata* effect (*Rechtskraft*) in favor of flexibility where circumstances warrant.[252] Only foreign judgments which are recognized in Germany may be altered by a German court. If the foreign judgment is not entitled to recognition, the parties must proceed from anew in Germany.[253]

Any alteration of a judgment must be based on a material change (*wesentliche Änderung*) in some factual circumstance on which the judgment was founded since the date of the last oral hearing on the judgment in question. For instance, a judgment for spousal support can be altered based on a post-judgment change in the financial circumstances of a former spouse if that spouse's financial circumstances was a ground for the award in the first place.[254]

A party seeking to alter a foreign judgment may institute an action for modification (*Abänderungsklage*) pursuant to ZPO §323.[255] The court determines the degree and nature of alteration according to the law of the jurisdiction originally rendering the judgment.[256]

251. See Ch. 9(F)(3) above on alteration of domestic judgments.

252. See Schack, §21(I), mn. 1001–1003.

253. Schack, §21(II)(2), mn. 1007–1009.

254. See Ch. 9(F)(3) above. According to the prevailing view, a party's move into a new state with a different cost of living can constitute a change in circumstances sufficient to support alteration of a foreign judgment. See Schack, §21(II)(2), mn. 1013.

255. Schack, §21(IV)(2), mn. 1019; Zöller/Vollkommer, §323, mn. 12. Grounds for alteration of judgment cannot be raised as affirmative defenses in proceedings on executions, but must be asserted in separate proceedings. See Federal Supreme Court, 6 *NJW-RR* 1155 (1991) (support claims).

256. Federal Supreme Court, 36 *NJW* 1978 (1983); Schack, §21(IV)(1), mn. 1015–1016; Zöller/Geimer, IZPR, mn. 34.

E. Proceedings in Aid of Foreign Jurisdiction

German procedural law recognizes obligations based on international comity as well as specific requirements of international conventions and treaties to respect the exercise of jurisdiction by the courts of other nations and to render reasonable assistance to parties involved in foreign litigation. The main areas in which German civil justice is invoked in aid of foreign jurisdiction are recognition of pendency of actions in foreign courts, service of foreign process in Germany, use of provisional measures in Germany to secure claims pending in foreign courts, and taking of evidence in Germany for use in foreign proceedings. By the same token, German litigants may expect corresponding cooperation in these areas from the governments and judicial systems of other states. As is the case with the other institutions of international civil justice, proceedings in aid of foreign jurisdiction are regulated by a mixture of German (and foreign) statute law, international conventions and treaties, and (most recently) by regulations of the European Union.

1. Recognition of Pendency of Foreign Litigation

Within Germany, once an action has become legally pending (*rechtshängig*) before one court, no other German court may take cognizance of the subject matter (*Streitgegenstand*) of the pending action. If an action with the same subject matter as an action pending elsewhere in Germany is filed, it must be dismissed on the ground of *lis alibi pendens*.[257] The doctrine implements policies of judicial economy by preventing courts from exercising competing jurisdictions.

The same considerations lead to a general willingness of German courts to recognize the defense of *lis alibi pendens* based on pendency in a foreign court, at least where there is a high likelihood that German courts would recognize the judgment of the court in question. As is the case within Germany, the key issues are the identity of the parties and the functional identity of the subject matter of the controversy. Of course circumstances requiring denial of recognition of a foreign judgment, such as lack of international jurisdiction, inad-

257. ZPO §261(3)(1). See Ch. 7(G) above for a discussion of pendency and its consequences.

equate service of process or *ordre public* may also serve as reasons for refusal to dismiss a German proceeding based on prior pendency of the case abroad.[258] Unless there appears to be a likelihood of recognition of the judgment (*positive Anerkennungsprognose*) the German court need not defer to the foreign proceeding.[259]

When an action becomes pending before a foreign court is generally determined by the law of the foreign jurisdiction.[260] The Brussels Regulation now provides, however, for a more uniform definition of pendency within the European Union.[261] According to the Brussels Regulation, pendency occurs when the document instituting the proceeding is lodged with the court, provided that the plaintiff does not fail to take any steps required to effect service on the defendant. If the document is one which must be served before being filed, then pendency occurs when the document is delivered to the authority responsible for service, provided that the plaintiff does not fail to file the document with the court.[262]

In some cases, such as within the EU, recognition of the pendency of foreign proceedings is required by treaty or regulation. Article 27 of the Brussels Regulation governs the situation where "proceedings involving the same cause of action and between the same parties"[263] are brought in the courts of dif-

---

258. See Ch. 12(C)(1) and (2) above on grounds for denial of recognition.

259. See Schack, §16(I)(2), mn. 752–755; Geimer, Part 11 (II)(1), mn. 2688; Federal Supreme Court, 39 *NJW* 2195 (1986). The German court may stay the proceeding (ZPO § 148) when the prospect of future recognition is unclear.

260. In Germany an action becomes pending upon service of the complaint on the defendant. ZPO §§261(I), 253(I); Ch. 7(G) above. In other countries pendency is often triggered by the filing of the complaint in the court. See Schack, §16(I)(1), mn. 756. This can mean that German plaintiffs will often lose the "race to the courthouse". For this reason some writers have argued in favor of modifying the traditional priority test. See, e.g., Geimer, Part 11 (VI), mn. 2701.

261. See BRJE Article 30. A similar provision is found in Article 11(4) of Regulation No. 1347/2000, OJ L 160, 30/06/2000, p. 19, 23 for family law matters.

262. BRJE Article 30. The English language version of the Brussels Regulation uses the term "seisin" rather than "pendency". The latter term is used herein in the interest of consistency within this work.

263. The term "cause of action" (stated in German as "*Klagen wegen desselben Anspruchs*") in the Brussels Regulation has a slightly broader connotation than "subject matter of the controversy" (*Streitgegenstand*) of German procedural law. See Ch. 9(F)(5) above. The European Court of Justice has given the term a broad reading as encompassing claims, regardless of form, that address the same core legal issue, rather then the more restrictive German construction of its corresponding concept. See European Court of Justice, Case 144/86, *Gubisch Maschinenfabrik v. Palumbo*, 1987 ECR 4861 (1987); Case 406/92, *The Tatry v. Maciej Rataj*, 1994 ECR I 5439 (1994); Federal Supreme Court, 134 BGHZ

ferent EU Member States. Article 27(2) requires that "where the jurisdiction of the court first seised is established, any court other than the court first seised shall decline jurisdiction in favour of that court."[264] Within the EU every court has the power to determine its own jurisdiction, and the courts of other states are required to honor that determination.[265] Only if the foreign court determines that it does not have jurisdiction may the German court go forward. Even actions apparently within the exclusive jurisdiction of the German courts are subject to this rule.[266]

The Brussels Regulation goes a bit further than German national law with respect to recognition of foreign pendency of claims related to claims asserted in a later German action. Under Article 28 if a "related action" is pending in the courts of another EU Member State, a German first-instance court may stay its proceedings, and may, on application of one of the parties, decline jurisdiction if the foreign court has jurisdiction over the claims presented to the German court and if its law permits joinder of such claims with the pending related claims.[267]

The strict provisions of the Brussels Regulation have raised the concern that potential defendants may seek to avoid facing relatively expeditious German procedure by initiating preemptive actions for declaratory judgment of non-liability (*negative Festellungsklage*) in other EU Member States where the pace of litigation is much more leisurely. Such actions have become colloquially known as "Italian torpedoes" and are sometimes resorted to in patent litigation to forestall and delay German actions for infringement.[268] Use of this tactic in extreme cases may risk liability for abuse of legal process (*Rechtsmissbrauchs*).[269]

201, 210 (1998); Schack, §16(I)(2)(e), mn. 762; Kropholler, Art. 27, mn. 3, 6–8 and for the corresponding German concept Ch. 9(F)(2)(a) above.

264. BRJE Article 27(2). Any court other than the court first seized must stay its proceedings until the jurisdiction of the court first seized is established. BRJE Article 27(1). See also Article 21 of the Lugano Convention.

265. See Ch. 12(B)(5) above.

266. Schack, §16(I)(2)(e), mn. 760. See also BRJE Article 29 providing that actions within the exclusive jurisdiction of several courts shall be determined by the first court in which they shall become pending.

267. Actions are "related" if they are "so closely connected that it is expedient to hear and determine them together to avoid the risk of irreconcilable judgments resulting from separate proceedings". BRJE Article 28(3).

268. See Court of Appeals of München, 44 *RIW* 631 (1998); Court of Appeals of Düsseldorf, 49 *GRURInt* 776 (2000).

269. See Schack, §16(I)(2)(e), mn. 762a; Kropholler, Art. 27, mn. 11; Hartley, "How to abuse the law and (maybe) come out on top: bad-faith proceedings under the Brussels Jurisdiction and Judgments Convention", in: Nafziger et al. (eds.), *Law and Justice in a Multistate World, Essays in Honor of Arthur T. von Mehren* (2002), p. 73. This liability may be

2. Service of Foreign Process

As indicated above[270] Germany's requirements for the form of notice of commencement of suit and the manner in which notice is to be given are relatively strict. Actual delivery of the suit papers to the defendant or a procedure calculated to afford the defendant with actual notice of the contents is generally required.[271] In many cases service of process initiating a German law suit must be made on a defendant who is not then to be found within Germany. Since actual service on the defendant is a prerequisite to suit (*Prozessvoraussetzung*) the German courts and lawyers must rely on courts and agencies in other countries to assist in making service there unless the foreign states permit service by registered mail with return receipt based on an international convention.[272]

By the same token, frequently courts and judicial agencies in other states have a need to effect service of process on natural or juristic persons found only within Germany. In most cases procedures for international service of process are provided by international convention or, within the European Union, by EU regulation.

The most important of these are the Hague Convention on Service Abroad of Judicial and Extra-Judicial Documents of November 15, 1965[273] and the European Union Regulation of May 29, 2000 on the Service in the Member States of Judicial and Extra-Judicial Documents in Civil or Commercial Matters.[274] Under the Hague Service Convention and the EU Service Regulation

---

based on BGB §826, the general provision of German tort law for intentional harm. See generally Mertens, in: *Münchener Kommentar zum Bürgerlichen Gesetzbuch*, 3rd ed. (1997), §826, mn. 172, 173; for early consideration of this issue see Stürner, "Der Justizkonflikt zwischen U.S.A. und Europa", in: Habscheid (ed.), *Der Justizkonflikt mit den Vereinigten Staaten von Amerika* (1986), pp. 3 ff., 53; Hopt, *Schadensersatz aus unberechtigter Verfahrenseinleitung* (1968).

270. See Ch. 12(C)(2)(a) above.

271. See Ch. 7(F)(5) above on service of process in connection with commencement of suit.

272. ZPO §183(1) and (3); for details see Ch. 7(F)(1)(d) above.

273. Hereinafter referred to as "the Hague Service Convention." The Convention is implemented within Germany by the Implementation Law for the Hague Convention on Service of Process Abroad of December 12, 1977(*Ausführungsgesetz zum Haager Übereinkommen über die Zustellung gerichtlicher und aussergerichtlicher Schriftstücke im Ausland in Zivil- und Handelssachen* or *AusfG*).

274. European Union Regulation No. 1348/2000, OJ L 160, 29/06/2000, p. 37 (hereinafter referred to as the "EU Service Regulation" or "Service Regulation"). The Service Regulation is currently implemented within Germany by the EU Service Regulation Implementation Law (*EG-Zustellungsdurchführungsgesetz* or *ZustDG*) of July 7, 2001, BGBl. I

respectively Germany is bound to provide assistance to other parties in accord with their terms and German courts and litigants have the benefit of their provisions for effecting valid service abroad.

In cases not covered by an international treaty or convention service of foreign process in Germany can proceed only by international comity. Absent an international treaty service of foreign process is limited to "unofficial service" (*formlose Zustellung*) upon a defendant willing to accept the papers as tendered. Compulsory service or substituted service is not available in the absence of international treaty.[275]

a. Service under the Hague Service Convention

The Hague Service Convention of 1965 covers service of process abroad in all forms of civil and commercial matters.[276] A party in a foreign state seeing to effect service of process in Germany must complete an application in a form prescribed by the Convention and forward the request to the Ministry of Justice for the German state in which service is to be effected.[277] The Ministry of Justice examines the application to determine whether execution of the request would harm the sovereignty or security of Germany. An applicant who

---

1536. According to the *Regierungsentwurf* (legislative proposal of the federal government) of April 9, 2003, which is likely to be adopted by the German parliament, the Implementation Law will be replaced by ZPO §§1067–1071. Together with proposed ZPO §§1072–1075 the provisions will form a new 11th title of the ZPO called "Judicial Cooperation within the European Union" (Justizielle Zusammenarbeit in der Europäischen Union). The provisions implementing the BRJE and the various Hague Conventions are not slated to be included in this new title.

275. See Regulation on Judicial Assistance in Civil Matters (*Rechtshilfeordnung in Zivilsachen* or *ZRHO*) §§68, 70(2); Schack, §13(III)(1), mn. 601. This regulation is not an EU Regulation, but rather a non-binding code of guidelines drafted by the Ministries of Justice of the individual states and the Federation. For details see Schack, §7(II), mn. 177.

276. Including civil claims for punitive damages. Even though German courts do, in principle, not recognize judgments awarding punitive damages (see Ch. 12(C)(2)(c) above), for purposes of service of process such actions are essentially "civil" and therefor service may be made under the Service Convention. See Court of Appeals of Düsseldorf, 45 *NJW* 3110 (1992) and Court of Appeals of München, 45 *NJW* 3113 (1992) affirmed by the Federal Constitutional Court, 48 *NJW* 649, 650 (1995); Stürner/Stadler, "Zustellung von "punitive damage" - Klagen an deutsche Beklagte nach dem Haager Zustellungsübereinkommen?", 10 *IPRax* 157 (1990); Juenger/Reimann, "Zustellung von Klagen auf punitive damages nach dem Haager Zustellungsübereinkommen", 47 *NJW* 3274 (1994). The same should be true for claims for multiple damages. For a very restrictive point of view see Merkt, *Abwehr der Zustellung von „punitive-damages"-Klagen* (1995).

277. Hague Service Convention, Article 3.

wishes to obtain official service (*förmliche Zustellung*) according to the requirements for such service in Germany must include a German translation of the documents to be served.[278] If unofficial service (*formlose Zustellung*) is sufficient no translation is required, but the person served is not required to accept the process and must be given the opportunity to take a look at the papers before deciding whether to accept them.[279]

The Ministry of Justice sends the papers to the court in the district where the defendant is located for the actual effectuation of service. The court then proceeds according to one of the methods authorized for service of process within Germany.[280] The return of service (*Zeugnis*) of the court is returned to the Ministry of Justice, which in turn forwards certification of completion of service to the requesting court or party. Germany has opted out of the provisions of the Hague Service Convention authorizing service of foreign process through the offices of the foreign consul or by mail.[281]

b. Service under the EU Service Regulation

Within the European Union service of foreign process is regulated by the EU Service Regulation of May 29, 2000.[282] This regulation parallels the basic scheme of the Hague Service Convention by which a Member State requested to effect service can designate a reception station for requests. It also allows individual states to opt out of direct service by parties or consular officials and to restrict service by mail.[283] Germany has designated the local courts as the reception stations for papers to be served within their respective districts.[284] Service by certified mail, return receipt requested, is allowed only if the doc-

---

278. Hague Service Convention, Article 5(3).

279. Hague Service Convention, Article 5(2); ZRHO §§67, 69. The consequences of rejection of papers unofficially served are primarily governed by the law of the jurisdiction in which the case is pending. If presentation of the papers to the defendant without acceptance suffices under that law, the defendant cannot safely reject such informal service, even if German law would not require acceptance. See Schack, §13(III)(2)(b), mn. 607. However noncompliance with the German standards of service of process might jeopardize recognition of any resulting judgment in Germany. See Ch. 12(C)(2)(a) above.

280. See Ch. 7(F) above for the permissible methods of service within Germany.

281. Implementation Law (*Ausführungsgesetz*) §6.

282. Germany has implemented the EU Service Regulation by the EU Service Implementation Law of July 9, 2001 (*EG-Zustellungsdurchführungsgesetz* or *ZustDG*). For a survey on service of process in Europe see Lindacher, "Europäisches Zustellungsrecht", 114 *ZZP* 179 (2001); Linke, "Die Probleme der internationalen Zustellung", in: Gottwald (ed.), *Grundfragen der Gerichtsverfassung - Internationale Zustellung* (1999), p. 95.

283. See European Service Regulation, Article 14(2).

284. ZustDG §4 (=ZPO-*Regierungsentwurf* §1069(2)).

ument is in the German language or the official language of the state of nationality of the addressee.[285]

c. *Substituted or Fictitious Service*

A recurrent problem with international service of process is the extent to which methods of substituted or fictitious service are to be recognized and implemented. In many cases in France a complaint against a non-resident defendant may be served on a local state's attorney who is deemed to be authorized to accept process for the absent defendant. At the request of the plaintiff the French court executor (*"huissier de la justice"*) is required to mail a copy of the papers to the defendant as well and to initiate parallel service under a convention or through diplomatic channels, but the service is in any event effective on delivery of the process to the official. This procedure, called *remise au parquet*, has caused some consternation in jurisdictions such as Germany where actual notification is considered a fundamental principle of fair judicial hearing.[286]

Until now the European Union has failed clearly to address the use of *remise au parquet* within a particular Member State, even when the defendant is a resident of another EU jurisdiction. To be sure, a default judgment which is not supported by actual notice and opportunity to defend need not be recognized or enforced by other Member States.[287] The terms of Article 19 of the European Service Regulation require that a judge stay a pending civil action against a foreigner for a limited time to allow the papers commencing the suit to be served on the defendant in accord with the law of the state of service.[288] Whether the provisions of the Service Regulation jeopardize the ongoing use of *remise au parquet* against foreigners is debated. If one takes the position that the notification which counts to initiate the suit is the notice to the designated official, and the notice to the absent party is only notice of the already perfected service in France, then this provision will not aid an absent defendant.[289] Both the EU Service Regulation and the Hague Service Convention

---

285. ZustDG §2 (=ZPO-*Regierungsentwurf* §1068(2)).

286. See Schack, §13 (III)(2), mn. 610; Geimer, Part 6 Chapter 1(XI), mn. 2092, 2093; Stürner, "Förmlichkeit und Billigkeit bei der Klagzustellung im Europäischen Zivilprozess", 47 *JZ* 325 (1992). Within the EU the *remise au parquet* might generally be considered offending EC Treaty Article 12(I) which provides that the Member States may not discriminate EU citizens of other Member States. See State Appeals Court of Karlsruhe, 45 *RIW* 538, 539 (1999).

287. See Ch. 12(C)(2)(a) above.

288. The Hague Service Convention Article 15 is similar.

289. See Schack, §13(III)(2)(b), mn. 609–612; Geimer, Part 6 Chapter 1(XI), mn. 2092–2093. Stürner, "Europäische Vollstreckung nach Zustellungsmängeln", in: Habscheid

permit an extraordinary appeal from a default judgment if actual notice did not reach the defendant. In such an appeal the defendant has the burden of showing that he had no actual knowledge of the commencement or pendency of the proceeding.[290]

d. Defects in Foreign Service

Under German procedural law defects in service of process are cured if the defendant actually receives the process and is able to act on it.[291] In general, if a defendant appears and does not contest service of process any defect in the service is waived.[292]

As a matter of principle the consequences of defective service of process for the ongoing proceeding are matters for the law of the state in which the case is pending, not the state in which service takes place. Thus, if foreign process is not correctly served in Germany, it is up to the foreign court to decide what, if any consequences flow from the failure. However, if the foreign judgment is to be recognized in Germany service should be adequate under German fundamental standards.[293]

There has been some debate about whether the general rule within Germany that defects of service of process will be cured upon actual receipt of the papers by the defendant applies to papers served abroad or to foreign papers served within Germany. Traditionally German case law has declined to apply the provisions of what is now ZPO §189 to cure defects in service of process abroad.[294] Some authors, however, argue that the policies supporting application of current ZPO §189 within Germany are equally pertinent to cases involving persons abroad, and that actual receipt of process abroad should cure defects in compliance with the technical requirements for international service.[295] On the other hand German doctrine regards service of process as an act of state. Especially direct service by mail may infringe foreign sovereignty if

(ed.), *Festschrift für Heinrich Nagel* (1987), p. 450 and with respect to the European Service Regulation Stadler, "Neues europäisches Zustellungsrecht", 21 *IPRax* 514, 517 (2001).

290. EU Service Regulation Article 19(4); Hague Service Convention Article 16.

291. ZPO §189.

292. ZPO §295.

293. See Ch. 12(C)(2)(a) above.

294. German Federal Supreme Court, 58 BGHZ 177 (1972); State Appeals Court of Hamm, 42 *RIW* 156 (1996). Current ZPO §189 was formerly ZPO §187. See Law on the Reform of the Service of Process of June 25, 2001 (*Zustellungsreformgesetz*), 2001 BGBl. 1206.

295. See, e.g., Schack, §13(IV), mn. 618–619; Geimer, Part 6 Chapter 2(IV), mn. 2102.

not permitted by foreign law or the foreign government. Infringements of international law cannot be cured by analogous application of German law construing ZPO §189 when well-established rules of international law or provisions of international conventions are lacking.

According to the European Court of Justice's construction of BRJE Article 34(2)[296] consequences of defective service are governed by the law of the deciding forum including international conventions. If the service of process does not meet the requirements of an international convention or the European Service Regulation, infringements of international or European law may only be cured by provisions and rules of international or European law. Where they are lacking national law cannot supplement international or European law by its own provisions to cure defects of service of process.[297] Insofar as international or European law makes references to the national law of the state where service is done,[298] provisions of national law may decide issues of defect service.[299] As a consequence direct service by mail or official service without translation cannot be cured and German courts will refuse to recognize and enforce American default judgments resulting out of defect service of process.

Within Europe Article 34(2) of the new Brussels Regulation may improve the opportunity to cure defect service. The European Court of Justice ruled under the old Article 27(2) of the Brussels Convention that proper service was an independent prerequisite of recognition of default judgments even when the defendant had actually received the process and was able to act on it in due time.[300] Furthermore the defendant was not obliged to appeal against the default judgment in the forum state in order not to lose his defense of improper service in the state of execution.[301] The wording of the new version of BRJE Article 34(2) overrules this severe point of view of the European Court of Justice liberalizing the strict requirements of proper service of process. The exact consequences of this change of European law are open.

---

296. Formerly Article 27(2) of the Brussels Convention; European Court of Justice, Case 305/88, Lancray v. Peters, 1990 ECR I 2725 (1990).

297. See Federal Supreme Court, 141 BGHZ 286, 302 ff. (1999); 120 BGHZ 305, 311 f. (1992); Stürner, 47 *JZ* 325 , 330 ff. (1992); Stürner/Bormann, 55 *JZ* 81, 87 (2000).

298. See Article 7(1) European Service Regulation; Article 5(1)(a) Hague Service Convention.

299. See Federal Supreme Court, 141 BGHZ 286, 302 ff., 303 (1999); Stürner/Bormann, 55 *JZ* 81, 87 (2000).

300. See European Court of Justice, Case 305/88, Lancray v. Peters, 1990 ECR I 2725 (1990).

301. European Court of Justice, Case 166/80, Klomps v. Michel, 1981 ECR 1593 (1981).

3. Provisional Measures to Secure Claims in Foreign Courts

Parties who are litigating in foreign courts may, under certain circumstances, make use of provisional measures such as attachment in Germany to secure foreign judgments that will be subject to recognition and execution in Germany. The procedures governing attachment in Germany make no distinction between domestic or foreign claimants. The requirement that the claim to be secured be one which can be reduced to a money judgment is satisfied by a foreign judgment recognizable in Germany.

A claimant who has a foreign action pending or contemplated, may apply to the attachment court (*Arrestgericht*) in Germany for attachment of property subject to its jurisdiction to secure the foreign judgment as recognizable in Germany.[302] On the other hand, the usual requirement that the application for attachment (*Arrestgesuch*) be brought in the court entertaining the case in chief can only be relaxed in favor of the court in which the property to be attached is located in "pressing cases" (*dringenden Fällen*).[303] The mere fact that the case in chief is pending in a foreign court would not be likely, by itself, to be a sufficiently pressing circumstance to justify proceeding in the local court where the property is located.[304]

A German court can entertain provisional measures to secure a judgment even when it may lack jurisdiction over the case in chief.[305] It is also argued that ZPO §917, which makes the prospect of execution outside the EU a sufficient ground for attachment in Germany applies not only to claims before German courts, but also to claims before courts in other states which will result in judgments recognizable in Germany.[306]

---

302. For the procedure on attachment and other provisional measures see Ch. 11(D) above.

303. ZPO §942.

304. See Schack, §8(VII)(2)(1), mn. 416.

305. See Geimer, Part 4 Chapter 8(XVIII), mn. 1203; Zöller/Vollkommer, §919. mn. 2; Schack, §8(VII)(2)(b), mn. 417–418. This is true even if another state's courts have exclusive jurisdiction over the claim in chief. Article 31 of the Brussels Regulation specifically authorizes application to "the courts of a Member State for such provisional, including protective, measures as may be available under the law of that State, even if, under this Regulation, the courts of another Member State have jurisdiction as to the substance of the matter." For recognition and enforcement see Ch. 12(C)(1) above.

306. See Schack, §8(VII)(2)(b), mn. 422.

If the claim is not pending in a German court or in some foreign court whose judgments are routinely recognized in Germany, the attachment court, on request of the defendant, can set a time within which the claim must be filed in a court which can issue a judgment that will be subject to recognition in Germany.[307] The court can also make an attachment subject to the creditor posting security for any damages that may be suffered by reason of the attachment.[308]

Provisional measures are frequently necessary in different kinds of family court proceedings which may involve international participants. Although the court can proceed expeditiously in such matters, generally it must have international jurisdiction of the parties or subject matter of the proceeding in order to render a provisional order.[309]

German courts may in appropriate cases enjoin persons subject to their jurisdiction from disposing of property located in other states *pendente lite*. However in practice preliminary attachment or other provisional measures in the jurisdiction where the affected property is located is the preferred course of action. As of the present time the so-called Mareva-injunction, or freezing order, in the sense of a negative restraint on foreign litigation enforced by contempt or other penalty, remains a creature of English jurisprudence and has found limited acceptance on the Continent.[310] Freezing orders are recognized and enforced by German courts against the litigating parties themselves, but generally not against third parties.[311]

4. Taking of Evidence for Use in Foreign Proceedings

Traditionally a state was under no obligation to compel persons within its jurisdiction to give evidence for use in foreign civil litigation. Efforts of the courts of a foreign state to obtain such evidence by any form of official means

307. ZPO §926. Stein/Jonas/Grunsky, §926, mn. 7; Zöller/Vollkommer, §926, mn. 10.

308. ZPO §921.

309. See Articles 2–8 of the new European Regulation on Jurisdiction, Recognition and Enforcement of Judgments in Family Matters.

310. For freezing orders see Dohmann, "Worldwide Mareva Injunction and the Enforcement of Foreign Judgments in England", in: P. Schlosser (ed.), *Materielles Recht und Prozessrecht - Recht der Internationalen Zwangsvollstreckung* (1992), p. 157; Zuckerman, "Mareva Injunctions and Security for Judgement...", 109 *L.Q.R.* 432 (1993); Stürner, "Einstweiliger Rechtsschutz", in: Storme (ed.), *Procedural Laws in Europe* (2003); pp. 143 ff., 163 ff.

311. See Court of Appeals of Karlsruhe, 1 *ZZP Int.* 91 (1996); Schack, §17 (3)(1)(f), mn. 823. One should keep in mind that provisional measures of a foreign court may be recognized only under the BRJE but not under German statute law. See Ch. 12(C)(1) above.

would be considered an affront to the sovereignty of the state in which such measures were carried out.[312] The only way such evidence could be obtained was through diplomatic channels, which in most cases proved to be a slow, expensive and unreliable route to the proof. Although ZPO §363 authorizes a German presiding judge to apply to the appropriate authority in a foreign state for a taking of evidence (*Aufnahme des Beweises*), in the absence of a treaty or other established cooperative relationship, it would be up to the officials of the foreign state to decide whether they would wish to cooperate.

This does not mean that courts are totally without power to gain access to proof located abroad. Parties to local proceedings can be required to produce documents within their possession, even though the documents may be located abroad.[313] A party with access to proof located abroad may be placed under an obligation to provide the proof on pain of an adverse decision on the affected issue.[314] Indeed, German nationals resident abroad remain subject to German jurisdiction and may be summoned by German courts to appear as witnesses in German proceedings without offending the sovereignty of the state in which they may be living or sojourning.[315] Witnesses who are foreign nationals living abroad may also be invited to give the testimony before a German consular official in their own country on a strictly voluntary basis as long as there is no threat of compulsion.[316] It is debated whether foreign witnesses may also be invited to come voluntarily to Germany to give their testimony in court. In practice German courts resort to the dubious solution of sending such invitations to foreign witnesses by ordinary mail in unmarked envelopes in order to avoid obvious conflict with the sovereignty of the foreign state.[317]

---

312. So, for example, a German judge could not travel uninvited to a foreign state to question a witness there, or even take a view of premises or things there that might be relevant to the decision of a German proceeding. See Schack, §15(VI)(1), mn. 709; Geimer, Part 8 Chapter 3(II)(1), mn. 2394; Bertele, *Souveränität*, pp. 404–518; Leipold, *Lex fori, Souveränität, Discovery* (1989), pp. 39 ff.; Stürner, "Die Gerichte und Behörden der U.S.A. und die Beweisaufnahme in Deutschland", 81 *Zeitschrift für vergleichende Rechtswissenschaft* 159, 211 (1982).

313. See Geimer, Part 3 Ch. 1(VII)(5), mn. 434; Stürner, in: Habscheid (ed.), *Justizkonflikt*, pp. 25 ff.

314. See Federal Supreme Court, 42 *JZ* 41 (1987) with note Stürner, p. 44; Stürner, in: Habscheid, *Justizkonflikt*, pp. 25 ff.

315. See Schack, §16(VI)(1)(b), mn. 715; Geimer, Part 3 Ch. 1(VII)(5), mn. 427.

316. See ZPO §363(2) (reception of evidence by the German consul); Federal Supreme Court, 37 *NJW* 2039 (1984); Schack, §16(VI)(1)(d), mn. 717.

317. For a very restrictive view see Federal Supreme Court, 37 *NJW* 2039 (1984) in which receipt of the written testimony of a witness in a foreign country without a letter of

The Hague Convention on Taking of Evidence Abroad[318] and the Brussels Regulation on Cooperation among the Courts of the Member States[319] have replaced the hazard and uncertainty of the traditional approaches to obtaining evidence abroad with procedures designed to afford easier access to foreign proof in most civil and commercial cases. As a party to the Hague Evidence Convention and as a Member State of the European Union subject to the Brussels Evidence Regulation Germany affords litigants in other states access to proof in Germany as authorized by these international arrangements. German litigants and courts can also make use of the Hague and Brussels Evidence procedures to obtain evidence from other signatories or Member States for use in German civil proceedings.[320]

---

request to the foreign authorities was regarded as an infringement of foreign sovereignty. See Stürner, in: Habscheid (ed.), *Justizkonflikt*, pp. 22 ff.

318. Hague Convention on Taking of Evidence Abroad in Civil and Commercial Matters of March 18, 1970. Hereinafter referred to as the "Hague Evidence Convention". The convention is implemented in Germany by §§7–14 of the Law Implementing the Hague Evidence Convention of December 22, 1977, BGBl. I, p. 3105 (*Ausführungsgesetz zum Haager Beweisübereinkommen [etc.]* or *AusfG*).

319. Brussels Regulation on Cooperation between the Courts of the Member States in the Taking of Evidence in Civil or Commercial Matters, European Union Regulation No. 1206/2001, OJ L 174, 28/05/2001, p. 1 (hereinafter referred to as the "Brussels Evidence Regulation" or "BER"). This Regulation shall apply from January 1, 2004. For a discussion see Hess/Müller, „Die Verordnung 1206/01/EG zur Beweisaufnahme im Ausland", 6 *ZZPInt* 149 (2001); Berger, "Die EG-Verordnung über die Zusammenarbeit der Gerichte auf dem Gebiet der Beweisaufnahme in Zivil- und Handelssachen (EuBVO)", 21 *IPRax* 522 (2001). According to the legislative proposal of the German federal government (*Regierungsentwurf*) of April 9, 2003, which is likely to be adopted by the German parliament, the BER will be implemented by ZPO §§1072–1075. Together with proposed ZPO §§1067–1071, the provisions will form a new 11th title of the ZPO called "Judicial Cooperation within the European Union" (*Justizielle Zusammenarbeit in der Europäischen Union*).

320. For a general discussion of the various methods of obtaining evidence located abroad see Stürner, "Die Gerichte und Behörden der U.S.A. und die Beweisaufnahme in Deutschland", 81 *Zeitschrift für vergleichende Rechtswissenschaft*, 159 (1982); Stürner, "Der Justizkonflikt zwischen U.S.A. und Europa", in: Habscheid (ed.), *Der Justizkonflikt mit den Vereinigten Staaten von Amerika* (1986), p. 3; P. Schlosser, *Der Justizkonflikt zwischen den U.S.A. und Europa* (1985); Junker, *Discovery im deutsch-amerikanischen Rechtsverkehr* (1987); Leipold, *Lex Fori, Souveränität, Discovery* (1989); Geimer, *Internationale Beweisaufnahme* (1998); Schabenberger, *Der Zeuge im Ausland im deutschen Zivilprozess* (1996); Mössle, *Extraterritoriale Beweisbeschaffung im internationalen Wirtschaftsrecht* (1990); Platto/Lee (eds.), *Obtaining Evidence in Another Jurisdiction in Business Disputes*, 2nd ed. (1993); Bertele, *Souveränität und Verfahrensrecht* (1998), pp. 404 ff.; Daoudi, *Extraterritoriale Beweisbeschaffung im deutschen Zivilprozess* (2000). A different problem is how evidence obtained through American pre-trial discovery may be used in German pro-

a. *Procedure for the Taking of Evidence Within the EU*

The Brussels Evidence Regulation is designed to provide a more or less seamless procedure by which a court in one Member State can seek the aid of a corresponding court in another Member State to obtain evidence from persons or things within its territorial jurisdiction for use in the requesting state. Within the EU the Brussels Evidence Regulation overrides the Hague Evidence Convention, to which most of the EU Member States are also parties.[321] The Regulation became effective July 1, 2001, but the procedures provided by the Regulation will not apply until January 1, 2004.[322]

The Brussels Evidence Regulation contemplates a procedure by which a "requesting court" of a Member State may lodge a direct request to a corresponding "requested court" of another Member State for assistance with the taking of evidence located within the jurisdiction of the requested court without having first to go through any central authority. The various Member States are required to prepare and exchange lists of courts capable of receiving evidence with descriptions of their respective jurisdictions.[323] Each Member State is also required to designate a "central authority" for dissemination of information among the courts of that state, addressing unusual and exceptional requests, and adjustment of difficulties.[324] Courts of a Member State are required to comply with requests for assistance only to the extent compatible with their own local law and procedure, and are not required to perform or permit activities that would be incompatible with local law or procedure. If

---

ceedings. See Eschenfelder, *Beweiserhebung im Ausland und ihre Verwertung im inländischen Zivilprozess: zur Bedeutung des US-amerikanischen Discovery-Verfahrens für das deutsche Erkenntnisverfahren* (2002).

321. BER Article 21(1). This does not prevent the Member States from concluding bilateral agreements providing for mutual assistance in the taking of evidence which are supplementary to and not incompatible with the Brussels Evidence Regulation. See Article 21. Because the BER is based on EC Treaty Article 65, Denmark is not bound by the Brussels Evidence Regulation.

322. BER Article 24(2).

323. BER Article 2(1) and (2). The lists are due on July 1, 2003. BER Article 22. In Germany, the local court (*Amtsgericht*) is designated as the corresponding court, where the taking of evidence will take place. See ZPO-Regierungsentwurf §1074(1).

324. BER Article 3. The designations are due by July 1, 2003, BER Article 22. In Germany, each state government determines the state's "central authority." ZPO-Regierungsentwurf §1074(3). It is probable that the ministries of justice in the various German states, currently designated as the coordinating authorities for requests for the taking of evidence under the Hague Evidence Convention, will be designated as the central authorities under the Evidence Regulation.

the evidence is not made available on a voluntary basis, the requested court is expected to employ such coercive measures as are offered by its regular procedures to obtain the evidence.[325]

The procedure is simple. Requests may be made only in connection with "judicial proceedings, commenced or contemplated."[326] A court desiring assistance in another Member State may simply request a court of the other state which has the evidence within its jurisdiction to receive the evidence in its behalf.[327] The request must comply with an official form and be set forth in the language of the requested court.[328] The request may seek that a witness be examined concerning a particular described subject matter or by specified questions. Request may also be made for production of documentary evidence or examination of a person or place as evidence for the requesting court.[329] The requesting court may specify special procedures for the reception of evidence, such as the administration of an oath, which are to be followed to the extent not incompatible with local proof-taking law or practice.[330] If the reception of evidence will involve special costs, such as for an expert opinion or for a special procedure requested, the requesting court may be asked to arrange for advance reimbursement of the costs.[331]

An important feature of the BER is the right of the parties and representatives of the requesting court to be present at the taking of evidence by the requested court.[332] The requesting court must designate the representatives and request that their presence and participation in the evidentiary proceeding be permitted. The requested court then advises the requesting court of the time

325. BER Articles 10(2) and 13.

326. BER Article 1(2).

327. BER Article 2(1). If the requested court does not have jurisdiction of the evidence sought, the request is to be forwarded to the court in the requested Member State that does have jurisdiction. BER Article 7(2).

328. For requests from other Member States see ZPO-Regierungsentwurf §1075.

329. BER Article 4.

330. BER Article 10(3).

331. In general Member States may not charge fees for reception of foreign evidence, BER Article 18(1). Advances of costs for expert testimony may be required. Costs are allocated among, advanced by, and taxed to the parties to the case in accord with the law of the requesting state in which the case is pending. BER Article 18(2) and (3).

332. BER Article 12. The requesting court can designate judicial personnel or others, such as experts, as its representatives, Article 12(3). For the arrangements that will obtain when German courts are the requesting court see ZPO-Regierungsentwurf §1073(1). According to the legislative proposal only the court or one of its members may be designated as representatives. Parties and experts would be permitted to participate in the way they could within Germany.

and place at which the evidence will be taken and the conditions under which the parties or representatives of the requesting court may participate. These conditions are governed by local law.[333]

If a person whose evidence is sought claims a valid privilege under the law of either the requesting state or the requested state, the requested court will not take the evidence. The applicability of a privilege of the requesting state may be determined in consultation with the requesting court.[334] Otherwise the only grounds for refusal to take the evidence requested are inapplicability of the Brussels Evidence Regulation to the matter at issue, incompleteness of the request, or incompatibility of the request with the judicial function of the requested state.[335]

The Brussels Evidence Regulation sets specific time deadlines by which the requested court is to respond to the request and within which the evidence is to be taken. The use of the phrases "without delay" and "by the swiftest possible means" indicates the legislative intent that the effect of the new Regulation should be to speed a process that has traditionally been associated with delay.[336] Responses to requests for the taking of evidence are due within 7 days of receipt and the requests are to be executed, at the latest, within 90 days of receipt.[337]

The Brussels Evidence Regulation has also introduced a new procedure by which a requesting court may ask for permission to receive the evidence itself in the requesting state. The evidence requested must be available on a voluntary basis, without the need for compulsion.[338] Such requests are to be processed through the central body authority of the requested state and are to be granted in the ordinary course unless the request is "contrary to fundamental principles of law" of the requested state.[339] The evidence may be re-

333. BER Article 12(4) and (5).

334. BER Article 14(1).

335. BER Article 14(2). Issues of competitive exclusive international jurisdiction between the states of the requesting and requested courts are not sufficient grounds for refusal to honor a request for taking of evidence. BER Article 14(3).

336. See BER Articles 6, 10(1).

337. BER Articles 7(1), 10(1). These time periods are extended if there is need for advance payment of costs or if the request is not complete and must be completed. See Articles 8 and 9.

338. BER Article 17(2). Any person to be examined as a witness must be reminded that the proceedings are voluntary. If compulsion is required to obtain the evidence, then the evidence must be taken by the courts of the state which exercises the compulsion.

339. BER Article 17(1), (4) and (5). The central authority of the requested state has 30 days to respond to the request.

ceived by a judicial officer of the requesting state or by a person designated by the court such as a court-appointed expert.[340] Procedures for receiving the evidence must be compatible with the law of the requested state. The requested state may also assign one of its own judges to attend and take part in the evidentiary proceedings in order to assure that local law is followed.[341] The evidence may be recorded by any means deemed sufficient by the requesting state and not incompatible with procedures of the requested state.

The Brussels Evidence Regulation also encourages the Member States to make use of electronic information technology not only for the transmission of requests and other inter-court communications, but also for the actual reception of evidence. For instance, a court in Germany can take evidence in another EU state for use in a German proceeding by teleconference or video-conference if facilities and the law of the other Member State permit.[342]

b. *Procedure under the Hague Convention on the Taking of Evidence Abroad*

Procedures for taking evidence under the Hague Evidence Convention[343] are somewhat more complicated and time-consuming than under the Brussels Regulation.[344] Courts of states which are parties to the Hague Convention may obtain assistance of German courts for the taking of evidence for use in foreign proceedings by filing an application for such assistance with the Ministry of Justice of the German state in which the evidence is to be received.[345]

340. BER Article 17(3). A German court may designate one of its members or a court-appointed expert to take the evidence abroad. See ZPO-Regierungsentwurf §1073(2).

341. BER Article 17(4).

342. BER Article 17(4).

343. The Convention will continue to govern within the EU until the procedures spelled out by the new Brussels Evidence Regulation are in force on January 1, 2004 and for Denmark and non-EU signatory states thereafter.

344. For a detailed analysis see Junker, *Discovery im deutsch-amerikanischen Rechtsverkehr* (1987), pp. 212–361 and pp. 405–422; Pfeil-Kammerer, *Deutsch-amerikanischer Rechtshilfeverkehr in Zivilsachen* (1987), pp. 171–394; Junker, "Der deutsch-amerikanische Rechtshilfeverkehr in Zivilsachen", 45 *JZ* 121 (1989); Paulus, "Discovery, deutsches Recht und das Haager Beweisübereinkommen", 104 *ZZP* 397 (1991); Stürner, "Rechtshilfe nach dem Haager Beweisübereinkommen für Common Law Länder", 37 *JZ* 521 (1981).

345. Hague Evidence Convention Article 2. Germany has designated the Ministries of Justice of the respective German states as the "central authorities" for the processing of requests for taking of evidence under the Hague Evidence Convention in their state courts.

The source of evidence must be accurately identified and the subject matter of the testimony clearly spelled out.[346]

The Ministry of Justice screens the requests for compliance with the Convention and compatibility with German law. Requests can be denied only if they would compromise German sovereignty or security or if the execution of the request would not be considered a judicial function in Germany.[347] If the request is found to be in order, the Ministry of Justice forwards it to the appropriate German court for the actual taking of the evidence. Since the Hague Convention also envisions that the parties or the requesting court may wish to be present at and participate in the taking of proof, the German court to which the request is referred must notify the requesting court of the time and place at which the evidence will be received so that the parties, their representatives or requesting court officials may attend and participate in the evidentiary proceedings.[348]

Although the court taking the evidence pursuant to a Hague Convention request is expected to use its customary measures of compulsion to obtain testimony, document production, etc., any privileges of the witness under the law of Germany or under the law of the requesting state must be honored.[349] Usually the form of testimony will follow that observed in German proceedings, but special formalities (such as administration of an oath or provision of a verbatim transcript) may be requested and will be observed if they do not conflict with German law.[350]

The Hague Evidence Convention also authorizes a procedure whereby foreign litigants can obtain evidence through their own consular offices in Germany.[351] A consul of a signatory state may take the evidence of its own

---

346. Hague Evidence Convention Article 3. If desired the precise questions to be posed to the witness may be set forth in the request. The request must be in the language of the requested state or in English or French unless the requested state has stated its unwillingness to receive requests in English or French, Article 4.

347. Hague Evidence Convention Article 12. In particular a signatory cannot deny the request of another signatory on the ground that the requested court has exclusive jurisdiction of the controversy for which the evidence is requested or that the requested state would not recognize the cause of action asserted in the proceeding.

348. See Hague Evidence Convention Articles 7, 8.

349. See Hague Evidence Convention Articles 10 and 11; Schack, §15(VI)(2)(c), mn. 728.

350. Hague Evidence Convention Article 9(2). For procedures for the taking of evidence under German law, some of which may not be the same as under American law, see Ch. 6(D)(1) (minutes of hearings), Ch. 7(L) (preparatory proceedings), Ch. 8(C)(7)(b) and (c) (expert testimony) and Ch. 8(C)(9)(a) (ordinary witness testimony).

351. Hague Evidence Convention Articles 15–18.

nationals within Germany so long as the evidence can be obtained without compulsion.[352]

A foreign consul may also take the voluntary evidence of German nationals and nationals of states other than his own if specifically authorized by a German state Ministry of Justice.[353] Fear of compromise of sovereignty has led Germany and many other countries to allow little use of this provision.[354] Currently Germany only permits consular officials of foreign states to receive evidence from nationals of their own states, not from German nationals or nationals of third countries.[355]

Finally, the Hague Evidence Convention authorizes the court of a signatory state to appoint a commissioner to go to another state to receive evidence if the evidence can be obtained without compulsion, provided that the foreign state has given either generalized or case-specific permission. Such a procedure can be useful if evidence is needed by an expert witness. Whether a judge of the court seeking the evidence should be appointed a commissioner to go and receive it in another jurisdiction is subject to some debate.[356] Germany has not given blanket permission for this activity and it can be assumed that individual permission would be rarely, if ever, granted.[357]

A signatory state may expressly authorize a consular official or a commissioner seeking evidence abroad to apply to the central authority of another signatory state (in Germany the Ministry of Justice of each state) for assistance in providing the evidence by compulsion. Such requests must be either generally or individually agreed to by the requested state.[358] Germany has not expressed its willingness to cooperate with such requests in any general regulation, presumably on the ground that the court-to-central authority route is sufficient to obtain compelled testimony. For the same reason it does not appear likely that cooperation would be forthcoming in response to individual requests from consuls or commissioners.

---

352. Hague Evidence Convention Article 15. A signatory state may condition this practice on receipt of permission from the host state.

353. Hague Evidence Convention Article 16.

354. See Law Implementing the Hague Evidence Convention (*Ausführungsgesetz zum Haager Beweisübereinkommen über die Beweisaufnahme in Zivil- und Handelssachen* or *AusfG)* §§11, 12.

355. See Hague Evidence Convention Articles 15, 16; Schack, §16(VI)(2)(c), mn. 731–733; Geimer, Part 3 Chapter 1(VII)(15), mn. 452.

356. See Schack, §15(VI)(2)(c), mn. 732.

357. See Law Implementing the Hague Evidence Convention § 12.

358. Hague Evidence Convention Articles 18, 19.

c. *German-American Issues Relating to the Taking of Evidence Abroad*

The Hague Evidence Convention was created to facilitate the conduct of civil law judicial proceedings for the reception of evidence[359] as well as the presentation of evidence at Anglo-American "trials." It was not originally designed to assist American-style pretrial discovery proceedings which are sometimes of extremely broad scope. Pretrial discovery, as it is known in the United States, is not a characteristic feature of German civil procedure and in some cases can contravene German public policy concerning the privacy of individuals and their business and personal affairs.[360] Indeed, Article 23 of the Hague Evidence Convention gives individual signatory states the option to opt out of the Convention with respect to requests to obtain pretrial discovery of documents as known in common law states. Germany and most of the other civil law signatories of the Convention have opted under Article 23 to deny or limit the use of the Convention by American litigants seeking document discovery.[361]

Contrary to the expectations of some of the European parties to the Convention, American litigants have been able in many cases directly to obtain pretrial discovery of documents and other evidence abroad. This has occurred despite the contrary policy of jurisdictions such as Germany, where such discovery can be seen as burdensome on parties, witnesses and the sov-

359. See Ch. 8(C) above.

360. See Ch. 7(L) above. German citizens enjoy a constitutional right of personal privacy (*Allgemeines Persönlichkeitsrecht*) derived from Articles 1 and 2 of the German Constitution. See Federal Constitutional Court, 53 *NJW* 1021 (2000). Any obligation to appear and argue in court may affect this right of privacy. German law of civil procedure attempts to limit the burden of being a party or witness in private disputes through the requirement of fact pleading and strict control of relevance. See Ch. 7(A)(4) and (L). For a detailed discussion see Stürner, *Die Aufklärungspflicht der Parteien des Zivilprozesses* (1975), §9, pp. 106 ff.; §13, pp. 193 ff. For fishing expeditions as a possible infringement of German "public order" Federal Supreme Court, 118 BGHZ 312, 323 f. (1992); Stiefel/Stürner, 38 *VersR* 829, 830 (1987). For a detailed analysis of the differing concepts of American and German protection of trade and business secrets see Stadler, *Der Schutz des Unternehmensgeheimnisses im deutschen und U.S.-amerikanischen Zivilprozess und im Rechtshi feverfahren* (1989); Kersting, *Der Schutz des Wirtschaftsgeheimnisses im Zivilprozess* (1995)

361. See German Law Implementing the Hague Evidence Convention §12. German Central Authorities may permit discovery of documents when the letter of request demands production of individually specified documents to prove contested facts which are strictly relevant to the case. Stürner, 81 *Zeitschrift für vergleichende Rechtswissenschaft* 159, 201 (1982); Junker, *Discovery*, pp. 296 f.; P. Schlosser, 101 *ZZP* 327, 330 f. (1988). No regulation of the Federal Ministry of Justice (Implementation Law §12(2)) has yet been enacted although many drafts have been proposed.

ereignty of foreign jurisdictions. The global economy has meant that many German entities are subject to the wide ranging international jurisdiction asserted by the American civil justice system. A German person or firm forced to litigate in the United States, either as plaintiff or defendant, is subject to the procedural regimen of the American court in which he finds himself. American courts assert the authority to require litigants to cooperate with discovery requests regardless of where the evidence sought may be found. Thus a German corporation which is party to a case in a United States court may be required to agree to depositions of its employees in Germany and to make production of documents or other evidence under its control in Germany, even though such procedures would be unavailable in domestic German litigation. A German litigant may even be required to disclose information which is privileged under German law but not protected under the law of the American jurisdiction that is the forum of the controversy. Non-compliance may result in discovery sanctions such as issue preclusion, costs awards, dismissal or default on claims, or in some cases contempt.[362]

The claim that pretrial discovery of documents and witness evidence abroad should take place solely under the Hague Evidence Convention was rejected by the United States Supreme Court in *Societe Nationale Industrielle Aérospatiale v. U.S. District Court.*[363] There the United States Supreme Court stated that American litigants are not relegated to the Hague Convention as the sole or even first means of obtaining evidence abroad. According to *Aérospatiale*, they can make use of other techniques to compel foreign litigants and persons subject to the jurisdiction of American courts to provide discovery that can not be had under the auspices of the Convention. The trial court must determine on a case by case basis whether a discovery measure would affront international comity or unfairly burden a foreign national or institution.

---

362. For a documentation of the described development see Stürner, 81 *Zeitschrift für Vergleichende Rechtswissenschaft*, 159 (1982); Stürner, in: Habscheid (ed.), *Justizkonflikt*, p. 3; Stürner, *Why are Europeans afraid to litigate in the United States?* (2001); P. Schlosser, *Der Justizkonflikt zwischen den USA und Europa* (1985).

363. 482 U.S. 522 (1987). A minority concurring opinion by Blackmun, Brennan, Marshall, O'Connor suggested that discovery under the Hague convention should be a rule of first resort. See Wright/Miller/Marcus, 8 *Federal Practice and Procedure*, 2nd ed., §2005.1. Among the numerous notes see Born, 57 *Law & Contemp. Probs.* 77 and from a European perspective Stürner, 42 *JZ* 988 (1987). For recent developments see Chalmers, 8 *Tul. J. Int.'l & Comp. L.* 189 (2000). For a comprehensive analysis of the application of American law to conduct outside the USA see Dodge, "Extraterritoriality and Conflict-of-Laws Theory: An Argument for Judicial Unilateralism", 39 Harv. Int'l L.J. 101 (1998).

This assertion of the "hegemony of American law" (*amerikanische Rechtshegemonie*)[364] has caused European jurisdictions including Germany to consider retaliatory measures aimed at curbing or frustrating extraterritorial effect of discovery measures in U.S.[365] Some commentators, however, suggest a less confrontational approach based on a possible amendment of the Hague Evidence Convention or some bilateral agreement to restrict extra-territorial discovery of evidence and documents in the hands of persons or entities not parties to the litigation while recognizing the reality that the actual parties to a case in the United States civil justice system will be required to abide by the rules of that system.[366]

d. Obtaining Foreign Evidence outside the EU and the Hague Evidence Convention for Use in German Proceedings

Most cases in which foreign evidence is required in a German civil proceeding can proceed under the Hague Evidence Convention or the Brussels Evidence Regulation. However these are not the exclusive means for German courts to obtain evidence in foreign states for use in German proceedings. As indicated above, witnesses resident in foreign states may be invited to appear at hearings for the taking of evidence in Germany, although their attendance may not be compelled.[367] Witnesses in foreign states not parties to the Hague

---

364. For this term see Stürner, in: *Der Justizkonflikt mit den Vereinigten Staaten von Amerika*, pp. 5 ff., 35 ff.

365. Blocking statutes of the European Union (Regulation Nō. 2271/96 of November 22, 1996, OJ L 309, 29/11/1996, p. 1) and of some Member States such as Great Britain and France forbid persons subject to American discovery in Europe from giving testimony not required by international treaty and provide "claw back" clauses in case of enforcement of punitive and multiple damages awards in the U.S. For a survey see Stürner, in: *Justizkonflikt*, pp. 27 f.; Grossfeld, *Internationales und Europäisches Unternehmensrecht*, 2nd ed. (1995), pp. 270 ff. (includes sample statutes); Schack, § 15, mn. 743; Geimer, Part 1 Chapter 5(I)(11), mn. 176; Bertele, *Souveränität*, pp. 518–547. Some authors discuss anti-suit injunctions; see Stürner, in: *Justizkonflikt*, pp. 30 f., 50 ff.; Schröder, "The Right not to be Sued Abroad", in: *Festschrift für Kegel* (1987), p. 523; Spiekhoff, "Die Klage im Ausland als Delikt im Inland", in: *Festschrift für Deutsch* (1999), p. 327; Krause-Ablass/Bastuck, "Deutsche Klagen zur Abwehr amerikanischer Prozesse?", in Lutter et al. (eds.), *Festschrift für Stiefel* (1987), p. 445.

366. See, e.g. Schack, §15(6)(3), mn. 744–745; Stürner, in: *Justizkonflikt*, pp. 43 ff.

367. For the prevailing opinion see Zöller/Greger, §377, mn. 1a. According to this view witnesses can also be requested to provide their testimony by written answers to questions posed by the court, again without threat of compulsion. ZPO §377(3). See Schack, §15(VI)(2)(b), mn. 720–721. But see the very restrictive point of view of the Federal Supreme Court, 37 *NJW* 2039 (1984) and Stadler, in: K. Schmidt (ed.), *50 Jahre Bundesgerichtshof: Festgabe aus der Wissenschaft*, Vol. III (2000), p. 645, 657.

Evidence Convention may give their testimony voluntarily to the German consul.[368] The German court can also follow the traditional route of requesting assistance from the foreign court system through diplomatic channels.[369] If such assistance is required the party designating such proof can be taxed with the job of preparing the necessary forms and documents to make the official request and with arranging the logistics of receiving the proof in the foreign jurisdiction.[370]

One can conceive of circumstances in which a German court can, in effect, require extra-territorial production of evidence by a party or even a witness associated with a party by advising the party of the consequences of failure to meet its burden of proof in its absence.[371] Such an exercise of indirect compulsion abroad by a court seeking evidence to make a fact finding in a judicial proceeding is not to be compared with the extra-territorial imposition of discovery obligations by parties to American litigation which has caused so much offense in civil law jurisdictions.

---

368. See Ch. 12(E)(4)(b) above on consular evidence under the Hague Evidence Convention.

369. See ZPO §363.

370. ZPO §364. The party designating the evidence (*Beweisführer*) is also required to advise the opponent of the time and place for taking the evidence if known.

371. Schack, §15(VI)(2)(b), mn. 722. Such a measure would most likely be employed if the party which has a degree of practical control over the evidence also has the burden of proof on the issue to which the evidence was relevant. If the party which has control over the evidence does not bear the burden of proof, German courts ordinarily would expect the opposing party to resort to the convention and would not exert any pressure of this kind to require such a party to make the absent witness available. See Federal Supreme Court, 42 *JZ* 41 (1987) with critical note Stürner, p. 44 (medical examination of a party in a foreign country, which has the burden of proof—power of the court to draw negative inferences in case of refusal is independent from the burden of proof).

CHAPTER 13

Some Comparative Observations

The primary purpose of this work has been to explain and analyze to an English-speaking readership the workings of modern Germany's system of civil justice, its legal structure, its participants, its rules and institutions as well as the way these elements function together to provide German litigants with legal adjudication of civil disputes. For this reason the authors have generally resisted the temptation to insert comparative observations at a number of points in the text where many readers would welcome comparative analysis. This book is primarily about the German civil justice system as a system, not how it compares with other justice systems in the modern world.

At the same time the experience of researching and writing this work has built on the authors' previous comparative law knowledge and experience. It would be wrong to close this volume without some discussion of the authors' impressions of the German civil justice system and some of its key elements in comparison with certain aspects of the Anglo-American system of civil justice, with which both authors are also familiar. Our final words will address the process of convergence among the German, other Western European, and the American civil justice system at the beginning of the 21st Century.

A. The Comparative Law Framework

Fruitful and effective comparison of law and legal institutions requires a certain discipline. Although it may be tempting to compare individual elements which have apparent similarity of form or function, such comparisons are of limited validity unless one first gives thought to the overall purposes which the system purports to serve and then to the role the element under comparison plays in conjunction with other elements of the system to achieve those purposes.[1]

It is now clear that the public policy role of civil justice within various modern democratic political economies varies to a considerable extent. The degree to which implementation of various important public policy objectives is consigned to private civil justice differs considerably between most Western European states and the United States of America. The particular social assignments of civil justice are not the same. Some countries rely on governmental and administrative initiatives to accomplish what others leave to privately initiated civil litigation. The degree of relative involvement of governmental institutions and private legal action may also differ among different states and systems.

For example, in the United States relatively weak governmental regulation of such matters as consumer product safety is complemented by a strong and vigorous civil litigation system that permits private litigants to hold manufacturers liable for damage caused by their products and thus incidentally deter them from the manufacture and sale of unsafe products. On the other hand, in Europe stronger governmental regulation of consumer product safety may reduce the need for private litigation to accomplish the same public purpose. Thus before one can compare the performance of a legal institution or any element thereof, one must ascertain what purposes the institution is expected to accomplish within the overall political economy of which it is a part.[2]

Within any system of law or justice one must also be careful about comparing individual elements of the system without sufficient consideration of the system as a whole. A policy that is accomplished by a particular element of one system may be addressed by a totally different element in another. Thus, when comparing how one system implements a particular policy of

---

1. Stressing the need to respect the even larger context of overall national culture, e.g., Chase, "American 'Exceptionalism' and Comparative Procedure", 50 *Am. J. Comp. L.* 277 (2002); Taruffo, "Transcultural Dimensions of Civil Justice", 23 *Comparative L. Rev.* 1 (2000). See also Stürner/Stadler, "Eigenarten der Prozessrechtsvergleichung - Special Features of Comparative Procedural Law", in: Gilles (ed.), *Transnationales Prozessrecht, Deutsche Landesberichte zur Weltkonferenz für Prozessrecht* (1995), pp. 263, 271 ff.; Stürner, "Procedural Law and Legal Cultures", in Gilles (ed.), *Prozessrecht und Rechtskulturen. XII World Conference of Procedural Law, Mexico City 2003* (2004).

2. This does not mean that one cannot discuss the relative efficacy of entrusting various social, political or economic policies to different private and public agencies and institutions. This kind of discussion is an aspect of the ongoing process of comparing political and social institutions in general.

civil justice, one must be sure to consider how the system functions as a whole to implement the policy, not how a particular element functions in comparison with other systems. In the words of a leading American comparatist,

> [E]ach system functions as a whole. Its general tendencies depend on the interaction in concrete situations of all of the elements discussed...Only after analyzing for each system the full range of historical, institutional and social facts here considered, can comparative generalizations be offered.[3]

For instance, in considering relative access to justice, it would not suffice to compare fee shifting in Germany with the "American rule" and the contingency fee system without taking into consideration the availability of legal aid in both systems as well as the cost to litigate in general. For this reason we believe that comparative observations belong at the end, not the beginning, of a comprehensive analysis of the entire system. To the extent that individual elements of a system are taken out for individualized comparison, one must keep in mind their context and other elements which complement them in this sense.[4]

Within the overall purposes to be accomplished by a civil justice system, one can identify several functions by which those purposes are accomplished. These functions appear to be more or less inherent in the concept of civil justice as it is known throughout the modern world. Reports and questionnaires in comparative studies of national civil justice systems are often structured around several principal functions or issues deemed fundamental to the process and institutions of civil justice.[5] While observers can differ as to the precise description of different functions of a civil justice system, there is general agreement as to many of the principle ones. Comparison of the way in

---

3. Von Mehren, "The Judicial Process: A Comparative Analysis", 5 *Am. J. Comp. L. 197* (1956). See also, Zweigert/Kötz, *An Introduction to Comparative Law, 3rd ed.* (1998), pp. 33 ff.; Rabel, *Aufgabe und Notwendigkeit der Rechtsvergleichung* (1925), reprinted in Rabel, *Gesammelte Aufsätze III* (1967). For a good survey on the most recent development of comparative law as a body of knowledge see Reimann, "The Progress and Failure of Comparative Law in the Second Half of the Twentieth Century", 50 *Am. J. Comp. L. 671* (2002).

4. See, e.g., von Mehren, *Law in the United States* (1988), pp. 83–104 (Comparison of role of consideration and offer and acceptance in contract doctrine).

5. See, e.g., Zuckerman, "Justice in Crisis: Comparative Dimensions of Civil Procedure", in: Zuckerman (ed.), *Civil Justice in Crisis* (1999), pp. 3–52; Snijders (ed.), *Access to Civil Procedure Abroad* (1996), pp. 1–24 ; Fazzalari (ed.), *Civil Justice in the Countries of the European Union* (1998).

which various systems accomplish these identified functions has become the method of comparative civil procedure law.[6]

After considering the respective purposes and roles of civil justice within German and Anglo-American political, economic and social culture, we compare the functional performance of the German civil justice system in accomplishing purposes which are common to both systems. These are in large part the adjudication of disputes between private parties by public process based on public norms. The functions we have chosen to compare are

1. Maintaining independence and credibility of the judicial institution;
2. Providing litigants with high quality determinations of fact and law;
3. Guaranteeing litigants procedural and systemic fairness;
4. Producing final enforceable decisions without undue delay and at reasonable cost;
5. Affording litigants reasonably free access to justice;
6. Contributing positively to the development and explication of the law;
7. Generating among litigants and the overall population confidence and satisfaction in civil justice and the rule of law.

The functions we have chosen are among those underlying the Principles of Transnational Civil Procedure currently under joint study by the American Law Institute and Unidroit.[7] We have attempted to condense the essence of some 31 principles from the ALI/Unidroit list into 5 of the 7 functions identified above and have added two others (Nos. 6 and 7 above) which seem of significance to the authors.[8]

It is possible to conceptualize and break down the civil litigation process even more systematically for comparative study.[9] While acknowledging the value of further systematic categorization for some purposes, we have chosen

---

6. For a discussion of this method see Zweigert/Kötz, § 3 II, pp. 33 ff.; Rheinstein, *Einführung in die Rechtsvergleichung*, 2nd ed. (1987), pp. 27 f.

7. See American Law Institute and UNIDROIT, *Principles and Rules of Transnational Civil Procedure* (Council Draft No. 2 of September 29, 2003, www.ali.org. Professor Stürner is the UNIDROIT Reporter for this project.

8. Of course there is bound to be overlap between categories in any list of functions or principles. For instance issues of cost, and delay clearly impact on access to justice, judicial independence is an aspect of procedural fairness, etc.

9. See, e.g., Gerber, "Comparing Procedural Systems: Toward an Analytical Framework", in: Nafziger et al. (ed.), *Law and Justice in a Multistate World; Essays in Honor of Arthur T. von Mehren* (2002), p. 665.

the loose functional categories mentioned above as a reasonable balance between the "forest" and the "trees" of civil justice systems.[10]

B. The Purposes and Roles of Civil Justice in Germany and the United States

As already discussed in Chapter 6 above, the primary purpose of institutions of civil justice in German political and economic culture is the fair, accurate and efficient vindication of private rights and interests based on the existing legal, political and social order.[11] This purpose is clearly also served by civil litigation in the courts of the United States and of practically every modern political economy.

In Germany litigation in the ordinary courts is generally not considered as a substitute or even a supplement for public regulation of economic and social actors such as manufacturers or public officials except to the extent that such regulation has been embodied in private rights.[12] On the other hand, in the United States the system of private civil justice is seen as an important element in the effective regulation of social and economic actors such as manufacturers of products, public officials, issuers of securities, environmental polluters, and the like.[13] Class actions and jury trials have been seen as im-

---

10. From the old proverb, "One must not lose sight of the forest for the trees."

11. See Ch. 6(A) above. Although in large part the parties are expected to understand their own interests and conduct the litigation with those interests in mind, the state also has an interest that the litigation proceed in a fair and accurate manner so that the law is appropriately construed and enforced. This conception of the civil justice system as an "arm of social aid" (*Glied sozialer Hilfe*) was developed during the 19th Century in Germany and was advanced by Franz Klein, the famous Austrian civil procedure scholar, at the turn of the 20th Century. It retains influence in Germany and many other jurisdictions. See, e.g., Wassermann, *Der soziale Zivilprozess* (1978), pp. 52–68; Damrau, "Der Einfluss der Ideen Franz Kleins auf den deutschen Zivilprozess", in: Hofmeister (ed.), *Forschungsband Franz Klein* (1988), p. 157, as to Germany and Cappelletti, "Social and Political Aspects of Civil Procedure—Reforms and Trends in Western and Eastern Europe", 69 *Mich. L. Rev.* 847, as to Europe as a whole.

12. On the other hand litigation in the Administrative Court (*Verwaltungsgericht*) does play an important role in keeping public officials accountable and their actions within legal and constitutional bounds.

13. See, e.g., Viscusi (ed.), *Regulation Through Litigation* (2002); Kagan, *Adversarial Legalism* (2001), pp. 18–25; Burbank/Silberman, "Civil Procedure Reform in Comparative Context: The United States of America", 45 *Am. J. Comp. Law* 675, 692 (1997); Damaska,

portant tools by which private litigants keep such actors "in line" with the public interest and public priorities.[14]

While it is acknowledged in Germany that ordinary civil litigation does often implement public policies affecting the interests of persons other than the parties, civil litigation is not conceived as an instrument to effect important public policy goals. "Public interest litigation" in the ordinary courts is more the exception than the rule.[15] On the other side of the Atlantic for at least a generation representative parties and public interest organizations have made aggressive use of the courts to implement goals that redound not to the benefit of a private party but to the interest of the public, or at least a cognizable subset thereof. Such litigation sometimes results in protective priorities different from those established by legally responsible public agencies. Although the intensity and effectiveness of such litigation has varied, its impact cannot be gainsaid.

Germany has an efficient and widespread system of medical care insurance and social welfare. Civil justice is not considered the primary means for persons who sustain personal injuries to obtain medical care and economic support. In the United States health insurance, unemployment insurance, and other forms of social welfare protection are considerably less adequate and far from universal. This means that often civil litigation is an injured person's sole hope to obtain funds for medical care or economic support.[16]

The Faces of Justice and State Authority (1986), pp. 71 ff., 98 ff.; Herbert Jacob et al. (eds.), *Courts, Law and Politics in Comparative Perspective* (1996).

14. This role of civil justice has been seen as one of the important reasons for retention of the institution of civil jury trial in the United States. See Adler, *The Jury* (1994), pp. 215–217; Stürner, *Why Are Europeans Afraid to Litigate in the United States?* (2001), pp. 16 ff., 18. For a discussion of the "privatization" of the enforcement of public norms and public policy by civil litigation and the class action mechanisms starting in the 1960s see Fiss, "The Political Theory of the Class Action", 53 *Wash. & Lee L. Rev.* 21 (1996); Resnik, "Money Matters: Judicial Market Interventions Creating Subsidies and Awarding Fees and Costs in Individual and Aggregate Litigation", 148 *UPA L.Rev.* 2119, 2144 ff. (2000); Sherman, "Group Litigation Under Foreign Legal Systems: Variations and Alternatives to American Class Actions", 52 *DePaul L. Rev.* 401, 402 (2002).

15. "Association suits" (*Verbandsklagen*) by consumer or environmental organizations in behalf of members and the public interest compose one significant exception. See Ch. 7(B)(5) above. Another exception is litigation in the Federal Constitutional Court by public officials and other public litigants. See Ch. 3(E) above for a brief discussion of the role and jurisdiction of the Federal Constitutional Court.

16. The interrelationship of these functions in the American legal culture raises fascinating debates about the nature of legal rights and the vindication of such rights in litigation. For an interesting analysis of this cultural debate in the context of a film about a mass-tort personal injury case see Sarat, "Exploring the Hidden Domains of Civil Justice, 'Naming, Blaming, and Claiming' in Popular Culture", 50 *DePaul Law Review* 425 (2000).

German civil justice does not purport to play any punitive or law enforcement role beyond the deterrence inherent in prompt and efficient enforcement of private rights. Damage awards are generally limited to actual damages sustained. As a matter of principle German law does not authorize awards of punitive damages.[17] Law enforcement going beyond the enforcement of private legal rights and punishment of wrongdoers is left to the criminal law and administrative regulation. In most American states civil justice retains the power to issue punitive damages awards against a defendant whose conduct has been particularly egregious.[18] The potential availability of such awards is often seen as a spur to parties or their lawyers to seek enforcement and vindication of rights under circumstances when actual damages might not be sufficient to support the effort.[19]

Although German civil justice proceedings are largely public[20] there is no particular policy of public education served by civil justice and its processes. Nor are civil proceedings expected to provide any element of drama, interest confrontation or "show". Such matters are left to political and policy debate in the media, in election campaigns and in other fora. In the United States, on the other hand, civil litigation can partake of high drama. Flamboyant trial lawyers use publicity and media exposure to make their claims bigger than life.

---

17. See Ch. 12(C)(2)(c) above.

18. These punitive awards can be substantial. For instance, in July 2000 a Florida jury awarded $144.8 billion in punitive damages in a class action brought in behalf of cigarette smokers against the tobacco industry. See *Engle v. RJ Reynolds Tobacco*, 2000 WL 33534572 (Fla. Cir. Ct. 2000). In 1994 a jury in Alaska issued an award of $5 billion against Exxon Corporation for the Exxon Valdez spill. These awards were later overturned on appeal. See *Ligget Group Inc. v. Engle*, 853 So. 2d 434 (Fla. App. 2003) and *In re Exxon Valdez*, 270 F. 3d 1215 (9th Cir. 2001) respectively.

19. See, e.g., Sunstein et al., *Punitive Damages; How Juries Decide* (2002) for a discussion of the manner in which juries' power to award punitive damages is exercised. For a discussion of the current debate in the United States over punitive damages see Daniels/Martin, "Myth and Reality in Punitive Damages", 75 *Minn. L. Rev.* 1 (1990). See also Klinck, "The Punitive Damages Debate", 38 *Harv. J. on Legis.* 469 (2001); "Developments—The Paths of Civil Litigation" (Part 3), 113 *Harv. L. Rev.* 1783 (2000); O'Connell, "The Case for Continuing to Award Punitive Damages", 36 *Tort and Insurance Law Journal* 873 (2001); Shores, "A Suggestion for Limited Tort Reform: Allocation of Punitive Damage Awards to Eliminate Windfalls", 44 *Ala. L. Rev.* 61 (1992); Pace, "Recalibrating the Scales of Justice Through National Punitive Damages Reform", 46 *Am. U. L. Rev.* 1573 (1997).

20. Unless otherwise provided (e.g. family cases or where specifically ordered for protection of participants) all plenary proceedings are open to the public. See Ch. 6(E)(2) above.

Televised live coverage of both criminal and civil trials brings the drama of litigation confrontation into the living-rooms of the American public.[21]

The purposes and roles of civil justice in German and American political, economic and social culture coincide to the extent that an important assignment of both systems is the prompt, efficient, fair and law-based adjudication of disputes between private litigants and the vindication and enforcement of private legal rights. It is in light of this common purpose that these systems can most fruitfully be compared.[22]

Consideration of the appropriate role of institutions of the courts and of civil justice within a modern democratic society and the various social and political purposes that civil justice can effectively serve is an important topic of political science. One can perhaps trace the different emphases of American and European civil justice systems to the American Declaration of Independence in which the revolting American colonists undertook to create a new kind of social order based on the individual's inalienable right to life, liberty and the pursuit of happiness. From that time forward Americans have been expected to pursue their own happiness and their state has been expected to support their right and initiative in this respect.[23]

In Europe personal freedom and the pursuit of individual happiness was never the basis of social order and structure. Beginning with enlightened despotism of the 18th Century, Europeans created structures and institutions of public welfare long before democratization of their governments or any recognition of individually enforceable human rights. The later democratization and development of the rule of law tended to establish individual human rights in terms of participation in these pre-existing institutions of communal welfare. Because of this development, enforcement of private rights against private litigants did not achieve the same significance in Europe as in the United States.

---

21. For a discussion of the extent to which modern media have developed the entertainment value of litigation, see, e.g., Friedman, "Lexitainment: Legal Process as Theater", 50 *DePaul Law Review* 539 (2000).

22. The meaning of "efficiency" of dispute resolution may depend to some extent on different cultural preferences. While German legal culture focuses on adjudication by court order, American legal culture prioritizes dispute resolution by settlement with the judgment as last resort. See James/Hazard/Leubsdorf, *Civil Procedure*, 5th ed. (2001), §6.7, pp. 381 ff.; Gross/Syverud, "Don't Try: Civil Jury Verdicts in a System Geared to Settlement", 44 *U.C.L.A. L. Rev.* 1 (1996). This may be a point not given sufficient consideration by Langbein, "The German Advantage in Civil Procedure", 52 *U. Chi. L. Rev.* 823 (1985).

23. See Damaska, *The Faces of Justice and State Authority* (1986), pp. 23 ff., 57 ff.; Lipset, *American Exceptionalism: A Double Edged Sword* (1996), pp. 31 ff.; Chase, 50 *Am. J. Comp. L.* 277, 280 ff.

Far more important was the enforcement of individual rights and entitlements with respect to those state institutions and agencies which administered programs of public well-being. Thus, fundamentally, the differing emphases in civil justice in Europe and the United States directly reflect the somewhat different roles of the state itself in the European and American social orders.

It can also be noted that most modern European constitutions seek to foster a degree of economic and social homogeneity within the population.[24] By contrast the American Constitution allows a degree of individual freedom that can result in wide economic and social disparities. One can speculate that as the economic and social homogeneity of Europe diminishes, greater and more frequent resort may be had to civil justice and that the global process of individualization may lead to greater significance for civil litigation in the enforcement of individual rights world wide. These questions are still open.

At the outset of this comparison we should address a question that has occasionally surfaced in connection with comparisons of German and American procedural law. To what extent do the institutions of American civil justice represent democratic elements of American political culture which should not be dispensed with in favor of institutions of a different kind of democratic tradition?[25] In our judgment it can fairly be said that the Amer-

---

24. See German Constitution Art. 20(1): "The Federal Republic of Germany is a democratic and *social* federation" (*"Die Bundesrepublik Deutschland ist ein sozialer und demokratischer Bundesstaat"*) and Art. 28(1)(1): "The constitutional order in the individual states must accord with the principles of the republican, democratic and *social* state under the rule of law within the meaning of this constitution" (*"Die verfassungsmässige Ordnung in den Ländern muss den Grundsätzen des republikanischen, demokratischen und sozialen Rechtsstaats im Sinne dieses Grundgesetzes entsprechen"*). See further Art. 6(4) (right of mothers to protection and care of the community); Art. 14(2) (Property to be used for the welfare of the community); Art. 3(3)(2) (no discrimination of disabled people). There are some decisions of the Federal Constitutional Court where the court construes constitutional rights in the light of this "principle of a social state", see Federal Constitutional Court, 22 BVerfGE 83, 86 ff. (1967) (right to legal aid); 33 BVerfGE 303 (1972) (access to universities); 50 BVerfGE 290 (1979) (worker participation); 68 BVerfGE 193 (1984) (public health insurance). See also Federal Supreme Administrative Court 1 BVerwGE 159 (1954); 52 BVerwGE 346 (1977) (constitutional requirement of public social welfare). For a survey see Degenhart, *Staatsrecht*, Vol. I, 18th ed. (2002), §4, mn. 424 ff.; Stein/Frank, *Staatsrecht*, 18th ed. (2002), §21, pp. 159 ff.; Maurer, *Staatsrecht I*, 2nd ed. (2001), §8(III), pp. 239 ff. See Treaty on the European Union 1992, Art. 2(1); European Treaty 1957/1997, Art. 2, 125ff., 136 ff., 152, 153, 158 ff. for provisions to further social welfare and homogeneity within the European Union.

25. For a discussion see, e.g., Redish, "The Adversary System, Democratic Theory, and the Constitutional Role of Self-Interest: The Tobacco Wars, 1953–1971", 51 *DePaul L. Rev.* 359, 364 ff. (2001).

ican civil justice system, with its heavy reliance on the private initiatives of parties and their lawyers to protect and vindicate legal rights, seems to reflect values of individualism and self-sufficiency that underlie American democracy as it has been practiced for the last two centuries. And certainly continental European civil justice systems seem to many Americans to represent a greater degree of reliance on state institutions to vouchsafe individual right and welfare than is the case under the American political system.[26] In the special case of Germany there may be a temptation to associate the collapse of German culture and society in the Third Reich with this kind of state-heavy political balance.[27] Suspicion of German institutions may also be subtly fueled by a sensed contemporary competition in culture, industry, science, and international business.

Our comparative study of German and American civil justice convinces us, however, that modern German civil justice embodies values of individual self-reliance which are generally fully consistent with a vigilant assertion and protection of individual rights by the citizens themselves. We say this for two reasons. First, the essentially adversarial character of the German civil process, the defining roles of lawyers and their clients, and the institutions which recognize and support individuals in their assertion and realization of their own rights are not that much different from the corresponding institutions of American civil justice.[28] Second, while we recognize that American civil justice, including jury trial, may reflect important democratic values in resolving major economic, social or even political interests which can be the subject of American civil litiga-

---

26. See Stürner, "Some Remarks on a New Joint Project of the American Law Institute and Unidroit", 34 *The International Lawyer* 1071, 1083 f. (2000).

27. See, e.g., Lord Simon in *National Society for the Prevention of Cruelty to Children*, 1972 Weekly Law Review 201; Marcus, "Malaise of the Litigation Superpower," in Zuckerman (ed.), *Civil Justice in Crisis* (1999), pp. 71, 101. The subtitle of the Marcus article "Judges Über Alles: The Rise of the Managerial Judge" is an allusion to the former first verse of the German National Anthem ("Deutschland über Alles"). These words were misused by the Nazis during the Third Reich and acquired the connotation of "Germany as the ruler of all" as opposed to their original meaning of "Germany, to its people most important of all."

The argument that the larger role of state institutions in German political culture may be associated with a national susceptibility to political extremism is critically discussed in detail by John H. Langbein, "The Influence of German Emigrés on American Law: The Curious Case of Civil and Criminal Procedure," in: Lutter et al. (eds.), *Der Einfluss deutscher Emigranten auf die Rechtsentwicklung in den U.S.A. und in Deutschland* (1993), pp. 320 ff., 328 ff. For German civil justice in the Third Reich see Ch. 2(F) above.

28. See especially Ch. 1(A) and (C), Ch. 6(A)–(C), Ch. 7(A) and (J), Ch. 8(A)–(C) above.

tion, the great bulk of civil litigation does not involve such confrontations, and the civil courts cannot realistically be considered the "front line" defenses for the preservation of democracy in modern society.

Thus, while we acknowledge a degree of past reluctance on the part of American reformers seriously to consider German contributions to the comparative law dialogue,[29] at present there seems to be no just reason for any approach other than a direct and forthright analysis based on fairness, accuracy, efficiency, and ultimately on shared values of democracy and individual rights.

C. Institutional Independence and Credibility

As suggested above an important function of a civil justice system is the maintenance of institutional independence and credibility of the civil justice system and its organs and participants. Provision of civil justice requires public participants free of corruption, political influence, or favoritism. It also requires courts and judges who are well trained and adequately funded to perform their work. It requires institutions that are durable and not subject to political winds and whims.

Although many citizens of the modern developed world would take these basic elements of a civil justice system for granted, it is not hard to think of states in which an independent judiciary, a funded justice system, and well-trained judges are non-existent.[30] Closer observation of states with long tra-

29. For the discussion on American-German comparison of procedural systems see Langbein, "The German Advantage in Civil Procedure", 52 *U. Chi. L. Rev.* 823 (1985); Gross, "The American Advantage: The Value of Inefficient Litigation", 85 *Mich. L. Rev.* 734 (1987); Bernstein, "Whose Advantage After All?: A Comment on the Comparison of Civil Justice Systems", 21 *U. C. Davis L. Rev.* 587 (1988); Allen/Köck/Riechenberg/Rosen, "The German Advantage in Civil Procedure: A Plea for More Details and Fewer Generalities in Comparative Scholarship", 82 *Nw. U. L. Rev.* 705 (1988); Langbein and Allen, "Trashing the German Advantage", 82 *Nw. U. L. Rev.* 763, 785 (1988); Reitz, "Grundlegende Unterschiede zwischen dem deutschen und dem U.S.-amerikanischen Zivilprozessrecht: Vorzüge, die sich ausschliessen?", 104 *ZZP* 381 (1991), English version in 75 *Iowa Law Review* 987 (1990); Stiefel/Maxeiner, "Civil Justice Reform in the United States", 42 *Am. J. Comp. L.* 147 (1994); Stürner, "U.S.-amerikanisches und deutsches Verfahrensverständnis", in: Lutter et al. (eds.), *Festschrift für Ernst C. Stiefel* (1987), p. 763.

30. One need only consider the former German Democratic Republic in which the institutions of civil justice functioned under the influence of the ruling political party. See Rüthers, *Geschönte Geschichten - geschonte Biographien* (2001). In many nation states serious and chronic under-funding undermines the independence as well as the competence

ditions of civil justice disclose some significant variations even with respect to these fundamental properties.[31]

1. Independence of the Judiciary

Both Germany and the United States enjoy long traditions of independent civil judiciaries. These traditions developed, to be sure, along different paths. In the thirteen original United States judges were politically appointed, but maintained the English tradition of judicial independence during service. During the 19th Century election of judges by popular vote became widespread in new states as well as in some of the original 13. More recent reforms have attempted to mitigate the politicization of judicial selection by such measures as the "Missouri Plan" and appointment processes with subsequent retention elections.[32]

In Germany the tradition of relative judicial independence finds its roots in the enlightened despotism of the era of Frederick the Great. During the 19th Century courts became progressively more independent from direct governmental influence, although membership in the judiciary tended to reflect a certain homogeneous upper class of citizens and even nobles. This was also the case during the Weimar Republic, which had a constitution guaranteeing complete independence of judges.

During the Third Reich the ordinary civil courts came under severe pressure from the totalitarian Nazi party, and the resistance of the judiciary was neither widespread nor successful.[33] As a consequence of the bad experiences

---

of the judiciary. In others nominally professional judges may be susceptible to undue political influence or favoritism. See, e.g., Garth, "Building Strong and Independent Judiciaries Through the New Law and Development; Behind the Paradox of Consensus Programs and Perpetually Disappointing Results", 52 *DePaul Law Review* 383 (2002); Solomon/Foglesong, *Courts and Transition in Russia* (2000), pp. 16–17 (overview).

31. For the United States and Europe see Stürner, "Europäische Justiz und Demokratie", in: Eberle et al. (eds.), *Festschrift für Winfried Brohm* (2002), p. 153; for a comparative survey Cappelletti, *Le Pouvoir des Juges*, 1990.

32. For a discussion of the various methods by which American judges are selected see Hazard/Taruffo, *American Civil Procedure* (1993), pp. 64-68.

33. Ordinary civil business was not, however, the main object of the Nazis' efforts to pervert the German justice system. Such efforts were more focused on the areas of criminal law and prosecution. For the role of the judiciary and lawyers in general in the "carrying out" of Nazi ideology in the field of civil law see the profound analysis of Rüthers, *Die unbegrenzte Auslegung - Zum Wandel der Privatrechtsordnung im Nationalsozialismus* (1968); id., *Entartetes Recht: Rechtslehren und Kronjuristen im Dritten Reich*, 2nd ed. (1989). See also Ch. 2(F) above.

during the Third Reich, complete judicial independence was an important priority in the reconstruction of Germany following World War II.[34]

In modern Germany judicial independence is guaranteed by the Constitution.[35] The Constitutional guarantee is implemented by statutory law and a judicial service system designed to make appointments and promotions primarily based on merit free of political influence.[36] Although most civil judges are employed and paid by the various German states, their role and function is primarily defined and regulated by federal law. With minor exceptions, such as honorary judges on commercial panels of the state district courts, civil judges are full-time professionals legally protected in their positions. Judges are reasonably well paid and do not have to resort to part-time outside employment to support themselves or their families.[37] There are effective mechanisms for the screening out and discipline of incompetent or dishonest judges by processes and decisions of independent courts.[38]

In a sense, the competent professional judge is the core element of the German system of public civil justice. German jurists celebrate the quality of their judiciary and safeguard it zealously.

This is not to say that politics play no role in the selection of German judges or in the decisions that they render. Political considerations do not count in an applicant's first appointment as a probationary judge in a German state court. On the other hand, judges on the Federal Constitutional Court and to a lesser extent the Federal Supreme Court are named by processes with strong

34. For a historical overview on the development of an independent judiciary see Kissel, *Gerichtsverfassungsgesetz - Kommentar*, 2nd ed. (1994), §1, mn. 13–24; Schulze-Fielitz, in: Dreier (ed.), *Grundgesetz - Kommentar* (2000), Art. 97, mn. 1–7; Simon, *Die Unabhängigkeit des Richters* (1975). For a comparative historical overview see Zätzsch, *Richterliche Unabhängigkeit und Richterauswahl in den USA und Deutschland* (2000), pp. 68–80.

35. Article 97 of the German Constitution provides that "Judges are independent and subject only to law." (*"Die Richter sind unabhängig und nur dem Gesetze unterworfen".*)

36. See Ch. 3(G) above.

37. The adequacy of judicial salaries also reduces temptation to corruption. Judges are allowed to earn outside income only from royalties on books, educational lectures, and service as neutral arbitrator. See Ch. 3(A) and (G)(3) above. A unique feature of German law is the practice of law professors serving as part-time judges on the state courts of appeals. This tradition may be an embodiment of the German attitude toward law as an essentially academic activity.

38. For an overview see Papier, "Die richterliche Unabhängigkeit und ihre Schranken", 54 *NJW* 1089, 1091 ff. (2001); Stürner, "Unabhängigkeit der Richter", 2003 *BRAK-Mitt.* No. 5 (2003). See Ch. 3(G) above.

political elements.[39] However once appointed German civil judges are insulated from political influence to a remarkable extent.[40]

In the United States judges are also as a matter of principle independent from political influence as well as other forms of favoritism or corruption. The method by which judges are selected and appointed varies among the different American states. In a large number of states judges are subject to popular election for fixed terms and must periodically stand for re-election. In those states the need to win election and solicit contributions for political campaigns from lawyers and potential litigants can cast doubt on the impartiality of these elected judges.[41] Politics also plays a role in the selection of judges in those states where they are appointed and in the American federal court system. In many states political influence on judicial appointments has been mitigated by the use of judicial qualifications panels which solicit applications and nominations and screen candidates. In any event, it is generally considered that judges who are appointed for life or for long terms tend to be more judicially independent than those who are required to stand for periodic popular election and raise political contributions to do so.[42] Federal judges, at least, are relatively well paid although the difference of income compared with well established practicing lawyers has increased in recent years.[43]

---

39. See Chs. 3(E) (Federal Constitutional Court) and 3(G)(2) (Federal Supreme Court) above. The same is true for chief judges (*Gerichtspräsidenten*) of higher German state appellate courts.

40. At the present there is a lively discussion on the appointments process and whether the process of "unpolitical" appointment of judges purely based on "merit" should be strengthened by increasing the role of sitting judges in the appointments process. See, e.g., Vosskuhle/Sydow, "Die demokratische Legitimation des Richters", 57 *JZ* 673 (2002); Röhl, "Selbstverwaltung für die Dritte Gewalt", 57 *JZ* 838 (2002); Papier, "Zur Selbstverwaltung der Dritten Gewalt", 55 *NJW* 2585 (2002); Hoffmann-Riem, *Modernisierung von Recht und Justiz* (2001); Mackenroth,"Die Qual der Wahl", *79 DRiZ* 214 (2001); Stürner, "Unabhängigkeit der Richter", 2003 *BRAK-Mitt.* No. 5 (2003).

41. This is particularly true in criminal cases, but can also be a matter for concern in civil litigation as well. See, e.g., Larkin, "Judicial Selection Methods: Judicial Independence and Popular Democracy", 79 *Denv. U. L. Rev.* 65 (2001); Barnhizer, "'On the Make': Campaign Funding and the Corrupting of the American Judiciary", 50 *Cath. U. L. Rev.* 361 (2001); Fabian, "The Paradox of Elected Judges: Tension in the American Judicial System", 15 *Geo. J. Legal Ethics* 155 (2001); Lay, *Law: A Human Process* (1996), pp. 128 f.

42. Levasseur, "Legitimacy of Judges", 50 *Am. J. Comp. L.* 43, 54 (2002): "Most observers regard appointments to provide the greatest degree of judicial independence. Once affirmed for a stated term, judges need not fear reprisals by voters or subtle threats by groups that would provide funding for election campaigns."

43. See ABA/Federal Bar Association (ed.), *Federal Judicial Pay Erosion—A Report on the Need for Reform* (2001), pp. 8 ff. In 2002, a United States district judge earned $154,700,

The practice of political election of judges and keeping them politically accountable by periodic re-election has been defended on the ground that American judges are expected to decide issues of widespread social and political significance and in so doing should reflect the political sentiments of the population.[44] This close political connection may correspond to the more political role of the American civil justice system as discussed above. This more political function of civil procedure has prioritized the democratic legitimacy of the judges and their judgments, while the "purer" version of the rule of law as traditionally emphasized in Germany results in a more detached and politically independent judiciary.[45]

We do not forget that a part of the function of case adjudication in American civil litigation is performed by juries of lay persons. While significant efforts are made to insure impartiality of the jurors in individual cases, their overall biases and indeed their competence to understand and intelligently decide the issues confided to them are very hard to predict or institutionally guarantee. We address the role of the American jury in civil litigation, however, when we discuss the quality of case determinations below.[46]

---

a federal circuit judge $159,100, see www.uscourts.gov/salarychart.pdf (June 25, 2003). The income of a U.S. district judge is the same as for a U.S. Senator or a member of the House of Representatives.

44. Larkin, "Judicial Selection Methods: Judicial Independence and Popular Democracy", 79 *Denv. U. L. Rev.* 65 (2001).

45. See Stürner, "Europäische Justiz und Demokratie", in: Eberle et al. (eds.), *Festschrift für Winfried Brohm* (2002), pp. 153, 160 f.; Rüthers, "Demokratischer Rechtsstaat oder oligarchischer Richterstaat?", 57 *JZ* 365 (2002); Hirsch, *Rechtsanwendung, Rechtsfindung, Rechtsschöpfung: Der Richter im Spannungsverhältnis von Erster und Dritter Gewalt* (2003).This also might be one reason why Germans accept without serious question the circumstance that a citizen of one German state (*Bundesstaat*) may be subject to the jurisdiction of the courts of another German state without the possibility of removing the case to a Federal court of first instance. Current political efforts to expand the concept of general acceptance of jurisdiction of courts of other political entities even to the level of the European Union may not be taking full account of the problem of democratic legitimacy of judicial power. See Stürner, in: *Festschrift für Winfried Brohm*, pp. 153, 163. For an analysis of the differing traditional concepts of law making and application see, e.g., Lawson, "Comparative Judicial Style", 25 *Am. J. Comp. L.* 364 (1977); Zweigert/Kötz, §18(II), p. 258.

46. See Ch. 13(D).

2. Training and Qualifications of Judges

Both the American and the German justice systems demand that prospective judges have the same formal education as the lawyers who appear before them.[47] German judges are selected primarily on merit based on their scores on the First and Second State Examinations and commence service as probationary judges promptly following their Second State Examinations, usually without having practiced as private lawyers. They are subject to periodic evaluation by senior judges and the chief judges of the courts on which they sit. Promotion is by the state ministries of justice based with the consent of state judicial conferences (*Präsidialräte*) and is based on seniority, the periodic evaluations and the candidates' reputations for judicial skill and temperament. Judges of the Federal Supreme Court are elected by a committee composed of the state Ministers of Justice and an equal number of deputies of the German Parliament with the approval of the Federal Minister of Justice.[48]

American judges are typically elected or appointed after some significant periods of activity as private practitioners or government lawyers. Traditionally an American jurist would undertake judicial service in her fifties or even later as the crowning element of her legal career. Competitive selection based on objective intellectual or experiential qualifications is usually strongly affected by political considerations, totally so in the case of elected judges. Thus, while American judges all share a baseline legal education to qualify as lawyers, there is no real guarantee of intellectual quality above this baseline in most cases. On the other hand, they bring with them their experience in the world of practice and in politics as well, to the extent the latter is properly relevant to their duties as judges.

Promotion of American judges is also by political appointment in the case of the federal judiciary and in many states, and by election in others. A judge's

47. In Germany the law provides that all lawyers have the same education as is required for appointment as a judge. See Ch. 4(C) above. In America there are no express educational qualifications to serve in the judiciary. In most cases judges are legally required to be qualified lawyers, and hence have received the education in order to qualify as lawyers. See, e.g., 4 Maine Revised Statutes §156(1)(a) (judge of the Maine District Court must be a "member of the bar of the State"). Although there is no express constitutional or statutory requirement of legal training for judges of the federal district and appeals courts, as a matter of unbroken tradition such judges have always been trained lawyers. There are statutes requiring that military and magistrate judges be qualified lawyers. See 10 U.S.C §826(b) and 28 U.S.C. §631 respectively.

48. See Ch. 3(G)(2) above.

perceived prior performance is cited as the basis for many promotionary appointments and may well play a role in elections to higher judicial office.[49]

Focusing on civil justice as the publicly provided means for vindication of private legal rights and enforcement of private obligations, both systems require appropriate base-line educational qualifications for judges. The German system relies on merit appointment of young jurists of high academic appointment who then are trained in successive judicial roles. The American system relies on experience in law practice and sometimes public life to prepare potential judges for their judicial roles.

The German system tends to produce judges of high technical quality and work discipline. It has been criticized for producing judges who tend to be relatively homogeneous and conformist and somewhat less likely to be innovative than their American counterparts.[50] They may also be hampered by their youth and lack of life experience in their early years of service, which may lead to some narrowness of outlook later on.

American judges tend to be of a wide range of intellectual quality and industriousness. Judicial appointment and promotion are not well correlated with intellectual ability or other objective measures of fitness for deciding civil cases. Some of them are able to supplement their intellectual abilities with practical wisdom gained from long experience out in "the real world." The variance in qualifications among judges can affect litigants in an arbitrary manner.

While both systems embody advantages and drawbacks, the German system once more may tend to provide a more consistent quality of judicial qualifications for civil case adjudication than is the case in most American jurisdictions. Making it possible for outstanding jurists to enter the judiciary after a significant period of private practice might add experience-based value to Germany judicial establishment.[51] To the extent that German civil justice addresses issues

49. See, e.g., Goldman, *Picking Federal Judges* (1997), pp. 350–351 commenting on a trend toward choosing highly qualified state court judges for appointment to the federal bench.

50. Flotho, "Richterpersönlichkeit und Richterauslese", 66 *DRiZ* 167, 170 (1988); Reimann, "Vom Deutschen Staatsdiener zum Amerikanischen Anwalt", 34 *JuS* 282 (1994); Allen, "The German Advantage in Civil Procedure: A Plea for More Details and Less Generality in Comparative Scholarship", 82 *Nw. U. L. Rev.* 705, 760 (1988); Fangmann/Zachert, *Gewerkschaftliche und Politische Betätigung von Richtern* (1986); Kaupen/Rasehorn, *Die Justiz zwischen Obrigkeitsstaat und Demokratie* (1971), p. 46.

51. There is nothing in the German Judges Law which prohibits appointment of ordinary judges after some period of law practice or other activity. Appointment of probationary judges right out of the Second State Examination is more a matter of long-estab-

with a political dimension, judges with significant life experience may be better equipped to serve than younger colleagues with greater technical ability.[52]

3. Sufficiency of Funding and Resources

There is scarcely a modern state that admits to funding its judicial establishment in a fully adequate manner.[53] However in the real world of underfunded judiciaries, both the German and the American judiciary seem to be relatively well off. Both seem to be given sufficient resources to perform their constitutional functions, even though additional resources are constantly needed and sought.

Germany appears to make a significantly larger proportional investment of public resources in the provision of civil justice than the United States or any individual American state. It is well known that Germany provides its citizens with many more professional judges per capita than does the United States.[54] While figures for support facilities for these judges, courthouses, and other accouterments of civil justice are not easily available, one would infer that they would also show a greater investment of public resources per capita on the part of Germany.

It also appears that Germany provides more funds for legal aid than the United States, at least on a per capita basis.[55] How this disparity affects relative access to justice in light of other complementary American institutions

---

lished tradition. It has long been possible for individuals to go back and forth between the judiciary and states attorneys offices (*Staatsanwaltschaft*). Recently suggestions have been made that the tradition be modified to permit greater access to the judiciary by mature private practitioners as well. See, e.g., Vosskuhle/Sydow, "Die demokratische Legitimation des Richters", 57 *JZ* 673, 680 (2002).

52. See Heldrich, "Juristen im Blickfeld der Soziologie", in: Horn et al. (eds.), *Europäisches Rechtsdenken in Geschichte und Gegenwart: Festschrift für Helmut Coing* (1982), Vol. 1, p. 525, 529.

53. See, e.g., Zuckerman, in: *Civil Justice in Crisis*, p. 8.

54. See Ch. 3(A) and (I)(2) above. A recent article estimated that Germany has more judges than the United States even on an absolute basis, 22,100 versus 21,500. This translates into a tremendous disparity per capita, 27 judges per 100,000 persons versus 9 judges per 100,000. See Clark, "Judiciaries in Distinct Legal Traditions", in: Nafziger et al. (eds.), *Law and Justice in a Multistate World—Essays in Honor of Arthur T. von Mehren* (2002), pp. 609, 611–612.

55. See Ch. 4(I) above on the German system of legal aid in civil matters. France and Germany invest approximately three times as much per capita in legal aid as do the United States. See Zuckerman, in: *Civil Justice in Crisis*, pp. 41–42; Johnson, "Equal Access to Justice: Comparing Access to Justice in the United States and Other Industrial Democracies", 24 *Fordham Int'l L. J.* 83, 96 (2000). It is estimated that in 2000 Germany spent an overall amount (including criminal matters) of 350 Mio. Euros in legal aid, which amounts to about 4,4 Euros per capita, see 32 *BRAK-Mitt.* 128, 130 (2001).

such the American rule on costs and the contingent fee can be debated.[56] However it does represent a significant public investment of resources in the quality of German civil justice.

These public investments, are, however, only half the picture. One of the salient operational differences between the German and the American systems of civil justice relates to the division of labor between public and private resources. The somewhat larger roles of German judges than American judges in civil case processing and adjudication are complemented by larger roles of private counsel in American litigation. It appears clear that American lawyers do more work and earn much larger fees than their German counterparts in most cases. This is because the American system expects them to do more than they are expected to do in German litigation. And the American system permits lawyers to be paid far more generously by contingent fees and hourly billing than most German lawyers receive according to the German statutory schedule of fees based on amounts in controversy.[57]

Unfortunately it is much harder to ascertain amounts paid by private parties than amounts of public expenditures. While the authors are under the impression that Americans in general devote more resources, private and public, per capita to civil justice than do Germans, there is no way such an impression can be documented with certainty. In any event, it is clear that in both Germany and America sufficient public resources are devoted to civil justice to permit the respective public organs of justice to function and discharge their responsibilities within the justice systems as a whole.[58]

D. Quality of Fact Finding and Application of Law

Effective vindication and enforcement of private rights requires a system that is capable of making accurate fact findings and correct applications of the

56. See Ch. 13(F) below.

57. See Ch. 4(H) above on fees in general and Ch. 9(E)(2) above on the computation of fees allowed in civil judgments. On January 1, 2001, there were 110,367 lawyers admitted to the bar in Germany, while there were about 1,005,842 lawyers admitted in the United States. In both countries the numbers have been growing steadily for years. See *Pressemitteilung der BRAK* of May 2, 2001 (www.brak.de/seiten/04_01_15.php); Marcus, "Malaise of the Litigation Superpower", in: Zuckerman (ed.), *Civil Justice in Crisis* (1999), p. 71, 82.

58. The relative allocation of responsibility between judges and lawyers, public and private resources, in civil litigation in Germany and the United States is discussed in greater detail in Ch. 13(D) below.

law in a large variety of civil disputes. If a system is not perceived as being capable of ascertaining the facts behind a controversy and applying the public norms to those facts to reach a credible decision litigants will lose faith in the system and in legal regulation of their transactions and relationships in general. Legal decisions which are based on accurate fact finding are likely to give correct economic and regulatory signals to the real world. Correct and consistent application of the law fosters predictability and assists potential litigants in their decision making. A reasonable level of factual accuracy and legal consistency are seen as core elements of a system of civil justice.[59]

Unfortunately measuring the factual accuracy of judicial fact finding is very difficult. To the extent that a judicial process seeks to make fact findings about past events, no one knows with certainty what the truth really is.[60] Once the event has occurred it disappears forever into the realm of recollection, history, myth and legend. Traces of the event may be preserved more or less accurately in documents and things connected with the event as well as the recollections of participants and observers. However the baseline, the event itself, is no longer there.

Thus efforts directly to gauge the quality of another entity's findings concerning past facts tend to be nothing more than "second guesses". The evaluator reviews the information available to the fact finder and asks herself if she would have come to the same conclusion, or if the first fact finder's conclusion seems "reasonable" or "understandable" in the evaluator's frame of reference. If the evaluator's factual conclusions from the information available coincide with those of the fact finder, the evaluator deems the fact findings to be of high quality. If the evaluator's factual conclusions differ, she is suspicious of the quality of the initial findings.[61]

---

59. Zuckerman, in: *Civil Justice in Crisis,* pp. 3–4: "In order to do justice, then, the court has to determine the true facts and then correctly apply the law to them. In Bentham's terminology, the purpose of procedure is rectitude of decision, which requires the correct application of the law to the true facts." To the extent that the purposes of civil justice are other than the vindication and enforcement of private rights, factual accuracy and legal consistency may be of less importance. For instance, if the purpose of a state's civil justice system is the implementation of a social-political agenda or the perpetuation of a particular social or economic status quo, then objective accuracy and consistency may be less important than the ability of the system to generate results implementing the agenda or preserving the social-political order.

60. Philosophers state in different ways that objective truth about past events is unknowable. Among American trial lawyers it is said that, "The truth is at the bottom of a bottomless pit". See Harr, *A Civil Action* (1995), p. 340, where this saying is attributed to Jerome Facher, Esq.

61. Of course this is the process followed by appellate courts in evaluating fact findings on appeal. In this comparison, a collegial reviewing court can bring the "second guesses"

Because of the fallibility of direct review of fact findings in litigated cases, not to speak of the labor involved in examining enough actual case files to get a reasonable sample, comparative law scholars do not attempt directly to measure the ability of a system to find facts accurately in litigated cases. Instead, the comparatists focus their attention on the resources and processes used by the system to reach fact findings. Are those processes ones which, as a matter of general experience, logic and common sense, are likely to generate accurate fact findings in the litigation context? If the system utilizes processes calculated to generate accurate and thorough fact findings, it is assumed that the findings resulting from that process tend to be reasonably accurate, at least over many cases. On the other hand, if the processes used by a system are not seen as effective for fact determination, it is assumed that in general, fact findings will not correlate well with reality.

And so, with respect to fact finding at least, comparison of the ability of the German and American civil justice systems to make accurate fact findings will have to focus on the apparent efficiency and quality of the processes of those systems rather than the actual accuracy of facts found in litigated cases.[62]

The situation is little better in the realm of application of the law. It is very hard directly to measure and compare the "quality" of various court's application of legal norms to facts found in litigated cases. To be sure, appellate courts are often more confident of their ability to "second guess" courts below on the law than they are on the facts. Perhaps one can get an indication of the general quality of a lower court's legal rulings in a number of cases by examining the percentage of reversals or modifications of those rulings on appeal. However direct evaluation of the quality or correctness of legal rulings would

---

of several judges to bear, thus increasing the credibility of its review. On the other hand, to the extent that the fact finder below had more immediate contact with the evidence (such as by personal observation of key witnesses), the reviewing court is likely to afford the previous fact finder's impressions some deference. See Ch. 10(D)(2) above for a discussion of the degree of deference afforded fact findings on appeal in Germany. In the United States fact findings of first instance judges and juries are afforded great deference and are rarely set aside on appeal. See Hazard/Taruffo, p. 178.

62. This is true for nearly all efforts to compare the efficiency of national fact finding mechanisms. See, e.g., Perrot, "Le droit à la preuve", in: Habscheid (ed.), *Effektiver Rechtsschutz und verfassungsmässige Ordnung* (1983), p. 91; Hay, Junker and Rüssmann, "Informationsbeschaffung für den Zivilprozess", in: P. Schlosser (ed.), *Die Informationsbeschaffung für den Zivilprozess - Die verfahrensmässige Behandlung von Nachlässen, ausländisches Recht und Internationales Zivilprozessrecht* (1996), pp. 1 ff., 63 ff., 137 ff.

require painstaking re-examination of numerous cases, an exercise far too laborious for a work of comparative law.[63]

As is the case with fact finding, the primary inquiry must focus on the processes and institutions for law application. Are these reasonably calculated and designed to result in careful, informed and consistent application of legal rules to facts found in litigated cases? If so, we can assume that they work as intended.

Although direct scientific measurement and comparison of the quality of fact finding and law application in multiple civil justice systems is not feasible in a work of this kind, some confirmation of a system's efficacy in these functions can be derived from the overall reputation of the system among the populations of litigants and lawyers served. If the lawyers and litigants have confidence in the system, it is likely that it is fulfilling these functions to a good extent. Failure of a system in either respect affecting a significant group of cases is likely to be reflected over time in the system's reputation in the perceptions of its regular users.[64]

1. Fact Finding

Many, although by no means all, litigated cases involve some dispute over the facts relevant to a determination of the controversy. An effective fact finding function is an important element of any civil justice system.

On the other hand, fact finding is an exercise that can become very costly and time consuming if a high level of apparent accuracy is an important goal. Constraints of cost and time cannot be ignored. Moreover, although facts always play a role in the resolution of legal disputes, under some systems they may tend to be of somewhat greater importance than under others. In the present context, it has been argued that fact finding and fact distinctions tend to be of somewhat greater importance in a common law system such as that of the United States than in a civil law system such as that of Germany.[65]

---

63. For a discussion of the problem of assessing the quality of appellate decisions in the context of judicial reform, Murray, "Maine's Overburdened Law Court—Has the Time Come for a Maine Appeals Court?", 52 *Me. L. Rev.* 44 (2000).

64. Broad-based surveys, how ever contestable they may be, might therefore have some value in the assessment of quality. See for an international overview Zuckerman, in: *Civil Justice in Crisis* (1999), pp. 3, 12–36.

65. See, e.g., Zweigert/Kötz, §18(IV), pp. 262 ff. Of course in any system there will always be cases which turn on very fine distinctions of fact. The contention is, however, that in common law systems there are likely to be more such cases than in civil law systems. The Federal Rules' broad pre-trial discovery can be seen as a direct consequence of this basic

Between America and Germany the debate on fact finding boils down to the judge-led German process with limited fact discovery and court-appointed expert witnesses as opposed to the attorney-conducted American process with relatively wide discovery and party-presented expertise at the case development and fact exposure stage and the German judge or tribunal as compared with the American single trial judge or civil jury at the fact finding stage.[66]

In a sense this is a comparison of extremes. Civil jury trial may be an institution in retreat even in the United States. Certainly only a tiny fraction of civil cases filed ever see trial by jury.[67] On the other hand, the institution of trial by jury has historically shaped the structure of the American civil process and established the roles of the participants. Thus it seems reasonable to include American civil jury trial in the fact finding comparison.

a. Case development and fact exposure

In American civil justice the investigation and uncovering of facts potentially relevant to adjudication of civil cases has been raised to a high art. American lawyers are not expected to have particularly comprehensive command of the relevant facts at the time they file suit. However they are given powerful tools of discovery to require the opposing party and third parties to provide potentially relevant information in the form of documents and things, interrogatory

---

distinction. See Stürner, "Discovery and Sanctions Against Non-Compliance", 2001 *Uniform L. Rev.* 871 (2001).

66. The comparisons between Germany and Great Britain are nowhere near as extreme. In Great Britain there is no jury trial in most civil cases and recent reforms have brought the fact finding process and the role of the lawyers and judge somewhat closer to the European model than the American. See Jolowicz, "The Woolf Report and the Adversary System", 15 *C.J.Q.* 198 (1996); id., "England and Wales", in: Fazzalari et al. (eds.), *Civil Justice in the Countries of the European Union* (1998), pp. 77, 100 ff.; Andrews, "A New Civil Procedural Code for England: Party-Control 'Going, Going, Gone'", 4 *ZZPInt* 3 (1999); Stürner, "Discovery and Sanctions Against Non-Compliance", 2001 *Uniform L. Rev.* 871, 874 f., 877, 882 (2001); id., "Anglo-American and Continental Civil Procedure—The English Reform as a Model for Further Harmonization?", lecture delivered at the conference on The ALI-UNIDROIT Principles and Rules of Transnational Civil Procedure, May 24, 2002, British Institute of International & Comparative Law (to be published in 2003).

67. For instance in the State of Massachusetts, less than 0.02% of all civil cases filed in all courts are decided by verdict of a jury. In most cases there is no right to jury trial. In many others jury trial is waived or the case is settled before it reaches trial or verdict. See Murray, "The Disappearing Civil Jury Trial in Massachusetts", (manuscript to be published in 2004.) For the state of civil jury trial in general see Sward, *The Decline of the Civil Jury* (2001); Marcus, "Malaise of the Litigation Superpower", in: Zuckerman (ed.), *Civil Justice in Crisis* (1999), pp. 71 ff., 81.

answers and deposition testimony and information about anticipated expert opinions. Fueled by contingency fee agreements with plaintiffs and hourly rates paid by defendants American lawyers can use the discovery and preparatory phases of civil cases to investigate, ascertain and expose potentially relevant facts to a great level of detail with relatively little interference from the judge. The theory is that the discovery process will so educate both parties about the facts of the case that they will be able to address the issues on which they differ in a more informed and thorough manner. In many cases the parties learn enough in discovery so that they can settle the case without further judicial intervention.

On the other hand the excesses of the American discovery process have become proverbial. There has long been the perception that much of routine as well as exceptional discovery is wasted effort which unnecessarily burdens the parties and the process in general. Discovery has sometimes become excessively adversarial, leading to bickering and controversy largely unrelated to the merits of the underlying case.[68] The discovery process permits one party to require the opponent to engage in activities which can be very costly and time consuming. This sometimes gives parties which can afford such activity an unfair advantage.

To date efforts to reform or control discovery in America have been unavailing. Frequent tinkering with the Federal Rules of Civil Procedure and even legislation have failed to make a difference.[69]

On the other hand, in Germany parties and their lawyers are expected to have developed their relevant factual assertions, at least, by the time they commence suit. They are also expected to be in a position to point to potential sources of proof for these factual assertions. Complaints are tested for suffi-

---

68. See, e.g., Brazil, "The Adversary Character of Civil Discovery: A Critique and Proposals for Change", 31 *Vand. L. Rev.* 1295, 1348 (1978); Schwarzer, "The Federal Rules, the Adversary Process, and Discovery Reform", 50 *U. Pitt. L. Rev.* 703, 703 (1989): "Discovery, originally conceived as the servant of the litigants to assist them in reaching a just outcome, now tends to dominate the litigation and inflict disproportionate costs and burdens. Often it is conducted so aggressively and abusively that it frustrates the objectives of the Federal Rules. It has been said that now lawyers must try their cases twice, once before trial and once at trial."

69. The Civil Justice Reform Act of 1990 was enacted in large part to curb discovery abuse and the resulting cost and delay in civil justice. For an analysis of the actual effect of this legislation, see Murray, "Civil Justice Reform in America: The 1990 Civil Justice Reform Act and its Consequences", 3 *ZZPInt.* 319 (1999); Marcus, "Retooling American Discovery for the Twenty-First Century: Toward a New World Order?", 7 *Tul. J. Int'l & Comp. Law* 153 (1999); Marcus, in: *Civil Justice in Crisis* (1999), pp. 71ff., 101ff; James/Hazard/Leubsdorf, *Civil Procedure*, 5th ed. (2001), §5.2, pp. 288ff.

ciency not only on their allegations, but also for the required citations to expected sources of proof. If there is no reasonable specification of potential proof for a factual allegation, the allegation may be ignored.[70] The court may, however, allow more general assertions of fact or less specific citations to sources of potential proof if the likely sources of proof are within the control of the opposing party or some third party.[71]

There is no discovery as such. But pretrial preparation can be addressed to obtaining the means of proving allegations in the pleadings, and the court can order production of documents and things not only by the parties, but also by third parties in the case preparation process as well as at plenary and evidentiary hearings.[72]

By becoming familiar with the parties' factual contentions and their anticipated sources of proof at an early stage of the proceeding, the German judge can take a role in the factual shaping of the case for decision. The judge can indicate which facts she considers irrelevant or unimportant. These facts need not be developed. On the other hand the judge can also provide the parties hints and feedback about areas of their fact contentions which need reinforcement, although the judge may not introduce new assertions of facts into the proceeding. While most of the proof must initially be proposed by one or the other parties, the judge has some ability to order proof and evidence on her own motion.[73]

While parties and their lawyers can and do conduct their own fact investigations during the case preparation phase, the lack of discovery tools combines with strong financial constraints to discourage such activities. The statutory fee schedule by which German lawyers are paid in litigated matters does

---

70. See Ch. 6(B)(2) and (3); Ch. 7(A)(4) and (J)(1); Ch. 8(C)(1)(a)–(c) above. However the judge would be expected to point out the deficiency to the party affected and give opportunity for the complaint to be amended or supplemented. See Ch. 6(C)(2) above on the court's duty to give hints and feedback.

71. See Ch. 7(J)(1) above.

72. See Ch. 7(L) and Ch. 8(c) above. The increased access to documents and things in the course of preparatory proceedings and the taking of evidence resulting from the most recent reforms in many respects implements ideas developed in the 1970s. See Stürner, *Die Aufklärungspflicht der Parteien des Zivilprozesses* (1976).

73. See Ch. 6(C); Ch.7(A)(4), (H), (J)(1) and (L); Ch. 8(C)(1)(b) and (c) above. In general, witnesses must be designated by one or the other of the parties, while the court can order production of documents, public records and reports, and expert testimony on its own motion. The court's ability to act on its own motion is somewhat expanded in family cases and other matters where there is a clear public interest in accurate fact finding in the case. See Ch. 11(A) and Ch. 11(E) above on special procedures in family cases and in cases within the court's non-contentious jurisdiction respectively.

not provide additional compensation for discovery or extensive and time-consuming preparatory activities.[74] Thus the impetus for most activity in preparing a case for plenary proceedings comes from the court and the lawyers tend to respond to the court's initiatives, directions, hints and feedback.[75]

The German preparatory process has the virtue of efficiency. The fact inquiry is concentrated on the facts which are likely to count with the fact finder early on in the process. The court is engaged, intellectually and otherwise, with what is going on. Waste of time on matter likely to be irrelevant is avoided.

On the other hand, in some cases where the facts may be complex and ill-understood by the parties (or the judge) at the outset of the case, the German process may not allow sufficient opportunity for detailed development and understanding of the facts. Although the German procedure bends over backward to insure that parties and their counsel have input at every stage of the proceeding, in some cases an engaged judge might prematurely focus the inquiry on a particular issue without permitting development of other issues or theories that could be important to a fully informed decision. In many cases a premature narrowing of the case by a first-instance judge can be remedied on second-instance appeal, which permits the introduction of new facts and evidence relevant to legal theories not considered below.[76]

b. Presentation and Reception of Evidence

An obvious and oft-cited difference between the German and American fact finding function is the manner in which factual proof is adduced and received by the fact finder.

In American courts facts presentation in both jury and non-jury cases is largely based on the jury trial model. The fact finder has no direct connection with the facts during the preparatory phases of the case. At most a judge may get an inkling of some of the relevant facts and the means to prove them by brief discussions with counsel at a pretrial conference, in a motion relating to discovery, or perhaps in papers filed on a motion for summary judgment.

---

74. See Ch. 8(C)(9)(a) above on witness preparation or coaching; Ch. 9(E)(2) above on statutory attorneys' fees.

75. See Ch. 7(E), (H) and (L) above for a discussion of the case preparation process. If the case has been set for preliminary hearing, the court sets the agenda for the hearing or hearings and the lawyers prepare to address the agenda as set by the court. The judges' various procedural orders fulfil the same function in cases prepared by written briefs.

76. See Ch. 10(D)(2) above on the circumstances under which new facts and legal theories may be introduced on second-instance appeal.

The facts are presented for the first time and in detail at the trial, where the parties' lawyers present in their opening statements detailed descriptions of the facts they respectively intend to prove. They then proceed to prove the facts by calling witnesses and presenting their testimony in question and answer form.[77] They also offer documentary evidence and "real evidence" consisting of things relevant to the matters at issue.[78] Each party has the right to object to evidence proposed by her opponent and to cross examine the witnesses called by the proponent. The entire process is regulated by intricate "rules of evidence" which regulate the kind of proof which may be received and the issues for which it may be considered.

The fact finder's role during the trial is essentially that of a passive audience viewing and hearing what is presented by the lawyers and their witnesses. Jurors are generally not permitted to ask questions of their own. While judges are permitted to pose questions of their own, they seldom do so. Both judge and jury rely on the opposing lawyers to present to them the facts which they will need to reach an informed decision on the facts.

There is also no opportunity for either judge or jury to give the lawyers any feedback on fact issues at any point prior to the rendition of judgment. In jury trial the jurors are forbidden from discussing the facts before all the evidence has been received and the judge has delivered his instructions on the applicable law. In non-jury trial it would be theoretically possible for a judge to advise counsel of her tentative view of the facts before the evidence were concluded, but in practice this almost never occurs. The judge remains a sphinx until the judgment is rendered.[79]

Parties can present expert witnesses on issues beyond the everyday knowledge of the fact finder, and such witnesses are allowed to give opinions

---

77. For the structure of a trial see James/Hazard/Leubsdorf, *Civil Procedure*, 5th ed. (2001), §7.3, pp. 389ff. Generally a lawyer will painstakingly prepare the witnesses she plans to present before they testify in order that their testimony be given as persuasively as possible.

78. In general admissible evidence must be portable enough to be brought into a courtroom. Although judges and juries are permitted to take "views" of premises, sites or bulky objects involved in litigation, such views are not considered evidence and fact finders are not supposed to base any fact finding directly on observations made during views. See Strong/Broun, *McCormick on Evidence, 5th ed.* (1999), §§216, 246; Murray, *Maine Evidence, 2000 Ed.* (1999), §616.4.

79. This particular kind of judicial restraint or reticence may spring from a desire to avoid an impression of prejudging the case before all of the evidence has been received. Typically one party presents all of her evidence on contested issues before the other is permitted to present any, and most judges believe that they should remain totally silent until they have heard the evidence presented by both sides.

which may include expert inferences from immediate facts. If there is a difference in opinion among the experts, the jury or judge as fact finder resolve the difference as they would with any other witness. There is some perception that a persuasive expert can be found to testify to almost any proposition—at a price.[80] Juries as well as judges are often not well equipped as a matter of education or specialized experience to choose between opposing expert opinions or determine the extent to which an expert opinion has merit and should be accepted. There is a perception that often the mode of presentation of otherwise incomprehensible expert testimony is more important than the content, and that plausible expert witnesses accompanied by flossy illustrative aids can have an exaggerated impact on credulous judges or juries.

Because of the participation of the lay jury, the process of presentation of evidence must be concentrated over a relatively brief period of time.[81] Although this constraint would not apply to non-jury cases, as a matter of practice, presentation of evidence in non-jury cases tends to follow the jury trial model. Usually the trial continues uninterrupted from start to finish, interrupted only by brief recesses during the day and at days ends and for weekends.

American trials are considered complex and highly demanding exercises for the participating lawyers, calling for a very high degree of skill. The complexity of the process, the role of the lay jury and the large roles of the lawyers in the presentation of evidence in a very concentrated and dramatic way lead to the perception that outcomes can be greatly influenced by the quality of a lawyer's presentation. Presentation of civil cases, particularly to juries, has become a specialty within the legal profession. Successful practitioners, particularly those who represent plaintiffs in personal injury, malpractice, products lia-

---

80. See, e.g., Langbein, "The German Advantage in Civil Procedure", 52 *U. Chicago L. Rev.* 823, 835 (1985): "At the American trial bar, those of us who serve as expert witnesses are known as 'saxophones'. This is a revealing term, as slang often is. The idea is that the lawyer play the tune, manipulating the expert as though the expert were a musical instrument on which the lawyer sounds the desired notes. I sometimes serve as an expert in trust and pension cases, and I have.... Money changes hands upon the rendering of the expertise, but the expert can run his meter only so long as his patron litigator likes the tune. Opposing counsel undertakes a similar exercise, hiring and schooling another expert to parrot the contrary position. The result is our familiar battle of opposing experts. The more measured and impartial an expert is, the less likely he is to be used by either side."

81. See, e.g., von Mehren, "The Significance for Procedural Practice and Theory of the Concentrated Trial: Comparative Remarks", in: Horn et al. (eds.), *Europäisches Rechtsdenken in Geschichte und Gegenwart; Festschrift für Helmut Coing*, Vol. 2 (1982), p. 364.

bility and similar cases, are the most highly compensated members of the American legal establishment.[82]

In Germany the parties and the lawyers introduce the relevant facts and means of proof in their pleadings and preparatory proceedings and present documents and tangible evidence to the court.[83] The court receives the documentary and other proof proffered by the parties. In some cases the court may order production of additional documents or tangible evidence on its own motion. The court also questions any witnesses nominated by either party with respect to factual assertions made by the parties. The court's questions initially allow the witness to relate the facts which the witness thinks are the most important, and then follow up to focus on those facts of most interest to the court.[84] It should be noted that in German, as well in other Continental-European civil proceedings, oral testimony of witnesses is generally of less significance than it is in the Anglo-American tradition of jury trial process. For instance, documentary and other tangible evidence is usually placed before the court without the intervention of a live witness. This circumstance, plus the fact that expert testimony is primarily supplied by court-appointed expert witnesses, diminish the importance of who actually asks the questions of those live witnesses who testify.

While recent and current policy seeks to concentrate hearings and avoid protracted series of hearings,[85] there is no requirement that all the evidence be presented at one time. Proof of facts can be received at all stages of the proceeding, commencing with the filing of the complaint and other initial proceedings.

The requirement that pleadings maintain a high level of particularity of factual allegation and identification of proof means that the court gets a pretty good idea of the parties' respective factual positions early on and can decide which facts are not contested and which ones are genuinely in dispute. If it

---

82. For the costs of jury trials and their significance in promoting settlements see James/Hazard/Leubsdorf, *Civil Procedure*, 5th ed. (2001), §6.3, p. 368.

83. In most cases this is a single judge (see Ch. 3(D)(2)(b) and Ch. 7(E)(1)), but sometimes in the state district courts and almost always in the state courts of appeals this is a panel of three judges. When a panel receives evidence typically one member, either the presiding judge or another judge, will take the laboring oar of doing most of the questioning on behalf of the panel. See Ch. 8(C)(7)(C) and (9)(a) above.

84. The court's ability to adduce proof at its own instance is not unfettered. Witnesses, for instance, can only be heard if they have been identified by one of the parties. See Ch. 8(C)(9)(a) above on the process of questioning in German evidentiary proceedings.

85. See Ch. 6 (C)(1), Ch. 7(E)(2), (H), (I) and Ch. 8(A)(2) above for a discussion of the principle of concentration of proceedings (*Konzentrationsmaxime*) and its expression in recent reforms.

turns out that there is no material fact in dispute, it may not be necessary to receive evidence at all and the case can be decided on the basis of the law.[86]

Thus, although German parties and their lawyers are active in the initial identification of relevant facts, and the identification of and presentation of evidence to support those facts, they are less active at the stage where the proof is actually received by the court than is the case with their Anglo-American counterparts. Lawyers can and do pose supplemental questions to prove their assertions of facts which were not sufficiently addressed by the witness in the course of the court's questioning.

There are no really significant evidentiary rules that screen out particular forms of evidence. The court is more or less untrammeled in its ability to consider practically all forms of proof for what they are worth in the circumstances of the case. In many cases documentary evidence seems to be afforded greater weight than oral testimony. This may come from the ease by which documentary evidence can be brought before the court and considered and from the perceived greater reliability of facts captured in documents over facts preserved only by human recollection. With few exceptions, however, any preference for documentary evidence seems to reflect rational weighting of its reliability under the circumstances rather than any prescribed preferential rule.[87]

There has been considerable debate in American comparative law literature over whether German lawyers are permitted to prepare non-party witnesses prior to their testimony in court.[88] As of the present time it appears clear that German lawyers can and, on occasion, do interview potential witnesses prior to nominating them in their pleadings in order to determine whether they have helpful testimony to offer. However they carefully refrain from any activity that smacks of "coaching" lest the court discredit the witness's anticipated testimony.[89] Another constraint on elaborate witness preparation is the fee struc-

86. See Ch. 7(A)(2)/(4), (J)(2)/(3) and Ch. 8(C)(1)(a)/(d) above. It is important to keep in mind that a party who fails to contest the facts alleged by the opposing party with the required level of particularity is deemed to have admitted the fact. In some cases such a presumption functions as a sanction for non-compliance with relatively strict pleading requirements.

87. See Ch. 8(C)(6) above for a discussion of documentary evidence and the relatively few issues on which documentary proof is given enhanced effect.

88. Compare Langbein, "The German Advantage in Civil Procedure", 52 *U. Chi. L. Rev.* 823, 834 (1985) with Allen/Köck/Riechenberg/Rosen, "The German Advantage in Civil Procedure: A Plea for More Details and Fewer Generalities in Comparative Scholarship", 82 *Nw. U. L. Rev.* 705, 721–22 (1988).

89. See Ch. 8(C)(9)(a) above for a discussion of the manner and extent of witness interviewing by German lawyers.

ture which does not provide additional compensation for preparatory work of this kind.

In Germany the primary means of presenting scientific, technical or specialized evidence outside ordinary knowledge and experience is through court-appointed expert witnesses.[90] Such witnesses are selected for conceded expertise and above all, impartiality. Their conclusions are presented in a way that allows the court, parties and counsel opportunity to challenge and test them. Parties may call their own expert witnesses, but their conclusions are deemed to be tainted by interest, and are of only secondary weight to the court.[91]

German judges tend to accept the conclusions of court appointed expert witnesses unless given good reason to doubt them. There is a perception that some courts appoint experts too readily on issues that could be decided by the court itself in the interest of easing the court's workload in cases with difficult disputes of fact.[92]

An important part of the process of reception of proof in Germany is the interplay between court and counsel concerning the inferences to be drawn from the evidence received. The Code of Civil Procedure requires that the court discuss the evidence received and the inferences likely to be drawn from the evidence before closing the plenary proceedings.[93] This apprises parties and counsel of the court's likely path of reasoning on the facts and gives the participants the opportunity of adducing additional arguments from the proof or even additional evidence to correct an apparent misconception.

It appears clear that the American system of civil justice places greater emphasis on a detailed and dramatic presentation of fact information than is the case in Germany. The American jury trial model allows and financially supports an unparalleled scope and volume of lawyer activity in the preparation and presentation of fact material. This can result in a very detailed and thorough exploration of even difficult factual issues.

The German system is somewhat more restrained in its investigation of the facts. Lawyers play important roles in identifying significant sources of evidence early on in the proceedings. Later the onus of fact finding activity is shared with the court, which shapes the direction and detail of the presentation of the facts to a considerable degree. In many cases where the facts are

---

90. See Ch. 8(C)(7)(b) above on court appointed expert witnesses.

91. See Ch. 8(C)(7)(b) and (C)(7)(d) above on the role of party experts.

92. See Ch. 8(C)(7)(d) above.

93. See Ch. 8(D)(2) above on the court's duty to discuss the evidence with counsel.

not especially complicated, this division of labor is quite efficient. The relevant facts are ascertained with a minimum of unnecessary partisan activity. In more complex cases, the limitations on lawyer activity inherent in the structure of the proceedings and the method of compensation may result in a less thorough and detailed development and presentation of relevant fact material than would be the case in American practice.[94]

On the other hand, the American process of presentation of evidence to a largely passive and inscrutable jury or judge may lead to uncorrected misconceptions on the part of the fact finders and unnecessary lawyer activity in proving facts which have already been established to the fact finder's satisfaction. The German process of feedback and dialogue between court, parties and counsel during and after the reception of evidence tends to avoid surprise misconceptions and foster efficiency and focus of the evidentiary proceedings on the issues really in dispute.

It must also be kept in mind that the American process of fact presentation by counsel must be fueled by fees of counsel. This raises not only the question of overall cost of operation of the system which is considered below,[95] but also the issue of inequality of resources to pay those fees. The system seems to work well where both parties are able to pay generous lawyers fees, either by contingent fee arrangements or on an ongoing hourly basis. However cases which will not support contingent fee arrangements and clients who cannot afford to pay large hourly-based fees will not result in the kind of lawyer fact presentation activity that is required by the American system. In such cases inequality of client resources can lead to injustice. And in cases where both clients are impecunious, the lack of resources can lead to impaired fact presentation and a failure of a reasonable exposition of the evidence on both sides. In Germany, where the reception of evidence is an activity shared by counsel and the court, and where fees are standardized to a great degree, a disparity in client resource seems likely to make less of a difference in the quality of the evidence received by the court.

In recent years as litigated cases ever more frequently involve fact issues outside the ordinary layperson's (or judge's) knowledge and life experience, a means to decide issues requiring expertise has become a more important component of civil justice. The American system of asking fact finders to choose between competing party-sponsored expert witnesses does tend to promote

94. Although civil litigation is considered an important part of the practice of the typical German lawyer, there has been no development of a specialist group of "super-star" litigators of exceptional skill who generate especially good results for their clients.

95. See Ch. 13(E)(1)(e) below.

deep and energetic exploration of scientific or technical issues. However it is questionable whether the fact finders have the competence to distinguish between the partisan presentations. The effect of disparity of party resources becomes exaggerated when expert witnesses are involved.[96]

The German system tends to place great reliance on the impartiality and professionalism of the expert witness. Judges tend to rely on court appointed experts to a great degree.[97] Challenging the position taken by a court-appointed expert is a decidedly uphill battle. When the issue is routine and the applicable expert opinion is relatively settled, a court-appointed expert system eliminates the need to resolve a divergence of opinion caused by the partisanship of party-hired expert witnesses. In such cases the German system tends to produce reliable expertise of good quality.

In those cases where the issue is a close one on which experts can differ in good faith, the particular slant of the person appointed may receive undue authority, and it may be difficult to challenge the expert even on legitimate grounds. There is the risk of a one-sided presentation of issues that may be less simple than they are made to seem by the highly credible court-appointed expert.

Viewed another way, American parties and their lawyers address factual assertions and the means to prove them initially during discovery and pretrial preparation, and then repeat much of this activity when they bring the evidence before the court or jury. This repetition is required because the jury and the judge are not privy to the facts and evidence as they are addressed and developed by the parties before the trial. While such repetition may result in a higher degree understanding the facts, the time and cost involved in a double-consideration of the facts is high.

This kind of doubling-up on proof of facts is avoided to a great extent by German procedure, in which the detailed development of the facts occurs only once as the case goes along. Recent reforms in English civil procedure may be moving in the same direction.[98] While German judge-oriented procedure does

96. See Ch. 13(E)(1) below for a discussion of the comparative cost of litigation including references to empirical data to the extent available.

97. See Bross, "Richter und Sachverständiger, dargestellt anhand ausgewählter Probleme des Zivilprozesses", 102 *ZZP* 413 (1989). See Ch. 8(C)(7)(d) above.

98. See Stürner, "Geschichtliche Grundlinien des europäischen Beweisrechts", in: Köbler et al. (eds.), *Europas universale rechtsordnungspolitische Aufgabe im Recht des dritten Jahrtausends - Festschrift für Alfred Söllner* (2000), pp. 1171, 1185 ff.; id., "Transnational Civil Procedure: Discovery and Sanctions against Non-Compliance", 2001 *Uniform. L. Rev.* 871, 882 (2001).

permit the repetition of proof at a hearing, or even on appeal, it has the flexibility to avoid unnecessary doubling of such activity in most ordinary cases.

c. *Analysis of Evidence and Fact Finding by the Court*

The presentation of the evidence to the fact finder and the reception of the evidence by the fact finder are not the end of the story. The important part is still to come. How does the fact finder analyze evidence to reach inferences and conclusions about facts in dispute?

In America the process by which juries find facts is shrouded in mystery. Jury verdicts do not contain any detailed explications of why the juries found the facts as they did.[99] In most cases the fact findings are implicit in simple mandates of "win or lose" or lump sum findings of damages. Nor are counsel or courts permitted to inquire into juries' processes of reasoning after they have rendered their verdicts.[100] The American "black box" system gains its legitimacy from the proposition that if the evidence presented to the jury is of high quality and reliability (as guaranteed by the rules of evidence) and the law as delivered to the jury by the judge in her charge is correct, the jury will do its job correctly and the verdict will be a rational reflection of the evidence and the law.

The assumption is that juries bring to the process of fact analysis the powerful tools of the combined common sense and life experiences of the several members of the jury panel. There is a widely held perception that in many cases juries reach the same result as judges would have reached from the same evidence.[101] Because juries do not have to justify their fact findings and are protected from later inquiry into their processes, it is believed that some juries may reach results by intuitive processes that would not bear rational explanation. In some cases there are suspicions that juries decide cases based on emotional issues and prejudices that should not play a part in a system of justice.[102]

---

99. This is hardly a surprise, considering the conditions under which juries serve, and the difficulty of drafting detailed explanations by committee.

100. This is an ancient taboo now embodied in Federal Rule of Evidence 606 and its many state counterparts. See *Tanner v. United States*, 483 U.S. 107 (1987).

101. The landmark study on which this perception is based was that of Kalven and Zeisel, where the authors found a correspondence of fact findings of about 75%. Kalven/Zeisel, *The American Jury* (1966), pp. 56–58. See further Joiner, *Civil Justice and the Jury* (1962), p. 201; Wissler et al., "Decisionmaking About General Damages: A Comparison of Jurors, Judges and Lawyers", 98 *Mich. L. Rev.* 751 (1999); James/Hazard/Leubsdorf, *Civil Procedure*, §7.7, pp. 400 ff. with further references.

102. Mistrust of jury trial therefore is the perhaps most significant reason why German and European companies fear being sued in America. See Stürner, "Some European Remarks on a New Joint Project of the American Law Institute and UNIDROIT", 34 *The In-*

Nor is the situation much better in cases which are tried to judges without juries. Although American judges are technically capable of explaining the basis for their findings of fact and inferences from the evidence, the jury trial tradition of unexplained fact findings tends to carry over to non-jury proceedings. Although U.S. federal judges are expected to set forth the facts which they have found in support of their decisions, there is no requirement that the court make findings to any particular level of specificity.[103] The extent to which a judge explains why she found particular facts to be proven is up to the individual judge. In many judicial opinions facts found are stated in conclusionary terms without any particular linking of those facts to the evidence adduced at trial.

Presumably professional judges are less likely to base decisions on emotional reactions or prejudices than are lay juries. On the other hand, in jurisdictions where judges are regularly elected to office, it is easy to imagine circumstances in which a judge might feel under some pressure to decide cases in ways pleasing to her electorate.

A jury brings community values to the fact finding process that are impossible to reflect in a purely logical exercise. On some issues, such as negligence, the jury's determination of what is "reasonable care" is informed by the experience of and reflects the view of the community. Awards of damages which are hard logically to quantify, such as damages for pain and suffering, carry the authority of community consensus of the worth of these injuries under the circumstances in question.[104]

Fact finding on matters of expertise is particularly fallible. Lacking a real understanding of the subject matter of experts' testimony, American juries and

---

ternational Lawyer 1071, 1074; id., *Why are Europeans Afraid to Litigate in the United States?* (2001), pp. 12 and 15: "It is the combination of broad discovery, jury trial, American rule of costs, contempt sanctions, big and busy American law firms, extraterritorial application of law and broad personal and subject matter jurisdiction which characterizes the American civil procedure in the eyes of European lawyers as a procedural monster which is feared because of its appetite, sharp teeth and capriciousness."

103. See, e.g., Federal Rule of Civil Procedure 52 (a). "It will be sufficient if the findings of fact and conclusions of law are stated orally and recorded in open court following the close of the evidence or appear in an opinion or memorandum of decision filed by the court." If a party desires more specific findings of fact, the party may move that the court's findings be amended or supplemented. In many states fact findings are not required at all unless a party requests them. See, e.g., Maine Rule of Civil Procedure 52(a) (fact findings are only required if a party moves for them within 5 days of entry of judgment).

104. See, e.g., Adler, *The Jury* (1994), p. 5; Chase, "American Exceptionalism and Comparative Procedure", 50 *Am. J. Comp. L.* 277, 288 ff. (2002).

judges may resort to extrinsic factors, such as form of presentation, invalid "common sense" analogues, or the relative likeability of the persons testifying in order to resolve conflicts in testimony between party experts.[105]

German judges approach fact finding with much more structure than American juries and somewhat more structure than American judges. Although they operate according to the principle of "free evaluation of evidence," by training as well as specific statutory mandate, they are required in their judgments to justify their fact findings in terms of the evidence received.[106] Discussion between court and counsel of the evidence and the likely inferences to be drawn from it during the course of evidentiary proceedings also contributes to transparency of a judge's fact finding function.[107] Finally, the knowledge that their fact findings will be subject to re-examination on appeal may give judges incentives to "get it right" on the first instance and avoid the embarrassment of modification or reversal of fact findings on appeal.[108]

In matters of expertise German judges tend to accept the opinions of their court-appointed experts, sometimes rather uncritically. Although judges are obliged to give reasons for their acceptance of an expert's conclusions if a party disagrees with them, in some cases judges accept expert advice even on matters that would ordinarily be considered matters of common sense and experience.[109]

In most first-instance cases German judges sit as single judges. Although three-judge panels in the state district court are hearing a diminishing percentage of first instance proceedings, in the more difficult cases the aggregation of knowledge and experience of the panel members seems likely to contribute to better fact finding.[110] Even three-judge panels, however, do not

105. See Adler, *The Jury*, pp. 126–127; *Wells by Maihafer v. Ortho Pharmaceutical Corp.*, 617 F. Supp. 262 (D. Ga. 1986); "Federal Judges v. Science", *New York Times*, Dec. 27, 1986, p. 22, col. 1.

106. See Ch. 8(D)(1) above on fact findings and justification in German civil judgments. In Germany there is a strong feeling that a detailed justification of the judge's factual conviction is an indispensable requirement for the control of judicial power. See, e.g., Weitzel, *Tatbestand und Entscheidungsqualität* (1990); Federal Constitutional Court, 47 *NJW* 2279 (1994).

107. See Ch. 8(C)(1)(e), (D)(2) and generally Ch. 6(C)(2) above on hints and feedback during and after evidentiary proceedings.

108. Whether the recent reform of second instance appellate procedure (see Ch. 10(D)(2) above) diminishes or increases these incentives may be an open question.

109. See Ch. 8(C)(7)(d) above on judicial evaluation of expert testimony. However such over-reliance on expert witness testimony can be grounds for reversal on appeal.

110. See Ch. 3(D)(2)(b) and Ch. 7(E)(1) above for a discussion of the division of caseload between single judges and three-judge panels in the state district court.

have the capacity to reflect community norms and values that comes from direct participation of a large number of lay persons in the fact finding as is the case with an American jury.[111] Fact finding on issues which do not lend themselves to rational analysis, such as the value of pain and suffering, cannot call on the authority of community consensus to supplement judicial reasoning. Awards for damages of this kind tend to be conservative and reflect precedent rather than the kind of intuitive consensus that comes from the jury process.

In some cases the method of training, selection and promotion of judges in Germany means that judges can be somewhat short on life experience and practical wisdom at the outset of their careers of judicial service. Life experience can be an important tool for the analysis and reconstruction of fact scenarios. Although assignments of judges in their first few years of service attempt to take their ages and levels of experience into account, it is not uncommon for judges in their late twenties or early thirties to have to grapple with difficult issues of parental responsibility in family cases without any relevant experience of their own to draw upon.[112]

Both the American system of fact finding by juries and the German system of fact finding by judges or panels of judges have undoubted strengths and weaknesses. To some extent it can be said that these respective systems represent cultural preferences rather than a conscious reflection of policy considerations in judicial fact finding.[113] On the other hand, it seems fairly safe to say that in today's increasingly crowded and complicated world, a judge-based fact finding system is likely to be the system of the future in both Germany and the United States.[114]

Although fact finding by juries continues to serve as a template for all American civil litigation, in fact, the actual occurrence of civil jury trial has become rare in the United States in all but the most extreme cases. In this respect the American civil justice establishment seems to be following the path

---

111. Honorary lay judges sit on commercial panels in the state district courts. See Ch. 3(D)(2)(c) above. Their participation brings some specialized "real world" expertise to these panels. However it can scarcely be said that they broadly represent community values and norms. On the other hand, lay judges may represent community values in some of the specialized courts such as labor courts, administrative courts, social welfare courts or tax courts. See Ch. 3(C) above.

112. See Ch. 3(G) and Ch. 13(C)(2) above.

113. For an American perspective see Chase, "Legal Processes and National Culture", 5 *Cardozo J. Intern'l & Comp. L.* 1 (1997).

114. For "commercial cases" excluding personal-injury and wrongful-death actions this is also the point of view of the ALI-UNIDROIT project on Principles and Rules of Transnational Civil Procedure, see Preface, Council Draft No. 2 of September 29, 2003, http://www.ali.org.

taken by other jurisdictions such as Canada and Australia which derive their legal systems from that of England. In these systems civil jury trial is all but extinct, as it has been in England itself since 1918.[115]

It is easy to point to various limitations of jury process which may be contributing to its demise. Some of the most obvious are the opacity of jury verdicts and the risk of extreme results. Perhaps more important are the tremendous cost and expense imposed on the parties by jury process and the rigidity imparted to the preparatory and fact finding proceeding by the participation of a lay jury.

The German experience strongly suggests that in most cases fact finding by engaged and informed judges can result in a more flexible, focused procedure and more predictable and transparent fact findings at a much lower cost. There may be some civil cases in which the role of community norms and values is so important as to justify a jury.[116] However it seems clear that in most cases Germans get better and more understandable fact finding from their judges than Americans from their juries.

American fact finding by judges, which has become the norm in a majority of litigated matters, remains to some extent under the influence of the jury trial pattern. American judges have not yet taken to the role of "managerial judges" although authorized to do so by rule and encouraged by legislation. Some reasons for this may be lack of contact with the facts at early stages of the litigation, high caseloads, and a tradition of restraint to avoid a perception of prejudgment.[117]

Although judicial opinions provide some transparency in fact finding, American judges have been generally somewhat reluctant to discuss their processes of reasoning from the evidence presented to their fact findings. This might be partly because they are protected in their findings by a very narrow scope of review on appeal. Another reason often given by judges for lack of explication of reasoning in their opinions is lack of time caused by excessive caseloads.

---

115. Jury trial in civil cases was suspended in England in 1918 as a war measure because of a shortage of jurymen. This suspension gradually evolved into abolition of jury trial for virtually all civil cases except for libel. See, e.g., Haines, "The Disappearance of Civil Juries in England, Canada and Australia", 4 *Defense Law Journal* 118 (1958). See also Denning, "What is Next in the Law", reprinted in: Glendon et al. (eds.), *Comparative Legal Traditions*, 2nd ed. (1994), p. 613.

116. For instance, in England, the jury has been retained to hear libel cases, in which community values and norms play important parts.

117. See, e.g., Murray, "Civil Justice Reform in America; The 1990 Civil Justice Reform Act and its Consequences", 3 *ZZPInt* 319 (1998).

d. Review of Fact Finding on Appeal

Appellate review provides an additional guarantee of the quality of fact findings in both Germany and the United States. However the scope of appellate review and the role played by appellate courts in correcting errors of fact finding differ significantly between the two systems.

Under the American tradition, first instance findings of fact are all but final in most cases. Jury verdicts are reviewed by a standard that permits appellate correction only when the appellate court is convinced that "no reasonable jury" could have made the finding in question from the evidence presented. Even findings made by judges sitting without juries are immune from challenge unless it appears that they are "clearly erroneous." Appellate courts, who do not hear witnesses themselves, defer to the trial court's on findings made from oral testimony and on issues such as witness credibility.[118]

In Germany recent reforms have attempted slightly to narrow appellate review of first instance fact findings.[119] Nonetheless, second-instance appellate review of matters of fact is quite broad. Appellate courts can and do question fact findings made below and hear or rehear testimony when there is a credible allegation that the court below misunderstood or misconstrued the evidence below.

Although it can be said that this more thoroughgoing review of facts on second-instance appeal means additional cost and delay in reaching final dispositions in civil cases, it plays an important role in reinforcing the fact finding function of the system as a whole. As is discussed below, the German system of engaged judges managing the evidentiary proceedings with little or no pretrial discovery can reach credible first instance judgments with very little delay and at relatively low cost.[120] However in some cases the German process can result in fact findings that may be premature or based on an incomplete understanding of the relevant facts and circumstances.

In many, if not most cases, the relatively expeditious German first instance procedure will result in fact findings which are accurate and satisfac-

---

118. See F.R.Civ. P. 52(a): In reviewing findings of fact made by a trial court, "due regard shall be given to the opportunity of the trial court to judge of the credibility of the witnesses". For a survey see James/Hazard/Leubsdorf, *Civil Procedure*, 5th ed. (2001), §12.9, pp. 766ff.; for the "clearly erroneous" standard see *Pullman-Standard v. Swint*, 456 *U.S.* 273, 287–289.

119. See Ch. 10(D)(2) above on the effect of recent reforms on review of fact findings on second-instance appeal.

120. See Ch. 13(E) below.

tory to the parties. In those cases the parties are served speedily and at low cost. However the German process of enhanced review of fact findings on appeal permits those litigants who are not satisfied with their first-instance dispositions to get the benefit of a more focused and thorough look at the facts in the second instance.[121] Such a second look at the facts, with the benefit of the experience of the first instance proceedings and the disclosed reasoning of the first instance judge, can be a very valuable means of correcting error. The cumulative effect of both instances can easily result in a better fact investigation than even an exhaustive concentrated first-instance process. These considerations led the German Parliament to retain the essence of the second-instance appellate review of facts in the 2001 civil justice reforms.[122]

As long as juries decide civil cases in America it is unlikely that appellate courts will exercise much appellate jurisdiction over their fact findings.[123] On the other hand, to the extent that American judges become more active and involved with the facts at early stages of the proceedings, and as such activity results in more rapid and efficient disposition of cases at the first instance, one can imagine that American appellate courts might increase their interest in and scrutiny of fact findings in the interest of maintaining quality of the system as a whole.

2. Application of the Law

Finding the relevant facts is only a part of the process of providing dispositions of high quality in individual cases. Once the court has determined "what likely happened", the court must then apply the relevant legal norms to that scenario of likely facts to reach a judicial disposition.

Again the American jury process presents a stark contrast to German procedure (and indeed to American procedure in non-jury dispositions). In the American jury process, either before or after the jury hears the evidence, the

---

121. See Stürner, "Eckpunkte einer Justizreform", 53 *NJW Beilage Heft 25*, 31f. (2000).

122. See Zöller/Gummer, *Zivilprozessordnung*, 23rd ed. (2002), §528, mn. 1; *Begründung der Bundesregierung zum ZPO-Reformgesetz* (comments of the government on the proposed reform of the ZPO), BT-Drs. 14/4722, p. 100 and *Bericht des Rechtsausschusses* (report of the judicial committee of the German parliament), BT-Drs. 14/6036, p. 157.

123. Except in the case of punitive damages, where one can observe a development towards more stringent appellate review. See *BMW of North America, Inc. v. Gore*, 517 U.S. 559, 116 S. Ct. 1589 (1996); James/Hazard/Leubsdorf, *Civil Procedure*, 5th ed. (2001), §7.29, p. 480; Eisenberg/Wells, "Punitive Awards After BMW, A New Capping System, and the Reported Opinion Bias", 1998 *Wis. L. Rev.* 387 (1998).

judge instructs the jury as to the likely applicable law in more or less general terms. These instructions are usually given orally, although recently there has been a trend to supplement the oral instructions with a written text. The content of what is told the jury about the law is discussed by the judge with the parties' lawyers beforehand and is frequently an issue on appeal. When the jurors retire to deliberate, they are supposed to apply the law as explained to them by the judge to the facts as they find them from the evidence. The verdict is usually rendered in opaque and conclusionary terms.

Although it is possible for an American judge to ask the jury to render a verdict consisting solely of fact findings, to which the judge then applies the law, such verdicts are quite rare.[124] When the fact finding to be made is anything more than a simple "yes or no" answer to a relatively simple question, it is usually easier to give the law to the jury than to devise questions which will provide the jury with the right scope and structure to give meaningful answers.

This system again relies on the assumption that if the jurors are told the correct law by the judge, they apply that law to the facts found in an informed and correct manner to reach their verdict. Legal constraints on inquiry into the thought processes of juries mean that there is little empirical evidence on the soundness of this assumption. Certainly extreme results in some cases lead to question whether the jury always faithfully follows the judge's instructions. How many verdicts actually represent a conscious and rational application of the declared law to the facts found and how many are the result of some other decision-reaching process is not known.

Application of the law is much simpler if no jury is involved. American judges sitting without jury deal with the law in a manner very similar to that used by their colleagues in Germany. They are expected to advert to the law applied in their opinions, which are subject to review on appeal. While there is no certainty that any judge decided a case for the reasons she said she did, the requirement that a judge explain and justify her application of the law does impart an important discipline which tends to insure reliable and consistent decision-making.

The extent to which a judge is responsible for an accurate application of law even when the parties do not suggest it varies among jurisdictions and

124. Such verdicts are termed "verdicts on special interrogatories". The judge, with the assistance of counsel, formulates a series of questions about the relevant facts at issue for the jury to answer. The judge then applies the law to the answers given by the jury. See F.R. Civ. P. 49; Wright/Miller, *Federal Practice & Procedure*, 2nd ed. (1995), Vol. 9A, §§2501–2520.

kinds of cases in America. In many cases a judge will not be responsible for applying a legal theory unless one or the other party has suggested it. In some cases the failure of a judge to apply the correct law is ground for reversal regardless of whether either party suggested that law during the proceedings below.[125]

The American system of appellate review in civil cases is well designed to correct errors in the application of law in the form of errors in a judge's charge to a jury or in the judge's application of legal doctrine to facts found in non-jury proceedings. Because of the opacity of jury deliberations and jury verdicts, there is no effective appellate review of the application of the law by juries.[126]

In Germany the mandatory structure of judicial judgments tends to make the determination of the applicable law and its application to the facts of the case both conscious and transparent.[127] German civil justice also operates according to the principle that the court is responsible for correct application of the law regardless of whether either party has called the correct law to the court's attention ("iura novit curia"). There is at least one, and sometimes two levels of appellate review of questions of law in first-instance judgments and decisions.

3. Overall Quality of Adjudication

It appears clear to us that both the German and the American systems of civil justice produce adjudications of consistently good quality in most cases. The German system with its heavy reliance on professional judges and court appointed experts likely has an edge in predictability and consistency of civil adjudications. In most civil cases the speedier and more inexpensive German process will produce fact findings of sufficient accuracy to insure appropriate dispositions. The limitations of the German system become more apparent in the larger more ambitious cases. In such cases, sometimes the enterprise and energy of the neutral judges and the contributions of counsel might result in a less than thorough exploration of really difficult factual and policy issues presented.[128]

In our judgment the American jury system also provides predictable and consistent outcomes in routines cases, although arguably at a considerably

125. See Friedenthal/Kane/Miller, *Civil Procedure*, 3rd ed. (1999), §13.4, p. 618ff.

126. For the problem of the general verdict see Friedenthal/Kane/Miller, §12.1, p. 549ff.

127. See Ch. 9(B)(3) above on the form of judgments.

128. See Stürner, "Some European Remarks on a New Joint Project of the American Law Institute and UNIDROIT", 34 *The International Lawyer* 1071, 1080 (2000); for a compromise Hazard/Taruffo/Stürner/Gidi, *Principles and Rules of Transnational Civil Procedure*, Introduction, The American Law Institute, Council Draft No. 2, (September 29, 2003), pp. 5 f.

higher economic cost than in Germany.[129] In the more unusual and extreme cases the participation of lay jurors and the opacity of their function can result in unpredictable and extreme results, which surely imposes an uncertainty cost on the system as a whole.[130]

On the other hand, the larger scope to lawyers' activity in fact development and case presentation permits an exhaustive investigation of issues of fact and a sophisticated development of fact distinctions. Finally, the function of the lay jury has the strength of incorporating community values in the civil justice process.

These respective areas of strength correspond to some extent to the expected role of civil justice in each countries respective social and economic culture. In Germany, where the assignment of civil justice is primarily the vindication of individual rights and normative adjustment of private disputes, consistency and predictability are all important. In the United States on the other hand, civil litigation plays a big role in regulating the respective social and economic relationships of business, government and individual citizens. The tradition of citizen participation on juries and the enlarged roles of parties and their lawyers in case presentation corresponds to this larger role of civil justice in public, private and economic life.

Putting aside the occasional extreme or unpredictable jury verdict on the one hand, and the occasional superficial or inadequately investigated fact finding on the other, it appears clear that both German and American civil justice consistently produce adjudications of high quality appropriate to the roles of the civil justice system in their respective political economies.

E. Delay and Cost

Both cost and delay are material elements evaluating the performance of institutions of civil justice. Justice which is available only at a high price or after long delays is "justice denied" to at least some affected parties. Reducing

129. This very high cost may be leading to a gradual abandonment of jury trial in cases involving modest amounts in controversy. See Sward, *Decline of the Civil Jury*, p. 137: "Jury trials take longer than bench trials, and both kinds of trials take longer than settlements or the resolution of cases on motions. There is, then, considerable incentive for actors within the system to resolve cases without juries, or even without trials".

130. For a discussion of jury competence in "complex cases" based on empirical research see the report of the Special Commission of the ABA Section on Litigation, *Jury Comprehension in Complex Cases* (1989); Sanders, "Scientifically Complex Cases, Trial by Jury, and the Erosion of Adversarial Process", 48 *DePaul L. Rev.* 355, 359 (1998).

both cost and duration of litigation has long been a policy priority in practically every modern nation state.[131]

In our view, German civil justice as presently administered, has the clear edge in terms of cost and even delay when compared with civil justice in the United States. It appears clear that in most cases German litigants can obtain judicial determinations of their legal claims at a fraction of the cost and within a shorter time than their American counterparts.

1. Cost of Litigation

The largest components of the costs borne by civil litigants are the fees and expenses of counsel, court fees, and other litigation expenses such as fees of expert witnesses. There are no reliable statistical compilations of these costs on an aggregate basis for either Germany or the United States. However the German statutory fee schedule on the one hand and the American practice of contingent-fee based representation in certain kinds of litigation on the other permit comparisons on the individual case level from which some systemic generalizations can be drawn.

Take, for instance, a simple personal injury case based on an automobile accident. Assume that the injured plaintiff is able to prove liability and damages which result in an award against the driver of the other car of $50,000 for medical expenses and pain and suffering.[132] Analyzing the principal cost components of counsel fees, court costs, and other miscellaneous expenses can give us an idea of the relative costs of litigation under the two systems.

a. Attorneys Fees

In both Germany and the United States the compensation of attorneys is likely to be the largest out of pocket cost for the litigating parties. In an Amer-

---

131. See, e.g., Zuckerman, in: *Civil Justice in Crisis*, p. 51: "The systems discussed in this volume vary, therefore, not in their central objective but in the way that they seek to provide correct decisions within a reasonable time and at an affordable cost. Although excessive delay and high cost have serious adverse effects on the efficacy of the system of justice, they have been persistent in most civil justice systems for a very long time. Every country boasts a long history of attempts to reduce delay and cost, yet few have been even moderately successful in reaching a sensible balance."

132. This assumption is somewhat artificial, since awards for pain and suffering in Germany tend to be considerably lower than such awards in the United States. Larger U.S. awards for the same injuries tend, however, to increase the overall costs of adjudication and the resulting disparity in cost between the two justice systems.

ican personal injury case usually the plaintiff's lawyer is paid on the basis of a contingency fee agreement under which the lawyer receives a percentage of any amount collected for the client in the litigation. Such arrangements generally run from 33 1/3% to 50% of the recovery, largely depending on the amount in controversy and the difficulty and contingency of the individual case. We can thus assume that the plaintiff's lawyer would get between $16,666 and $25,000 of the $50,000 recovery in our typical case.[133]

Defense counsel in American civil personal injury cases are typically paid on an hourly basis by their insurance company clients. Their charges thus vary depending on the amount of activity in the case. In the less than 3% of the cases which go to trial and verdict it is not unusual for hourly defense counsel fees to exceed the amounts received by the plaintiffs' lawyers, especially if the ultimate recoveries are modest in amount or even zero.[134]

What has been ascertained is that as a rule, the amount expended by defendants for their civil representation is not less than that paid out by plaintiffs on contingent fee arrangements.[135] Thus, while the pattern of payments

---

133. It should be acknowledged that the contingent fee system means that plaintiff's counsel receives compensation only in those cases which result in a net recovery. An estimate of the average amount paid for representation of plaintiffs in personal injury cases would require the amounts paid to lawyers from cases with net recoveries to be spread over the entire body of cases brought, including those resulting in small recoveries or no recoveries at all.

134. If the amount recovered were zero the defense counsel would receive full payment from its client and the plaintiff's attorney, operating on a contingent fee arrangement, nothing.

135. See Kritzer, "The Wages of Risk: The Returns of Contingency Fee Legal Practice", 47 *DePaul L. Rev.* 267 (1998); Jay, "The Dilemmas of Attorney Contingent Fees", 2 *Geo. J. Legal Ethics* 813, 826 (1989): "A somewhat helpful indicator of what occurs in the typical case is found in studies that compare the legal fees spent by both plaintiffs and defendants in tort cases. One study, which unfortunately is dated, shows that the effective hourly wages of plaintiffs' attorneys paid on a contingent basis are not much higher than the hourly wages of the defense counsel.... Other research indicates that the overall attorneys' fees for plaintiffs in tort cases are actually much less than those spent by defendants (this does not compare effective hourly rates for attorneys, however)." This seems to be in line with empirical studies showing that the hours spent or at least the hours effectively billed are in general closely related to the amount in controversy or the importance of the case to the client. See Willging/Stienstra/Shapard/Miletich, "An Empirical Study of Discovery and Disclosure Practice Under the 1993 Federal Rule Amendments", 39 *B.C.L.Rev.* 525, 531 (1998); McKenna/Wiggins, "Empirical Research on Civil Discovery", 39 *B.C.L.Rev.* 785, 793 (1998). The same should be true for the relatively new method of task-based billing which seems to be a shift towards a fixed fee system. See Rotunda,"Moving From Billable Hour to Fixed Fees: Task-Based Fees and Legal Ethics", 47 *U. Kan. L. Rev.* 819 (1999). Task-based billing

differs in individual cases, defense counsel as a group receive about the same compensation per case as to their counterparts on the other side.[136]

Applying this overall assumption to our hypothetical case, it can be estimated that the cost for representation of the defendant could well be in the realm of $16,666 to $25,000, and perhaps more if the case went to trial.

Taking only attorneys fees, it appears that the cost of counsel for both parties of litigating a medium-sized personal injury case to adjudication can amount to a sum equalling from two-thirds to 100% of the amount ultimately awarded.[137]

In Germany, on the other hand, the compensation of the lawyers for both parties would be determined by the Federal Attorneys Fee Law (*Bundesrechtsanwaltsgebührenordnung* or *BRAGO*) and its fee schedules.[138] Assuming that the case proceeded through first instance judgment and included the taking of evidence, each lawyer would be entitled to compensation based on three fee units at an amount in controversy of 50,000 Euro.[139] At a per fee unit amount of 1046 Euro, the plaintiff's attorney would be entitled to 3138 Euro and the defendant's lawyer to a like amount. The combined attorneys fees for both parties in obtaining the adjudication would be some 6276 Euro, or about 13% of the amount in controversy.[140]

It is true that smaller amounts in controversy generate relatively larger fees even to the point that the combined lawyers fees can exceed relatively modest recoveries or very small amounts in controversy.[141] However it appears

---

is being introduced primarily by commercial purchasers of legal services such as insurance companies. See Rickerson, "Law Firms Profit Increase With Strategic Legal Management", 68 *Defense Counsel J.* 228 (2001).

136. There may be an exception for the so-called "big hitter" plaintiffs' lawyers who may be in a class by themselves because they only handle cases with likely large damages awards.

137. Obviously there are economies of scale in litigation. One could anticipate some reduction in the relationship of the lawyers fees to the amount awarded for larger awards. If the amount awarded were $5 million, one could anticipate that both the plaintiff's and the defendant's lawyers fees would amount to a smaller share of the recovery than would be the case if the recovery were in the $50,000–$500,000 range.

138. See Ch. 4(H) above on the Attorneys Fee Law in general, and Ch. 9(E)(2) above on the computation of attorneys fees in judgments.

139. See BRAGO §31. This assumes parity of the Euro and the Dollar.

140. These fees would ultimately be borne by the parties in the proportion that the outcome reflected vindication of their respective positions. See Ch. 9(E)(2) above on the allocation of attorneys fees in civil judgments.

141. So, for instance, if the parties litigated to judgment with an amount in controversy of 600 Euro and the plaintiff recovered 300 Euro, counsel for both parties would be entitled to compensation at 45 Euro per fee unit resulting in total counsel fees nearly equal to the amount recovered.

clear that up and down the scale German lawyers' s fees represent a much smaller absolute and relative litigation cost than is the case in the United States.

b. Court Fees and Costs

The picture is somewhat different with respect to the fees charged by courts for entertaining civil proceedings. It appears clear that Germany attempts to require the parties to bear a somewhat greater amount and proportion of the costs expended by public institutions for the provision of public justice than is the case in the United States.

In America by tradition and custom courts charge only nominal fees for entertaining and even adjudicating civil cases. The filing fee for a civil case in the United States District court is currently $150 regardless of the amount in controversy.[142] This is in line with the cost of filing a civil case in the courts of general jurisdiction of most of the American states. While it is true that some jurisdictions impose additional fees or costs for particular judicial services such as jury trial, in general such fees are nominal to very moderate in amount and do not increase with the amount in controversy.[143] Such costs and fees represent a trifling proportion of the budgets of both state and federal courts. Although in contrast to attorneys fees, court costs and fees are generally taxed to the loser if the case is decided, they are not a significant factor in litigation tactics or decisions. In our hypothetical case we could expect that the parties together would have expended less than $250 on all forms of court costs other than expert witness fees.[144]

In Germany, on the other hand, civil litigants are expected to pay meaningful court costs for the right to conduct civil litigation in the various state and federal courts. Court costs are based both on the amount in controversy and on the amount of judicial activity required to bring the case to resolution.[145] In our

---

142. See 28 U.S.C. §1914(a).

143. See, e.g., Maine Schedule of Court Fees—Web Page of Maine Supreme Judicial Court, www.courts.state.me.us/rules_forms_fees/filing_fees.html (Fee for entry of action in Superior Court—$100, additional fee for exercising right to jury trial in civil cases—$300). There are sometimes nominal costs for filing appeals. Other court costs may include the costs of service of process, copies of papers, filing of judgments, etc. All of these are nominal in amount.

144. In most American jurisdictions, expert witness fees are at least in part classified as court costs for the purpose of cost shifting even though the experts are selected and paid directly by the respective parties. For more details see Ch. 13(E)(1)(c) below.

145. See Ch. 9(E)(1)(a) above on the basis for computation of court costs in judgments.

hypothetical case, assuming an amount in controversy of 50,000 Euro, the plaintiff would have been required to advance a basic court cost of three fee units each of 456 Euro for a total "suit fee" (*Prozessgebühr*) of 1368 Euro at the time of filing the complaint.[146] Additional fees would be associated with any provisional measures sought or independent hearings for the reception of evidence.

The clear cost advantage enjoyed by German litigants with respect to attorneys fees must thus be tempered by the higher levels of costs they are required to pay to their courts. The net balance of combined costs continues, however, to favor Germany.

c. *Other Litigation and Expert Witness Expense*

Litigation clearly imposes costs to parties other than the amounts they are required to pay the courts and their lawyers. There is no attempt to measure or compare the costs to the parties from having to attend court themselves, costs of uncertainty of outcome, time cost of money, or other costs borne directly by the parties by virtue of participating in civil litigation.

There is one additional area of cost, however, that should be mentioned. Modern litigation almost always involves the presentation of expert testimony. Unlike ordinary witnesses, who both in Germany and in the United States are expected to appear in court to give their evidence for nominal compensation, expert witnesses are fully and adequately compensated for the preparation and rendition of their expert opinions.

As indicated above, in the United States, the parties retain, prepare and present their own expert witnesses on the issues in the case which require expertise. Frequently the fees and expenses of these witnesses are substantial.[147] In recent times, the widespread use by experts of elaborate visual teaching has added an entire new element of cost associated with their appearances. While the fees and expenses of expert witnesses are initially borne by the party who presents them, in most American jurisdictions there is provision for shifting at least a part of the expenditures for expert witnesses to the losing party as a component of "court costs".[148] When this occurs, the expert witness fees, or

---

146. Court Costs Law (*Gerichtskostengesetz or GKG*) §12, Attachment 1.

147. Although most commentators condemn the practice, in some cases experts as well as attorneys are engaged on contingent fee arrangements. See Note, "Contingency Fees for Expert Witnesses in Civil Litigation", 86 *Yale L. J.* 1680 (1977); Patterson, "Conflicts of Interest in Scientific Expert Testimony", 40 *Wm. and Mary L. Rev.* 1313, 1331, n. 73.

148. See 28 U.S.C. §1920; 14 MRSA §1502-C. Pursuant to FRCP 54(d) and 28 U.S.C.A. §1920(3) only the ordinary statutory witness fees as fixed by 28 U.S.C.A. §1821 (attendance fee of $40 per day, travel expenses and subsistence allowance) are taxed against the loser.

portions of them included as court costs, are generally by far and away the largest component of the amount to be taxed.

In a simple personal injury case the plaintiff would typically call at least one expert medical witness to document the plaintiff's injury and the extent of ongoing impairment or need for treatment. If damages are controverted, the defendant would likely call its own doctor to give an opinion on these issues. Assuming that both sides called expert witnesses in our $50,000 personal injury case, it could be assumed that each doctor would charge fees in the order of $2500 for examination of the plaintiff, preparation for trial, and for testifying.[149] The court or jury would draw its conclusion of the amount of impairment or need for ongoing treatment from consideration of the differing testimony of the two experts.

In Germany expertise is usually provided by one or more court appointed expert witnesses.[150] On the assumption that our case presented a single issue requiring expertise, ordinarily one would expect a single court appointed expert. The court would usually accept the expert's testimony with whatever insights or qualifications the parties or their lawyers were able to suggest. At the same level of compensation, the total expenditure for expertise would be on the order of 2500 Euro, approximately half of the amount that would be expected in U.S. litigation.

d. Other Private or Public Costs?

Any cost comparison between German and American civil justice is not complete without consideration of public expenditures for civil justice. Reliable, comprehensive data from which direct comparisons can be made is extremely difficult to obtain.[151] Judicially related expenditures in public budgets in both countries are very difficult to break out, particularly if one seeks to isolate expenditures for civil justice. Nor is there correspondence between categories of public expenditures among the myriad organs of state and federal government in both countries.

Gross budgets associated with the judiciary appear to be a slightly larger proportion of public expenditures in Germany than in either the United States

---

See *Crawford Fitting Company v. J.T. Gibbons, Inc.*, 107 S.Ct. 2494, 482 U.S. 437 (1987); Wright/Miller/Kane, *Federal Practice and Procedure*, 3rd ed., Vol. 10, §2678, p. 477.

149. For want of a better source, this figure comes from the experience of Professor Murray in many years of civil litigation practice. The fees would likely be higher if either expert were subject to pretrial deposition by the other side.

150. See Ch. 8(C)(7) above.

151. See Ch. 3(J)(3) above.

or most American states. Germany's apparently higher per capita public expenditure for justice parallels its well known high number of judges per capita.[152] Even in the absence of precise figures it appears that in Germany the public bears a larger share of the cost of providing justice in civil cases than does the public in America.

While this somewhat larger level of public expenditure should be taken into account in comparing the cost of civil justice in both countries, when spread over the caseloads of the respective court systems, the additional public cost of justice in Germany pales in comparison with the additional private cost of justice in the United States.

e. *The Overall Cost Picture*

The high cost of civil justice in the United States has long been a subject of critical comment and calls for reform. Reduction of the excessive cost of American civil justice was a prime goal of the most recent attempt at comprehensive legislative reform at the federal level, the Civil Justice Reform Act of 1990.[153] High cost is cited as a serious drawback in virtually every comparative commentary on American civil justice.[154] High private cost of civil justice has a serious negative effect on access to justice by the indigent and the provision of cost-effective legal aid.

On the other hand, the cost of civil justice appears to be relatively reasonable in Germany. While cost reduction is a goal for every justice system, in Germany costs to litigants of securing civil justice appear to be under control. To the extent that reduction of party costs has meant increase in public costs, any increase in public costs appears to be reasonable in terms of private resources saved.

An authoritative analysis of the cost differences between American and German institutions of public justice is far beyond the scope of this work. However an overview of both systems can support some tentative generalizations.

---

152. See Ch. 3(A) and (I)(2) above for a discussion of the number of judges per capita in Germany compared with roughly corresponding figures for the United States and the United Kingdom.

153. For a discussion of the Civil Justice Reform Act of 1990 and followup evaluations of its effectiveness see Murray, "Civil Justice Reform in America, The 1990 Civil Justice Reform Act and its Consequences", *3 ZZPInt 319*, (1999).

154. See, e.g., Marcus, "Malaise of the Litigation Superpower", in: Zuckerman (ed.), *Civil Justice in Crisis* (1999), pp. 92–95. The American tort system has been estimated to cost more than twice as much per capita as the tort systems of other industrialized countries. See, e.g., Galanter, "Real World Torts: An Antidote to Anecdote", 55 *Md. L. Rev.* 1093, 1141 (1996). How much of the high cost of the American tort system stems from the size of awards to victims as opposed to costs of the system itself has not been broken down.

The German system appears to limit and contain the largest components of private litigation costs by somewhat limiting the scope of lawyer activity and by seriously limiting lawyer compensation. While it is true that nothing prevents lawyers and their clients from agreeing on counsel fees higher than those provided in the Attorneys Fee Law, the losing party is required to reimburse fees only to the extent authorized by the Attorneys Fee Law.[155] This provides a practical cap on attorneys fees in most cases at the statutory levels.[156]

The German system also allocates the work between judge and lawyer in a way so as to maximize the efficiency of both key elements in most cases. The lawyers work with their clients in preparing the allegations and the proof to substantiate them before the proceedings are commenced. However once the case is in court, the judge plays a dynamic role in shaping and streamlining the case and sorting out the factual proof needed to decide it. Proof of the greater economic efficiency of this approach over the party and lawyer dominated American litigation process is at the anecdotal stage.[157]

The American system permits parties to come to court only scantily prepared. Comprehensive pretrial discovery permits exhaustive development of the relevant fact scenarios and the means to prove them, but at great cost in terms of adversarial lawyer activity. The marshalling and presentation of the facts in dramatic oral proceedings to passive fact finders also requires a great deal of lawyer activity that is minimized in German evidentiary proceedings.

While it cannot be gainsaid that this investment of party and lawyer resources does result in a more thorough and exhaustive explication of the facts than typically takes place in a German case, one must ask whether such activity is cost justified in the ordinary civil case. German parties seem to be at least as satisfied with the quality of the justice they receive as American litigants are with theirs.[158] It is tempting to conclude that by allocating so much of the burden of responsibility for case development and presentation to private counsel, by giving them so much procedural scope within which to fulfill this responsibility, and by compensating them on a more or less open-

---

155. But note that conditional compensation based on a favorable outcome and contingency fees are not permitted! See Ch. 4(H) above.

156. See Ch. 4(H) above on the relationship of attorneys fees to the statutory fee schedules.

157. For an effort to make a comparison of cost and efficiency by measuring various inputs to processing the same case under both systems, see Murray, "A Comparative Law Experiment", 8 *Ind. Int'l & Comp. L. R.* 231 (1998).

158. See Ch. 13(H) below.

ended basis for doing the work, the American civil justice system imposes on litigating parties unnecessarily high costs in most cases.

On the other hand, it is also clear that Americans expect that their system will perform public policy functions not undertaken by civil justice in Germany. At least a part of the caseload of American courts consists of cases that simply would not be brought in Germany.[159] Large and complex cases which address important issues of public policy or mass compensation may have social and even political consequences for American society as a whole which can justify very high expenditures by the interests involved. The functions of public education, and dramatization of confrontations of rights and interests within society may be worth some additional expenditure on the part of persons benefitted by such education or dramatization.

Any comparison of the cost-efficiency of the German and American civil justice systems on an overall basis is further complicated by the fact that in America civil justice fulfils public functions of compensation and income redistribution that are performed by social insurance and welfare programs in Germany. A meaningful comparison of the cost of this function would have to include the costs of operation and ongoing development of these systems in Germany, which would offset, at least in part, the higher civil justice costs borne by individual private parties in the United States.

So far as concerns the caseload in common to both systems, those cases where the function of the justice system is the vindication of private legal rights according to public norms, it appears to us that the German system offers clear cost advantages on an overall basis.

2. Duration of Proceedings.

Unreasonable delay has traditionally been considered along with excess cost as a serious cause for dissatisfaction with the performance of civil justice systems. "Justice delayed is justice denied" has meaning in Germany as well as the United States.[160] Reduction of the duration of civil proceedings has long been a goal of judicial reform not only in America and Germany, but in practically every civil society.[161]

---

159. See Ch. 13(A) above.

160. The German expression is "Delayed justice gives stones instead of bread." (*Verspätete Gerechtigkeit gibt Steine statt Brot*).

161. See, e.g., Zuckerman, in: *Civil Justice in Crisis*, p. 51: "Although excessive delay and high cost have serious adverse effects on the efficacy of the system of justice, they have been persistent in most civil justice systems for a very long time. Every country boasts a

At the current time considerable progress has been made in the reduction of delay in both Germany and, at least in many kinds of cases, in the United States as well. At a time when litigants in some modern states have to wait years to obtain first-instance judgments in contested cases requiring evidentiary proceedings, Germans and Americans have relatively swift recourse to justice. During 1996 in Germany the average time between filing of a complaint and the issuance of a first instance judgment was 4.6 months in the local courts and 6.5 months in the state district courts.[162]

In the United States the picture is complicated by significant differences among the many American justice systems. A 1991 study of 39 urban state trial courts found that most courts needed more than one year to conclude the average case. In twelve of the courts about 90 per cent of cases were disposed of within two years of filing and in one court only 1 per cent of cases were two years old. In three courts more than 50 per cent of cases needed more than two years and in one court of those 96 per cent of cases were not concluded within one year.[163] Tort cases generally took more time than contract cases.

The results of a statistical portrait based on the data of the Civil Trial Court Network, a joint project of the National Center for State Courts and the Bureau of Justice Statistics, are somewhat better.[164] In 1996 the average case in state courts of first instance needed 340 days, in Federal District Courts 420 days (without asbestos cases 302 days). Cases with jury trials were concluded within 751 days in state courts and within 588 days in federal courts. The presence or absence of a jury trial clearly influenced the duration of a case according to this evaluation.[165]

In both Germany and the United States the durations of civil proceedings can be extended by appeals. For many cases the first-instance judgment is not the end of the road for the litigants.

Somewhat surprisingly the German percentage of civil cases that are appealed is not much higher than the corresponding percentage in the American

---

long history of attempts to reduce delay and cost, yet few have been even moderately successful in reaching a sensible balance".

162. Gottwald, "Civil Justice Reform: Access, Cost, and Expedition. The German Perspective", in: Zuckerman (ed.), *Civil Justice in Crisis* (1999), pp. 207, 211 f.

163. See Goerdt/Lomvardias/Gallas, *Reexamining the Pace of Litigation* (1991), pp. 37ff.; Marcus, "Malaise of the Litigation Superpower", in: Zuckerman (ed.), *Civil Justice in Crisis* (1999), pp. 71 ff., 90f. with further references.

164. See Eisenberg/Goerdt/Ostrom/Rottman, "Litigation Outcomes in State and Federal Courts: A Statistical Portrait", 19 *Seattle University Law Review* 433 (1996), Tables 6 and 7.

165. But see Goerdt et al., *Reexamining the Pace of Litigation* (1991), p. 45.

federal court system.[166] In Germany the average time from filing to disposition of appeals was recently measured as 5.4 months in District Courts and between 8.5 and 5.4 months (family cases) in State Appeals Courts.[167] The average duration of appeals in the American Federal Court system is 11.4 months.[168]

The 2001 reforms in Germany were aimed at least in part at strengthening the first instance and reducing the number and duration of appeals. Whether the reforms as enacted will have this effect remains to be seen. However it does seem clear that the result of current German policy is that relatively simple cases can reach judgments which the parties will both accept relatively fast, and that more complex and contentious matters will continue to require more time to reach final resolution via the appellate process. It also seems clear that although German civil justice has traditionally been viewed as generous with appellate remedies, currently the rate and duration of appeals in Germany is very similar to the rate and duration of appeals in the United States.

3. The Impact of Likely Reform

It is hard to gauge whether either the American or the German civil justice systems can or will undertake further measures aimed at reduction of cost or delay in civil cases. In the United States high costs in many kinds of cases continue to be seen as serious reform issues. On the other hand, making any significant progress in cost reduction will likely require real change in fundamental institutions of civil justice. The biggest factor in cost, the institution of jury trial, and the resulting economic inefficiencies in case preparation and presentation, is dear to the American legal culture. Although it has been nibbled at over the years, any effort to fundamentally alter or abolish it would meet serious political opposition. One can perhaps anticipate continued attrition in actual jury trials and development of alternative ways for judges to function more efficiently as the jury archtype begins to fade.

Little comprehensive reform activity can be expected as well in Germany. Comprehensive reforms aimed at reducing cost and delay were considered,

166. In 1996, 11 per cent of local court civil judgments and 16 per cent of state district court first instance civil judgments went into second instance appeal. See Gottwald, in: *Civil Justice in Crisis*, p. 207, 224. See also Ch. 3(K) above with similar data for 1998. In 1989, 13 per cent of Federal District Court terminations were appealed. See Marcus, "Malaise of the Litigation Superpower", in: Zuckerman (ed.), *Civil Justice in Crisis*, p. 115 Appendix 3.6. One can assume that the percentage of judgments of American state courts of first instance that are appealed would be of the same order of magnitude.

167. See Ch. 3(K) above. The figures are for 1998.

168. See Marcus, in: *Civil Justice in Crisis*, p. 115 Appendix 3.7.

and in part adopted in 2001. Experience under these reforms will be accumulated before further reforms are considered.

F. Access to Justice

In recent years greater attention has been focused in comparative civil justice studies on the degree to which litigants of all levels of economic ability have access to civil justice. A civil justice system which is not reasonably accessible to all who have legal rights to litigate or protect is seriously deficient by modern day standards.[169]

Litigating in any system of civil justice involves private costs. Thus indigent litigants are almost always at a disadvantage in litigation. The question is the extent to which the processes of the system are designed and resources are provided to indigent litigants in order to minimize this disadvantage.

The American system, with its dependence on party-supported lawyer activity for fact development and case presentation, poses severe challenges for indigent litigants. The high private cost of litigating in America may set a threshold which many litigants cannot surmount.

Plaintiffs with apparently meritorious claims for severe personal injuries or other losses which would generate awards of money damages can often obtain access to justice via contingent fee arrangements with their lawyers.[170] Generous damages awards mitigate the impact of dividing the recovery with counsel.

The contingent fee system does little to help claimants who are seeking relief other than money damages or for defendants. Such parties are effectively barred from access to American civil justice and often must protect their interests in other ways.[171]

Legal aid is provided in a variety of forms ranging from legal services programs which provide representation via staff attorneys, to various programs of representation by volunteer attorneys. It is very difficult to measure the total amount of legal aid being provided by formal programs and informal contri-

---

169. See, e.g., Zuckerman, in: *Civil Justice in Crisis*, pp. 3, 9 f.; Woolf, *Access to Justice* (1995) (comprehensive report on reform of English civil justice system).

170. Under the contingent fee system lawyers screen cases both for their likely merit, and for a source of a cash recovery from which the contingent fee can be paid. If either is not present, contingent fee representation is generally not possible.

171. For instance, uninsured indigent defendants are not often sued, since they are unlikely to be able to pay damages from which contingent compensation could be paid to the plaintiff's lawyers.

bution of services by volunteer attorneys.[172] However the general perception is that only a fraction of the need for legal services is being met.[173]

The large role of party counsel in American civil justice also makes the provision of effective legal aid both difficult and expensive. Successful use of the American civil justice system requires a lot of activity of competent, often specialist counsel for both parties. Although the model of traditional American legal aid programs has been to attempt to provide such counsel or the resources to pay such counsel to indigent litigants, the goal of adequate representation for every litigant with a potentially meritorious case has never been reached or even approached.

Currently American reformers are considering the possibility of reconfiguring parts of the American civil justice system to permit access to and use of the system with less or even no participation by counsel. Recent upsurges of litigants who appear without counsel because they simply cannot afford lawyers have led to measures designed to make the courts more "user friendly" to such litigants.[174] In some jurisdictions lawyers are beginning to "unbundle" services provided to clients in the hope that in many matters clients might be able to proceed on their own with less than full-scale representation by counsel.[175] The effect of these and similar developments is to transfer more of the burden of providing civil justice in individual cases to the publicly supported neutrals in the system, namely the judge and court staff.

In Germany the barriers to indigent litigants are in general not so high. Restrictions on the role and compensation of lawyers make it easier for clients

---

172. In recent years amounts expended by federally supported legal services programs have been in the range of $300 million annually. However this does not include additional expenditures by state and locally supported programs and the contributions of volunteers. The Equal Justice Library has estimated the U.S. total expenditure for legal aid services to be in the neighborhood of $600 million during 1998. See www.equaljusticelibrary.org/international/comparative.asp; Johnson, 24 *Fordham Int'l L. J.* 83 (2000).

173. See, e.g., a recent study in the State of Maine, which concluded that only about 20% of indigent residents' need for legal services is being met by existing programs and institutions. Representation in various forms of civil litigation, especially family related matters, is a major component of the need of indigent persons for legal services. See Rau, "The Unmet Legal Needs of the Poor in Maine: Is Mandatory Pro Bono the Answer", 43 *Maine L. Rev.* 235, 237 (1991).

174. E.g., Arizona courthouse kiosks, Massachusetts Task Force for Unrepresented Litigants.

175. See, e.g., Maine Bar Rule 3.4(i) adopted effective July 1, 2001 authorizing provision of "unbundled" legal services under some circumstances; Feature, "A La Carte Legal Services: Follow These New 'Limited Representation' Rules to Offer an Unbundled Menu to Clients with Limited Needs, Limited Means", 16 *Maine Bar Journal* 156 (2001).

to proceed without counsel in many cases and to hire counsel when they must.[176] The rules of procedure as well as the active and engaged role of the German judges make it feasible for clients to appear pro se, which they do in about a third of local court cases.[177]

The German legal aid program appears to be somewhat more successful than its American counterpart in meeting the needs of litigants who do require representation by counsel. While it is difficult to estimate the total amount expended for legal aid in Germany, one can infer that the amount per capita likely exceeds the corresponding figure for the United States.[178] Legal aid funds also go further in Germany because litigation depends on lawyer activity to a lesser extent than in the United States, because lawyers compensated with legal aid funds receive reduced fees, and because successful legal aid litigants sometimes get their fees reimbursed by the other party.

Legal aid is not available to every indigent litigant in Germany. The requirement that the litigant's position be one of likely merit as determined by the judge can be a significant barrier to claims which, for one reason or another the judiciary does not wish to encourage. The absence of legal aid for the determination of eligibility for legal aid means that this threshold has to be surmounted by the litigant alone, in some cases assisted gratis by a lawyer in anticipation of paid legal aid representation.[179] On the other hand, practically every system of dispensing legal aid has some standard of merit, and the German standard does not seem more restrictive than in most other jurisdictions.[180]

---

176. See Ch. 6(B)(4)(b) above on pro se litigants in German courts. In family cases in the local courts and in all cases in the state district courts representation by counsel is mandatory.

177. For instance, many legal filings may be made orally through the clerk's offices, judges interact directly with parties, and there are no intricate rules of evidence. See Ch. 7(A)(1) above on form of the complaint and Ch. 8(B) above on judge-party interaction and the informality of evidentiary proceedings.

178. See Ch. 4(I)(3) and Ch. 13(C)(3) above on the level of expenditures for legal aid in Germany and its relationship to expenditures in other countries.

179. See Ch. 4(I)(2) above for a discussion of the application of this requirement in preliminary proceedings.

180. Until recently legal aid was available in the United Kingdom to all litigants who were able to convince their lawyers to take their cases. Recent reforms have required lawyers seeking approval of legal aid-funded representation to certify to the probable merit of their clients' positions. See Sommerlad, "The Implementation of Quality Initiatives and the New Public Management in the Legal Aid Sector in England and Wales: Bureaucratization, Stratification and Surveillance", 6 *Int'l J. Legal Prof.* 311 (1999); Sanderson/Sommerlad, "Exploring the Limits to the Standardization of the Expert Knowledge of Lawyers: Quality and Legal Aid Reforms in the United Kingdom", 52 *Syracuse L. Rev.* 987 (2002).

Giving due recognition to the strong commitment of Germans to funding access to justice for almost all potential litigants, it appears that the major reason for the difference in access to civil justice in Germany and in the United States comes from the structure of the systems themselves. The high reliance of the American system on the activities of private counsel creates an almost insuperable hurdle to access to justice for all but well-heeled litigants and those who will become funded by damages awards.[181] By making greater use of neutral resources in the provision of justice the German system makes it possible for litigants to participate at lower cost and for legal aid to provide legal representation when it is required for effective participation.

The relative predictability of judgments and in particular, the moderate size and predictability of statutory attorneys fees have fostered the development and widespread use of legal costs insurance in Germany.[182] Such insurance can give access to justice to middle-income litigants who might otherwise have difficulty raising significant lawyers' fees and facing the possibility of having to pay the other party's fees. Such insurance is all but unknown in the United States, likely because of the unpredictability of litigation on the jury model and the large amounts and extreme variability of lawyers' fees in litigated matters.

The handwriting seems to be on the wall. To afford all potential litigants access to civil justice in America will require massive systematic reforms designed to reduce the cost of participation in that system. Very likely this will result in some shift of the effort required for processing and determination of civil cases from the parties and their lawyers to neutral agencies and the decision maker itself. Otherwise it is hard to see how the United States will be able to afford the resources necessary to give all its citizens access to court.[183]

---

181. Recent studies suggest that civil justice in the United States has priced itself out of the range of even middle-income litigants. Marcus, "Malaise of the Litigation Superpower", in: *Civil Justice in Crisis*, p. 93; The Brookings Institution, *Justice for All: Reducing Costs and Delay in Civil Litigation* (1989), p. 6: "A majority of judges and lawyers agree that the high costs of litigating in America unreasonably impede access to the civil justice system by the ordinary citizen. Furthermore, they believe that the civil justice system today gives an unfair advantage to 'large interests' with greater resources." See also Levin/Colliers, "Containing the Cost of Litigation", 37 *Rutgers L. Rev.* 219 (1985).

182. See Ch. 4(J) above on legal cost insurance in Germany.

183. In England, with a civil justice system resembling that of the United States, the cost of trying to provide legal aid to all eligible litigants far exceeded amounts expended in either the United States or Germany and ultimately exceeded England's ability to afford it. See Sanderson/Sommerlad, "Exploring the Limits to the Standardization of the Expert Knowledge of Lawyers: Quality and Legal Aid Reforms in the United Kingdom", 52 *Syracuse L. Rev.* 987, 991 (2002): "During the 1980s, concern began to be expressed about the mounting cost of providing legal aid, and about the difficulty of supervising the work of

G. Development and Explication of the Law

The role of civil justice in the ongoing development and explication of the law is perhaps less frequently acknowledged than other systematic purposes and goals. However it is an important assignment of the civil justice system in both Germany and the United States.

Judicial decisions form the very fabric of the common law in jurisdictions with the Anglo-American tradition of justice. In the United States court decisions in civil cases, both at the trial and the appellate level have led to the development of new legal doctrine and the education of parties and the population as a whole on their evolving legal rights and responsibilities.[184]

Although Germany is considered a civil law "code" jurisdiction, judicial decisions in civil cases play an important role in development and explication of doctrine. This is particularly true of the decisions of the Federal Constitutional Court, which has applied very general constitutional provisions to create substantive rights and procedural requirements.[185]

---

the many lawyers providing legal services at government expense. The result was a process of reform, which began with the removal of the administration of the scheme from the profession's regulatory body, the Law Society, and its replacement by the quasi-autonomous Legal Aid Board.

In the 1990s, under the aegis of the Legal Aid Board, the reform continued with the introduction of quality assurance procedures that involved the 'franchising' of Legal Aid providers. In order to obtain a franchise, forms would have to meet the 'transaction criteria' that prescribed standards for all areas of legal service provided under the scheme.The Access to Justice Act 1999 represented the culmination of this process of regulatory reform, which has transformed the legal aid system in England and Wales. The Act replaced civil legal aid with the Community Legal Service fund. It also created the Criminal Defense Service (hereinafter CDS). The Legal Aid Board (hereinafter LAB) was replaced by the Legal Services Commission (hereinafter LSC), which has responsibility for both the CDS and the Community Legal Service (hereinafter CLS). Both schemes are cash limited and Regional Legal Services Committees have been created with the primary function of assisting in the allocation of limited funds by defining priority need in their areas."

184. A well-known example of the common law in action is the decision of the New York Court of Appeals authored by Chief Judge Cardozo in *McPherson v. Buick Motors Co.*, 216 NY 382 (1916) which established negligence liability for defective products regardless of the contractual relationship of the parties.

185. See, e.g., Diederichsen, "Das Bundesverfassungsgericht als oberstes Zivilgericht - ein Lehrstück juristischer Methodenlehre", 198 *AcP* 171 (1998). See Ch. 3(F) and Ch. 10(H)(3) above.

In both jurisdictions civil litigation functions to teach the parties and others affected by the result of civil cases the norms and requirements of the law thereby increasing general understanding of the law and legal culture.

One development which may affect the law development and explication role of courts in the United States is the very high proportion of cases which are settled prior to court decision. In some jurisdictions this proportion is above 90%. While settlement is considered to be a desirable resolution for most civil cases, question has been raised about whether all or even most settlements in American civil cases represent reasoned approximations of potential results.[186] To the extent that a large number of cases are settled because of exhaustion or inequality of party resources or other extraneous factors, the role of civil litigation in the conservation, development and explication of the law may suffer.

H. Overall Public Satisfaction and Confidence

The satisfaction and confidence of the public in its system of civil justice is an important pillar of a stable civil society. Confidence in the system that preserves and vouches safe private rights and legally protected interests fosters vigorous economic activity and social stability. Uncertainty or even cynicism about the reliability or integrity of institutions of civil justice, on the other hand, exacts heavy social and economic costs to deal with uncertainty and provide alternative means of protecting rights and interests.

Fundamentally both Germany and the United States exhibit relatively high levels of public satisfaction and confidence in their systems of civil justice. There is no evidence of the corrosion of corruption of the judiciary or its institutions. Both jurisdictions host large and active legal professions. The rule of law is well established and is considered effective in civil matters in both Germany and the United States.

On the other hand, for some time there has been a consciousness that all is not right with civil justice in America. Literature discussing issues in the civil justice arena tends to be rather critical than enthusiastic. There are calls for reform of a number of important American justice institutions. Some

---

186. See Galanter/Cahill, "'Most Cases Settle'; Judicial Promotion and Regulation of Settlements", 46 *Stanford L. Rev.* 1339 (1994). For a discussion of case settlement in Germany see Ch. 11(I)(1) above.

commentators have suggested that reform of American civil justice might profit from the examples of civil law jurisdictions, particularly Germany.[187]

While the precise nature of these complaints and concerns vary, many of them address the high cost, procedural intricacy and substantive unpredictability of a justice system based on the template of trial by jury. While the participation of the jury in civil dispositions is reassuring to some, to others it is irrational and disquieting. For every citizen who is glad to have his civil fate in the hands of his peers, there is another who finds such a fate to be seriously unfair. As cases become more complex and involve issues of science and technology, public appreciation of the limitations of juries as fact finders appears to become more widespread.

Other reasons for Americans' expressed public concern with the performance of their civil justice seem to cluster around issues of cost and efficiency. Lawyer costs are too high and consume too large a portion of the dispute resolution dollar. Litigation takes too much time and involves too much unproductive activity. Participation in litigation, particularly civil discovery proceedings is onerous and burdensome to the clients.

At the same time, fundamental reform of American civil justice has been slow in coming. All of the main institutions and processes of which Americans complain remain intact. Some attribute the lack of effective reform activity to an underlying public satisfaction with American civil justice despite surface quibbles and complaints. Others blame strongly entrenched interest groups of litigation professionals who prosper under the current conditions and have vigorously opposed meaningful change.

In Germany, on the other hand, there appears to be widespread satisfaction and confidence with the performance of civil justice.[188] The recent comprehensive reform initiative was perceived more as a refinement of a system that functioned well before the reforms rather than a fix for a system that was seriously broken.

That is not to say that German commentators are not interested in making further improvements to civil justice in Germany. For instance, thought is being given to the selection, training and promotion of judges. Should initial selection be deferred and the pool of potential judges be expanded to bring

187. See Langbein, 52 *U. Chi. L. Rev.* 823 (1985); Murray, "What America Can Learn from German Civil Justice", Newsletter of the *Deutsch-Amerikanische Juristenvereinigung* (1999). For further references see Ch. 13(B) above.

188. See, e.g., Zuckerman, in: *Civil Justice in Crisis*, p. 3, 31: "...unlike in most other countries reviewed in this volume, [in Germany] there is a high degree of public confidence in, and satisfaction with, the administration of civil justice."

more diversity and life experience into the judiciary? Does the "complete jurist" approach to legal education produce the best lawyers as well as the best judges? Could a reform of the administrative organization of German courts strengthen the independence and efficiency of the judiciary?[189] The debate continues. However in general, perceived problems in the system are seen as susceptible to minor adjustments of civil justice institutions rather than requiring any fundamental rebuilding. It is also clear that German jurists have very little interest in any wholesale importation of institutions and practices of American civil justice into Germany.

I. Convergence in European and American Civil Justice Systems

It is easy to conclude that judge-centered systems of civil justice such as the German system and civil justice systems based on the jury trial model of which the American system is the current archetype differ diametrically in underlying principle and practical approach. Some have suggested that these differences are fundamental and that there is little common ground for comparison and even less likelihood of actual convergence in either theory or practice.[190]

More recent study and the experience over the last 50 years since the rebirth of modern Germany suggest, however, that the German and American systems represent points on a continuum of optional political designs for justice institutions and of roles for their participants. It is clear that within the privileged western world, of which both Germany and the United States are parts, most important values of politics, economy, culture and society are common ones shared by all nation states and their political economies. To the extent that civil justice systems fulfil similar roles in modern political economies, their func-

---

189. See the initiative of the Association of German Judges 90 *DRiZ* 5 (2002) and its detailed description by B. Kramer, "Das Neue Steuerungsmodell und die Unabhängigkeit der Richter", 114 *ZZP* 267 (2001); id., "Modernisierung der Justiz: Das Neue Steuerungsmodell", 54 *NJW* 3449 (2001); Hoffmann-Riem, *Modernisierung von Recht und Justiz* (2001), pp. 209 ff. For a critical analysis see Papier, "Zur Selbstverwaltung der Dritten Gewalt", 55 *NJW* 2585 (2002); Stürner, "Unabhängigkeit der Richter", 2003 *BRAK-Mitt.*, No. 5 (2003). For a first report on reforms of court administration of labor courts, see Francken, "Das Neue Steuerungsmodell und die Arbeitsgerichtsbarkeit", 20 *NZA* 457 (2003).

190. For a more detailed discussion see Stürner, 34 *The International Lawyer* 1071 (2000); id., "Transnational Civil Procedure", VI (NS) *Uniform L. Rev.* 871 (2001).

tions can be studied and fruitfully compared. As society in general evolves it is not surprising that there are signs of convergence of previously very different institutions.

One can think of convergence on at least two levels. First, in some respects converging changes in the overall structure of society can lead to changes in the purpose and role for civil justice within that society. Second, if the purpose and role of civil justice becomes much the same in two different political economies, one can then anticipate an actual convergence of the institutions of civil justice to reflect the most efficient means of carrying out their assigned role.

1. Convergence in the Purpose and Role of Civil Justice

As societies change and develop the purpose and role of various institutions within those societies change as well. This is certainly true of the institutions of civil justice. For instance, when the former German Democratic Republic merged with the Federal Republic of Germany in 1990 the role of civil justice rapidly expanded in the former GDR territory to replace socialist institutions that were discarded. On a less dramatic level, when an administrative or regulatory mechanism is adopted to address a particular social problem such as environmental pollution or purity of foods and drugs, this new remedy can, in whole or in part, replace previously existing remedies founded solely on private law and provided through the civil justice system.[191]

In politics and government, the only thing that is constant is constant change. As governments experiment with various mechanisms to deal with social, economic and political problems, one can anticipate that experience will show some remedies to be more successful than others in implementing and safeguarding basic values and common interests. Over time experience will lead to the most efficient means to deal with the important social and economic problems.[192]

As the basic structure and mix of social and political institutions tends to converge, the role and function of civil justice within this mix will tend to

191. A well-known example of this phenomenon is the introduction of workers' compensation in the American states at the end of the 19th century.

192. This activity has been cited as one of the strengths of American federalism, which preserves for the various states important roles in development of private as well as public law. The various states' experiments with legal and institutional solutions to social problems have been called a "laboratory of democracy". This process is not necessarily a fast one. History, cultural values, such influences as religion, political personalities and chance all play important roles in the speed and short-term direction of political evolution.

become more similar among nation states. The process of harmonization can be accelerated by such enterprises as the European Union, where conscious efforts are being made to rationalize differing approaches to common problems among the member states. However in a larger sense and over a longer time frame, political and social evolution encompasses the entire western world which includes both Europe and the United States.[193] It can be anticipated that the various political entities of the western community of political, cultural and economic values will gradually evolve toward a more or less similar allocation of roles and functions of the various organs and institutions of their civil governments. Such factors as local conditions, culture, history, language and the like will affect the degree of harmonization and prevent complete homogenization. But the principles of evolution suggest that over time all governmental structures will tend to approach the structure that experience shows best implements and safeguards the basic values which all social groups share.

Indeed, over the last half-millennium within the Western Hemisphere there has been a remarkable convergence among self-governing nation states on matters of basic governmental structure and the allocation of powers and responsibilities to foster identified common values of freedom, economic vitality, and self-determination. Five hundred years ago what is now Europe and the United States included all forms of social organization from despotic monarchies, to various forms of incomplete democracies, to theocracies and to communes. It is now accepted by all western nations that governmental powers should be divided between an executive, a legislature and a judiciary, that persons should have resort to civil justice to vindicate private rights, and more recently, that courts play a role in maintaining and safeguarding the proper relationship between citizens and their governmental institutions.

Within the broad area of justice there is now consensus that civil justice should be separated from criminal justice,[194] that it should be accessible to citizens, that it should be dispensed by neutrals, that justice should be based on law and not on bribery, political influence or raw power. This consensus is likely to continue to grow as communication and dialogue exposes differences to discussion and as informed citizens choose government institutions to address conditions of human life on earth that fundamentally are very similar throughout the western world.

---

193. Over an even longer time frame one can anticipate a process of convergence involving the entire globe as common values become accepted by everyone.

194. The continuance of punitive damages in the United States suggests that this separation is not yet complete in all societies. See Ch. 12(C)(2)(c) and Ch. 13(B) above.

2. Convergence in Civil Justice Institutions

As the general consensus on the role and purpose of civil justice in modern society becomes more widespread, procedures and institutions of civil justice will continue to evolve in light of this growing common view of its purpose and function. There is no doubt that different institutions can continue to fulfil general purposes and functions which are similar. Yet one can anticipate that if a particular approach seems to fulfil these purposes and functions more efficiently and at less cost there will be a tendency for all systems to move in that direction. Tradition, localism, vested interests in existing systems will be hurdles. But ultimately one can expect that systems of civil justice will evolve into that form which best accomplishes the functions expected of it at the least cost.

As intercourse among modern nation-states increases, the process of evolution can be expected to accelerate. Within the European Union there has been remarkable progress toward harmonization of very different civil justice regimes over a relatively short 30-year time span. The recent reform of English civil justice, which now seems to be strongly converging with that of Continental Europe,[195] has confounded many a die-hard fan of "Common Law forever!" The previous half-century saw a similar convergence in civil justice procedures and institutions among the various American states, whose disparate civil justice systems dramatically converged following the adoption of the Federal Rules of Civil Procedure.[196]

America and Europe share the same cultural heritage and cherish the same political ideals. Their economies are becoming increasingly intertwined. Modern western culture is no respecter of national borders. As the world continues to become smaller it is not too much to expect that over time there will be significant convergence between the institutions of civil justice in America and Europe.

3. Signs of Convergence to Date

Acknowledging that there are major differences in the forms and institutions of civil justice in the United States and Germany, nonetheless, one can see signs of some convergence already. Commentators and courts in the United States are

---

195. See Andrews, "A New Civil Procedure Code for England: Party-Control 'Going, Going, Gone'", 4 *ZZPInt* 3 (1999); Stürner, "Zur Struktur des europäischen Zivilprozesses", in: Gottwald/Roth (eds.), *Festschrift für Ekkehard Schumann* (2001), p. 491.

196. See Millar, *Civil Procedure of the Trial Court in Historical Perspective* (1952), Ch. VI, pp. 52ff., 62.

beginning to discuss the advantages of court appointed expert witnesses and urge greater use of neutral experts.[197] Scholars and reformers in Europe are studying forms of collective litigation, including the American class action, with a view to expanding such activities in European justice systems.[198] Some commentators are beginning to write about the similarities of American and European civil justice rather than the differences.[199] There is now significant evidence that ever growing international consensus on the values, roles and purposes of civil justice is gradually resulting in functional convergence of the systems which provide it. Without discussing the various forms of convergence any detail, recent changes in the role of the American judge on the one hand, and growing interest in more intense fact development and discovery in Europe may deserve brief discussion.

a. The Changing Role of the Judge in the United States

In the United States there is now widespread recognition that civil litigation cannot be left to the untrammeled will of the parties and their lawyers, and that judges should play larger roles in shaping civil cases for determination. Reformers write of the need for "managerial judging" to control the excesses of partisan counsel and to focus attention on the issues that matter.[200]

---

197. See, e.g., F. R. Ev. 706; Green, "The Complete Courthouse", in: *Dispute Resolution Devices in a Democratic Society* (1985), pp. 44–54; *Daubert v. Merrell Dow Pharmaceuticals, Inc.*, 509 U.S. 579 (1993) (recommending use of court-appointed expert witness to assess qualifications of party-nominated experts).

198. See, e.g., Jürgen Basedow et al. (eds.), *Die Bündelung gleichgerichteter Interessen im Prozess* (1999). This study ultimately recommends against adopting of American-style class action practice in Europe, but suggests easing of venue and other restrictions on joining of similar claims pending in different courts. See also, Sherman, "Group Litigation Under Foreign Legal Systems: Variations and Alternatives to American Class Actions", 52 *DePaul L. Rev.* 401 (2002). For the recent European and German development in the field of collective litigation see Ch. 7(B)(5).

199. See, e.g., von Mehren, "Some Comparative Reflections on First Instance Civil Procedure: Recent Reforms in German Civil Procedure and the Federal Rules", 63 *Notre Dame L. Rev.* 609 (1988); Sherman, "The Evolution of American Trial Practice Towards Greater Congruence with Continental Trial Practice", 7 *Tul. J. Int'l & Comp. L.* 125 (1999).

200. The Civil Justice Reform Act of 1990 sought to foster managerial judging in United States District Courts. See Murray, "Civil Justice Reform in America; The 1990 Civil Justice Reform Act and its Consequences", 3 *ZZPInt* 319 (1998); Kakalik et al., *Discovery Management: Further Analysis of the Civil Justice Reform Act Evaluation Data* (1998). Since then the call for more active management of litigation by judges has continued. See, e.g., Marcus, in: *Civil Justice in Crisis,* p. 71, 110:

> Despite the absence of hard evidence that various forms of case management have desirable consequences, there is sufficient basis for confidence that judges can bring about improvement by taking more interest in their civil cases. Faced with

Judicial officers meet with counsel at various kinds of pretrial conferences, scheduling conferences, and discovery conferences designed to identify issues, and rationalize proceedings in the early stages of the litigation. Disposition of cases by summary judgment has increased. Gradually American judges seem to be shedding their traditional passive umpireal roles and taking more responsibility for how cases develop.

In the ordinary civil courts individual judges are beginning to depart from the passive-umpire role associated with jury trials in order to take a more active part in the conduct of non-jury proceedings. Some civil non-jury trials are beginning to resemble corresponding proceedings in Europe.[201] Appellate hearings and oral arguments on questions of law have functioned in very similar ways for some time now.

Activist judging appears to have taken the best hold in newly formed courts and tribunals which do not have traditions of jury trial. For instance, administrative law judges which provide a first level of judicial review the actions of administrative agencies often appear to function more like German judges than their American counterparts on the benches of the more traditional courts. This is particularly true of judges of courts in which the role of counsel is likely to be circumscribed or absent. For instance, in many Social Security appeals neither the claimants nor the agency will be represented by attorneys. The judges review the case record, question the witnesses and talk directly with the parties in a manner very similar to that of their counterparts in the social welfare courts in Germany.

> potentially growing demands on their time and stable or shrinking resources, judges can be expected to continue to be active in trying to control litigation. Although arguments can be made about the importance of leaving parties in control of their litigation, the general American reality in connection with case management is that the choice is between freedom for lawyers and authority for judges. By and large, objectors to judicial case management have been lawyers who formerly had unrestrained latitude to control their cases. Moreover, many lawyers welcome the involvement of the judge and support more rather than less judicial supervision.

See also, Resnik, "Changing Practices, Changing Rules: Judicial and Congressional Rulemaking on Civil Juries, Civil Justice, and Civil Judging", 49 *Ala. L. Rev.* 133 (1997) (questioning the value of managerial judging).

201. See Peckham, "The Federal Judge as a Case Manager", 69 *Cal. Rev.* 770 (1981); Resnik, "Managerial Judges", 96 *Harv. L. Rev.* 376 (1982); Braun, *Die Rolle des Federal District Court Judge im Verhältnis zu den Parteien* (1986). This is particularly true of trials involving litigants who are not represented by counsel such as Social Security hearings before administrative law judges and small claims proceedings. See Sherman, 7 *Tul. J. Int'l & Comp. L.* 125, 138.

The movement to managerial judging in ordinary civil cases in the United States is hampered by three practical constraints. First is the traditional division of responsibility between judge and jury requiring that all determinations of disputed fact be reserved to the jury.[202] Judges are not permitted to make preliminary determinations of disputed facts or take action that will influence the ultimate fact finding by the jury.[203] They must thus avoid managerial measures that might somehow affect the fact presentation to and determination by the jury.

Second, the current structure of American civil justice does not give judges the information they need in order to take a more active role in case preparation and fact finding. Parties file sketchy notice pleadings that are frequently amended to conform to the results of discovery. The discovery process is entirely conducted by the parties and their lawyers. The judge does not participate and does not even receive the material produced or discovered. Judges attempting to act managerially require counsel to prepare and file informative memoranda summarizing their positions and identifying facts and issues in dispute.[204] A special procedure on motions for summary judgment has been devised to apprise judges of the fact scenario sufficiently so that they can act on an informed basis.[205] However these more or less ad hoc measures are not a substitute for thoroughgoing knowledge of the facts and legal contentions at issue from the earliest stage of the proceeding.[206]

---

202. This division of responsibility is often constitutionally required. See, e.g., United States Constitution, 7th Amendment ("In Suits at common law, where the value in controversy shall exceed twenty dollars, the right of trial by jury shall be preserved, and no fact tried by a jury, shall be otherwise re-examined in any Court of the United States, than according to the rules of the common law."); Constitution of the State of Maine, Article 1, §20 ("In all civil suits, and in all controversies concerning property, the parties shall have a right to a trial by jury, except in cases where it has heretofore been otherwise practiced....").

203. Unlike their counterparts in the United Kingdom, American judges do not even share their impressions of the evidence with the jury.

204. See, e.g., M. R. Civ. P. 16(d)(2) requiring the filing of pretrial memoranda prior to a pretrial conference. The federal counterpart does not expressly require filing of pretrial memoranda. However local rules, scheduling orders and long established practice in most U.S. District Courts have had the same effect.

205. See F.R. Civ. P. 56(c)–(g). For a critique of excessive use of the summary judgment procedure see Miller, "The Pretrial Rush to Judgment: Are the 'Litigation Explosion,' 'Liability Crisis' and Efficiency Clichés Eroding Our Day in Court and Jury?", 78 *N.Y.U. L. Rev.* 982 (2003).

206. Compare Ch. 7(A)(2), (E), (L) and Ch. 8(C)(1)(a) above on the function of particularized pleading of facts and identifying sources of proof in Germany.

Finally, Americans have staffed their courts at a level that does not permit judges to spend very much time per case. American judges carry much higher caseloads than their European counterparts. While this is consistent with their very restricted traditional role, if American judges are to step in and actively manage civil cases, there will have to be many more of them.[207] Thus, although the idea of managerial judging is alive and appears to be taking hold in the United States, effective and practical implementation of the concept will require more thoroughgoing reform of the American civil justice system.[208]

b. *Experiments with Fact Discovery in Europe*

Thoughtful European commentators have recognized that American civil discovery procedures may lead to the uncovering of relevant fact information that is not available to European fact finders, particularly in complex and difficult cases.[209] At the same time, Europeans recoil from the high costs and well-known excesses of American discovery practice. Indeed, in the United Kingdom, recent reforms have tended to restrict, rather than enlarge discovery.[210]

Without signaling any likelihood of wholesale adoption of American civil discovery, in recent years German civil justice reformers have taken some cautious first steps at enlarging access to fact information for courts and litigants in civil litigation. The most significant of these steps are the 2001 amendments to Sections 142 and 144 of the Civil Procedure Code. Courts may now require non-parties as well as parties to produce documents and things for inspection in connection with civil cases based solely on their relevance to the issues raised for decision. While this broadened power is to be exercised by the court,

207. For instance, the number of judges per capita in the United States has been estimated at 9 per 100,000 inhabitants, as compared with 27 per 100,000 inhabitants in Germany. See Clark, "The Relative Importance of Judiciaries in Distinct Legal Traditions", in: Nafziger et al. (ed.), *Law and Justice in a Multistate World; Essays in Honor of Arthur T. von Mehren* (2002), pp. 609, 611, Table 1. Americans file at least as many civil actions per capita as do Germans. See Ch. 3(A),(J)(2) and (K); Ch. 13(C)(3) above.

208. For a discussion of how these constraints may have frustrated the intent of the Civil Justice Reform Act of 1990 see Murray, "Civil Justice Reform in America; The 1990 Civil Justice Reform Act and its Consequences," 3 ZZPInt 319 (1998).

209. See, e.g., P. Schlosser, "Die lange deutsche Reise in die prozessuale Moderne", 46 *JZ* 599 (1999); Katzenmeier, "Aufklärungs- und Mitwirkungspflichten der nicht beweisbelasteten Partei im Zivilprozess", 57 *JZ* 644 (2002); Stürner, *Die Aufklärungspflicht der Parteien des Zivilprozesses* (1976), §4, pp. 17ff. (English discovery).

210. This has been done by strengthening the "strict relevance" rule of discoverability and making discovery in many kinds of cases subject to approval by a judicial officer. See Woolf, *Access to Justice, Interim Report* (1995), Ch. 21, nos. 21–23, 28.

not the parties, presumably parties will not hesitate to request the court to invoke it if they are aware of the existence of material in the hands of the opponent or of third parties that may be of value to their cases.[211]

This reform represents the latest step in a progressive development from the traditional German position that parties and the court could obtain documentary evidence in the hands of private persons, including opposing parties, only if they had independent substantive right to possession of or access to the material. Traditionally there was no right to require production of non-public documents by an adverse party or third party solely because of their relevance to some issue in the litigation.[212] The flexibility of German procedure on the reception of various forms of factual proof allows such production to be ordered at relatively early stages of the proceedings, when the lawyers can use the information obtained in their preparations for later proceedings.[213]

While it is too early to assess any practical experience with this extension, it is likely that it will function as a useful tool to extend the fact finding power of court and parties alike without unduly burdening third parties or the litigation process itself.

4. The Future of American Civil Jury Trial

It is clear that the largest impediment to convergence between American and German civil justice is the American institution of trial by jury in civil cases. Of course one can state the issue in the reverse, namely that the leading barrier to more complete convergence is the lack of civil jury trial in Germany.[214] However it is now clear even to the most diehard enthusiast of the

---

211. For a discussion of this development in the context of preparatory and plenary/evidentiary proceedings, see Ch. 7(L), Ch. 8(C)(4) and Ch.8 (C)(6)(b) respectively above.

212. See Ch. 7(L), Ch. 8(C)(4) and (6)(b) above for a discussion of production of documents and other evidence in the hands of parties and third parties in German civil litigation.

213. See Ch. 7(L) above. This kind of joint participation of court and lawyers in early discovery and development of facts tends to erode the distinction between discovery and reception of evidence. A similar development appears to be taking place in England where judges are taking larger roles in what was formerly considered party discovery in preparation for a later trial. See Stürner, "Transnational Civil Procedure", VI (NS) *Uniform. L. Rev.* 871, 882 (2001).

214. There is, of course, no jury trial in civil cases anywhere in Continental Europe, or, for that matter anywhere else in the world, except for remnants in England, Canada, and other former English colonies.

American jury trial tradition, that it is the United States, not Germany or Europe, which is the "odd man out" in the modern world of civil justice.

The United States stands alone in the modern world in its continued use of juries to decide civil cases. Great Britain, the originator of the modern-day jury trial, has abandoned it for all but a tiny minority of civil cases for over three-quarters of a century.[215] The process has fallen into general disuse as well in Great Britain's former colonies such as Canada, Australia, and New Zealand. Only in the United States is civil justice still dispensed according to a template of trial by jury.

This work is not intended as a critique of American civil jury trial. At the same time, it is worth noting that the institution appears to be in serious decline even in the United States. While the virtues of jury trial continue to be extolled by many American legal scholars as well as by most film and television writers, in practice American litigants are "voting with their feet" and resorting to trial by jury in ever decreasing numbers. Today the overwhelming majority of civil proceedings brought in United States courts are either settled or are disposed of by some kind of decision by a judge rather than a jury verdict.[216]

Under these circumstances it may not be untoward to ask how long jury trial can continue to define the structure, roles and procedures of American civil litigation? As lawyers, judges and litigants become less familiar with jury trial's unique processes, one can expect that they will be more receptive to procedural forms that would otherwise be inconceivable in a jury-trial environment. To the extent that these procedures, such as a larger role for the judge in case development and presentation of evidence, prove to contribute to a just, speedy and inexpensive determination of civil cases, one can expect that

---

215. See Landsman, "The Civil Jury in America: Scenes from an Unappreciated History," 44 *Hastings L.J.* 579, 582 (1993):

> The jury's origins are a matter of substantial scholarly uncertainty. Orthodox opinion, strengthened by the writings of great legal scholars such as Maitland... Thayer,... has held that the jury was a Norman import, brought to England by William the Conqueror and his minions after their victory at Hastings in 1066. More recent scholarly work by Dawson... and others has shifted attention to the Anglo-Saxon antecedents of Norman jury procedure. Modern scholars have argued persuasively that important precursors to the jury existed in England prior to the Conquest and likely played a significant part in inducing Englishmen to place their trust in the jury trial mechanisms proffered by the conquerors.

See also Sward, *The Decline of the Civil Jury* (2001), pp. 72 f.; Millar, *Civil Procedure of the Trial Court in Historical Perspective*, §4, pp. 20 f.

216. See, e.g., Murray, "The Disappearing Massachusetts Jury Trial," (manuscript to be published in 2004); Sward, *The Decline of the Civil Jury*, pp. 12 f.

their adoption and use may over time contribute to the abandonment of the old jury trial procedures.[217] It is entirely conceivable that jury trial may persist for some time in certain classes of cases, such as some kinds of product liability and mass tort litigation, which involve confrontation of major social and economic interests on a scale which will justify the expense and procedural burden associated with jury trial process.[218]

5. The Role of International Commercial Arbitration

For some time now lawyers entering into contractual relationships spanning jurisdictions, economies and cultures have avoided national justice systems by specifying international commercial arbitration for resolving disputes between them arising out of their contractual relationships. Over the last three decades international commercial arbitration has grown in importance and acceptance. Now arbitration centers based in Paris, London, New York, Hong Kong, Singapore, and most other major centers of world commerce administer private civil justice for subscribing parties.

International commercial arbitration agreements permit the parties to select their judges and wide latitude in devising appropriate procedures for fact determination. Law is either chosen by contract, or by the arbitral tribunal based on conventional choice of law doctrine.[219] The New York Convention

217. This appears to be what happened in Canada and Australia, where jury trial remains technically available for many civil cases, but is rarely if ever used. Procedures in these jurisdictions are more and more based on the judge as fact finder.

218. Carrington, "The Seventh Amendment: Some Bicentennial Reflections", 1990 *U. Chi. Legal F.* 33 (1990); Farrar-Myers/Myers, "Echoes of the Founding: The Jury in Civil Cases as Conferrer of Legitimacy", 54 *SMU L. Rev.* 1857 (2001); George Priest,"Justifying the Civil Jury", in: Litan (ed.), *Verdict: Assessing the Civil Jury System* (Brookings 1993), p. 103 at p. 108:

> The Kalven and Calabresi treatments provide the strongest defense of the substantive role of the civil jury as a decision-making institution. According to this view, civil juries are appropriate for the reduction of disputes that require the application of complex societal values. Similarly, in cases of extreme sensitivity or controversy, the discontinuous jury may better appear as society's voice, and, when decisions are extremely difficult and require judgments inherently impossible to defend—deciding that one person rather than another should live, for example—the decision-making authority should operate aresponsibly, without offering reasons and, *a fortiori*, not subject to review since there are no superior grounds or principles from which to review the decision.

219. In the past arbitral tribunals would frequently decide cases based on the "lex mercatoria", a kind of international common law of commerce which the tribunal could derive from a wide variety of sources. This practice is yielding to more conventional choice

makes arbitral awards enforceable in almost every jurisdiction of commercial significance.[220]

Although international commercial arbitration grew out of the civil law culture of Western Europe, in recent years Anglo-Americans have become eager converts to its processes. Procedures which traditionally resembled those of civil law courts such as those of France or Germany, have gradually evolved to include elements associated with lawyer-run litigation in the United States. Now it is not uncommon to hear American style declarative or "suggestive" cross-examination in international arbitral proceedings. Frequently such proceedings include some sort of pre-hearing discovery, the presentation of party experts, and other English or American litigation elements.[221]

There continues to be a wide variety of procedures employed in international arbitration proceedings. However in cases that involve both Anglo American and continental European participants, there appears to be a movement toward a compromise procedure containing elements of both families of civil justice systems. Frequently one sees arbitral statements commencing or defending proceedings which resemble in particularity and detail the kinds of pleadings which initiate law suits, say, in German courts. By the same token, the arbitral tribunals themselves tend to resemble European civil courts. The arbitrators are likely to be lawyers or academics of high academic standing and respect. There is no development of anything resembling an American civil jury.

On the other hand, in many cases some form of party discovery has become common. The discovery usually involves production of documents and perhaps oral depositions of the parties. Third party discovery is much less common.[222] In almost every case the scope of discovery is under the strict control of the arbitral panel.

---

of national law or international convention such as the UN Convention on the International Sale of Goods.

220. The result is that often arbitral awards are more easily enforced abroad than the judgments of national courts.

221. Reed/Sutcliffe, "The 'Americanization' of International Arbitration?", 2 *Mealey's Int'l Arb. Q. L. Rev.* 3 (2001). For an example of Anglo-American influence on international arbitration proceedings see the Rules on the Taking of Evidence in International Commercial Arbitration of the International Bar Association as adopted on June 1, 1999 (www.ibanet.org/pdf/rules-of-evid-2.pdf), which represent a remarkable compromise between continental and Anglo-American traditions.

222. This is partially because arbitral tribunals usually have no authority over third parties. However in most jurisdictions, it is possible to obtain judicial assistance in securing discovery from third parties in aid of arbitral proceedings. See, e.g., Uniform Arbitration Act §17 (National Association of Commissioners on Uniform State Laws 2000); UNCI-

The progress and development of most arbitrations tends to follow a model similar to that of litigation in Germany.[223] The arbitrators, either acting as a panel or through the presiding officer, are apprised of the issues and likely relevant facts early on, and tend to guide the proceedings to focus on those issues which seem of importance to them. Although there is no statutory duty to provide hints and feedback as in Germany, many arbitrators will let counsel know their tentative thinking processes and what is bothering them as the case develops.

Hearings tend to involve both arbitrators and party counsel in the questioning of witnesses and presentation of evidence. Exclusionary rules of evidence, such as the hearsay rule, are generally not applied. Usually both arbitrators and parties or their lawyers will question the witnesses. The order may depend on whether the presiding officer comes from the European or American legal tradition.[224]

Arbitral proceedings make use of single tribunal-appointed experts as well as experts retained and presented by the parties. The procedure used depends on the nature of the issue requiring expertise as well as the legal traditions of the arbitrators and participants.

International commercial arbitration awards are carefully reasoned and written documents explaining the findings and reasoning of the tribunals. The authority of international arbitration and its appeal to potential parties depends in large part on the quality of its findings and determinations. Organizations sponsoring and administering international arbitration proceedings frequently attempt to exert some quality control over the written arbitral awards.[225] Although court review of arbitral awards is typically limited, poorly reasoned or inadequately explained arbitral dispositions are not good refer-

---

TRAL Model Law on International Commercial Arbitration §27. See Ch. 11(H)(3) above on judicial assistance to arbitration proceedings in Germany.

223. This is also true of the procedure of the specialized London Commercial Court. See Lewis, "Dispute Resolution in the London Market", 64 *Prac. L. Inst.* 67, 69 (1992).

224. Arbitrators trained in European legal tradition generally lead off with the questioning, allowing counsel for the parties to follow up, and often conduct some form of cross examination. American-trained arbitrators will frequently defer to counsel for the parties for the initial rounds of questioning, but will follow up with their own questions on issues not clarified to their satisfaction by the preceding questions by the lawyers. See Elsing/Townsend, "Bridging the Common Law–Civil Law Divide in Arbitration", 570 *Prac. L. Inst. / Lit.* 635 (2002).

225. For instance, the International Chamber of Commerce, in Paris, requires that every award of an ICC tribunal be reviewed by personnel attached to its Court of Arbitration before the award is issued. See Article 27 ICC Rules On Arbitration (1998).

ences for an arbitral organization when parties are considering dispute resolution entities to name in future contracts.

Because international arbitration is employed only when specified in a pre-dispute contract between the parties, there are large classes of litigation which rarely if ever are subject to arbitration. Most tort cases, for example, involve litigants with no pre-existing contract relationship, and would not come to arbitration.[226]

The significance of international commercial arbitration is that it is serving as a laboratory for hybrid and converging procedures which utilize litigation elements from both traditions. Over many cases, one can expect that procedures which show themselves as effective, fair and cost-efficient will tend to be adopted over procedures that embody outmoded tradition or serve special economic interests. While it is too early to speak definitively based on the experience in international commercial arbitration, there are signs that lawyers from civil law and common law cultures can adapt to compromise procedures that make sense in view of common goals and purposes for their dispute resolution process.

6. The Recent Reforms in England

The prospect of future convergence between German-style civil justice and Anglo-American civil justice systems got a significant boost by the Woolf civil justice reforms recently enacted in the United Kingdom. In 1992 Lord Woolf, was commissioned to conduct a comprehensive study of civil justice in England and Wales, and to report to Parliament, the bench and bar, and the public at large, with proposals for reforms to improve the quality and reduce cost and delay associated with civil justice in those jurisdictions. A Preliminary Report in 1995 was followed by a national debate and a final Report in 1996.[227] Legislation and new court rules have now implemented many of the Woolf recommendations.[228]

Many of the new measures adopted by Parliament and the courts appear to move English civil justice significantly in the direction of continental Eu-

226. It is possible, of course, for parties to an existing dispute to chose arbitration to resolve it. However at that point it is likely that one party or the other will sense that its interests will be better served by a national court system which will make it difficult to obtain the necessary agreement to arbitrate.

227. Woolf, *Access to Justice: Interim Report to the Lord Chancellor on the Civil Justice System in England and Wales* (1995); Woolf, *Access to Justice: Final Report* (1996).

228. Civil Procedure Rules 1998. See May (ed.), *Civil Procedure, Vol. I and II* (Spring 2003) ("White Book"); Plant/Rose (eds.), *Blackstone's Guide to the Civil Procedure Rules* (1999).

ropean systems.[229] In particular, the new emphasis on judicial management of cases, the strict limits on party discovery, and the increased use of court-appointed experts, all resonate more with German civil justice than with civil litigation in the United States or with the brand of civil justice previously carried on in Great Britain.

It is still too soon to gauge how quickly traditional roles and divisions of work and responsibility between judges and lawyers will be affected by these new reforms. However over time it can be expected that the face of English justice will bear a greater resemblance to justice as practiced elsewhere within the European Union than traditional common law aficionados ever deemed possible.[230] These changes in the jurisdiction that was the main source of the American civil justice tradition show that there is real potential for convergence between common law–civil law systems in our current era.[231]

7. The Proposed Transnational Principles of Civil Procedure

Another positive sign for international convergence in civil justice systems can be found in the ongoing work of the American Law Institute and UNIDROIT in the development and refinement of Transnational Principles of Civil Procedure. This project shows that thoughtful academics and practitioners from both the common law and the civil law traditions can agree on many fundamental principles of civil justice which should be followed by all regimes and should be expected by international parties when litigating in any forum.

The current project is an outgrowth of an effort originally sponsored by the American Law Institute to develop a regime of court rules to govern certain kinds of litigation between international parties. Initially the ALI proposed to develop a single set of rules of procedure that could be adopted internation-

229. For an outstanding treatise on the new rules see Andrews, *English Civil Procedure: Fundamentals of the New Civil Justice System* (2003).

230. For a historical survey on this development see Stürner, "Transnational Civil Procedure", VI (NS) *Uniform L. Rev.* 871 (2001); id., "Zur Struktur des europäischen Zivilprozesses", in: Gottwald/Roth (eds.), *Festschrift für Schumann* (2001), p. 491; id., "Geschichtliche Grundlinien des europäischen Beweisrechts", in: Köbler/Heinze/Hromadka (eds.), *Festschrift für Söllner* (2000), p. 1171.

231. For more details of the new face of English civil justice in the light of harmonization see Andrews (ed.), *Principles and Rules of Transnational Civil Procedure* (forthcoming 2003) with papers and contributions of a congress organized by the British Institute of Comparative Law.

ally, either by convention or by national enactment, to govern contract and commercial litigation in national courts between natural or corporate citizens of different countries.[232] After ALI reporters[233] working with an Advisor Committee had generated a Preliminary Draft of the proposed rules, the ALI approached UNIDROIT about the possibility of international sponsorship and adoption. UNIDROIT in turn commissioned an evaluation of the ALI Preliminary Draft to inform its consideration of the ALI joint-sponsorship proposal. In 1999 UNIDROIT joined the project.[234]

Since then the original project to develop transnational rules of civil procedure has evolved into a collaborative effort to identify principles of civil procedure which ought to be applied to international cases in national courts, without necessarily requiring or expecting that these principles will be embodied in a particular rules format. As a result of ongoing work by the reporters, informed by presentations and discussions at meetings with academics and practitioners all over the globe, a body of some 40 Principles of Transnational Civil Procedure has been proposed.[235] The original Rules, since modified, now serve as an example of how the Principles can be implemented in a rules format.

It is too early to know whether and how the draft Principles will actually be adopted or implemented as a framework for civil litigation in national court systems. To the extent that the Principles are influential in the ongoing process of judicial reform, the process of convergence will be accelerated.

8. The Face of Civil Justice in the Future

The temptation to use comparative perspectives to try to predict developments in the future is sometimes overwhelming. At the beginning of the 21st Century civil justice is on the move. Significant change in institutions of civil justice with which we have long been familiar seem almost inevitable.

---

232. See, e.g., Hazard, "From Whom No Secrets Are Hid", 76 *Texas Law Review* 1665 (1998).

233. Professors Geoffrey C. Hazard, Jr. and Michele Taruffo.

234. The evaluation was performed by Professor Rolf Stürner, one of the authors of this work. See the English report on the results of this feasibility study by Stürner, 34 *The International Lawyer* 1071 (2000); in German 112 *ZZP* 185 (1999) and in French 60 *Revue internationale de droit comparé* 845 (2000). When UNIDROIT joined the project as co-sponsor, Professor Stürner was appointed Co-reporter from UNIDROIT. The other author of this book, Professor Peter Murray, is a member of the consultative group of the ALI.

235. See American Law Institute/UNIDROIT, *Principles and Rules of Transnational Civil Procedure*, Council Draft No. 2 (September 29, 2003), www.ali.org.

The strongest influence for change in national civil justice systems is globalization of commerce and the increasing interaction of persons and commercial entities from different national economies. This is not limited to the traditional kind of international transactions, consciously undertaken by mercantile firms in international trade. Now even the most ordinary consumer products and even services are peddled and consumed in an international marketplace. In both Germany and the United States one need only to consider the proportion of cars, drugs, movies, or music-CD's that originate from abroad in order to appreciate this phenomenon. Services ranging from financing of multimillion dollar or euro projects to rendering consumer computer and software support are also rapidly becoming internationalized. National borders are mattering less and less in the international economy.

We believe that these irreversible tendencies will inevitably lead to the harmonization of those civil justice regimes that affect international intercourse, and perhaps more slowly, to the harmonization of civil justice systems in general. What will be the result of this harmonization?

It can fairly be said that principles and features of the German Civil Justice system have influenced the development of civil justice in a large part of the world.[236] At the same time, the American system holds sway in the world's largest single commercial economy and has tremendous influence as a result of American economic dominance. It is our view that civil justice will be dispensed in the world of the future in a form that embodies the best principles and features from both systems.

Our comparative study of German and American civil justice suggests that the system of the future will expect judges to take larger roles in the preparation, shaping and "management" of most civil cases than they have traditionally taken in America. Developments in England as well as attempted reforms in the United States appear to point clearly in this direction. The Transnational Principles make case management by the judge a central principle of modern civil justice.[237] The proposition that greater use

---

236. For a survey and many details see Habscheid (ed.), *Das deutsche Zivilprozessrecht und seine Ausstrahlung auf andere Rechtsordnungen* (1991) (with contributions from Stürner, Jelinek, Walter/Meier, Trocker, Rouhette, Kohl, Ekeløf, Smith, Stefánsson, Michelsen, Möller, Németh, Sawczak, Jedrzejewska, Beys, Kuru, Miguel di Alonso, Barbosa Moreira, Fisch, Vakamura and Ho).

237. See ALI/UNIDROIT Transnational Principles and Rules of Civil Procedure - Council Draft No. 2 (September 29, 2003), Principle 14:

14. Court Responsibility for Direction of the Proceeding

14.1 Commencing as early as practicable, the court should actively manage the proceeding, exercising discretion to achieve disposition of the dispute of neutral resources can focus party energy on the key issues and thereby increase efficiency in civil litigation appears to be well understood and accepted.

We expect that the jury trial template will gradually be abandoned in ordinary civil cases, perhaps not without a struggle.[238] The world as a whole is too skeptical over the validity of jury processes in normal civil cases to expect that it will ever be generally accepted abroad.[239] Even in America the institution appears to be in serious practical decline.[240] The abandonment of the jury trial model for most cases will enable ordinary civil proceedings to be structured to save cost and time and to reduce the burden on counsel and the associated costs.

On the other hand it is likely that litigation of the future will include some form of fact discovery, likely conducted under closer court supervision than is currently the American practice. Recent reforms of German civil procedure have taken a small step toward a form of discovery by authorizing the court to order a party or a third party to produce documents or things for inspection by the court.[241] International arbitration proceedings in which facts are in serious dispute now typically include pre-hearing discovery procedures based on American models.[242] Traditionally German civil practice would mitigate potential injustice from the disclosure of unexpected evidence at the plenary stage by continuing the proceedings to allow time for response.[243] The reformed procedure allows a form of discovery that may reduce surprise and any resulting need for continuance. At least in complicated cases a degree of

---

> fairly, efficiently, and with reasonable speed....
>
> 14.2 To the extent reasonably practicable, the court should manage the proceeding in consultation with the parties.
>
> 14.3 The court should determine the order in which issues are to be resolved, and fix a timetable for all stages of the proceeding, including dates and deadlines. The court may revise such directions.

238. Haddon, "Rethinking the Jury", 3 *Wm. & Mary Bill Rts. J.* 29 (1994); Cecil et al., "Citizen Comprehension of Difficult Issues: Lessons from Civil Jury Trials", 40 *Am. U. L. Rev.* 727 (1991).

239. See Schack, *Einführung in das amerikanische Zivilprozessrecht*, 3rd ed. (2003), pp. 62 f.; Zuckerman, in: *Civil Justice in Crisis* (1999), pp. 3 ff., 20 f., 47 ff.

240. See Ch. 13(I)(4) above, Sward, *The Decline of the Civil Jury*, p. 145.

241. ZPO §142, 144. See Ch. 7(L), Ch. 8(C)(4), Ch. 8(C)(6)(b) and Ch. 13(I)(3)(b) above.

242. Elsing/Townsend, "Bridging the Common Law—Civil Law Divide in Arbitration", 670 *Prac. L. Inst. / Lit.* 635 (2002); Weigand, "Discovery in der Internationalen Schiedsgerichtsbarkeit", 38 *RIW* 361 (1992).

243. See Ch. 8(D)(2) above.

discovery could perhaps lead to a more thorough development of the facts than was feasible under the traditional procedure.

It also appears likely that lawyers litigating in the future may well exercise greater roles and responsibilities than is currently the case in Germany. Active German judges and severe restrictions on lawyer compensation combine to limit the creative energy that German lawyers are able or willing to invest in civil litigation. Even in countries such as Germany where administrative agencies and social welfare programs fulfil many of the functions left to private litigation in America, there is likely to be more "rights based" litigation in the future.[244] Damages awards in German courts are inching upward to more closely approximate current day notions of the value of pain and suffering , or the freedom from pain and suffering. This in turn has led to the development of litigation financing options which resemble the contingency fee arrangements that fuel American litigation.[245] The widespread existence of legal costs insurance permits Germans to spread legal costs and thereby bear larger costs of counsel.

In the international free market of arbitration procedures typically lawyers perform a larger role and receive a greater proportion of the overall litigation budget than is the case in ordinary German litigation process. German litigants who can afford it currently sometimes contract with their counsel for compensation in excess of that which they can recover under the standard statutory fee schedule. This practice suggests that such litigants believe it worth their while to compensate their lawyers for exertions greater than would be expected under the statutory compensation scheme.

The general tendency in recent years toward relaxation of strict governmental control of professional activities can be expected to lead to some relaxation of restrictions on German lawyers' compensation and resulting increases in activity of German lawyers in cases where increased activity will be of value to their clients.[246]

One question about civil justice of the future that remains unanswered is how future justice systems will assure access to high-quality civil justice for litigants of little or no means. In the United States, which relies on its civil justice system for some purposes fulfilled by governmental and social programs

---

244. See Ch. 7(B)(5) above on the development of collective litigation and the German Lawyers' Association 2002 recommendation that group actions be instituted for securities litigation: *Verhandlungen des 64. Deutschen Juristentages*, Vol. II/1 (2002), pp. P1 ff., P89.

245. See Ch. 4(J) above on commercial financing of litigation costs based on contingencies. It continues to be far from clear whether contingent financing of attorneys fees and costs will catch on in Germany.

246. See Ch. 4(E)(3) above.

in other countries, the problem of affording access to justice to all remains acute. England, which tried to provide its litigants with very generous civil legal assistance, has found that it could not afford it, and has had to cut back. The German model is also expensive despite a judicially administered threshold test of likely merit.

It appears likely that systems in which a greater share of the work required in litigation is done by neutrals can provide legal assistance to litigants at lower cost than can systems which require a great deal of activity on the part of private counsel. Thus, as American civil justice systems of the future may tend to expect more of their judges, the resulting smaller roles of counsel may be more easily filled by publicly funded legal resources. Whether increased efficiencies can ever bring the costs of legal aid to a level where public willingness to fund such costs will suffice to meet the need seems highly questionable based on experience to date. Affording access to justice for all will thus continue to be a challenge to our ingenuity as well as our humanity.

Brief Bibliography

I. English Language Literature on German Civil Justice

Anke Freckmann and Thomas Wegerich, *The German Legal System*, London 1999, pp. 124–179

Walther J. Habscheid, "Germany", in: Elio Fazzalari (ed.), *Civil Justice in the Countries of the European Union*, Padova 1998, pp. 155–188

Benjamin Kaplan, Arthur Taylor von Mehren, and Rudolf Schäfer, "Phases of German civil procedure", 71 *Harvard L. Rev.* 1193–1268, 1443–1472 (1958)

Harald Koch and Frank Diedrich, *Civil Procedure in Germany*, The Hague 1997, Munich 1998

John H. Langbein, "The German Advantage in Civil Procedure", 52 *U. Chi. L. Rev.* 823 (1985)

Hans Schima and Hans Hoyer, "Ordinary Proceedings in First Instance. Central European Countries", in: *International Encyclopedia of Comparative Law*, Vol. XVI: Civil Procedure (Mauro Cappelletti ed.), Ch. 6 III., pp. 101–140

Arthur Taylor von Mehren, "Some Comparative Reflections on First Instance Civil Procedure: Recent Reforms in German Civil Procedure and the Federal Rules", 63 *Notre Dame L. Rev.* 609 (1988)

Stephen O'Malley and Alexander Layton (in collaboration with Thomas Försterling), "Federal Republic of Germany", in: Stephen O'Malley and Alexander Layton (eds.), *European Civil Practice*, 2nd ed., London 2003

Gerhard Robbers, *An Introduction to German Law*, Baden-Baden 1998, pp. 328–341

Peter Smits and Marc Ynzonides, "German Civil Procedure", in: Henricus J. Snijders (ed.), *Access to Civil Procedure Abroad*, Munich, London et al. 1996, pp. 277–311

Astrid Stadler, "Introduction to German Civil Procedural Law", in: Werner Ebke and Matthew W. Finkin (eds.), *Introduction to German Law*, Den Haag 1996, pp. 357–381

Georg A. Wittuhn and Ralf Stucken, "Germany", in: Christian T. Campbell (ed.), *International Civil Procedures*, London 1995, pp. 271–325

II. Principal German Treatises and Commentaries

Adolf Baumbach, Wolfgang Lauterbach, Jan Albers, and Peter Hartmann, *Zivilprozessordnung*, commentary, 61st ed., Munich 2003

Fritz Baur and Rolf Stürner, *Zwangsvollstreckungs-, Konkurs- und Vergleichsrecht, Vol. 1, Einzelvollstreckungsrecht* (debtors and creditors law), 12th ed., Heidelberg 1995. - *Vol. 2, Insolvenzrecht* (bankruptcy law), 12th ed., Heidelberg 1990

Wolfgang Grunsky, *Zivilprozessrecht*, 11th ed., Munich 2003

Othmar Jauernig, *Zivilprozessrecht*, 28th ed., Munich 2003

Wolfgang Lüke, *Zivilprozessrecht*, 8th ed., Munich 2003

Münchener Kommentar zur Zivilprozessordnung, commentary, 2nd ed., Munich 2000, 2001, 2002

Hans-Joachim Musielak (ed.), *Kommentar zur Zivilprozessordnung*, commentary, 3rd ed., Munich 2003

Leo Rosenberg, Karl Heinz Schwab, and Peter Gottwald, *Zivilprozessrecht*, 15th ed., Munich 1993

Leo Rosenberg, Hans Friedhelm Gaul, and Eberhard Schilken, *Zwangsvollstreckungsrecht* (debtors and creditors law), 11th ed., Munich 1997

Kurt Schellhammer, *Die Arbeitsmethode des Zivilrichters* (The methodological approach of the judge in civil matters), 14th ed., Heidelberg 2002

Friedrich Stein and Martin Jonas (eds.), *Zivilprozessordnung*, commentary, 21st ed., Tübingen 1993–2002, 22nd ed., Tübingen 2002 et seq.

Heinz Thomas and Hans Putzo (eds.), *Zivilprozessordnung*, commentary, 25th ed., Munich 2003

Richard Zöller (ed.), *Zivilprozessordnung*, commentary, 23rd ed., Cologne 2002

Index